Becoming a Helper

EIGHTH EDITION

Marianne Schneider Corey
Consultant

Gerald Corey
California State University, Fullerton
Diplomate in Counseling Psychology
American Board of Professional Psychology

CENGAGE

Australia • Brazil • Canada • Mexico • Singapore • United Kingdom • United States

CENGAGE

Becoming a Helper, **8th Edition**
Marianne Schneider Corey,
Gerald Corey

Product Team Manager: Carolyn Henderson-Meier

Product Manager: Julie Martinez

Product Assistant: Juleah Morehouse

Manager, Content Delivery: Andrea Wagner

Content Manager: Vanessa Desiato

Learning Design Manager: Jessica Badiner

Learning Designer: Emily Lehmann

Marketing Director: Kristen Hurd

Art Director: Marissa Falco

IP Analyst: Deanna Ettinger

Production Service: Lumina Datamatics Ltd.

Cover Image: Stuart Monk/Shutterstock.com

Compositor: Lumina Datamatics Ltd.

Library of Congress Control Number: 2019939822

Student Edition:

ISBN: 978-0-357-36627-1

Loose-leaf Edition:

ISBN: 978-0-357-36632-5

Cengage
200 Pier 4 Boulevard
Boston, MA 02210
USA

Printed at CLDPC, USA, 07-22

To you, our readers.
We hope this book will help you
make a significant difference
in the lives of others.

CONTENTS

ABOUT THE AUTHORS

Jean Bogroff

Marianne Schneider Corey is a licensed marriage and family therapist in California and is a National Certified Counselor. She received her master's degree in marriage, family, and child counseling from Chapman University. She is a Fellow of the Association for Specialists in Group Work and was the recipient of this organization's Eminent Career Award in 2001. She received the Lifetime Achievement Award from the American Mental Health Counselors Association in 2011. She holds memberships in the American Counseling Association, the American Group Psychotherapy Association, the Association for Specialists in Group Work, the Association for Counselor Education and Supervision, the Western Association of Counselor Education and Supervision, and the National Organization for Human Services.

Marianne has been involved in leading groups for different populations, providing training and supervision workshops in group process, facilitating self-exploration groups for graduate students in counseling, and cofacilitating training groups for group counselors and weeklong residential workshops in personal growth. Both Marianne and Jerry Corey have conducted training workshops, continuing education seminars, and personal-growth groups in the United States, Germany, Ireland, Belgium, Mexico, Hong Kong, China, and Korea.

In addition to *Becoming a Helper,* Eighth Edition (2021, with Gerald Corey), which has been translated into Korean and Japanese, Marianne has coauthored the following books with Cengage Learning:

- *Issues and Ethics in the Helping Professions,* Tenth Edition (2019, with Gerald Corey and Cindy Corey), which has been translated into Japanese, Chinese, and Korean
- *Groups: Process and Practice,* Tenth Edition (2018, with Gerald Corey and Cindy Corey), which has been translated into Korean, Chinese, and Polish
- *I Never Knew I Had a Choice,* Eleventh Edition (2018, with Gerald Corey and Michelle Muratori), which has been translated into Chinese
- *Group Techniques,* Fourth Edition (2015, with Gerald Corey, Patrick Callanan, and Michael Russell), which has been translated into Portuguese, Korean, Japanese, and Czech

Marianne has made educational video programs (with accompanying student workbooks) for Cengage Learning: *Groups in Action: Evolution and Challenges DVD and Workbook* (2014, with Gerald Corey and Robert Haynes); and *Ethics in Action: DVD and Workbook* (2015, with Gerald Corey and Robert Haynes).

Marianne and Jerry have been married since 1964. They have two adult daughters, Heidi and Cindy, two granddaughters (Kyla and Keegan), and one grandson (Corey). Marianne grew up in Germany and has kept in close contact with her family and friends there. In her free time, she enjoys traveling, reading, visiting with friends, bicycle riding, and hiking in the mountains and the desert.

Gerald "Jerry" Corey is Professor Emeritus of Human Services and Counseling at California State University at Fullerton. He received his doctorate in counseling from the University of Southern California. He is a Diplomate in Counseling Psychology, American Board of Professional Psychology; a licensed psychologist; and a National Certified Counselor. He is a Fellow of the American Psychological Association (Division 17, Counseling Psychology; and Division 49, Group Psychotherapy); a Fellow of the American Counseling Association; and a Fellow of the Association for Specialists in Group Work. Other memberships in professional organizations include the American Group Psychotherapy Association; the Association for Counselor Education and Supervision; the Western Association of Counselor Education and Supervision; and the National Organization for Human Services. Jerry received the Lifetime Achievement Award from the American Mental Health Counselors Association in 2011, the Eminent Career Award from ASGW in 2001, and the Outstanding Professor of the Year Award from California State University at Fullerton in 1991. He teaches courses in group counseling, theories of counseling, and ethics in counseling. He is the author or coauthor of 16 textbooks in counseling currently in print, along with more than 60 journal articles and book chapters. Several of his books have been translated into other languages. *Theory and Practice of Counseling and Psychotherapy* has been translated into Arabic, Indonesian, Portuguese, Turkish, Korean, and Chinese. *Theory and Practice of Group Counseling* has been translated into Korean, Chinese, Spanish, and Russian.

During the past 45 years Jerry and Marianne Corey have conducted group counseling training workshops for mental health professionals at many universities in the United States as well as in Canada, Mexico, China, Hong Kong, Korea, Germany, Belgium, Scotland, England, and Ireland. In his leisure time, Jerry likes to travel, hike and bicycle in the mountains and the desert, and drive his grandchildren and friends in his 1931 Model A Ford. Marianne and Jerry have been married since 1964. They have two adult daughters (Heidi and Cindy), two granddaughters (Kyla and Keegan), and one grandson (Corey).

Gerald Corey has six books published by the American Counseling Association, the most recent being *The Art of Integrative Counseling*, Fourth Edition (2019). Jerry is coauthor (with Michelle Muratori, Jude Austin, and Julius Austin) of *Counselor Self-Care* (2018); he is coauthor (with Barbara Herlihy) of both *Boundary Issues in Counseling: Multiple Roles and Responsibilities*, Third Edition (2015) and *ACA Ethical Standards Casebook*, Seventh Edition (2015). He is coauthor (with Robert Haynes, Patrice Moulton, and Michelle Muratori) of *Clinical Supervision in the Helping Professions: A Practical Guide*, Second Edition

(2010); and he is the author of *Creating Your Professional Path: Lessons From My Journey* (2010).

Other publications by Gerald Corey, all with Cengage Learning, include:

- *Theory and Practice of Counseling and Psychotherapy*, Enhanced Tenth Edition (and *Student Manual*) (2021)
- *Issues and Ethics in the Helping Professions*, Tenth Edition (2019, with Marianne Schneider Corey and Cindy Corey). This work has been translated into Chinese, Japanese, and Korean.
- *Groups: Process and Practice*, Tenth Edition (2018, with Marianne Schneider Corey and Cindy Corey). This work has been translated into Chinese, Korean, and Polish.
- *I Never Knew I Had a Choice*, Eleventh Edition (2018, with Marianne Schneider Corey and Michelle Muratori). This work has been translated into Chinese, Indonesian, Korean, Polish, Russian, and Vietnamese.
- *Theory and Practice of Group Counseling*, Ninth Edition (and *Student Manual*) (2016). This work has been translated into Arabic, Bulgarian, Chinese, Russian, Spanish, and Turkish.
- *Group Techniques*, Fourth Edition (2015, with Marianne Schneider Corey, Patrick Callanan, and J. Michael Russell). This work has been translated into Czech, Japanese, Korean, and Portuguese.
- *Case Approach to Counseling and Psychotherapy*, Eighth Edition (2013)

He has also made several educational DVD programs on various aspects of counseling practice: (1) *Ethics in Action: DVD and Workbook* (2015, with Marianne Schneider Corey and Robert Haynes); (2) *Groups in Action: Evolution and Challenges DVD and Workbook* (2014, with Marianne Schneider Corey and Robert Haynes); (3) *DVD for Theory and Practice of Counseling and Psychotherapy: The Case of Stan and Lecturettes* (2013); (4) *DVD for Integrative Counseling: The Case of Ruth and Lecturettes* (2013, with Robert Haynes); (5) *DVD Lecturettes for Theory and Practice of Group Counseling* (2012); (6) *MindTap Video Program for Theory and Practice of Group Counseling* (2020); and (7) *MindTap Video Program, Counseling Gwen, for Theory and Practice of Counseling and Psychotherapy* (2021). All of these video programs are available through Cengage Learning.

PREFACE

Many books deal with the skills, theories, and techniques of helping. Yet few books concentrate on the problems involved in becoming an effective helper or focus on the personal difficulties in working with others. In writing this book, we had in mind both students who are planning a career in human services, counseling, social work, psychology, couples and family therapy, or related professions and helpers who have just begun their careers. This book provides a general overview and introduction, and you will likely take a separate course on each chapter topic we present here. Our aim is to introduce you to these topics in such a way that you will look forward to learning more about the issues we raise. We intend this book to be used as a supplement to textbooks dealing with helping skills and with counseling theory and practice. *Becoming a Helper* has proved useful for introductory classes in the fields of human services, counseling, and social work, as well as for courses such as prepracticum, practicum, fieldwork, and internship.

In this book we focus considerable attention on the struggles, anxieties, and uncertainties of helpers. In addition, we explore in depth the demands and strains of the helping professions and their effects on the practitioner. In Chapter 1 readers are challenged to become aware of and examine their motivations for seeking a career in the helping professions. We assist readers in assessing what they will get from their work. Throughout the book, we keep the focus on how helpers may be affected by the problems they face and the choices they make in service to their clients.

Chapter 2 addresses the importance of helpers knowing themselves and encourages readers to explore their family-of-origin experiences, focusing on how earlier relationships continue to influence the quality of later ones. We explore how helpers can understand the developmental transitions in their own lives and discuss the implications of this self-understanding when working with transitional phases in the lives of clients.

Values are an integral part of the client–helper relationship, and we devote considerable attention to an analysis of how values influence the helping process in Chapter 3. We develop the thesis that the job of helpers is not to impose values but to help clients define their own value system. It is essential that counselors-in-training become aware of their values on a variety of topics. We explore the belief systems of helpers and discuss the positive and negative effects that a variety of beliefs and assumptions can have on one's practice.

Special consideration is given to understanding and working with diverse client populations whenever this topic is relevant. In addition, Chapter 4 addresses a range of diversity issues. Beginning and seasoned helpers encounter common problems in their work related to dealing with resistance, transference and countertransference, and clients who are sometimes perceived as "difficult," and we address these critical topics in Chapter 5.

Chapter 6 provides an overview of the stages of the helping process, with a brief discussion of the skills and knowledge required to be a successful helper at each of these stages. The focus of this discussion is not just on skill development but also on the personal characteristics that enable helpers to be effective. Because helpers ask clients to examine their behavior to understand themselves more fully, we ask helpers to be equally committed to an awareness of their own lives. Without a high level of self-awareness, a helper may obstruct clients' progress, especially when these clients are struggling with issues the helper has avoided facing.

Chapter 7 is an overview of various theories with the emphasis on key concepts and practical applications. There is a discussion of an integrative approach to counseling practice, which offers guidelines on how to select a theoretical orientation.

Forming a sense of ethical awareness and learning to resolve professional dilemmas is a task facing all helpers. In Chapter 8 we raise a number of challenges surrounding current ethical issues as a way to sensitize readers to the intricacies of ethical decision making. A few of these topics include informed consent, confidentiality and privacy, documentation, and malpractice and risk management. Chapter 9 is devoted to learning how to manage boundaries, both personal and professional, and how to ethically perform multiple roles.

We challenge students to take a proactive stance in their educational program in Chapter 10. Being proactive applies to selecting field placements and internships as well as to getting the most from supervision. Therefore, we offer some practical strategies for ensuring quality experiences in fieldwork and profiting from supervision.

In Chapter 11 we discuss the group process and the value of working with groups in human services work. Emphasis is on the tasks of group leaders at each of the stages of a group. Chapter 12 describes ways of working in the community and various forms of community intervention. Chapter 13 deals with stress, burnout, impairment, and self-care. The emphasis is on how to monitor yourself to prevent burnout and how to design a personal self-care program aimed at keeping you alive both personally and professionally.

Chapter 14 explores crisis management in the personal and professional lives of counselors. The relatively new field of disaster mental health is discussed along with strategies for helping in times of natural and human-caused disasters. This chapter provides readers with an understanding of how crisis situations affect both clients and helpers, a plan for learning to better handle crises in a helper's life and work, and interventions that can help clients cope with crises in their lives.

Although this book should be useful to any student planning to enter the helping professions, our backgrounds are in the field of counseling, and this orientation comes through in this book. Therefore, those who want to work in the counseling aspects of the human services are likely to find this book especially meaningful. We have tried to write a personal book that will stimulate both thought and action. At the end of each chapter we encourage readers to commit to some specific action that will move them closer to their goals.

What's New in the Eighth Edition of *Becoming a Helper*?

For the 8th edition, each chapter has been carefully reviewed and updated to present the current thinking, research, and trends in practice. For every chapter, we have added learning objectives. The following chapter-by-chapter list of highlights outlines some sample material that has been added, updated, expanded, and revised for the 8th edition.

Chapter 1: Are the Helping Professions for You?

- Updated information on the various helping professions
- Updated suggestions for creating one's professional journey

Chapter 2: Helper, Know Thyself

- Revised section on how professional practice can affect a helper's personal life
- Revised and expanded section on individual and group counseling for self-understanding
- Revised material on countertransference on the helper's part

Chapter 3: Knowing Your Values

- Substantial revisions with increased emphasis on helpers identifying and learning to manage their values to avoid unduly influencing clients
- Increased emphasis on seeking supervision and consultation when maintaining objectivity becomes a problem
- New discussion on referral not being an option for dealing with value conflicts
- Commentary on recent legislation that allows counselors to deny services based on their personal or religious convictions
- Revised material on addressing the concerns of LGBTQI people
- Increased emphasis on bracketing personal values in counseling relationships
- Revised section on religious and spiritual values

Chapter 4: Understanding Diversity

- Introduction to how a social justice orientation relates to a multicultural perspective
- Revised sections on examining cultural assumptions and cultural values
- Revision of section on multicultural counseling competencies
- New section on cultural competence as a lifelong learning process
- Updated literature on understanding people with disabilities
- New material on social justice competencies
- Updating of CACREP 2016 multicultural training standards

Chapter 5: Common Concerns of Beginning Helpers

- Updated literature on transference and countertransference
- Alternative perspectives on understanding client defensiveness, ambivalence, and resistance
- Revised discussion on knowing when and how to make referrals

Chapter 6: The Helping Process

- Updated discussion of the stages of change
- Revision and update of the stages in the helping process

Chapter 7: Theory Applied to Practice

- Addition of suggested reading for each of the theories
- Revision of discussion on the Adlerian approach
- Expansion of goals of existential therapy
- New material on relapse prevention
- A new section on mindfulness and acceptance approaches in psychotherapy
- A new section on motivational interviewing
- A new section on feminist therapy
- Updated information on evidence-based practice as a trend in clinical work
- Updated and expanded coverage of an integrative perspective on counseling
- New discussion of the future of psychotherapy integration

Chapter 8: Ethical and Legal Issues Facing Helpers

- Introduction of the concept of fear-based ethics versus concern-based ethics
- Introduction of the concept of mandatory ethics versus aspirational ethics
- Updated codes of ethics of the various professional organizations
- Minor revision of confidentiality and privacy in a technological world
- Revision and expansion of risk-management strategies

Chapter 9: Managing Boundary Issues

- Discussion of shifts in thinking about multiple relationships
- Updated codes of ethics on managing boundaries and multiple relationships
- New material on multiple relationships in military settings
- Expanded and updated coverage on boundary issues in small communities
- Expanded discussion of the cultural context in the intersection of personal and professional relationships
- Updated and expanded section on social media and boundaries
- Discussion of the latest ethics codes on bartering and gift giving

Chapter 10: Getting the Most From Your Fieldwork and Supervision

- Expanded discussion on vicarious liability and strict liability
- Updated and expanded section on informed consent in supervision
- Discussion of how one's personal relationships can be affected by involvement in fieldwork
- Expanded discussion of multiple roles and relationships and how they can be managed so that these relationships do not result in exploitation of supervisees

Chapter 11: Working With Groups

- New section on groups for veterans and people in the military
- New section on creating a bereavement group
- Updated and expanded discussion of experiential group training experience
- Increased emphasis on multicultural issues and social justice themes in group work

Chapter 12: Working in the Community

- More emphasis on the multiple roles of community workers
- Updated treatment of the scope of the community approach

Chapter 13: Stress, Burnout, and Self-Care

- Updated literature on identifying self-defeating internal dialogue
- More emphasis on changing distorted and self-distorted ways of thinking
- Increased discussion of risks associated with vicarious traumatization
- New material on stress associated with a personal crisis
- Revised discussion of self-care as an ethical mandate rather than a luxury
- More on ethics codes on impairment
- New material on characteristics of an effective self-care action plan
- New section on therapeutic lifestyle changes that promote wellness
- More emphasis on benefits of mindfulness
- New material on how meditation can sharpen our thinking patterns
- New discussion on the importance of self-compassion and how this can be a route to caring about others
- Increased emphasis on physical activity and exercise as ways of caring for ourselves
- Expanded discussion on developing an exercise program
- New section on diet and nutrition as a form of self-care
- New section on role of relationships and well-being
- Updated and expanded coverage on religious/spiritual involvement and meaning in life
- New section on providing service to others as a lifestyle pattern
- New discussion on the role of recreation in self-care

Chapter 14: Managing Crisis: Personally and Professionally

- Updated literature on stress and crisis in the helping professions
- Understanding crisis both personally and professionally
- How crisis situations affect individuals
- Revised discussion on ways stress and emotional fatigue can lead to burnout
- Updated literature on action plans for implementing self-care routines
- Expanded and updated discussion of posttraumatic growth following a traumatic event
- How to help clients refocus through self-talk and building resilience
- Introduction to the field of disaster mental health
- The value of a safety plan with clients who pose a risk for suicide
- Revised section on disaster mental health counseling

Supplements

MindTap

Becoming a Helper comes with MindTap, an online learning solution created to harness the power of technology to drive student success. This cloud-based platform integrates a number of learning applications ("apps") into an easy-to-use and easy to access tool that supports a personalized learning experience. MindTap combines student learning tools—readings, multimedia, activities, and assessments—into a singular Learning Path that guides you through your counseling course. All the activities have been newly tagged to CACREP standards and Learning Objectives. This MindTap includes:

- "Why Am I Here?" Polling Activities
- Helper Studio Activities
- Exercises and "You Decide" Case Studies
- A variety of curated video and role play activities, including content from the *Ethics in Action*, and a new video program on the helping professions.
- "Did I Get It?" Chapter Quizzing
- "What Does This Mean to Me?" Reflection Activities

Instructor's Resource Manual

An *Instructor's Resource Manual* is available for this edition. It contains suggestions for teaching the course, course objectives, key terms, class activities to stimulate interest, PowerPoint slides, a test bank for all chapters, reflection and discussion questions, and online test items. The instructor can choose from the many multiple-choice, true-false, matching, and short essay questions provided. These materials can be accessed through the instructor's companion site at login.cengage.com. Faculty can access the ancillaries that accompany this text by contacting a Cengage Learning sales representative.

Ethics in Action Video Program and Workbook

An integrated learning package titled *Ethics in Action: Video Program and Workbook* (third edition, 2015) is available to enhance the eighth edition of *Becoming a Helper.* The *Ethics in Action* Video Program is designed to bring to life the ethical issues and dilemmas counselors often encounter and to provide ample opportunity for discussion, self-exploration, and problem solving of these issues and dilemmas. The vignettes are based on a weekend workshop coled by Marianne Schneider Corey and Gerald Corey for a group of counseling students, which included challenging questions and lively discussion, role plays to bring the issues to life, and comments from the students and the Coreys. Additional material on the video program is designed to provide a self-study guide for students who are also reading this book. This educational program is divided into three parts: (1) Ethical Decision Making, (2) Values and the Helping Relationship, and (3) Boundary Issues and Multiple Relationships. This interactive self-study program challenges students to deal with the complexity of ethical issues and encourages reflection on their perspectives on each of the issues presented. By viewing the video program and completing the exercises, students will be in a better position to get involved in class discussions. At the end of several chapters in *Becoming a Helper* are suggested activities and guidelines for integrating the *Ethics in Action* video program with this textbook. The more students become involved in this learning package, the more their understanding of ethical practice will be enhanced.

Acknowledgments

In preparation for this revision, a survey was conducted with responses from 50 instructors, all of whom have used *Becoming a Helper* within the last two years. The feedback of from this survey was helpful in guiding our revision process, especially by focusing our attention on the range of courses for which this book is selected, including counseling, human services, psychology, and social work. Michelle Muratori, of Johns Hopkins University, reviewed the manuscript and also consulted with us with the revisions of both the previous edition and the current revised edition.

Appreciation goes to the following people who reviewed selected chapters of the eighth edition of *Becoming a Helper*:

Jude Austin, Mary Hardin-Baylor University (Chapters 10 & 11)
Julius Austin, Tulane University (Chapters 10 & 11)
James Robert Bitter, East Tennessee State University (Chapter 2)
Jamie Bludworth, Arizona State University (Chapter 10)
Sherry Cormier, West Virginia University (Chapters 3, 6, 10, 11, 13, & 14)
Robert Haynes, Borderline Productions (Chapter 14)
Barbara Herlihy, University of Texas at San Antonio (Chapters 3, 4, 8, 9, & 14)
Ed Neukrug, Old Dominion University (Chapters 1, 4, & 14)
Ted Remley, Our Lady of Holy Cross University (Chapter 10)
Mark Stebnicki, East Carolina University (Chapters 4 & 14)

We thank Julie Martinez (product manager, Counseling, Human Services, and Social Work) and Vanessa Desiato (associate content manager) who facilitated moving this revision into production. We also thank Susan Cunningham for preparing the index. As always, we appreciate the dedicated effort of Kay Mikel, the copy editor of this book, who helps us keep this book concise, practical, and reader friendly.

Marianne Schneider Corey
Gerald Corey

CHAPTER 1

Are the Helping Professions for You?

Learning Objectives

1. Recognize your motives for becoming a helper.
2. Identify whether a helping career is for you.
3. Identify the attributes of an ideal helper.
4. Describe what is involved in selecting an educational and career path.
5. Describe the main areas of focus for key helping professions.
6. Assess your attitudes and beliefs about the helping process.

Focus Questions

1. What has attracted you to the helping professions? Who in your life has influenced your decision to consider becoming a professional helper? What major events in your life have contributed to your desire to enter this field?
2. What is your main motivation for wanting to be a helper? What personal needs of yours are likely to be met through this work?
3. Think of a time when you needed help from a significant person in your life or from a counselor. What did you most want from this person? What did he or she do that either helped or hindered you?
4. At this time in your life, how prepared (from a personal standpoint) do you feel you are to enter one of the helping professions? In what ways do you feel prepared and in what ways do you feel unprepared?
5. What can you do to make your educational program more meaningful and derive the maximum benefit from your academic courses?
6. If you were applying to a graduate program or for a job in the field, how would you respond to these questions on the application form or in an interview: "What qualities, traits, attitudes, values, and convictions are central to being an effective helper?" "How might these personal characteristics be either assets or liabilities for you as a helper?"
7. If you were to pursue a career in one of the helping professions, what kind of work appeals to you? What clients or populations do you think you would like to work with? What kind of human services work do you expect would bring you the greatest meaning and satisfaction?
8. What personal strengths do you have that will assist you in your work as a helper? What personal limitations might hinder your work? How might you go about working to improve those limitations?

9. How can you learn more about what is involved in a particular helping profession of interest to you?
10. What role do you think your values will play in selecting a career in the helping professions?

Aim of the Chapter

The Learning Objectives at the beginning of each chapter will guide your reading, and the Focus Questions will help you personalize the content you are about to read. We believe the best way to assist you in understanding your own beliefs and attitudes about the helping role is to encourage you to be an active learner and to engage with the material in a personal way. We do not expect you to have clarified all of your thoughts about these topics before reading the chapter, nor do we expect you to be able to answer all of the questions we pose. Developing competence as a helper is an ongoing process that requires many years of supervised practice and introspection. Many of you are just beginning your educational program and may have had little or no contact with clients. The questions we raise are designed to spark self-reflection as you embark on your journey of becoming a helper.

As you consider a career in one of the helping professions, you are probably asking yourself these questions:

- Are the helping professions for me?
- Will I know enough to help others when I start my first practicum?
- Will I be able to work effectively with people who are very different from me?
- Will a career in helping others be too emotionally intense for me?
- Will I be able to secure a job?
- Will my career provide me with financial security?
- Will I be able to apply what I am learning to my job?
- Will this career be satisfying for me?
- For which specific profession am I best suited?
- How do I select the best school and training program?

This book is intended to help you answer these and other questions about your career. The focus is on *you* and on what you need personally and professionally to be the best helper possible. We also emphasize the realities you are certain to face when you enter the professional world. You will be best able to cope with the demands of the helping professions if you get an idea now of what lies ahead. In addition to presenting the obstacles that you may encounter, we also point out the joys and rewards of making a commitment to helping others as a way of life. Perhaps one of the most meaningful rewards for helping professionals is the opportunity to assist people in creating their own paths.

We begin this chapter by inviting you to examine your reasons for wanting to become a helper. To help you clarify your personal and professional motivations, we share our own experiences as beginning helpers and demonstrate that learning to become a helper is a process that involves both joys and challenges. This chapter also introduces you to the attributes of an effective helper. There is no one pattern of characteristics that identifies "ideal helpers," but we encourage you to think about the characteristics you possess that could either help or hinder you in your work with others.

Most students have questions about which professional program will best help them attain their career objectives, and we explore the differences among various educational routes. Although you may think you know the career path you want to pursue, we encourage you to keep your options open while you are reading this book and taking this course. You will probably hold several different positions within the career that you eventually choose. For example, you may begin by providing direct services to clients in a community agency but later on shift to administering programs.

Finally, keep in mind as you read this book that we use the terms **helper** and **human service professionals** interchangeably to refer to a wide range of practitioners, some of which include social workers, counselors, clinical and counseling psychologists, couples and family therapists, pastoral counselors, mental health nurses, school counselors, rehabilitation counselors, and community mental health workers.

LO1 Examining Your Motives for Becoming a Helper

In choosing a career in the helping professions, it is imperative that you reflect on the reasons you are considering entering this field. For many of us, becoming a helper satisfies some of our personal needs, such as the need to make a difference in the lives of others. It is gratifying to know that we can make a significant difference, especially when people do not have a great deal of hope that they can change or have faith in themselves to create a better life. You can be a change agent for such people and facilitate their belief in themselves. As you reflect on the needs and motives we discuss in this section, ask yourself, "How do my personal needs influence my ability to be an effective helper?"

Typical Needs and Motivations of Helpers

Our students and trainees have had a variety of motivations for pursuing careers in the helping professions. We want you to recognize your motivations and needs and to become aware of how they influence the quality of your interactions with others. Let's examine some of the reasons you may have for becoming a helper.

The need to make an impact. Perhaps you hope to exert a significant influence on the lives of those you serve. You may have a need to know that you are making a positive difference in someone's daily existence. Although you recognize that you will not be able to change everyone, you are likely to derive satisfaction from empowering individuals. When clients are not interested in changing, are afraid to make changes, or do not want your help, you may become frustrated. If your worth as a person is too dependent on your need to make a difference, you are likely to become disillusioned and disappointed. This may lead you to disengage from your role as a helper and ultimately reduce your effectiveness. Your professional work is one source for finding meaning in your life, but we hope it is not your only source of satisfaction. Becoming overly invested in clients can lead to blurred boundaries and burnout. As helpers we may facilitate, guide, empower, educate, and support clients, but it is important to remember that the power and decision to change rests within the client. One of our key obligations as helping professionals is to honor the self-determination of those we serve.

The need to reciprocate. The desire to emulate a role model sometimes plays a part in the decision to be a helper. Someone special—perhaps a teacher, mentor, or a therapist—may have influenced your life in a very special way, or the influential person may be a grandmother, an uncle, or a parent. Practicing therapists often acknowledge that they were greatly influenced by their experience in their own personal therapy to seek the education needed to become competent professionals. The phrase "paying it forward" illustrates this idea.

The need to care for others. You may have been a helper from a early age. Were you the one in your family who attended to the problems and concerns of other family members? Do your peers and friends find it easy to talk to you? If you are a "natural helper," you may have sought training to improve and enhance your talent. Many of our students are adult children of alcoholics who adopted the role of peacemaker in their families. Although this pattern is not necessarily problematic, it is important that such helpers become aware of their dynamics and learn how they function in both their personal and professional lives. Helpers who were peacemakers in their family of origin may be unaware of how their aversion to conflict influences their interactions with others and may inadvertently steer clients away from examining unpleasant feelings such as anger and resentment. If this pattern of peacemaking is left unexamined, it could detract from their ability to provide quality care to others.

One of the pitfalls of being a caregiver to significant people in your life is that very often no one attends to your needs. As a result, you may not have learned to ask for what *you* need. You can easily become personally and professionally burned out, or emotionally exhausted, if you do not learn to ask for help for yourself. Learning to say "no" and setting personal limits and boundaries are crucial components of self-care. Natural caregivers often struggle with these limits.

It is crucial to strike a healthy balance between taking care of others and taking care of yourself. Skovholt and Trotter-Mathison (2016) emphasize the importance of sustaining the personal self and developing professional resiliency. They caution helping professionals to become aware of the dangers of one-way caring in their professional lives. You need to rely on your sense of self as your primary instrument and take care to preserve and protect yourself so you can continue to be effective with clients.

The need for self-help. An interest in helping others may stem from an interest in dealing with the impact of your own struggles. The wounded healer can be authentically present for others searching to find themselves. If you have struggled successfully with a problem, you are able to identify and empathize with clients who come to you with similar concerns. For example, you may have experienced the difficulties of growing up in an abusive family and remain sensitive to this early wounding. In your professional work, you are likely to encounter a number of individuals with similar struggles. Some women who were involved in abusive relationships may become counselors who specialize in working with battered women. Some men who were abused as children develop particular professional interests in counseling abused children and youth. Addictions counselors may be recovering from an addiction themselves, or they may have grown up with an alcoholic or drug-addicted parent.

Stebnicki (2009a) believes that professionals who have experienced a wounded spirit need to be open to questioning their own spiritual health so they can be of assistance to their clients as they struggle with existential concerns of loss, grief, trauma, and stressful life events. He reminds us that "remembering emotions related to such painful events and re-creating an internal emotional scrapbook can be extremely painful and difficult for both clients and counselors, especially for counselors new to the helping profession" (p. 54).

Sometimes individuals who are psychologically impaired study to become helpers in an attempt to understand how to resolve their own problems. If you do not attend to your own healing, it is unlikely that you will be effective in helping others. Furthermore, engaging in intense work with others can stimulate and intensify your own pain. If clients' stories saturated with themes of anxiety, depression, grief, loss, or traumatic stress mirror your own personal struggles, *empathy fatigue* may ensue (Stebnicki, 2008; also see Chapter 14 in this book). Before you attempt to deal with the lives of others, examine your own life situation. Doing this introspective work will increase your self-awareness and help you to avoid the trap of imposing a hidden agenda on your clients. For example, a female counselor who works with women who are victims of partner abuse may try to work out her own unfinished business and conflicts by giving advice and pushing these clients to make decisions they are not yet ready to make. Because of her unresolved personal problems, she may show hostility to a controlling partner. She might make the assumption that what "worked" for her will work for everyone.

The need to be needed. Very few helpers are immune to the need to be needed. It can be psychologically rewarding to have clients say that they are getting better because of your influence. These clients are likely to express their appreciation for the hope that you have given them. You may value and get a great deal of satisfaction from being able to take care of other people's wants. Satisfying this need is perhaps one of the greatest rewards of being a helper. It is not necessary to deny that you like being wanted, approved of, and appreciated. However, if this dynamic is consistently in the forefront, it can overshadow the needs of your clients. An unhealthy dependence can be cultivated by a helper's need to be needed. We do not want clients to terminate counseling before their needs are met, but we also do not want them to remain in counseling long after they have met their therapeutic goals. One of our primary aims as helpers is to empower clients to help themselves. When clients leave counseling because they are functioning well and their therapeutic needs have been satisfied, we can consider that a success!

If you depend exclusively on your clients to validate your self-worth, you are on shaky ground. In reality, many clients will not express appreciation for your efforts, nor will some of them make changes in their lives. Furthermore, agencies often provide feedback only when your performance does not meet the expected standards. No matter what you accomplish, the institution may expect more of you. Eventually, you may realize that whatever you do it is not enough. Wanting to feel appreciated for what you are doing for others is certainly understandable, but being able to evaluate and reinforce yourself for the work you have done is an essential component of self-care for effective helpers.

The need for recognition and status. You may have hopes of gaining recognition and acquiring a certain degree of status, in addition to a certain income level. If you work in an agency, however, many of the consumers of the services you offer will be economically disadvantaged. You may be working with mandated clients who are on probation or incarcerated; people living in poverty who are dealing with addictions or chronic mental illness, racism, and other forms of oppression; or clients who have lost their job or are having difficulties finding employment. This work may not bring you the financial rewards and the recognition you seek; however, your efforts may be deeply rewarding in other ways and are desperately needed in society. As one counselor put it: "This work carries its own set of rewards and benefits that I personally find far more meaningful than money and status. From my experience, when these clients are able to find change and healing, it is huge and life-changing and has a ripple effect that improves their lives and that of their children and families." There are many opportunities for those who continually work to enhance their education and training, and it is possible to work with marginalized client populations and still earn a living.

Conversely, you may work in a setting where you can enjoy the status that goes along with being respected by clients and colleagues. If you have worked hard and are good at what you do, accept the recognition you have earned. You can be proud yet still be humble. If you become arrogant as a result of your status, you may be perceived as unapproachable, and clients as well as coworkers may be put off by your attitude. You also may come to accept far more credit for your clients' changes than you deserve. Some clients will put you on a pedestal, and you may come to like this position too much. You may be playing an important role in helping to facilitate change in your clients' lives, but they are the ones who are doing the hard work both during and outside of sessions. If you want your self-esteem to rest on a solid foundation, it is necessary for you to look within yourself to meet your status needs rather than looking to others to provide you with affirmations that you are indeed a worthwhile person, whether by verbal acclaim or by financial gain.

The need to provide answers. Some students seem to have a need to give others advice and to provide "right answers." They may say that they feel inadequate if friends come to them with a problem and they are not able to give them concrete advice. Yet their friends may really need to be listened to and cared for rather than to be told "what they should do." Although you may find satisfaction in influencing others, it is important to realize that your answers may not be best for them. Many times there is not a "correct" answer at all. As a helper, your purpose is to provide direction and to assist clients in discovering their own course of action. If your need to fix it by providing advice and answers sometimes gets in the way of effectively relating to others, we suggest that you explore this in personal counseling.

The need for control. Related to the need to provide others with advice and answers is the need to control others. All of us have some need for self-control and may also have the need to control others at times. For example, parents of young children understandably need to exercise some degree of control for safety reasons. However, some of us have a great, if not excessive, need to control what others are thinking, feeling, and doing. Ask yourself these questions: Are you convinced that some people should think more liberally (or more conservatively)? When people are angry, depressed, or anxious, do you sometimes tell them that they should not feel that way and do your best to change their state of mind? Do you at times have a strong need to change the way people who are close to you behave, even if what they are doing does not directly affect you? If you feel a strong need to provide solutions to every problem a client presents, you are meeting your own needs rather than working in the best interest of your client. Although some helpers have a need to control under the guise of being helpful, it can be a productive exercise to reflect on what the outcomes might be if you gave more control to those you encountered. Is your role to control the lives of others, or is it to teach others how to regain effective control of their own lives?

How Your Needs and Motivations Operate

We often say that in the ideal situation your own needs are met at the same time that you are meeting your clients' needs. Most of the needs and motives we have discussed can work either for or against a client's welfare. If you are unaware of your needs, however, there is a much greater likelihood that your own needs will determine the nature of your interventions. If you are attempting to work through conscious or unconscious personal conflicts by focusing on the problems of others, for example, there is a greater chance that you will unconsciously use your clients to meet your own needs. In addition, you may be in trouble if some of these needs assume such a high priority that you become obsessed with them. For instance, if your need for control is so high that you consistently attempt to determine the path that others take, you could easily interfere with your clients' development of independence and self-determination.

In many counseling programs, instructors expect their students to examine their own vulnerabilities, struggles, and faulty beliefs as part of the process of becoming effective helpers. These programs are based on the premise that it is as much the "wounded" parts of us as the "healthy" parts that drive us to become helpers. Students are asked to examine the ways in which their personal issues and psychological histories will be an asset or a liability in their future professional work.

Helpers who meet their own needs at the expense of their clients are depriving their clients of the quality of care to which they are entitled. One guiding principle we find useful is to remain invested in the client's *process* rather than the *outcome.* If a client is considering divorce, for example, and if our values are strongly against divorce, we help the client explore the pros and cons of either choice, but we remain neutral with respect to the client's final decision.

As helpers, it is important to remember that it is our clients—not us—who have to live with the consequences of the decisions that are made.

As you reflect on the needs we have discussed, think about how they might either enhance or interfere with your ability to help others. If you have not yet worked with clients, recall your actions in situations with friends or family members who were struggling with some problem. How did you respond to them when they were looking for the best course of action? Do your best to identify how any of these needs can become problematic if you deny them, become obsessed with them, or meet them at the expense of others.

It is unlikely that any single motive drives you; rather, needs and motivations are intertwined and can change over time. Even though your original motives and needs change, your desire to be a helper may remain unchanged. Because personal development is an ongoing process, we suggest that you periodically reexamine your motives for being a helper. It can be a valuable tool toward self-awareness and client welfare.

Our Own Beginnings as Helpers

This is a personal book in two ways. It is personal in that we encourage you to find ways to apply the book to yourself. In addition, we have written the book in a personal manner, sharing our own views and experiences whenever we think it is appropriate and useful. As a concrete illustration of how personal motives and experiences can affect career choice, we discuss some of our own motivations for becoming helping professionals and remaining in the field.

Beginning a helping career is not always easy and can involve anxiety and uncertainty. Although at this point we certainly feel more confident than when we were beginning our careers, we have not forgotten our own struggles. We, too, had to cope with many of the fears and self-doubts discussed in the previous pages. By sharing our own difficulties with you, we hope to encourage you not to give up too soon.

At this point in our professional lives, we continue to take time to reflect on both what we are giving and what we are getting through our varied work projects.

Marianne Corey's Early Experience

I was a helper long before I studied counseling in school. From childhood on I responded to the needs of my brothers and sisters. At age 8, I was made almost totally responsible for my newborn brother. I not only took care of him but also attended to other members of an extended family.

My family owned a restaurant in a German village, and I worked there at a very young age. The restaurant, which was in our home, was the meeting place for many of the local men. These men came to socialize, as well as to eat and drink. For hours they would sit and talk, and I was taught that I had better listen attentively. Furthermore, I learned that I should not repeat the personal conversations and gossip to other townspeople. At this early age I learned three very important skills: attentive listening, empathic understanding, and confidentiality. The men frequently shared their war experiences, and I saw how much healing took place for them by being able to tell their stories. I was profoundly affected by the changes I observed in these men. Even now, as a counselor, I am aware of the healing properties people experience when they reveal their painful stories to an empathic listener.

In my own life I overcame many obstacles and exceeded my dreams. As a result, I am often successful in challenging and encouraging my clients not to give up too soon when limits are imposed on them. Through my work I derive a great sense of satisfaction when I have been instrumental in the lives of individuals who are willing to take risks, to tolerate uncertainty, to dare to be different, and to live a fuller life because of their choices. When clients show appreciation for our work together, I encourage them to take credit for their hard work that resulted in the changes they value.

In my life now I find it easy to give to my friends, family, and community as well as to clients. It seems natural to me to give both personally and professionally. It continues to be a struggle for me to find a good balance between giving to others and taking care of myself. Although I am considered a good giver, I realize that I am not as good when it comes to making my needs known and asking for what I want.

It is interesting for me to compare my cultural conditioning and early role in my family with my development as a professional caregiver. Although I seemed to assume the role of caring for my brothers and sisters "naturally," I did not feel quite as natural when I began formal helping. In my first practical experiences as part of my undergraduate program in behavioral sciences, I had my share of self-doubt.

In one of my earlier internships I was placed in a college counseling center. I remember how petrified I was one day when a student came in and asked for an appointment and my supervisor asked me to counsel this client. The feedback that I received later from my supervisor on how confident I had appeared was very incongruent with what I had felt. Here are some of the thoughts that ran through my head as I was walking to my office with this client: "I'm not ready for this. What am I going to do? What if he doesn't talk? What if I don't know how to help him? I wish I could get out of this!" In my self-absorption I never once considered any of my client's feelings. For instance, how might he be approaching this session? What fears might he be having?

I was much more aware of myself than of my clients. I took far too much responsibility, put too much pressure on myself to "do it right," and worried a lot about what harm I might do. I did not allow my clients to assume their rightful share of the responsibility for making changes. I often worked much harder than they did, and sometimes it seemed that I wanted more for my clients than they wanted for themselves. I think I had a tendency to exaggerate my capacity for causing harm because of my fears and insecurities as a helper. When I shared with my supervisor my concern about feeling overwhelmingly responsible for the outcomes of our sessions and about hurting my clients, she responded, "You are assuming more power than you have over your clients." When some of my colleagues were beginning helpers, they too expressed feelings similar to the concerns and anxieties I just described. If you are a new counselor, you should probably be concerned if you do *not* feel some anxiety as you begin your work with clients.

Another time I told my supervisor that I had doubts about being in my profession, that I was overwhelmed by all the pain I saw around me, and that I was concerned that I was not helping anybody. I remember being very emotional and feeling extremely discouraged. My supervisor's smile surprised me. "I would be very concerned about you as a helper," he said, "if you never asked yourself these kinds of questions and were not willing to confront yourself with these feelings." In retrospect, I think he was telling me that he was encouraged for me because I was acknowledging my struggles and was not pretending to be the all-competent counselor who was without fears.

As a beginning counselor I was acutely aware of my own anxieties. With experience I learned to be better at being present with my clients and entering their world. Although I am not anxiety-free, I am less self-conscious as I practice therapy. Furthermore, although I take responsibility for the counseling process, I do not see myself as totally responsible for what goes on in a session, and I am usually not working harder than my clients.

At one time I wanted to abandon the idea of becoming a counselor and instead considered teaching German. I was very aware of comparing myself with professionals who had years of experience, and I thought I should be as effective as they were. I eventually realized that my expectations were extremely unrealistic: I was demanding that I immediately be as skilled as these very experienced people. I had been giving myself no room for learning and for tolerating my rudimentary beginnings.

One of my professional activities now is working with beginning helpers. I find that they are often in the same predicament I was in when I began working with others. These students seem focused on how much I know and how easy interventions seem to come to me. By contrast, they feel discouraged with their lack of knowledge and with how much they have to struggle to find "the right thing to say." They usually sigh with relief when I tell them about some of my beginnings and admit that I do not see myself as an expert but as someone who has a certain amount of expertise in counseling. I want most to convey to them that learning never stops, that beginnings are difficult and, at times, discouraging.

Jerry Corey's Early Experience

When I was in college studying to become a teacher, I hoped to create a different learning climate for students than I was experiencing as a learner. I wanted to help others, and it was important for me to make a difference. I recognize now that the need to make a significant difference has been a theme for most of my professional life. As a child and as an adolescent, I did not feel that my presence made that much difference. In many ways, during my early years, I felt that I did not fit anywhere and that I was invisible. I was surrounded by a large, extended immigrant Italian family who often spoke in their native language, which I did not understand. There was a good deal of pain attached to feeling ignored, and one of my early decisions was not to let myself be ignored. This took the form of me becoming a nuisance, which of course resulted in negative attention. In college I experienced some success and found some positive routes to being recognized. Later, when I began my teaching career, I began to see that I could make a difference, at least within the confines of my classroom. In addition to helping students enjoy learning, I also received personal satisfaction from knowing that I was a useful person, which was quite different from my perception of myself during my youth.

At the beginning of my career as a counseling psychologist, I did not feel confident, and I often wondered whether I was suited for the field. I recall the times my supervisor and I were coleaders of a group as being particularly difficult. I felt incompetent and inexperienced next to my supervisor, who was an experienced helper. Much of the time I did not know what to say or do. It seemed that there was little place for me to intervene because my coleader was so effective. I had many doubts about my ability to say anything meaningful to the members. It just seemed that my supervisor was so insightful and so skillful that I would never attain such a level of professionalism. The effect of working with an experienced group leader was to heighten my own sense of insecurity and inadequacy. In retrospect, however, I realize that this was an invaluable learning experience.

Another thing that I found difficult was practicing individual counseling in a university center. When I began as a practicing counselor, I frequently asked myself what I could do for my clients. I remember progress being very slow, and it seemed that I needed an inordinate amount of immediate and positive feedback. If a client was still talking about feeling anxious or depressed after several weeks of sessions, I immediately felt my own incompetence as a helper. I frequently found myself thinking: "How would my supervisor say this? What would he do?" I even caught myself copying his gestures, phrases, and mannerisms. Many times I felt that I did not have what it took to be an effective counselor, and I wondered if I had pursued the wrong path.

I often had no idea what, if anything, my clients were getting from our sessions. Indications of whether clients were getting better, staying the same, or getting worse were typically very subtle. What I did not know at the time was that clients need to struggle as a part of finding their own answers. My expectation was that they should feel better quickly, for then I would know that I was surely helping them. I also did not appreciate that clients often begin to feel worse as they give up their defenses and open themselves to their pain. When I saw clients expressing their fear and uncertainty about their future, it brought out my own lack of certainty that I could help them. Because I was concerned about saying "the wrong thing," I often listened but did not give too many of my own reactions in return.

Even though it is uncomfortable for me to admit this, I was more inclined to accept clients who were bright, verbal, attractive, and willing to talk about their problems than clients who seemed depressed or unmotivated to change. I encouraged those I considered to be "good and cooperative clients" to come back. As long as they were talking and working, and preferably letting me know that they were getting somewhere with our sessions, I was quick to schedule other appointments. Those clients who seemed to make very few changes escalated my own anxiety. Rather than seeing their own part in their progress or lack of it, I typically blamed myself for not knowing enough and not being able to solve their problems. I took full responsibility for what they did during the session. It never occurred to me that the fact that they did not return for another session might have said something about them and their unwillingness to change. I had limited tolerance for uncertainty and for their struggle in finding their own direction. My self-doubts grew when they did not show up for following appointments. I was sure that this was a sign that they were dissatisfied with what they were getting from me.

I particularly remember encouraging depressed clients to make an appointment with one of the other counselors on the staff. I learned in my own supervision that working with depressed clients was difficult for me because of my reluctance to deal with my own fears of depression. If I allowed myself to really enter the world of these depressed clients, I might get in touch with some of my anxiety. This experience taught me the important lesson that I could not take clients in any direction that I had not been willing to explore in my own life. Had I not challenged my fears and self-doubts, I am quite certain I would have missed out on many of the meaningful and enjoyable facets of my work.

A lesson I learned from my professional pursuits is the importance of persisting, even in the absence of external validation. Although it is difficult to persist when reinforcement from significant others is not forthcoming, I gradually began to learn to look to myself for the kind of approval I had sought from others. The work I did in my personal counseling provided meaningful insights and helped me to accept that I probably would not be as effective as I expected to be when I first began this work. The challenging and constructive feedback I received from friends and family members also helped me to accept some truths and make some significant behavioral shifts.

My hope is that you will not give up when you experience self-doubts; instead, challenge whatever might be holding you back. Sometimes you will be excited about your future as a counseling professional, and at other times you may be discouraged and wonder if it is all worth the effort. If you are willing to continue exploring your personal life, you will be in a better position to assist others as they struggle with making decisions in their life.

LO2 Is a Helping Career for You?

As is clear from our accounts, both of us had self-doubts, and the same seems to be true of many of our colleagues when we talk about our early beginnings in the helping professions. What we all have in common is our willingness to challenge our self-doubts. If you keep the question of whether you want to pursue a helping career open, you are bound to have periods of self-doubt. At times, you may feel excited about the prospects of your career choice, and at other times you may feel hopeless and discouraged. Be tolerant of these ambivalent feelings. Do not make the decision whether to pursue a helping career based on your initial experiences. Remain open to the pattern of consistent feedback you receive from faculty members, supervisors, and your peers. In some situations, you may hear that you are not suited for a particular field. Such feedback is certainly hard to accept. But if someone has concerns about your entry into a helping profession, be willing to listen and to consider what that person has to say. Your first inclination may be to decide that the person does not like you, yet the advice may be in your best interest. If you hear such a recommendation, ask for specific reasons for this evaluation and find out what alternatives the person can suggest to you.

As you read about our personal journeys and the evolution of our professional careers, we hope you have been thinking about your own personal journey and the kind of professional path you want to create for yourself. Take time to reflect on some of these questions: What major turning points have you experienced in your life? What are your aspirations at this time? What is your vision, and who has encouraged you thus far? What challenges do you face in making your vision a reality? Our hope is that you will not lose sight of your vision, even when you meet with detours along the road. Believe in yourself in spite of self-doubt, find sources of support to help you get through tough times, and work hard to achieve your career goals. If you are willing to remain open and apply the effort needed to change, you may find that your limitations can become your assets.

The inclination to give up too soon is often greatest when you first have to apply what you have learned in your courses to a situation in the real world, such as a practicum. Chances are that you will find that what worked in the lab does not work so well in real-life helping situations. In the lab you may have worked with fellow students who role-played clients who were cooperative. Now you are facing some clients who, no matter how hard you try, are not responding to you. It takes time and experience to learn how to apply your knowledge of theories and techniques to actual situations. At first your attempts at helping may seem artificial and rehearsed. You will probably be more aware of this artificiality than your clients will be. Again, allow yourself time to gain a greater sense of ease in applying what you have learned and in functioning in your role as a helper.

LO3 Portrait of the "Ideal Helper"

Imagining the characteristics of the "ideal helper" can be a useful exercise, but even the most effective helpers cannot meet all of these criteria. If you try to match the ideal picture we are about to paint, you could be needlessly setting yourself up for failure and frustration. But it is surely possible to become a more effective helper if you are aware of areas that you need to strengthen. You can improve your existing skills and acquire new ones. You can integrate knowledge that will enhance your abilities. You can make personal changes that will enable you to be more present and effective as you intervene in the lives of your clients. With these possibilities in mind, consider this picture of a helper who is making a significant difference:

- You are committed to an honest assessment of your own strengths and weaknesses. You recognize that who you are as a person is one of the most important instruments you possess as a helper.
- You recognize that the quality of the therapeutic relationship is more predictive of success than any particular theory, intervention, or technique.
- You have a basic curiosity and are open to learning. You realize what you do not know, and you are willing to take steps to fill the gaps in your knowledge.
- You have the interpersonal skills needed to establish good contact with other people, and you can apply these skills in the helping relationship.

- You genuinely care for the people you help, and this caring is expressed by doing what is in their best interest. You are able to deal with a wide range of clients' thoughts, feelings, and behaviors.
- You realize that change is typically hard work, and you are willing to stay with clients as they go through this difficult process. You are able to enter the world of your clients and see the world through their eyes rather than imposing your own vision of reality on them.
- You realize that clients often limit themselves through a restricted imagination of possibilities for their future. You are able to invite clients to dream and to take the steps necessary to fulfill their dreams. You know that you cannot inspire clients to do in their lives what you are unable or unwilling to do in your own life.
- You are willing to draw on a number of resources to enable clients to fulfill their goals. You are flexible in applying strategies for change, and you are willing to adapt your techniques to the unique situation of each client.
- In working with clients whose ethnic or cultural background is different from your own, you show your respect for them by not fitting them into a preconceived mold. You challenge the biases and assumptions that you hold about individuals from particular groups and are committed to broadening your view and learning more about different cultural perspectives. You remain respectfully curious about all the clients you meet and actively engage with those who differ from you on the basis of race, ethnicity, gender, sexual orientation, ability/disability, socioeconomic status, and religious background.
- You are willing to speak up about the inequities that exist in society that have a negative impact on your clients. You embrace your obligation as a social justice advocate to fight for the needs of those who are marginalized and oppressed and to empower them.
- You take care of yourself physically, mentally, psychologically, socially, and spiritually. You do in your own life what you ask of your clients. As you encounter problems in your own life, you view them as opportunities for growth and actively face your challenges in a courageous manner.
- You realize that personal growth is a lifelong journey, and you are committed to engaging in the self-reflection necessary to make changes in your personal life.
- You question life and engage in critical self-examination of your beliefs and values. You are aware of your needs and motivations, and you make choices that are congruent with your life goals. Your philosophy of life is your own creation, not one that has been imposed on you.
- You have established meaningful relationships with at least a few significant people.
- Although you have a healthy sense of self-love and pride, you are not self-absorbed, nor are you arrogant.

Our intent in presenting this list is not to overwhelm you but to provide you with some characteristics that are worthy of reflection. You might be telling yourself that you lack many of these characteristics. An unskilled helper can become a skilled one, and all of us can become more effective in touching the lives of the clients we encounter. In addressing the question "Are the helping professions for me?" you are encouraged to use this book as a catalyst for honest self-reflection.

We also strongly encourage you to question and interview people in the helping professions from a variety of settings to assist you in exploring the possibilities of a future as a helper. Ask about their journey into their chosen profession and the struggles they encountered along the way.

Many training programs offer some self-exploration experiences in which students can become more aware of how their personal attributes manifest themselves in relationships. Practicum and internship seminars typically provide opportunities for you to focus on ways in which your personal style influences your ability to establish helping relationships with clients. If your program does not offer formal personal-growth experiences, seek these resources in the community. Much of the rest of this book deals with the interplay between you as a person and your work as a professional helper. Our underlying assumption is that the best way to prepare for a dynamic career is to appreciate the richness of your own being and to be able to use your own life experiences in your evolution in the helping professions.

Investing in Your Educational Program

At the beginning of your educational program, you may feel that you will have to remain in school forever to do what you want professionally. However, if you are enjoying and gaining from the experience, you will likely be surprised at how soon you complete your program. The key is to be personally involved in your educational program and to see a connection between your formal studies and your personal and professional goals. Think about how much time and energy you are prepared to devote to making your education meaningful. It may help to consider your education as an investment, and then decide what you can do to get the most from this investment. Most of all, find ways to enjoy the process.

Investments are often evaluated by their cost-benefit ratio. The cost of your educational investment includes not just money but your time and energy as well. Look at the potential benefits of this investment, including what you hope to gain. Ask yourself if what you are putting in (costs) is worth what you hope to get out of it in return (benefits). What are the benefits of putting a great deal of yourself into your formal studies? What will taking responsibility for your education cost you in terms of time taken away from other facets of your life?

Learning to Cope With the System

You will encounter external and internal barriers to achieving your goals and maximizing your potential as learners and professional helpers. We have found that students, as well as professionals, often underestimate the ways in which they do have power. For example, we know of a student who was responsible for changing several unfair practices within her academic institution merely by raising her concerns and bringing them to the attention of the faculty and administrators. Many systems impose limitations, and you will be challenged to learn how to work creatively within them without sacrificing your integrity. People often are so busy that they fail to question the practices and procedures within the systems in which they work. It can be empowering to question and strive to change these institutions and systems.

You will undoubtedly face a number of challenges in your educational program, a few of which involve grades, requirements, courses, and evaluation.

You may feel anxious about being evaluated and think that grades are not an accurate measure of your learning. It is a mistake to assume that grading stops when you graduate from a university. There are reviews and evaluation practices on all levels in the professional world. In a business, for example, your supervisors rate you and determine whether you get a promotion or a raise. If you are a professional, both your clients and your place of work will evaluate your performance.

Students sometimes assume that there are worlds of difference between the roles they play in college and the roles they will assume as professionals. Many of the traits that you have as a student will most likely carry over into your behavior as a worker. If you have great difficulty in showing up for classes regularly, for example, you are likely to carry this habit into your work appointments. Getting a position in a community agency is a highly competitive effort. If you hope to gain entry into the professional world, it is essential that you be prepared to cope with the realities of the marketplace.

We ask our students to think about their time in school as a long job interview. The connections you make in school and the reputation you build for yourself are critical in gaining access to future jobs and professional opportunities. How you performed as a learner will undoubtedly influence how strongly your professors state their degree of support or their recommendation for opportunities you may pursue in your professional life.

LO4 Selecting a Professional Program and Career Path

In this section we introduce you to a range of considerations in selecting your educational program and your career in the helping professions. We encourage you to think about how the following topics apply to you: the rewards of being a helper, creating realistic expectations and testing them, and deciding which educational and professional route to pursue.

The Joys and Rewards of Being a Helping Professional

Your involvement in working intimately in the lives of others can yield many benefits and gifts to you personally. In very few other kinds of work do you have as many opportunities to reflect on the quality of your own life. Helping others can provide you with the satisfaction of knowing that you are making a significant difference to others, which in itself enhances the meaning of life.

Create Realistic Expectations

Students planning to enter one of the helping professions sometimes create an unrealistic picture of the profession. In their minds, they may envision themselves as being able to help anyone who comes to them. Although having ideals and goals to strive for is part of being a helper, it is easy to paint an unrealistic picture of what your career as a helper will be like. You need to engage in ongoing reality testing to maintain a balanced outlook. You can test your vision by talking to various practitioners in many different settings. Ask them to tell you what they do in a typical week. Inquire about their motivations for choosing and remaining in the helping professions. Ask especially about the rewards, joys, challenges, demands, and frustrations of their work.

When you begin fieldwork, you will be able to test many of your ideas and expectations against the real world of work. This is a good time to again reflect on your motives and needs for considering helping as a career. Observations in various field settings and practical experience working with different client populations will provide a more accurate picture of how your career is likely to satisfy your needs for becoming a helper in the first place. If you find yourself in a program that you really do not like, consider whether it is worth it for you to stay in the program. Be sure you evaluate the overall direction of the program rather than a specific course or requirement that you do not like.

Deciding Which Educational and Professional Route to Take

At this point, you may not even be certain you want to pursue a career in the helping professions. If you are enrolled in a 2-year community college program in human services, you may be wondering whether it would be best for you to get a job to gain experience once you have completed your program and to return to school later for further study. A wide range of human services jobs is available, including social service assistants, outreach workers in the community, work with parolees or in prison settings, work with the physically challenged, addictions counseling, and a host of positions in community agency settings.

It is generally true that the higher your educational level the more career options you have. Human services programs at the bachelor's degree level train students for entry into a wide range of jobs, some of which include family and children's services, youth corrections, crisis shelters, career counseling, youth programs, residential treatment centers, mental health units, senior citizens centers, nursing homes, and agencies for people with disabilities.

If you are enrolled in a master's program in counseling, social work, or psychology, you are probably thinking of what you need to do to obtain your master's degree. Many of you will want to accrue the supervised hours of internship experience required for your goal of becoming a licensed professional counselor, a licensed marriage and family therapist, or a licensed clinical social worker. You may be wondering whether to pursue a doctoral program now or add that to your long-range plans. There are many paths open to you, and you will need to choose the career path that best suits you.

Whether you are an undergraduate or a graduate student, you probably have had some concerns about selecting the right program. We encourage students to be open to new ideas, especially when participating in fieldwork placements. There are no absolute guidelines or perfect choices, and you do not need to have a specific career goal in mind when you enter a program. Gather program material from several universities and talk with professors and students. Talking with professionals about their work experience can also broaden your perspective. Ask about the specific educational and practical background that they most value. In selecting a program, ask yourself these questions: "Will the program give me what I need to do the work I want to do? Does the orientation of the program fit with my values? Am I compatible with the program?"

You can take many routes as a helper in human services: social worker, psychiatric technician, couples and family therapist, mental health counselor, psychologist, or school counselor. Each of these professional specialties has a different focus, yet all have in common working with people. Much depends on what you want to do, how much time you are able to invest in a program, where you want to live, and what your other interests are.

At the undergraduate level, human services programs train practitioners for community agency work. Human service professionals generally carry out specific roles and functions under the supervision of clinical social workers, psychologists, and licensed counselors. At the master's degree level, students can choose among various types of programs, some of which include school counseling, mental health counseling, addiction counseling, rehabilitation counseling, counseling psychology, clinical psychology, couples and family therapy, and clinical social work. Each specialization has its own perspective and emphasizes different roles and functions for practitioners.

Regardless of which of the helping professions interests you the most, you are likely to discover many different positions within an area of specialization. Do not become overly anxious about making the "right decision" or delay making any choice because you cannot decide which career or program to pursue. View your professional life as a developmental process, and explore new possibilities as you gain additional work experience.

LO5 Overview of Some of the Helping Professions

As you read about the various specialty areas of practice described in this section, think about the characteristics that fit best with your own expectations. Each specialty has much to recommend it, but you probably will find yourself drawn more to one than to the others. The professional organization for each specialty is described, and we have provided contact information for these organizations to facilitate further inquiries about membership, conferences, and the code of ethics of the organization.

Social Work

This specialization attends not only to the inner workings of a person but also to an understanding of the person in the environment. A master's program in **social work** (MSW) prepares students broadly for casework, counseling, community intervention, social policy and planning, research and development, and administration and management. The coursework tends to be broader than that in counseling and focuses on developing skills to intervene and bring about social change on levels beyond the individual. Although clinical social workers are engaged in assessment and treatment of individuals, couples, families, and groups, they tend to view environmental factors as contributing strongly to an individual's or a family's problems. In addition to academic courses, a supervised internship is part of the social worker's preparation for either direct or indirect social services.

National Association of Social Workers (NASW). NASW membership is open to all professional social workers, and there is a student membership category.

The NASW Press, which produces *Social Work* and the *NASW News* as membership benefits, is a major service in professional development. NASW also provides a number of pamphlets on relevant topics. Further information about NASW can be found on their website: www.socialworkers.org.

Couples and Family Counseling

The specialization of **couples and family therapy** is primarily concerned with relationship counseling. It deals with assessing and treating clients from a family-systems perspective. Students in a master's or a doctoral program in couples and family therapy take a variety of courses in assessment and treatment, as well as theory courses. They also do extensive supervised fieldwork with children and adults, couples, and families. Many master's degree programs in counseling offer a specialization in relationship counseling or couples and family therapy. Components of the training program include the study of systems theory, an examination of family of origin, and an emphasis on ethical and professional issues specific to working with couples and families. Most states have licensure for marriage and family therapists. To become a licensed marriage and family therapist, minimal requirements include a master's degree along with a number of internships hours and passing an examination. Those who pursue a degree with a specialization in couples and family therapy need to make a paradigm shift from an individual context to a systemic way of thinking.

American Association for Marriage and Family Therapy (AAMFT). The AAMFT has a student membership category. The organization sponsors a conference each year. For membership applications or for further information, refer to their website: www.aamft.org.

International Association of Marriage and Family Counselors (IAMFC). IAMFC members have the opportunity to have online discussions and to network with others who have similar research interests. Topics of interest include blended families; counseling offenders; separation and divorce counseling; substance abuse; mediation; MFT training; gay, lesbian, bisexual, and transgender issues; military families; sexual offenders; systemic interventions in mental illness; survivors of sexual abuse; family interventions in schools; multicultural counseling; and families and violence. For further information, refer to their website: www.iamfc.org.

Clinical and Counseling Psychology

Although clinical and counseling psychology are different specializations, there are no rigid boundaries separating their professional functions so we discuss them together. Although you can be licensed as a social worker, counselor, and couples and family therapist with a master's degree, this is not the case if you wish to refer to yourself as a psychologist. Both counseling and clinical psychology require a doctorate for licensure. **Clinical psychologists** focus on assessment, diagnosis, and treatment procedures of mildly to severely disturbed people. They interview clients and write case studies. **Counseling psychologists** assist relatively healthy people in solving developmental problems and functioning more effectively. They help clients find and use information to make better personal, educational, and occupational choices. Professional psychologists in both specialties often offer psychotherapy to individuals, couples, families, and groups; they may teach or conduct research. Both specializations focus on evaluation of treatments and programs and help clients develop action plans. Clinical and counseling psychologists often work in the same settings.

American Psychological Association (APA). The APA is the largest scientific and professional organization representing psychology in the United States and has a Student Affiliates category rather than student membership. Each year in August the APA holds a national convention. For further information, refer to their website: www.apa.org.

American Counseling Association (ACA). The ACA has created state branches, regional leadership units, and chartered 19 specialty divisions. For nearly 70 years, ACA has maintained a *Code of Ethics* for professional counselors that is recognized by licensure boards and courts of law across the United States. In addition, the ACA has advocated in the public policy arena at the state and federal level on behalf of the counseling professional, students, and clients served by professional counselors. Student memberships are available to both undergraduate and graduate students enrolled at least half-time or more at the college level. The organization sponsors a national convention each year and also offers webinars. The ACA resource catalog provides information on various aspects of the counseling profession as well as detailed information about membership, journals, books, home-study programs, video and DVD programs, and liability insurance. For further information, refer to their website: www.counseling.org.

Licensed Professional Counselor

The main licenses available in most states include licensed professional counselor, licensed mental health counselor, licensed clinical social worker, licensed psychologist, and licensed marital and family therapist. To qualify for a license, an applicant generally must first secure a graduate degree (or level determined by the licensing board) in the professional area of specialization. Beyond the degree, a minimum number of hours of supervised clinical work is required, and the applicant must pass both a written and sometimes an oral examination.

Licensure statutes determine and govern professional practice, specifying what the holder of the license can do. A person with a professional license is assumed to have minimal competence in the general practice of clinical work. A state license in counseling is permission from a particular state to practice as a counselor and to call oneself a licensed counselor. The names of state licenses for counselors vary from state to state. Some examples are Licensed Professional Counselor (LPC), Licensed Professional Clinical Counselor (LPCC), Licensed Mental Health Counselor (LMHC), and Licensed Clinical Professional Counselor (LCPC). It is important to become familiar with the coursework and supervision requirements for licensure in the state in which you intend to practice, as these requirements vary from state to state.

Licensure assures the public that practitioners have completed minimum educational programs, have had a certain number of hours of supervised training, and have gone through some type of evaluation and screening. Licenses do not, and probably cannot, ensure that practitioners will competently do what their licenses permit them to do. The main advantages of licensure are protection of the public from grossly unqualified and untrained practitioners and formal representation to the public that practitioners are part of an established profession.

American Mental Health Counselors Association (AMHCA). The AMHCA is a growing community of approximately 6,200 clinical mental health counselors. Their mission is to enhance the profession of clinical mental health counseling through licensing, advocacy, education, and professional development. AMHCA strives to be the national organization representing licensed clinical mental health counselors and state chapters, with consistent standards of education, training, practice, advocacy, and ethics. Recognized as a national division of the ACA until 2019, the AMHCA is now an independent organization. The ACA achieved passage of state licensure in all 50 U.S. states and its territories in 2019, and it continues to work collaboratively with the AMHCA on issues of common concern. For further information, refer to AMHCA's website: www.amhca.org.

School Counseling

Accreditation guidelines for school counseling have been implemented over the past 20 years, which has moved school counseling forward in terms of accountability as a helping profession. All states now require a master's degree in school counseling, and professional organizations advocate and lobby for legislative initiatives and the establishment of credentialing.

School counselors perform a wide variety of roles and functions in elementary, middle, and secondary schools, including individual counseling, group guidance, group counseling, consultation, advocacy, and coordination. In addition to working with students, many school counselors consult with teachers, administrators, and, at times, with parents. School counselors work with students on a variety of educational issues, including personal and social counseling. From a multicultural perspective, school counselors have the challenge of advocating for all students, sensitizing the school community to cultural diversity issues, and establishing a comprehensive developmental counseling program.

American School Counselors Association (ASCA). The ASCA is the major professional organization devoted to school counseling. The ASCA has a code of ethics and a student membership category. For additional information, refer to their website: www.schoolcounselor.org.

Rehabilitation Counseling

Rehabilitation counseling focuses on person-centered programs and services for people with medical, physical, mental, developmental, cognitive, and psychiatric disabilities to help them achieve their personal, career, and independent living goals in the most integrated setting possible. The profession itself is founded on humanistic values and the belief that each person has unique cultural attributes. Rehabilitation counseling is a holistic and integrated program of medical, physical, psychosocial, and vocational interventions (Commission on Rehabilitation Counselor Certification [CRCC], 2014). Rehabilitation counselors use career, vocational, mental health, case management, and counseling strategies to empower people with chronic illnesses or disabilities to achieve their maximum level of independence and psychosocial adjustment through personally fulfilling, socially meaningful, and functionally effective interaction with their environment. For additional information on the rehabilitation counseling profession, refer to their website: www.crcertification.com.

Drug and Alcohol Counseling

Addiction is one of the main public health issues in the United States today. Substance abuse counselors are actively involved in education, prevention, intervention, and treatment for various addictions. Practitioners in the field provide treatment in a variety of settings: private and public treatment centers, residential treatment facilities, hospitals, private practice, and community agencies.

National Association of Alcohol and Drug Abuse Counselors (NAADAC). NAADAC is the major national professional organization devoted to ethical standards for addiction professionals. NAADAC's mission is to lead, unify, and empower addiction-focused professionals to achieve excellence through education, advocacy, knowledge, standards of practice, ethics, professional development, and research. For additional information, refer to their website: www.naadac.org.

Human Service Professionals

Many people are in need of support and psychological assistance other than, or in addition to, counseling and psychotherapy. These clients, sometimes called **consumers**, are often helped by people with an undergraduate or graduate degree in psychology, sociology, or a related field. More recently, many of these helpers have an associate, bachelor's, master's, or doctoral degree in **human services** (Neukrug, 2016a). Although not licensed therapists, **human service practitioners** assist in the difficult work with clients who may be struggling with mental health issues and are in need of assistance with daily living skills. Sometimes these practitioners are supervised by licensed counselors, social workers, or psychologists.

Human service professionals (which include educators, students, and human service practitioners) are generalists with broad training that encompasses skills from counseling, psychology, and social work (Woodside & McClam, 2019). They hold a variety of jobs, including case worker, case manager, community organizer, community planner, community outreach worker, crisis counselor, parole officer, advocate, mental health aide, substance abuse counselor, social work assistant, alcohol or drug abuse counselor, mental health technician, child care worker, and residential assistant, to name just a few (Moffat, 2011). Their focus is on support and basic psychological aid rather than in-depth counseling and psychotherapy. Some social service agencies have discovered that human service practitioners provide services as well as, or more effectively than, highly trained licensed professionals for these clients. Only a limited number of licensed professionals are available to work with the vast number of individuals seeking mental health and daily living skills assistance, and human service practitioners are bridging this gap in the social service field.

National Organization for Human Services (NOHS). The National Organization for Human Services is made up of members from diverse educational and professional backgrounds with the mission of fostering excellence in human services delivery through education, scholarship, and practice. Regular membership is open to educators and practitioners, and student memberships are available. NOHS schedules a conference each year. For further information, refer to their website: www.nationalhumanservices.org.

Values to Consider in Choosing Your Career Path

People generally go through a series of stages when choosing a career path. Information from practitioners and professors can help you define a professional direction. But you cannot rely solely on the advice of others when making your career decisions. In today's world, it is increasingly important to become a generalist. Your chances of gaining employment in a managed care system are greater if you are able to work with a range of client populations in a variety of problem areas. Although you may develop expertise in an area of specialization, flexibility is often necessary to meet the changing demands in the marketplace.

Ultimately you must decide for yourself which path is likely to best tap your talents and bring you the most fulfillment. In your career decision-making process, consider your self-concept, motivation and achievement, interests, abilities, values, occupational attitudes, socioeconomic level, parental influence, ethnic identity, gender, and any physical, mental, emotional, or social disabilities. Your values will affect your choice of a career path, and it is important to assess, identify, and clarify your values to match them with your career aspirations.

Your **work values** pertain to what you hope to accomplish in an occupation. Work values are an important aspect of your total value system. Recognizing those things that bring meaning to your life is crucial in finding a career that has personal value for you. A few examples of work values include helping others, influencing people, finding meaning, prestige, status, competition, friendships, creativity, stability, recognition, adventure, physical challenge, change and variety, opportunity for travel, moral fulfillment, and independence. Because certain work values are related to certain occupations, they can be the basis of a good match between you and a position.

To clarify some of these work values, ask yourself these questions:

- Do I like working with a wide range of people?
- Am I able to ask for help from others when I am faced with problematic situations?
- Do I value doing in my own life what I encourage others to do in theirs?
- How do I feel about offering help to others with their problems?
- Am I interested in organizing, coordinating, and leading others in work projects?
- Do I value working on projects I have designed, or do I tend to look to others to come up with ideas for projects with which I can become involved?

Your values and interests are intertwined; knowing them can help you identify areas of work where you will find the most personal satisfaction.

Suggestions for Creating Your Professional Journey

In *Journeys to Professional Excellence*, Bemak and Conyne (2018) introduce 12 leaders in the fields of psychology and counseling who share their personal and professional journeys. They talk about how they chose their career paths, what challenges they have faced, what factors contributed to their successes and failures, how they balance their personal and professional lives, and what advice they have for those entering the helping professions. We highly recommend this book as you think about the kind of professional journey you would like to create.

Here are some ideas for you to consider as a way to actively create your personal and professional journey:

- Look for opportunities to challenge your perceptions of your limitations and focus on what you can do.
- Ask for help when you need it, both personally and professionally.
- Find a group of people who are supportive and can offer you encouragement.
- Seek out at least one mentor and form networks with others in the helping professions.
- Seek supervision and be open to feedback and learning regardless of the stage of your career.
- Remain connected to those people who mean the most to you in your life. Take time for your family and close friends.
- Strive to integrate your personal and professional journeys. Commit to taking care of yourself in all ways. If you hope to care for others, you need to take care of yourself.
- Learn about people from cultures different from your own and strive to acquire cultural competencies.
- Be your genuine self. Learn from others and integrate that into who you are.
- Listen to your intuitive voice and create your own path.
- Value your mistakes along the way as they provide opportunities for growth and change.
- Establish both long-term and short-term goals.
- Recognize that obstacles, disappointments, and failures can teach you valuable lessons.
- Maintain a sense of humor.
- Realize that you can make a significant difference. Become an agent of individual and social change.
- Work hard and set high standards for yourself.
- Join a professional organization and attend conferences.
- Read, discuss, reflect, and keep a personal journal.
- Develop interests outside of the counseling field.
- Identify your sphere of influence, and act when you have the power to do so.
- Identify your strengths and seek out self-exploration and therapeutic experiences.
- Dare to dream and have the courage to pursue your passions.

At times in your training, you may feel discouraged, and it may be difficult to focus on what is really important. Review this list, and use it as a way to regain your momentum. Reflect on the points that most speak to you. What kind of future do you want for yourself, both personally and professionally? Begin taking action now on your journey toward the future.

LO6 Self-Assessment: An Inventory of Your Attitudes and Beliefs About Helping

Self-assessment is an ongoing process for all helping professionals. Completing this inventory will help you clarify your beliefs and values. The inventory is designed to introduce you to issues and topics presented in this book and to stimulate your thoughts and interest. You may want to complete the inventory in more than one sitting, giving each question your full concentration.

This is not a traditional multiple-choice test in which you must select the "one right answer." Rather, it is a survey of your basic beliefs, attitudes, and values on specific topics related to the helping process. For each question, write in the letter of the response that most clearly reflects your viewpoint at this time. In many cases the answers are not mutually exclusive, and you may choose more than one response if you wish. In addition, a blank line is included for each item so you can provide a response more suited to your thinking or qualify a chosen response.

Notice that there are two spaces before each item. Use the space on the left for your answer at the beginning of the course. At the end of the course, take this inventory again, placing your answer in the space on the right. Cover your initial answers so you won't be influenced by how you originally responded. Then you can see how your attitudes have changed as a result of your experience in this course.

____ ____ 1. **Effective helpers.** The personal characteristics of helpers are
a. not really that relevant to the helping process.
b. the most important variable in determining the quality of the helping process.
c. shaped and molded by those who teach mental health workers.
d. not as important as the skills and knowledge helpers possess.
e. ________________________________

____ ____ 2. **Personal traits.** Which of the following do you consider to be the most important personal characteristic of a good helper?
a. Willingness to serve as a model for clients
b. Courage
c. Openness and honesty
d. A sense of being "centered" as a person
e. ________________________________

____ ____ 3. **Self-disclosure.** I believe helpers' self-disclosure to their clients
a. is essential for establishing a relationship.
b. is inappropriate and merely burdens the client.
c. should be done rarely and only when helpers feel it would be of benefit to clients.
d. is useful to reveal how helpers feel toward their clients in the context of the professional relationship.
e. ________________________________

____ ____ **4. Fees.** If I were working with a client who could no longer continue because of his or her inability to pay my fees, I would most likely
a. be willing to see this person at no fee, but in return expect him or her to do some type of volunteer work in the community.
b. give my client the names of several referrals.
c. suggest some form of bartering of goods or services for therapy services.
d. adjust my fee to whatever the client could afford.
e. ______________________

____ ____ **5. Change.** Which of the following factors is most important in determining whether the helping process will result in change?
a. The kind of person the helper is
b. The skills and techniques the helper uses
c. The motivation of the client to change
d. The theoretical orientation of the helper
e. ______________________

____ ____ **6. Key attribute of effective helpers.** Which of the following do you consider to be the most important attribute of an effective mental health practitioner?
a. Knowledge of the theory of counseling and behavior
b. Skill in using techniques appropriately
c. Genuineness and openness
d. Ability to specify a treatment plan and evaluate the results
e. ______________________

____ ____ **7. Fieldwork.** With respect to a fieldwork placement,
a. I do not feel at all ready to participate in fieldwork.
b. I would treat it like a job.
c. I expect to limit myself to working with the kind of clients that I think I want to eventually work with in a job position.
d. I want to work with clients that I think would be a challenge for me.
e. ______________________

____ ____ **8. Effectiveness as helper.** To be an effective helper, I believe I
a. must have an in-depth knowledge of my client's cultural background.
b. must be free of any personal conflicts in the area in which the client is working.
c. need to have experienced the same problem as the client.
d. must be aware of my own needs and motivations for wanting to enter the helping field.
e. ______________________

____ ____ **9. Helping relationship.** With regard to the client–helper relationship, I think
a. the helper should remain objective and anonymous.
b. the helper should be a friend to the client.
c. a personal relationship, but not friendship, is essential.
d. a personal and warm relationship is not essential.
e. ______________________

____ ____ 10. **Being open and honest with clients.** I should be open and honest with my clients
a. when I like and value them.
b. when I have negative feelings toward them.
c. rarely, if ever, so that I will avoid negatively influencing the client–helper relationship.
d. only when it intuitively feels like the right thing to do.
e. ________________________________

____ ____ 11. **Ethical decision making.** If I were faced with an ethical dilemma, the first step I would take would be to
a. talk to my supervisor or seek consultation.
b. attempt to solve the problem myself.
c. identify the nature of the problem or problems.
d. talk to my client and strive to involve him or her in working through this dilemma.
e. ________________________________

____ ____ 12. **Dealing with inadequate supervision.** If I were not getting the kind of supervision I thought I needed and want, my inclination would be to
a. make the best of the situation and not cause any trouble.
b. demand that my supervisor provide adequate supervision.
c. learn assertiveness skills and consistently ask for what I need by way of supervision.
d. suggest that my peers and I form our own peer-supervision group to talk about the concerns we are facing.
e. ________________________________

____ ____ 13. **Competence.** If I were an intern and was convinced that my supervisor was encouraging trainees to take on clients with problems beyond their level of education and competence, I would
a. first discuss the matter with the supervisor.
b. ask my supervisor to give me extra help and perhaps work with me directly.
c. ignore the situation for fear of negative consequences.
d. refuse to engage in delivering any services that I thought were beyond my level of competence.
e. ________________________________

____ ____ 14. **Cultural competence.** Practitioners who work with culturally diverse groups without having multicultural knowledge and skills
a. are certainly not going to be able to provide effective services.
b. are probably guilty of unethical behavior.
c. will need to acquire the knowledge and skills by taking a course, reading, or engaging in continuing education.
d. are making themselves vulnerable to a malpractice suit.
e. ________________________________

____ ____ **15. Dealing with difficult clients.** If I were working with a difficult and resistant client, my approach would likely be to
a. discuss my reactions to my client's behavior with him or her.
b. keep my reactions to myself and figure ways that I might get the upper hand with my client.
c. discuss strategies for reaching difficult clients with a supervisor or colleague.
d. strive to honor and respect the resistances my client displays and encourage my client to explore his or her attitudes and behaviors.
e. ______________________________

____ ____ **16. Being ready.** I won't feel ready to offer professional help to others until
a. I have completed the program I am now in.
b. I have developed a specialization that will make me an expert in a particular area.
c. I feel very confident and know that I will be effective.
d. I have become a self-aware person and developed the ability to continually reexamine my own life and relationships.
e. ______________________________

____ ____ **17. Managing attractions.** If a client evidenced strong feelings of attraction or dislike for me, I think I would
a. immediately want to discuss this matter in my supervision.
b. not have a clue as to how to respond.
c. quickly refer my client to another professional.
d. engage in self-disclosure, letting my client know how I was affected by what he or she said to me.
e. ______________________________

____ ____ **18. Diversity.** Practitioners who counsel clients whose sex, race, age, social class, or sexual orientation is different from their own
a. will constantly be tested by these clients, which will make trust almost impossible.
b. need to understand the meaning of the differences between their clients and themselves.
c. are likely to be very effective if they are willing to acquire a range of knowledge and skills that will enable them to become culturally competent helpers.
d. are probably not going to be effective with such clients because of these differences.
e. ______________________________

____ ____ **19. Value priorities.** When I consider being involved in the helping professions, I value most the
a. money I expect to earn.
b. status and recognition that will be associated with the job.
c. knowledge that I will be intimately involved with people who are searching for a better life.
d. opportunity to give back to the community.
e. ______________________________

____ ____ **20. Value judgments.** With respect to making value judgments in the helping relationship, I believe helpers should

a. feel free to make value judgments about their clients' behavior.
b. actively teach their own values when they think clients need a different set of values.
c. remain neutral and keep their values out of the helping process.
d. encourage clients to question their own values and decide on the quality of their own behavior.
e. ______________________________

____ ____ **21. Helper key tasks.** Helpers should

a. teach desirable behavior and values by modeling them for clients.
b. encourage clients to look within themselves to discover values that are meaningful to them.
c. reinforce the dominant values of society.
d. very delicately, if at all, challenge clients' value systems.
e. ______________________________

____ ____ **22. Making referrals.** I would refer a client to another professional if

a. I were convinced that I was no longer able to be effective with this client for any reason.
b. I didn't have much experience working with the kind of problem the client presented.
c. any sort of conflict of values existed between my client and me.
d. the client seemed resistant and was not willing to be open to my suggestions.
e. ______________________________

____ ____ **23. Confidentiality.** Regarding confidentiality, I believe

a. there is little hope that trust will be established unless clients can be guaranteed absolute confidentiality.
b. it is ethical to break confidence when there is reason to believe that a client will do harm to someone else or will harm him- or herself.
c. it is essential for me to discuss in detail the purpose and limits of confidentiality at the first session with a client.
d. it is ethical to inform the authorities when a client is breaking the law.
e. ______________________________

____ ____ **24. Sex with former clients.** A sexual relationship between a *former* client and a therapist is

a. ethical if the therapist can prove that the relationship will not harm the former client.
b. considered ethical 5 years after the termination of the professional relationship.
c. ethical only when client and therapist discuss the issue and agree to the relationship.
d. never ethical, regardless of the time that has elapsed.
e. ______________________________

____ ____ 25. **Accepting gifts.** If a client were to offer me a gift, I would
a. possibly accept it, but only after fully discussing the matter with my client.
b. never accept it under any circumstances.
c. accept the gift only if this was the termination of our professional relationship.
d. accept the gift if gift-giving were a part of the client's culture and if refusing the gift would be insulting to my client.
e. ______________________________

____ ____ 26. **Spiritual and religious values.** With respect to the role of spiritual and religious values in the helping process, I would be inclined to
a. do my best to keep my own values out of the professional relationship for fear that I would unduly influence my client.
b. recommend to my client that he or she think about how spirituality or religion could bring new meaning to his or her life.
c. avoid introducing such topics in a session unless my client initiated this discussion.
d. routinely conduct an assessment of my client's spiritual and religious beliefs during the intake session.
e. ______________________________

____ ____ 27. **Goals of helping.** Regarding the issue of who should select goals in the helping process, I believe
a. it is the helper's responsibility to select goals.
b. it is the client's responsibility to select goals.
c. the responsibility for selecting goals should be a collaborative venture by both client and helper.
d. the question of who selects the goals depends on what kind of client is being seen.
e. ______________________________

____ ____ 28. **Social justice counseling.** Counseling from a social justice perspective involves addressing the realities of oppression, privilege, and social inequities. This implies
a. being aware of sociopolitical forces that have influenced my clients.
b. teaching my clients how to become advocates for themselves.
c. assisting people in gaining full participation in society.
d. assuming an advocate role if I am to make a difference.
e. ______________________________

____ ____ 29. **Advocacy competence.** To become a competent client advocate, a helper must
a. be aware of his or her own beliefs, attitudes, and biases as they relate to social and political factors influencing marginalized and underserved populations.
b. have the courage to speak out against injustices.
c. engage in considerable reflection before taking action.
d. assess whether to engage in social advocacy action.
e. ______________________________

____ ____ 30. **Internet counseling.** Regarding the practice of counseling via the Internet, I believe
a. the practice is fraught with ethical and legal problems.
b. this is a form of technology with real promise for many clients who would not, or could not, seek out face-to-face counseling.
c. it is limited to dealing with simple problems because of the inability to make an adequate assessment.
d. will eventually replace traditional face-to-face counseling.
e. ________________________________

____ ____ 31. **Unethical behavior.** I consider the most unethical form of therapist behavior to be
a. abandoning a client.
b. becoming sexually involved with a client.
c. imposing my values on a client.
d. accepting a client who has a problem that goes beyond my competence.
e. ________________________________

____ ____ 32. **Bartering.** I believe bartering with a client in exchange for therapy services
a. depends on the circumstances of the individual case.
b. should be considered if the client has no way to pay for my services.
c. is almost always a poor idea.
d. should not be undertaken without prior consultation to explore the possible harm to the client.
e. ________________________________

____ ____ 33. **Responsibility to the community.** Concerning the helper's responsibility to the community, I believe
a. the helper should educate the community concerning the nature of psychological services.
b. the central role of a helper is that of a change agent.
c. it is appropriate to function as an advocate for underrepresented groups in the community.
d. helpers should become involved in helping clients use the resources available in the community.
e. ________________________________

____ ____ 34. **Working in systems.** When it comes to working in institutions or a system, I believe
a. I must learn how to survive with dignity within a system.
b. I must learn how to subvert the system so that I can do what I deeply believe in.
c. the institution will stifle most of my enthusiasm and block any real change.
d. I cannot blame the institution if I am unable to succeed in my programs.
e. ________________________________

____ ____ **35. Philosophical conflicts.** If my philosophy were in conflict with that of the institution I worked for, I would

a. seriously consider whether I could ethically remain in that position.

b. attempt to change the policies of the institution by any means possible.

c. agree to whatever was expected of me in that system so that I would not lose my job.

d. quietly do what I wanted to do, even if I had to be devious about it.

e. ______________________________

By Way of Review

Near the end of each chapter we list some of the chapter's highlights. These key points serve as a review of the messages we have attempted to get across. After you finish each chapter, we encourage you to spend a few minutes writing down the central issues and points that have the most meaning for you.

- Become active in getting the most from your education. No program is perfect, but you can do a lot to bring more meaning to your course of study.
- Just as you are evaluated and graded in your educational program, you will be evaluated in the professional world. Evaluation can create stress, but it is part of your educational program and your future career.
- Remain open to the question of whether a career in one of the helping professions is right for you. In deciding whether to pursue one of the helping professions, do not give up too soon. Be prepared for doubts and setbacks.
- Although the "ideal helper" does not exist in reality, a number of behaviors and attitudes characterize effective helpers. Even though you might not reach the ideal, you can strive to reach your own goal.
- It is essential that helpers examine their motivations for going into the field. Helpers meet their own needs through their work, and they must recognize these needs. It is possible for both client and helper to benefit from the helping relationship.
- Some of the needs for going into the helping professions include the need to be needed, the need for prestige and status, and the need to make a difference. These needs can work both for you and against you in becoming an effective helper.
- In selecting an educational program, follow your interests. Be willing to experiment by taking classes and by getting experience as a volunteer worker.
- Investigate various specialty areas in the helping professions before committing to a particular path. Visit the websites of the professional organizations or associations of each of these specializations to clarify your thinking about your career direction.
- Be willing to seek information about careers in mental health from others, such as professionals in the field and faculty members, but realize that ultimately you will decide which career path is best for you.

- Do not consider the selection of a career as a one-time event. Instead, allow yourself to entertain many job possibilities over your lifetime.
- Realize that you must have a beginning to your career. Be patient, and allow yourself time to feel comfortable in the role of helper. You don't have to be the perfect person or the perfect helper. Be mindful of the fact that developing competence as a helper is an ongoing process that takes many years of supervised practice and introspection.
- Your career as a professional helper can be highly beneficial to you personally. In very few other kinds of work do you have as many opportunities to reflect on the quality of your own life and have opportunities to make a significant difference in the lives of others.

What Will You Do Now?

After each chapter review, we provide concrete suggestions you can put into action. These suggested activities grow out of the major points developed in the chapter. Once you have read the chapter, we hope you will find some way to develop an action program. If you commit yourself to doing even one of these activities for each chapter, you will become more actively involved in your own learning.

1. If you are an undergraduate and think you would like to pursue a graduate program, select at least one graduate school to visit and talk with faculty members and students. If you are in a graduate program, contact several community agencies or attend a professional conference to determine what kinds of positions will be available to you. If you have an interest in obtaining a professional license, contact the appropriate board early in your program to obtain information on the requirements.
2. Ask a helper whom you know about his or her motivations for becoming a helper and for remaining in the profession. What does this person get out of helping clients?
3. Conduct an interview with a mental health professional who works in a position similar to the one you hope to obtain. Before the interview, develop a list of questions that you are interested in exploring. Write up the salient points of your interview, and share the results in your class.
4. The career-guidance center in your college or university probably offers several computer-based programs to help you decide on a career. If you are interested in a more comprehensive self-assessment that describes the relationship between your personality type and possible occupations or fields of study, we strongly recommend that you take the *Self-Directed Search* (SDS), which is available online at Psychological Assessment Resources (www.self-directed-search.com). The SDS takes 20 to 30 minutes to complete. Your personalized report will appear on your screen.
5. Think of ways you can apply what you read. Decide on something specific, a step you can take now that will help you become actively engaged in a positive endeavor. After reading this chapter, for example, you could decide to reflect on your own needs and motives for considering a career in the helping professions. Review some significant turning points in your life that might have contributed to your desire to become a helper.

6. If you are in a training program, now is an ideal time to become involved in professional organizations. Become an active student member in at least one of the organizations described in this chapter. By joining a professional organization, you can take advantage of its workshops and conferences, often at a reduced rate. Membership also puts you in touch with other professionals with similar interests, gives you ideas for updating your skills, and helps you make excellent contacts. Check out the websites of the professional organizations described in this chapter to see what they have to offer, to learn about their mission, and to download their code of ethics.
7. Obtaining a master's degree or a doctoral degree in counseling, counselor education, social work, psychology, or couples and family counseling may be the beginning of your educational journey as a mental health professional, not the final destination. If you hope to establish even a part-time private practice, or to work in some positions in mental health agencies, you need to secure a license to practice. Licenses and credentials usually do not specify the clients or types of problems practitioners are competent to work with, nor do they specify the techniques that counselors are competent to use. Most licensing regulations do specify that licensees are to engage only in those therapeutic tasks for which they have professional competence, but it is up to the licensee to put this rule into practice. Each state has different continuing education requirements beyond the core curriculum required by the state. This makes reciprocity between states more complicated. If you are interested in securing more information about the licensure process, research the specific licenses available in your state and the requirements for making application for these licenses. What are the requirements for licensure as a social worker, marriage and family therapist, licensed professional clinical counselor, and other specializations? Compare the basic requirements to obtain a license in various professions.
8. We cannot stress enough the value of keeping a journal as an adjunct to reading this book and taking this course. Write in your journal in a free-flowing and unedited style. Be honest, and use journal writing as an opportunity to get to know yourself better, to clarify your thinking on issues raised in each chapter, and to explore your thoughts and feelings about working in the helping professions. At the end of each chapter, we provide a few suggestions of topics for you to reflect on and include in your journal writing. For this chapter, consider these areas:
   - Write about your main motives for wanting to become a helper. How do you expect your needs to be satisfied through your work?
   - Write about factors that have influenced your conception of what it means to be a helper. Who are your role models? What kind of help did you receive?
   - Spend some time thinking about the attributes of the ideal helper. What are your personal strengths that could enable you to become a more effective helper? How can you determine how realistic your expectations are about the profession you want to enter?
   - What are your thoughts about selecting an educational and professional route to pursue? Write about your work values that you might consider in choosing a career path.

9. Attend a professional state, regional, or national conference offered by one of the various professional organizations. Attending as a student has numerous benefits, such as developing a network for jobs, field placements, and meeting colleagues with similar interests.
10. Bring your completed self-assessment inventory to class to compare your views with those of others in the class. Such a comparison might stimulate some debate and help get the class involved in the topics to be discussed. In choosing the issues you want to discuss in class, circle the numbers of those items that you felt most strongly about as you were responding. You may find it instructive to ask others how they responded to these items in particular.
11. At the end of each chapter we provide some suggestions for further reading. For the full bibliographic entry for each of these sources, consult the *References* section at the back of the book. For a discussion on a wide array of issues confronting those in the helping professions, see Kottler (2017). For comprehensive coverage of topics such as development of a professional identity, ethical standards, basic process skills, approaches to counseling, and the making of a professional counselor, see Kottler and Shepard (2015) and Neukrug (2016a, 2016b). For wisdom on a variety of topics for new counselors, see Yalom (2003). For accounts of professional journeys of various counselor educators and practitioners, see Bemak and Conyne (2018) and Corey (2010).

CHAPTER 2

Helper, Know Thyself

Learning Objectives

1. Articulate the value of self-exploration experiences for helpers.
2. Provide a rationale for the importance of personal therapy for human service practitioners.
3. Describe how understanding your family of origin is key in your development as a professional helper.
4. Explain how life transitions are a part of life-span development.
5. Describe the key developmental tasks from infancy to late adulthood.

Focus Questions

1. To what degree do you believe it is possible for people to change long-established behavior patterns? What do you think the process of change has been for you?
2. What importance do you place on self-exploration as part of the process of becoming a helper? To what extent does critical thinking have a place in your growth and development?
3. How much do you know about your family of origin's influence on your development? How familiar are you with the life experiences of your parents, your grandparents, and other extended family?
4. In what ways have the experiences within your family of origin affected your current relationships? How might these same experiences influence your role as a professional helper? Can you identify any unresolved issues between you and your family that might affect your professional work?
5. What unfinished business in your personal life could present difficulties for you in working with clients with a range of problems? What steps can you take to address these issues?
6. What life experiences can you draw from to understand the diverse range of client problems you will encounter?
7. As you reflect on the developmental patterns in your life, how well have you dealt with the effects of key transition periods? What events have most influenced your present attitudes and behavior?
8. Your current life is largely a result of the earlier choices you have made. What is one early choice that has particularly affected the kind of person you are today?

9. In addition to academic coursework, what do you think it would take for you to be able to effectively work with a family?
10. What age group would you find most challenging to counsel? What would be difficult for you in working with this age group?

Aim of the Chapter

Most of us were raised in families that included at least one parent or parental figure, a certain amount of structure, and a set of rules designed to help us cope with life and meet the challenges we faced. Many problems your clients will bring to counseling are grounded in their experiences as children growing up in their families. To be an effective helper, you need to recognize the ways in which your own family of origin has influenced you and how your early background may influence your professional work. Whether you plan to work with individuals, groups, couples, or families, it is important to be familiar with your family-of-origin issues. Your perceptions and reactions to clients are often influenced by your personal experiences with your own family. If you are unaware of these sensitive areas, you may misinterpret your clients or steer them in a direction that will not arouse your own anxieties. If you are aware of emotional issues that activate your defensiveness, you can avoid getting entangled in the problems of your clients.

The material we present in this chapter is personal and can assist you in examining many dimensions of your family experience. We ask you to unravel the mystery of your connection with your family of origin so you can develop a richer appreciation for the many ways you have been influenced by the patterns established during childhood. This knowledge will help you guard against countertransference in your practice. We cannot stress this message enough—***helper, know thyself***. If you want to be a therapeutic agent in the lives of others, you must know yourself and, when necessary, be able to heal yourself.

One way we train beginning helpers is to assist them in focusing on their own development as a person. We ask counselors-in-training to read about certain life themes, to think about their own development and turning points, and to recall key choices they have made. These themes include dealing with developmental transitions through childhood, adolescence, and adult life; experiences with friendships; love and intimate relationships; loneliness and solitude; death and loss; sexuality; work and recreation; and the meaning in life. These are some of the themes clients bring into counseling sessions, and if you have a limited awareness of your own struggles, you may not be an effective helper. In training workshops, counselors-in-training discover the impact of their life experiences on clients and how clients' life experiences can affect them.

Impact of Professional Practice on the Helper's Life

Both new and experienced practitioners may find it difficult to make a clear distinction between their personal life and their professional life. Helpers hear painful stories day after day, and they must become self-aware and learn to work through their own pain in a constructive manner to remain effective in their professional work. Self-knowledge is a good place to begin. Practicing self-care on a regular basis and maintaining healthy boundaries in your personal and professional life are strategies that may help to prevent burnout or compassion fatigue. Consistently ignoring your own needs or downplaying the importance of your feelings and reactions will surely increase your chances of succumbing to these conditions. (Burnout and self-care are addressed in detail in Chapter 13.)

Unless you have identified your own sources of vulnerability and to some extent worked through experiences that may have left you psychologically wounded, you may be constantly triggered by the stories of your clients. Old wounds can be opened, affecting both your personal and professional life. Therapeutic practice can reactivate your earlier experiences and reawaken unresolved needs and problems. It is important for you to be willing to deal with your personal issues when they are triggered through your work with others.

Case example: Therapy that triggers personal pain.

Nancy, a beginning counselor working in an agency, is asked to colead a grief group for adults. Nancy believes there is a real need for this work, and she is enthusiastic in accepting the coleadership role. She lost her husband in a tragic manner, yet she feels that she has allowed herself to fully experience the pain of his death and has accepted the loss. She works very well with the members in her group as the sessions begin. She is compassionate, supportive, and empathic, and she is able to help them work through some of their pain. After a few weeks, however, Nancy notices that she is no longer looking forward to the group sessions. She feels somewhat depressed and finds herself becoming apathetic toward the members.

Your stance. If you found yourself dreading to meet with a group you had been enthusiastic about leading only a short time ago, what would you do? How would you get to the bottom of these confusing feelings? Would you seek advice from colleagues or personal therapy? Would you continue to lead this group?

Discussion. Although some of Nancy's old wounds were healed, exposure to the intense pain of so many other people has reopened these wounds. By putting her own emotions "on hold," either in or out of the group, she is likely to become ineffective as a helper. She has ignored her vulnerability to the pain of her loss and her need to express and work through this pain as it is being reexperienced. This numbing has led to Nancy's depression and her inability to work effectively with her clients. In addition, Nancy's clients may interpret her withdrawal as meaning she has lost interest in them because of something they did wrong, which would be harmful to their own therapy.

Reexperiencing old pain does not necessarily mean that Nancy will become ineffective in working with this type of group. Quite the contrary. If she accepts the fact that she is still wounded and explores these feelings, she can heal her own wounds as she is facilitating the healing process in others. She can model the ongoing nature of grief work and teach the members that although the pain will never completely be erased it can become less controlling. If it is appropriate, Nancy may share her present reactions and feelings. However, even if she chooses not to reveal her experiences to the group, she can use her experiences as a bridge to connect with the struggles of others.

It may be wise for Nancy to seek personal therapy to address her depression and feelings of numbness and apathy. If she continues this type of involvement over a long period, it is likely that she will experience burnout.

Case example: The resurfacing of old wounds.
Maria, who was raised by an abusive father, decided to pursue therapy as a young adult to address her unresolved personal pain. She remained in therapy for a year and terminated with her therapist when she felt she had gained sufficient insight into her childhood trauma. Years later, Maria became a social worker and was hired by the Department of Children and Family Services. On one occasion, Maria's supervisor pointed out to her that she seemed to be quick to remove children from their homes and less inclined than her colleagues to recommend family preservation services.

Initially Maria felt defensive upon hearing this feedback, but she soon realized she was experiencing countertransference with several of the families in her caseload. This realization triggered a particularly painful memory involving her father, which resulted in a panic attack the next time she met with certain clients. This event prompted Maria to make an appointment with a therapist. She realized that her unfinished business was interfering with her ability to function effectively as a social worker, and she felt compelled to return to therapy.

Your stance. If you were in Maria's shoes, how would it be for you to receive this feedback from your supervisor? If you found yourself having similar countertransference reactions toward several of your clients, what would you be inclined to do? What do you think the potential consequences would be if Maria had not addressed her psychological wounds that had resurfaced?

Discussion. Just as in Nancy's case, Maria perceived herself to be emotionally equipped to function effectively as a helper. She did not recognize that she was experiencing countertransference and still had unfinished business of her own. To her credit, Maria was able to lower her defensiveness and heed the important feedback from her supervisor. Although her decision to return to therapy may have been motivated largely by her desire to be a more effective social worker, her commitment to reexamine these wounds is likely to result in personal growth that will enhance the quality of her life and her personal relationships as well.

LO1 Value of Self-Exploration for the Helper

You may discover that working with individuals or families resurrects themes in your life, some of which may previously have been outside your conscious awareness. If you are unaware of issues stemming from your family experiences, you are likely to find ways to avoid acknowledging and dealing with these potentially painful areas with your clients. As your clients confront events that trigger their pain, memories of your own pain may be activated. For instance, you may still have a great deal of hurt over your parents' divorce. At some level, you may believe the divorce was your fault or that you could have done something to keep your parents together. If you are counseling a couple considering divorce, you may want to steer them toward remaining married for the sake of the children. You are giving them solutions that originate from your reservoir of hurt. On some level, you could be protecting the children from the pain of your situation that you have yet to fully realize or appreciate. It is important to recognize that your capacity to facilitate the healing forces in others is based on your willingness to experience your own wounds and bring about healing for yourself.

Identifying and resolving unfinished business related to your family of origin allows you to establish relationships that do not repeat negative patterns of interaction. As you review your family history in this chapter, you will no doubt gain some insights into patterns that you have "adopted" from your family of origin. Your own therapy helps you to understand how these past conflicts are still affecting you.

As you begin to practice counseling, you might become aware that you are taking on a professional role that resembles the role you played in your family. For example, you may recognize a need to preserve peace by becoming the caretaker of others. During your childhood, you may have assumed adult roles with your own parents by trying to take care of them. Now, as you begin your professional work, it is possible that you could continue the pattern of taking more responsibility for the changes your clients make than they do.

Transference and countertransference are common in the therapeutic process. **Transference** generally has roots in a client's unresolved personal conflicts with significant others. Because of these unresolved concerns, the client may perceive the helping professional in a distorted way, bringing past relationships into the present relationship with the counselor. Transference can lead a client to gain insight into how he or she operates in a variety of relationships. The counterpart to the client's transference feelings toward a helper is the helping person's **countertransference**; that is, emotional-behavioral reactions toward a client that originate from some part of the helper's life. Consider your own possible sources of countertransference. If you have fears about dying or the aging and death of your parents, for example, it is quite possible for you to encounter difficulty in working with older people. The struggles of these clients can activate unconscious processes in you that, if left outside your awareness, can interfere with your ability to be truly helpful. How you deal with a client's transference is crucial.

If you are unaware of your own dynamics, you may miss important therapeutic issues and be unable to help your clients resolve the feelings they are bringing into the professional relationship with you. One clue that you may have unresolved issues is when you find yourself becoming *emotionally reactive* (Kerr & Bowen, 1988); that is, you have an almost automatic, reflexive emotional trigger that seems out of character for you. Emotional reactivity may not present itself as an aggressive or negative feeling, such as anger, frustration, or irritation. If you have affectionate or sexual feelings toward your client, a need to protect one or more people in a couple or family, or you want to stand up for one person against another, these countertransference feelings are also a kind of emotional reactivity.

Many situations in a family can plant the seeds for potential countertransference: growing up in a home with the unpredictability of violence, conflicts that were never addressed, secrecy that was protected at all costs, fears surrounding incest, absence of any boundaries, and significant events (such as grave illness or the death of a family member) that were ignored on a psychological level. If you felt that no matter how much you did, it was never quite enough to win your mother's approval, for example, you may now be very finely attuned to the judgments of women who remind you of your mother. If you allowed your father to completely affirm or deny your value as a person, you may be very sensitive to what male authority figures think of you. You might give them the power to make you feel either competent or incompetent. As a child, if you often felt rejected, you may now create situations in which you feel like the one who is left out and just does not fit. Conversely, you may always have been appreciated and now think this should continue in all situations and at all times. You can identify these kinds of situations in your own counseling sessions and get help in working through areas in your life where you may be psychologically stalled. (Transference and countertransference are discussed in further detail in Chapter 5.)

Case example: The cost of unmanaged countertransference.

Mirek experienced the trauma of losing his younger brother to a heroin overdose several years ago. At the time of his brother's death, he vowed to become a substance abuse counselor and to do a much better job treating addicts than those counselors who "did not do enough," in his opinion, to prevent his brother from relapsing and overdosing. Mirek did not consider himself to be the one in his family with "the problem," so he never participated in his own personal therapy.

Mirek felt he could be an effective counselor and save 100% of his clients from the same fate as his brother. He was hired at a substance abuse treatment facility and soon found himself working increasingly long hours and being available to his clients almost all of the time. When his supervisor told him he needed to establish better boundaries with his clients and protect his time, he became enraged and told her that denying clients' access to help whenever they want it is a terrible policy. As he stormed out of her office, he said: "If my clients overdose because I am not there when they need me, you will be the one to blame!" He was written up for being insubordinate and was given the clear message that he needed to address his issues in therapy if he wanted to continue his employment at the facility.

Your stance. How do you think Mirek's countertransference got in his way as a helper? Was his reaction a reflection of his own unfinished business related to his brother's overdose, or did he have a valid point to question his supervisor's directive to develop firmer boundaries as a helper? What are appropriate boundaries to set with clients? As a helper, do you think clients should have access to you 24 hours a day, seven days a week?

Discussion. It is extremely distressing when a client overdoses or harms him- or herself, and it is natural to want to do whatever is within our power to prevent such an event from happening. It is important to be available to clients, but we must also establish appropriate boundaries if we are to remain effective in our professional role. Mirek is operating on the mistaken belief that if he "does enough" as a helper he can prevent others from overdosing. Even the most successful addictions counselors cannot save all of their clients from self-destructive outcomes.

It is likely that some of the blame and the anger Mirek has projected onto the treatment community reflects his own repressed guilt for "not doing enough" to help his troubled sibling. Mirek's unmanaged countertransference jeopardized his professionalism at the treatment facility, and his inappropriate response to his supervisor could have cost him his job, a setback at a more personal level. If Mirek decides to pursue his own therapy, he will have an opportunity to process the grief he undoubtedly still has related to his brother's death. Through his therapy, Mirek may realize that he was not responsible for his brother's behavior and choices, which could alleviate his guilt and help him recognize that his clients are also making their own choices. By working through the unconscious processes that distorted his view of a helper's role, Mirek will be better able to assist future clients in their own recovery.

LO2 Using Individual and Group Counseling for Self-Understanding

When you become aware of bringing patterns that originated from your personal experiences into your professional life, individual and group counseling can provide a safe place to explore and talk about painful memories that are often associated with these personal experiences. Ideally, consider participating in a combination of individual and group therapy because the two approaches to therapy complement each other.

Personal therapy is a valuable component for the growth of students in the helping professions. Personal therapy can improve the emotional and mental functioning of mental health professionals, and it is an empirically supported path toward self-development (Norcross & VandenBos, 2018). Individual therapy provides you with an opportunity to look at yourself in some depth. As a part of your internship experience, you may experience a reopening of old emotional wounds when you engage in intensive work with your clients. Your therapeutic work may bring to the surface feelings of unexpressed and unresolved grief over significant loss or challenge gender perspectives and cultural stereotypes with which you were raised. Personal counseling can support healthy growth and development as well as provide an avenue for remediation when needed. If you are in personal counseling while you are doing your internship, you can bring your issues to your therapy sessions. In your own therapy, you can explore your motivations for becoming a helper. Your appreciation for the courage your clients will require in their therapeutic journey will be enhanced through your own experience as a client. In addition, we believe personal therapy is a basic part of ongoing self-care. As professional helpers, we are often in the role of giver; to preserve our vitality, we need to create spaces in which the "giver" can be supported. Ethical practitioners make a commitment to maintaining their well-being.

Multiple reasons underlie the importance of personal therapy for human service professionals. Counseling can be valuable in limiting countertransference, ensuring that your personal issues do not get in the way of working effectively with clients. Exploring your own issues in counseling increases self-awareness, improves your ability to deal more effectively with your own emotional reactions, sharpens your counseling skills, decreases the possibility of unethical work, increases empathy, and enhances your skills in creating a therapeutic alliance (Kalkbrenner, Neukrug, & Griffith, 2019; Neukrug, Kalkbrenner, & Griffith, 2017).

Large-scale studies show that the majority of mental health professionals have participated in their own therapy and rate their experiences in personal therapy quite positively (Orlinksy & Ronnestad, 2005; Orlinsky, Schofield, Schroder, & Kazantzis, 2011). Ronnestad, Orlinsky, and Wiseman (2016) list benefits of psychotherapy for *therapists as people* that include "positive increments in self-awareness, self-knowledge, self-understanding, self-care, and self-acceptance as well as reduction in symptoms and improved relationships and personal growth generally" (p. 230). Personal therapy can be instrumental in increasing empathy, enhancing warmth and relational skills, expanding our awareness of transference and countertransference processes, and reducing the likelihood of burnout or unethical behavior (Orlinsky et al., 2011).

Self-reported outcomes of personal therapy gathered by Norcross (2005) reveal positive gains in multiple areas, including self-esteem, work functioning, social life, emotional expression, intrapersonal conflicts, and symptom severity. The impact of one's personal therapy is generally more formative than traditional coursework. The bulk of evidence attests to its evidence-based position in the formation of therapists (Norcross & VandenBos, 2018). Specific lasting lessons practitioners gain from their personal therapy most frequently pertain to interpersonal relationships and the dynamics of psychotherapy. A key lesson is appreciating the importance of learning how to deal with transference and countertransference.

Experiencing our own personal therapy provides a basis for understanding and compassion for our clients. We gain a greater appreciation of how challenging it is for clients to come to us and the courage it takes for them to reveal intimate aspects of their lives. Participating in our own therapy is a way for us to learn how to establish and maintain a working alliance and how to deal with the challenges and uncertainties involved in therapeutic work (Ronnestad et al., 2016). Wise and Barnett (2016) identify engaging in personal psychotherapy on a periodic basis as a self-care strategy and as a form of positive self-development. Personal therapy is one of the ways to maintain self-care and competence throughout your career.

Group counseling provides another pathway to self-awareness. Group therapy provides an opportunity for you to hear and consider feedback from others. A group experience can help you become aware of your interpersonal style and give you a chance to experiment with new behaviors in a group setting. The reactions you receive from others can help you identify personal attributes that may be either strengths or limitations in your work as a helper. Many of the patterns you acquired as a child may still be problematic for you today. You could do useful work in group therapy on any unresolved issues you have with your parents, with family rules that you have accepted, or in situations where you feel stuck. Victoria, a master's student training to be a marriage and family therapist, explains how engaging in both individual and group therapy enhanced her self-understanding:

> I cannot imagine not having my own therapy. I began my therapy prior to even entering the program and have continued it for several years now. During this last year, I also have been engaging in group therapy, which is a useful complement to my individual therapy. I appreciate therapy both for my own

growth and for the benefit of my clients. My personal therapy allows me to use myself and my intuitions as a powerful therapeutic tool in understanding the client's experiences, and it also enables me to connect deeply with clients. Client material often illuminates areas of work for me. Because I have weekly sessions with my own therapist, I am able to deal with these issues as they arise. I can temporarily put aside my own emotional vulnerabilities through this awareness, and be more fully present with my clients. I have often experienced a parallel process with my clients, and their work inspires my own, which increases my effectiveness.

As Victoria's personal account reveals, therapy—be it individual, group, or family—is not just for treatment purposes or for curing deeply rooted personality disturbances. We see therapy as an avenue for continuing to deepen your self-understanding and for looking at the ways in which your needs are related to your work. Becoming involved in some form of intensive self-exploration therapy can motivate you to assess your needs and motives for becoming a helper, which are outlined in Chapter 1. Committed helping professionals are open to engaging in lifelong self-exploration as the need presents itself. Practitioners must recognize and deal with their personal problems as they surface to safeguard their clients. What is important is that therapists seek personal therapy *before* distressing life situations lead to impairment.

We recommend that you involve yourself in therapeutic experiences that increase your availability to your clients. There are many ways to accomplish this goal: individual therapy, group counseling, consultation with trusted colleagues, continuing education (especially of an experiential nature), keeping a personal journal, and reading.

Although both individual and group therapy are valuable routes to gaining a deeper knowledge of yourself, other less formal avenues to personal and professional development can also be explored. As a counselor-in-training, you may not be able to participate in personal therapy, for both practical and economical reasons. Other routes to personal development include reflecting on the meaning of your life and work; reading and journal writing; participating in peer groups; remaining open to the reactions of significant people in your life; traveling and immersing yourself in different cultures; engaging in spiritual activities, such as meditating; participating in physical challenges; and spending time with your family and friends. By participating in various forms of self-exploration, you can gain firsthand knowledge of what your clients are likely to experience. This process will increase your respect for clients and their struggles. If you have not experienced the joys and pains of growth that result from a therapeutic relationship, how can you guide and support others on their journey?

LO3 Working With Your Family of Origin

Some programs in marital and family therapy require students to take a family-of-origin course. The assumption is that future practitioners need to understand the influence of their own **family of origin** before they engage in professional work with individuals, couples, and families. Some states mandate such a course as a requirement for licensure as a couples and family therapist. It is well for training programs to provide family-of-origin work for students as part of their growth group experiences (Bitter, 2014). One study demonstrated that graduate students highly valued genogram work as part of their counselor training (Lim, 2008). The genogram, a graphic representation of one's family of origin, is an effective psychosocial tool in counselor training. "It provides the opportunity for trainees to examine preconceived notions about self and the world, to critically evaluate the stories that have shaped them, and to make decisions about new ways of being and relating" (p. 42). By exploring the dynamics of their own family of origin, helpers can relate more effectively to themes presented by families they encounter in clinical practice.

Genogram work is a formal process, and it helps to have a guide (see McGoldrick, 2011a, 2016; McGoldrick, Gerson, & Petry, 2008). Genograms provide a structure, or frame, for family stories of emotional significance. They may start out as a simple map of squares (for men) and circles (for women) with lines of connection, but they evolve into a complex picture of issues, emotional reactions, and coping strategies that permeate generations. Many people enhance their genogram with family pictures, art, or even video.

Here is the start of Jim's genogram:

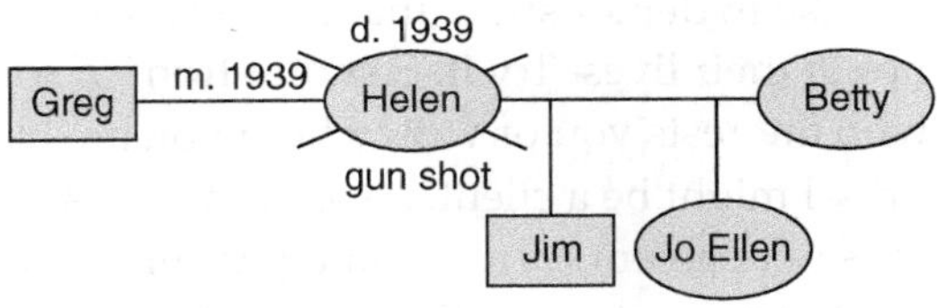

In these first few pieces of Jim's genogram, what stands out to you? What questions come to mind that might have some bearing on how Jim sees himself, his life, and the relationships between men and women? Are you at all interested in how the death of Greg's first wife, Helen, happened? Do you think that event colored Greg's picture of self or marriage? What do you think Betty knew or felt about that death? Did it carry over into Jim's life, and if so, how?

Lawson and Gaushell (1991) recommend that training programs address candidates' family issues before admitting them to a program. They suggest requiring a family autobiography as part of the application materials. This would yield useful information concerning intergenerational family characteristics that would have a relationship to a helper's ability to work with families. Lawson and Gaushell emphasize these intergenerational family characteristics of counselor trainees:

- Clinicians who have resolved negative family experiences are better able to assist their clients, especially those with whom they have issues in common.
- It is essential that trainees be given assistance in identifying and addressing their own problematic family issues to enhance their psychological functioning and their effectiveness as helpers.
- Unmet needs in early family experiences later manifest themselves in intense and conflicting ties with these family members.
- Helpers' early roles as peacemakers create later ambivalence regarding intimacy with significant others.
- Counselor trainees' experiences in their families of origin can lead to difficulties in their current relationships.

Identifying Your Issues in Your Family of Origin

A great deal of the following discussion of one's family of origin is based on the contributions of **Virginia Satir**, one of the pioneers in family therapy. When Satir was 5 years old, she remembers hearing her parents talking and wanting to know what they were up to. In workshops, Satir often mentioned that this was when she decided to be a "detective on parents." Later she viewed herself as a detective who sought out and listened for the reflections of self-esteem with her clients. Her therapeutic work convinced her of the value of a strong, nurturing relationship based on interest and a fascination with those in her care.

Family therapists generally assume it is inevitable that they will encounter some of the dynamics of their family of origin in the families they treat. Satir used to say that if she walked into a room with 12 people she would meet everyone she ever knew. When you are counseling a couple or a family, many people are participating in this interaction. In other words, you do not always perceive individuals with a fresh and unbiased perspective. The more you are aware of these patterns, the greater the benefit to your clients. It is crucial that you know to whom you are responding: to the individual in front of you or to a person from your past.

Satir used this exercise to demonstrate that people are constantly revisiting friends and loved ones in their lives. Try it. Stand in front of someone (Person A) in your current life who interests you or with whom you are having some difficulty. This individual might be a client, an associate, a family member, or a friend. If the person is not present, you can imagine him or her. Take a good look at this person and form a picture on the screen of your mind. Now, let a picture of someone in your past come forward (Person B). Who comes to mind? How old are you, and how old is Person B? What relationship do you, or did you, have with this individual you are remembering? What feelings are linked with this relationship? What did you think about Person B? Now, reexamine your reactions to Person A. Do you see any connection between what Person A is evoking in you and the past feelings evoked by Person B? You can apply this exercise by yourself through the use of imagery when you have intense emotional reactions to other people, especially if you do not know them well. This exercise can help you begin to recognize the effects past relationships may have on your here-and-now responses (Satir, Banmen, Gerber, & Gomori, 1991). Perhaps what is most important is simply to be aware of ways in which you are carrying your past into present interactions.

In this section, we invite you to identify as many family-of-origin experiences as possible and to reflect on how these life experiences are likely to have an influence on *who* and *what* you are at this point. You are not necessarily determined by your earlier experiences, and they do not have to serve as the template for your current significant relationships. You can shift your perspective, but only if you have recognized and dealt with your experiences. If you are working with a family, moreover, you will have an experiential starting point to invite them to look at their functioning as a system and as individuals within the family.

Much of the remainder of this section is based on our perspective on family history, which is a modification and integration of material taken from several sources: (1) Adlerian lifestyle assessment methods (Corey, 2013a; Mosak & Shulman, 1988; Powers & Griffith, 2012); (2) Satir's communication approach to working with families (Satir, 1983, 1989; Satir & Baldwin, 1983; Satir, Bitter, & Krestensen, 1988; see also Bitter, 2014); (3) concepts of family systems (Bitter, 2014; Goldenberg, Stanton, & Goldenberg, 2017; Nichols & Davis, 2017); (4) genogram methods (McGoldrick, 2011a, 2016; McGoldrick et al., 2008); and (5) family autobiography methods (Lawson & Gaushell, 1988). As you read the following material, try to personalize the information. We are primarily providing you with ways to understand and work with your own family material and secondarily offering you a basis for understanding the individuals and families in your professional work.

Your family structure. Some of the many patterns of family life include nuclear, extended, single-parent, grandparent-grandchild, divorced, adoptive, same-sex parents, children raised outside the family, and blended families. The term **family structure** also refers to the social and psychological organization of the family system, including factors such as birth order and the individual's perception of self in the family context. Expand your awareness of your family of origin by thoughtfully answering these questions:

- In what type of family structure did you grow up? Did the structure of your family change over time? If so, what were these changes? What were some of the most important family values? What most stands out for you about your family life? How do these experiences affect you today?
- What is your current family structure? Are you still primarily involved in your family of origin, or do you have a different family structure? If you do, what roles do you play in your current family that you also enacted in your original family? Have you carried certain patterns from your original family into your current family? How do you see yourself as being different in the two families?
- Draw a genogram or a diagram of your family of origin. Include all the members, and identify their significant alliances. Identify the relationships with each person that you had as a child and your relationships with each member now.
- Make a list of the siblings, from oldest to youngest. Give a brief description of each (including yourself). What most stands out for each sibling? Which sibling is most different from you, and how? Which is most like you, and how?
- How would you describe yourself as a child in your family of origin? What were some of your major fears? hopes? ambitions? What was school like for you? What was your role in your peer group? Identify any significant events in your physical, sexual, and social development during childhood.
- Identify a personal struggle of yours. How has your relationship with your family contributed to the development and perpetuation of this struggle? What options are open to you for making substantial changes? What are a few ways in which you can be different in your family?
- Make a list of strengths you have. How has your family contributed to the development of these strengths?

Parental figures and relationships with parents. Your parents were central figures in your development whether you felt a loving connection with them or felt deprived of any connection. Their presence or absence during your formative years had a profound effect on your development. If your father or mother was absent from your early family life, did any surrogate figures emerge? If you grew up in a single-parent family, did this one parent play the role of both mother and father? You may have grown up in a family with two parents of the same gender. What did you learn about yourself and the world? How did others react to you having same-gender parents? How did society norms toward your parents affect your life then and today?

If you grew up in a heterosexual two-parent family, what did your parents teach you through the behavior they modeled about family life? Spend some time thinking about your parental figures and your relationships with them. Focus on what you learned from observing and interacting with your parents, on what you observed in their interactions with each other. How did they fight or solve problems? How did they express affection for one another? Who made the decisions and in what way? Who handled the money and family finances? How did each parent interact with each child? How did each of your siblings view and react to your parents?

Describe your father (or the person who substituted for him). What is or was he like? What were his ambitions for each of the children? How did you view him as a child? How did you view him as you got older? How do you view him now? How are you like him? How are you unlike him? What does your father say when he compliments you or when he criticizes you? What was his advice to you as a child? What is his advice to you now? What could you do to disappoint him now? What can you do to please him? What was his relationship to his children? What is his current relationship to your siblings? What sibling is the most like your father, and in what ways? What did your father tell you (either directly or indirectly) about yourself? life? death? love? sex? marriage? men? women? your birth? What is it about you or your behavior that you would not want him to know? If you are in a committed relationship, what similarities do you see between your partner and your father?

Now describe your mother. Use the same list of questions and ask each of them about your mother (or the person who substituted for her). Create a sketch of how you viewed your mother.

Your parents or those who raised you have been the "air-traffic controllers" of your life. They launched you, guided you, and helped you survive. They are the people on whom you depended for survival, and you may feel less than grown up in relation to them. You may find yourself acting the way you did as a child when you are with them as opposed to functioning as a psychological adult. It is important to remember that the last relationships that many people work out are those with their parents.

Becoming your own person. From the perspective of those who grow up in cultures that value autonomy and individualism, a healthy person achieves both a psychological separateness from and a sense of intimacy with his or her family. Psychological maturity is not a fixed destination that you reach once and for all; rather, it is a lifelong developmental process achieved through reexamination and resolution of internal conflicts and intimacy issues with loved ones. You do not find yourself in isolation; rather, the process of self-discovery is bound up with the quality of your relationships to others in connection. Becoming your own person does not mean "doing your own thing" irrespective of your impact on those with whom you come in contact.

It is possible to assume responsibility by doing for yourself what you expected others to do for you as a child. If you are becoming a separate being, you still maintain connections, reach out to others, share with them, and give yourself in your relationships. Being an integrated person means that you recognize the many and varied aspects of your being, that you accept both positive and negative sides, and that you do not disown parts of yourself.

The notions of independence, autonomy, and self-determination are Western values, and they tend to reduce the importance of the family of origin. In more collectivist societies, family bonds and unity are given more emphasis than self-determination and independence. In many Chinese American families, filial piety, or obedience to parents and respect and honor for them, is highly valued. Allegiance to one's parents is expected from a son, even after he marries and has his own family. A son may have difficulty with the notion of being his own person beyond the limits of his family role and may continue to think of himself first as a son. For such a person, individuation is neither ideal nor particularly functional. The concept of individuation and separation from his family can easily lead to conflicts in his family relationships. He will discover who he is more easily within the family context than outside of it. It is quite clear that cultural values play a key role in adopting behaviors that reflect an individualistic or collectivistic spirit. At this point, reflect on these questions:

- How has your cultural upbringing influenced the importance you place on values such as striving for autonomy and independence or striving for interdependence and harmony with your family? Which values stemming from your culture do you want to retain? Are there any of these values you want to challenge or modify?
- To what extent do you see yourself as having a distinct identity and as being psychologically separate from your family of origin? To what extent are you psychologically connected with your family of origin? Are there any aspects of this relationship that you want to change? Are there aspects that you would not be comfortable changing or would want to remain the same? Explain your answer.

Coping with conflict in the family. If you have difficulty dealing with conflict in your current relationships, one reason may be that conflict was not addressed in direct ways in your family of origin. You may have been taught that conflict was something to be avoided at all costs. If you observed that conflict had no resolution in your family or that people would simply not speak to each other for weeks after a conflict, you are probably fearful when conflicts emerge. Conflicts belong to the whole family, although parents at times portray their children as the problem. The key to successful relationships lies not in the absence of conflict but in recognizing its source and being able to cope directly with the situations that lead to conflict. Conflicts that are denied tend to fester and strain relationships. In fact, when patterns related to family conflict are left unexamined, history tends to repeat itself in subsequent generations. For instance, if your parents resorted to emotionally cutting off those who disagreed with them, you may follow this pattern in your adult relationships. Or you may have internalized the message that if you disagree with people they will cut you out of their life. This could lead to a pattern of compromising your own opinions and beliefs just to keep the peace in relationships. Whatever pattern emerges, becoming aware of the way conflict was communicated and handled in your family of origin will help you understand the impact it has on how you deal with conflict now. How was conflict expressed and dealt with in your family? What were its sources? What was your role? Were you encouraged to resolve conflict directly with others? Did you feel safe in voicing your opinion in disputes between you and members of your family? What messages did your family learn from the culture at large about conflict and its resolution? How were these messages transmitted to you?

The Family as a System

Families have certain rules governing interactions. These **family rules** are not simple commandments, such as what time children need to be home after a date. They also include unspoken rules, messages given by parents to children, injunctions, myths, and secrets. These rules are often couched in terms of "do's" or "don'ts": "Do behave at all times." "Do be perfect." "Don't shame your family." "Don't be disloyal to your family." "Don't question adults or authority figures." "Don't confront your parents, but do what you can to please them." "Don't talk to outsiders about your family." It is impossible for children to grow up without some rules or injunctions, and on the basis of them, children make early decisions. They decide either to accept family rules or to fight them. "Children are to be seen but not heard." "Have fun only when all the work is finished." When parents feel worried or helpless, they tend to dictate rules in an attempt to control the situation. These family rules initially assist children in handling anger, helplessness, and fear. They are intended to provide a safety net for children as they venture into the world (Satir et al., 1988).

Consider some of the major do's and don'ts that you heard growing up in your family and your reactions to them.

- What are a few messages or rules that you accepted?
- What are some rules that you fought against?
- What early decisions do you deem most significant in your life today? In what family context did you make these decisions?
- Do you ever hear yourself giving the same messages to others that you heard from your parents?

Virginia Satir (1983) recognized that the family rules we learned were often in a form that lacked choice and were impossible to implement. "I must never get angry" is an example of this kind of family rule; so is "I must always be the best" or "I must always be kind." Cognitive therapists might want clients to challenge words like "must" and "always" and "never" as irrational, but Satir preferred to engage clients in a rules transformation process. This is how the transformation process goes:

1. Start with the rule as learned: "I must never get angry."
2. Change the "must" to "can": "I can never get angry." It's still a problematic statement, but at least it has *choice* in it.
3. Change the "never" or "always" to "sometimes": "I can sometimes get angry." Now this rings with truth. The next step is to personalize it.
4. Think of at least three situations in which it would be OK for you to get angry. For example, I can get angry: when I see and experience injustice toward others, when other people presume to know what I think or feel and speak for me, or when I see cruelty to animals. Note that being angry at these times does not require you to be emotionally reactive or explosive. There are many ways to express anger without damaging your heart with explosiveness.

What rules did you learn in your family? You may not even have heard them out loud; rules often are enacted and controlled through family responses to behavior. See if you can identify three family rules that were part of your upbringing, and then go through Satir's rules transformation process for each one.

In healthy families there are fewer rules, and they are applied consistently. The rules are humanly possible, relevant, and flexible (Bitter, 1987). According to Satir and Baldwin (1983), the most important family rules are those that govern individuation (being unique) and sharing information (communication). These are the rules that influence the ability of a family to function in open ways and to allow all members the possibility for changing. Satir notes that many people develop a range of styles as a means for coping with stress resulting from the constrictions of family rules.

Bitter (2014) contrasts a functional family structure with one that is dysfunctional. In **functional families**, each member is allowed to have a separate life as well as a shared life with the family group. Different relationships are given room to grow. Change is expected and invited, not viewed as a threat. When differentiation leads to disagreements, the situation is viewed as an opportunity for growth rather than an attack on the family system. The structure of the functional family system is characterized by freedom, flexibility, and open communication. All the family members have a voice and can speak for themselves. In this atmosphere, individuals feel support for taking risks and venturing into the world.

By contrast, **dysfunctional families** are characterized by closed communication, by the poor self-esteem of one or both parents, and by rigid patterns. Rules serve the function of masking fears about differences. They are rigid and are frequently inappropriate for meeting a situation. In unhealthy families, the members are expected to think, feel, and act in the same way. Parents attempt to control the family by using fear, anger, punishment, guilt, or dominance. Eventually, the system breaks down because the rules are no longer able to keep the family structure intact. This can lead to intense stress.

When stress is exacerbated because of the breakdown of the family system, members tend to resort to defensive stances. Bitter (1987, 2014) describes how congruent people cope with stress. They do not sacrifice themselves to a singular style in dealing with it. Instead, they transform stress into a challenge that is met in a useful way. Such people are centered, and they avoid changing their colors like a chameleon. Their words match their inner experience, and they are able to make direct and clear statements. They face stress with confidence and courage because they know that they have the inner resources to cope effectively and to make sound choices. They feel a sense of belongingness and a connectedness with others. They are motivated by the principle of social interest, which means that they are not interested merely in self-enhancement but are aware of the need to contribute to the common good.

Think about this discussion of how family rules are manifested in both functional and dysfunctional family structures. Rather than labeling your own family as "functional" or "dysfunctional," think about specific aspects within your family system that may not have been as healthy as you wish. Also think about those aspects of your family life that were helpful, functional, and healthy. Apply the discussion of family structures and family rules to your own experiences. We recommend several books that will provide you with more detailed information on this topic: Satir (1983), Satir (1989), and Satir and Baldwin (1983).

Family secrets can also influence the structure and functioning of a family. Secrets can be particularly devastating because that which is hidden typically assumes greater power than that which is out in the open. Generally, it is not what is openly talked about that causes difficulty in families but what is kept hidden. If there are secrets in the family, children are left to figure out what is going on in the home. Did you suspect that there were secrets in your family? If so, what was it like for you to perpetuate the secrecy? to divulge the secrets? What do you think that secrecy did to the family atmosphere?

Significant developments in your family. You might find it useful to describe your family's life cycle. Chart significant turning points that have characterized your family's development. One way to do this is to look at family photo albums to see what the pictures reveal. Let them stimulate memories and reflections. As you view pictures of your parents, grandparents, siblings, and other relatives, look for patterns that can offer clues to family dynamics. In charting transitions in the development of your family, reflect on these questions:

- What were the crisis points for your family?
- Can you recall any unexpected events?
- Were there any periods of separation due to employment, military service, or imprisonment?
- Who tended to have problems within the family? How were these problems manifested? How did others in the family react to the person with problems?
- In what ways did births affect the family?
- Were there any serious illnesses, accidents, divorces, or deaths in your family? If so, how did they affect individual members in the family and the family as a whole?
- Was there a history of physical, sexual, or emotional abuse? If so, how did that affect individuals within the family unit and the family as a whole?

Looking into these areas can enable you to determine the forces that have changed you, and this in turn will help you work with clients.

Proceed With Caution

If there has not been severe trauma in your family, simply reflecting on the questions we have raised that deal with your family history can be therapeutic by itself, even though it may be accompanied by some turmoil. If you decide to carry the process a step further and interview members of your family, being sensitive to their feelings and reactions will go a long way toward reducing the chances that you will alienate family members.

In Chapter 4, you will learn that it is essential to be sensitive to cultural themes in the lives of your clients and their families and that you might lose certain clients if you do not demonstrate an understanding of how their culture affects their choices and actions. Apply this general principle as you approach members of your family. Be sensitive to the cultural rules of your family structure, and consider how concepts such as roles, rules, myths, and rituals operate in your family. If your family is religious, much of your cultural influence may be reflected in the religion your family embraced.

In some families, a mother or father would be offended if a child were to seek information from a family member. A Japanese graduate student approached his father to interview him as part of his family autobiography assignment. The father was reluctant to engage in any significant sharing of family material despite the student's insistence that getting this knowledge was important for him. Explain to family members your reasons for asking these questions.

In doing a review of your family history, be prepared for the possibility of a crisis developing, either for you or within your family. Doing this level of work may lead to a number of surprises and discoveries for which you are not prepared. One student discovered that she had been adopted. She was faced with dealing with anger and disappointment over not having been told. You may learn of family secrets, or you may learn that your "ideal family" is not as perfect as you thought. You may well find that your family has both functional and dysfunctional aspects. Many of the students who were enrolled in a personal-growth group with one of us (Marianne) became anxious or depressed by what they were learning about both themselves and their family system in their other classes and felt a need to talk about how they were being affected.

You may well discover that the sources of information are scarce, even about your grandparents. For example, I (Jerry) know precious little about my father's life before he and my mother married. From my father, I have some knowledge about his difficult beginnings in this country. At the age of 7, he and his brother came from Italy to New York. His father (whom I know almost nothing about) brought the two children to this country after his wife died. Again, there is scant information about my father's mother. I don't even know how she died. Apparently, my grandfather's intentions were to have a relative in this country care for his boys, yet this relative was unable to do so because of other family responsibilities. This led to my father's placement in an orphanage. I recall some stories he told me about the loneliness of his childhood in the institution and how difficult it was coming to this country not being able to speak a word of English. What is striking to me is how little I do know about my father's side of the family, and this in itself reveals how much material was denied and was kept secret. Because my father died over 50 years ago, I have had to look for bits of information from my mother about my father's history and also to relatives who knew something about his life.

In contrast, Marianne's family history is easily traced back to the early 1600s. For many years, I (Marianne) have heard rich stories that formed the tapestry of my family's history. As I grew up in an extended family in a German village, many relatives and townspeople revealed information about several generations. I did become aware of one pattern from my father's side. Someone in the family would typically get angry, and an emotional cutoff would result in which certain people would never speak to each other again. This teaches me how family patterns often repeat themselves for several generations. Although we cannot change another person, we do have power over how we allow ourselves to be affected by the actions and decisions of others.

Doing this level of self-exploration is a must if you intend to work with families. Committing yourself to this task will better enable you to appreciate what client family members go through when they are in therapy with you. We encourage you to stick with the process of discovery, preferably under supervision. It helps to be able to talk to someone about what you are learning.

Change does not come about without some pain and anxiety. Your commitment to exploration and change may bring discomfort to significant people in your life. Being involved in a training program as a helper involves some risks to your current relationships. Your parents, siblings, spouse, children, or other relatives may be threatened by some of your changes. You may believe in the value of recognizing pain and dealing with it, and as a result of your changed perspective you may want your parents or siblings also to adopt a new outlook and change their ways. Perhaps they have avoided pain and are not interested in disturbing this pattern. Even if facing their situation could lead to basic changes and a fuller existence, it is not for you to decide that they should be any different than they are now.

As a result of what you are learning about human relationships in your program, along with positive changes you are making in your life, it can be difficult for you to see family members who seem to settle for a limited existence, if not a destructive lifestyle. You might ask, "How can I help other families in trouble if I cannot help my own family?" If you burden yourself with the thought that it is your task to change members of your family, you will end up feeling frustrated.

A graduate student in a counseling program approached one of us and said he felt burdened in putting to use in his own family what he was learning in his courses. Asked what he hoped to accomplish for a weekend therapeutic group aimed at self-exploration, he said: "I feel an urgency to resolve all my problems with my family by the end of this weekend workshop. After all, how can I help my future clients solve their problems if I have problems within my family?" Although this student was encouraged in his attempt to deal with his problems, he was setting himself up for failure by trying to meet an unrealistic expectation. Even more of a burden was his belief that it was his place to get significant people in his life to change. If people within his family were not motivated to make certain changes, he needed to realize that he would never be able to do it for them—no matter how talented he was. What he could do was to focus on himself and be true to himself, which in itself could be an invitation for them to change.

He could talk about the changes he had made. He could also let others know how he was affected by some of their behaviors and, as well, what kind of relationship he would like with them.

The point is to avoid adopting an attitude that others should change. Patience and respect are critical. To make changes in your life, you probably had to get through layers of your own defenses. It took both time and patience for you to allow yourself to become more vulnerable and open to new possibilities. Allow this same space for others in your life to consider their changes.

LO4 Understanding Life Transitions

In this section, we discuss major life themes at the various stages of human development from infancy through old age. **Personal transformation** demands an awareness of how you dealt with developmental tasks in the past and how you are now addressing these issues. By drawing on your own life experiences, both past and present, you are in a better position to appreciate the struggles of your clients, which enables you to intervene more effectively with them.

Our goal is for you to reflect on your life transitions and the significant decisions you made at those junctures. It is a major challenge to work through an upheaval such as marriage or divorce, the birth or death of a family member, losing a job, or retiring. All of these transition points test your ability to handle uncertainty, to leave what is known and secure, and to take a new direction in life.

In 2017 the American Psychological Association produced a report titled *Multicultural Guidelines: An Ecological Approach to Context, Identity, and Intersectionality*. Guideline 8 refers to developmental stages and life transitions:

> Psychologists seek awareness and understanding of how developmental stages and life transitions intersect with the larger biosociocultural context, how identity evolves as a function of such intersections, and how these different socialization and maturation experiences influence worldview and identity.

By understanding the challenges at each period of life, you will understand how earlier stages of personality development influence the choices you continue to make in life. There is great variability among individuals within a given developmental phase. Your family of origin, culture, race, gender, sexual orientation, and socioeconomic status all influence the way in which you experience the developmental process. Chronological age is only one index in considering emotional, physical, and social age.

LO5 A Theoretical Basis for Understanding Life Stages

There are many theoretical approaches to understanding human development, each of which provides a somewhat different conceptualization of the stages from infancy to old age. These theories provide a road map to understanding how people develop in all areas of personal functioning. We address three alternative perspectives on lifelong personality development in this section: we describe a model that draws on Erik Erikson's (1963, 1982) psychosocial theory of human development; incorporate Thomas Armstrong's (2007) "gifts" of each of the stages of life; and highlight some major ideas about development from the self-in-context approach, which emphasizes the individual life cycle in a systemic perspective (McGoldrick, Carter, & Garcia-Preto, 2011b).

The **systemic perspective** is grounded on the assumption that how we develop can best be understood through learning about our role and place in our family of origin. The systemic view is that individuals cannot really be understood apart from the family system of which they are a part.

We describe nine stages of development from infancy to old age by pointing out the **psychosocial tasks** for each phase. We also briefly describe potential problems in personality development if these tasks are not mastered. Acute and chronic illness during any period of life can disrupt the transition through the different life stages. For example, juvenile diabetes may disrupt normal childhood experiences; spinal cord injury, cancer, and HIV/AIDS can disrupt midcareer and social development. It is essential to recognize how your own development can be either an asset or a liability in your efforts to help others. As you read and reflect on these stages of development, ask yourself how well you have mastered some of the major psychosocial tasks at each period of your development.

Erikson's (1963, 1982) model is holistic, addressing humans inclusively as biological, social, and psychological beings. **Psychosocial theory** provides a conceptual framework for understanding trends in development; major developmental tasks at each stage of life; critical needs and their satisfaction or frustration; potentials for choice at each stage of life; critical turning points or developmental crises; and the origins of faulty personality development, which lead to later personality conflicts. Erikson's theory holds that we face the task of establishing equilibrium between ourselves and our social world at each stage of life.

Erikson describes human development over the entire life span in terms of various stages, each marked by a particular crisis to be resolved. For Erikson, **crisis** means a turning point in life, a moment of transition characterized by the potential to go either forward or backward in development. Critical turning points in our lives are influenced by a variety of biological, psychological, and social factors. Although we may not have direct control of some key elements of our development, such as early experiences and genetics, we have choices about how we interpret these experiences and use them to further our growth. At key turning points in life, we can either successfully resolve the basic conflict or get stuck on the road to development. These turning points represent both dangers and opportunities: crises can be viewed as challenges to be met or as catastrophic events that simply happen to you. Each developmental stage builds on the psychological outcomes of earlier stages, and individuals sometimes fail to resolve the conflicts and thus regress. To a very large extent, an individual's current life is the result of earlier choices; life has continuity.

In *The Human Odyssey: Navigating the Twelve Stages of Life*, Thomas Armstrong (2007) maintains that every stage of life is equally significant and necessary for the welfare of humanity. Each stage of life has its own unique **gift** to contribute to the world. Armstrong believes that we should take the same attitude toward nurturing the human life cycle as we do toward protecting the environment from global warming and other threats. He argues that by supporting each of the developmental stages, we are helping to ensure that people are given care and helped to develop to their fullest potential.

McGoldrick, Carter, and Garcia-Preto (2011b) have criticized Erikson's theory of individual development for underplaying the importance of the interpersonal realm and connection to others. Contextual factors have a critical bearing on our ability to formulate a clear identity as an individual and also to be able to connect to others. The **self-in-context perspective**, as described by McGoldrick and colleagues, takes into account race, socioeconomic class, gender, ethnicity, and culture as central factors that influence the course of development throughout the individual's life cycle. These factors influence a child's beliefs about self and ways of being emotionally connected with others. For healthy development to occur, it is necessary to establish a clear sense of our unique selves in the context of our connection with others at each stage of life.

Infancy

In **infancy**, birth to age 1, the basic task is to develop a sense of trust in self, others, and the environment. The infant is a vibrant and seemingly unlimited source of energy (Armstrong, 2007). The core struggle at this time is for **trust versus mistrust** (Erikson, 1982). If the significant persons in an infant's life provide the needed warmth and attention, the child develops a sense of trust. This sense of being loved is the best safeguard against fear, insecurity, and feelings of inadequacy.

If there is an absence of security in the home, personality problems tend to occur later. Insecure children come to view the world as a potentially frightening and dangerous place. They have a fear of reaching out to others, a fear of loving and trusting, and an inability to form or maintain intimate relationships. Rejected children learn to mistrust the world and view it largely in terms of its ability to do them harm. Some of the effects of rejection in infancy include tendencies in later childhood to be fearful, insecure, jealous, aggressive, hostile, and isolated. To illustrate the negative impact of starting out life on a foundation of mistrust, consider the case of Lionel who spent the first several months of his life being raised by neglectful parents before going into foster care. As an adult, Lionel is extremely guarded when he is around others, convinced that they are going to disappoint him. He pushes others away, especially intimate partners, by isolating himself whenever they get too close.

Daniel Goleman (1995) believes that infancy is the beginning point for establishing **emotional intelligence**, which he defines as the ability to control impulses, empathize with others, form responsible interpersonal relationships, and develop intimate relationships. He identifies the most crucial factor in teaching emotional competence as timing, especially in our family of origin and in our culture of origin during infancy. He adds that childhood and adolescence expand on the foundation for learning a range of human competencies. Later development offers the critical windows of opportunity for acquiring the basic emotional patterns that will govern the rest of our lives.

Reflections and application. As you reflect on the developmental tasks during this stage, think about the foundation you had during your earliest years and how these experiences either prepared you or handicapped you for the tasks you now face in your life. Consider these questions: What did you learn from your family of origin about how to be in the world? Do you have difficulty trusting others? Are you able to trust yourself and your ability to make it in the world? Do you have fears that others will let you down and that you have to be very careful about how much you show of yourself?

Early Childhood

The most critical task of **early childhood**, ages 1 to 3, is to begin the journey toward autonomy. The core struggle at this time is for **autonomy versus shame and doubt** (Erikson, 1982). By progressing from being taken care of by others to being able to care for one's own needs, children increase their understanding of interdependence and develop a sense of emotional competence, which involves delaying gratification.

Children who fail to master the task of establishing some control over themselves and coping with the world around them develop a sense of shame and feelings of doubt about their capabilities. Parents who do too much for children hamper their development. If parents insist on keeping children dependent, these children will begin to doubt the value of their own abilities. During this period, it is essential that feelings such as anger be accepted rather than judged. If anger is not accepted, children may not be able to deal with anger in their interpersonal relationships later in life. They will become adults who feel they must deny all of their "unacceptable" feelings.

Reflections and application. Some helpers have trouble recognizing or expressing angry feelings. Thus, they also have trouble allowing their clients to have these "unacceptable" feelings and may steer clients away from these feelings. If this description fits you, are you able to see any alternatives other than withdrawing from anger? One way you could behave differently is to remain in the room physically and psychologically as a client directs his anger toward you. Later, during a supervision session, you can deal with the fears that were evoked in you. If these feelings and attitudes get in the way of dealing with your clients, you may need to address this in your personal therapy.

Preschool

During the **preschool** years, ages 3 to 6, children seek to find out what they are able to do. The core struggle at this time is for **initiative versus guilt** (Erikson, 1982). According to Erikson, the basic task of the preschool years is to establish a sense of competence and initiative. Preschoolers begin to learn to give and receive love and affection, learn basic attitudes regarding sexuality, and learn more complex social skills. According to Armstrong (2007), the gift of this stage of life is *playfulness*. When young children play, they re-create the world anew. They take *what is* and combine it with *what is possible* to fashion new events. If children are allowed realistic freedom to choose their own activities and make some of their own decisions, they tend to develop a positive orientation characterized by confidence in their ability to initiate and follow through. According to the self-in-context perspective, this stage ushers in the awareness of "otherness" in terms of gender, race, and disability. A key task is to increase trust in others (McGoldrick et al., 2011b).

If children are unduly restricted or not allowed to make decisions for themselves, they develop a sense of guilt and ultimately withdraw from taking an active stance toward life. To illustrate this, suppose Debo learned during her preschool years that she had no say in what she was allowed to wear or what games she was allowed to play. As an adult, Debo has adopted a passive and avoidant style. Debo feels guilty when she is forced to make decisions because she is afraid she may make the wrong choice.

During this period the foundations of gender-role identity are laid, and children begin to form a picture of appropriate masculine and feminine behavior. At some point both women and men may want to broaden their conception of what kind of person they want to be. However, early conditioning often makes the expansion of the self-concept somewhat difficult. Many people seek counseling because of problems they experience in regard to their gender-role identity.

Reflections and application. As you read and apply the developmental tasks of this stage to your own life, look for patterns in your present attitudes and behavior that could be traced to your preschool years. Consider some of these questions: Have you become the kind of woman or man you want to be? Where did you acquire your standards of appropriate gender-role behavior? What conflicts from your childhood affect you today? Do your present behaviors and current conflicts indicate areas of unfinished business?

Middle Childhood

Erikson (1982) states that the major struggle of **middle childhood**, ages 6 to 12, is **industry versus inferiority**. The central task is to achieve a sense of industry; failure to do so results in a sense of inadequacy. Children need to expand their understanding of the world and continue to develop an appropriate gender-role identity. The development of a sense of industry includes focusing on creating goals, such as meeting challenges and finding success in school. According to Armstrong (2007), *imagination* is a key gift during the first half of this stage. The sense of an inner subjective self develops, and this sense of self is alive with images taken from the environment. During the second half of this stage, *ingenuity* is a key characteristic. Older children acquire a range of social and technical skills that enable them to deal with the increasing pressures they are facing.

From the self-in-context view, this is a time when children increase their understanding of self in terms of gender, race, culture, and abilities. There is an increased understanding of self in relation to family, peers, and community. A key task is developing empathy, or being able to take the perspective of others (McGoldrick et al., 2011b).

Children who encounter failure in their early schooling often experience major handicaps later in life. Those children with early learning problems may begin to feel worthless. Such feelings often dramatically affect their relationships with their peers, which are also vital at this time. Problems that can originate during middle childhood include a negative self-concept, feelings of inferiority in establishing and maintaining social relationships, conflicts over values, a confused gender-role identity, dependency, a fear of new challenges, and a lack of initiative. For example, one lasting psychological effect of Bronwyn's underachievement in school during her middle childhood years is her deep-seated belief as an adult that she does not have much to offer as a person and that she is not important. She avoids most personal and professional situations that may require her to take risks because she does not believe she can achieve any meaningful goals.

Reflections and application. What were some of the highlights of the first few years in school for you? Did you feel competent or incompetent as a learner? Did you see school as an exciting place to be or as a place that you wanted to avoid? What were some of the specific ways in which you felt that you were successful or that you were a failure? What attitudes did you form about your competence as a person during your early school years? Think of some significant people in your life at this time who affected you either positively or negatively. Attempt to recall some of their expectations for you, and remember the messages they gave you about your worth and potential. How might this be influencing you today?

Adolescence

Adolescence, ages 12 to 20, is a period of searching for an identity, continuing to find one's voice, and balancing caring of self with caring about others. The core struggle is over **identity versus identity confusion** (Erikson, 1982). Armstrong (2007) describes the unique gift of this stage of life as *passion*. A powerful set of changes in the adolescent body is reflected in sexual, emotional, cultural, and spiritual passion and a deep inner zeal for life. From the self-in-context perspective, key developmental tasks include dealing with rapid body changes and body image issues, learning self-management, developing one's sexual identity, developing a philosophy of life and a spiritual identity, learning to deal with intimate relationships, and an expanded understanding of self in relation to others (McGoldrick et al., 2011b).

For Erikson (1963, 1982), the major developmental conflicts of adolescence center on the clarification of who you are, where you are going, and how you are getting there. The struggle involves integrating physical and social changes. Adolescents may feel pressured to make career choices early, to compete in the job market or in college, to become financially independent, and to commit themselves to physically and emotionally intimate relationships. Peer-group pressure is a major force, and it is easy to lose oneself by conforming to the expectations of friends. With the increasing stress experienced by many adolescents, suicidal ideation is not uncommon.

During the adolescent period, a major part of the identity-formation process consists of separation from the family system and establishment of an identity based on one's own experiences. The process of separating from parents can be an agonizing part of the struggle toward individuation. Although adolescents may adopt many of their parents' values, to individuate they must choose these values freely as opposed to accepting them without thought.

Reflections and application. Take a few moments to review some of your adolescent experiences. How did you feel about yourself during this time? In reviewing these years, how might your experiences work for or against you in dealing with your clients? Think about your degree of independence and interdependence during your adolescence. Focus on what gave meaning to your life. Also, ask yourself these questions: At this time in my life, did I have a clear sense of who I was and where I was going? What major choices did I struggle with during my adolescent years? As you review this period, focus on how your adolescent experiences affected the person you are today.

Early Adulthood

According to Erikson (1982), we enter **early adulthood**, ages 20 to 35, after we master the adolescent conflicts over identity. Our sense of identity is tested anew in adulthood, however, by the core struggle for **intimacy versus isolation**. The ability to form intimate relationships depends largely on having a clear sense of self. Intimacy involves sharing, giving ourselves, relating to another based on our strength, and a desire to grow with that person. If we think very little of ourselves, the chances are not good that we will be able to give meaningfully to others. The failure to achieve intimacy often results in feelings of isolation from others and a sense of alienation. Judith is a prime example of a young woman who failed to develop a strong sense of self as a result of her earlier struggles. She tries to act the way she thinks others want her to act in a desperate attempt to gain love, approval, and acceptance, but she invariably ends up feeling lost and alone. She has had a number of intimate partners, but they seem to distance themselves from her after a short time.

Armstrong (2007) identifies the principle of *enterprise* as a key characteristic of this stage of life. For young adults to accomplish the tasks facing them (such as finding a home and a partner or establishing a career), enterprise is required. This characteristic serves us well at any stage of life when we go into the world to make our mark.

The major aim of early adulthood is being able to engage in intimate relationships and find satisfying work. Some developmental issues include caring for self and others, focusing on long-range goals, nurturing others physically and emotionally, finding meaning in life, and developing tolerance for delaying gratification to meet long-range goals (McGoldrick et al., 2011b).

As we leave adolescence and enter early adulthood, our central task is to assume increased responsibility and independence. Although most of us have moved away from our parents physically, not all of us have done so psychologically. To a greater or lesser degree, our parents will have a continuing influence on our lives. Cultural factors play a significant role in determining the degree to which our parents influence our lives. For example, in some cultures developing a spirit of independence is not encouraged. Instead, these cultures place a prime value on cooperation with others and on a spirit of interdependence. In some cultures, parents continue to have a significant impact and influence on their children even after they reach adulthood. Respect and honor for parents may be values that are extolled above individual freedom by the adult children. In these cultures, the struggle for autonomy may be to define one's place in the family rather than to separate from it.

Autonomy, a key developmental task of early adulthood, refers to mature self-governance. If you are an autonomous person, you are able to function without constant approval and reassurance, are sensitive to the needs of others, can effectively meet the demands of daily living, are willing to ask for help when it is needed, and can provide support to others. You are at home with both your inner world and your outer world. Although you are concerned with meeting your needs, you do not do so at the expense of those around you. You are aware of the impact your behavior may have on others, and you consider the welfare of others as well as your own self-development. Making decisions about the quality of life you want for yourself is partly what autonomy is about. Autonomy also entails your willingness to accept responsibility for the consequences of your choices rather than placing the responsibility on others if you are not satisfied with the way your life is going. Furthermore, achieving a healthy balance between independence and interdependence is not something you do at a given time once and for all. The struggle between autonomy and interdependence begins in early childhood and continues throughout life.

In writing about genuine maturity from the self-in-context perspective, McGoldrick and colleagues (2011b) remind us that the ultimate goal in Western societies is to develop a mature, interdependent self. We are challenged to establish a solid sense of our unique self in the context of our connection to others. This systemic perspective is based on the assumption that maturity requires the ability to empathize, communicate, collaborate, connect, trust, and respect others.

Reflections and application. If you are a middle-aged or older person, what decisions did you make in early adulthood, and how do you think those decisions would influence the way you might work with clients? Do you have any regrets about the choices you made? How do you think your own struggles (or lack of them) would affect you in working with clients who have problems deciding for themselves what they want to do personally and vocationally?

Middle Adulthood

Middle adulthood, between ages 35 and 55, is characterized by a "going outside of ourselves." The core struggle at this time is for **generativity versus stagnation** (Erikson, 1982). It is a time for learning how to live creatively with ourselves and with others, and it can be the time of greatest productivity in our lives. This is a period when people are likely to engage in a philosophical reexamination of their lives, which may result in reinventing themselves in their work and in their involvement in the community (McGoldrick et al., 2011b). Armstrong (2007) refers to *contemplation* as the gift of middle adulthood. People in midlife reflect on the deeper meaning of their lives, which is an important resource that can be drawn on to enrich life at any age. Other tasks include nurturing and supporting one's children, partner, and older family members. A challenge is to recognize accomplishments and accept limitations. Generativity includes being creative in one's career, finding meaningful leisure activities, and establishing significant relationships in which there is giving and receiving.

As is true with any stage, there are both dangers and opportunities during this time. Some of the dangers include slipping into secure, but stale ways of being, and failing to take advantage of opportunities for enriching life.

Many individuals experience a midlife crisis, when their whole world seems to be unstable. During middle age, there is sometimes a period of depression. When people begin to see that some of their visions have not materialized, they may give up hope for a better future. A problem of this period is the failure to achieve a sense of productivity, which then leads to feelings of stagnation. It is important that individuals realize the choices they have in their life and see the changes they can make rather than giving in to the feeling that they are victims of life's circumstances. At age 48, Steve has realized that his dream of rising up the corporate ladder is probably not going to happen. He has had the same middle management position for several years and repeatedly has been overlooked for promotions. Steve is angered by the success of his younger colleagues but doesn't consider looking for another job because he is certain that remaining in his current position is his only option.

Reflections and application. If you have reached middle adulthood, what struggles and decisions could you draw on as a resource? If you have not yet reached middle age, what would you most want to have accomplished in your life by this time? What would be your expectations for your relationships? What would you want from your work? How might you go about keeping yourself alive and avoiding predictable ruts?

Late Middle Age

Erikson does not differentiate between middle age and late middle age, but instead has one general stage that spans the period from the mid-30s to the mid-60s. For Armstrong (2007), the gift of this period is *benevolence.* Through their example, others are able to learn ways of striving to make the world a better place. McGoldrick and colleagues (2011b) differentiate between these two phases of middle age. For them, **late middle age**, ages 55 to 70, is a time when many adults are beginning to consider retirement, pursuing new interests, and thinking more about what they want to do with the rest of their lives. It is a period for taking up new interests, which may be increasingly possible as child rearing or financial responsibilities fade in importance. During this time, people become more aware of the reality of death, and they may reflect more on whether they are living well. It is a time for reevaluation and a time when people are at the crossroads of life. They may begin to question what else is left, and they may establish new priorities or renew their commitments. Late middle age is a period when people reach the top of the mountain and become aware that they must begin the downhill journey. They might painfully experience the discrepancy between the dreams of their younger years and the harsh reality of what they have actually accomplished with their life so far. A challenge during this period of life is coming to terms with the reality that not everything could be done. People face the challenge of letting go of some of their dreams, accepting their limitations, giving up dwelling on what they cannot do, and instead, focusing on what they *can* do (McGoldrick et al., 2011b).

Many people in their mid-50s have reached their peak in terms of status and personal power, and this can be a satisfying time of life. Adults at this stage often do a lot of reflecting, contemplating, refocusing, and evaluating of themselves so they can continue to discover new directions.

Reflections and application. For a moment, reflect on a few personal and professional accomplishments you would most want to realize by the time you reach late middle age. If you could create a new direction at this time in your life, what might it look like?

Late Adulthood

Late adulthood, age 70 onward, is characterized by the core struggle for **integrity versus despair** (Erikson, 1982). Encountering the death of parents and losses of friends and relatives confronts us with the reality of preparing ourselves for our own death. A basic task of late adulthood is to complete a life review in which we put our life into perspective and come to accept who we are and what we have done. From Armstrong's (2007) perspective, people in late adulthood give the gift of *wisdom*. Older adults represent the source of wisdom that exists in each of us, which helps us avoid the mistakes of the past and reap the benefits of life's lessons. This is also a time in life when spirituality may take on a new meaning and provide us with a sense of purpose, even as we face a growing dependence on others (McGoldrick et al., 2011b). Prevalent themes for people during late adulthood include loss; loneliness and social isolation; feelings of rejection; the struggle to find meaning in life; dependency; feelings of uselessness, hopelessness, and despair; fears of death and dying; grief over others' deaths; sadness over physical and mental deterioration; and regrets over past events. Today, many of these themes characterize people in their mid-80s more than people in their 60s and even 70s.

People who succeed in achieving ego integrity are able to accept that they have been productive and that they have coped with whatever failures they faced. Such people are able to accept the course of their lives, and they do not endlessly ruminate on all that they could have done, might have done, and should have done. In contrast, some older people fail to achieve ego integration. They are able to see all that they have not done, and they often yearn for another chance to live in a different way. Florence, age 72, is plagued with regrets about the friendships she lost over the years due to her decision to invest all of her time with her husband, James, who passed away 2 years ago. She also regrets passing up opportunities to develop hobbies or to pursue a career. If she had it to do all over again, she would be more assertive and tell James that she needs to pursue friendships and interests outside of their relationship.

Late adulthood has changed just as dramatically as the earlier middle-age stages. As is the case for each of these developmental stages, there is a great deal of individual variance. Many 70-year-olds have as much energy as many middle-aged people. How people look and feel during late adulthood is more than a matter of physical age; it is largely a matter of attitude. To a great degree, vitality is influenced by state of mind more than by mere chronological years lived.

Reflections and application. If you have not reached old age, imagine yourself at that time of life. What would you like to be able to say about your life? What kind of relationships would you most hope to be able to have established at this time in your life? Focus especially on your fears of aging and also on what you hope you could accomplish by this time. What do you expect in these later years? What are you doing now that might have an effect on the kind of person you will be when you are old? Can you think of any regrets you will be likely to express? As you anticipate growing older, think about what you can do today to increase the chances that you will be able to achieve a sense of integrity as an older person. Are you cultivating interests and relationships that can become a source of satisfaction in later years?

If you find yourself postponing many things that you would like to do now, ask yourself why. Assess the degree to which you are satisfied with the person you are becoming today. Finally, assess your present ability to work with older clients. If you yourself have not reached this age, what experiences could you draw on as a way of understanding the world of an older client? Even though you might not have had some of the same experiences, do you see how you can relate to some of their feelings that are very much like your own?

Most of us can look back in our lives and remember enough to reflect effectively on our past transitions and experience, but we are able to look forward only about 10 years beyond our current age. If you are in late adolescence or early adulthood, interview older people at different developmental stages to gain a better understanding of what lies ahead. Listen with your heart. What can these people teach you about life and about what is yet to come?

It is critical to understand and reflect on the turning points in your own life so you will have a framework for working with clients. Self-exploration and self-understanding is a continuous process. You will need to know yourself if you hope to become a therapeutic agent in the lives of others. As we tell our own students, "You won't be able to take clients any further than you have been willing to go in your own life."

By Way of Review

- Some training programs offer family-of-origin work for students as a way for them to come to a fuller appreciation of how their family experiences have influenced who and what they are. This training enables helpers to relate more effectively to the families they will meet in their clinical practice.
- To increase your effectiveness when working with families, it is essential that you unravel the mystery of your connection with your family of origin and that you become aware of ways you continue to play out patterns established during childhood.
- When interpreting the meaning of your experiences growing up in your family, it is useful to think about the structure of your family, your relationships with your parents and siblings, key turning points for your family, and the messages your parents conveyed.
- Being a professional helper often reopens your own psychological wounds. If you are not willing to work on your unfinished business, you might reconsider whether you want to accompany clients on their journey of dealing with their past wounds.
- Personal counseling, both individual and group work, is of value in increasing your self-awareness and providing you with an opportunity to explore your unresolved conflicts. By becoming involved in your own counseling, you can gain increased insight into personal issues that could intrude in your work.

- Family therapy and personal therapy can illuminate your own areas of transference and countertransference and broaden your vision of how your family-of-origin experiences have served as a template for later interpersonal relationships. Your experience with the therapeutic process can increase your awareness of certain patterns of thinking, feeling, and behaving.
- Each of the stages of life represents a turning point when individuals are challenged with the fulfillment of their destinies. Both helpers and clients need to realize that personal transformation entails the willingness to tolerate pain and uncertainty. Growth is not generally a smooth process but involves a degree of turmoil.
- At each stage of life there are choices to be made. Your earlier choices have an impact on the kind of person you are now.
- Specific tasks and specific crises can occur from infancy through old age. Review your own developmental history so that you have a perspective in working with the developmental struggles of your clients. You will be in a better position to understand your clients' problems and to work with them if you have an understanding of your own life experiences and vulnerabilities.
- How you cope with crises in your own life is a good indication of your ability to help your clients work through theirs. If you face and deal with your problems with all the resources available to you, you can be present for clients who are in crisis. Your understanding of ways to tap internal resources can serve you as you guide clients in discovering their resources for change.

What Will You Do Now?

1. As a basis for discovering more about your family of origin, interview your parents and any others who knew you well as you were growing up. You can ask each of these people a specific list of questions about yourself. The point of this exercise is for you to gather information about events or situations that can assist you in getting a fuller picture of your childhood. What does each person remember the most about you? Are you able to detect any themes in what the people you interview recall about you?
2. Develop a list of questions to help you understand what it was like for your parents as they were growing up. For example, you might ask your parents what their relationships with their parents were like at ages 6, 14, or 21. The aim of the exercise is not to put them on the spot or to get them to divulge secrets, but to better understand the hopes, goals, concerns, fears, and dreams your parents had as children, adolescents, and young adults. You might talk with your parents about how their early experiences influenced them as parents. Discuss with them any patterns you see between them and yourself.
3. If possible, consider interviewing your grandparents. Again, in thinking about questions you would like them to address, be sensitive to how they might respond to sharing personal facets of their lives. You might simply ask them to share any events or memories that they would feel comfortable disclosing. Rather than simply asking them questions, consider sharing with them significant memories you have of them as you were growing up.

What did they teach you? What similar patterns do you see that have been handed down from your grandparents, to your parents, to you, and to your children, if any?

4. Consider starting a personal journal or scrapbook that will compile significant information about your family of origin. In putting this project together, focus on the self-exploration questions raised in this chapter. You might even include material that reflects turning points in your life. For example, you might include a poem you wrote or a greeting card you received—anything that seems meaningful to you. In doing this project, it would be useful to include pictures of you and your parents, siblings, grandparents, other relatives, and friends. Include any input from your parents, grandparents, and other relatives that will provide details of your family-of-origin experiences. Look for themes and patterns that will give you a clearer picture of the forces that still influence you today.
5. Much of this chapter provides you with material for reflection about how your family-of-origin experiences influence the person you are today. Spend some time thinking about what you learned about yourself *personally* by reading this chapter. Are there any personal issues that you see as being unresolved and that you are committed to exploring? If so, write about this unfinished business in your journal. How might your own unresolved personal issues affect your ability to work with individuals who are struggling with concerns pertaining to their family?
6. Write down a list of resources for personal growth and ways of increasing your self-awareness. Think of some avenues that would promote self-exploration on your part. Are you willing to pursue any of these resources and engage in further personal growth beyond the requirements of the course you are taking?
7. Remember a time in your life that was either the most difficult (painful) or the most exciting (joyful). What did you learn from these experiences? If this time occurred during childhood, talk with someone you knew well as a child about what he or she remembers of you. What are the implications of these experiences in your own life for you as a helper? How might some of your life experiences affect you as you work with others who are like you? different from you?
8. Reflect on some of your life experiences that you think will facilitate your work with clients. Use your journal to record a few key turning points in your life. Can you think of one or two times when you were faced with making a major decision? If so, how might this turning point still have an influence on your life? What lessons did you learn from making this decision, and how might this experience better enable you to identify with the struggles of clients?
9. In small groups, spend some time exploring how your experiences with your family are likely to influence your work with families and with individuals as well. What are some of your attitudes about family life that will surface in your professional work?
10. For the full bibliographic entry for each of these sources, consult the References at the back of the book. For a self-in-context developmental approach that emphasizes an individual life cycle in a systemic perspective, see McGoldrick, Carter, and Garcia-Preto (2011b). See Armstrong (2007) for

a discussion of the stages of development in the life cycle. For an overview of development through life from a psychosocial perspective, see Newman and Newman (2015). For a comprehensive and well-written book on family therapy, see Bitter (2014). For themes and choices dealing with childhood, adolescence, and adulthood, refer to G. Corey, Corey, & Muratori (2018).

Ethics in Action Video Exercises

11. In video role play 2, Dealing With Anger: A Protective Brother, the client (Richard) reports that his sister is dating an Asian man. Richard is angry and says he is not going to let that happen. He adds that his sister is not going to mess with his family like that. The counselor (Nadine) asks Richard if he thinks his sister should live to make him happy. He says, "My sister is going to do what I say and that's just it!" This vignette shows how a counselor's own unfinished personal issues can get in the way of counseling a client who is expressing anger. Identify and discuss the ethical issues you see played out in this vignette. Reenact the role play by having several students take the role of counselor to show alternative perspectives.
12. Video role play 5, Giving Advice: Taking Charge, illustrates how a counselor's lack of self-awareness can be problematic. The counselor (Nadine) is giving an abundance of advice. She is telling her client (John) that he needs to take charge and decide what is the right way to treat his children. When counselors focus on telling clients what they should be doing, it is a good idea to consider whether countertransference issues may be blocking the therapeutic process. Role-play how you might deal with John's concerns about how he is treating his children. Show how you might deal with a client who asks for your advice.
13. In video role play 7, Family Values: The Divorce, the client (Janice) has decided to leave her husband and get a divorce. She tells her counselor (Gary) that she doesn't want to work on her marriage anymore. Janice says that she is tired of her husband's anger and moods. The counselor responds: "I hate to hear that. What about your kids? Who will be the advocate for them?" She says, "If I am happy, they will be happy. I will take care of my kids." The counselor concludes by asking, "Is divorce the best way to take care of your children?" It is clear that the counselor has an agenda for the client and is focused on the welfare of her children. The client feels misunderstood and does not think the counselor is helping her. In small groups, discuss the main ethical issues in this case. If you were Janice's counselor, what kind of questions would you ask of Janice, if any?

    Put yourself in this situation with a client similar to Janice. Your client is experiencing a great deal of ambivalence about getting a divorce, even though she tells you she is convinced that her marital situation is hopeless. She pleads with you to tell her whether she should remain married or get a divorce. What approach might you take? Have one student role-play the confused client who is searching for an answer and ask several students to give different ways of proceeding with this client.

CHAPTER 3

Knowing Your Values

Learning Objectives

1. Describe how helper values operate in the counseling process.
2. Discuss the ethical issues involved in imposing helper values.
3. Explain the reasons a referral is not an answer for resolving value conflicts.
4. Explain the implications of significant court cases on value conflicts.
5. Identify ways oppression and discrimination are associated with sexual orientation.
6. Explain how values are sometimes related to gender-role identity.
7. Discuss the role of spiritual/religious values in the helping process.
8. List several guidelines for dealing with end-of-life issues.

Focus Questions

1. To what degree are you aware of your core values and how they could affect the way you work with clients?
2. Is it possible for you to interact with clients without making value judgments? Do you think it is ever appropriate to make value judgments? If so, under what circumstances?
3. Can you be true to your own values and at the same time respect your clients' choices, even if they differ from yours?
4. Do you tend to influence your friends and family regarding "right" choices? If so, what are the implications for the way you are likely to function as a helper?
5. To what extent can you support clients in making their own decisions, even if you believe they would be better served by following a different path?
6. What key values do you believe are essential to the helping process? How would you communicate these values to your clients?
7. Why do you think the imposition of a counselor's values is an ethical issue?
8. What is one particular value you might find challenging in your work with clients?
9. What do you think is involved in counselors managing their values as they work with a diverse range of clients?
10. Do you think a referral is ever an ethical answer in resolving a value conflict with a client?

Aim of the Chapter

The helping professions involve value-laden processes. We must respect our clients' worldview and understand their value system to be of help to them and to be agents of change and empowerment. Even if we hold a very different set of values, our ethical obligation is to assist clients in meeting therapeutic goals consistent with their worldview and values, not our own. It is our clients who have to live with the consequences of the changes they make in counseling, not us.

To assist you in clarifying your values and identifying ways in which they might interfere with effective helping, we describe a range of practical situations you may encounter. Value issues pertaining to multicultural populations are of special importance, and Chapter 4 is devoted to this topic. In this chapter, you are encouraged to critically evaluate the possible impact of your personal values on your clients, the effect your clients' values may have on you, the conflicts that can arise if you and your clients have different values, and the importance of learning to effectively manage these conflicts.

LO1 Role of Values in Helping

Values are embedded in therapeutic theory and practice. Levitt and Moorhead (2013) contend that values not only enter the counseling relationship but can significantly affect many facets of the relationship. Counselors are expected to be able to set aside their personal beliefs and values when working with a wide range of clients. Although helpers may not agree with the values of some clients, counselors are expected to respect the rights of clients to hold their own views. Effective helpers must learn to work with a variety of clients with diverse worldviews and values.

Complete the following self-inventory as a way of focusing your thinking on the role your values will play in your work. As you read each statement, decide the degree to which it most closely identifies your attitudes and beliefs about *your role as a helper*. Use this code:

3 = This statement is true for me.
2 = This statement is not true for me.
1 = I am undecided.

____ 1. I believe it is my task to challenge a client's philosophy of life.

____ 2. I could work objectively and effectively with clients who have values that differ sharply from my own.

____ 3. I believe it is both possible and desirable for me to remain neutral with respect to values when working with clients.

____ 4. Although I have a clear set of values for myself, I feel quite certain that I could avoid unduly influencing my clients to adopt my beliefs.

____ 5. It is appropriate to express my views and expose my values as long as I do not impose them on clients.

____ 6. I might be inclined to subtly influence my clients to consider some of my values.

____ 7. If I discovered sharp value conflicts between a client and me, I would consider referring the client.

____ 8. I have certain spiritual and religious views that would influence the way I work.

____ 9. I would not have any difficulty counseling a pregnant woman who wanted to explore abortion as one of her alternatives.

____ 10. I have certain views pertaining to gender roles that might affect the way I counsel.

____ 11. I would not have problems counseling a gay couple on relationship concerns.

____ 12. I see the clarification of a client's values as a crucial task in the helping process.

____ 13. My view of family life would influence the way I would counsel a couple considering divorce.

____ 14. I would have no trouble working with a woman (man) who wanted to leave her (his) children and live alone, if this is what my client decided.

____ 15. I have generally been willing to critically evaluate my values.

____ 16. I might be willing to work in individual counseling with a client who is in a committed relationship and is having an affair, even if the client is not willing to disclose the relationship to his or her partner.

____ 17. I feel quite certain that I can separate my personal values from my professional values in working with clients in an objective way.

____ 18. I think I will work best with clients who have values similar to mine.

____ 19. I think it is appropriate to pray with my clients during a session if they request this of me.

____ 20. If I had a conflict of values with a client, I would talk about this with my client.

There are no "right" or "wrong" answers to these statements. The inventory is designed to stimulate your thinking on how your values are likely to influence the way you carry out your functions as a helper. Select a few items and talk with a fellow student about your views. As you read this chapter, assume an active stance, and think about your position on the value issues we raise.

LO2 Avoiding Imposing Values

The clients with whom you work ultimately have the responsibility of choosing what values to adopt, what values to modify or discard, and what direction their lives will take. Through the helping process, clients can learn to examine values before making choices. You may believe it is a good practice to disclose some of your values as you work with clients. If you are thinking of disclosing your values, it is critical that you assess the impact this might have on your client. Ask yourself these questions: Why am I disclosing and discussing my values with my client? What therapeutic benefit will my disclosure have for my client? How vulnerable is my client to being unduly influenced by me? Is my client too eager to embrace my value system? It is important that you avoid disclosing a particular value you hold as a way to steer your client toward accepting a value orientation consistent with your own. As you will discover again and again in this chapter, the counseling process is about the *client's values*, not the helper's values.

Even if you think it is inappropriate to impose your values on clients, you may unintentionally influence them in subtle ways to subscribe to your values. If you are strongly opposed to abortion, for example, you may not respect your client's right to consider abortion. On the basis of your convictions, you may subtly (or not so subtly) direct your client toward choices other than abortion. Practitioners cannot be completely objective and value-free (Shiles, 2009), but helpers must learn to separate their personal values from the counseling process. Kocet and Herlihy (2014) describe this process as **ethical bracketing**: "intentional setting aside of the counselor's personal values in order to provide ethical and appropriate counseling to all clients, especially those whose worldviews, values, belief systems, and decisions differ significantly from those of the counselor" (p. 182). It is essential that you take into consideration the ways you may influence your clients, either intentionally or unintentionally. Francis and Dugger (2014) emphasize that counselors are ethically responsible to monitor the various ways they may communicate their values to clients "and be aware of how the power differential that exists within each counseling relationship may result in the imposition of their values" (p. 132).

Some well-intentioned practitioners think their task is to help people conform to acceptable and absolute value standards. It is no easy task to avoid communicating your values to your clients, even if you do not explicitly express them. What you pay attention to during counseling sessions will direct what your clients choose to explore. The methods you use will provide them with clues to what you value. Your nonverbal messages give them indications of when you like or dislike what they are doing. Because your clients may feel a need to have your approval, they may respond to these clues by acting in ways that mirror your values instead of developing their own inner direction.

Refusing to work with clients simply because you do not agree with their values is unethical. We encourage you to consider this from the client's perspective. Imagine having the courage to seek help for a personal struggle only to be informed that the therapist will not accept you as a client due to a particular value you hold that may or may not be related to your presenting concern. It would be natural to feel offended, angry, and rejected. If you have low self-esteem and feel rejected by this therapist, you may feel even worse about yourself and give up on the idea of seeking therapy from a different helper. As you can see, referring clients due to value differences can harm clients.

Our Perspective on Values in the Helping Relationship

From an ethical perspective, it is imperative that helpers recognize the impact their values have on the way they work with clients. If you pay attention to your clients and why they are coming to see you, you will have a basis for inviting a discussion on how values influence your clients' behaviors.

Our position is that the helper's main task is to provide those who seek aid with the motivation needed to look at what they are doing, determine the degree to which what they are doing is consistent with their values, and consider whether their current behavior is meeting their needs. If clients conclude that their lives are not fulfilled, they can use the helping relationship to reexamine and modify their values or their actions, and they can explore a range of options that are open to them. Counseling is about working with clients within the framework of *their* value system. People seeking help must determine what they are willing to change and the ways they may want to modify their behavior.

Dealing With Value Conflicts

Your task is to help clients explore and clarify their beliefs and apply their values to solving their problems. The American Counseling Association (ACA, 2014) states this clearly:

> Counselors are aware of—and avoid imposing—their own values, attitudes, beliefs, and behaviors. Counselors respect the diversity of clients, trainees, and research participants and seek training in areas in which they are at risk of imposing their values onto clients, especially when the counselor's values are inconsistent with the client's goals or are discriminatory in nature. (Standard A.4.b.)

When you find yourself struggling with an ethical dilemma over value differences, the best course to follow may be to seek consultation in working through the situation so the appropriate standard of care can be provided (Kocet & Herlihy, 2014). Supervision is a useful way to explore value conflicts with clients. If you are having difficulty maintaining objectivity regarding a certain value, consider this your problem rather than the client's. Perhaps personal counseling will help you understand why your personal values are intruding in your professional work.

LO3 Referral Is Not an Answer to Resolving Value Conflicts

How do you know *when* and *how* to refer? How will the client be affected by a referral? Why would you want to refer? What kind of referral might be most appropriate? What if few referral resources are available? Herlihy and Corey (2015d) state that "referring a client due to a value conflict constitutes a discriminatory referral, which is unethical" (p. 194). Referring clients should not be used as a convenient solution when you are faced with value conflicts.

It is possible to work through a conflict successfully through a process of self-reflection. What is it about a client or a particular value difference that makes it difficult for you to work with the client? What barriers within you are making it difficult to separate your personal values from your professional responsibilities? Is it necessary that you and your client share a common set of values in a particular area? Mental health practitioners are sometimes too eager to suggest a referral rather than explore how they could work with a client's problem. Shiles (2009) notes that far too little has been written about situations in which referring a client is inappropriate, unethical, and may constitute an act of discrimination. For example, inappropriate referrals have been made for clients with differing religious beliefs, sexual orientations, or cultural backgrounds. Referrals should be limited to situations in which you do not have the competence or have not developed a particular skill set to help that individual with her or his concerns. The overuse of client referrals among mental health practitioners often involves discriminatory practices that are rationalized as ways to avoid practicing beyond one's level of competence.

LO4 Significant Court Cases on Value Conflicts

In two court cases, conservative Christian counselors-in-training filed suit against their public universities over the requirement that students avoid imposing their personal and moral values on clients.

Ward v. Wilbanks. In *Ward v. Wilbanks* (2010), Julea Ward, a master's degree student in counseling, filed suit against her university (Eastern Michigan University) over the requirement that she should be expected to counsel a client even in cases of major value conflicts. Ward frequently expressed a conviction that her Christian faith prevented her from affirming a client's same-sex relationship or a client's heterosexual extramarital relationship. During the last phase of her program in 2009, Ward was enrolled in a practicum that involved counseling clients and was randomly assigned to counsel a gay client. She asked her faculty supervisor to either refer the client to another student or to allow her to begin counseling and make a referral if the counseling sessions involved discussion of his relationship issues. Ward was told that refusing to see a client on the basis of sexual orientation was a violation of the ethics code for the counseling profession and therefore was not ethically acceptable. The counseling program initiated an informal and then a formal review process examining the reasons for Ward's request for a referral. The program offered her a plan for remediation so that she could keep her values separate from the counseling relationship, but she refused any plan for remediation on the grounds that this was a violation of her basic rights.

Ward was dismissed from the program and later sued the university in U.S. District Court, claiming that the dismissal violated her religious freedom and her civil rights. The district court ruled that the university was justified in dismissing Ward for violating provisions of the code of ethics that prohibit discrimination based on race, religion, national origin, age, sexual orientation, gender, gender identity, disability, marital status/partnership, language preference, or socioeconomic status. The court also ruled that the university was justified in enforcing a legitimate curricular requirement, specifically that counseling students must learn to work with diverse clients in ways that are nondiscriminatory.

The Alliance Defending Freedom (ADF) is a legal organization that defends individuals and organizations whose conservative religious views or actions are challenged in various arenas of public life. With help from the ADF, Ward appealed her case to the United States Court of Appeals for the Sixth Circuit, which sent the case back to district court for a jury trial. To avoid a costly trial, the case was settled out of court. As part of the settlement, the ADF dropped their demands that the university's curriculum, policies, and practices be changed. (For more information about this case, see Dugger & Francis [2014]; Herlihy, Hermann, & Greden [2014]; and Kaplan [2014]).

Keeton v. Anderson-Wiley. Jennifer Keeton was a counseling student at Augusta State University (ASU). In *Keeton v. Anderson-Wiley* (2010), Keeton actively sought to impose her religious and moral values on clients whose behavior she deemed to be morally wrong. She consistently maintained that she "condemned homosexuality" based on her interpretation of biblical teachings.

She stated her intention to recommend "conversion therapy" to gay clients and to inform them that they could choose to be straight. The faculty had concerns that Keeton would be unable to separate her personal religious views on sexual morality from her counseling practice. She was presented with a remediation plan, which she did not carry out, and she was dismissed from the training program. The federal appeals court upheld the right of the university to enforce standards expected of students in a counseling program, even when a student objects on religious grounds. (For a critical review of the ethical and legal implications of using religious beliefs as the basis for refusing to counsel certain clients, see Herlihy et al. [2014]).

Lessons learned. Kaplan (2014) asserts that *Ward v. Wilbanks* is the most important legal case for the counseling profession in the last 25 years. In his discussion of the ethical implications of *Ward v. Wilbanks*, Kaplan makes several salient points:

- Practitioners may not deny professional services to an individual belonging to a legally protected class based on the counselor's values.
- Referrals are appropriate on the basis of lacking skills-based competency. The focus of ethical referrals is on the needs of the client, not the values of the counselor.
- To avoid client abandonment, a referral should be considered as an option of last resort.
- The counselor's obligation to an individual begins at the first contact, not at the first session.

Dugger and Francis (2014) were on the faculty of Eastern Michigan University at the time of the lawsuit. They have addressed the lessons they learned from *Ward v. Wilbanks* and offer the following recommendations:

- It is crucial to have policies and procedures in place before a lawsuit is filed.
- Training programs should clearly articulate expectations for student behavior and performance based on ethical practice, identify consequences for failing to meet these expectations, and spell out due process procedures available to students.
- Training programs are expected to closely adhere to the policies and procedures they have in place.

Implications of court cases and legislation. Some political groups and lawmakers are retaliating against policies and ethics codes that prohibit discrimination on the basis of religion and sexual orientation by passing "freedom of conscience" clauses. For example, Arizona's Senate Bill 1365 ensures that mental health professionals will not put their licensure status in jeopardy by denying services to clients on the basis of sincerely held religious beliefs. This bill was signed into law by the governor of Arizona in May 2012. Similar bills have been introduced and passed in other states, but counselors must embrace the ethics code of their profession to conform to best practice standards.

The state of Tennessee passed controversial legislation in 2016 that would allow mental health practitioners in that state with "sincerely held principles" to deny services without risk of legal consequences to potential clients who identify as lesbian, gay, bisexual, or transgender. This discriminatory bill under the guise of "religious freedom" seeks to protect conservative therapists from certain 2014 changes in the American Counseling Association's *Code of Ethics*. As long as reluctant practitioners refer the client to another qualified professional, the bill states that they will be protected from licensure suspensions and any legal penalties. Supporters claim the bill protects the rights of therapists by allowing them to refer individuals to more appropriate professionals. Opponents claim that this legislation is part of a wave of bills around the country that legalizes discrimination against lesbian, gay, bisexual, and transgender people.

Wise and her colleagues (2015) maintain that these legislative initiatives (such as the bills enacted in Arizona and Tennessee) limit the ability of educators to train students to provide competent care to diverse client populations. Such legislative actions are potentially in conflict with the ethical commitment to nondiscrimination outlined in the ethical standards for the APA, the ACA, the AAMFT, and the NASW. In light of the contentious court cases and legislative actions, Wise and her colleagues (2015) call for training programs to take a proactive approach to conscience clauses rather than assume a reactive stance. They recommend that students who are entering a program indicate explicit agreement with nondiscrimination policies.

We fully agree that counselor training programs have a responsibility to be clear with prospective students about what is expected of them as ethical practitioners. Students enrolling in a program should be told from the outset that trainees cannot ethically discriminate against clients because of a difference in values or refuse to work with a general category of clients. Students need to be aware of these fundamental aspects of the code of ethics as these requirements will influence their development as counselors and will affect their participation in the program.

Mental health professionals should be able to work effectively with the diversity of worldviews, beliefs, and cultural identities they will encounter; conscientious objection acts clearly violate the letter and spirit of the ethics codes of the helping professions. If counseling students are not willing to learn to work with the wide range of clients they will encounter, we suggest that they reconsider whether counseling is the right profession for them.

In the remainder of this chapter, we consider some value-laden issues that you might encounter in your work with a range of client populations. These areas include concerns of lesbian, gay, bisexual, transgender, and gender nonconforming individuals; family values issues; gender-role identity issues; religious and spiritual values; abortion; sexuality; and end-of-life decisions.

LO5 Concerns of LGBTQI People

The concept of human diversity encompasses more than racial and ethnic factors; it encompasses all forms of oppression, discrimination, and prejudice, including those directed toward people on the basis of their age, gender, socioeconomic status, religious affiliation, disability, and sexual orientation. Working with lesbian, gay, bisexual, transgender, queer or questioning, and intersex (LGBTQI) individuals often presents a challenge to counselors who hold conservative religious values. When serving LGBTQI individuals, counselors must be aware of the attitudes and beliefs they hold that can either enhance or inhibit their counseling effectiveness with these populations. A counselor who works with LGBTQI people has a responsibility to understand the special concerns of these individuals and is ethically obligated to develop the knowledge and skills to competently deliver services to them (Corey, 2019).

Homosexuality and bisexuality were assumed to be a form of mental illness for more than a century. In 1973 the American Psychiatric Association stopped labeling **homosexuality**—a sexual orientation in which people seek emotional and sexual relationships with same-gendered individuals—as a form of mental illness. It is generally considered unacceptable to use the term *homosexual* in clinical practice because it can be associated with a pathological stigma (Kocet, 2019). The mental health system had finally begun to treat the *problems* of gay, lesbian, bisexual, and transgender people rather than treating *them* as the problem. Kocet (2019) notes that the literature in the mental health field is clear and consistent: LGBTQI individuals are not mentally disordered. Although LGBTQI people may suffer with anxiety, depression, or posttraumatic stress, their sexuality or gender identify is not the cause of their mental health diagnosis; instead it is the result of societal and cultural biases, stigma, and harassment from a society that does not embrace the continuum of gender identity.

Heterosexism is a worldview and a value system that can undermine the healthy functioning of the sexual orientations, gender identities, and behaviors of LGBTQI individuals. Helpers need to understand that heterosexism pervades the social and cultural foundations of many institutions and often contributes to negative attitudes and discrimination toward people who are not heterosexual or do not meet the socially accepted standards of stereotypical gender roles and behaviors. Therapists must begin by challenging their own personal prejudices, biases, fears, attitudes, assumptions, and stereotypes regarding sexual orientation if they hope to understand the ways in which prejudice, discrimination, and multiple forms of oppression are manifested in society toward LGBTQI people. When working with LGBTQI clients, it is imperative that counselors become aware of their own privilege, marginalization, and potential biases, which could have a negative impact on the counseling relationship (Ginicola, Filmore, & Smith, 2017).

Despite the advances in understanding sexual orientation, bias and misinformation continue to be widespread in society, and many LGBTQI people face social stigmatization, discrimination, microaggressions, and violence. Unless helpers are conscious of their own assumptions and possible countertransference, they may project their misconceptions and fears onto their clients. Some counselors and counselors-in-training consider same-sex relationships to be immoral. Such attitudes of a counselor have the potential of bringing harm to LGBTQI clients who have the right to expect that they can talk about their intimate relationship concerns in therapy without fearing that their counselor will be judgmental (Herlihy et al., 2014).

Imagine you are counseling a man who is gay and wants to talk about his relationship with his partner and the difficulties they have communicating with each other. As you work with him, you become aware that it is difficult for you to accept his sexual orientation. You find yourself challenging him about this rather than concentrating on the issues he brings forward. You are so focused on his sexual orientation, which goes against what you think is morally right, that you and your client both recognize that you are not helping him. What steps could you take in addressing these value differences? Are you willing to explore the impact of your values on your interventions with this man during your supervision?

Helping professionals who have negative reactions to the LGBTQI community are likely to impose their own values and attitudes, or at least to convey strong disapproval. Identify and examine any myths and misconceptions you might hold, and understand how your values and possible biases regarding sexual orientation are likely to affect your work as you consider the cases that follow.

Case example: Confronting loneliness and isolation.

Consider how your values are likely to influence the way in which you would work with Eric, a 33-year-old gay man. You are doing an intake interview with Eric, who tells you that he is coming to counseling because he often feels lonely and isolated. He has difficulty in intimate relationships with both men and women. Once people get to know him, Eric feels they will not accept him and somehow won't like him. During the interview, you discover that Eric has a lot of pain regarding his father, with whom he has very little contact. He would like a closer relationship with his father, but being gay stands in the way. His father has let him know that he feels guilty that Eric "turned out that way." He just cannot understand why Eric is not "normal" and why he can't find a woman and get married like his brother. Eric mainly wants to work on his relationship with his father, and he also wants to overcome his fear of rejection by others with whom he would like a close relationship. He tells you that he would like those he cares about to accept him as he is.

Your stance. What are your initial reactions to Eric's situation? Considering your own values, would you expect to have any trouble establishing a therapeutic relationship with him? In light of the fact that he lets you know that he does not want to explore his sexual orientation, would you be able to respect this decision? As you think about how you would proceed with Eric, reflect on your own attitudes toward gay men. Would your attitude be different if this client was not a gay man but rather was a lesbian? Think about some of the issues you might focus on in your counseling sessions with Eric: his fear of rejection, pain related to his relationship with his father, desire for his father to be different, difficulty in getting close to both men and women, sexual orientation, and values. With the information you have, which of these areas are you likely to explore with Eric?

Case example: Caught in a conflictual situation.

Margie waits several months after starting counseling to tell you that she is a lesbian. Although she has talked about her feelings of anxiety and depression during every session, she has held back on disclosing the underlying source of her debilitating symptoms—her fear of being alienated from her family if she tells them that her roommate, Sheila, is actually her partner. Margie's parents hold conservative values and in her presence have openly condemned others who identify themselves as gay or lesbian. She is certain that coming out to them would devastate them and cause them to disown her. At the same time, Margie is experiencing increasing pressure from Sheila to introduce her to her family as her partner. Stuck between wanting to please her partner and wanting to be accepted by her family, Margie is very conflicted, which is exacerbating her anxiety and depression. She tells you that she was afraid to reveal her sexual orientation to you earlier because she feared you may have a similar reaction to her news as she expects her family would have. She ultimately decided to tell you because she couldn't hold it in any longer and needed to tell someone.

Your stance. How would it be for you to hear this from Margie? What might you be inclined to say to her? How would your own values influence your perceptions of Margie's situation and affect the way you intervened in her case? Consider how you would react internally to the conflictual situation that Margie is experiencing and how you would support her in working through it. This would be a critical time to engage in self-reflection to ensure that you would not be tempted to impose your values on Margie regardless of the particular beliefs or values you hold. If your values are similar to those of Margie's family, what measures can you take to ensure that you work effectively with her and that your biases don't contaminate the therapeutic process? Would you be able to focus on the issues Margie presents and not the value conflict you have with her?

Discussion. Counselors are not exempt from the influence of negative societal stereotyping and prejudice toward LGBTQI people. Many LGBTQI people internalize the negative societal messages they receive, which causes them to experience psychological pain and conflict.

You may tell yourself and others that you accept the right of others to live their lives as they see fit, yet you may have trouble when you are in an actual encounter with a client. There could be a gap between what you can intellectually accept and what you can emotionally accept. This is something to examine in your supervision sessions and perhaps in your personal counseling.

Understanding the Needs of LGBTQI Clients

Helpers who work with LGBTQI people are ethically obligated not to allow their personal values to intrude into their professional work. The ethics codes of the ACA (2014), the APA (2017a), the AAMFT (2015), and the NASW (2017) clearly state that **discrimination**, or behaving differently and usually unfairly toward a specific group of people, is unethical and unacceptable. From an ethical perspective, practitioners must become aware of their personal prejudices and biases regarding sexual orientation. This is particularly important when a client discloses his or her sexual orientation after the helping relationship is firmly established. In such situations, judgmental attitudes on the part of the helper can seriously harm the client. Of course, these biases and prejudices can be harmful when they are communicated to the client, either directly or indirectly, at any point in counseling.

The Association for Lesbian, Gay, Bisexual and Transgender Issues in Counseling (ALGBTIC, 2008) recognizes that helping professionals need to be well versed in understanding the unique needs of this diverse population. ALGBTIC has developed a set of specific competencies for trainees (available on their website) to help them examine their personal biases and values regarding LGBTQI individuals. Helpers who acquire these competencies are in a position to implement appropriate intervention strategies that ensure effective service delivery to this client population.

ALGBTIC (2009) has also developed *Competencies for Counseling With Transgender Clients,* which is geared toward counselors who work with transgender individuals, families, groups, or communities. These competencies are based on a wellness, resilience, and strength-based approach, and it is felt that counselors are in a unique position to make institutional change that can result in a safer environment for transgender people. This begins with counselors creating a welcoming and affirming environment for transgender individuals and their loved ones. Counselors must respect and attend to the whole individual, and they should not simply focus on gender-identity issues.

You might well be unaware of your client's sexual orientation until the therapeutic relationship has been established. Or a client who has been involved in only heterosexual relationships may begin to question his or her affectional orientation well into the therapeutic process. This client may need to spend time in counseling exploring his or her affectional orientation to find inner peace, and you must be able to competently facilitate this process. If you expect to provide services in a community agency or any other setting with diverse client populations, you need to have a clear idea of your own values relative to issues associated with sexual orientation. As a way of clarifying your values pertaining to sexual orientation, complete the following inventory, using this code:

3 = I agree, in most respects, with this statement.
2 = I am undecided in my opinion about this statement.
1 = I disagree, in most respects, with this statement.

____ 1. Lesbian, gay, and bisexual clients are best served by lesbian, gay, and bisexual helpers.

____ 2. A gay or lesbian counselor is likely to push his or her values on a heterosexual client.

____ 3. I would have trouble working with either a gay male couple or a lesbian couple who wanted to adopt children.

____ 4. Sexual identity is a choice.

____ 5. A lesbian, gay, bisexual, or transgender person can be as well adjusted (or poorly adjusted) as a heterosexual person.

____ 6. I would have no difficulty being objective in counseling lesbian, gay, bisexual, or transgender clients.

____ 7. I have adequate information about referral sources in the local gay community.

____ 8. I feel a need for specialized training and knowledge before I can effectively counsel lesbian, gay, bisexual, and transgender clients.

____ 9. I expect that I would have no difficulty conducting family therapy if the father were gay.

____ 10. I think that lesbian, gay, bisexual, and transgender people of color are subject to multiple forms of oppression.

After you finish the inventory, look over your responses to identify any patterns. Are there any attitudes that you want to change? Have any of your attitudes been modified as a result of this discussion? Are there any areas of information or skills that you are willing to acquire?

A recommended resource for a more comprehensive discussion on this topic is *Affirmative Counseling With LGBTQI+ People* (Ginicola, Smith, & Filmore, 2017).

Family Values

The value system of helpers has a crucial influence on the formulation and definition of the problems they see in a family, the goals and plans for therapy, and the direction the therapy takes. Helpers have their own values pertaining to marriage, the preservation of the family, divorce, same-sex marriages, gender roles and the division of responsibility in the family, adoption of children by same-gender couples, child rearing, and extramarital affairs. Helpers may take sides with one member of the family against another; they may impose their values on family members; or they may be more committed to keeping the family intact than are the family members themselves. Helpers who, intentionally or unintentionally, impose their values on a couple or a family can do considerable harm. Wilcoxon, Remley, and Gladding (2013) maintain that therapists who work with families need to be aware that their personal values are significant aspects of their professional work, and they caution therapists to avoid imposing their values on clients. It is not the helper's role to decide how members of a family should change. The role of the therapist is to help family members see more clearly what they are doing, to help them make an honest evaluation of what their present patterns are, and to encourage them to make the changes they deem necessary. Consider the following case examples.

Case example: Counseling a mother who is restless.

Veronika has lived a sheltered life. She was married at 17, had four children by the age of 22, and is now going back to college at age 32. She is a good student—excited, eager to learn, and discovering all that she had missed. She finds that she is attracted to a younger peer group and to professors. She is experiencing her "second adolescence," and she is getting a lot of affirmation that she did not have before. At home she feels unappreciated, and the members of her family are mostly interested in what she can do for them. At school she is special and is respected for her intellect.

Veronika is close to a decision to leave her husband and her four children, ages 10 to 15. Veronika comes to see you at the university counseling center and is in turmoil over what to do. She wants to find some way to deal with her guilt and ambivalence.

Your stance. How do you react to Veronika's statement that she is considering leaving her husband and her four children? Would you encourage her to follow her inclinations? If Veronika gave this matter considerable thought and then told you that, as painful as it would be for her, she needed to leave her family, would you be inclined to encourage her to bring her entire family in for some counseling sessions? For a moment, consider your own value system. What values might you impose, if any? If Veronika said that she was leaning toward staying married and at home, even though she would be resentful, what interventions might you make? If a parent or spouse had left you at some point, how might this experience affect you in working with Veronika?

Discussion. Your values as a helper have the potential to influence the outcome of therapy, and it may be difficult to refrain from making any judgments in this case. If you think Veronika should be true to herself and follow her heart no matter the cost, you may encourage her to act on her impulse to leave her family before she has fully processed her options and contemplated the potential repercussions. As Veronika examines her own values, she may discover that she can improve her family situation by establishing boundaries with her husband and children so that her needs are no longer neglected.

Case example: A family in crisis.

A wife, husband, and three adolescent children come to your office. The family was referred by the youngest boy's child welfare and attendance officer. The boy is acting out by stealing and is viewed as the problem person in the family.

The husband is in your office reluctantly. He appears angry and unapproachable, and he lets you know that he doesn't believe in this "therapy stuff." He makes excuses for the boy and says he doesn't see that there is much of a problem, either in the marriage or in the family.

The wife tells you that she and her husband fight a lot, that there is much tension in the home, and that the children are suffering. She is fearful about what might happen to her family. She is concerned about supporting herself and her three children if she were to separate from or divorce her husband.

Your stance. How would you be affected by this family? What course of action would you take? How would your values pertaining to family life influence your interventions with this family? Would you expose your own values in this case, even if the family members did not ask you? If they asked you what you thought of their situation and what you thought they should do, what would you say?

Discussion. It is imperative to remain mindful of the power inherent in your professional role at all times. Even if you are careful not to impose your values in working with this family in crisis, what you say is likely to be influenced by your core values. If you believe the wife should be more assertive with her husband in this situation, you might encourage her to challenge him. Such a strategy could endanger the relationship, and you must be mindful of the anger issues between the parents and how this may escalate. A key task for this counselor is to find ways to encourage the father to participate and to engage the whole family in the therapy experience.

Case example: Confronting infidelity.

A couple seeks your services for marital counseling. The husband has confessed to his wife that he is having an affair, and the incident has precipitated the most recent crisis in their relationship. Although the wife is highly distraught, she wants to stay married. She realizes that their marriage needs work and that there is a lack of emotional connection between the two of them, but she thinks it is worth saving. They have children, and the family is well respected and liked in the community.

The husband wants to leave, yet he is struggling with conflicting feelings and is not sure what to do. He is very confused and says he still loves his wife and children. He is aware that he is going through some kind of midlife crisis, and each day he comes up with a different decision. His wife is in pain and is uncertain about what actions to take.

Your stance. What are your values pertaining to affairs in a committed relationship? What would you want to say to each partner? Should a helper counsel a couple to stay together or get divorced? In thinking about the direction you might pursue with this family, consider whether you have ever been in this situation yourself in your own family. If so, how do you think this experience would affect the way you worked with the couple? If one partner expressed confusion and desperately wanted an answer, and was hoping that you would point him or her in some direction, would you be inclined to do so or to tell either of them what to do?

Discussion. It is helpful to remind yourself that the clients will live with the consequences of their decisions, not you. As much as they may want you to tell them what direction to take, your task is to empower your clients to make their own decisions *when* they are ready to make them. The unraveling of an intimate relationship is painful for those involved, and you may be inclined to lessen their pain by steering them in a particular direction, especially when they seem to be stuck and are asking for your guidance in making a decision. By exercising patience with the process and modeling that for your clients, you will help them to explore their options fully before taking action. More therapeutic work needs to be done before a clear direction will become apparent to either of them. It is important for the couple to decide the option that they can best live with going forward.

LO6 Gender-Role Identity Issues

All helpers need to be aware of their values and beliefs about gender. Helpers who work with couples and families can practice more ethically if they are aware of the history and impact of gender stereotyping as it is reflected in the socialization process in families, including their own. The way people perceive gender has a great deal to do with their cultural background. You can become a more effective practitioner if you are willing to evaluate your beliefs about appropriate family roles and responsibilities, child-rearing practices, multiple roles, and nontraditional careers for women and men. With self-reflection, it is possible for you to become more culturally sensitive, gender sensitive, and to avoid imposing your personal values on individuals, couples, and families.

Case example: Challenging the traditional role as a mother.

John and Emma recently entered couples therapy for help resolving conflict over Emma's recent return to work after several years as a full-time mother and homemaker. Both report that they "argue a lot about this issue." John states that he prefers to have Emma stay home full time and care for their two young children and the household responsibilities. Emma reports feeling happier when she works part time and contributes financially to the family. It also allows them to hire extra help for household tasks and child care. She loves her work and the social interactions with her colleagues and does not want to give it up. John believes mothers are better for children than babysitters, and because he has the greater earning capacity, Emma should be the one to stay home. Emma states her perception that it is more important for children to have a happy mother than a full-time mother, and her desire to have an outside work interest above and beyond her family should not be tied to income. Both John and Emma are very invested in their relationship, but they can't get past this hurdle.

Your stance. How would your own personal values regarding parenting and gender roles influence your assessment and approach to working with John and Emma? What are the ethical boundaries regarding the therapist's values in such a case? How do you avoid imposing your own beliefs and persuading or directing this couple?

Discussion. If you have strong personal values about gender roles in marriage and family, it might be easy for you to impose your own values in this case. Alignment, collusion, and triangulation are all unhealthy possible outcomes when counselors insert their own values into these discussions. A belief that women should have choices and not be bound by traditional family roles might lead you to align with Emma and try to persuade or convince John of this. Conversely, a view that children should have a mother at home versus another caregiver may lead you to try to convince Emma she needs to be home and to abandon her personal goals, resulting in alignment with John. It is unethical for the therapist to determine the goals of the individuals involved, with the exceptions of abuse and danger.

Case example: Parenting in a traditional family.

Fernando and Elizabeth describe themselves as a "traditional couple." They are in marriage counseling with you to work on the strains in their relationship arising from rearing their two adolescent sons. The couple talk a lot about their sons. Both Elizabeth and Fernando work full time outside the home. Besides working as a school principal, Elizabeth has another full-time job as mother and homemaker. Fernando says he is not about to do any "women's work" around the house. Elizabeth has never really given much thought to the fact that she has a dual career. Neither Elizabeth nor Fernando shows a great deal of interest in examining the cultural values and stereotypes that they have incorporated. Each of them has a definite idea of what women and men "should be." Rather than talking about their relationship or the distribution of tasks at home, they focus their attention on troubles with their sons. Elizabeth wants advice on how to deal with their problems.

Your stance. If you become aware of the tension within this couple over traditional gender roles, will you call it to their attention in your counseling with them? Do you see it as your job to challenge Fernando on his traditional views? Do you see it as your job to encourage Elizabeth to want more balance of responsibilities in their relationship? If Fernando is from a Latino background, could his views on "women's work" reflect the values of his family of origin? Would you want to learn about the role relationships of Elizabeth's parents? Would you want to explore the cultural values each learned while growing up? If you were counseling this couple, what do you think you would say to each of them? How would your values influence the direction in which you might go? What bearing would your own gender-role conditioning and your own views have on how the counseling process might unfold?

Discussion. If you will be working with couples and families, it is essential that you appreciate the fact that gender-role stereotypes serve a purpose and are not easily modified. As a helper, your role is to guide your clients in the process of examining their gender-role attitudes and behaviors if doing so is relevant to the problem for which they are seeking your services. Effective communication between you and your clients can be undermined by stereotypical views about how women and men think, feel, and behave. You need to be alert to the particular issues women and men struggle with and the ways their own views about gender keep them locked in traditional roles. You can offer assistance to both female and male clients in exploring and evaluating cultural messages they received about gender-role expectations. Without deciding what changes they should make, you can facilitate awareness on the part of your clients, which can open up new possibilities for making self-directed choices.

In a classic journal article, Margolin (1982) provides some recommendations on how to be a nonsexist family therapist and how to confront negative expectations and stereotyped roles in the family. One suggestion is that helpers should examine their own behavior and attitudes that would imply sex-differentiated roles and status. For example, helpers can show their bias in subtle ways by looking at the husband when talking about making decisions and looking at the wife when talking about home matters and rearing children. Margolin also contends that practitioners are especially vulnerable to the following biases: (1) assuming that remaining married would be the best choice for a woman, (2) demonstrating less interest in a woman's career than in a man's career, (3) encouraging couples to accept the belief that child rearing is solely the responsibility of the mother, (4) showing a different reaction to a wife's affair than to a husband's, and (5) giving more importance to satisfying the husband's needs than to satisfying the wife's needs. Margolin raises two critical questions for those who work with couples and families:

- How does the counselor respond when members of the family seem to agree that they want to work toward goals that (from the counselor's vantage point) are sexist in nature?
- To what extent does the helper accept the family's definition of gender-role identities?

LO7 Religious and Spiritual Values

There is a growing awareness and willingness today to explore spiritual and religious beliefs and values in counseling and in training programs for helpers (Dobmeier & Reiner, 2012; Hagedorn & Moorhead, 2011; Johnson, 2013). Religion and spirituality are oftentimes part of the client's problem, and they can also be part of the client's solution to a problem. Spiritual values help many people make sense out of the universe and the purpose of their lives. Because spiritual and religious values can play a major part in human life, these values should be viewed as a potential resource in the helping relationship rather than as something to be ignored (Johnson, 2013). Exploring spiritual or religious values with clients can be integrated with other therapeutic tools to enhance the helping process, if doing so is what clients want.

Counselors cannot ignore a client's spiritual and religious perspective if they want to practice in a culturally competent and ethical manner (Johnson, 2013; Robertson & Young, 2011; Young & Cashwell, 2011a, 2011b). Johnson (2013) believes spiritually informed therapy is a form of multiculturalism.

Johnson contends that a client-defined sense of spirituality can be a significant avenue for connecting with the client and can be an ally in the therapeutic change process. However, he admits that not all clients are interested in discussing spiritual or religious concerns. With such clients, it is important to avoid imposing a spiritual perspective on them. Helpers need to acquire the skills of listening for how clients talk about existential concerns of meaning, values, mortality, and being-in-the-world. Some clients do not talk explicitly about spirituality, but existential themes tend to emerge in therapy. By listening to the unique ways clients make sense of their lives and derive meaning, helpers can remain open to how clients define, experience, and access whatever helps them stay connected to their core values and their inner wisdom. Asking questions about a client's religious or spiritual background at the outset of the professional relationship conveys their potential relevance to the helping process (Barnett & Johnson, 2011). If counselors do not raise questions about a client's spiritual or religious values and concerns during assessment, the client may be hesitant to bring up these concerns in treatment.

In clarifying your values pertaining to religion and counseling, consider these questions: Does an exploration of religion or spirituality belong in formal helping relationships? Is the helping process complete without a spiritual dimension? If a client's religious needs arise in the therapeutic relationship, is it appropriate for a therapist in a secular setting to deal with them? Do you have to hold the same religious beliefs, or any beliefs at all, to work effectively with clients who have religious struggles?

Even if spiritual and religious issues are not the focus of a client's concern, these values may enter into the sessions indirectly as the client explores moral conflicts or grapples with questions of meaning in life. Can you keep your spiritual and religious values out of these sessions? How do you think they will influence the way you counsel? If you have little belief in spirituality or are hostile to organized religions, can you be nonjudgmental? Can you empathize with clients who view themselves as being deeply spiritual or who feel committed to the teachings of a particular religious institution?

Johnson (2013) believes that therapists would do well to spend time reflecting on their own spiritual identity and journey, especially on experiences that were emotionally intrusive and fostered reactivity. If therapists understand and have worked through their spiritual emotional baggage, they can listen to their clients without becoming emotionally reactive or trying to impose their personal agenda on clients. Helpers are in a position to assist their clients in exploring spiritual or religious concerns.

It is important that we do not neglect the beliefs and concerns of people who identify as nonreligious (Sahker, 2016). Individuals experiencing spiritual or religious struggles may seek therapy when they decide to leave the religion of their family of origin. These clients may want a safe place to discuss their doubts and distress related to internal conflicts involving nonbelief. Some who have left the religion of their family of origin experience rejection by family members, and clients often want to express and explore the pain they experience as a result of their choice. The assessment process is crucial in identifying any religious or spiritual concerns, both positive and negative, that an individual may have. If clients say they want to talk about these matters, helpers should be able to meet their needs (Corey, Corey, & Corey, 2019).

Case example: Finding comfort in spirituality.

Peter has definite ideas about right and wrong, as well as sin, guilt, and damnation; and he has accepted the teachings of his fundamentalist faith. When he encountered difficulties and problems in the past, he was able to pray and find comfort in his relationship with his God. Lately, however, he has been suffering from chronic depression, an inability to sleep, extreme feelings of guilt, and an overwhelming sense of doom that God is going to punish him for his transgressions. He consulted his physician and asked for medication to help him sleep better. The physician and his minister both suggested that he seek counseling. At first Peter resisted this idea because he felt strongly that he should find comfort in his religion. With the continuation of his bouts of depression and sleeplessness, he hesitantly comes to you for counseling.

He requests that you open the session with a prayer so that he can get into a proper spiritual frame of mind. He also quotes you a verse from the Bible that has special meaning to him. He tells you about his doubts about seeing you for counseling, and he is concerned that you will not accept his religious convictions, which he sees as being at the center of his life. He inquires about your religious beliefs.

Your stance. Would you have any trouble counseling Peter? He is struggling with trusting you and with seeing the value in counseling. What are your reactions to some of his specific views, especially those pertaining to his fear of punishment? Do you have reactions to his strong fundamentalist beliefs? Would you be able to work with him objectively, or would you try to find ways to sway him to give up his view of the world? If you have definite disagreements with his beliefs, would that be an obstacle to working with him? Would you challenge him to think for himself and do what he thinks is right? How could you challenge yourself not to allow your views to influence him?

Discussion. Ethical practice requires that you avoid indoctrinating clients with a particular set of spiritual or religious values. You have an ethical responsibility to be aware of how your beliefs affect your work and to make sure you do not unduly influence your clients. Assume that you have a religious orientation, yet you believe in a God who loves whereas Peter believes in a God he fears. You discuss the differences in the way the two of you perceive religion. Yet you also say that you want to explore with him how well his religious beliefs are serving him in his life and also examine possible connections between some of his beliefs and how they may be contributing to his symptoms.

As you think over your own position on the place of spiritual and religious values in the helping relationship, reflect on these questions:

- Is it appropriate to deal with religious issues in an open and forthright manner as clients' needs are presented in the helping process?
- Do clients have the right to explore their religious concerns in the context of the helping process?
- If you have no religious or spiritual commitment, how could this hinder or help you in working with diverse clients?
- Are you willing to refer a client to a rabbi, minister, imam, priest, or other religious leader if the client has questions you are not qualified to answer?

Attention to spirituality can be part of an integrated and holistic effort to help clients resolve conflicts and improve health, as well as to find meaning in life (Shafranske & Sperry, 2005). The beliefs, values, and faith systems of clients are often sources of support in difficult times, and they can be used by the counselor to help the client in the healing process (Francis, 2016).

Case study: Counseling and spirituality.

Guiza is a student intern who feels deeply committed to spirituality and also claims that her religious faith guides her in finding meaning in life. She does not want to impose her values on her clients, but she does feel it is essential to at least make a general assessment of clients' spiritual/religious beliefs and experiences during the intake session. One of her clients, Alejandro, tells Guiza that he is depressed most of the time and feels a sense of emptiness. He wonders about the meaning of his life. In Guiza's assessment of Alejandro, she finds that he grew up without any kind of spiritual or religious guidance in his home, and he states that he is agnostic. He never has explored either religion or spirituality; these ideas seem too abstract to help with the practical problems of everyday living. Guiza becomes aware that she is strongly inclined to suggest to Alejandro that he open up to spiritual ways of thinking, especially because of his stated problem with finding meaning in his life. Guiza is tempted to suggest that Alejandro at least go to a few church services to see if he might find any meaning in doing so. She brings her struggle to her supervisor.

Your stance. Consider Guiza's situation as you reflect on how your values can influence your approach with clients. When, if ever, would you recommend to your client that he or she talk to a minister, priest, rabbi, or other faith leader? If you sought consultation from your supervisor, what key issues would you most want to explore and clarify? Could you maintain your objectivity? Would you consider suggesting a referral because of your problems with respect to the spiritual or religious beliefs and values of your client?

Discussion. You may experience conflicts in values with your clients in the spiritual realm. Holding a definite system of religious values is not a problem, but wanting your clients to adopt your values is problematic. Without blatantly pushing your values, you might subtly persuade clients toward your religious beliefs or lead them in a direction you hope they will take. Conversely, if you do not place a high priority on spirituality and do not view religion as a salient force in your life, you may not be open to assessing your client's religious and spiritual beliefs.

Case study: Resolving a value conflict.

Yolanda is a devout Catholic. After a marriage of 25 years, her husband left her. She has now fallen in love with another man and very much wants a relationship with him. But because her religion does not recognize divorce, Yolanda feels guilty about her involvement with another man. She sees her situation as hopeless, and she cannot find a satisfactory solution. Living alone for the rest of her life scares her. But if she marries the man, she fears that her guilt feelings will eventually ruin the relationship because her church may not recognize the marriage as legitimate.

Your stance. Consider these questions as a way to clarify how your values could affect your work with Yolanda. Do you know enough to inform Yolanda of the options available to her in terms of being remarried in a Catholic church? Would you recommend that Yolanda talk to a priest? Why or why not? If Yolanda asked you what she should do or what you think about her dilemma, how would you respond?

Discussion. There are many paths toward fulfilling spiritual or religious needs, and it is not the helper's task to prescribe any particular pathway. However, we think it is the helper's responsibility to be aware that spirituality or religion is a significant force for many clients. It is especially important for a practitioner to pursue spiritual or religious concerns if the client initiates them. Practitioners need to be finely tuned to the client's story and to the purpose for which he or she sought professional assistance. It may also be important to have referral sources available for specific needs of clients.

Case study: A case of karma?

Pratiksha, a Hindu woman, comes to therapy to address her depression and anxiety. She has a daughter with a physical disability, and when her siblings share good news about the accomplishments and success of their own children, she becomes upset. She loves her nieces and nephews and is happy about their success, but their successes remind her of her daughter's limitations. In conversations with her siblings, she rarely talks about her daughter. She feels ashamed of her daughter's limitations, which intensifies her feelings of guilt. Pratiksha believes that the suffering both she and her child are experiencing in this life are due to karma. She is convinced that she and her daughter must have behaved badly in a former life to deserve this punishment.

Your stance. As Pratiksha's therapist, how would you respond to her conviction that she and her daughter are being punished in this life for transgressions in a previous life? Would you convey understanding and acceptance of her belief system, or would you be inclined to challenge this belief? If you challenge her belief, might you run the risk of imposing your own values on her and conveying the message that her Hindu values make no sense? On a personal level, how would you react to this case?

Discussion. It is important to respect the client's religious views, and to listen to Pratiksha's interpretation of how karma is functioning in her life. As her therapist, you might ask Pratiksha to consider alternative ways of thinking about her daughter's disability that will help her to feel more optimistic and hopeful. For instance, rather than viewing her daughter's disability as a punishment, Pratiksha may come to feel that this is an opportunity for her to learn important life lessons on a spiritual level.

It is important to empathize with Pratiksha's internal experience. If you choose to intervene by having Pratiksha reframe the meaning of her daughter's condition within the framework of her religious and cultural values, you need to consider the timing of this intervention. If this intervention is introduced prematurely, it could leave Pratiksha feeling invalidated. It is crucial that this client be given the opportunity to fully express her concerns without feeling judged so a warm and trusting therapeutic environment can be established. Having the time and space to process her feelings about her daughter with an empathic listener may go a long way in helping her to resolve her feelings of shame and guilt.

Abortion

Helpers may experience a value clash with their clients on the issue of abortion. Clients who are exploring abortion as an option often present a challenge to helping professionals, both legally and ethically. From a legal perspective, mental health professionals are expected to exercise "reasonable care"—acting in accordance with what is expected of professionals—and if they fail to do so, clients can take legal action against them for negligence.

We suggest that you familiarize yourself with the legal requirements in your state that impinge on your work with clients, especially if you are in a position of working with minors who are considering an abortion. The matter of parental consent in working with minors varies from state to state. It is also important to know and apply the policies of the agency or school where you work.

In working with clients who are facing choices around unplanned pregnancy, it can be useful to invite them to talk about the value systems they hold and in what ways these values support or conflict with the choices they are considering. When clients seem stuck over making a difficult decision, counselors sometimes attempt to make this decision for clients or to give them advice. It is crucial for the counselor to help the client explore her options while being sure to use the client's frame of reference for the discussion. Would you be able to provide an unbiased atmosphere where clients can consider options without being influenced by your beliefs and values?

Case study: Balancing contradictory advice.

Connie, a 19-year-old college student, seeks your assistance because she is contemplating having an abortion. Some of the time she feels that ending the pregnancy is the only answer; other times she feels that she wants to have the child. She is also considering the option of having her child and giving it up for adoption. Connie contemplates telling her parents but is afraid they would have a definite idea of what she should do. She is unable to sleep and feels guilty for putting herself into this situation. She has talked to friends and solicited their advice, and she has received many contradictory recommendations from them. Connie lets you know that she is not at all sure of what she should do and asks you to help her.

Your stance. With the information you have, what are some things you would say to Connie? Think about your values pertaining to abortion. Would you dissuade her from having an abortion and suggest other options? To what extent do you think you could keep your values out of this session? Sometimes we hear students say that they would refer a pregnant client who was considering an abortion to another professional because of their values. They would not like to sway the woman, and they fear that they could not remain objective. Does this apply to you? If a client in treatment with you for some time became pregnant and indicated she was considering getting an abortion, what would you do?

Discussion. Deciding whether to terminate a pregnancy or to give birth to a child, and then whether to keep the child or place it for adoption, are major life decisions. Connie's case illustrates the confusion and stress common to women who find themselves in a similar predicament. She has a relatively narrow window of time in which to make a decision that is likely to have a significant impact throughout her life. Because of the urgency of making a decision, Connie may need to engage in focused exploration that involves a psychoeducational component. By examining the implications of all the potential options, while keeping her values (not the therapist's values) at the forefront of discussion, Connie will be in a better position to make an informed decision.

If a helper has difficulty honoring the decision that a client makes with regard to keeping a child or having an abortion, the helper should consider raising this issue in supervision or consultation rather than burdening the client with it. Making a referral because you have a value-based conflict with this client would be considered unethical.

Sexuality

Consider your values with respect to sexuality, as well as how you acquired them. How comfortable are you in discussing sexual issues with clients? Are you aware of any barriers that could prevent you from working with clients on sexual issues? How would your experiences in sexual relationships (or the lack of them) influence your work with clients in this area? Would you promote your sexual values? For example, if a teenage client was acting out sexually and this behavior was in large part a form of rebellion against her parents, would you confront her behavior? If a teenage client took no birth-control precautions yet was sexually active with multiple partners, would you urge him or her to use birth control, encourage abstinence, recommend that he or she be more selective in choosing sexual partners, encourage the client to consider the consequences of his or her action, or pursue a different course?

Although you may say that you are open-minded and that you can accept sexual attitudes and values that differ from your own, it may be that you are inclined to try to change clients who you believe are involved in self-destructive practices. Assess your attitudes toward casual sex, premarital sex, teen sexuality, and extramarital sex. What are your attitudes toward monogamy? What do you consider to be the physical and psychological hazards of sex with more than one partner? How would your views on this issue influence the direction you would take with clients in exploring sexual concerns?

When you have made this assessment, ask yourself whether you would be able to work objectively with a person who had sexual values sharply divergent from yours. If you have very conservative views about sexual behavior, for example, will you be able to accept the liberal views of some of your clients? If you think their moral values are contributing to the difficulties they are experiencing in their lives, will you be inclined to persuade them to adopt your conservative values?

From another perspective, if you see yourself as having liberal sexual attitudes, how do you think you would react to a person with conservative values? Assume your unmarried client says that he would like to have more sexual experiences but that his religious upbringing has instilled in him the belief that premarital sex is a sin. Whenever he has come close to having a sexual experience, his guilt prevents it from happening. He would like to learn to enjoy sex without feeling guilty, yet he does not want to betray his values. What would you say to him? Could you help him explore his own value conflict without contributing to his dilemma by imposing your own values?

You may work with clients whose sexual values and behaviors differ sharply from your own, and you may struggle with managing your own values with these clients. It is unethical to refer a client because of your difference in values, and likewise it is unethical to impose your values on your clients. Consider the following case and reflect on how your sexual values may influence your work in this setting.

Case study: Sexuality in a group home for the disabled.

You are a social worker in a group home for disabled adults and discover that some of the residents are having sexual intercourse with each other. Although these clients are adults, you wonder if their parents or conservators need to be contacted.

Your stance. What would your initial reaction be if you discovered that clients were having sexual relations with each other in the group home? How might you react if the parents expressed strong disapproval and demanded that the group home staff take action to prevent sexual activity? If certain clients expressed their love for each other and made it clear that they were going to continue pursuing a sexual relationship regardless of their parents' approval, what would you do? Given the disability status of these adults, what are the legal implications in this case?

Discussion. There are several factors to consider in this case. If you were the helper in this setting, you would do well to raise these questions: Why are my values entering into this situation? Could I bracket my values so that they do not interfere with the clients' decisions and behaviors? What is the policy of the agency on this matter? What legal considerations might I want to discuss with a supervisor at the agency? Reflect on the vulnerability of the people in the group home, especially if abuse or coercion is taking place. In this situation, discussing these questions with a colleague and a supervisor would be an important step to take.

End-of-Life Decisions

Psychological services are useful for healthy individuals who want to make plans about their own future care. Such services are also beneficial to individuals with life-limiting illnesses, families experiencing the demands of providing end-of-life care, and bereaved individuals. With growing public support and continuing efforts by states to legalize physician-assisted suicide, it is likely that an increasing number of clients will seek professional assistance in making end-of-life decisions. It is essential to know the laws in your jurisdiction and state and to be familiar with the ethical guidelines of your professional organization concerning an individual's freedom to make end-of-life decisions. Seek legal consultation in cases involving a client's request for more explicit assistance with hastened death.

Some of you will be faced with assisting clients in making end-of-life decisions, including deciding whether to take active steps to hasten death. As a helper, you need to be willing to discuss end-of-life decisions when clients bring such concerns to you. If you are closed to any personal examination of this issue, you may interrupt these dialogues, cut off your clients' exploration of their feelings, or attempt to provide your clients with your own solutions based on your personal values and beliefs.

Some end-of-life decisions are made more broadly than is the case with physician-assisted suicide. Some individuals will refuse all treatment as a choice of ending life. This option should not be considered as a passive approach because some action must be taken or not taken to allow death to occur. In this situation, does a helper have an ethical responsibility to explore the client's decision to refuse treatment? Even though it is not against the law to refuse treatment, the client may have made this decision based on misinformation. A counselor could help the client assess the nature of the information upon which his or her decision was based.

Gamino and Bevins (2013) identify a host of ethical challenges and dilemmas that counselors may need to consider regarding end-of-life care: respecting client autonomy; assessing an individual's capacity for decision making; honoring advance directives; respecting an individual's cultural values; maintaining confidentiality; dealing with medical futility; establishing and maintaining appropriate boundaries; and including families in the scope of care. In addressing these ethical issues, practitioners should assist their clients in making decisions within the framework of their clients' own cultural beliefs and value systems. Counselors must struggle with the ethical quandaries of balancing the need to protect client rights to autonomy and self-determination with meeting their ethical and legal responsibilities regarding end-of-life care. They must be prepared to work with both those who are dying and their family members.

Cultural considerations also affect the relationship helpers have with people who are near the end of life (Kwak & Collet, 2013). Cultural beliefs influence decisions about many concerns related to the end of life. Although it is not possible to be fully informed about every cultural group, counselors are expected to engage in discussions about the beliefs of the dying person and family members early in the process as a way to be prepared for times when culture intersects with the counseling process (Werth & Whiting, 2015).

LO8 Guidelines for Dealing With End-of-Life Issues

For helpers who ask for assistance in clarifying and exploring end-of-life decisions, Werth and Holdwick (2000) provide these guidelines:

- Assess your personal values and professional beliefs regarding the acceptability of rational suicide.
- As a part of the informed consent process, give prospective clients information about the limitations of confidentiality as it applies to assisted death, if applicable.
- Make full use of consultation throughout the process.
- Keep risk-management-oriented notes.
- Consult the ethics codes and state laws that apply.
- Assess your clients' capacity to make reasoned decisions about their health care.
- Review clients' understanding of their condition, prognosis, and treatment options.
- Involve physicians in this process, as counselors may not fully understand these medical issues.

- Strive to include clients' significant others in the counseling process.
- Assess the impact of external coercion on clients' decision making.
- Determine the degree to which clients' decisions are congruent with their cultural and spiritual values.

Consider these guidelines as you contemplate your own position with respect to key questions on end-of-life decisions. Do individuals have a right to decide whether to live or die? Do some individuals who are in pain have a difficult time distinguishing between ending their life and ending their suffering? If so, do you feel ethically obligated to help clients clarify whether they merely want their suffering to end or whether they truly have a desire to end their life? Are you aware of the laws of your state and the ethical standards of your professional organization concerning an individual's freedom to make end-of-life decisions? If your personal or professional value system is not accepting of an individual ending his or her own life, how might your beliefs get in the way of assisting your client who may be struggling with this decision? What could you do to manage a conflict in values between you and your client?

Case study: The right to choose to die.

A man in his 30s, Andrew, discovers that he has tested positive for HIV. Some of his friends have died from AIDS, and he sees nothing ahead for him except a bleak future. He has been your client for several months and has been successfully exploring other issues in his life. Andrew is clearly leaning in the direction of ending his life before he becomes very ill. Andrew is rational, and he believes that taking this action would be reasonable and in accord with his basic human rights. How would you begin a discussion with Andrew about his future?

Your stance. AIDS was once a deadly disease, and people suffered from a social stigma as well as debilitating illness. With the medications available today, HIV has become a chronic and manageable condition, and Andrew can live a long and full life. As a mental health worker, would you attempt to help Andrew understand that he can live? Would you explore with Andrew the fears that have led him to consider ending his life? What is the role of mental health professionals in working with a person considering some form of hastened dying? Is it the proper role of the helper to steer the client in a particular direction? Is your role to prevent Andrew from taking actions that would hasten his death?

Discussion. What is your position on an individual's right to decide about matters pertaining to living and dying? Is this issue now more complicated by the fact that this condition can be successfully managed? Should he be prevented from ending his life, even if it means taking away his freedom of choice? It is your responsibility to clarify your own beliefs and values pertaining to end-of-life decisions so you can assist your clients in making decisions within the framework of their own belief and value systems. Once you understand your own perspective on end-of-life decisions, you can focus on the needs and personal values of your clients.

Case study: Confronting the right to die.

Esmeralda, who is in her early 40s, is suffering from advanced rheumatoid arthritis. She is in constant pain, and many of the pain medications have serious side effects. This is a debilitating disease, and she sees no hope of improvement. She has lost her will to live and comes to you, her therapist of long-standing, and says: "I am in too much pain, and I don't want to suffer anymore. I don't want to involve you in it, but as my counselor, I would like you to know my last wishes." She tells you of her plan to take an overdose of pills, an action she sees as more humane than continuing to endure her suffering.

Your stance. Think about how your values might influence your interventions in this case. To what degree can you empathize with Esmeralda's desire to end her life? What role would your beliefs play in your counseling? Would you want to be kept alive at all costs, or might you want to end your life? Would you feel justified in doing so? What would stop you?

Discussion. Mental health counselors must understand their own values and attitudes about end-of-life options (such as clients' autonomy and their right to participate in hastening their own death). In addition, counselors need to understand their role in the decision-making process of clients who may choose to hasten their dying process (Bevacqua & Kurpius, 2013). Do you have an ethical and legal responsibility to prevent Esmeralda from carrying out her intended course of action? Do you think you would be able to find meaning through suffering in an extreme circumstance? If you were in full agreement with her wishes, how would this influence your intervention?

Case study: The counselor's legal duty to report.

Josh, a 65-year-old former client of William Park, returns to see him. He is now widowed, his only child is dead, and he has no living relatives. He has been diagnosed with a slow, painful, terminal cancer. Josh tells William that he is contemplating ending his life but would like to explore this decision. William fears being put in a bind because of the potential legal requirement to report him if he decides to end his life. Josh comes weekly, discusses many things with his therapist, and talks lovingly of his deceased wife and daughter. He thanks William for his kindness and his help throughout the years. He has made up his mind to end his life in the next few days, and after a last farewell he goes home.

Your stance. Do you think William should make a report as a way to protect Josh? What would you do in this case? Explain your position in the context of your own values regarding end-of-life decisions. Do you see any conflict between ethics and the law in this case?

Discussion. Suppose you felt like ending your life even after trying various ways of making your life meaningful. Imagine you felt as if nothing worked and that nothing would change. What would you do? Would you continue to live until natural causes ended your life? Do you believe that *any* reason would justify you taking your own life? How might your personal decision process influence how you assist clients in their decision making?

By Way of Review

- There are numerous areas in which your values can potentially conflict with the values of your clients. Ethical practice dictates that you seriously consider the impact of your values on your clients and that you learn how to manage any value conflicts you may have with clients.
- Ultimately, it is the responsibility of clients to choose in which direction they will go, what values they will adopt, and what values they will modify or discard.
- It is not the helper's role to push clients to adopt the personal values of the helper.
- Students and practicing counselors have a right to embrace their own personal and moral values, but it is crucial that they do not use their personal values as a yardstick by which to measure the validity of the values of their clients.
- Simply because you do not embrace a client's values does not mean that you cannot work effectively with the person. By bracketing your personal values from your professional duties, you are being objective, nonjudgmental, and respecting your client's right to autonomy.
- Referring a client may be inappropriate, unethical, and may constitute an act of discrimination. Client referrals among mental health practitioners who hold specific, rigid values often involve discriminatory practices that are rationalized as ways to avoid harming the client or practicing beyond one's level of competence.
- Counselors who work with LGBTQI clients have a responsibility to understand the special concerns of these individuals and are ethically obligated to acquire the knowledge and skills to competently deliver services to them.
- With self-reflection, it is possible for helpers to become more culturally sensitive and more gender sensitive and to avoid imposing their personal values on individuals, couples, and families.
- In two Supreme Court cases, the university's right to require students to comply with nondiscrimination guidelines in counseling clients were found not to infringe on the students' rights to religious freedom. Students in both cases were offered remediation but declined this educational assistance in clarifying the boundaries of their personal values when counseling clients with different values.
- Several states have added freedom of conscience clauses to legislation to ensure that the licensure status of mental health professionals will not be in jeopardy if they refuse services to clients on the basis of sincerely held religious or personal values.
- Clients facing decisions due to an unplanned pregnancy can be invited to talk about the value systems they hold and how their values support or conflict with the choices they are considering.
- Assess your own sexual attitudes and values, and ask yourself whether you would be able to work objectively with a person whose sexual values are very different from your own.

- With continuing efforts by states to legalize physician-assisted suicide, an increasing number of clients may seek professional assistance in making end-of-life decisions. Know the laws in your jurisdiction and state, and consult the ethical guidelines of your professional organization regarding end-of-life decisions.

What Will You Do Now?

1. Spend some time reflecting on the role you expect your values to play in your work with a range of clients. How might your values work for you? Against you? Reflect on the source of your values. Are you clear about where you stand on the value issues raised in this chapter? In your journal, write some of your thoughts about these questions. Under what circumstances would you be inclined to share and perhaps explore your values and beliefs with your clients? Can you think of situations in which it might be counterproductive for you to do so?
2. Consider a personal value that could get in the way of your being objective when working with a client. Choose a value that you hold strongly, and challenge it. Do this by going to a source that holds values opposite to your own. If you are strongly convinced that abortion is immoral, for instance, consider going to an abortion clinic and talking with someone there. If you are uncomfortable with issues pertaining to sexual orientation because of your own values, go to a LGBTQI organization on campus or in your community and talk with people there. If you think you may have difficulty with religious values of clients, find out more about a group that holds religious views different from yours.
3. Mental health practitioners are sometimes too eager to suggest a referral rather than explore how they could work with a client's problem. In small groups, discuss how you would handle a situation in which you encountered a value conflict but could not refer your client. What steps would you take to ensure that you were providing quality services to your client and were not imposing your values on him or her?
4. For the full bibliographic entry for each of the sources listed here, consult the References at the back of the book. For books dealing with the role of spiritual values in the helping process, see Cashwell and Young (2011), Frame (2003), and Johnson (2013). For an excellent treatment on end-of-life issues, see Werth (2013a).

Ethics in Action Video and Workbook Exercises

5. For supplemental activities that accompany this chapter, see Part Two: Values and the Helping Relationship of the *Ethics in Action* DVD and Workbook program or the online program. Complete the response to each of the vignettes and bring your completed responses to class for discussion.
6. In video role play 8, Sexuality: Promiscuity, the client (Suzanne) is having indiscriminate sexual encounters, and her counselor (Richard) expresses concern for Suzanne when he learns about her sexual promiscuity.

Richard then focuses on how Suzanne's behavior plays out the recurring theme of abandonment by her father, but Suzanne doesn't see the connection. If you were Suzanne's counselor, how would you deal with the situation as she presents it? What ethical issues does this role play illustrate? Is it ethically appropriate for you to strongly influence your client to engage in safer sex practices, even if she did not ask for this? Demonstrate how you would approach Suzanne through role playing.

7. In video role play 9, Being Judgmental: The Affair, the client (Natalie) shares with her counselor that she is struggling with her marriage and is having a long-term affair. The counselor (Janice) says, "Having an affair is not a good answer for someone—it just hurts everyone. I do not think it is a good idea." How would your values influence your interventions in this situation? In what value areas pertaining to relationships might you have difficulty maintaining objectivity? Are there situations in which you might want to get your client to adopt your values?

   This vignette can be useful in small group discussions and also in role playing. Have one student role-play the counselor and show how he or she might work with Natalie. In a second role play, have one student become the counselor's supervisor and demonstrate what issues the supervisor might explore with Janice.

8. Video role play 10, Imposing Values: A Religious Client, portrays a conflict of values between the client and the counselor. The client (LeAnne) thinks prayer should be the answer to her personal problems. She doesn't believe she is hearing the Lord clearly. Her counselor (Suzanne) has some trouble understanding what religion means to LeAnne, and Suzanne has difficulty working within LeAnne's religious framework in the counseling relationship. Instead, Suzanne comments that she feels she is in competition with God and the client's religion. Suzanne wants her client to put more faith in the counseling process rather than relying on her religion to solve her problems.

   In small groups discuss some of these questions: Is it ethical for you to challenge your client's belief in the power of prayer and her reliance on God to solve her problems? Explain. If a client introduces spiritual or religious concerns, what ethical issues arise if the counselor does not want to explore these concerns with the client? If LeAnne were your client, how might you proceed with her? What concerns do you have, if any, about your ability to remain objective with LeAnne if she wants to talk about finding her answers in her religion?

9. In video role play 11, Value Conflict: Contemplating an Abortion, the values of the client and the counselor clash. The client (Sally) is considering an abortion and the therapist (Lucia) has difficulty with this possible decision. Lucia feels uncomfortable because of her belief that life begins at conception, and she tells Sally that she will have to get some consultation to sort out her thinking.

In small groups, discuss the ethical issues involved in this situation. How do you imagine Sally feels about her counselor's responses? What are your thoughts about a counselor disclosing her beliefs about abortion to the client? Would it be ethical for this counselor to suggest a referral because of this value conflict? This would be a good case to role-play and show various ways of dealing with the client. When should a counselor seek supervision and consultation if value conflicts arise with a client?

10. In video role play 12, Counselor Disapproval: Coming Out, the client (Conrad) discloses his homosexual orientation. Conrad states that this is something he is struggling with, mainly because it is not accepted in his culture or in his religion. The client admits that he trusts his counselor (John) and that it feels good to be able to make this disclosure. Conrad wants his counselor's help in coming out to his friends and family. John is not receptive and says, "Are you sure this is the best thing for you?" Then John discloses that he does not approve of homosexuality, emphasizing that he does not see this as "being very healthy." Conrad reacts negatively to John's judgmental attitude and lack of acceptance of who he is as a person.

In small groups discuss some of these questions: How does John's disclosure of his values affect the client–counselor relationship? If you were John's supervisor, what would you want him to look at? If you were the counselor in this situation, how would you respond to Conrad? If the counselor were to refer Conrad because of a value conflict, this would be a discriminatory referral, which is unethical. What steps can the counselor take, short of referral, to work effectively with this client?

11. In video role play 13, An Ethical and Legal Issue: End-of-Life Decision, the client (Gary) tells his counselor that he just found out he is HIV-positive and is seriously considering ending his life. The counselor (Natalie) tells Gary that she can't believe what she is hearing. Natalie is doing her best to persuade Gary not to take his life. She tells him that he is taking the easy way out if he chooses to end his life. She asks him if he has a plan. Natalie suggests that he think about his family and other options. She lets Gary know that he may be in a crisis state and not able to make a good decision.

Can you see any potential conflict between the ethical and legal issues in this situation? If you were Gary's counselor, would you respect his decision to end his life, or would you attempt to influence him to search for alternatives to suicide? After discussing the issues involved in this case, practice role playing the way you might deal with Gary.

CHAPTER 4

Understanding Diversity

Learning Objectives

1. Describe the components of a multicultural perspective on helping.
2. Explain the concept of cultural tunnel vision.
3. Discuss a range of cultural values and assumptions in the helping process.
4. Describe the ethical issues in working with people with disabilities.
5. Discuss the steps for acquiring competence in multicultural counseling.
6. List several social justice competencies.
7. Describe several components of multicultural training.

Focus Questions

1. How much thought have you given to your own cultural background, and how has it influenced you?
2. How prepared are you to work with client populations that differ from you significantly in a number of ways (age, gender, culture, race, ethnicity, sexual orientation, socioeconomic status, and educational background)?
3. What values do you hold that could make it difficult for you to work with clients who have a different worldview? What biases and assumptions do you hold about individuals who look, think, feel, and behave differently from you?
4. How might you respond if a client wondered out loud if you will be able to help him because of differences in worldview or culture?
5. How much involvement have you had with people with disabilities? How do you generally feel in their presence? What personal characteristics or experience do you have that could facilitate your work with this population?
6. What are some societal stereotypes pertaining to people with disabilities? How could you work to change these beliefs in your community?
7. What can you do to increase your knowledge and awareness of diverse cultural groups? As you learn about different cultural groups, how can you avoid stereotyping individual members within these groups?
8. How do you relate to the idea of cultural competence being a process that continues throughout your career rather than a goal that can be achieved within a short time frame?

9. How prepared are you to advocate for clients who have been oppressed or marginalized in society? What are the most challenging aspects for you in assuming the role of social advocate?
10. What are the first steps you could take to expand your current attitudes and worldview?

Aim of the Chapter

Most helpers encounter a wide variety of clients in their work. At this point in your development as a helper, it is imperative that you are open to learning how to establish contact with individuals who differ from you in various ways. You do not need to share the same worldview or the same background as your client, nor is it necessary for you to experience the same life circumstances to form an effective therapeutic alliance. However, it is necessary for you to have a range of experiences upon which to draw in understanding the human condition. Universal human themes link people together, but it is crucial to acknowledge our differences as well.

Your openness to learn from the lessons that life has presented to you, your respect for contrasting perspectives, your interest in understanding the diverse worldviews of the clients you will meet, and your willingness to advocate for those who have been oppressed are critical attitudes and skills. Even if you have grown up in a monocultural context, you can learn about people with a worldview different from your own. Through concerted efforts on your part, it is possible to expand your current attitudes and views.

To function effectively as a helper, you must familiarize yourself with your clients' cultural attitudes and realize how cultural values operate in the helping process (see Chapter 3). By understanding how your own cultural background has contributed to who you are, you have a basis for understanding other viewpoints. All helpers need to seriously consider these issues, regardless of their racial, ethnic, or cultural background.

You will probably take a course in cultural diversity, which is likely to emphasize the changing demographics in society and the urgent need for helpers to develop cultural competence. In that course, you will surely be expected to examine the ways in which many members of society have been marginalized and discriminated against. It is also likely that you will explore the critical concepts of power and privilege in a personal way and that you will learn how to broach differences in your conversations with clients. Although exploring these themes and topics may at times take you out of your comfort zone, it can be enlightening and can help broaden your vision of the world. By honoring cultural diversity, you can formulate alternative perspectives and develop appropriate tools for working with diverse client populations.

LO1 A Multicultural Perspective on Helping

We look at **multicultural helping** from a broad perspective and do not limit our consideration of this topic to race and ethnicity. Pedersen (2000) defines cultural groups by *ethnographic* variables (nationality, ethnicity, language, and religion), *demographic* variables (age, gender, and place of residence), *status* variables (educational and socioeconomic background), and formal and informal *affiliations*. According to Pedersen, the multicultural perspective provides a conceptual framework that both recognizes the complex diversity of a pluralistic society and suggests bridges of shared concern that link all people, regardless of their differences. This perspective looks at both the unique dimensions of a person and the common themes we share with those who are different.

Multicultural counseling "can be operationally defined as the working alliance between counselor and client that takes the personal dynamics of the counselor and client into consideration alongside the dynamics found in the cultures of both of these individuals" (Lee, 2019b, p. 5). Effective multicultural counseling defines contextual goals consistent with the life experiences and cultural values of clients and balances the importance of individualism versus collectivism in assessment, diagnosis, and treatment (Sue & Sue, 2016).

In this chapter, we deal with both multiculturalism and diversity perspectives. **Multiculturalism** puts the focus on ethnicity, race, and culture. We interpret the word **culture** broadly to include differences in gender, age, religion, economic status, nationality, physical capacity or disability, and affectional or sexual orientation. **Diversity** refers to individual differences on a number of variables that place clients at risk for discrimination. Both multiculturalism and diversity have been politicized in the United States in ways that have often been divisive, but these terms can equally represent positive assets in a pluralistic society. **Cultural pluralism** recognizes the complexity of cultures and values the many forms of diversity.

When you become a helper, you will encounter many individuals from cultures different from your own. You may consult textbooks, websites, and other sources about your clients' culture to be prepared to work effectively with them. It may surprise you to learn that your path to becoming a culturally competent helper begins with an exploration of how your own cultural heritage and values might affect the counseling process. Lee (2019b, p.10) describes the conceptual framework of multicultural counseling competency by addressing three key questions:

1. "Who am I as a cultural being?"
2. "What do I know about cultural dynamics and how they may influence my client's worldview?"
3. "How do I promote client mental health and well-being in a culturally competent manner?"

Becoming and remaining multiculturally competent entails a great deal of work, study, and clinical experience. Lee (2019a, pp. 18–19) identifies some guidelines for facilitating a working alliance between counselor and client in the helping process:

- Consider cultural factors in any counseling interaction.
- Examine and evaluate your cultural baggage, your cultural privilege, your biases, and the relevance of your theoretical orientation in working with diverse clients.
- Avoid stereotypes or adopting a monolithic perspective.
- Be open to learning about other cultures; be willing to learn from culturally diverse clients.
- Be willing to make a commitment to advocacy and social justice.

The Need for a Multicultural Emphasis

In the past few decades, we have seen an increased awareness on the part of the helping professions to address the special issues involved in working with people of various cultures. Because of the changing demographics in the United States, a conceptual framework is needed to help professionals deliver competent services to clients from culturally diverse backgrounds (Lee, 2019b). Cultural factors are an integral part of the helping process, and culture influences the interventions we make with our clients. Whether we are aware of it or not, Pedersen (2008) claims that culture controls our lives and defines reality for each of us. Adopting a multicultural perspective enables us to think about diversity without polarizing issues into "right" or "wrong." Depending on the cultural perspective from which a problem is considered, there can be several appropriate solutions. In some cases, a similar problem may have very different solutions depending on the client's culture. For example, helpers may encourage some clients to express feelings of hurt to parents but respect other clients' practice of restraint in self-expression so as not to offend their elders.

An effective multicultural counselor respects the needs and strengths of diverse client populations and recognizes the experiences of these clients. However, it would be a mistake to perceive individuals as simply belonging to a group. The differences between individuals within the same group are often greater than the differences between groups. Pedersen (2000) indicates that individuals who share the same ethnic and cultural background are likely to have sharp differences. Not all Native Americans have the same experiences, nor do all African Americans, all Asian Americans, all Euro-Americans, all women, all older adults, or all people with physical or intellectual disabilities. Helpers, regardless of their cultural background, must be prepared to deal with the complex differences among individuals from a variety of groups.

Pedersen (2000) believes multicultural awareness can increase the quality of your life, and it can also make your job easier. Adopting a perspective that cultural differences are positive attributes that add to relationships will expand your ability to work with diverse client groups. We hope you will view the tapestry of culture woven into the fabric of all helping relationships not as a barrier to break through but as a garment that provides comfort in your clients' search for meaning.

Ethical Dimensions in Multicultural Practice

Recognizing diversity in our society and embracing a multicultural approach in the helping relationship have become fundamental tenets of professional codes of ethics, and the ethics codes specify that discrimination by helping professionals is unethical. Most ethics codes mention the practitioner's responsibility to recognize the special needs of diverse client populations. Lee (2015) maintains that counselors must address diversity in a way that is both culturally responsive and ethically responsible. Those counselors who are unaware of cultural dynamics and their impact on client behavior are at risk of practicing unethically.

Becoming an ethical and effective helper in a multicultural society is a continuing process. Effective **multicultural counseling** evolves from three primary practices. First, helpers must be aware of their own assumptions, biases, and values about human behavior, and of their own worldview. Second, helpers need to become increasingly aware of the cultural values, biases, and assumptions of diverse groups in our society, and come to an understanding of the worldview of culturally different clients in nonjudgmental ways. Third, with this knowledge helpers will begin to develop culturally appropriate, relevant, and sensitive strategies for intervening with individuals and with systems (Lee, 2019b; Sue & Sue, 2016).

Discrimination in providing services is often linked to racial and cultural factors, socioeconomic class, and gender, and discrimination and misdiagnosis can be due to biased attitudes on the part of practitioners (Dolgoff, Loewenberg, & Harrington, 2009). For example, people in lower socioeconomic classes consistently receive more severe diagnoses than do individuals in higher socioeconomic classes. Discrimination involves more than simply refusing to offer services to certain client groups; it can take any one of these forms:

- Being unaware of one's own biases and how they can inadvertently be communicated to clients.
- Being unaware that some of the theories studied during a training program may be culture bound.
- Being unaware of differences in cultural definitions of health and illness.

Lack of awareness can lead helpers to engage in unintentional racism, which can be extremely damaging to clients.

Unfortunately, many people of color are subjected to **racial microaggressions**: "brief and commonplace daily verbal, behavioral, or environmental indignities, whether intentional or unintentional, that communicate hostile, derogatory, or negative racial slights and insults" (Sue et al., 2007, p. 271). These "racial microaggressions are not limited to White–Black, White–Latino, or White–Person of Color interactions. Interethnic racial microaggressions occur between people of color as well" (p. 284). Microaggressions related to a person's gender, sexual orientation, or disability may have equally powerful and potentially destructive effects. For example, consider the counselor who continues to steer the conversation to the societal challenges faced by her client with cerebral palsy when the client has come for help in addressing anxiety related to his relationships, conflicts with a sibling or parent, or grieving the loss of a loved one.

Cultural differences are real, and they influence all human interactions. All counseling is multicultural in nature, as both client and counselor bring their unique histories and culture into the counseling process (Lee, 2019b). Clinicians may misunderstand clients of a different gender, race, ethnicity, age, social class, or sexual orientation. If practitioners fail to integrate these diversity factors into their practice, they are infringing on the client's cultural autonomy and basic human rights, which will reduce the chance of establishing an effective helping relationship. It is important to be able to deal with all aspects of diversity. For some clients, religious values are important. Other clients may focus on gender or age discrimination. By paying attention to what a client is saying, helpers can discover which aspects of a client's identity are most salient for this person at this time.

Cardemil and Battle (2003) believe that openly discussing race and ethnicity is one way to actively include a multicultural element in counseling, and a way to strengthen the therapeutic alliance and promote better therapeutic outcomes. For example, the counselor might say: "Today we have been talking about your sense that many of your coworkers are prejudiced. What has this conversation with me been like for you? What has it been like for you to share experiences of discrimination with a White therapist who hasn't had those kinds of experiences?" (p. 282). Day-Vines and colleagues (2007) refer to this as **broaching behavior** and stress the importance of having "a consistent and ongoing attitude of openness with a genuine commitment by the counselor to continually invite the client to explore issues of diversity" (p. 402). Race may contribute to the client's presenting problem, and acknowledging this can be instrumental in establishing a working therapeutic relationship.

LO2 Overcoming Cultural Tunnel Vision

Our work with students in a human services training program has shown us that students often struggle with **cultural tunnel vision.** Many students are unaware of the difficulty of dealing with clients who have a cultural background different from their own. They may have limited cultural experiences, and in some cases, they see it as their role to transmit their values to their clients. Some make inappropriate generalizations about a particular group of clients. For example, some students-in-training may assert that certain groups of people are unresponsive to psychological intervention because of a lack of motivation to change. This perceived lack of motivation might reflect cultural differences, the clients' ambivalence about change, or hesitance to seek support from someone outside their family system. Clients also may distrust the professional helping process due to past experiences with discrimination and oppression.

It is worth repeating that all helping relationships are multicultural. Both those providing help and those receiving help bring to their relationship attitudes, values, and behaviors that can vary widely. One mistake is to deny the importance of these cultural variables; another mistake is to overemphasize such cultural differences to the extent that helpers lose their spontaneity and thus fail to be present for their clients. We need to understand and accept clients who have a different set of assumptions about life, and we need to be alert to the likelihood of imposing our own worldview. In working with clients with different cultural experiences, it is important that we resist making value judgments for them.

The **culturally encapsulated counselor,** a concept introduced by Wrenn (1962, 1985), exhibits the characteristics common to cultural tunnel vision. Think about how broad your own vision is as you consider these traits of culturally encapsulated counselors:

- Define reality according to one set of cultural assumptions
- Show insensitivity to cultural variations among individuals
- Accept unreasoned assumptions without proof or ignore proof because that might disconfirm their assumptions
- Fail to evaluate other viewpoints and make little attempt to accommodate the behavior of others
- Remain trapped in one way of thinking, resist adaptation, and reject alternatives

Encapsulation is a potential trap that all helpers are vulnerable to falling into. If we accept the idea that certain cultural values are supreme, our refusal to consider alternatives limits us. If we possess cultural tunnel vision, we are likely to misinterpret patterns of behavior displayed by clients who are culturally different from us. Because of this lack of understanding, we may label certain client behaviors as resistant, we may make an inaccurate diagnosis of a particular behavior as maladaptive, or we may impose our value system on the client. For example, some Latinas might resist changing what we could view as dependency on their husband. If we work with Latina clients, we need to appreciate that Latino tradition tells these women that it is never appropriate to leave one's husband, even if he is unfaithful. If we are unaware of this traditional value, we could make the mistake of pushing such women to take an action that will violate their belief system.

Case example: Looking through a narrow lens.

Marcia, a school counselor, personally believes that students develop healthier self-esteem when they engage in sports and have a balanced course load that does not consume too much time outside of the classroom. Min-jun and his family recently moved to the United States from South Korea so the children could prepare for admission to a top U.S. university. During their first meeting, Min-jun informs Marcia that he would like to take a large number of Advanced Placement (AP) courses and join some academic clubs. He is not interested in participating in sports as an extracurricular activity. Marcia strongly discourages Min-jun from taking so many AP courses and suggests that he join the baseball or soccer team rather than focus so heavily on academic clubs. Min-jun defers to Marcia's authority and politely agrees to her recommendations, but he leaves her office feeling concerned about how well prepared he will be to get into a top university.

Your stance. If you were in Min-jun's situation, how might you feel if your school counselor imposed an agenda on you that did not take your cultural values into consideration? What might you be inclined to say to Marcia if she was your colleague and you noticed that she was basing her recommendations largely on her own assumptions and life experiences?

Discussion. Although Marcia's intentions are good and her recommendations are meant to help bolster Min-jun's self-esteem and promote his development as a well-rounded individual, she is not taking this student's cultural context into account. It is important to note that Min-jun's family relocated to the United States so that he and his sister could avail themselves of academic opportunities, which reflects the family's value on education. Marcia is also failing to take into account how competitive college admissions have become at top tier universities where Min-jun plans to apply. Given Min-jun's respect for authority, it is unlikely that he will challenge Marcia's recommendations.

Honoring Clients' Cultural Values

Culture is a vital part of who we are as human beings. Conveying the message to clients (either explicitly or implicitly) that they need to abandon this vital part of themselves and embrace the dominant culture is antithetical to what we stand for as helpers. Harboring an agenda for clients to conform to cultural standards that conflict with their own values is insensitive, if not unethical, and could lead clients to terminate from counseling prematurely. A particular behavior may be acceptable in one culture but unacceptable, or perhaps even illegal, in another culture (e.g., particular child-rearing practices); helpers need to remain nonjudgmental when assisting clients who are navigating these issues.

Chung and Bemak (2012) coined the term **political countertransference** to describe a helper's personal reaction to the political context in which he or she works with clients. For example, a helper may have a strong personal reaction to a highly charged political issue such as terrorism, abortion, immigration reform, shutdown of the government, or gay marriage. Helpers must monitor their reactions and be aware of the potential impact of their political countertransference on their clients. This awareness is particularly important during this time of polarization around multiple political issues in our society.

Realize that there is no sanctuary from cultural bias. We tend to carry our biases around with us, yet we often do not recognize this fact. It takes a concerted effort and vigilance to monitor our biases and value systems so that they do not interfere with establishing and maintaining successful helping relationships.

Cultural Values and the Helping Process

Many of the theories and practices of the helping process discussed in Chapters 6 and 7 are grounded in core value orientations of mainstream American culture. Hogan (2013) characterizes these underlying values as emphasizing the patriarchal nuclear family; keeping busy; measurable and visible accomplishments; individual choice, responsibility, and achievement; self-reliance and self-motivation; change and novel ideas; competition; direct communication; materialism; and equality, informality, and fair play. The degree to which these value orientations fit clients from other cultures needs to be carefully considered by human services practitioners.

Some writers in the multicultural field are critical of the strong individualistic bias of contemporary theories and the lack of emphasis on broader social contexts such as families, groups, and communities (Chung & Bemak, 2012; Zalaquett, Ivey, & Ivey, 2019). Intervention strategies based on Western assumptions may not be congruent with the values of some clients and may perpetuate forms of injustice and institutional racism. Clients from oppressed groups may be slow to form trusting relationships with counselors, and mental health professionals may have difficulty identifying with these clients if they ignore the history or context of this distrust. Seeking professional help is not typical for people from certain cultural backgrounds, and helpers need to expand their perception of mental health practices to include support systems such as family, friends, community, self-help programs, faith healing practices, and occupational networks. Mental health providers must be willing to redefine their professional roles and adapt their practices to better suit the client's worldview, life experiences, and cultural identity (Chung & Bemak, 2012).

Some time ago we presented a series of workshops in Hong Kong for human services professionals. This gave us the opportunity to rethink the relevance of applying some of our approaches to working with Chinese clients. Almost all the participants in these workshops were Chinese, but some of them had obtained their graduate training in social work or counseling in the United States. These professionals struggled with retaining values basic to their Chinese heritage while integrating the counseling approaches they had studied in the United States.

In talking with these practitioners, we learned that they pay more attention to the family than to individuals' interests in their interventions. Many told us that they had to demonstrate patience and understanding with their clients. They saw it as essential to form a trusting relationship before engaging in confrontation. Although this necessity applies to counseling in general, it seems especially important for clients from diverse cultural groups.

Case example: Considering cultural differences.*

A counselor, Doug, receives a telephone request from the oldest male in a traditional extended family that had recently migrated from a northern state in India. Kishore is requesting counseling concerning his younger sister, who is having difficulty adjusting to their new country and has recently tried to run away from her family. He states that there is disagreement between his sister, Savita, and the rest of her family about whom she should marry. Doug's usual practice would be to respond positively to the inquiry but to insist on the potential client speaking directly to him to arrange an appointment.

Doug wonders what he should do in these circumstances, particularly in view of the cultural differences. It becomes clear that the brother intends to attend the counseling sessions with his younger sister, Savita. This is contrary to Doug's usual practice of seeing clients alone. He hesitates before deciding whether to accept these arrangements.

Your stance. If you were the counselor in this situation, how would you respond to this phone call? Consider these issues in forming your opinion:

- What are the indications of cultural differences between the counselor and the prospective clients?
- Who is the client?
- How far should the counselor go in adapting his usual practices to respond to these cultural differences?
- How does the available ethical guidance from your professional counseling organization help or hinder you in responding to these circumstances?

Discussion. This case study directs attention to potential tensions between cultural competence and meeting other ethical requirements. The ethical guidance issued by most professional associations requires cultural sensitivity and competence and warns against prejudice. However, the ethics codes seldom offer more precise instructions on how to achieve these requirements, nor do they provide advice on how to resolve conflicts between any adaptations made in response to cultural differences and other ethical requirements.

The most significant cultural feature of this case is that Kishore is reaching out beyond the family for help. Typically, within his culture problems are resolved or contained within the family, and there is great reluctance to communicate the private business of the family to outsiders. If the problem is of such significance

*We thank Tim Bond, University of Bristol, UK, and Lina Kashyap, Tata Institute of Social Sciences, Mumbai, India, for contributing this case study.

that it justifies breaking the family's privacy, the counselor should recognize the seriousness of this request and the family's sense of concern and vulnerability in requesting help in this way. They are taking a major step outside their cultural norms. One of the first challenges for the counselor is to recognize the scale of risk that the family is taking and the significance of responding in a culturally appropriate way in order to offer a sense of reassurance and safety.

The second culturally significant feature is that the request for counseling is from the oldest male, who has responsibility for the well-being of all family members. This creates new challenges for the counselor who will need to balance being respectful of the oldest male's responsibility while working with other members of the family who will also be expected to defer to the oldest male. Kishore's desire to be present in the counseling sessions may be interpreted as his way of communicating his care and concern for his sister or as a way of exercising control. It is unlikely that this will become clear in an initial phone call, and it may take several sessions before the balance between care and control and the nature of the relationship between brother and sister becomes apparent.

As the counselor, Doug is faced with a critical decision about whether to start his work on the basis suggested by the brother or to attempt to ensure that Savita both wants counseling and is seen on her own to ascertain her wishes. The first might be more culturally appropriate for his client, and the second more respectful of a sense of individual autonomy and women's rights. As Doug has little information about Savita's views about her situation, he may decide to offer an initial meeting with both of them to discuss their situation and to agree on how he will work with them. A single meeting may not be sufficient to enable Savita to speak freely; her cultural background may encourage reticence over speaking freely, or even at all, in the presence of men. A tradition of modesty may discourage her from making eye contact with a stranger who is male. Doug will have to be sensitive and patient to win her trust sufficiently for her to communicate her views. He may want to keep an open mind as to whether a female counselor would be more appropriate if Savita is to become the primary client.

Doug's multicultural competence may be tested in other ways. Actions can be as important as words in providing a sense of security across cultural differences. One of the ways in which he might open the meeting would be to offer a cup of tea or water as a culturally appropriate way of demonstrating a respectful welcome, even if offering refreshments is not his normal practice with clients.

At some point Doug will need to decide who constitutes the "client." This is both an ethically and professionally significant decision that cannot be made without taking cultural values into account. Professional ethical guidance for counselors tends to be based on assumptions about nuclear families and the rights of all family members to be autonomous. The basic unit of ethical concern is the individual. These are culturally specific assumptions characteristic of North America and some areas of Europe, including Britain. In extended family systems, the basic unit of ethical concern may be the family as a whole rather than any individual within it. From this perspective, it could be a mistake to understand the request for help in personal terms relating to the two named individuals. Instead, it may be better understood as a request on behalf of the whole family, including other significant unnamed people such as the mother or an older sister.

Deciding how to interpret the request and its implications for establishing how to deliver the counseling is likely to be one of the primary tasks of the initial assessment. It is also ethically significant. Should the counselor work with the autonomy of the family as whole, even if this is at the expense of individual autonomy, or prioritize individual autonomy at the expense of family identity? How the counselor should position himself with respect to existing family structures and gender relationships is another challenging issue that will require careful consideration throughout the counseling relationship. When a counselor is working with people from an unfamiliar cultural background, there is a strong case for obtaining appropriate cultural mentoring in addition to any external therapeutic support or supervision. Some professional bodies strongly recommend or require this additional cultural mentoring.

The decision about who is the client will determine how the counselor approaches issues of informed consent, whose consent ought to be sought, and the management of confidentiality between family members. The emphasis on consent that is characteristic of most professional ethics codes may fail to convey the level of respect that is the intended ethical purpose of this practice. Many counselors would consider it to be good practice to discuss these issues with the prospective clients to determine their wishes before making a final decision about how to proceed. The extent to which such discussions are possible and desirable will depend on the degree of urgency and purpose for which counseling is being sought.

Many of the helping professions express doubts about how far an ethical principle founded on respect for individual autonomy can adequately address the needs of people from a collectivist culture. Could a professional ethic that emphasizes the principle of respect for individual autonomy in itself be culturally insensitive and exclude people who hold other cultural values?

LO3 Examining Your Cultural Assumptions

Culturally learned basic assumptions, whether we are aware of them or not, significantly influence the ways in which we perceive and think about reality and how we act. A willingness to examine such assumptions opens doors to seeing others from their vantage point rather than from a preconceived perspective. Helpers often unwittingly make cultural assumptions on a variety of topics. Review the basic cultural assumptions that influence you and determine how you might be imposing your views. What forces have shaped your basic assumptions? Are you open to considering the relevance of such assumptions in working with clients who are different from you? Reflect on how your understanding of these issues is likely to influence your work with clients.

Assumptions about self-disclosure. Self-disclosure is highly valued in counseling, and most helpers assume that no effective helping can occur unless clients reveal themselves in the helping relationship. One way to facilitate meaningful disclosure on the part of clients is for helpers to model appropriate self-disclosure. Ivey, Ivey, and Zalaquett (2018) comment that helper self-disclosure can increase client self-disclosure, create trust between counselor and client, and establish a more equal relationship in the interview.

Unless clients work through the obstacles to some level of disclosure, they may not be able to participate fully in the helping relationship. However, you can recognize and appreciate that some of your clients will struggle in letting you know the nature of their problems. This struggle in itself is a useful focus for exploration. Rather than expecting such clients to disclose freely, you can demonstrate respect for their values and at the same time ask them what they want from you and why they are seeking counseling. With your support and encouragement, clients can sort through their values and socialization pertaining to self-disclosure and decide the degree to which they want to change.

Some forms of helping place less stress on verbal disclosure, such as music therapy, occupational and recreational therapy, and other forms of activity therapy. Helpers can also assume an advocacy role for the client in the system, can help clients build on their natural sources of support, or can teach clients to use the resources within the community. As you will see in Chapter 12, a number of community-based interventions may be more appropriate for some clients than traditional approaches to helping.

Assumptions about nonverbal behavior. Clients can disclose themselves in many nonverbal ways, but cultural expressions are prone to misinterpretation. Personal space requirements, eye contact, handshaking, dress, formality of greeting, perspective on time, and so forth all vary among cultural groups. Mainstream Americans often feel uncomfortable with silence and tend to fill in quiet gaps with words. In some cultures, in contrast, silence indicates a sign of respect and politeness. You could misinterpret a quiet client's behavior if you did not realize that the client might be waiting for you to ask questions. It is good to keep in mind that there are no universal meanings of nonverbal behaviors.

You may have been systematically trained in a range of microskills: attending, open communication, observation, hearing clients accurately, noting and reflecting feelings, and selecting and structuring, to mention a few (Ivey et al., 2018). Although these behaviors are aimed at creating a positive therapeutic relationship, individuals from certain ethnic groups may have difficulty responding positively or understanding the intent of the counselor's attitudes and behavior. The helper whose confrontational style involves direct eye contact, physical gestures, and probing personal questions may be seen as offensively intrusive by clients from some other cultures.

In American middle-class culture, direct eye contact is usually considered a sign of interest and presence, and a lack thereof is interpreted as evasiveness. It is common for individuals to maintain more eye contact while listening and less while talking. Some research indicates that African Americans may reverse this pattern by looking more when talking and slightly less when listening. Among some Native American and Latino groups, eye contact by the young is a sign of disrespect. Some cultural groups generally avoid eye contact when talking about serious subjects (Ivey et al., 2018). Clearly, helpers who pathologize a client's lack of eye contact may not be understanding or respecting important cultural differences. Helpers must acquire knowledge of a wide range of cultural differences to reduce the probability of miscommunication, misdiagnosis, and misinterpretation of nonverbal behaviors.

Assumptions about trusting relationships. Many, but not all, Americans of European background tend to form quick relationships and to talk easily about their personal life. This characteristic is often reflected in a helper's style, and the helper may expect the client to approach their relationship in an open and trusting manner. Doing this is very difficult for some clients, however, especially given that they are expected to talk about themselves in personal ways to a stranger. It may take some time to develop a meaningful working relationship with a client who is culturally different from you.

Assumptions about self-actualization. Helping professionals commonly assume that it is important for the individual to become self-actualized. But some clients are more concerned about how their problems or changes are likely to affect others in their life. In collectivistic cultures the individual exists in relation to others, and one of the guiding principles is achievement of collective goals. Likewise, Native Americans judge their worth primarily in relation to how their behavior contributes to the harmonious functioning of their tribe. Emphasis is on social relatedness and the interconnectedness of all things. Shared experiences are used as a means of healing individuals, which occurs only in the context of relationship with others (McWhirter & Robbins, 2014).

Assumptions about directness and assertiveness. Although some cultures prize directness, other cultures see being direct as a sign of rudeness and as something to be avoided. If you are not aware of this cultural difference, you could make the mistake of interpreting a lack of directness as a sign of being unassertive rather than as a sign of respect. Getting to the point immediately is valued in some cultures, but other cultures value less direct styles of communication. It is easy to put the responsibility on the client when the therapy interventions do not work. However, if therapists cannot connect to clients using the techniques in which they were trained, it is their responsibility to find other ways to work with their clients.

If you are operating from an individualistic orientation, you are likely to assume that your clients are better off if they can behave in assertive ways, such as telling people what they think, feel, and want. It is critical to recognize that being direct and assertive is just one way of being; counselors should avoid assuming that assertive behavior is the norm and is desirable for everyone. Certain clients might be offended if it were automatically assumed that they would be better off if they were more assertive. For example, assume that you are working with a woman who rarely asks for what she wants, allows others to decide her priorities, and almost never denies a request or demand from anyone in her family. If you worked hard at helping her become an assertive woman, it could very well create conflicts within her family system. If she changed her role, she might no longer fit in her family or in her culture. Therefore, it is crucial that both you and your clients consider the consequences of examining and modifying cultural values.

One way to respect your clients is to listen to what they say they value. Ask your clients what behaviors are and are not working in their lives. If clients tell you that being indirect or unassertive is problematic for them, then this should be explored. However, if such behaviors are not posing difficulty for them, you need to monitor how your biases may be operating when you attempt to change clients in directions that they are not interested in pursuing. Asking your clients what they want from you is a way of decreasing the chances that you will impose your cultural values on them. On this point, consider the following case.

Case example: Is listening to your client enough?

Mac, a successful psychologist, has concerns about much of the multicultural movement. He sees it as more trendy than useful. "I do not impose my values. I do not tell clients what to do. I listen, and if I need to know something, I ask. How am I to know whether a Japanese American client is more American than Japanese or vice versa unless I ask him? My belief is that the client will tell you all you need to know."

Your stance. What is your reaction to Mac's attitude? How would you determine the level of acculturation of a client of yours? What is your reaction to Mac expecting his client to educate him on culture issues?

Discussion. We react not so much to what Mac says as to what is implied by what is said. Certainly, it is important for clients to tell counselors what they need to know. However, Mac seems to downplay the necessity for ongoing education and sensitivity to cultural issues, which might enable him to ask more effective questions. It is not the responsibility of Mac's clients to educate him. Listening to our clients is not enough; we also need to be formally and informally educated.

Challenging Your Stereotypical Beliefs

Although you may assume you are without bias, stereotypical beliefs could well affect your practice. **Stereotyping** involves assuming that the behavior of an individual will reflect or be typical of that of most members of his or her cultural group. This assumption leads to statements such as these: "Asian American clients are emotionally repressed." "African American clients are suspicious and will not trust professional helpers." "White people are arrogant." "Native Americans have very low motivation." Lee (2019b) emphasizes the importance of challenging stereotypical beliefs. "An important component of any cross-cultural encounter is the ability to get beyond stereotypes and ensure that one sees people as individuals within a cultural context" (p. 9).

Sue (2005) contends that **modern racism** is often subtle, indirect, and unintentional, which allows people to remain oblivious to its existence. According to Sue, racism frequently operates outside the level of conscious awareness. Helpers who view themselves as being without any stereotypes, biases, and prejudices are most likely underestimating the impact of their socialization. Such helpers can be even more dangerous than those who are more open about their biases and prejudices.

According to Pedersen (2000), this form of racism emerges unintentionally from well-meaning and caring professionals who are no more or less culturally biased than segments of the general public. He believes that unintentional racists must be challenged either to become intentional racists or to modify their attitudes and behaviors. The key to changing the unintentional racist lies in examining basic underlying assumptions, such as those we described earlier.

In addition to cultural stereotypes, some stereotypes are associated with special populations, such as people with disabilities, older people, and people who are homeless. Statements that lump together individuals within a group reflect a myth of uniformity. In your professional work, you need to realize that there are variations within cultural groups and that such differences may be at least as important as those among different groups. In your attempt to be culturally sensitive, be careful to avoid further stereotyping of certain groups.

Although cultural differences both among and within groups may be obvious, it is important not to go to the extreme of focusing exclusively on the differences that can separate us. In working with mental health professionals in foreign countries, we have become even more convinced that there are some basic similarities among the peoples of the world. Universal experiences can bind people together. Although personal circumstances differ, most people experience the pain of making decisions and attempting to live with integrity in the world. It is essential to be respectful of the real cultural differences that exist, and it is equally important that we not forget the common denominators of all people.

Expanding Your Awareness of Cultural Assumptions and Values

Try to identify some of your cultural assumptions and values as you think about these questions:

- As a helper, is it necessary that you share the cultural background of your client to be effective?
- How might your own experiences with discrimination help or hinder you in working with clients who have been discriminated against?
- What stereotypes are you aware of having?
- Will your values help or hinder you in forming a helping relationship with individuals who do not share your values?

LO4 Understanding People With Disabilities*

Part of understanding diversity involves understanding how ability and disability are relevant factors in the delivery of human services. In ways similar to people of color, people with disabilities have to face prejudice, hostility, lack of understanding, and discrimination on the basis of their physical appearance and perceived emotional or mental abilities. DePoy and Gilson (2004) point out that diversity categories such as race, ethnicity, and gender fall under a similar analytic lens. Individuals without disabilities frequently view people with disabilities through the same distorted spectacles with which they see others who differ from them. The clarity of a helper's vision can be impaired by myths, misconceptions, prejudices, and stereotypes about people with disabilities.

It is important to recognize the potential of people with disabilities. Helpers' attitudes are a key factor in successfully intervening in the lives of people with disabilities. Dispelling myths and misconceptions when helping people with

*We want to acknowledge Mark Stebnicki, professor in the Department of Addictions and Rehabilitation at East Carolina University, for his consultation with us and helpful input in revising this section on understanding people with disabilities.

disabilities achieve their goals can be just as necessary as when working with people who have addiction issues, intense marital conflicts, or are survivors of extraordinary, stressful, and traumatic events.

Examining Stereotypes Pertaining to Physical Disabilities

People with physical disabilities do not want to be labeled with language such as "crippled," "afflicted," "special," or "handicapped." Many advocates believe that the environment itself, both physical and social, and others' negative attitudes toward people with disabilities are the real handicapping conditions (Smart, 2019). Historically, much of the language used to refer to "the disability experience," as portrayed in the print and electronic media, has communicated a condescending attitude toward people with disabilities. For example, the term *mental retardation* began as a medical term and appeared in the *Diagnostic and Statistical Manual of Mental Disorders* (American Psychiatric Association, 2000), but over time it was repeatedly misused in our society in a hurtful and derogatory way. In response to this, Rosa's Law was passed to replace the old designation with the term *intellectual disability*. The revised *DSM-5* (American Psychiatric Association, 2013a) now places "intellectual disabilities" under the category of Neurodevelopmental Disorders. People with spinal cord injuries also have been stereotyped as being "physically or mentally deficient" in some way, which has profound implications for socialization, employment outlook, self-esteem, and basic independent functioning (Marini, 2007). Overall, people with disabilities remain the most disenfranchised group in almost every society, regardless of their ethnicity. People with disabilities are often unemployed and underemployed, and many live below the poverty line (Olkin, 2016). Olkin states that people with disabilities generally report psychosocial issues more than physical barriers as major impediments in living with a disability. People with disabilities are often underserved in the counseling field, but this is beginning to change as awareness and advocacy efforts improve. One growing trend in some states is to provide community-based counseling for people with severe disabilities, bringing the services to people who otherwise could not access therapy in traditional office settings.

Individuals without disabilities often try to hide their feelings of awkwardness in the presence of a person with a disability through exaggerated attention and kindness. Helpers may have learned a variety of negative messages about disability, and they may experience some initial discomfort. It is essential for helpers to demonstrate a willingness to examine their own attitudes when they are working with people who have any kind of disability. A critical aspect of self-awareness is to recognize, understand, and manage one's countertransference in working with clients with disabilities (Olkin, 2016).

Although people with disabilities share some common concerns, there is considerable diversity among people with physical disabilities. As with any special population with which you work, it is important that you identify your assumptions. For example, you could assume that certain careers might be out of reach for a client with a disability. But to make this assumption without checking it out with your client is tantamount to limiting his or her options. Smart (2019) notes that many of our assumptions about individuals with disabilities are inaccurate and may impede the helping process because they may further stereotype the client. This would be a good time for you to reflect on any stereotypes that you may have toward people with disabilities and to scrutinize some of your assumptions.

A major role of practitioners who work with people with disabilities is to help these individuals to understand the prejudice and discrimination that surrounds disability. According to Palombi (Cornish, Gorgens, Monson, Olkin, Palombi, & Abels, 2008), people with disabilities often experience many of the same prejudices and kinds of discrimination as other underrepresented groups. Attitudinal barriers by people without disabilities are much greater than barriers to employment or even physical and architectural barriers. For instance, people with chronic medical or physical conditions (e.g., cerebral palsy, multiple sclerosis) who have articulation, speech, or communication difficulties are often perceived as having an intellectual disability. A visible physical disability may also be perceived by professionals as a mental or physical incapacity, requiring a heavy reliance on personal caregivers and overall dependence rather than independence.

Professional helpers need to understand the ultimate harmful costs to the individual because many people with disabilities integrate negative societal stereotypes and attitudes into their self-esteem and self-concept. It is crucial that helpers recognize their own biases and address them; failing to do so may result in perpetuating attitudinal barriers based on ignorance, false beliefs, and prejudice (Cornish et al., 2008). Helpers need to be able to assist their clients who have a disability develop an understanding of the impact that societal stereotypes have on their view of themselves.

Pushing Through Perceived Limitations

If you work with people with disabilities, you must develop attitudes and intervention skills that will enable your clients to recognize the strengths and resources they possess. The kinds of help people with disabilities need may encompass a broad range of services. Primarily, these individuals could benefit from psychosocial adjustment services with the intention of optimizing their level of independent functioning, developing positive coping skills, cultivating resiliency strategies, and achieving optimal levels of wellness. Some clients may need help finding community resources to enable them to participate fully in the workforce. Others may need counseling to overcome the anxiety and depression that is often present when it looks like all of life has been turned on its head in a single moment. The rehabilitation plan should be highly individualized and presented in such a way that each person can reach his or her optimal level of medical, physical, psychological, emotional, vocational, and social functioning. People with disabilities often have complex issues; it is best not to judge these clients or their needs based on your first meetings with them. Although many people with disabilities do want and need counseling that addresses the impacts of their disability, it is a mistake to assume this. For example, a 27-year-old woman who has been blind since birth may feel offended if the counselor continues to focus on her blindness; she adjusted to this condition as a child. The helper who focuses on the disability may be the one who is blind to the totality of the human being in front of her. Actively listen to the client's presenting concern because it could have little to do with her disability. She has other attributes as well, such as being a mother, a child, or a sibling; having a job or career; and being a partner. The disability is but one aspect of the person's life, and it may not be a significant concern when counseling this client.

Smart (2019) indicates that individuals with disabilities are becoming advocates for themselves and asserting their rights to counseling services in all specialty areas and practice settings. To provide ethical and effective services to individuals with disabilities, Smart believes that obtaining a broad knowledge of the disability experience is essential. Cornish and her colleagues (2008) state that professionals are not being adequately trained to provide services to clients with disabilities despite the likelihood that they will work with this population, and they may not be able to provide ethical and competent care. Practitioners must engage in self-reflection to accurately determine whether they are competent to provide services to people with disabilities.

Mackelprang and Salsgiver (2009) provide these guidelines for practice with people with disabilities:

- Operate on the assumption that people are capable or potentially capable.
- Critically evaluate the assumption that the problem with disability lies with the person and that individuals with disabilities must be changed before they can function adequately in society.
- Recognize that people with disabilities often face discrimination and oppression, as do other minority groups. Realize that your interventions might well involve political advocacy and actions on your part to eliminate policy barriers that prevent individuals from accessing society's benefits.
- Empower people with disabilities with interventions based on the assumption that these individuals have the right to control their own lives. (pp. 436–438)

When working with people with disabilities, use people-first language (e.g., a client *with* cerebral palsy spastic quadriplegia, not the quadriplegic client), keep abreast of current terminology used for disabilities to demonstrate respect (e.g., intellectual disability rather than mental retardation), seek knowledge about disability etiquette (e.g., wheelchairs are often considered an extension of the individual, and it is rude to lean on the wheelchair or hang things from the handles without permission), and avoid mentioning the disability at all unless it is pertinent to the current situation because no single attribute defines a person. It is of the utmost importance to ask clients directly about their experience and their preferences when referring to their disability.

Case example: Challenging our perceptions.

I (Marianne) gave a talk to people with disabilities at a residential facility. The kinds of questions they raised were not any different from those of other groups that I have addressed, and many of the residents emphasized that they were no different from people without disabilities. Later, I asked a staff member at this institution to ask a few residents this question: "What would you like to tell helpers in training about yourself to assist them in better dealing with special populations?" Some of the residents gave these responses:

- "I would like them to know that I want to be treated as a normal person even though I am in a wheelchair. Look at the person, not at the wheelchair. Don't be afraid of us."
- "I'm a very good person. I'm a very smart person. I have a disability, but I also have intelligence."
- "I can think and feel just like a normal person."

The staff member said a great deal in very few words in a letter to me about her perceptions of the people she helps:

> They have lived in institutions for most of their adult lives. They say they are no different from people without disabilities, but I think that they have enormous hearts. The people I have known have no prejudice and are very loving and giving. They also have a greater appreciation for the very simple things in life that most of us take for granted each day. They are unique individuals and I feel fortunate to have worked with them.

Your stance. Consider your own attitudes and assumptions about people you meet who have disabilities. Do you go out of your way to "help" these individuals? Do you conveniently "avoid" getting too close to them? How might your own reactions affect your work as a helper with this population?

Discussion. Societal attitudes are slowly changing as well-known individuals demonstrate a basic truth—having a disability does not mean that the person is disabled. Most of us are familiar with the Special Olympics, in which people with physical disabilities participate at the highest levels. Indeed, many people who are not so well known are challenging themselves to reach phenomenal goals in their daily lives. Such individuals continue to teach us about ourselves and the capacity of the human spirit to overcome any obstacle. And what about clients who have a disability but who lack hope and want to give up? If helpers accept their hopelessness and despair, they will be of little therapeutic value to their clients. Human services professionals need to discover their clients' strengths and work toward empowerment.

LO5 Multicultural Counseling Competencies

The helping professions continue to emphasize a monocultural approach to training and practice, leaving many helpers ill prepared to deal effectively with cultural diversity (Sue & Sue, 2016). Although referral is sometimes an appropriate course of action, it should not be viewed as a solution to the problem of inadequately trained practitioners. Lee (2015) contends that unethical conduct with culturally diverse clients is often due to a lack of counselor competence. Lee adds that cultural ignorance should not be an excuse for unethical counseling practice. Students in the mental health professions, regardless of their racial or ethnic background, should receive training in multicultural helping. Although it is unrealistic to expect you to have an in-depth knowledge of all cultural backgrounds, it is feasible to have a comprehensive grasp of general principles for working successfully with cultural diversity. If you are open to the values inherent in a diversity perspective, you will find ways to avoid getting trapped in provincialism, and you will be able to challenge the degree to which you may be culturally encapsulated (see Wrenn, 1985).

Sue and his colleagues (1982; Sue, Arredondo, & McDavis, 1992) developed a conceptual framework for **multicultural counseling competencies** and standards in three areas. The first area deals with the helper's beliefs and attitudes about race, culture, gender, and sexual orientation. The second dimension involves knowledge and understanding of the worldview of the helper and specific knowledge of the diverse groups with whom he or she works. The third area deals with skills and intervention strategies needed to serve diverse client groups. Arredondo and her colleagues (1996) operationalized these competencies, and Sue and his colleagues (1998) extended multicultural counseling competencies to individual and organizational development. Sue and Sue (2016) have summarized the multicultural competencies as they apply to practice. These multicultural competencies have been endorsed by the Association for Multicultural Counseling and Development (AMCD), by the American Counseling Association (ACA), by the Association for Counselor Education and Supervision (ACES), and by the American Psychological Association (APA). The most recent version of the competencies, *Multicultural and Social Justice Counseling Competencies,* was developed by the Multicultural Counseling Competencies Revisions Committee (Ratts, Singh, Nassar-McMillan, Butler, & McCullough, 2016). This document provides a framework for the effective delivery of services to diverse client populations. The American Psychological Association (2017b) also developed a diversity document, *Multicultural Guidelines: An Ecological Approach to Context, Identity, and Intersectionality.*

The essential attributes of **culturally skilled helpers**, compiled from these sources, are presented next. You can use this checklist to identify areas of *multicultural competence* you now possess as well as areas in which you need to acquire additional knowledge and skills.

Beliefs and Attitudes of Culturally Skilled Helpers

Put a check mark in the box before each of the beliefs and attitudes in this section that you think you already hold or each area of awareness that you already possess.

With respect to beliefs and attitudes, culturally skilled helpers …

- ☐ become aware of their own personal culture and how they might come across to those who differ from them in a multitude of ways.
- ☐ are aware of how their own cultural heritage, gender, class, ethnic identity, sexual orientation, disability, and age shape their values, assumptions, and biases related to identified groups.
- ☐ gain awareness of their personal and culture biases toward individuals or groups other than their own.
- ☐ do not allow their personal biases, values, or problems to interfere with their ability to work with clients who are different from them.
- ☐ believe that cultural self-awareness and sensitivity to one's own cultural heritage are essential for any form of helping.
- ☐ are aware of their negative and positive emotional reactions toward others that may prove detrimental to establishing collaborative helping relationships.

- ☐ have moved from being culturally unaware to knowing their cultural heritage.
- ☐ learn about the ways in which they are both alike and different from the person they are helping.
- ☐ seek to examine and understand the world from the vantage point of their clients.
- ☐ become aware of how any aspect of diversity (age, disability, race, ethnicity) can become a target of negative behaviors.
- ☐ are able to recognize the limits of their multicultural competence and expertise.
- ☐ respect clients' religious and spiritual beliefs and values.
- ☐ recognize their sources of discomfort with differences that exist between themselves and others.
- ☐ welcome diverse value orientations and diverse assumptions about human behavior and, thus, have a basis for sharing the worldview of their clients as opposed to being culturally encapsulated.
- ☐ do not maintain that their cultural heritage is superior and are able to accept and value the many forms of diversity.
- ☐ are able to identify and understand the central cultural constructs of their clients and to avoid applying their own cultural constructs inappropriately to people with whom they work.
- ☐ respect indigenous helping practices and respect help-giving networks within the community.
- ☐ monitor their functioning through consultation, supervision, and further training or education.
- ☐ understand that mainstream Western helping strategies might not fit all people or all problems and realize how they may need to adapt their interventions to the needs of their clients.

Knowledge of Culturally Skilled Helpers

Put a check mark in the box before each type of knowledge in this section that you think you already possess.

With respect to knowledge areas, culturally skilled helpers …

- ☐ possess knowledge about their own racial and cultural heritage and how it affects them personally and in their work.
- ☐ possess knowledge and understanding about how oppression, racism, prejudice, discrimination, and stereotyping affect them personally and professionally.
- ☐ do not impose their values and expectations on clients from differing cultural backgrounds and avoid stereotyping clients.
- ☐ strive to understand the worldviews, values, and beliefs of those with whom they work.
- ☐ understand the basic values underlying the helping process and know how these values may clash with the cultural values of diverse groups of people.
- ☐ are aware of the institutional barriers that prevent some individuals from utilizing the mental health services available in their communities.

- ☐ have knowledge of the potential bias in assessment instruments and use procedures and interpret findings keeping in mind the cultural and linguistic characteristics of clients.
- ☐ possess specific knowledge and information about the particular individuals with whom they are working.
- ☐ are knowledgeable about communication style differences and how their style may clash with or foster the helping process with people from different cultural groups.
- ☐ are knowledgeable about the community characteristics and the resources in the community as well as those in the family.
- ☐ learn about the basics of family structure and gender roles of groups with whom they work.
- ☐ understand how people in various cultures feel about asking for professional help.
- ☐ have knowledge about sociopolitical influences that impinge upon the lives of ethnic and racial minorities, including immigration issues, poverty, racism, stereotyping, stigmatization, and powerlessness.
- ☐ view diversity in a positive light, which enables them to meet and resolve the challenges that arise in their work with a wide range of client populations.
- ☐ know how to help clients make use of indigenous support systems. In areas where they are lacking in knowledge, they seek resources to assist them.

Skills and Intervention Strategies of Culturally Skilled Helpers

Put a check mark in the box before each of the skill areas in this section that you think you already possess.

With respect to specific skills, culturally skilled helpers …

- ☐ take responsibility for educating their clients to the way the helping process works, including matters such as goals, expectations, legal rights, and the helper's orientation.
- ☐ familiarize themselves with relevant research and the latest findings regarding mental health and mental disorders that affect diverse client populations.
- ☐ are willing to seek out educational, consultative, and training experiences to enhance their ability to work with culturally diverse client populations.
- ☐ assess their level of cross-cultural and personal-cultural competence and do what they can to become a culturally competent helper.
- ☐ are open to seeking consultation with traditional healers or religious and spiritual leaders to better serve culturally different clients, when appropriate.
- ☐ use methods and strategies and define goals consistent with the life experiences and cultural values of their clients and modify and adapt their interventions to accommodate cultural differences.
- ☐ establish rapport with and convey empathy to clients in culturally sensitive ways.
- ☐ have the ability to design and implement nonbiased and effective interventions for clients from identified groups.

- ☐ are able to initiate and explore issues of difference between themselves and their clients, when it is appropriate.
- ☐ are not limited to only one approach in helping but recognize that helping strategies may be culture bound.
- ☐ are able to send and receive both verbal and nonverbal messages accurately and appropriately.
- ☐ are able to exercise institutional intervention skills on behalf of their clients.
- ☐ become actively involved with individuals outside of the office (community events, celebrations, and neighborhood groups) to the extent possible.
- ☐ are committed to understanding themselves as racial and cultural beings and are actively seeking a nonracist identity.
- ☐ actively pursue and engage in professional and personal-growth activities to address their limitations.
- ☐ consult regularly with other professionals regarding issues of culture to determine whether or where referral may be necessary.

Reflection questions. Now that you have completed the checklist, summarize and think about the implications of your current level of awareness, knowledge, and skills. As a way to assess your present level of multicultural competence, reflect on the following questions:

- Are you familiar with how your own culture has a present influence on the way you think, feel, and act? What steps could you take to broaden your base of understanding, both of your own culture and of other cultures?
- Are you able to identify your basic assumptions, especially as they apply to diversity in culture, ethnicity, race, gender, class, religion, disability, age, and sexual orientation? To what degree are you clear about how your assumptions are likely to affect your practice as a helper?
- How open are you to being flexible in applying the techniques you use with clients?
- How prepared are you to understand and work with clients of different cultural backgrounds?
- To what degree are you now able to differentiate your own cultural perspective from that of a person from another culture?
- To what degree is your academic program preparing you to gain the awareness, knowledge, and skills you will need to work with diverse client populations?
- What kinds of life experiences have you had that will better enable you to understand and counsel people who have a different worldview?
- Can you identify any areas of your personal-cultural biases that could inhibit your ability to work effectively with people who are different from you? If so, what steps might you take to challenge your biases?

Recognizing Your Own Limitations

As a culturally skilled helper, you have the ability to recognize the limits of your multicultural competency and expertise. It is not realistic to expect that you will know everything about the cultural background of people with whom you will work. There is much to be said for letting your clients teach you about relevant aspects of their culture. Ask clients to provide you with the information you will need to work effectively with them. In working with culturally diverse individuals, it helps to assess the degree of acculturation and identity development that has taken place. This is especially true for individuals who have had the experience of living in another culture. They often have allegiance to their own home culture but find certain characteristics of their new culture attractive. They may experience conflicts when integrating the values from the two cultures in which they live. These core struggles can be productively explored in the context of a collaborative helping relationship.

We encourage you to accept your limitations and to be patient with yourself as you expand your vision of how your culture continues to influence the person you are today. It is not helpful to overwhelm yourself with all that you do not know or to feel guilty over your limitations or parochial views. You will not become a more effective and culturally skilled helper by expecting to be completely knowledgeable about the cultural backgrounds of all your clients, by thinking that you should have a complete repertoire of skills, or by demanding perfection. Instead, recognize and appreciate your efforts toward becoming a more diversity-competent helper.

Cultural Competence as a Lifelong Learning Process

Acquiring cultural competence is a lifelong learning process that includes formal training, self-reflection, and questioning what is occurring in cross-cultural therapeutic partnerships. Cultural competency involves more than self-awareness and knowledge; it entails acquiring skills for effective multicultural intervention. Counselors entering cross-cultural helping relationships need to develop techniques and skills consistent with the life experiences and cultural values of their clients (Lee, 2019b). Culturally competent helpers are continually developing attitudes and beliefs, knowledge, and skills that enable them to work more effectively with diverse clients. They realize that they can never say they have achieved an ultimate level of competency (Corey, Corey, & Corey, 2019). Culturally competent practitioners adapt and incorporate various therapeutic approaches to address the multiple facets of each client's unique needs and life experiences. They are attuned to both interpersonal and intrapersonal factors that foster the therapeutic relationship (Chu, Leino, Pflum, & Sue, 2016). For an in-depth discussion of becoming a culturally competent practitioner, see *Multicultural and Social Justice Counseling Competencies: A Blueprint for the Profession* (Lee, 2019c).

LO6 Social Justice Competencies

Understanding that oppression and discrimination operate in the lives of our clients is fundamental to ethical practice, and we must translate this awareness into various forms of social action. We can play a significant role in making society a better place by challenging systemic inequities. The **social justice perspective** is based on the premise that oppression, discrimination, privilege, and social inequities do exist and have a negative impact on the lives of many people from diverse cultural groups. Broadly constructed, **social justice** involves access and equity to ensure full participation in the life of a society, particularly for those who have been systematically excluded on the basis of race/ethnicity, gender, age, physical or mental disability, education, sexual orientation, socioeconomic status, or other characteristics of background or group membership. For us to be able to effectively work with a range of people from diverse backgrounds, it is critical that we acquire competencies in the social justice perspective, and that we also incorporate these competencies into our practice. Lee (2018b) conceives of social justice as "a *shared journey*, that first and foremost needs to take place inward with self-reflection, self-awareness, self-empowerment, and self-change, in order to create the fertile ground upon which social change can blossom" (p. 249).

The social justice perspective reflects a valuing of fairness and equal treatment for marginalized and devalued individuals and groups of people who do not share equally in society. Counseling practices rooted in social justice aim to challenge inherent inequities in social systems. Social justice goes beyond raising awareness and focuses on issues of oppression, privilege, power relations, and social inequities. Counselors as agents of social change possess the awareness, knowledge, and skills to intervene, not only at the individual level but also at the systemic level (Lee, Baldwin, Mamara, & Quesenberry, 2018).

Chung and Bemak (2012) refer to social justice work as a **fifth force**; it entails a paradigm shift beyond the individual and represents a proactive concern with advocacy and social change. For instance, a helper who is invested in social justice may become active in a local organization that addresses the issue of voter suppression during election time. "Being an advocate requires the core counseling skills and multicultural competencies, along with energy, commitment, motivation, passion, persistence, tenacity, flexibility, patience, assertiveness, organization, resourcefulness, creativity, a multisystems and multidisciplinary perspective, and the ability to deal with conflict and negotiate and access systems" (p. 175).

Sustained efforts on a large-scale need to be made in advocating for oppressed groups, but you can also promote social justice in small ways in everyday life. Although acquiring multicultural and social justice competencies and working toward social change might seem like an ambitious undertaking, each of us can take small steps toward bringing about social change. For example, when a coworker in the break room or a "friend" on Facebook makes an insensitive comment about someone from a marginalized group, you have an opportunity to be a social justice advocate by commenting on the biased remarks you are hearing. Counseling for social justice is the next logical evolutionary step from multicultural counseling. Social justice work involves a move from understanding the experiences of oppressed groups toward social action with the goal of achieving social equity for marginalized or disenfranchised individuals (Lee et al., 2018). Developing social justice competence, like multicultural competence, is not achieved once and for all. It is best to think of competence in these areas as part of a lifelong journey in developing attitudes and behaviors that will equip you to best serve a wide range of client groups.

LO7 Multicultural Training

The standards established by the Council for Accreditation of Counseling and Related Educational Programs (CACREP, 2016) require that training programs provide curricular and experiential offerings in multicultural and pluralistic trends, including characteristics within and among diverse groups nationally and internationally. Social justice principles, concepts, and practices should be infused throughout the training curriculum. CACREP standards call for supervised practicum experiences that include people from the environments in which the trainee is preparing to work. It is expected that trainees will study ethnic groups, subcultures, the changing roles of women, sexism, urban and rural societies, cultural mores, spiritual issues, and differing life patterns. Lee (2018c) emphasizes that students must be provided with opportunities to acquire multicultural and social justice competencies. This competence is predicated on (1) counselor self-awareness, (2) an understanding of the client's worldview, (3) an understanding of how privilege affects the counseling relationship, and (4) developing advocacy intervention skills at the individual, group, institutional, and societal levels.

To enable helpers to utilize a multicultural perspective in their work, we support specialized training through formal courses and supervised field experiences with diverse client populations. We believe a self-exploratory class should be required for trainees in the helping professions to help them better identify their cultural and ethnic blind spots. In addition to enabling students to learn about cultures other than their own, such a course could offer opportunities for trainees to learn more about their own race, ethnicity, and culture.

A good program should include at least one course dealing exclusively with multicultural issues and people from diverse backgrounds. However, reliance on a single course designed to address the interface of professional ethics, multicultural counseling competence, and social justice counseling issues is not adequate for assisting counselors with the demands they will face (Bemak & Chung, 2007). In addition to a separate course, a broad range of ethical decision-making skills related to multicultural counseling should be integrated throughout the curriculum and infused in all aspects of the training program. For example, a fieldwork or internship seminar can introduce ways that helping strategies can be adapted to the special needs of diverse client populations and show how some techniques may be quite inappropriate for culturally different clients. The integration of multiculturalism and gender awareness can certainly be a thread running through relevant formal courses. In addition, there could be at least one required field placement or internship in which trainees have multicultural experiences. Ideally, the supervisor at this agency will be well versed in the cultural variables of that particular setting and also be skilled in cross-cultural understanding. Further, trainees should have access to both individual and group supervision on campus from a faculty member.

Supervised experience, along with opportunities for trainees to discuss what they are learning, is the core of a good program. We encourage you to select supervised field placements and internships that will challenge you to work on gender issues, cultural concerns, developmental issues, and lifestyle differences. You will not learn to deal effectively with diversity by working exclusively with clients with whom you are comfortable and whose culture is familiar to you. You can learn a great deal by going out into the community and interacting with diverse groups of people who face myriad problems. Through well-selected internship experiences, you will not only expand your own consciousness but will increase your knowledge of diverse groups. This will provide a basis for acquiring intervention skills.

An effective multicultural training program includes the components of awareness, knowledge, skill development, and experiential interaction, all of which are integrated in actual practice. As you have seen, awareness of personal attitudes and of attitudes toward diverse client populations is integral to becoming an effective helper. From a knowledge perspective, helpers need to understand what makes a diverse population unique. They need to know what behavior is acceptable within the diverse population and how this behavior differs from that of other groups.

Skill development is a necessary but not sufficient component of learning to work with diverse populations. The skills themselves are not unique, but the ways in which these skills are applied to particular clients should be the focus of training. Effective training will pay sufficient attention to each of these domains. If any of them are neglected, helpers are at a disadvantage.

Training programs have come a long way in the past several years, but they still have some way to go to equip helpers with the knowledge and skills required to meet the needs of diverse clients. As a student, you can take some small, yet significant steps toward recognizing and examining the impact of your own cultural background and learning about cultures different from your own. Deciding to act upon even a few of the suggestions given in this chapter is one way to move in the direction of becoming a culturally skilled helper.

By Way of Review

- Multiculturalism recognizes and values diversity in helping relationships and calls on helpers to develop strategies that are culturally appropriate.
- A multicultural perspective considers specific values, beliefs, and actions related to race, ethnicity, gender, age, ability, religion, language, socioeconomic status, sexual orientation, political views, and geographic region. Multicultural counseling, broadly conceptualized, considers the personality dynamics and cultural backgrounds of both helper and client in establishing a context in which they can interact meaningfully.
- To function effectively with clients of various cultures, helpers need to know and respect specific cultural differences and realize how cultural values operate in the helping process.
- Be aware of any tendencies toward cultural tunnel vision. If you have limited cultural experiences, you may have difficulties relating to clients who have a different view of the world. You are likely to misinterpret many patterns of behavior displayed by these clients.
- Broaching the topic of race and ethnicity is one way to actively include a multicultural element in counseling; it can strengthen the therapeutic alliance and promote better therapeutic outcomes.

- Many diverse clients have come to distrust helpers associated with the establishment or with social service agencies because of a history of unequal treatment.
- It is important to pay attention to ways in which you can express unintentional racism through your attitudes and behaviors. One way to change this form of racism is by making your assumptions explicit.
- Microaggressions related to a person's gender, sexual orientation, or disability can be as powerful and potentially destructive as are racial microaggressions.
- Helpers must be committed to continually monitoring their political countertransference so their biases and assumptions do not contaminate the therapeutic process.
- In working with people from other cultures, avoid stereotyping and critically evaluate your assumptions about the use of self-disclosure, nonverbal behavior, trusting relationships, self-actualization, and directness and assertiveness.
- Helpers must demonstrate a willingness to examine their own attitudes when working with people who have any kind of disability.
- Many individuals with disabilities are able to achieve a high degree of success; keep your focus on clients' potential rather than their perceived limitations.
- Effective multicultural helpers have been identified in terms of the specific knowledge, beliefs and attitudes, and skills they possess.
- Social justice, the *fifth force* in the helping professions, addresses issues of oppression, privilege, and social inequities. Helping professionals need to take an active stance in addressing social justice issues that are manifested in society by acquiring social justice competencies.
- Acquiring and refining multicultural and social justice competencies should be thought of as a lifelong developmental process that requires ongoing self-reflection, training, and education.
- Helpers who view differences as positive attributes will be most likely to meet and resolve the challenges that arise in multicultural helping situations.

What Will You Do Now?

1. If your program does not require a course on cultural diversity, consider taking such a course as an elective. You might also ask if you can sit in on some class sessions in various courses that deal with specific populations. For example, in one university these are a few of the courses offered: The Black Family, The Chicano Family, American Indian Women, The African Experience, The Chicano and Contemporary Issues, Afro-American Music Appreciation, The White Ethnic in America, Women and American Society, The Chicano Child, and Barrio Studies.
2. On your campus you will probably find a number of student organizations for particular cultural groups. Approach some members of one of these organizations for information about the group. See if you can attend one of their functions to get a better perspective on their culture.

3. Think of ways to broaden your cultural horizons. Go to a restaurant, social event, faith-based service, concert, play, or movie that will expose you to a culture that you are unfamiliar with or that you would like to learn more about. If possible, attend this activity with a person from a cultural background that is different from your own. Ask this person to teach you about salient aspects of his or her culture.
4. If your grandparents originally came from another country, interview them about their experiences growing up in their culture. If they are bicultural, ask them about any experiences with combining both cultures. What have been their experiences in assimilation? Have they retained their original cultural identity? What do they most value in both cultures? Do what you can to discover the ways in which your cultural roots have some influence on your thinking and behavior today. In Chapter 2 you were introduced to the importance of discovering how your family of origin continues to influence you. This exercise can help you develop a richer appreciation of your cultural heritage.
5. Helpers are likely to encounter clients with a variety of disabilities. Some broad types of disabilities include mobility disabilities, visual disabilities, deafness, developmental disabilities, psychiatric disabilities, and cognitive disabilities. In groups of three or four, select a broad category and research the kinds of help available in your community for people with this type of disability. What additional services would benefit this population? Present your findings in class.
6. For the full bibliographic entry for each of the sources listed here, consult the References at the back of the book. For a good overview of counseling strategies and issues for various ethnic and racial groups, consult Atkinson (2004). See Chung and Bemak (2012) for an excellent treatment of the social justice perspective in the helping professions. See Lee (2018a) for various perspectives on counseling for social justice. See Lee (2019c) for a useful treatment of multicultural issues in counseling. See Ratts and Butler (2019) for a treatment of multicultural and social justice competencies. Sue and Sue (2016) have written a comprehensive text on counseling diverse client populations, and they provide a framework for developing cultural competency in the areas of cultural awareness, knowledge acquisition, and skill development.

Ethics in Action Video Exercises

7. In video role play 3, Challenging the Counselor: Culture Clash, the client (Sally) directly questions the counselor's background. She says that she didn't expect the counselor (Richard) to be so young and seemingly inexperienced. She presses him further about whether he knows much about the Chinese culture.

   Assume you are the counselor, and your client directly questions you about your background, wondering if you are able to understand her life experience and thus help her. When you consider the range of differences between you and your client, what specific differences concern you the most?

Role-play a situation where a clash between you and a client might develop (such as a difference in age, race, sexual orientation, or culture).

8. In video role play 6, Multicultural Issues: Seeking More From Life, the client (Lucia) is presenting her struggle, which can be understood only to the extent that the counselor (Janice) understands her client's cultural values. In this case, Lucia is struggling with a decision of what she wants to do with her life. Her parents would like her to stay at home and take care of her children. She asks Janice how she might be able to help her. The counselor lets Lucia know that the most important thing is that she is at peace with whatever decision she makes. This situation can be role-played in class or in a small group and used as a springboard for discussion of what it takes for a counselor to be able to ethically and effectively counsel diverse clients.

CHAPTER 5

Common Concerns of Beginning Helpers

Learning Objectives

1. Identify self-doubts about becoming a helper.
2. Explain the differences between transference and countertransference.
3. Describe signs for recognizing countertransference.
4. Explain ways of dealing with resistance therapeutically.
5. Identify types of clients who may be a challenge to work with effectively.
6. List five guidelines for dealing effectively with ambivalence.
7. Describe competence from an ethical and legal perspective.
8. Explain when making a referral is appropriate.

Focus Questions

1. What client behaviors do you anticipate to be the most problematic for you? Why?
2. As a helper, how can you best deal with clients exhibiting difficult behavior (e.g., those who act in a passive-aggressive, unmotivated, or withdrawn manner)?
3. How can you maintain an appropriate distance from your clients' problems while remaining open and sensitive to their struggles?
4. How can you deal with your own reactions, which may be stimulated by working with a wide range of clients?
5. What do you generally do when a friend or family member displays a difficult behavior? How would your reaction be different if a client exhibited this behavior?
6. What aspects from your past are likely to affect your ability to work with certain types of clients?
7. What behaviors or attitudes would cause you to want to refer clients to another professional?
8. What do you think your job would be like if you had a caseload composed of clients like yourself?
9. How willing are you to examine your own personal concerns as part of your professional development?

Aim of the Chapter

Chapter 2 stressed the importance of helper self-knowledge and how helpers can use their own life experiences as a way to better understand those with whom they will work. In this chapter, we look at ways you are likely to be personally affected by your work as a helper. Your capacity and willingness to be open to what is emerging inside of you as you encounter defensive behavior in your clients is the theme of this chapter.

As a helper, you will encounter a range of special concerns throughout your career, but some problems will be particularly daunting for you. It is critical that you understand and learn how to deal effectively with the feelings that some of your clients have toward you and the corresponding feelings that they evoke in you. Even experienced helpers show an interest in learning creative ways to deal with difficult clients, especially people who are highly defensive. In this chapter, we address the important issues of transference, countertransference, and understanding and managing your own feelings and actions as you work with clients with whom you have difficulty. Some of the case examples are complex and require a high level of knowledge and skill. Begin to think about how you might eventually deal with cases like these.

Some helpers become too invested in getting well-defended clients to change, and they fail to be aware of their own dynamics and reactions as they interact with clients they perceive as being difficult. It can be productive to pay as much attention to yourself as you do to your clients. Do not think that you should know exactly what to do in every complex situation. In your program, you will have many opportunities to learn and practice the skills that can be applied to demanding situations. Your supervised field placement activities and your supervisory sessions are ideal places to talk about the concerns raised in this chapter as well as to practice various intervention skills.

This chapter will probably raise more questions than it answers. There are no simple solutions to the many complex situations that you may encounter in your helping relationships. Seasoned counselors and therapists also find the task of helping clients work through their multilayered issues to be challenging, if not perplexing, at times. We hope you will give yourself the latitude to not expect to have all the answers. Our purpose is to introduce you to a range of common concerns that beginning helpers typically face.

LO1 Exploring Self-Doubts and Fears

Students in human services and counseling programs sometimes bring up fears, perfectionist strivings, and other personal concerns. Students often express their anxiety over the prospect of facing clients. They ask themselves: What will my clients want? Will I be able to help them? What if I don't know what to say? Will they want to come back? Realize that anxiety can be a normal reaction to facing a new or threatening situation. Too much anxiety can render an intern unable to pay attention to the client, however; so it is critical for helpers to learn how to manage their anxiety. Another concern of many students and practitioners is their expectation that they must be able to help all clients. They often burden themselves with the belief that they cannot afford to be less than perfect, lest they make a mistake and hurt a client.

In practicum and internship courses, we frequently hear statements of self-doubt from those who are beginning to help others. Apply these statements to yourself, and decide to what degree you see them as your concerns using the following scale:

5 = I strongly agree
4 = I agree
3 = I neither agree nor disagree
2 = I disagree
1 = I strongly disagree

____ 1. I am afraid my clients will suffer from my mistakes and my uncertainty in knowing what to do.

____ 2. I often feel I should know more than I do.

____ 3. I feel uncomfortable with silences in counseling situations.

____ 4. It would be difficult for me to deal with overly demanding clients.

____ 5. I am likely to have trouble working with clients who are not motivated to change or who are mandated to come to me for counseling.

____ 6. I expect that I may have trouble deciding how much of the responsibility for change is mine and how much is my client's.

____ 7. I am concerned that I may have trouble being myself and trusting my intuition when I practice counseling.

____ 8. I am afraid of conflict and confrontation, and I think this might be a problem when helping others.

____ 9. I worry that my clients will think I am incompetent because I am a beginner.

____ 10. I am not sure how much of my personal reactions I should reveal in counseling sessions.

____ 11. I worry that I may overidentify with my client's problems to the extent that they become *my* problems.

____ 12. I expect that I will want to give advice to those whom I counsel.

____ 13. I am concerned that I will lack the knowledge and skills to work with clients whose values and culture are different from my own.

____ 14. I am apprehensive about whether my clients will like and approve of me.

____ 15. I am afraid that I will become so consumed with my clients' issues that I will feel overwhelmed and eventually burn out.

Now go back and select the issues that represent your greatest concerns. What negative messages are you telling yourself, and how might you begin to critically evaluate them if they are not serving you well?

LO2 Transference and Countertransference

You may have pinpointed concerns and fears that could influence your ability to work effectively with clients in your responses to the checklist. Certainly a major concern of many helpers, both personally and professionally, is being able to deal constructively with their clients' reactions to them. A central task is to know when your reactions are being triggered by your own internal conflicts rather than resulting from the dynamics of your clients.

Various Forms of Transference

In previous chapters, you were introduced to the concepts of transference and countertransference; this chapter addresses these topics in more detail. You will recall that your experiences with your family of origin may influence the manner in which you will be able to manage feelings a client may project onto you. **Transference** often operates on the unconscious level and involves clients projecting onto a helper past feelings or attitudes they had toward significant people in their lives.

Transference typically has its origins in early childhood and constitutes a repetition of past material in the present with the therapist. This pattern causes a distortion in the way clients perceive and react to the counselor. Clients may view you with a mixture of positive and negative feelings. At different times the same individual may express love, affection, resentment, rage, dependency, and ambivalence. Transference feelings take place even in the practice of brief counseling. It is essential to understand what transference means and how to deal with it skillfully and therapeutically.

In our training workshops for students and mental health practitioners, we explore examples of difficult client behaviors that participants present to us. We stress the importance of understanding the functions that these behaviors serve for individuals, examining the payoffs of a client's defensive style and understanding how it is an attempt to cope with anxiety. Rather than focusing on the dynamics of difficult clients and ways of dealing with them, we devote attention to assisting helpers in becoming aware of, understanding, and exploring their own reactions. We encourage those whom we teach to approach challenging or defensive behaviors with interest and respect rather than with impatience and judgment.

Here are some examples of transference situations that you are likely to encounter. Ask yourself what your response might be to a client's feelings toward you and what feelings are likely to be evoked in you.

Clients who perceive you in distorted ways. Some clients will perceive you as an idealized parent. They may have an expectation that you will take care of them in ways that their parents never did. In considering clients who make you into a parent and want you to adopt them, ask yourself these questions: How comfortable or uncomfortable am I with clients who attribute to me unrealistic traits and attributes? How do I feel when people have unrealistic expectations of me?

Other clients may immediately distrust you because you remind them of a former spouse, a critical parent, or some other important figure in their life. For example, consider the female client who is assigned to a male therapist and lets him know that she has little regard for men. The men in her life have been untrustworthy, and because her therapist is male, he, too, might well betray her. If you had a client who prejudged you on the basis of earlier experiences, how would you react? Are you able to recognize your client's behavior as a transference reaction and deal with it nondefensively? How would you respond if no matter how positive your interactions are with her, she continues to tell you that you will eventually let her down?

Some clients will not let themselves trust you because they experienced abandonment in early childhood and are sure you will abandon them as well. They are superimposing past experiences on you. Assume that a client of yours comes from a divorced family. She is somehow convinced that she caused her parents to separate. Because she was abandoned in the past and remembers the pain of that time in her life, she is wary of frustrating you lest you also abandon her. In working with such a client, consider these questions: What can I do to convince her that I do not intend to abandon her? What are my reactions to being told that I am going to be like her parents?

Clients who experience political transference. Transference can also be rooted in clients' past negative experiences and attitudes toward other people and institutions. You may encounter clients who view you as part of a system that has oppressed them, or you may remind them of an individual who is part of a group that has mistreated them. In **political transference**, clients project onto helpers reactions to the political context that has shaped their experience (Chung & Bemak, 2012). For instance, suppose you are a mainstream American school counselor who is meeting with an Arab American male student who has been the target of cyberbullying. His American peers have maliciously accused him of being a terrorist, which has led him to feel depressed and anxious. Because you are also part of the dominant group, this young man may believe that you also harbor racist feelings toward him and are stereotyping him. He may not trust you based on his past experiences with other mainstream Americans who have assaulted his integrity and have offended him deeply. How would you be inclined to react to this student if he expressed hostility toward you, reflecting his defensiveness? What if he seemed intimidated by you or seemed fearful about self-disclosing? How would that make you feel, and how would you react?

Clients who adulate you. Some clients will make you the object of their affection. They are convinced that they would not have the problems they are faced with now if they could find a person like you who would unconditionally accept them. How would you respond to this kind of adulation? Could your client's reactions distort or enhance your self-perceptions?

Clients who make unrealistic demands on you. Some clients make no decisions without first finding out what you think. They may want to know if they can call you at any time. They may request that you extend the allotted time for their sessions. They talk about how close they feel to you and would like to be your friend. They want you to affirm them and tell them that they are special. Even though you may intellectually understand the nature of these unrealistic demands, how do you imagine such demands would affect you? In what ways could you help such clients see the connection between how they are treating you and how they treated some significant person in their past?

Clients who respond with intense anger toward you. Some clients will lash out at you with displaced anger. They will be annoyed with you if you confront them. These clients let you know that they resent you when you give them your observations and reactions to their behavior. Recognize that you are probably getting more of this client's anger than you deserve, and avoid getting into a debate with the person. If you take the client's reactions to you too personally, you are bound to react defensively. As a helper, how do you deal with your feelings toward a person who behaves in this way? With this kind of client, you may need to express and deal with your own feelings with a supervisor or a trusted colleague.

Understanding and Working With Transference Therapeutically

These illustrations of transference behaviors demonstrate how essential it is for you to gain awareness of your own needs and motivations. If you are unaware of your own dynamics, you will get lost in your clients' projections and dynamics. You are likely to avoid focusing on key issues and instead attempt to defend yourself. Paying attention to your own feelings about a client who imposes on you and makes unreasonable demands of you will give you a sense of how significant people in this client's life are affected by his or her behavior.

It is a mistake to think that all feelings your clients have toward you are simply transference. At times clients may be realistically angry with you because of something you have done or said or not done. Their anger does not have to be an irrational response triggered from past situations. If you answer your phone during a session with a client, for example, she may become angry with you over the interruptions and your lack of presence. Her anger could be a justifiable reaction and not one that should be "explained away" as a mere expression of transference.

Likewise, clients' affection for you does not always indicate transference. It could be that they genuinely like some of your traits and enjoy being with you. Of course, some helpers are quick to interpret positive feelings as realistic and negative feelings as distortions. You can err both by being too willing to accept unconditionally whatever clients tell you or by interpreting everything they tell you as a sign of transference.

When clients appear to work very hard at getting the counselor to reject them, it can be useful to explore what they are getting from this self-defeating behavior or how what they are doing serves them. Handled properly, clients can experience and express feelings toward you that more properly belong to others who have been significant in their lives. When these feelings are explored therapeutically, clients become aware of how they are keeping old patterns functional in many of their current relationships. By paying attention to how your clients behave and react to you, you can begin to understand how they react to significant others in their lives.

Transference can be worked with productively in the therapeutic relationship. By bringing early memories through to the relationship with the counselor, clients are able to gain insight into how their past relationships with significant others have resulted in unresolved conflicts that influence their present relationships. "Because transference involves a type of reliving of clients' early relationships in the present, the therapist's observations and feedback can help them to see, understand, and appreciate their own contributions to the situation"

(Safran, Kriss, & Foley, 2019, p. 39). Person-centered therapists and Gestalt therapists have a different view of the therapeutic relationship and do not find the concept of transference to be therapeutically useful in their work with clients.

Working With Transference in Group Counseling

In a group setting, we have found it useful to have the participants gradually become aware of their transference reactions to each other and to the group leaders. At the beginning of a group, we ask members to pay particular attention to people in the room whom they notice most. We facilitate the process of members' increasing their awareness of others by asking these questions:

- Who are you most aware of in this group?
- Are you finding yourself drawn to some people more than to others?
- Do some people seem especially threatening to you?
- Are you finding yourself making quick assumptions about others? For example, "He looks judgmental." "She's intimidating me." "I think I can trust him." "I definitely want to stay away from her." "It looks as if these three people are a clique."

We pay particular attention to group members who have strong reactions to a person they hardly know. It is common for people to "see" in others some of the very traits they disown in themselves. This process of projection forms the basis of transference. Although we ask the participants to become aware of their first reactions to others, we do not ask them to reveal these thoughts or to respond to others too quickly. Instead, we suggest that participants share their reactions after they have had some chances for interaction. By disclosing such persistent positive or negative responses, they have opportunities to come to a deeper understanding of aspects of themselves that they were unaware of and how quickly they make assumptions about people.

A therapeutic group provides a context for increasing awareness of certain patterns of psychological vulnerability. Members of a group can gain insight into the ways their unresolved conflicts create certain patterns of dysfunctional behavior. By focusing on what is going on within a group session, the group provides a dynamic understanding of how people function in out-of-group situations. This insight may include coming to an understanding of how they were affected by important figures in their childhood and how they now act around people who are significant to them. With this new insight, people are able to catch themselves when old patterns become evident in their daily interactions. Rather than responding automatically, they are now able to respond in different ways. Thus a man who treats most women in authority roles with deference can stop himself from making them into representations of his mother. He can then respond to different women more as they really are.

LO3 Understanding and Dealing With Countertransference

Transference tends to evoke reactions in the helper, and these reactions can become problematic if they result in **countertransference**: the therapist's unconscious emotional responses to a client that produce a distorted perception of the client's behavior. This phenomenon occurs when there is inappropriate affect, when counselors respond in highly defensive ways, or when they lose their objectivity in a relationship because their own conflicts are triggered. It is important to be alert to the possibility of countertransference and to guard against unrealistic reactions helpers may have toward their clients that interfere with their objectivity. If you want to be effective in your helping efforts, it is essential that you consider countertransference as a potential source of difficulties. You do not have to be problem free, but it is crucial that you understand how your own problems and countertransference can affect the quality of your relationships with clients.

Countertransference is not always harmful. You can use all of your reactions in therapeutic ways, assuming that you eventually become aware of the sources of your countertransference. Remember that we are considering countertransference from a broader perspective than the psychoanalytic view of countertransference as being merely a reflection of an individual's unresolved internal conflicts that need to be overcome as a prerequisite to working effectively with a client. In current practice, countertransference refers to all of the therapist's thoughts and feelings toward clients, whether prompted by the clients themselves or by events in the helper's own life. As mentioned, **political countertransference** can even be evoked by the helper's reactions to highly charged political issues (Chung & Bemak, 2012). Countertransference involves the therapist's total emotional response to a client including feelings, reactions, associations, fantasies, and fleeting images (Safran et al., 2019). Rather than being considered problematic, countertransference can be viewed as a way to understand the client's experience and thus can provide valuable information for both the client and the practitioner.

The helper's task is to attend to the feelings he or she is experiencing in relationship to the client and then to identify the sources of these emotional reactions. It is essential that counselors monitor their feelings during their sessions with clients and use their responses as a source for understanding clients and helping them to understand themselves. When counselors' personal issues are brought into awareness, the chances increase that their countertransference will be managed appropriately, which means that their reactions are less likely to interfere with the helping relationship. Counselors can achieve a better understanding of their own dynamics and countertransference phenomena through supervision, personal reflection, and being a client in their own personal therapy. Countertransference awareness is not a one-time event; it is an ongoing and evolving process.

Simply having feelings toward a client does not automatically mean that we are having countertransference reactions. We may feel deep empathy and compassion for some of our clients as a function of their life situations. Countertransference occurs when our needs become too much a part of the relationship or when our clients trigger old wounds of ours. Just as our clients will have some unrealistic reactions to us and will project onto us some of their unresolved personal matters, so too can we have unrealistic reactions to them.

One example of countertransference can be seen with the helper (Trudy) who divorced 15 years ago after having an affair. Trudy still feels some regret about her behavior, but she tends to avoid thinking about it and has never engaged in any personal work. Trudy now encounters a client who is involved in an affair and finds herself judging and disapproving of this client's behavior. Trudy disconnects from her client because the material is too threatening for her to face. This kind of reaction to countertransference can harm the client.

Intimate partner violence (IPV) often triggers countertransference issues for helpers who have a history of IPV as well as for those who do not. A counselor with her own history of IPV may feel shame and self-blame, and these feelings may reside just below consciousness. Listening to the client brings her own experiences near the surface, and the therapist may find herself judging her client's behavior based on her own decisions. A helper without personal IPV experience also may struggle to relate to the client due to subconsciously resisting the idea that IPV could happen to anyone, and the thought of being that vulnerable and a victim is too threatening to accept. For a more detailed discussion on IPV, see *It Could Happen to Anyone: Why Battered Women Stay* (LaViolette & Barnett, 2014).

We ask you to look at how your own attitudes, behaviors, and reactions to clients may, at times, actually foster defensiveness in them. Without being overly self-critical or blaming yourself, examine your reactions to those with whom you work to determine how what you are doing can either decrease or escalate the problematic behaviors your clients manifest. As a helper, it is crucial that you be willing to look at the part you may play in contributing to problematic behaviors manifested by clients. It is a useful practice to take an objective inventory of the various ways that you affect the client and the therapeutic relationship. What parts of yourself do you dislike or struggle to acknowledge that could later interfere in connecting with a client with similar dynamics?

If you use your own feelings as a way of understanding yourself, your client, and the relationship between the two of you, these feelings can be a positive and healing force. Even though you may be insightful and self-aware, the demands of the helping profession are great. The emotionally intense relationships that develop with your clients can be expected to bring your unresolved conflicts to the surface. Because countertransference may be a form of identification with your client, you can easily get lost in the client's world. When this happens, your ability to be helpful is limited. Below are some illustrations of countertransference:

- *"Let me help you."* Your client has had a very difficult life. No matter how hard he tries, things don't work out, despite his best efforts. You find yourself going out of your way to be helpful to this client to the extent that he becomes dependent on you. Your intervention might be more comforting to you than it is beneficial to the client.
- *"I hope he cancels."* You are intimidated by a client's anger directed at you or others. When you are in the presence of this client, you are not yourself but are self-conscious and guarded. When he cancels a session, you find yourself relieved.
- *"If only you saw things my way!"* You are working with a client who holds diametrically opposite views on social and political issues that you feel passionate about. You are convinced she would be much happier and healthier if she looked at the world through your lens. You find yourself thinking about this client throughout the week, hoping she will change her views.

- *"My own reactions are getting in my way."* Sometimes your clients will express pain and show tears. This anguish may make you anxious because it reminds you of some past or present situation in your life that you would rather avoid. You may intervene, asking questions in an attempt to stop the client's feelings. It is important to realize that such interventions are motivated by bringing comfort to the helper, not by doing what is in the best interest of the client.
- *"You are too much like me."* Some of your clients are bound to remind you of some of the traits that you would rather not acknowledge in yourself. Even if you do recognize certain traits, you may find it disconcerting to work with clients who talk about problems and situations that are very much like your own. A client may be a compulsive workaholic, for example, and you may see yourself as working too hard. You might find yourself spending a lot of energy getting this client to slow down and take it easy.
- *"You remind me of someone I know."* Your clients will often remind you of significant people in your own life. Put yourself in each of these situations, and imagine how you would respond and to whom you are responding when you have reactions to a client:

    1. Your partner has had an affair and has left you for another person. You are faced with a client who is having an affair and is contemplating leaving his or her partner of many years.
    2. You have been a rape victim, and your client discloses that she has been raped. Or your client informs you that he raped a woman years ago.
    3. You were abused as a child, and your client tells you, after several months, that he was incarcerated because he had abused his own children.
    4. You have just dealt at home with a rebellious teenage daughter, and your first client for the day is a very hostile adolescent.
    5. You lost a grandfather, but you have never really gone through a mourning process and come to terms with his death. One of your older male clients is in poor health and almost dies. As he talks about his feelings, you are extremely uncomfortable and find yourself unable to respond to him. You attempt to reassure him that he will be all right.
    6. You grew up in a household with a single mother who struggled financially because your father was too busy pursuing his heroin addiction. Your new client has visible hypodermic needle tracks on his arms from years of heroin addiction, and you find yourself repeatedly distracted as you look at his arms and remember your own disturbing interactions with your father.
    7. Your mother was critical, demanding, and perfectionistic. You have an older female client who exhibits some of these same characteristics. You find yourself feeling especially anxious before her sessions, spending more time on your appearance than you normally would, and you begin to notice that you avoid challenging this client when it would be indicated therapeutically.

No one is immune to countertransference, and it is crucial that you be alert to its subtle signs. You may find that certain clients evoke a parental response in you.

Their behavior can bring out your own critical responses to them. Knowing this about yourself enables you to work through some of your own projections or places where you are strongly affected.

Among the most vulnerable to the effects of countertransference may be those caregivers who work with the seriously ill or dying. These caregivers are continually confronted with the reality of death. In their work they watch people around them die. Unless these caregivers are able to process their reactions, this work will take an emotional toll on them. Unless you have explored your feelings about death, loss, separation, and grief, your feelings will continue to be activated as you work with clients. In our experience in training students, we find that many of them have difficulty working with people who are terminally ill or with older people because of the constant reminder of their own mortality.

Empathy fatigue, a form of countertransference, can result from helpers being exposed to the pain that clients express, especially if counselors are not aware of their own unresolved personal issues (Stebnicki, 2008). According to Stebnicki, counselors can easily experience intense feelings of being overwhelmed by listening to multiple client stories of grief, stress, loss, and trauma. Counselors can get lost in clients' themes of trauma and pain. As a defense, helpers may dissociate and distance themselves from their clients' overwhelming feelings of grief and helplessness. Empathy fatigue can be a route to burnout and impairment, which is discussed in detail in Chapter 14.

You probably will not be able to eliminate countertransference altogether, but you can learn to recognize manifestations of countertransference and deal with countertransference reactions as *your problem* rather than your client's problem. Countertransference becomes problematic when it is not recognized, understood, monitored, and managed. Recognizing countertransference is the most important first step in learning how to manage it. Here are some additional signs to watch for in recognizing your own countertransference:

- You become intensely irritated by certain clients.
- With some clients you continually run overtime.
- You find yourself wanting to lend money to some unfortunate clients.
- You feel like adopting an abused child.
- You quickly take away pain from a grieving client.
- You usually feel depressed after seeing a particular client.
- You are developing sexual feelings toward a client.
- You tend to become bored with some clients.
- You often work much harder than your client.
- You get overly emotional with a certain client.
- You give a great deal of advice and want your clients to do what you think they should do.
- You are quick not to accept a certain type of client, or you suggest a referral even though you have little information about the client.
- You find yourself lecturing or debating with some clients.
- You need approval or admiration from certain clients.
- You find yourself paying special attention to your appearance on days you see a particular client.
- You daydream or struggle to focus with certain clients.

Remember that it is not the feelings that are the problem; rather, it is the behavior generated by certain feelings that we need to be concerned about. To manage countertransference, you must have a receptive attitude and welcome self-awareness. Accept whatever feelings you are experiencing without feeling guilty or judgmental.

When you begin to realize that certain topics or issues stimulate heightened feelings or specific reactions on your part, strive to understand what is contributing to your excessive or inappropriate responses. Your own supervision will be a central factor in learning how to deal effectively with both transference and countertransference reactions. You can become more aware of your own manifestations of countertransference by focusing on yourself in your supervision sessions. Rather than talking exclusively about a client's problem, spend some time talking about what is going on with you when you are in a session with a particular client who triggers your countertransference. It may be productive to process your countertransference reactions with a supervisor, but avoid blaming your client for the reactions you are having.

Ongoing supervision will enable you to accept responsibility for your reactions and at the same time prevent you from taking full responsibility for directions that your clients take. In addition to supervision, personal therapy is a pathway to self-knowledge that can provide insights you can apply in working with transference and countertransference phenomena. Your ability to gain self-understanding and to establish appropriate boundaries with clients is fundamental to managing and effectively using your countertransference reactions. It is well to remember that helping others change will certainly also change you. It can be useful to practice a **parallel process**, in which helpers temporarily put their reactions aside and later process them in their own therapy, which can benefit both client and helper. If you are unwilling to resolve your own personal problems and conflicts, you will not have much credibility when you ask your clients to explore their deeper concerns.

Working With Clients Who Manifest Problematic Behavior

Professional helpers and students alike are concerned with how to handle "difficult clients." They hope to learn techniques for making these clients less troublesome, for these clients tax them personally and professionally. There are no simple techniques. In our workshops, we help participants become aware of and understand their own reactions to behavior they view as being problematic, and we teach ways of constructively sharing their reactions with clients.

As we address concerns helpers often experience in working with clients who pose a challenge for them, we are conscious of the language we use and attempt to avoid labeling clients. When helpers encounter obstacles in forming a working alliance with clients, they sometimes refer to them as being "resistant" or "difficult" clients. Calling people who are seeking help "difficult" can involve a blaming element, so it is good to keep in mind that the helper's goal is to approach clients with empathy, compassion, and a healthy curiosity aimed at uncovering the complexities of what contributes to those difficult behaviors.

Attitude Questionnaire on Understanding and Working With Problematic Behavior Displayed by Clients

Take a few minutes to complete this self-inventory to examine your attitudes toward resistance and problematic behaviors exhibited by clients. Indicate your position on each statement using the following scale:

1 = strongly agree
2 = slightly agree
3 = slightly disagree
4 = strongly disagree

____ 1. Challenging clients force me to reflect on and explore my own unresolved problems that get in the way of being an effective helper.

____ 2. Problematic behavior is best approached with a sense of interest.

____ 3. Negative attitudes on the part of clients generally lead to ineffective results in the helping process.

____ 4. When I encounter clients' reluctance, it generally gets me to question my part in contributing to this behavior.

____ 5. Involuntary clients will rarely benefit from professional helping relationships.

____ 6. When clients are silent, this is almost always a lack of willingness to cooperate with treatment.

____ 7. Client defensiveness is often a sign of handling a transference relationship poorly.

____ 8. The most effective way of dealing with client defensiveness is to be highly confrontational with clients.

____ 9. One way of working with challenging clients is to pay attention to my own feelings.

____ 10. Labeling or judging clients who exhibit difficult behavior tends to entrench this behavior.

Now look over your responses and try to identify patterns in your perceptions of resistance and difficult behavior. At this point, how does problematic behavior from clients generally affect you, and how can you effectively deal with this?

LO4 Handling Resistance With Understanding and Respect

Most clients will test you in some way to determine whether the relationship with you will be safe. It is essential that you encourage your clients to express their hesitations and anxieties. A helper can explore with clients how they are experiencing each session, beginning at the initial meeting. Unless the helper asks clients about any potential problems with the helping process, their concerns will likely remain unspoken. Most clients will experience ambivalence and defensiveness at various times in the helping process. Clients are likely to have mixed feelings regarding staying in a safe zone versus taking the risk of letting you know them. This ambivalence can be explored in the helping relationship to the benefit of the client.

From a psychoanalytic perspective, **resistance** is defined as the individual's reluctance to bring into conscious awareness threatening material that has been previously repressed or denied. It can also be viewed as anything that prevents individuals from dealing with unconscious material. From a broader perspective, resistance can be viewed as behavior that keeps us from exploring personal conflicts or painful feelings. Resistance can be thought of as ways we attempt to protect ourselves from anxiety and defend ourselves from pain, and thus it serves a function.

There are various ways of viewing resistance, and some helpers interpret resistance in a judgmental way. By reframing the concept, we can use what appears to be resistance in a therapeutic way. Learn to respect resistance and various forms of avoidance, and strive to understand the meaning of these behaviors. Teyber and Teyber (2017) suggest that counselors can understand the client's reluctance as an outdated coping strategy that at one time served a self-preservative and adaptive function but is no longer useful. By honoring clients' resistance, helpers are able to appreciate the fact that a particular coping strategy was the best possible response to a difficult situation. Both helpers and clients can recognize that some resistance makes good sense when it is understood in context.

The perspective of motivational interviewing. People who seek counseling are often ambivalent about making behavioral changes, and their motivation may ebb and flow during their therapeutic journey; motivational interviewing provides guidelines for facilitating attitudinal and behavioral changes. **Motivational interviewing (MI)** is a humanistic, client-centered, directive counseling approach in which the therapeutic relationship is central to understanding the change process (Miller & Rollnick, 2013). When clients are contemplating making changes in their lives, concerns and fears about changing are common, and reluctance to change is a normal and expected part of the therapeutic process. What appears to be low motivation may in fact reflect clients' ambivalence about changing. *Motivational interviewing* promotes acceptance and compassion for this ambivalence and is a useful way to explore a client's ambivalence (Naar & Safren, 2017). A central goal of *motivational interviewing* is to increase internal motivation to change based on the personal goals and values of clients. As individuals become ready to change, it is likely that their intrinsic motivation will increase. Have you ever wanted to change something about yourself or your life but held back and didn't make this change? If so, what stopped you from taking action?

Your clients will come to trust you, and let down some of their guard if you approach their reluctance with understanding, compassion, regard, and respect. Part of respecting resistance means that you appreciate the functions these defenses serve. In the therapeutic relationship, clients can learn to become self-accepting rather than blaming themselves and adopting a critical attitude. There are times when people need their defenses to survive a crisis situation. At such times, you need to be supportive rather than insist that your clients surrender their protection.

Perhaps the key to understanding clients' various forms of defensive behavior is in paying attention to your countertransference, which is evoked by behaviors on the part of the client. You cannot afford to have a fragile ego as a professional helper. Give your clients some latitude, and strive not to respond defensively to any problematic behavior they might display. If you keep in mind that your clients are coming to you for help, you may be able to be more patient with them.

Learning not to take defensive behavior of clients personally. In dealing with clients who display problematic or defensive behaviors, monitor your responses to their behavior, and do your best to avoid assuming a defensive stance. Clients whom you perceive as being difficult or challenging may contribute to your own feelings of self-doubt and incompetence and bring out your feelings of inadequacy and frustration. If you too quickly become annoyed with these clients, you are likely to cut off avenues of reaching them and a tense situation is likely to worsen. If clients exhibit initial distrust, do not take their behavior in a personal way but view this as a sign of strength and recognize ways you can utilize clients' cautiousness in the helping process. Clients have their own reasons for lack of cooperation and for refusing the help that they have sought. The helper and the client need to discover what these reasons are and address them in the helping relationship. Your task is to approach difficult clients in a different way and work cooperatively with them so that they might learn new and more adaptive ways of coping.

We hope you will avoid labeling clients as "resistant" or "difficult" and instead describe the behaviors you are observing. When you view clients as being scared, overwhelmed with grief, cautious, or hurt, you can reframe any problematic behavior pattern they may manifest. By simply changing the word "resistant" to more descriptive and nonjudgmental terminology, your own attitude toward clients who appear to be "difficult" may change. As you change the lens through which you perceive clients' behaviors, it will be easier for you to adopt an understanding attitude and encourage clients to explore the meaning of their reluctance.

Instead of viewing difficult behavior as something designed to make your work impossible, try to approach such behavior with a genuine sense of interest and curiosity. If your client Enrique exhibits hostile behavior, consider reframing this experience: "It's interesting how hard Enrique is trying to get me to not like him. I wonder how his behavior is serving a purpose and whether he could find another way to get what he wants more directly." Or consider Maribel, a client who sits silent for much of each session: "Maribel seems scared. Her silence during the sessions may be due to her lack of understanding of how to ask for help with her problems." Describe how you see your clients behaving toward you and invite them to explore the meaning of their behavior. It may be appropriate to let them know how certain of their behaviors are affecting you. After this declaration of your personal reactions, clients are more likely to explore alternative ways of getting what they want from you and from others.

LO5 Types of Clients Who May Pose a Challenge to You

If you want to be effective with clients who present a challenge to you, develop patience and give them room to maneuver. Establish whether clients are interested in changing patterns of behavior that they perceive as problematic.

If clients assert that they do not want to change a certain behavior, or that this behavior is not a problem in their outside life, your efforts to facilitate change may be in vain.

While working with clients whom you perceive as being problematic, do not put the exclusive focus on them. Rather than constantly paying attention to the problematic behaviors manifested by your clients, reflect on your reactions to your clients. See what these reactions tell you, both about yourself and about your client. Regardless of which specific behavior a client exhibits, it is essential that you understand your own countertransference. Certain clients are more difficult for you because they evoke your countertransference reactions. Think about which of the characteristics of difficult clients described in the following pages would provide the greatest challenge to you.

Involuntary clients. There are many kinds of involuntary clients. Some are sent by the court, others are sent by their parents, others come in under duress with an intimate partner, and some will be referred to you by another helper. Involuntary clients may have little motivation to change and may see little value in the help you offer. A client who is not seeing you voluntarily can be difficult to engage. Sometimes clients are reluctant to seek help because of their misconceptions about what the helping process entails, or they may have had negative experiences with counseling. How you approach such clients will determine the degree to which they will become more or less cooperative.

A typical involuntary client is Yuri, who attends your therapy group because he was found guilty of driving under the influence. His main motivation in coming to this class is to satisfy the judge's order. He figures that attending class is better than going to jail. Although he is willing to come to the sessions, he tells you that he doesn't believe he has a problem. Rather, his intoxication was due to a series of unfortunate circumstances. By validating his feelings and providing information about the services you offer, Yuri may become more cooperative and interested. Yuri did make a choice to attend therapy rather than to go to jail. Helping Yuri to recognize that he made this choice may enable him to feel more in control and responsible for his own path. This recognition frequently results in more active participation. Together you can make a contract specifying the willingness you both have to work productively. Many clients mandated to treatment, such as Yuri, do make significant changes.

Clients who are silent and withdrawn. Clients who say very little almost always evoke anxiety. Imagine this client sitting in your office: He looks down at the floor much of the time, responds politely and briefly to your questions, and does not volunteer any information. For you the session seems to last forever, and you feel as though you are getting nowhere. You might ask, "Do you want to be here?" He will reply, "Sure, why not?" If you ask him what he wants to change in his life and what he wants to talk about, he will say that he doesn't know.

Is it your responsibility to get this client talking? Are you taking his silence personally? Are you thinking of ways to draw him out? Before you assume an inordinate amount of responsibility, or before you judge his silence unfavorably, attempt to put his silence in some context. You might ask yourself, and at times your client, what makes it difficult to talk? The reasons for his silence could be any of the following: He is frightened. He sees you as the expert and is waiting for you to ask a question or tell him what to do. He feels intimidated; he may be rehearsing every thought and critically judging his every reaction. He feels shame over asking for help. He is responding to past conditioning of "being seen but not heard." His culture may put a value on silence. He may have been taught to listen respectfully and merely to answer questions. Furthermore, your client may be quiet and invisible because this pattern served to protect him as a child. He may withhold information and limit his words because they have been used against him in the past. In other words, silence should not always be interpreted as a refusal to cooperate with your attempts to help. Some clients respond better to less verbal forms of therapy, such as through the use of expressive arts therapy or sand tray therapy. Many teenage clients struggle with traditional face-to-face therapy and are much more at ease talking while also playing a game.

Silent clients in a group counseling situation can affect you and the other members in many ways. You may judge yourself, thinking that if you knew the right things to say and do, your client would open up and talk fully. You could do the talking for your client or constantly draw him out. It might be helpful to say something like this: "I notice that you are very quiet in this group. You seem to pay attention to what other group members are saying, yet I rarely hear from you. How is it for you to be in this group?" If this client does not interpret his silence as a problem, maybe you will be working in vain in trying to change him. This group member may have many reasons for being quiet. If he does see his silence as a problem, you can explore with him the ways in which this behavior is problematic. If you assume full responsibility for bringing him out, he never has to struggle with the reasons underlying his silence.

Clients who talk excessively. The opposite of the client who rarely talks is the person who talks excessively. Some clients tend to get lost in telling stories. They provide you with every detail so they won't be misunderstood. However, you may be left wondering what the point of the story is. Instead of talking about how they are affected by a particular situation, they overwhelm people with information that is not relevant.

Consider the case of Jianni, who inundates you with detailed information. Any attempt you make to slow her down results in her telling you that she wants to be sure that you understand what she is saying. Jianni keeps talking because she is likely to feel anxious if she slows down and experiences some of the things she is talking about.

In working with Jianni, you might feel overwhelmed and not know how to intervene. Although she is talking about painful situations, she is doing so in a very detached and rehearsed style. You might have reservations about interrupting her, out of fear of cutting her off. One of your functions is to help Jianni gain awareness into how her behavior might serve as a defense. Here are a few examples of some helpful comments you might make:

- I notice that when you speak of your relationship with your mother you tear up. Then you quickly change the subject and talk about another matter.
- You said a lot just now. Take a few moments to reflect on what has the most importance for you.

- Would you be willing to stop talking, and tell me what you are aware of at this moment?
- You are making a real effort to give me a lot of details so I can understand you better. I want to understand you, yet the many details you provide make it difficult for me to hear what you are trying to tell me.
- If you had to express in one sentence all that you have been trying to tell me, what would you say?

If you are having reactions to a client like Jianni who overwhelms you with words, such as noticing that you have a hard time staying with her, it could be therapeutic to deal with your own reactions. Chances are that Jianni is affecting many people in her life in much the same way she is affecting you. This is an opportunity for her to get feedback on how she comes across and for her to determine if she wants to do anything different. If you chronically suppress your reactions and pretend that you are listening with unconditional positive regard, you are reinforcing her talkativeness.

Clients who overwhelm themselves. Clients often have a multitude of problems and overwhelm themselves by wanting to attend to these problems all at once. They rapidly describe one problem after another, and in doing so they may appear panicked and unable to focus. As a helper, you need to intervene and slow down their process. As with other forms of unsuccessful communication, explore with clients who overwhelm themselves how to better manage some of the problems they are encountering. It can be helpful to say something like this: "I know there are many things that you feel are pressing on you today. I suggest you sit quietly for a moment and reflect on what it is that you most want from this session. Select the one concern that is most pressing to you at this time." With these clients, it is also useful to begin sessions with a brief relaxation or meditation exercise to help calm and focus them for the session.

Clients who often say "Yes, but . . ." You will encounter clients who give you an abundance of reasons why your interventions won't work. As a helper, you may have doubts that you can be of any assistance. No matter what insights or hunches you share or what suggestions you make, the client quickly responds with an objection. Some illustrations of the client responses that work against your best efforts to be of help are given below:

> **Helper:** I recommend that you bring your wife to one of your counseling sessions.
> **Client:** I agree that it might help, but my wife would feel very threatened. My wife will never change! I'm willing to talk to her, but I don't think it would help.
> **Helper:** When I suggest something that could be of help to you, are you aware that you give reasons why my suggestion would not work?
> **Client:** You don't understand my situation. I try to change, but there are just so many things that keep me from changing.

When you are trying to help such clients, there is a tendency to become easily discouraged. It doesn't take much to get irritated. Even though you are willing to help this client, he is convinced that he cannot be helped. Eventually you may feel helpless and be inclined to give up. When you sense that you are working harder than your client is working, it may be time to renegotiate with him what he wants and why he is coming to see you.

Clients who deny needing help. Some people do not see that they have a problem. They may come to a couples counseling session wanting to help their spouse but be unwilling to see their part in the troubled relationship. It is not likely to be productive for you to attempt to convince these clients that they have a problem when they insist otherwise.

For example, if you ask Roy what he wants from you, he will probably reply: "My wife wanted me to come to counseling, and I'm here for her sake." You may be able to get through to Roy if you take his word for it and accept his view that he is not the one with the problem. By asking him how he is being affected by his wife's problems, you may eventually get to problems that he wants to deny. Another alternative is to ask him how it is for him to come to your office. If he replies by saying, "Oh, it's fine," you could respond, "What were you thinking as you approached the office?" Or you could ask: "You say you're here to help your wife. What are some of the areas that you think she needs help with?" Or you could say: "You tell me that you don't have any problems and that your wife made you come here today. How do you respond to her demands that you join her today? Might this be a problem for you?"

Clients who manifest passive-aggressive behavior. Certain clients have learned to defend themselves from hurt by dealing with people indirectly. They use hostility and sarcasm as a part of their style of avoiding. They are highly evasive when they are confronted. If you explain your reactions, they are likely to say: "Well, you really shouldn't feel this way. When I made that remark, I was just kidding. You take me too seriously."

Some common signs of clients who exhibit **passive-aggressive behavior** are as follows: They often arrive late. They say little. You see reactions on their faces, yet they assure you that everything is fine. They giggle when you talk. They raise eyebrows, frown, sigh, shake their head, look bored, become distracted with their cell phones, and show other nonverbal reactions yet deny that anything is going on with them. They chronically draw attention to themselves, and when they have the attention, they do little with it.

Clients who behave in passive-aggressive ways may be hard to deal with. It is not helpful to label them and to interpret their behavior by saying, "You are passive-aggressive." It is hard to deal directly with such behavior because of its elusive quality. However, you will certainly have reactions to clients who make hostile remarks or who offer sarcasm. One way of cutting through this indirect behavior is to be aware of what it brings up in you and to describe your reactions. Avoid making judgments, but describe the behavior you see and tell the clients how their behavior is affecting you. It is also useful to ask them if they are aware of their behavior and to tell you what it means. For example, you might say: "When I talk, I have noticed that you sometimes smile, or roll your eyes, or turn around. I find myself reacting to you and wonder if there is something you want to say to me." This comment gives the client an opportunity to be more direct and to interpret his or her own behavior.

To monitor your own transference reactions, here are some questions to put to yourself: Do certain clients who display hostility remind me of any people in my life? What do I feel like when people are not direct and I sense that there are some things they are not telling me? Is it timely and appropriate for me to describe my reactions to the hostility I perceive from my clients?

Clients who rely primarily on their intellect. Some individuals block out feelings and present themselves primarily in intellectual ways. Any time they get close to an emotion, they find a way to evade the feelings and turn to a safer cognitive zone. They constantly try to figure out why they have a problem. They are adept at self-diagnosis and theorizing abstractly about the nature of their dysfunctions. As long as they function primarily on an intellectual level, they know they are safe. If they allow themselves to feel jealousy, pain, depression, anger, or any other emotion, they do not feel safe. To avoid experiencing anxiety, they have learned to insulate themselves from feelings.

Do not insist that such clients get to a feeling level. You can let them know how it is for you to be with them when they show little affect, but it is not helpful to try to strip away their defense. When they feel ready to let go of it, they will do so. Think about the ways in which you are affected in dealing with a woman who remains very cerebral. If you are successful in getting her to give up her protection, will you be able to help her? Will you be able to be present for this person when she lowers her defenses and gets in touch with years of repressed feelings? Will you be overwhelmed by her pain? If you are not able to be present when she expresses her fear, will this prove to her that people are not to be trusted with her emotions?

Clients who use emotions as a defense. The opposite of clients who use their intellect as a defense are clients who often emote. These clients use their emotions as a defense. Their behavior may put you in a bind. You may have trouble trusting their emotions. You may become annoyed, feel manipulated, or suspect that they are not sincere.

When you are with these clients, reflect on what they bring out in you. It is possible that some of your highly emotional clients remind you of people in your life who manipulated you with their emotions. For example, a sister might have succeeded in making you feel guilty when she cried and stormed out of the room. Now, as you work with clients who exhibit some of these behaviors, you may feel a lack of compassion for them and, in turn, wonder whether you have a problem with empathy.

LO6 Guidelines in Dealing Effectively With Ambivalence and Reluctance

Learn to listen attentively and with respect as clients express their fears, reservations, ambivalences, and reluctances. Think about ways you can intervene when clients exhibit problematic behavior or give signs of resistance. Here are some guidelines for you to consider:

- Express your reactions to clients respectfully.
- Avoid responding to sarcastic remarks with sarcasm or to hostile comments with hostility.
- Provide clients with necessary information so they can get the most from the helping process.

- Encourage clients to explore their fears and hesitations rather than expecting immediate trust.
- Avoid judging a client; instead, describe the behavior you are observing that tends to be self-defeating.
- State observations and hunches in a tentative way as opposed to being dogmatic.
- Be sensitive to clients who are culturally different from you without stereotyping a client because of his or her culture.
- Monitor your own countertransference reactions.
- Avoid using your knowledge, expertise, and power to intimidate those seeking help.
- Do not take clients' reactions in an overly personal way.

When we talk about dealing with difficult client behaviors in workshops, participants are always interested in learning specific strategies for dealing with the type of client behavior they find most frustrating. In our discussion here, we have avoided suggesting techniques that might change clients. Instead, we put the focus on you, as a person and as a helper. You cannot directly change clients who are manifesting defensive behaviors, but you can learn significant lessons about the dynamics of their behavior as well as better understand your own defenses.

Focus on why your clients have come to you, what they hope to get, and how you can teach them better ways of fulfilling their needs. If you respond in a negative manner to clients who exhibit negative behaviors, it will hamper your effectiveness with them. If you resist the temptation to attack their defenses, and if you avoid labeling or judging them, the chances of their defenses being lowered increase.

LO7 Striving for Competence

It is common for beginning helpers to have doubts about their general level of competence. In fact, it is not at all unusual for even experienced mental health practitioners to wonder seriously at times whether they have the personal and professional abilities, knowledge, and skills needed to work with some of their clients. It is more troubling to think of helpers who rarely question the adequacy of their skills. In thinking about the matter, you may range from one extreme to the other, at times being plagued with self-doubts and at other times thinking that you can deal with any problem a client presents.

Competence is both an ethical and a legal concept. From an *ethical* perspective, competence is required of practitioners if they are to protect and serve their clients. Even though mental health professionals may not intend to harm clients, incompetence is often a major contributing factor in causing harm. From a *legal* standpoint, incompetent practitioners are vulnerable to malpractice suits.

Striving for competence is a lifelong endeavor. It is best to think of competence as a process rather than as something we achieve once and for all. You may achieve competence in a particular field, but you need to take steps to maintain this level of knowledge and skills throughout your career. One of the most important steps toward maintaining your competence is to engage in collegial consultation with other professionals throughout the duration of your career, especially when you go into new areas of practice.

LO8 Knowing When and How to Make Referrals

All of the professional codes of ethics spell out that you should not practice beyond the limits of your competence. Assessing competence is not an easy task. Many people who complete a doctoral program lack the skills or knowledge needed to carry out certain therapeutic tasks. Obviously, a degree alone does not guarantee competence for any and all helping services. In your role as a helper, you will work with a wide spectrum of clients in very diverse settings, which requires different skills and competencies. You need to assess how far you can safely go with clients, when to seek consultation, and when to refer clients to other professionals. Careful self-monitoring is an effective way to ensure that you are providing quality services. It is important to learn when to consult another professional if you have not had extensive experience working with a particular problem.

When faced with clients displaying problematic behaviors such as those described in this chapter, you might well doubt your competence and be inclined to make a referral. The ethics codes of most professional organizations stipulate that making referrals, when appropriate (such as lacking competence), is a responsibility of the professional helper. For example, the National Association of Social Workers (2017) provides this guideline:

> Social workers should refer clients to other professionals when the other professionals' specialized knowledge or expertise is needed to serve clients fully or when social workers believe that they are not being effective or making reasonable progress with clients and that other services are required. (1.16.a.)

It is imperative that you make skillful referrals when the limits of your competence are reached. Your clients deserve to understand the reason for the referral, and you will need to learn how to make this referral in such a manner that your client will be open to accepting your suggestion rather than feeling rejected or abandoned. A client's failure to make progress with you is another reason to consider a referral. When referral becomes necessary, it is generally recommended to provide the client with three referral options.

Clients can be negatively affected when you too quickly refer them. We hope you will not see the answer for working with challenging clients, on a routine basis, as referring them to another professional. If you follow the practice of referring all clients with whom you have difficulty, you might soon have very few clients! It is a good idea to think about the reasons that motivate you to suggest a referral. If you recognize a pattern of frequent referrals, then you may need to examine your reasons for doing so.

In cases where you have limited experience, it is especially important to be open to consulting another professional as a way to acquire or upgrade your skills. We hope that you can say to a client, "I don't know what to do, but I know where we can get some help." Beginning helpers sometimes believe that they must always know what to do, and they hesitate to let their clients know that they might not be sure how best to proceed. Although we do not expect you to know everything, we certainly expect that you can learn much under supervision.

Keeping Current

Your academic program will provide some basic training, yet it is essential to find ways of extending your education beyond graduation. To assume that your skills never deteriorate or that you know everything you need to know upon graduation is not realistic. Your knowledge and skills will soon be outdated unless you take steps to keep abreast of new developments. Unless you engage in lifelong learning, your professional knowledge may decline drastically, even if you are in the early phase of your career (Taylor & Neimeyer, 2016). Some useful ways to combat knowledge obsolescence and maintain competence are to be willing to consult with other professionals throughout your career, participate in peer consultation groups, engage in self-directed learning, and attend professional conferences. Learning never ends, and new clients present new challenges. You also may need to seek supervision and consultation when working with various client populations and emerging areas of concern.

Some current issues in the helping professions that are receiving increased attention are methods of dealing with substance abuse and eating disorders; working with oppressed populations including gay, lesbian, bisexual, and transgender clients and people with physical, cognitive, intellectual, and psychiatric disabilities; traumatic stress; helping survivors of natural and manmade disasters; domestic violence; physical, psychological, and sexual abuse of children; abuse of older people and spouses; HIV/AIDS; conflict resolution skills; parent education; adolescent suicide; school violence and mass shootings; serving culturally diverse client populations; and legal and ethical issues. Many professions have mandatory continuing-education requirements for relicensing or recertification of their members. Take advantage of in-service and continuing-education programs to learn about emerging trends. You can keep abreast of developments by taking specialized courses and workshops that deal with particular client groups and current interventions. When continuing education is tailored to your personal and professional needs, it can keep you on the cutting edge of your profession.

Another way of keeping informed of developments in your field is through reading. In addition to professional journals and books dealing with your specific subject of interest, novels and nonfiction works about other cultures can contribute to your continuing education.

Perhaps the best way of keeping yourself up to date is to be involved in a professional network with colleagues who are willing to learn from one another as well as assume a teaching role. Colleagues can offer both the challenge and the support for practitioners to adopt a fresh perspective on problems they encounter in professional practice. Networking among professionals also provides a consistent avenue for identifying and addressing sources of negative feelings and loss of objectivity. An excellent way to develop this network is by joining the professional organization that most interests you and by attending the state, regional, and national conferences offered by this organization (see Chapter 1).

By Way of Review

- Effective helpers must become aware of clients' transference and of their own countertransference. Neither of these factors is to be eliminated but is to be understood and attended to therapeutically.
- Countertransference refers to the unrealistic reactions therapists have toward clients that are likely to interfere with their objectivity. One way of becoming more aware of your potential for countertransference is by being willing to seek your own therapy. Another way is by focusing in your supervisory sessions on yourself and your reactions to clients.
- Defensive behavior and reluctance take many forms, and it is necessary to understand the ways in which they protect clients. Not all cautiousness or reluctance stems from stubbornness on the part of the client. Some can be caused, or at least contributed to, by the attitudes and behaviors of helpers.
- The goal in a helping relationship is not to eliminate defensive behavior but to understand what functions it serves and to use it as a focus for exploration.
- A useful way of looking at the concept of resistance is to view it through the lens of those who practice motivational interviewing (MI) where it is viewed as a normal part of the therapeutic process.
- Clients display many types of difficult behaviors, and some of them will evoke your own countertransference reactions. When this happens, you are now part of the problem. Instead of allowing your countertransference to interfere with the quality of the therapeutic work with your clients, take the opportunity to engage in personal work to effectively process your own unfinished business.
- Competence is both an ethical and a legal concept, and striving for competence is a lifelong journey.
- Ethics codes explicitly state that it is unethical to practice outside the boundaries of your competence. It is essential that you be able to make an accurate assessment of your knowledge and skills to determine your ability to effectively work with a particular client. You need to learn what clients you can best work with and to know when a referral is appropriate.
- Either as an intern or on your job, you may be asked to take on clients or to provide therapeutic strategies that are beyond the scope of your training and experience. Learn to be assertive in staying within your limits.
- Graduation from a training program does not signal the end of learning but merely the beginning of a process of professional growth and development. To maintain your effectiveness, continuing education is a necessity.
- One of the best ways of keeping on the cutting edge of one's profession is to become involved in a peer-consultation group that affords professionals opportunities to share their concerns and learn from one another. Through peer groups, helpers can actively contribute to their own personal and professional development and that of their colleagues.

What Will You Do Now?

1. Envision a client who would be extremely difficult to counsel and reflect on the ways this client could present problems for you. What makes this case a difficult one for you? What do you think you would do if you actually had this person as a client? What might you do if you felt that you could not work with him or her?
2. Reflect on the kinds of defensive behavior that you see within yourself. How open are you to accepting your limitations? If you were a client in counseling, what defenses to changing might you develop? What do you think it would be like if your clients were very much like you? Talk with a friend about this subject as a way of confirming (or contradicting) your views.
3. Look over the descriptive list of difficult client behaviors and identify specific kinds of client behaviors you would find most difficult to deal with in a helping relationship. In your journal, write down what you can learn about yourself from your reactions to certain behaviors displayed by clients.
4. If you work in an agency, a school, or another setting, you may encounter resistance to change and defensiveness among your colleagues and supervisors rather than with your clients. In small groups, discuss how you might handle such situations. Take turns role-playing how you might approach a defensive colleague.
5. In small groups explore what you think the criteria should be for determining whether a therapist is competent. Make a list of specific criteria, and share it with the rest of the class. Are you able as a class to identify some common criteria for determining competence?
6. In small groups explore the topic of when and how you might make a referral. Role-play a referral, with one student playing the client and another playing the counselor. After a few minutes the "client" and the other students can give the "counselor" feedback on how he or she handled the situation.
7. Look again at the inventory at the beginning of the chapter that helped you identify your self-doubts and fears pertaining to your role as a helper. Select one or two of these concerns and write about them. What are some steps you might take in dealing with your greatest concerns?
8. Review the attitude questionnaire on working with reluctant and difficult clients. Write down your ideas about how you might become more therapeutic in dealing with reluctant and difficult clients.
9. For the full bibliographic entry for each of the sources listed here, consult the References at the back of the book. For an in-depth discussion of honoring the client's resistance, see Teyber and Teyber (2017). For another perspective on reframing resistance by addressing ambivalence toward change, see Miller and Rollnick (2013).

CHAPTER 6

The Helping Process

Learning Objectives

1. Describe the elements involved in the stages of change model.
2. Explain why brief interventions are popular in the helping professions.
3. Discuss how a therapeutic alliance is basic to any form of helping.
4. Describe how the assessment process is crucial in identifying clients' problems.
5. Explain the value of a collaborative partnership between client and counselor in creating therapeutic goals.
6. Discuss two ways of encouraging clients to take action to make basic changes in their life.
7. Discuss what is involved in a successful termination of a helping relationship.

Focus Questions

1. What beliefs do you have about the capacity of people to change? Who is responsible for change in the helping relationship?
2. How is your philosophy of human nature related to your approach to working with people who seek your help?
3. What basic beliefs do you hold about the helping process? How do you think these beliefs influence your practice?
4. Which of your assets, strengths, and resources can you draw on in establishing helping relationships?
5. If a client appeared to be getting little from a helping relationship with you, what questions could you ask yourself and your client?
6. How does knowledge about the stages of helping influence what you do with a client? What is the helper's role at various stages in the helping process?
7. What guidelines would you use for challenging clients? What is an appropriate balance between challenge and support?
8. How important is helper self-disclosure in the helping relationship? What guidelines would you use to determine when self-disclosure is appropriate?
9. How would you work with clients to formulate goals for the helping relationship? What role do clients have in identifying personal goals and in achieving these goals?
10. What guidelines would you use for effective termination?

Aim of the Chapter

The purpose of this chapter is to help you clarify your role as a helper at various stages in the helping process. We look at the skills and knowledge you need and the personal characteristics that are required to apply those skills. We identify specific skills that are especially relevant for the various stages in a helping relationship and ask you to assess your current level of skill development. Our basic assumption is that the kind of person you are and the attitudes you bring to the helping relationship are the major determinants of its quality.

In our view, you need to integrate knowledge, skills, and the person you are to be an effective helper. Knowledge alone is insufficient, yet without it you cannot become an effective helper. If you focus mainly on acquiring skills and neglect theory and knowledge, these skills will have little value. Effective helpers must be sensitive to the interpersonal dimension of the helping process to productively apply their skills and knowledge in each situation. Helpers who have little self-awareness are at best skilled technicians with a limited ability to make a difference in the lives of clients. Helping is more than technique; it is also an expression of who the helper is. The helping professions are based on scientific knowledge that practitioners are able to use in creative and personal ways. In short, the process of helping is both an art and a science.

In this chapter, we assist you in clarifying your thinking about helping by raising a number of questions about your style as a helper: How can you best determine the appropriate balance of focusing on feeling, thoughts, and behaviors? What is the optimal balance between providing a great deal of structure and providing only minimal structure? Do you believe clients are capable of finding their own solutions to problems? How can you best create and maintain a collaborative working relationship with your clients?

Your View of the Helping Process

Your view of the helping process is largely a function of your beliefs about human nature and about how people change. Before you accept a position in any setting, it is essential that you understand the philosophy of the agency because this influences the manner in which the agency functions. You might work in a state facility that emphasizes behavior-modification strategies or for a counseling service that offers only brief forms of therapy. You might work at an agency where you are expected to use the *Diagnostic and Statistical Manual of Mental Disorders* ([*DSM-5*], American Psychiatric Association, 2013a) to arrive at a specific diagnosis for each client you see, sometimes in the very first session. One purpose of this chapter is to help you identify and clarify your views on how helping can best occur.

The Impact of Our Beliefs on Our Work

Our views and beliefs about human nature are very much related to the helping strategies we will employ with our clients. If we see people as basically good, for example, we will trust that our clients can assume responsibility for the direction of their lives. If we see human nature through a negative lens, we may regard it as our duty to correct people's flawed nature.

Effective helpers hold positive beliefs about people; have a healthy self-concept; ground their interventions in a theoretical rationale; are respectful of cultural differences; are able to fully listen and understand; and possess empathy, congruence, warmth, compassion, genuineness, and positive regard. They test their beliefs and examine whether their interventions are expressions of their core beliefs and assumptions about how people change. Effective helpers value their clients and take a collaborative stance. In contrast, ineffective helpers tend to be rigid and judgmental, telling clients how to think and how to solve their problems. Ineffective helpers do not see their clients as having the means to control their own lives. As you think about your qualities as a helper, review the characteristics of the "ideal helper" we described in Chapter 1.

If we expect the best in people, they are likely to give us their best. If we treat people as though they have the capacity to understand and resolve their problems, they are more likely to find answers within themselves. By developing a collaborative partnership with our clients, we are telling them that they can use the helping relationship as a pathway to re-creating their lives. Conversely, if we assume that people generally resist change, we might increasingly see behavior that confirmed our expectations. We would be fostering a self-fulfilling prophecy in our clients that reinforced our assumptions. Ask yourself these questions: Do I tend to form quick judgments about people and make generalizations based on limited experience? Am I willing to seriously examine the assumptions that I make, and am I open to changing some of them? Have my assumptions changed over time? Being willing to question the origin of our assumptions and modify them, if necessary, enhances our growth as a helper.

Learning to Critically Evaluate Assumptions

A few years ago, we provided a series of in-service training workshops at a state institution. Although we had the good fortune to meet and work with some dedicated and effective helpers, we also encountered some judgmental and ineffective helpers who seemed to think that their patients could do nothing right. A few workers at the institution were quite outspoken in their beliefs that these patients were resistant to therapy, were not motivated to change, and were only putting in their time as ordered by the court. If the clients did not talk during the sessions, they were labeled "resistant"; if they did talk, they were often viewed as "manipulative."

In our training workshops we urged the staff members to suspend their judgments at least during the time they were providing therapy. We encouraged them to give their patients a chance to show something more of themselves than the problem with which they had become identified. If staff members were open to discovering other facets of the patient's personality, they might discover struggles in the patient's life with which they could identify. We asked these helpers to carefully assess their assumptions that seemed nontherapeutic and to be open to the possibility that they could begin to see clients and the helping process in a different light.

If you are making some of the assumptions we have described, think about how they might determine the way you approach clients. Your beliefs about yourself, the people with whom you work, and the nature of the helping process are often more subtle than the assumptions we have highlighted. Whether your beliefs are subtle or extreme, however, you tend to behave on the basis of them. If you do not trust your clients to understand and deal with their problems, you will use strategies to get them to accept your assessment and to follow your prescriptions.

After identifying your assumptions, you can begin to see how your attitudes are being expressed in your behavior. Then you are advised to assess how well such attitudes and behaviors are working for you and are helping your clients. We suggest that you examine the source of your beliefs regarding an individual's capacity to make substantial changes and your beliefs regarding the role of the helper–client relationship in bringing about change. Think through, clarify, and question these beliefs in an ongoing process of self-examination.

You may not have clear beliefs about the helping process if you are just beginning your training. You may have incorporated your beliefs in an uncritical and unconscious manner and not tested them to determine whether they are valid or functional. If you have lived in a sheltered environment and have rarely stepped outside of your social and cultural group, you may not even be aware of how narrow your belief system is. It is possible to live in an encapsulated environment and thereby "see" only what confirms your existing belief system. This is known as **confirmatory bias**.

One good way to identify and clarify your beliefs is to put yourself in situations that may enable you to question your beliefs. If you have limited contact with alcoholics, for instance, learn about Alcoholics Anonymous and attend a meeting. If you have limited experience with certain cultural and ethnic groups, volunteer or do fieldwork placements with a culturally diverse population. If you are aware that you hold stereotypes about older adults, volunteer to work in a board and care home for older people. Direct contact with populations that are unfamiliar to you is the best way to learn about people whom you might have stereotyped. Approach these situations with an open mind and avoid simply looking for evidence to support your prior judgments. A stance of openness will enable you to develop a different orientation toward helping.

LO1 Our Beliefs About the Helping Process

It took us some time to learn that there is no one right way to approach clients. Instead of looking for the right thing to do or say, we strive to follow what we think is a productive path to pursue with a client. In this process we trust our intuition and develop our own ways of working. If our hunches about a client are incorrect, that quickly becomes apparent if we pay attention to the relationship. We continually relearn that it is important to talk with clients about what we think is going on between us, which is known as the skill of **immediacy**. For example, if we have a hunch a client is engaging in storytelling to avoid talking about something else that is extremely painful, we might say to this client: "As you are telling this painful story, I am noticing how unemotional you seem to be. What are you aware of right now?"

At times, when we have trouble relating to a particular client, this person is reflecting some dimension within ourselves that we are reluctant to accept.

It can be helpful to imagine our clients as mirrors that reflect some aspect of our being. The Jungians call this concept **shadow aspects**. We do not necessarily need to change anything, but it does help to recognize patterns we have in common with our clients. For example, a helper (Claire) struggles to relate to a client who exhibits attention-seeking behaviors, such as being overly competitive with a sister to the detriment of the relationship. (This client puts her sister down to feel better about herself, frequently one-ups her sister in accomplishments, and even started dating her sister's boyfriend.) Inwardly, Claire may be feeling some level of resentment, which leads to a feeling of disconnection with the client. If Claire is able to engage in self-exploration in a curious and nonjudgmental way, she may find that her reaction is based on not liking that same core dynamic within herself. During college Claire went to great lengths to maintain a 4.0 GPA, and anyone who knew her would have characterized her as an overachiever with strong perfectionist tendencies. On the surface, the two individuals may seem different, but ultimately both share the core dynamics of experiencing a need for external validation to feel good and worthy about themselves. If Claire can attain self-awareness in this area, she will have the opportunity to benefit from a **parallel process** by engaging in her own therapy work outside of sessions while working with this client in sessions. What parts of yourself do you dislike or have difficulty acknowledging that could later interfere in connecting with a client with similar dynamics?

We do not accept the full responsibility for deciding what the focus of a helping relationship will be. Rather than working very hard to figure out what clients should want, we ask them frequently what it is they want. We often ask: "Is what you are doing working for you? If not, what are you willing to do to change it?" If their current behavior is generally serving them well, they may not feel a strong need to change a particular style. We encourage them to look at the price they could be paying for behaving the way they are, and then the decision whether to change is up to them. We do not see it as our task to decide for our clients how they should live their lives; rather, our role is to encourage them in making a self-assessment and then deciding for themselves what they most want to explore in the professional relationship with us.

After a sufficient amount of time has passed, if clients appear to be getting little from the helping relationship, we examine our part in this outcome by asking ourselves about our involvement and willingness to risk with this client. We may also ask the client, "Is something I am doing making it difficult for you to make progress?" In addition, we explore with the client his or her part in the lack of progress. We recognize that we cannot make clients want to change, yet we can create a climate where together we look at the advantages and disadvantages of making certain changes. We see the helping process as a collaborative endeavor in which both parties share the responsibility for making change happen.

Employing motivational interviewing (MI) strategies (see Chapters 5 and 7) can be an effective way to help mobilize clients to make the changes they claim they want to make. Rather than viewing reluctance to change in a pathological manner and labeling the client "difficult," think of resistance as a normal response to having mixed feelings about making changes.

It is important to assess an individual's stage of change or "readiness to change." In the transtheoretical model, behavior change is conceptualized as a process that evolves over time. By exploring a client's ambivalence and posing questions that elicit change talk, the helper may be successful in helping the client move through the five stages of change outlined by Krebs, Norcross Nicholson, and Prochaska (2019):

1. *Precontemplation stage.* The client has no intention of changing a behavior pattern in the foreseeable future.
2. *Contemplation stage.* The client is aware of a problem and considering overcoming it but has not yet made a commitment to take action.
3. *Preparation stage.* The client intends to take action in the near future and reports some small behavioral changes.
4. *Action stage.* The client take steps to modify his or her behavior, experiences, or environment to solve the problem.
5. *Maintenance stage.* The client works to consolidate the gains made during the action stage and to prevent relapse.

It is therapeutically useful to meet clients wherever they are in the change process and facilitate a dialogue that will help them move forward. Helping clients examine the different sides of their ambivalence may increase their motivation to change. Think of ambivalence as an expected part of the process of change, and view it as a resource in the helping process (Cormier, Nurius, & Osborn, 2017). Here are some questions that may help clients who seem mired in ambivalence:

- What about your current behavior or situation is *not* working for you? What concerns do you have about it?
- How would you like things to be different a year from now?
- What are the best results you could hope for if you changed? Are there any potential undesirable results from changing that concern you?
- How important would you say it is for you to make the changes we discussed? On a scale of 1 to 10 (1= not important; 10 = very important), where would you say you are?

LO2 Brief Interventions

If you work in an agency setting, you will likely be expected to be skilled in making **brief interventions**, which refers to a variety of time-sensitive, goal-directed, efficiency-oriented methods; these methods can be incorporated in any theoretical approach (Hoyt, 2015). You will need to learn a number of time-limited, solution-focused, structured, effective strategies that can empower clients to make specific behavioral changes they desire. The emphasis is on making relatively quick assessments of clients' problems and designing brief interventions geared more to relief of problematic symptoms than to intensive self-exploration aimed at long-term behavioral change. Brief therapy traditionally involves 12 to 25 sessions, depending on client circumstances (Miller & Marini, 2009), but it can be limited to fewer sessions, perhaps even to 1 or 2 sessions. At times, even one session can be enough to get a client back on track. Practitioners with varying theoretical orientations suggest the utility of single-session therapy in certain cases.

Experts polled about the future of psychotherapy foresee short-term therapy (5–12 sessions) and very short-term therapy (1–3 sessions) as increasing in popularity in the next 10 years (Norcross & Beutler, 2019; Norcross, Pfund, & Prochaska, 2013). Miller and Marini (2009) describe some of the main characteristics of the brief therapy model. Emphasis is on discovering the immediate concerns clients describe at the first session. The therapist attempts to answer this question: "Why has this client decided to seek counseling at this time?" Practitioners who operate from a brief therapy model are actively involved from the beginning, establish a collaborative relationship with clients, are ever mindful of termination, summarize each session, and with clients devise homework to be carried out between the sessions. Clients are invited to consider returning to counseling months or even years after termination if they want assistance in dealing with future life adjustment or developmental challenges.

A brief approach is a stark contrast to long-term therapy geared to self-exploration, gaining insight into how the past is connected to present problems, and exploring intrapsychic conflicts. This change in the focus of helping will have an impact on your role as a helper. You will be required to develop interventions tailored to short-term and specific behavioral change. In addition to short-term interventions aimed at a variety of client problems, you may be expected to participate in prevention programs such as social skills training, stress management, parent education, vocational counseling, couples counseling, and wellness programs.

Consider how you can maximize short-term strategies aimed at teaching clients problem-solving skills they can apply to their current and future problems. Ask yourself how you can most effectively balance quality care with cost-containment requirements in an agency where you work. Whether the client is engaged in long-term therapy or brief therapy, view each session as if this may be the only one. If you only had one session with this client, what would you most want to accomplish? Shifting your thinking toward maximizing the effectiveness of each session can produce remarkable results. As you read about the stages of helping in the next section, reflect on how you would apply the range of skills described if you were to work in a setting that required you to think in terms of brief interventions.

Stages of the Helping Process

This section is designed to help you determine your assets and liabilities as a potential helper. We present a conceptualization of approaches to skills development based on the work of a number of authors, including Cormier (2016), Cormier, Nurius, and Osborn (2017), DeJong and Berg (2013), Egan and Reese (2019), Ivey, Ivey, and Zalaquett (2018), James and Gilliland (2017), and Teyber and Teyber (2017). Our focus is on presenting a model that describes the stages in the helping process and the major tasks facing helpers at each of these stages. The skills development model offers a general framework of the phases of the helping process and is not linked to any particular theoretical approach. You can apply any of the current theories of counseling (see Chapter 7) to this model of helping.

Egan and Reese (2019) describe the stages of the helping model by framing these stages in the context of the following basic client questions:

1. *What is going on?* What are the problems, concerns, or unused opportunities that I most want to explore?
2. *What does a better future look like*? In what ways do I want my life to be different? What do I need or want? What are the changes I most want to make? What am I willing to pay for what I want?
3. *How do I get what I need or want?* What are some possible paths to my goals? What plan will help me make my preferred picture a reality? How can I turn planning and goal setting into an action plan that leads to success? Now that I know where I want to go, how do I get there?

In each stage, the question provides the focus for that stage of the helping process. These themes help clients move forward in coping with their personal concerns and in developing opportunities for change.

At each stage in this process, helpers have different roles and tasks requiring specific skills. There is considerable overlap among the functions at each of these stages. Rather than thinking of this model as discrete steps that flow in linear order, it is best to think of it as a circular process of decision making. Ivey, Ivey, and Zalaquett (2018) point out that a circle has no beginning and no end and can be used as a symbol of an egalitarian relationship in which the client and the helper form a partnership in working on mutually agreed-upon concerns.

The helper's theoretical orientation greatly influences what occurs at the various stages. Not all clients will feel comfortable with the stages as presented, regardless of cultural background, nor will all clients progress through all of the stages. Issues of rapport, structuring, defining problems, establishing goals, and assessing progress will be important for the duration of the helping relationship. The framework we provide will help you assess your ability to engage others in a helping relationship.

As we describe each of these stages, we focus on *you as a helper.* Assess your own qualities to determine your interest and ability in helping others. Realize that the helping relationship is not just a technical process but a deeply personal human endeavor. As a helper, you will be actively involved with those with whom you are working by drawing on what you know, by applying skills and interventions in a timely and appropriate manner, and by using yourself as a person in creating meaningful relationships with clients or others you help. This is true whether you are involved in the counseling or the administrative aspects of the helping professions. The human relations skills we describe are crucial for all helpers in all settings. If you are unable to apply some basic human relations skills, chances are slim that you will be able to create and maintain adequate rapport with your clients. Although the main emphasis of our discussion is on these skills as they apply to counseling relationships, you can apply them to a variety of other interpersonal situations in your personal life as well.

LO3 Stage 1: Establishing a Working Relationship

The therapeutic relationship is the foundation for effective counseling, healing, growth, and change, and this has been increasingly recognized in the field. Many studies demonstrate that the quality of the therapeutic alliance is a main predictor of positive therapy outcomes and behavior change (Meichenbaum, 2017; Naar & Safren, 2017). The main task of this first stage of helping is to work toward building a quality **therapeutic alliance**, in which therapist and client work in partnership to achieve agreed-upon goals. This working alliance is essential to addressing the tasks of each stage. An effective therapeutic relationship fosters a creative spirit that focuses on developing techniques aimed at increasing awareness, which enables clients to change their thinking, feeling, and behaving. Comprehensive discussions of the therapeutic relationship can be found in *Psychotherapy Relationships That Work: Volume 1* (Norcross & Lambert, 2019) and *Psychotherapy Relationships That Work: Volume 2* (Norcross & Wampold, 2019).

People often seek professional assistance when they realize they are not dealing with problem situations in a satisfactory manner. Helpers are expected to create a relationship in which clients can reveal their story, identify what they want to change, and attain a new method of dealing with their problems. Some people seek counseling because they struggle with self-doubt, feel trapped by their fears, and suffer from some form of loss. Some people reach out for professional support because they are battling depression, anxiety, addictions, or other mental health issues. Returning veterans and their families often seek counseling to deal with posttraumatic stress disorders (PTSD). Some issues may be rooted in biological or psychological causes, but others stem largely from environmental or sociopolitical sources. Clients from marginalized and oppressed groups may have endured discrimination in its various forms and may have been the target of hate crimes. These individuals are likely to seek counseling to deal with the effects of trauma, abuse, disenfranchisement, and a host of other injustices.

Many enter counseling to improve relationships. Others seek help because they are not living as effectively as they would like or because something is missing in their life. Some seek deeper meaning and purpose. They may feel caught in a meaningless job, experience frustration because they are not living up to their own goals and ideals, or feel dissatisfied in their personal lives. In short, they are not managing their lives as well as they might. Two general goals of helping arise from these assumptions: one goal relates to clients' managing their lives more effectively and the other relates to clients' abilities to deal realistically with problems and develop opportunities (Egan & Reese, 2019).

Working with involuntary clients. Not all clients seek counseling voluntarily. Involuntary clients may be unwilling to accept help, and they may not even believe anyone can help them. Working with involuntary clients can be extremely difficult, especially when they exhibit high levels of defensiveness. It is not uncommon for helpers working with involuntary or mandated clients to describe them as being in denial and minimizing the actions and attitudes that got them into trouble. The first task for these counselors is to help these individuals decrease their defensiveness so they will be receptive to the counseling process and willing to work on their issues. Dealing with their hesitation and doubts, rather than ignoring these feelings and attitudes, is one of the best ways to begin with an involuntary client.

Clients mandated to treatment may feel anger, frustration, indignation, shame, anxiety, and fear. Instilling hope and demonstrating respect for the individual, regardless of the behaviors that prompted being mandated to treatment, are an excellent beginning for this counseling relationship. Building a strong therapeutic alliance and relationship is of paramount importance. Mandated clients do not differ from voluntary clients in this regard: both benefit from the trust, safety, and rapport of a strong relationship and use it as a springboard for future work. Attributes of effective counselors—such as being nonjudgmental, genuine, empathic, accepting, and exhibiting unconditional positive regard—are especially important when working with the mandated population; this goes a long way toward establishing and maintaining the therapeutic relationship.

Developing trust with mandated clients may be more challenging than it is with voluntary clients because these individuals may have a lifetime of abuse and other breaches of trust to overcome. Involuntary clients often say the correct words without working toward change. Helpers need to learn how to distinguish empty words from genuine change. Often, mandated clients need to repeat treatment efforts multiple times before they are able to achieve long-term change. Even during these less successful treatment attempts, counselors are planting seeds that may eventually bear fruit in some form or fashion. Many helpers who specialize in these populations report that the extra efforts are worthwhile and ultimately play a part in the healing process for these clients.

To address any barriers to creating a working relationship, we must be able to recognize the signs of defensiveness and resistance (see Chapter 5), both in our client and in ourselves. It is important to understand the many meanings of client reluctance and not to interpret it as a sign of failure on the client's part or as our failure as helpers. If we are primarily concerned with defending ourselves against the various forms of defensive behavior we will encounter with clients, we deprive these clients of opportunities to explore the real meanings of their behavior. It helps to think of resistance as something that both the counselor and client are engaged in. It is not a one-person operation, rather it is more accurate to think of two-way resistance and think of it as an interpersonal construct that describes the dynamics between the client and the helper (Cormier et al., 2017).

One way of not reacting defensively to a client's problematic behavior and of exploring its meaning is illustrated by the following example. You are seeing an involuntary client for the first time. She is extremely hostile and lets you know that she neither wants nor needs your help. She questions your abilities as a counselor. As an effective helper, you cannot indulge yourself in feelings of rejection. However, in a nondefensive way you can explore with this client her unwillingness and her difficulty in seeing you. If you are patient, you may discover that this client has some very good reasons not to trust a professional like you. She may have felt betrayed by a counselor, and she may fear that the information she gives to you will be used against her at some future time. She may regard you as part of the larger system that has treated her unfairly. For excellent discussions on working nondefensively with client resistance, reluctance, and ambivalence, see Cormier, Nurius, and Osborn (2017), Egan and Reese (2019), Miller and Rollnick (2013), and Teyber and Teyber (2017).

Creating a climate for change. In our work with both voluntary and involuntary client populations, our clients' willingness to engage in self-exploration has a lot to do with the kind of climate we establish during the initial sessions. If we work too hard, ask too many questions, and offer quick solutions, clients have little incentive to participate. Our role is to create a collaborative partnership in which clients assume a fair share of the responsibility for what takes place both inside and outside the session. During the early sessions, we can greatly assist clients by teaching them how to assess their own problems and address questions such as "What do you most need to be working on?" and "What personal issues, if successfully addressed, would make a difference in your life?"

Establishing the relationship. To create an effective helping relationship, it is of paramount importance to assist clients in becoming aware of their assets and strengths rather than concentrating on their problems, deficits, and liabilities. For clients to feel free to talk about themselves, we need to provide attention, active listening, and empathy. Clients must sense our respect for them, which we can demonstrate by our attitudes and behaviors. We reveal an attitude of respect for our clients when we are concerned about their well-being, view them as able to exercise control over their own destiny, and treat them as individuals rather than stereotyping them. We show clients that we respect them through our behavior, such as actively listening to and understanding them, suspending critical judgment, expressing appropriate warmth and acceptance, communicating to them that we understand their world as they experience it, providing a combination of support and challenge, assisting them in cultivating their inner resources for change, and helping them consider the specific steps needed to bring change about.

Genuineness is another key ingredient in establishing a productive working alliance with clients. Being genuine does not mean acting on any impulse or saying everything that we think or feel. We can be genuine with our clients when we avoid getting trapped in a professional role; are open and nondefensive, even if we feel threatened; and show a consistency between what we are thinking, feeling, and valuing and what we reveal through our words and actions. These questions are typically asked at the initial session:

- What brings you here?
- What has been going on in your life recently that prompted you to seek professional help at this time?
- What did you do when you faced problems before this time?
- Have you experienced counseling before, and if so, what was that like?
- What expectations do you have regarding the helping process?
- What are your hopes, fears, and reservations?
- What would you most like to accomplish in these sessions?

In establishing a therapeutic relationship, helpers must be able to give their full attention to the other person. If helpers are preoccupied with their own agenda, it will be difficult to understand the experiential world of another person. A helper's presence is truly a gift to a client. At this time, assess the qualities you possess that will either help or hinder you in assuming the client's internal and subjective frame of reference. Consider these questions:

- Are you able to attend to what clients are telling you both verbally and nonverbally and grasp the core messages? Do you pay attention mainly to *what* (content) people tell you, or do you also notice *how* (process) they deliver their messages?
- Are you able to set aside your own biases for a time and attempt to enter the client's world? For example, if you are opposed to abortion on the basis of your own religious beliefs, are you able to bracket your values when working with a client who is considering an abortion and help her reach her own decision?
- Are you able to remain focused on the issues that your clients want and need to explore?
- Are you able to communicate your understanding, empathy, and acceptance to your clients?
- Are you able to work nondefensively with clients who appear guarded? Are you able to help these individuals work through their reluctance and explore their issues more deeply?

Although it may seem deceptively simple to merely listen to others, understanding the world as others see it is demanding. Respect, genuineness, and empathy are best considered as a "way of being," not as techniques to be used on clients. We might interfere with clients' willingness to express themselves if we put forth too much effort in trying to be real. For example, we may want to prove to clients that we too struggle with our own problems. To demonstrate our humanness, we may take the focus away from our clients and put it on ourselves by telling detailed stories about our life. It is a good practice to ask ourselves why we are making this kind of self-disclosure and the degree to which it may or may not be benefiting the client.

Establishing a working relationship with clients implies that we are genuine and respectful in behavioral ways, that the relationship is a two-way process, and that the clients' interests are supreme. This means that we avoid doing for clients what they are capable of doing for themselves. In establishing rapport and a collaborative relationship with clients, the helper needs to master basic helping skills such as attending, listening, reflecting, clarifying, formulating questions, getting significant details, asking open questions, summarizing, paraphrasing, noticing nonverbal behavior, and attending to the evolving process. Useful discussion of these basic interviewing and counseling skills can be found in Cormier (2016), Cormier, Nurius, and Osborn (2017), DeJong and Berg (2013), Egan and Reese (2019), Ivey, Ivey, and Zalaquett (2018), Miller and Rollnick (2013), and Young (2013).

Educating clients and obtaining informed consent. The process of educating clients about how to get the most from the helping relationship, addressing their questions, and clarifying their expectations are routes to ethical and effective practice. Create a balance between giving clients too much and not enough information. Provide clients with the opportunity to talk about what they hope to gain from being in counseling. For clients to feel trusting enough to meaningfully express themselves, they need to have at least some minimal information about the nature of the helping relationship. During the early sessions, discussion should be guided by clients' concerns, interests, and questions.

Therapists may want to explore with clients questions such as these: How is confidentiality protected, and what are the limits of confidentiality? How does the therapeutic process work? What is the primary role of a helper? What is the approximate length of the counseling process? How will termination be handled? What are the main rights and responsibilities of a client? What are some of the main benefits and risks of counseling? Of course, not all these topics can be addressed in one session. Educating clients and obtaining informed consent begins at the first session and continues throughout the duration of the helping process in one way or another. We discuss the topic of informed consent more fully in Chapter 8. For a more completed discussion of informed consent, see Corey, Corey, & Corey (2019).

LO4 Stage 2: Identifying Clients' Problems

During the second stage, the central task is to gather information, conduct an assessment, identify the client's problems and resources, and assist clients in setting goals. Typically, people become clients either because they recognize they need outside help to understand and cope with their problems or because someone else suggests, or in some instances mandates, professional intervention. Clients often need assistance in identifying and clarifying aspects of their lives that are not working for them. The helper's role is to assist clients in identifying problem situations or missed opportunities for full development.

As soon as possible in the helping process it is crucial to teach clients how to identify and clarify problem areas and how to acquire problem-solving skills they can apply in a variety of difficult situations in everyday living. The helper's role is not to identify the nature of clients' problems but to assist them in doing this themselves. In a sense, from the very first meeting we can be most helpful to clients by encouraging them to look within themselves for resources and strengths they can draw on to better manage their lives. Effective helpers also put clients in touch with external resources within the community that can help them meet the demands of daily living. For instance, if a low-income client needs affordable health care and food stamps, an effective helper would assist this client in contacting the appropriate services and making sure that her basic needs are met. The confidence our clients have in us will increase if they are convinced that we appreciate the resources both within themselves and in their external world.

By understanding our client's cultural background, we are doing a great deal to build upon the therapeutic working relationship that was begun at the initial session. We must have some understanding of our client's basic beliefs and values if we hope to be useful to this person. If we are not aware of the central values that guide our client's behavior and decisions, our client will soon pick up on this and likely not return for further sessions. (See Chapter 4 for a more detailed discussion of the importance of understanding clients' cultural values.)

Understanding the environmental context. Clients may come to you not to resolve internal conflicts but to better understand and deal with external stressors in their environment. Some people who seek your services may need your assistance in linking them to resources within their community. They may need legal assistance or your help in coping with day-to-day survival issues such as getting a job, arranging for child care, or taking care of a dependent parent. Clients in a crisis situation require immediate direction in finding external resources to cope effectively with the crisis.

As you listen to your clients, do not assume that they simply need to adjust to problematic situations. They may feel frustration and anger due to societal factors such as being discriminated against in their workplace because of their age, gender, race, religion, disability, or sexual orientation. You will do them a major disservice if you encourage them to adjust to their situation by settling for injustices in an oppressive environment. Support your clients in their efforts to take action within their community to bring about change. Of course, to do this means that you must assume a variety of helping roles: educator, advocate, social change agent, and influencer of policymaking. A more detailed discussion of your role in influencing change within the community is presented in Chapter 12.

Conducting an initial assessment. **Assessment** consists of evaluating the relevant factors in a client's life to identify themes for further exploration in the counseling process. This assessment does not necessarily have to be completed during the intake interview or even the early phase of helping, nor does it have to be a fixed judgment that the helper makes about the client. To obtain the most accurate results from an assessment, it is first necessary to have established rapport and structured the relationship, which is a task for the first stage. Ideally, assessment is a collaborative effort that is part of the interaction between client and helper. Both should be involved in discovering the nature of the person's presenting problem, a process that begins with the initial sessions and continues until the professional relationship ends. Here are a few questions that are helpful to consider during this early assessment phase:

- What appears to be going on in this person's life at this time?
- What are the client's main assets and liabilities?
- What coping strategies is the client currently using, how effective are they, and what kinds of supplemental coping strategies would most benefit this client?
- Who are the significant people in the client's life? Can they be relied upon for support?
- Is this a crisis situation, or is it a long-standing problem?
- Does this client need stabilization or exploration?
- What is the client primarily seeking from the therapeutic relationship, and how can it best be achieved?
- What major internal and external factors are contributing to the client's current problems, and what can be done to alleviate them?
- In what ways can an understanding of the person's cultural background shed light on developing a plan to deal with these problems?
- How might cultural differences between the client and the helper affect the helping process?
- What significant past events appear to be related to the client's present level of functioning?
- What are the prospects for meaningful change, and how will it be determined that change has occurred?

Helpers will develop tentative hypotheses, which they can share with their clients as the process evolves. Additional information is bound to emerge in time, which may call for a modification of the original assessment. This process of assessment does not necessarily have to result in classifying the client under some clinical category. Instead, helpers can describe behavior as they observe it and encourage clients to think about its meaning. In this way assessment becomes a process of thinking about issues *with* the client rather than the assessment being made solely by the professional. This kind of assessment is vital to the interventions that are selected, and it helps practitioners in conceptualizing a case. Consider using assessment instruments when conducting an initial assessment. The use of assessment instruments can provide a broader picture of the person, and using instruments appropriately during the early phase of helping can identify substance abuse and trauma in a person's life (Ed Neukrug, personal communication, October 1, 2018).

Diagnosis, which is sometimes part of the assessment process, consists of identifying a pattern of symptoms that leads to a specific diagnosis described in the *Diagnostic and Statistical Manual of Mental Disorders* (*DSM-5*; American Psychiatric Association, 2013a), the official guide to a system of classifying psychological disorders. The *DSM-5* is the standard reference for distinguishing one form of mental disorder from another; it provides specific criteria for classifying emotional and behavioral disturbances and describes the differences among the various disorders. In addition to describing cognitive, affective, and personality disorders, the *DSM-5* also deals with a variety of other disorders pertaining to developmental stages, learning, trauma, substance abuse, moods, sexual and gender identity, eating, sleep, impulse control, and adjustment. The rationale for using this traditional diagnostic approach is to enable the therapist to plan treatments tailored to the special needs of the client. Both assessment and diagnosis are intended to provide direction for the treatment process.

Whether diagnosis should be part of psychotherapeutic practice is a controversial issue. Some mental health professionals see diagnosis as an essential step in any treatment plan, but others oppose a diagnostic model on the assumption that *DSM* labels stigmatize people. Although you may not yet have had to face the practical question of whether to diagnose a client, you will probably need to come to terms with this issue at some point in your work. More and more agencies now rely on initial assessments and a *DSM* diagnosis for reimbursement purposes. Because most agency settings require some form of official assessment and diagnosis, being able to carry out these functions competently is likely to be an integral part of your job responsibilities.

In our view, diagnosis does not have to be a matter of categorizing clients; rather, practitioners can think more broadly, describe behavior, and think about its meaning. In this way, diagnosis becomes a process of thinking *about* the client *with* the client. Diagnosis can be viewed as a general descriptive statement identifying a client's style of functioning, and like informed consent, thinking diagnostically is an ongoing process.

Psychological distress needs to be considered within the framework of biological and developmental factors, but environmental factors must be considered as well. Although the stressor may be located within the individual, the broader systemic and cultural contexts must be considered for meaningful assessment.

For example, the distress of depression is generally the result of the interaction of the person in the environment. Depression in women or in people from some cultural groups can result from cultural racism or sexism. Individuals who have been discriminated against may experience depression as a result of environmental factors. It is important for clinicians to understand the various ways that depression is often associated with the racism or sexism that marginalized groups routinely experience in their daily lives (Zalaquett, Fuerth, Stein, Ivey, & Ivey, 2008). The inclusion of culture-related issues such as race, ethnicity, gender, sexual orientation, disability, and spirituality is essential for accurate assessment and diagnosis.

Even though you may not find diagnosis necessary or useful in your practice, it may behoove you to know enough about diagnosis to refer a client. For example, once you have made a diagnosis of a client who is chronically depressed with possible suicidal tendencies, you are in a position to make an appropriate referral if you do not have the competence to work in this problem area. Likewise, the ability to recognize disorders such as schizophrenia is ethically important in order to make appropriate referrals to a psychiatrist for medication, if needed.

Helping clients gain a focus. Some people who come for help feel overwhelmed with a number of problems. By trying to talk about everything that is troubling them in one session, they also may manage to overwhelm the helper. It is necessary to provide a direction for the helping efforts, enabling both the client and the helper to know where to start. To achieve this focus, it is essential to make an assessment of the major concerns of the person seeking help. You could say to a client who presents you with a long list of problems, "We won't be able to deal with all your problems in one session. What was going on in your life when you finally decided to call for help?" Here are some other focusing questions: At this time in your life, what seems most troublesome to you? You say that you often wake up in the middle of the night; what do you find yourself thinking about? When you don't want to get up in the morning, what is it that you most want to avoid? If you could address only one problem today, which one would you pick?

As helpers, we can be instrumental in encouraging clients to tell their story and to explore their key issues in terms of their experiences, feelings, and behaviors. By focusing on what is salient in the present and by avoiding dwelling on the past, we can assist clients in clarifying their own problems and opportunities for change. A participant in one of our training workshops commented that she was beginning to see the fine line that exists between the therapeutic value of telling one's story versus overwhelming people by getting lost in talking about oneself. She also learned that the purpose of a client disclosing personal information is not to satisfy the helper's curiosity. Client self-disclosure can provide a sense of the person's struggles, which will aid the helper in identifying a direction for the sessions.

Reflect for a moment on the degree to which you are able to facilitate the process of your clients' being able to tell some aspect of their life story. Do you let clients tell their story, or do you get impatient and want to interrupt them? Do you encourage clients to tell stories in great detail out of curiosity? Do you have a tendency to get lost in the details of their story and miss the essence of their struggle? Are you able to inquire with open-ended questions that help clients flesh out meaningful stories?

Identifying exceptions to one's problems. As the helping relationship deepens and clients present us with information about their life, we can help them identify and overcome their own distortions. This is a good time to encourage clients to identify exceptions to their problem-saturated lives. We might ask them what they can do and have already done to deal with their problems. They can be guided in focusing on possible solutions rather than continuing to define themselves in light of their presenting problems. By reconceptualizing a particular problem, we can assist clients in acquiring a new perspective that will lead to action. We can challenge clients who see very few options to developing a variety of alternatives in coping with a given problem. We can help them distinguish between what they can do and what might be difficult for them to do, and we can invite them to stretch their boundaries. We can also encourage clients to make choices for themselves and to be willing to accept responsibility for their decisions. By providing clients with support and challenge, we are able to facilitate their process of change. For a more detailed treatment of the topic of identifying exceptions to one's problems, see DeJong and Berg (2013).

LO5 Stage 3: Collaboratively Creating Goals

In the third stage, the helper and the client collaboratively establish goals by determining the specific changes desired by the client. It is the helper's role to assist clients in formulating meaningful goals. If clients hope to make changes, they have to be willing to go beyond talking and planning; they must translate their plans into action.

Goals are desired outcomes of the helping process that are agreed upon by the helper and the client. From a strengths perspective, the helper pays particular attention to what clients do well and to their resources. When clarifying goals, helpers might ask questions like these: What would you like to achieve from our work together? Where would you like to be in your life at this time? What specific feelings, thoughts, and behaviors are you most interested in changing? What would you like to reduce or eliminate from your life? What qualities would you like to acquire that you do not now have? What do you imagine the ideal solution would be to the problems you have presented? How might things be different if you were able to eliminate a key problem from your life? What kind of future do you most want for yourself?

Brian is a young worker who comes to you because he wants help in getting into college. Consider how you might assist Brian in setting his goals. He has put off applying to colleges for several years, and the thought of actually being accepted scares him. However, his job dissatisfaction is so great that it has begun to affect his personal life. Test results show that Brian is performing far below his intellectual abilities. In his work with you, Brian discovers that he has accepted some early messages from his parents that he is ignorant and would never amount to anything, and they attributed his early difficulties in school to laziness. His insight that he unconditionally accepted these early messages has been important. As a helper, we could make a mistake by focusing on his feelings about his parents and endlessly exploring the reasons he feels inadequate. We will better serve this client by helping him define the steps toward his goal. At this stage he is aware of what has stopped him so far in accomplishing his goals. He knows that he must acquire better reading and writing skills before he can successfully compete in college. Now he has clarified a new set of goals, and his task is to identify the specific steps to take in accomplishing them.

Clients need to state their goals in such a manner that both they and the helper will know what changes are desired and both will have a framework to assess the degree to which these goals are being attained. Establishing, refining, and revising goals takes time and continued effort, but doing so will give direction to the helping process. After goals are collaboratively established, it is critical to devise alternative approaches to deal with the identified problems. Guide clients in a brainstorming process to create perspectives that are in line with their values and can lead to action. It is important that these goals be measurable, be realistic in terms of the resources of the client, and be chosen by the client. Sometimes it is not possible for clients to make a desired change, but even in these cases clients can be empowered. Clients can choose how they perceive, interpret, and react to their situation, which can reduce their stress.

A problem-solving approach. The need of helpers to solve problems for others could easily block them from hearing what clients want to communicate. A common mistake we have observed with trainees is a tendency to short-circuit the exploration of feelings of clients and move too quickly to solving their presenting problem. Clients often struggle with expressing their feelings and thoughts about a problem. Helpers who focus on a "fix-it" orientation can obstruct the helping process when they fail to acknowledge this struggle.

If we are too intent on providing solutions for every problem, it is possible that we are preoccupied with our own needs for being a competent helper who wants to see results. We may be uncomfortable with the client's struggle or emotions, and we may push for resolution without proper exploration. If we were this kind of helper in the case of Brian, we would have spent no time listening and exploring his deep feelings of inadequacy. We would not have assisted him in examining what had kept him time and again from succeeding academically. With our problem-solving orientation, we would have urged him to apply prematurely for college. If Brian had not had an opportunity to express and explore his fears and self-doubts and if he had not acquired any insights into his own part in setting himself up to fail, it is unlikely that he would succeed in college.

Develop a systematic way of incorporating cognitive, affective, and behavioral goals as a starting point for counseling. Take time to reflect on the following questions to clarify your thoughts on the kinds of goals you want to establish with your clients:

- How could you make establishing therapeutic goals a collaborative process between you and your client?
- How does your theoretical orientation influence your view of therapy goals?
- What are your goals for the helping process?
- What would you do if your goals for the helping process conflicted with your client's goals?

- How could you best manage a value conflict between you and your client?
- What challenges do you expect to face in assisting your clients in the development of specific goals for the helping process?
- What importance do you place on expecting your clients to develop both short- and long-term goals?
- How could you help clients who have ill-defined goals formulate meaningful and clear goals for their therapy sessions?

LO6 Stage 4: Encouraging Client Exploration and Taking Action

The fourth stage of helping deals with exploring alternatives, identifying strategies for action, choosing which combination of strategies will best meet the client's goals, and putting these plans into a realistic action program. One of the tasks of this phase is to facilitate generalization and transfer of learning from the sessions to daily life.

Once the goals of the helper–client relationship have been identified, it becomes necessary to decide on the various avenues by which these goals can be accomplished. Knowing *what* you want to change is the first step, and knowing *how* to bring about this change is the next step. Helpers first assist clients in developing and assessing action strategies for making their vision a reality. To work toward changing a client's thoughts, feelings, and behaviors, it is generally necessary to explore alternatives and confront incongruities. This stage of helping may be the longest, and at times this stage involves a lengthy exploration of an individual's dynamics. The helper's task is to explore possibilities and to assist the client in finding new ways to act more intentionally and effectively in the world (Ivey et al., 2018). Confrontation (or challenging) and self-disclosure can further client self-exploration, lead to new insights, and encourage clients to take action to achieve their personal goals. Collaboratively create a plan of action through discussion in the sessions, then formulate the steps needed to carry out the plan in daily life. Finally, evaluate how well the plan is working, and make adjustments when necessary.

Confronting (or challenging) clients. A helper needs to acquire the skills of caring and gentle confrontation of clients' behaviors as a way to enable them to move forward. **Confrontation** should not be viewed as aggressive or as destructive of a supportive relationship. This process invites individuals to look at the discrepancies, incongruities, denials, distortions, excuses, defensive behaviors, and evasions that prevent them from taking action to change their lives. Some helpers see it as producing defensiveness and withdrawal in clients. Or they may view it as an adversarial stance between them and their clients, which can lead to premature termination of the helping relationship. Helpers sometimes see confrontation as a negative act with destructive potential and avoid it at all costs, even though it is the very thing they need to provide an impetus for change. There are many misconceptions about the purpose and value of confrontation, and we agree with Egan and Reese (2019) that **challenging** clients more accurately describes this process. A lack of challenge often results in stagnation. Without some degree of challenge, clients are likely to persist with self-defeating behavior and develop no new perspectives or skills to make change possible. Helpers cease being effective catalysts to others' growth if all they offer is support.

Ask yourself if you are willing to challenge others when this may be useful. If you find it difficult to challenge others, it is important to understand why. It could be that you want to be liked and approved by your clients. You might fear that they will be angry with you or will not return. Even though challenging others might not be easy for you, it is a vital skill in moving clients beyond the mere "talking-about" phase of their counseling. It is not abnormal to feel anxious about challenging others or being confronted by others. Even though you may be uncomfortable, one of the ways to develop skills in challenging is by doing what is difficult.

Challenging clients effectively entails focusing on their awareness of what they are thinking, feeling, and doing. In other words, you describe what you observe. For example, you may say to a client, "When you talk about the hurtful names your father used to call you, I notice that you are smiling. This seems incongruent with the sadness and hurt I imagine you may be feeling. Are you aware of this tendency? What do you suppose this is about for you?" Sometimes helpers observe a pattern in clients' storytelling, and it can be useful to share your observation about this pattern. For example: "Both times when you mentioned how your mother embarrassed you in front of others, you immediately followed with a positive statement about her and said that she is really such a good mother. Are you aware of this pattern? What do you think this might say about you?" This kind of statement pattern could indicate many things: guilt over saying anything negative about his mother, a need to protect his mother's image, a need for the therapist not to think poorly of his mother, a pervasive pattern of making excuses for others, or low self-esteem. Despite the temptation to provide insights to clients, they should be encouraged to develop their own insights. Clients are the experts on their own life, and if they are able to see what they are doing, they can develop new perspectives on their life situation. They are also influenced to make changes based on this self-understanding. Ideally, the challenging is not done exclusively by the helper; rather, the client learns the value of *self-challenging*. A helper can assist clients in developing the capacity for self-challenge that they will need in working through their problems.

Here are some suggestions for making challenges to clients effective. Know your motivations for challenging a client. Is it because you want to more deeply understand another, or is it because you want to control the other person? Do you care about your relationships with clients? You must earn the right to make confrontational statements. Challenge clients only if you feel an investment in them and if you have the time and effort to continue building the relationship with them. If you have not yet established a working relationship with a client, your challenging is likely to be received defensively, and rightly so. The degree to which you can challenge your clients depends on how much they trust you.

Be willing to be challenged yourself. If you model a nondefensive stance in the counseling relationship, your clients will be much more willing to listen to what you tell them. Before you challenge others, imagine being the recipient of what is said. The tone and your general manner of giving your message will have a lot to do with how others hear you. It is also useful to present your challenges in a tentative manner, as opposed to issuing a dogmatic pronouncement. Challenging is your chance to inspire clients to look at what they most want to change in themselves and what seems to be interfering with this change.

Challenging, or confrontation, is not intended to attack the defenses of clients; rather, it invites them to examine their problematic behaviors and keep moving toward more effective behavior. Challenges should not be absolute statements concerning who or what others are. Here is an example of a confrontation that would be certain to arouse a client's defensiveness and evoke resistance: "I'm impatient with hearing you complain every week about how horrible your life is. I don't think you really want to change." Here is an intervention that could lead to a more productive exploration of the client's difficulties: "I have noticed that you talk quite often about how difficult things have been for you. What do you think makes it difficult for you to take the initial steps to bring about some changes in your life?"

Faced with a client who keeps making excuses for not showing up to scheduled job interviews, in an effective challenge you might say: "You have talked at length about how being employed makes you feel better about yourself and gives your life meaning. I find it interesting that you have not attended several job interviews over the past few weeks. What can you tell me about that? I wonder if your decision to not show up is a way to exercise control over the outcome. What is your fear about what would happen if you attended the interviews?" By exploring the client's reluctance to take steps in the direction of his goal, he may be much more inclined to gain insight into his fears and get unstuck than if you challenged him with "What are you thinking! Blowing off interviews is a sure way to remain helpless and unsuccessful. I know you can do better, so why aren't you?" Such a statement is likely to escalate his defensiveness.

Likewise, in counseling a couple it would be unproductive to tell a husband to "Be quiet and listen to what she has to say!" This comment might silence him for the rest of the session, but it would be more helpful to describe what you saw going on between the two of them: "You say you want your wife to tell you how she feels about you, yet you've interrupted her several times and told her why she should not feel the way she does. Are you aware of this? Describe your wife's behavior, rather than labeling it. Would you be willing for the next few minutes to let her talk and not think about what you're going to say in return? When she's finished, I'd like you to tell her how you're affected by what she has said. Focus more on you, and tell her about you." People who are talked to in a caring way are less likely to be defensive if they are told what effect they have on others rather than simply being judged and labeled.

You can invite clients to consider strengths they possess but may not be using. Emphasizing strengths is usually more fruitful than dwelling on weaknesses. It helps to be specific: avoid sweeping judgments and focus on concrete behaviors. Remember to describe to clients what you see them doing and how this behavior affects you. It is also useful to encourage a dialogue with clients, and your sensitivity to their responses is a key factor in determining the degree to which they will accept the challenges you present to them.

Here is an example of a helper's challenge to a client who is not making the best use of her strengths: "For several weeks now you've made detailed plans to reach out to a friend. You say that when you do reach out to people they usually like you, and you have no reason to fear that this friend will reject you. Yet you have not made contact with her, and you have many reasons for not doing so. Let's explore what is keeping you from contacting her."

To make the issue of challenging more concrete, we present examples of other styles of challenging. The first statement illustrates an ineffective challenge; this is followed by an effective challenge alternative.

- "You're always so cold and aloof, and you make me feel distant from you." A more effective statement is: "I feel a distance between us, and I am interested in exploring this. This relationship between us is important to me. Sometimes in our sessions I feel you disconnect, and I wonder if you get this feedback in the outside world too?"
- "You're always smiling, and that's not real." A more effective statement is: "Often when you say you're angry, you're smiling. I have a hard time knowing whether you are angry or happy. Are you aware of this?"
- "If I were your husband, I'd leave you. You're full of hostility, and you'll destroy any relationship." A more effective statement is: "Anger is a perfectly normal human emotion, but it can result in destructive or harmful behavior. I feel startled by the intensity of your anger, and occasionally I even feel fear because of your angry behaviors. Many of the things you say are hurtful and create distance between us. Is this something you are aware of and would like to change?"

In the ineffective statements, the people being addressed are being told how they are, and in some way are being discounted. In the effective statements, the helper doing the talking is revealing his or her perceptions and feelings about the client and is reporting how the person's behavior is affecting him or her.

If you want to learn more about challenging clients, we recommend *The Skilled Helper* (Egan & Reese, 2019); *Intentional Interviewing and Counseling: Facilitating Client Development in a Multicultural Society* (Ivey et al., 2018); and *Interviewing and Change Strategies for Helpers* (Cormier et al., 2017).

Using helper self-disclosure appropriately. Appropriately and timely disclosing aspects of yourself can be a powerful intervention in working with clients and facilitating a process of their self-exploration. It is a mistake to think of self-disclosure in terms of "all" or "none"; it can best be viewed on a continuum. There is a distinction between a helper's self-disclosing statements (disclosing personal information about oneself) and self-involving statements (revealing personal thoughts, feelings, and reactions to the client in the context of here-and-now aspects of the helping relationship). Therapist self-disclosure refers to therapist statements that reveal something personal about the therapist's life or person outside of therapy (Hill, Knox, & Pinto-Coelho, 2019). Self-involving statements, referred to as *immediacy*, lead to a discussion of the therapeutic relationship by both therapist and client in the here-and-now, as well as processing client–therapist interactions (Hill et al., 2019).

Letting our clients know how we are affected by what they are saying and doing is frequently more useful to them than revealing aspects of our personal life.

If you are having a difficult time listening to a client, for example, it could be useful to let the person know this by saying: "I've noticed at times that it's difficult for me to stay connected to what you're telling me. I'm able to follow you when you talk about yourself and your own feelings, but I find myself losing interest when you go into great detail about all the things your daughter is doing or not doing." In this statement, the client is not being labeled or judged, but the helper is giving his reactions about what he hears when his client tells stories about others. An example of an unhelpful response would be "You're boring me!" This response is a judgment of the client, and the helper assumes no responsibility for his own lack of interest.

It can be therapeutic to talk about ourselves if doing so is for a client's benefit, but it is not necessary to reveal detailed stories of our past to form a trusting relationship with others. Inappropriate self-disclosure of our personal problems to our clients can easily distract them from productive self-exploration. Examine the impact your disclosures have on others. If your self-disclosing behavior prevents clients from exploring their issues, it may be time to consider your own therapy or supervision.

Some helpers use self-disclosure inappropriately as a way of unburdening themselves. They take the focus away from clients and direct it to their own concerns. If our feelings are very much in the foreground and inhibit us from fully attending to a client, it may be helpful to let the client know we are distracted and it is our problem, not the client's. Depending on our relationship with the client, we might share some aspects about our own situation, or we might simply reveal that what the client is struggling with touches us personally, without going into too much detail.

Identifying and assessing action strategies. Insight without action is of little value. Self-understanding and seeing a range of possible alternatives can be significant in the change process, but clients also need to identify specific actions they can take and are willing to carry out in everyday living. Clients often do not accomplish their goals because they devise strategies that are unrealistic. One function of helping at this stage is to assist clients in thinking of many possibilities to achieve their goals. Together, helpers and clients come up with a range of alternatives for coping with problems, assess how practical these strategies are, and decide on the best plans for action. Helpers have the task of guiding clients to recognize the skills they need to put goals into action.

The process of creating and carrying out plans enables people to begin to gain effective control over their lives. This is clearly the teaching phase of the helping process, which is best directed toward providing clients with new information and assisting them in the discovery of more effective ways of getting what they want and need. Throughout this planning phase, the helper continually urges clients to assume responsibility for their own choices and actions.

Wubbolding (2000, 2011, 2017) writes about the central place of planning and commitment in any change process, emphasizing that when clients make plans and follow through they are taking charge of their lives by redirecting their energy and making action choices. According to Wubbolding (2017), effective plans have several characteristics that can be summarized in the acronym SAMIC^3.

A results-centered plan is not complicated; it is *simple*. To achieve the desired result, the plan must be *attainable* and realistically doable. It is *measurable*, answering the question, "precisely when will I follow through on my plan?" "I" stands for *immediate*. It is important to implement the plan as soon as possible. The most effective plan is one *controlled* by the planner and not dependent on other individuals or outside circumstances. Ideally, the counselor, choosing a self-care behavior, makes a firm *commitment* to implement the plan. A *consistent* plan, repeated regularly, is required to achieve desired goals. Other specific guidelines for effective plans are listed below:

- The plan should be within the limits of the motivation and capacities of each client. Plans should be realistic and attainable. Helpers do well to caution clients about plans that are too ambitious or unrealistic. A realistic action plan for the first week working with a client with agoraphobia is that the client chooses to practice the progressive muscle relaxation learned in session every day and agrees to journaling for 10 minutes daily. It would be unrealistic to plan that the client will leave the house to go to the bank this week.
- Good plans are simple and easy to understand. Although plans need to be concrete and measurable, they should be flexible and open to modification as clients gain a deeper understanding of the specific behaviors that they want to change. An initial action plan for a client struggling with methamphetamine addiction might include abstaining from all substances; attending three Narcotics Anonymous meetings per week (Mondays, Thursdays, and Saturdays at 7:00 p.m.); calling a sponsor daily; avoiding all people, places, and things associated with previous methamphetamine use; actively working the 12 steps beginning with the first step; practicing deep breathing and meditation daily; and attending counseling sessions weekly.
- The plan should involve positive action and should be stated in terms of what the client will do. A client working to improve her self-esteem agrees to the following: "Each day this week I will say out loud the affirmation 'I am lovable and worthy of great joy.' I will also use the thought-stopping technique of picturing the stop sign every time I am aware of my negative self-talk statements, such as 'I am not good enough.' Then I will replace that negative self-defeating thought with my affirmation."
- It is useful to encourage clients to develop plans that they can carry out independently. Plans that are contingent on what others will do lead clients to sense that they are not steering their own ship but are at the mercy of others. A client with depression symptoms commits to walking 30 minutes per day at 5:00 p.m. The client does not include her husband in the plan because she would then need to rely on her husband, which would limit her independent ability to carry out the plan.
- Good plans are specific and concrete. Clients can develop specificity when helpers raise questions such as "what?" "where?" "with whom?" "when?" and "how often?" A client whose goal is weight loss suggests a general plan to exercise more often. By asking narrowing questions, the client's plan can become specific and measurable: walk on the treadmill at his local gym for 45 minutes every weekday before work, and meet with his personal trainer every Saturday morning at 9:00 a.m.

- Effective plans are repetitive and ideally are performed daily. For people to overcome symptoms of depression, anxiety, negative thinking, or psychosomatic complaints, it is essential to replace these symptoms with new patterns of thinking and behaving. Each day, clients might choose a course that will lead to a sense of being in charge of their life.
- Plans should be done as soon as possible. Helpers can ask questions such as "What are you willing to do today to begin to change your life?" "You say you'd like to stop depressing yourself. What are you going to do now to attain this goal?"
- Effective planning involves process-centered activities. For example, clients may state that they will do any of the following: apply for a job, write a letter to a friend, take a yoga class, substitute nutritious food for unhealthy food, devote 2 hours a week to volunteer work, or take a vacation they have been wanting.
- Before clients carry out their plan, it is a good idea for them to evaluate it to determine if it is realistic, attainable, and reflective of what they need and want. After the plan has been carried out in real life, it is useful to evaluate it again. Helpers can raise the question with the client, "Is your plan helpful?" If the plan does not work, it can be reevaluated and alternatives can be considered.
- For clients to commit themselves to their plan, it is useful for them to firm it up in writing.
- Part of developing a plan for action involves a discussion of the main costs and benefits of each strategy as well as a discussion of the possible risks involved and the chances for success. It is the helper's task to work with clients in constructively dealing with any hesitations they might have to formulating plans or carrying them out.

Resolutions and plans are meaningless unless there is a decision to carry them out. It is crucial that clients commit themselves to a definite plan that they can realistically accomplish. The ultimate responsibility for making plans and following through on them rests with the client. It is up to each client to determine ways of carrying these plans outside the helping relationship and into the everyday world. Effective helping can be the catalyst that leads to self-directed, satisfying, and responsible living.

Carrying out an action program. Clients are encouraged to see the value in actively trying new behavior rather than being passive and leaving action to chance. One way of fostering an active stance by clients is to formulate clear contracts. In this way clients are continually reminded about what they want and what they are willing to do. Contracts are also a useful frame of reference for evaluating the outcomes of helping. Discussion can be centered on how well the contract is being met and what modifications of it might be in order.

If certain plans do not work out well, this is a topic for exploration in a subsequent session. For example, if a mother does not follow through with her plan to deal with her son who is getting in trouble in school, the counselor can explore with her what stopped her from carrying it out. Contingency plans are also developed. The counselor might role-play different ways the mother could deal with setbacks or with her son's lack of cooperation. In this way clients learn how to deal with reverses and how to predict possible obstacles to their progress.

Relapse prevention is an integral part of the final phase of therapy. At times, it is inevitable that clients will revert to old patterns and experience self-defeating thoughts and behaviors. It is a good practice to explore possible stumbling blocks and ways to cope with them. The point is not that clients never experience setbacks but that they become aware of when they slip into old familiar patterns that no longer work for them. Clients can think about difficulties they might face in sticking with their plans and ways to address any lapses. The goal of relapse prevention is to help clients maintain the gains they have made by using what they learned in counseling when they need it in the future (Dobson & Dobson, 2017).

LO7 Stage 5: Termination

Termination, the fifth stage, assists clients in maximizing the benefits from the helping relationship and deciding how they can continue the change process. During this stage, clients consolidate their learning and make long-range plans. A helper's role at this time is to prepare clients for termination, to encourage them to express any feelings or thoughts about ending the relationship, to review what they have accomplished, and to identify and discuss future plans.

Just as the initial session sets the tone for the helping relationship, the ending phase enables clients to maximize the benefits from the relationship and decide how they can continue the change process. As a helper, our goal is to work with clients in such a way that they can terminate the professional relationship with us as soon as possible and continue to make changes on their own. As mentioned earlier, in settings where brief therapy is the standard, it is especially important that termination and issues pertaining to restrictions on time be addressed at the initial session. If an agency policy specifies that clients can be seen for only six sessions, for example, clients have a right to know this from the outset.

Working in a short-term context, the final phase of the helping process should always be in the background. With brief interventions, the goal is to teach clients, as quickly and efficiently as possible, the coping skills they need to live in self-directed ways. Our overriding goal is to increase the chances that our clients will not continue to need us. It is critical to remember that if we are effective helpers we will eventually "put ourselves out of business"—at least with our current clients. We need to keep in mind that our role is to get clients working effectively on their own, not to keep them dependent on us for help. If we can teach our clients ways of finding their own solutions to problems, they can use what they have learned dealing with their present concerns when any future problems occur.

Preparing clients for termination. In cases of structured, time-limited counseling, clients need to be informed from the beginning about the approximate number of sessions available. Although clients may cognitively know there are a limited number of sessions, emotionally they may deny this restriction of their counseling experience. Termination should be discussed at the first session and be explored as necessary throughout the course of the helping relationship. In this way, termination does not come as a surprise to the client.

The limitation of time can help clients establish short-term, realistic goals for the helping process. Toward the end of each session, we can ask clients the degree to which they see themselves reaching the goals they have established. By reviewing the course of treatment, clients are in a position to identify what is and is not working for them in the helping process. Each session can be assessed in light of having a specific number of sessions devoted to accomplishing preset goals.

Ideally, termination is the result of a mutual decision by the client and the helper that the goals of the helping process have been accomplished. Effective termination provides clients with closure to their experience as well as a clear sense of what they need to do to continue this momentum in daily life.

Terminating when clients are not benefiting. Ethical standards state that it is improper to continue a professional relationship if it is clear that a client is not benefiting. Assessing whether the client is really being helped can be difficult. Consider this example: You have been seeing a client for some time who typically reports that she has nothing to talk about in the sessions. You have talked to her about her unwillingness to disclose much of herself in the counseling sessions. The client agrees yet continues her behavior. Finally, you suggest termination because, in your opinion, she is not benefiting from the counseling relationship. The client is reluctant to terminate despite her lack of involvement in the sessions. What would you do if you were confronted with this situation?

When a client who is not making progress does not wish to terminate, Younggren and Gottlieb (2008) suggest an open, collaborative stance on the part of the therapist. When a client does not seem to be benefiting from treatment, it is critical that the therapist explore with the client the reasons for the lack of progress. However, ultimately it is the therapist's responsibility to determine whether further progress is likely to occur or if termination is in order.

Helpers need to be careful not to jump to the conclusion *too quickly* that the client is not making progress. During the early stages of the training process, it is common for some helpers to want "immediate success" with their clients. A novice helper dealing with his or her own self-doubt and insecurities could prematurely suggest that a client is not making progress. This could be upsetting and even damaging to the client's self-esteem. Before determining that a client is not making adequate progress, it is wise for the novice helper to discuss this in supervision.

Taking steps to avoid fostering dependency. Helpers can foster clients' dependent attitudes and behaviors in many subtle ways. Sometimes helpers actually prevent clients from ending a professional relationship. Instead of helping clients find their own direction, helpers may do too much for them, which results in clients assuming too little responsibility for action and change. Although our clients may temporarily become dependent on us, clinical and ethical issues arise if we foster their dependency and prevent their progress. Ask yourself these questions as a way of determining the degree to which you could encourage either dependent or independent behavior:

- Do I have a hard time terminating a case? Do I have trouble "losing" a client? Am I concerned about a reduction in my income?
- Do I encourage clients to think about termination of the professional relationship, and do I assist them in preparing for termination?

- Might I need some clients more than they need me? Do I have a need to be needed? Am I flattered when clients express dependency on me?
- Do I challenge clients to do for themselves what they are able to do? How do I respond to clients when they press me for answers?
- To what degree do I encourage clients to look within themselves for potential resources to find their own answers?

Some helpers may foster dependence in their clients as a way of feeling important. When clients become passive and ask for answers, these helpers respond too quickly with problem-solving solutions. Such actions may not be helpful in the long run because clients are being reinforced to depend on you. Our main task as helpers is to encourage clients to rely on their own resources. By reinforcing the dependency of our clients, we are telling them that we do not trust that they can help themselves or that they can function independently of us.

Skills for ending the helping relationship. Basically, the interventions for endings pertain to assisting clients in consolidating their learning and determining how they can proceed once they stop coming in for treatment. Here are some considerations for effectively accomplishing these tasks:

- We remind clients of the approaching ending of the sessions. This should be done a couple of sessions before the final one. We might ask clients to think about any unfinished business they have and what they would most like to talk about in the final two meetings with us. We frequently can ask at a session prior to the last one, "If this were our last meeting, what would you want to talk about?"
- If we are not limited to a specified number of sessions, one option is to space out the final few sessions. Instead of meeting weekly, our client might come in every 3 weeks. This schedule allows more opportunity to practice and to prepare for termination.
- We review the course of treatment with clients. What lessons did clients learn, how did they learn them, and what do they intend to do with what they have learned? What did they find most helpful in the sessions? What was less helpful in the course of treatment? What were their greatest struggles, and what did they do to work through those challenges? What did they think about their own participation in this process?
- It is good practice to encourage clients to talk about their feelings of separation. Just as they may have had fears about seeking help, they may have different fears about ending the work with us.
- Examine your own feelings about endings. Helpers are often ambivalent about letting go of clients. It is possible to hold back clients because of our own reluctance to terminate with a client, for whatever reason. It is essential that we reflect on the degree to which we may need our clients more than they need us.
- It is a good idea to have an open-door policy, meaning that clients might be encouraged to return at a later time should they feel a need for further learning. Although professional helping is best viewed as a terminal process, at a later period of development clients may be ready to deal with a new set of problems or concerns in ways they were not willing to do when they initially began counseling. Clients may need only a few sessions to get refocused.

- Those who have participated in counseling have acquired some needed skills and resources for continuing the process of personal growth. Assisting clients to translate their learning into action programs is one of the most important functions during the action phase and the ending phase of helping. If clients have been successful, the ending stage is a *commencement*; they now have some new directions to follow in dealing with problems as they arise. For this reason, discussing available programs and making referrals are especially timely toward the end of our work with clients. In this way, the end leads to new beginnings.

By Way of Review

- Skills and knowledge are important in becoming an effective professional, but personal qualities are equally important in determining our success as helpers. Our own life experiences play a vital role in our ability to be present and to be effective in working with clients.
- Your view of the helping process is largely a function of your beliefs about human nature and about how people change. It is essential that you clarify your beliefs about what brings about change.
- It is natural and expected for clients to experience a certain degree of ambivalence about change. Motivational interviewing is one approach that may help clients progress through the stages of change.
- Brief interventions are widely used today. They emphasize time-limited, solution-focused, structured, effective strategies that empower clients to make specific behavioral changes they desire.
- Effective helpers hold positive beliefs about people; have a healthy self-concept; ground their interventions in values; and possess empathy, congruence, warmth, compassion, genuineness, and unconditional positive regard.
- Generalizations that helpers make about clients tend to foster a self-fulfilling prophecy within clients. If helpers view clients as being highly dependent and unable to find their own way, they will most likely live up to this expectation.
- Mandated or involuntary clients may exhibit resistance toward entering the counseling relationship. If we expect these clients to be difficult and resistant, we are likely to see more of these behaviors. If we have positive expectations about their ability for change and growth, we are more likely to find ways to encourage these clients to benefit from the therapeutic relationship.
- There are five stages in the helping process. Stage 1 is the time for creating rapport and establishing the therapeutic alliance. Stage 2 consists of helping clients identify and clarify their problems. In Stage 3 the client and the helper collaboratively create goals. Stage 4 involves encouraging clients to engage in deeper self-exploration and develop an action plan aimed at change. This is a time to take action and to assist clients in translating what they have learned in counseling to everyday life situations. Stage 5 deals with termination and the consolidation of learning. Specific helper strategies are required at each of these stages. Developing these skills takes time and supervised practice.

What Will You Do Now?

1. Identify a few of your key beliefs and assumptions that stand out after you have read this chapter. To examine how you acquired these beliefs and assumptions, talk with someone you know who tends to hold similar beliefs. Then seek out somebody with a different perspective. With both of these people, discuss how you developed your beliefs.
2. Consider the skills needed for effective helping, and select what you consider to be your one major asset and your one major limitation, and write them down. How do you see your main asset enabling you to be an effective helper? How might your main limitation get in the way of working successfully with others? What can you do to work on the area that limits you? You might ask people you know well to review your statements about yourself. Do they see you as you see yourself?
3. As part of a class assignment, write a one-page essay that describes your personal view of what helping is about. How would you approach writing this essay if the reader is a layperson who knows little about the helping process? How would your essay be modified if the reader is a potential employer or clinical supervisor?
4. After reflecting on your beliefs about people and about the helping process, write some key ideas in your journal pertaining to the role that your beliefs play in the manner in which you might intervene in the lives of clients. How do your beliefs influence the suggestions you make to clients? How are your beliefs the groundwork for the strategies from which you will draw in dealing with client populations?
5. As you review the stages of the helping process, ask yourself what you consider to be your most important tasks at each of the different stages. Write in your journal about some of the challenges you expect to face when working with people at each of these stages. For example, might termination be a difficult process for you? Would you have difficulty appropriately sharing your life experiences with your clients? Might you have difficulty challenging clients? What can you do to develop the personal characteristics and skills you will need to effectively intervene at each of the stages of helping?
6. For the full bibliographic entry for each of these sources, consult the References at the back of the book. For comprehensive overviews of stages in the helping process, descriptions of systematic skill development, and intervention strategies, see Cormier (2016), Cormier, Nurius, and Osborn (2017), DeJong and Berg (2013), Egan and Reese (2019), Ivey, Ivey, and Zalaquett (2018), James and Gilliland (2017), Teyber and Teyber (2017), and Young (2013).

CHAPTER 7

Theory Applied to Practice

Learning Objectives

1. Provide a general framework for theory applied to practice.
2. Explain how a thinking, feeling, and behaving model can serve as an integrative approach to counseling practice.
3. Describe the key concepts and techniques of psychoanalytic approaches.
4. Describe the key concepts and techniques of experiential and relationship-oriented approaches.
5. Describe the key concepts and techniques of cognitive behavioral approaches.
6. Discuss the major categories that are a part of mindfulness approaches to therapy.
7. Describe the key concepts and techniques of postmodern approaches.
8. Explain the unique ways family systems approaches differ from individual counseling.
9. Explain practical ways to develop an integrative approach to counseling practice.
10. Describe how evidence-based practice fits into the future of integrative psychotherapy.

Focus Questions

1. Why is theory relevant to practice?
2. The psychodynamic approaches emphasize understanding how childhood experiences influence the person you are today. Do you value understanding the past as a key to the present? How might you work with a client from the perspective of the past? the present? the future?
3. The experiential approaches stress the value of a client's direct experience rather than being taught by the counselor. How much do you trust a client's ability to lead the way in a helping relationship?
4. In the experiential approaches, the client–counselor relationship is the most important determinant for therapeutic outcomes. What specific things can a helper do to form a collaborative working relationship with a client?
5. The cognitive behavioral approaches give primary attention to how thinking influences the way we feel and act. To what extent do you value focusing on a client's thinking processes?

6. The postmodern approaches de-emphasize the therapist-as-expert and view the client as the expert. What do you think of this position?
7. Family systems approaches consider the functioning of the whole family rather than that of a single individual. What unique value do you see in working with a client's issues based on his or her family of origin? How much emphasis would you give to family-of-origin work when meeting with clients?
8. What are the advantages and disadvantages of brief models of therapy? How do brief, solution-focused intervention strategies fit the requirements of managed care programs?
9. How do you determine whether an intervention you are planning to use is suitable for the client?
10. What do you understand by developing your own integrative perspective on the helping process? What do you think it would take to be able to effectively integrate some basic concepts and techniques from various theoretical orientations?

Aim of the Chapter

The purpose of this chapter is to provide you with a brief overview of some of the major theories of counseling that have applicability to a variety of helping relationships. We consider the role of theory as a guiding factor for practicing effectively. You will be introduced to the following five general theoretical orientations: psychodynamic models, experiential and relationship-oriented approaches, cognitive behavioral therapies, the postmodern approaches, and the family systems perspective. We also present our own integrative approach, emphasizing the role of thinking, feeling, and acting in human behavior, which is based on selected ideas from most of the theories presented in this chapter.

Your theoretical orientation provides a map for making interventions, and developing this perspective takes considerable time and experience. A theory provides a structure for organizing information you get about a client, designing appropriate interventions, and evaluating the outcomes. We stress the importance of developing a personal stance toward counseling that fits the person you are and is flexible enough to meet the unique needs of the client population with which you work. The main objective of this chapter is to stimulate your thinking about how to design a framework for practice.

LO1 Theory as a Roadmap

There are many theoretical approaches to understanding what makes the helping process work. Different practitioners might work in a variety of ways with the same client, largely based on their theory of choice. Their theory will provide them with a framework for making sense of the multitude of interactions that occur within the therapeutic relationship. Some helpers focus on feelings, believing that what clients need most is to identify and express feelings that have been repressed. Other helpers emphasize gaining insight and explore the reasons for actions and interpret clients' behavior. Some are not much concerned about having clients develop insight or express their feelings. Their focus is on behavior and assisting clients to develop specific action plans to change what they are doing. Other practitioners encourage clients to focus on examining their beliefs about themselves and about their world; they believe change will result if clients can eliminate faulty thinking and replace it with constructive thoughts and self-talk.

Helpers may focus on the past, the present, or the future. It is important to consider whether you see the past, present, or future as being the most productive avenue of exploration. This is more than just a theoretical notion. If you believe your clients' past is a crucial aspect to explore, many of your interventions are likely to be designed to assist them in understanding their past. If you think your clients' goals and strivings are important, your interventions are likely to focus on the future. If you are oriented toward the present, many of your interventions will emphasize what your clients are thinking, feeling, and doing in the moment.

Each of these choices represents a particular theoretical orientation. Attempting to practice without having an explicit theoretical rationale is like flying a plane without a flight plan. If you operate in a theoretical vacuum and are unable to draw on theory to support your interventions, you may flounder in your attempts to help people change.

Theory is not a rigid set of structures that prescribes, step by step, what and how you should function as a helper. Rather, we see theory as a general framework that enables you to make sense of the many facets of the helping process, providing you with a map that gives direction to what you do and say. Your theory needs to be appropriate for your client population, setting, and the type of counseling you provide. A theory is not something divorced from you as a person. At best, a theory becomes an integral part of the person you are and an expression of your uniqueness.

LO2 Our Theoretical Orientation

Neither of us subscribes to any single theory in its totality. Rather, we function within an integrative framework that we continue to develop and modify as we practice. We draw on concepts and techniques from most of the contemporary counseling models and adapt them to our own unique personalities. Our theoretical orientations and styles of practice are primarily a function of the individuals we are. Our conceptual framework takes into account the *thinking*, *feeling*, and *behaving* dimensions of human experience.

We value approaches that emphasize the *thinking* dimension. We typically challenge clients to think about the decisions they have made about themselves. Some of these decisions may have been necessary for their psychological survival as children but now may not be functional. We want clients to be able to make necessary revisions that enable them to be more fully themselves. One way we do this is by asking clients to pay attention to their "self-talk." Here are some questions we encourage clients to ask themselves: How are my problems caused or exacerbated by the assumptions I make about myself, about others, and about life? How do I contribute to or intensify my problems by the thoughts and beliefs I hold? How can I begin to free myself by critically evaluating the sentences I repeat to myself? Many of the techniques we use are designed to tap clients' thinking processes, to help them think about events in their lives and how they have interpreted these events, and to work on a cognitive level to change certain belief systems.

Thinking is only one dimension that we pay attention to in our work with clients. The *feeling* dimension is also extremely important. We emphasize this facet of human experience by encouraging clients to identify and express their feelings. Clients are often emotionally frozen due to unexpressed and unresolved emotional concerns. If they allow themselves to experience the range of their feelings and talk about how certain events have affected them, their healing process is facilitated. If individuals feel listened to and understood, they are more likely to express more of the feelings that they have kept to themselves.

Thinking and feeling are vital components in the helping process, but eventually clients must express themselves in the *behaving* or *doing* dimension. Clients can spend many hours gaining insights and expressing pent-up feelings, but at some point they need to get involved in an action-oriented program of change. Their feelings and thoughts can then be applied to real-life situations. Examining current behavior is the heart of the helping process. We tend to ask questions such as these: What are you doing? What do you see for yourself now and in the future? Does your present behavior have a reasonable chance of getting you what you want, and will it take you in the direction you want to go? If the emphasis of the helping process is on what people are doing, there is a greater chance that they will also be able to change their thinking and feeling.

In addition to highlighting the thinking, feeling, and behaving dimensions, we help clients consolidate what they are learning and apply these new behaviors to situations they encounter every day. Some strategies we use are contracts, homework assignments, action programs, self-monitoring techniques, support systems, relapse prevention tools, and self-directed programs of change. These approaches all stress the role of commitment on the clients' part to practice new behaviors, to follow through with a realistic plan for change, and to develop practical methods for carrying out this plan in everyday life.

The existential approach is the foundation of our integrative approach to counseling, and it underlies our integrated focus on thinking, feeling, and behaving. We both operate on the assumption that counseling is a life-changing process and that we each can be the architects of our own lives. We invite people to look at the choices they *do* have, however limited they may be, and to accept responsibility for choosing for themselves. We help clients discover their inner resources and learn how to use them in resolving their difficulties. If clients don't like the design of their present existence, they can take steps to revise the blueprints. We do not provide answers for clients, but we facilitate a process that leads clients toward greater awareness of the knowledge and skills they can draw on to solve both their present and future problems. We believe counseling is a journey in which the therapist is a guide who facilitates client exploration.

We realize that choices available to people are oftentimes limited, and their freedom may be restricted by external factors. The unfortunate reality is that many clients have had to contend with oppressive conditions such as racism, discrimination, sexism, and poverty; it is important for helpers to do more than assume that clients are capable of changing their internal world. Helpers also have a role to play in bringing about change in the external environment when societal or community conditions are directly contributing to a client's problems.

Individuals cannot be understood without considering the various systems that affect them—family, social groups, community, church, and other cultural forces. For the helping process to be effective, it is critical to understand how individuals influence and are influenced by their social world. Effective helpers need to acquire a holistic approach that encompasses all facets of human experience.

As we work with an individual, we are not consciously thinking about what theory we are using. We adapt the techniques we use to fit the needs of the individual rather than attempting to fit the client to our techniques. In deciding on techniques to introduce, we take into account an array of factors about the client population. We consider the client's readiness to confront an issue, the client's cultural background, the client's value system, and the client's trust in us as helpers. A general goal that guides our practice is helping clients identify and experience whatever they are feeling, identifying ways in which their assumptions influence how they feel and behave, and experimenting with alternative modes of behaving. We have a rationale for using the techniques we employ, and our interventions generally flow from some aspects of the theories that we describe in the remainder of this chapter.

One way to understand how the various major theoretical orientations apply to the counseling process is to consider five categories under which most contemporary systems fall. These are (1) the *psychodynamic approaches,* which stress insight in therapy (psychoanalytic and Adlerian therapy); (2) the *experiential* and *relationship-oriented approaches,* which stress feelings and subjective experiencing (existential, person-centered, and Gestalt therapy); (3) the *cognitive behavioral approaches,* which stress the role of thinking and doing and tend to be action-oriented (behavior therapy, rational emotive behavior therapy, cognitive therapy, and reality therapy); (4) the *postmodern approaches*, which stress a collaborative and consultative stance on the therapist's part (solution-focused brief therapy, motivational interviewing, narrative therapy, feminist therapy); and (5) *family systems approaches,* which stress understanding the individual within the entire system of which he or she is a part.

Although we have separated the theories into five general groups, this categorization is somewhat arbitrary. Overlapping concepts and themes make it difficult to neatly compartmentalize these theoretical orientations. Most training programs at the graduate level require students to take a semester-long theory course that describes each theory in great depth. Our purpose here is to provide an overview of the focus of each of these approaches by outlining their basic assumptions, key concepts, therapeutic goals, therapeutic relationship, techniques, multicultural applications, and main contributions to the helping process.

LO3 Psychodynamic Approaches

Psychodynamic approaches provide the foundation from which many diverse theoretical orientations have sprung. Although most helpers will not have the training to practice psychoanalytically, this point of view is useful in gaining an understanding of client dynamics and how therapy can assist clients in working through some deeply engrained personality problems. Psychoanalytic therapy has progressed far beyond Freud; many contemporary forms of relational psychoanalysis can be adapted to brief therapeutic approaches.

Along with Freud, Alfred Adler was a major contributor to the development of the psychodynamic approach to therapy. Although influenced by many of Freud's ideas, Adler developed a very different approach to therapy. Adlerians put the focus on reeducating individuals and reshaping society. Adler was the forerunner of a subjective approach to psychology that focuses on internal determinants of behavior such as values, beliefs, attitudes, goals, interests, and the individual perception of reality. He was a pioneer of an approach that is holistic, social, goal oriented, systemic, and humanistic. As you will see, many of Adler's key concepts are found in other theories that emerged later in time.

Psychoanalytic Approach

Overview and basic assumptions. The **psychoanalytic approach** rests on the assumption that normal personality development is based on dealing effectively with successive psychosexual and psychosocial stages of development. Faulty personality development is the result of inadequately resolving a specific developmental conflict. Practitioners with a psychoanalytic orientation are interested in the client's early history as a way of understanding how past situations contribute to a client's present problems.

Key concepts. The psychoanalytic approach is an in-depth and generally longer-term exploration of personality. Some of the key concepts that form this theory include consciousness and unconsciousness, dealing with anxiety, the functioning of ego-defense mechanisms, and the developmental stages throughout the life span.

Therapeutic goals. A primary goal is to make the unconscious conscious. Restructuring personality rather than solving immediate problems is the main goal. Childhood experiences are reconstructed in therapy, and these experiences are explored, interpreted, and analyzed. Successful outcomes of psychoanalytic therapy result in significant modification of an individual's personality and character structure.

Therapeutic relationship. Psychoanalytically oriented therapists try to relate objectively with warm detachment. Both transference and countertransference are central aspects in the relationship. The focus is on resistances that occur in the therapeutic process, on interpretation of these resistances, and on working through transference feelings. Through this process, clients explore the parallels between their past and present experience and gain new understanding that can be the basis for personality change.

Techniques. All techniques are designed to help the client gain insight and bring repressed material to the surface so that it can be attended to in a conscious way. Major techniques include maintaining the analytic framework, free association, interpretation, dream analysis, analysis of resistance, and analysis of transference. These techniques are geared to increasing awareness, acquiring insight, and beginning a working-through process that will lead to a reorganization of the personality.

Multicultural applications. The psychosocial approach that emphasizes turning points at various stages of life has relevance for understanding diverse client populations. Therapists can assist clients in identifying and dealing with the influence of environmental situations on their personality development. The goals of brief psychodynamic therapy are to provide a new understanding for current problems. With this briefer form of psychoanalytically oriented therapy, clients can relinquish old patterns and establish new patterns in their present behavior.

Contributions. The theory provides a comprehensive and detailed system of personality. It emphasizes the legitimate place of the unconscious as a determinant of behavior, highlights the significant effect of early childhood development, and provides techniques for tapping the unconscious. Several factors can be applied by practitioners who are not psychoanalytically oriented, such as understanding how resistance is manifested and can be therapeutically explored, how early trauma can be worked through successfully, and understanding the manifestations of transference and countertransference in the therapy relationship. Many other theoretical models have developed as reactions against the psychoanalytic approach.

Suggestions for further reading. A useful book for an overview of this approach is *Brief Dynamic Therapy* (Levenson, 2017).

The Adlerian Approach

Overview and basic assumptions. According to the **Adlerian approach**, people are primarily social beings, influenced and motivated by societal forces. Adlerian therapy rests on a central belief that our happiness is largely related to social connectedness. Because we are embedded in a society, we cannot be understood in isolation from that social context. We are primarily motivated by a desire to belong. Human nature is viewed as creative, active, and decisional. The approach focuses on the unity of the person and on understanding the individual's subjective perspective. The subjective decisions each person makes regarding the specific direction of this striving form the basis of the individual's lifestyle (or personality style). The **lifestyle** consists of our beliefs and assumptions about others, the world, and ourselves; these views lead to distinctive behaviors that we adopt in pursuit of our life goals. We can shape our own future by taking risks and making decisions in the face of unknown consequences. People who seek counseling are not viewed as being "sick"; rather, they are seen as being discouraged and functioning on the basis of self-defeating and self-limiting assumptions. Clients require encouragement to correct mistaken perceptions of self and others and to learn to initiate new behavioral interaction patterns.

Key concepts. Consciousness, not the unconscious, is the center of personality. The Adlerian approach is based on a growth model and stresses the individual's positive capacities to live fully in society. Adler saw humans as creative beings who possess strengths and abilities to effectively meet the problems of living. The theory is characterized by seeing unity in the personality, understanding a person's world from a subjective vantage point, and stressing life goals that give direction to behavior. **Social interest**, the heart of this theory, involves a sense of identification with humanity, a feeling of belonging, and a concern with bettering society. **Inferiority feelings** often serve as the wellspring of creativity, motivating people to strive for mastery, superiority, and perfection. People attempt to compensate for both imagined and real inferiorities, which helps them overcome handicaps.

Therapeutic goals. Counseling is a collaborative effort, with client and therapist working on mutually accepted goals. Change is aimed at both the cognitive and behavioral levels. Adlerians are mainly concerned with challenging clients' mistaken notions and faulty assumptions. Working cooperatively with clients, therapists try to provide encouragement so that clients can develop socially useful goals. Some specific goals include fostering social interest, helping clients overcome feelings of discouragement, changing faulty motivation, restructuring mistaken assumptions, and assisting clients to feel a sense of equality with others.

Therapeutic relationship. The client–therapist relationship is based on mutual respect, and both client and counselor are active parties in a relationship between equals. Through this collaborative partnership, clients recognize that they are responsible for their behavior. The emphasis is on examining the client's lifestyle, which is expressed in everything the client does. Therapists frequently interpret this lifestyle by demonstrating connections between the past, the present, and the client's future strivings.

The therapeutic process involves placing emphasis on the individual's lifestyle—the cognitive framework or schema from which the individual attempts to understand life and to make behavior choices. More specifically, the therapist seeks to ascertain the faulty, self-defeating perceptions and assumptions about self, others, and life that maintain the problematic behavioral patterns the client brings to therapy.

Techniques. Adlerian therapists have developed a variety of cognitive, behavioral, and experiential techniques that can be applied to a diverse range of clients in a variety of settings and formats. Adlerians are not bound to follow a specific set of procedures, which gives them a great deal of freedom in working with clients in ways that are uniquely suited to their own therapeutic style. Some specific techniques they often employ are attending, encouragement, confrontation, summarizing, interpreting experiences within the family, early recollections, acting as if, catching oneself, suggestion, and homework assignments.

Multicultural applications. The interpersonal emphasis of the Adlerian approach is most appropriate for counseling people from diverse backgrounds. The approach offers a range of cognitive and action-oriented techniques to help people explore their concerns in a cultural context. Adlerian practitioners are flexible in adapting their interventions to each client's unique life situation and are guided by what is in the best interests of the client. Adlerian therapy is an encouragement-focused counseling approach that has a psychoeducational focus, a present and future orientation, and is a brief, time-limited horizon. These characteristics make the Adlerian approach suitable for working with a wide range of client problems.

Contributions. One of Adler's most important contributions is his influence on other therapy systems. There are significant linkages between Adlerian theory and most of the present-day theories. Indeed, Adler's ideas are a part of many other psychological schools, such as family systems approaches, Gestalt therapy, reality therapy, rational emotive behavior therapy, cognitive therapy, person-centered therapy, solution-focused brief therapy, and existential therapy. These approaches are all based on a similar concept of the person as purposive and self-determining and as striving for growth and meaning in life.

Suggestions for further reading. An excellent resource on this approach is *Adlerian Therapy* (Carlson & Englar-Carlson, 2017). For further discussions of Adlerian therapy, see Corey (2021, chap. 5), Neukrug (2018, chap. 4), Prochaska and Norcross (2018, chap. 3), Watts (2019), and Wedding and Corsini (2019, chap. 3).

LO4 Experiential and Relationship-Oriented Approaches

Therapy is often viewed as a journey taken by counselor and client, a journey that delves deeply into the world as perceived and experienced by the client. This journey is influenced by the quality of the person-to-person encounter in the therapeutic situation. The value of the therapeutic relationship is a common denominator among all therapeutic orientations, yet some approaches place more emphasis than others do on the role of the relationship as a healing factor. This is especially true of the existential, person-centered, and Gestalt approaches. These **relationship-oriented approaches** (sometimes known as **experiential approaches**) are all based on the premise that the quality of the client–counselor relationship is primary, with techniques being secondary. The experiential approaches are grounded on the premise that the therapeutic relationship fosters a creative spirit of inventing techniques aimed at increasing awareness, which enables clients to change some of their patterns of thinking, feeling, and behaving.

Some of the key concepts common to all experiential approaches that are believed to be related to effective therapeutic outcomes include the following:

- The quality of the person-to-person encounter in the therapeutic situation is the catalyst for positive change.
- The counselor's main role is to be present with clients during the therapeutic hour. This implies that the counselor has good contact with the client and is centered.
- Clients can best be invited to grow by a counselor modeling authentic behavior.
- A therapist's attitudes and values are at least as critical as his or her knowledge, theory, or techniques.
- Counselors who are not sensitively tuned in to their own reactions to a client run the risk of becoming technicians rather than artists.

- The I-Thou relationship enables clients to experience the safety necessary for risk-taking behavior.
- Awareness emerges within the context of a genuine meeting between the counselor and the client, or within the context of I-Thou relating.
- The basic work of therapy is done by the client. The counselor's job is to create a climate in which the client is likely to try out new ways of being.

These somewhat overlapping notions give a sense of the paramount importance of the therapeutic relationship. Counselors who operate in the framework of the relationship-oriented therapies are much less anxious about using the "right technique." Their techniques are most likely designed to enhance some aspect of the client's experiencing rather than being used to stimulate clients to think, feel, or act in a certain manner.

The Existential Approach

Overview and basic assumptions. The **existential perspective** holds that we define ourselves by our choices. Although outside factors restrict the range of our choices, we have some freedom because we control our attitudes and behavior. Because we have the capacity for awareness, we have freedom, yet with this freedom comes responsibility for the choices we make. People seeking therapy often have led a **restricted existence**, functioning with a limited degree of self-awareness. The therapist's job is to assist clients in becoming aware of how they are living so they can consider changes they may want to make. As an outgrowth of the therapeutic venture, clients are able to recognize patterns of living that are no longer useful for them, and they begin to accept responsibility for changing their future.

Key concepts. There are six key propositions of existential therapy: (1) We have the capacity for self-awareness. (2) Because we are basically free beings, we must accept the responsibility that accompanies our freedom. (3) We have a concern to preserve our uniqueness and identity; we come to know ourselves in relation to knowing and interacting with others. (4) The significance of our existence and the meaning of our life are never fixed once and for all; instead, we re-create ourselves through our projects. (5) Anxiety is part of the human condition. (6) Death is also a basic human condition, and awareness of it gives significance to living.

Therapeutic goals. The principal goal is to work with clients in recognizing their role in creating the kind of life they presently have. The existential approach places primary emphasis on understanding clients' current experience, *not* on using therapeutic techniques. Existential therapists believe that we are capable of self-awareness, which is the distinctive capacity that allows us to reflect and to decide. With this awareness, we become free beings who are responsible for choosing the way we live, and thus we create our own destiny. The notions of freedom and responsibility challenge us to redesign our lives and to accept responsibility for choosing for ourselves. However, making choices gives rise to existential anxiety, another basic human characteristic, which is heightened when we reflect on the reality of death. Facing the inevitable prospect of eventual death gives the present moment significance as we become aware that we do not have forever to accomplish our goals. The reality of death is a catalyst that can challenge us to create a life that has meaning and purpose.

Therapeutic relationship. The client–therapist relationship is of paramount importance because the quality of the I-Thou encounter offers a context for change. Instead of prizing therapeutic objectivity and professional distance, existential therapists value being fully present, and they strive to create caring relationships with clients. Therapy is a collaborative relationship in which both client and therapist are involved in a journey into self-discovery.

Existential therapy and person-centered therapy place central prominence on the person-to-person relationship. Both of these approaches emphasize striving to maintain an equal-power relationship and an attitude of unconditional positive regard. Client growth occurs through a genuine encounter. A key factor influencing the outcome of therapy is the quality of the therapeutic relationship.

Techniques. Existential therapy reacts against the tendency to view therapy as a system of well-defined techniques; it affirms looking at those unique characteristics that make us human and building therapy upon them. Primary emphasis is on understanding the client's current experience. Existential therapists are free to adapt their interventions to their own personality and style, as well as paying attention to what each client requires. Therapists are not bound by any prescribed procedures and can use techniques from other therapeutic models. Interventions are used in the service of broadening the ways in which clients live in their world. Techniques are tools to help clients become aware of their choices and their potential for action.

Multicultural applications. Because the existential approach is based on universal human themes, and because it does not dictate a particular way of viewing reality, it is highly applicable when working in a multicultural context. In working with cultural diversity, it is essential to recognize the commonalities and similarities among clients. Themes such as relationships, finding meaning, anxiety, suffering, and death are concerns that transcend the boundaries that separate cultures. Clients in existential therapy are encouraged to examine the ways their present existence is being influenced by social and cultural factors. From a social justice perspective, the freedom to choose needs to be viewed within the context of environmental realities such as discrimination and oppression.

Contributions. The person-to-person therapeutic relationship lessens the chances of dehumanizing therapy. The approach has something to offer counselors regardless of their theoretical orientation. The basic ideas of this approach can be incorporated into practice regardless of the counselor's particular theory. It provides a perspective for understanding the value of anxiety and guilt, the role and meaning of death, and the creative aspects of being alone and choosing for oneself.

Suggestions for further reading. An excellent resource on the existential approach is *Existential-Humanistic Therapy* (Schneider & Krug, 2017). For further discussions of existential therapy, see Corey (2021, chap. 6), Deurzen (2010, 2012), Elkins (2009, 2016), Neukrug (2018, chap. 5), Prochaska and Norcross (2018, chap. 4), and Wedding and Corsini (2019, chap. 8).

The Person-Centered Approach

Overview and basic assumptions. Person-centered therapy was originally developed by Carl Rogers in the 1940s as a reaction against psychoanalytic therapy. Based on a subjective view of human experience, the **person-centered approach** emphasizes the client's resources for becoming self-aware and for resolving blocks to personal growth. It puts the client, not the therapist, at the center of the therapeutic process. It is the client who primarily brings about change. Rogers did not present his approach as being a final model, and he expected the theory and practice to evolve over time. By participating in the therapeutic relationship, clients actualize their potential for growth, wholeness, spontaneity, and inner-directedness.

Key concepts. A key concept is that clients have the capacity for resolving life's problems effectively without interpretation and direction from an expert therapist. Clients are able to change without a high degree of structure and direction from the therapist. This approach emphasizes fully experiencing the present moment, learning to accept oneself, and deciding on ways to change.

Therapeutic goals. A major goal is to provide a climate of safety and trust in the therapeutic setting so that the client, by using the therapeutic relationship for self-exploration, can become aware of obstacles to growth. The client tends to move toward more openness, greater self-trust, and more willingness to evolve as opposed to being a static entity. The client learns to live by internal standards as opposed to taking external cues for what he or she should become. The aim of therapy is not merely to solve problems but to assist a client's growth process to enable him or her to better cope with present and future problems.

Therapeutic relationship. The person-centered approach emphasizes the attitudes and personal characteristics of the therapist and the quality of the client–therapist relationship as the prime determinants of the outcomes of therapy. The qualities of the therapist that determine the relationship include genuineness, nonpossessive warmth, accurate empathy, unconditional acceptance of and respect for the client, permissiveness, caring, and the ability to communicate those attitudes to the client. Effective therapy is based on the quality of the relationship between therapist and client. The client is able to translate his or her learning in therapy to outside relationships with others.

Techniques. Because this approach stresses the client–therapist relationship as a necessary and sufficient condition leading to change, it specifies few techniques. Techniques are always secondary to the therapist's attitudes. The approach minimizes directive techniques, interpretation, questioning, diagnosis, and collecting history. It maximizes active listening and hearing, expressing empathy, reflection of feelings, and clarification.

Multicultural applications. The emphasis on universal, core conditions provides the person-centered approach with a framework for understanding diverse worldviews. Empathy, being present, and respecting the values of clients are essential attitudes and skills in counseling culturally diverse clients. Person-centered counselors convey a deep respect for all forms of diversity and value understanding the client's subjective world in an accepting and open way.

Contributions. One of the first therapeutic orientations to break from traditional psychoanalysis, the person-centered approach stresses the active role and responsibility of the client. It is a positive and optimistic view and calls attention to the need to account for a person's inner and subjective experiences. Emphasizing the crucial role of the therapist's attitude, this approach makes the therapeutic process relationship-centered rather than technique-centered.

Suggestions for further reading. A useful book for an overview of this approach is *Person-Centered Psychotherapies* (Cain, 2010).

Gestalt Therapy

Overview and basic assumptions. **Gestalt therapy** is an experiential and existential approach based on the assumption that individuals and their behavior must be understood in the context of their present environment. The therapist's task is to facilitate clients' exploration of their present experience. Awareness, choice, and responsibility are cornerstones of practice. Clients carry on their own therapy as much as possible by doing experiments designed to heighten awareness and to engage in contact. Change occurs naturally as awareness of "what is" increases. Heightened awareness can also lead to a more thorough integration of parts of the client that were fragmented or unknown. Gestalt therapy pays attention to *process* as well as content. This approach is phenomenological because it focuses on the client's perceptions of reality and is existential because it is grounded in the notion that people are always in the process of becoming, remaking, and rediscovering themselves.

Key concepts. This approach focuses on the here-and-now, direct experiencing, awareness, bringing unfinished business from the past into the present, and dealing with unfinished business. Other concepts include energy and blocks to energy, contact and resistance to contact, and paying attention to nonverbal cues. Clients identify their own unfinished business from the past that is interfering with their present functioning by reexperiencing past situations as though they were happening in the present moment.

Therapeutic goals. The goal is attaining awareness and greater choice. Awareness includes knowing the environment and knowing oneself, accepting oneself, and being able to make contact. Clients are helped to note their own awareness process so that they can be responsible and can selectively and discriminatingly make choices. With awareness the client is able to recognize denied aspects of the self and proceed toward reintegration of all its parts.

Therapeutic relationship. This approach stresses the I-Thou relationship. The focus is not on the techniques employed by the therapist but on who the therapist is as a person and the quality of the relationship. Factors emphasized include the therapist's presence, authentic dialogue, gentleness, direct self-expression, and a greater trust in the client's experiencing. There is a creative spirit of suggesting, inventing, and carrying out experiments aimed at increasing awareness. The counselor assists clients in experiencing all feelings more fully and letting them make their own interpretations. Technical expertise is important, but the therapeutic engagement is paramount. Rather than interpreting the meaning of experience for clients, the therapist focuses on the "what" and "how" of their behavior.

Techniques. Although the therapist functions as a guide and a catalyst, presents experiments, and shares observations, the basic work of therapy is done by the client. Therapists do not force change on clients; rather, they create experiments within a context of the I-Thou dialogue in a here-and-now framework. These experiments are the cornerstone of experiential learning. Although the therapist suggests the experiments, this is a collaborative process with full participation by the client. **Gestalt experiments** take many forms: setting up a symbolic dialogue between a client and a significant person in his or her life; assuming the identity of a key figure through role playing; reliving a painful event; exaggerating a gesture, posture, or some nonverbal mannerism; or carrying on a dialogue between two conflicting aspects within an individual.

Multicultural applications. Gestalt therapy can be used creatively and sensitively with culturally diverse populations if interventions are used flexibly and in a timely manner. Gestalt practitioners focus on understanding the person and not on the use of techniques. Experiments are done with the collaboration of the client and with an attempt to understand the background of the client's culture.

Contributions. Gestalt therapy recognizes the value of working with the past from the perspective of the here-and-now. This orientation emphasizes doing and experiencing as opposed to merely talking about problems in a detached way. Gestalt therapy gives attention to nonverbal and body messages, which broaden the field of material to be explored in a helping relationship. It provides a perspective on growth and enhancement, not merely a treatment of disorders. The method of working with dreams is a creative pathway to increased awareness of key existential messages in life.

Suggestions for further reading. A useful and current resource on this approach is *Gestalt Therapy* (Wheeler & Axelsson, 2015). For further discussion of Gestalt therapy, see Corey (2021, chap. 8), Neukrug (2018, chap. 6), Prochaska and Norcross (2018, chap. 6), and Wedding and Corsini (2019, chap 9).

LO5 Cognitive Behavioral Approaches

This section describes some of the main **cognitive behavioral approaches**, which include behavior therapy, rational emotive behavior therapy, cognitive therapy, and reality therapy. It also includes an introduction to the third wave of behavior therapy approaches known as mindfulness and acceptance therapies. Although the cognitive behavioral approaches are quite diverse, they do share these attributes: (1) a collaborative relationship between client and therapist, (2) the premise that psychological distress is largely a function of disturbances in cognitive processes, (3) an emphasis on changing cognitions to produce desired changes in affect and behavior, and (4) a time-limited and educational treatment focusing on specific target problems. The cognitive behavioral approaches are based on a structured, psychoeducational model, and they tend to emphasize the role of homework, place responsibility on the client to assume an active role both during and outside of therapy sessions, and draw from a variety of cognitive and behavioral techniques to facilitate change. Cognitive behavioral practitioners are concerned with teaching clients how to be their own therapist. Typically, a therapist will educate clients about the nature and course of their problem, about the process of cognitive therapy, and how thoughts influence emotions and behaviors. The educative process includes providing clients with information both about their presenting problems and about *relapse prevention*, which consists of ways to deal with the inevitable setbacks clients are likely to experience as they apply what they are learning to daily life. Of all the therapeutic models, the cognitive behavioral therapies have gained most in popularity and are increasingly being used as the basis for practice with a wide variety of client populations, with a multitude of problems, and in many different settings.

Behavior Therapy

Overview and basic assumptions. Behavioral approaches assume that people are basically shaped by both learning and the sociocultural environment. Due to the diversity of views and strategies, it is more accurate to think of behavioral therapies rather than a unified approach. The central characteristics that unite the diversity of views of the field of behavior therapy are a focus on observable behavior, current determinants of behavior, learning experiences to promote change, and rigorous assessment and evaluation. A basic assumption of the behavioral perspective is that most problematic cognitions, emotions, and behaviors have been learned and that new learning can modify them. Although this modification process is often called "therapy," it is more properly an educational experience in which individuals are involved in a teaching/learning process.

Key concepts. **Behavior therapy** emphasizes current behavior as opposed to historical antecedents, precise treatment goals, diverse therapeutic strategies tailored to these goals, and objective evaluation of therapeutic outcomes. Therapy focuses on behavior change in the present and on action programs. Concepts and procedures are stated explicitly, tested empirically, and revised continually. There is an emphasis on measuring a specific behavior before and after an intervention to determine if, and to what degree, behaviors change as a result of a procedure.

Therapeutic goals. A hallmark of behavior therapy is the identification of specific goals at the outset of the therapeutic process. The general goals are to increase personal choice and to create new conditions for learning. An aim is to eliminate maladaptive behaviors and to replace them with more constructive patterns. Generally, client and therapist collaboratively specify treatment goals in concrete, measurable, and objective terms. In helping clients achieve their goals, behavior therapists typically assume an active and directive role. Although the client generally determines *what* behavior will be changed, the therapist typically determines *how* this behavior can best be modified.

Therapeutic relationship. Although the approach does not place primary emphasis on the client–therapist relationship, a good working relationship is an essential precondition for effective therapy. The skilled therapist can conceptualize problems behaviorally and make use of the therapeutic relationship in bringing about change. The assumption is that clients make progress primarily because of the specific behavioral techniques used rather than by the relationship with the therapist. The therapist's role is to teach concrete skills through the provision of instructions, modeling, and performance feedback. Therapists tend to be active and directive and to function as consultants and problem solvers. Clients must also be actively involved in the therapeutic process from beginning to end, and they are expected to cooperate in carrying out therapeutic activities, both in the sessions and outside of therapy.

Techniques. Behavior therapy differs from other therapies in that it is brief, active, directive, collaborative, and focused on factors maintaining problem behaviors rather than on factors that may have triggered a problem initially. Assessment and diagnosis are done at the outset to determine a treatment plan. Behavioral treatment interventions are individually tailored to specific problems experienced by clients. Any technique that can be demonstrated to change behavior may be incorporated in a treatment plan. A strength of the approach lies in the many and varied techniques aimed at producing behavior change, a few of which are relaxation methods, systematic desensitization, in vivo desensitization, flooding, assertion training, and self-management programs.

Multicultural applications. Behavioral approaches can be appropriately integrated into counseling with culturally diverse client populations when culture-specific procedures are developed. The approach emphasizes teaching clients about the therapeutic process and stresses changing specific behaviors. By developing their problem-solving skills, clients learn concrete methods for dealing with practical problems within their cultural framework.

Contributions. Behavior therapy is usually a short-term approach, and it has wide applicability. It emphasizes research into and assessment of the techniques used, thus providing accountability. Specific problems are identified and explored, and clients are kept informed about the therapeutic process and about the gains being made. The approach has demonstrated effectiveness in many areas of human functioning, and the concepts and procedures are easily grasped. The therapist is an explicit reinforcer, consultant, model, teacher, and expert in behavioral change.

Suggestions for further reading. For further discussion of behavior therapy, see Corey (2021, chap. 9), Craske (2017), Dobson and Dobson (2017), Kazantzis, Dattilio, and Dobson (2017), Ledley, Marx, and Heimberg (2018), and Wedding and Corsini (2019, chap. 6).

Rational Emotive Behavior Therapy

Overview and basic assumptions. Albert Ellis is considered the father of rational emotive behavior therapy (REBT) and the grandfather of cognitive behavior therapy. **Rational emotive behavior therapy** rests on the premise that thinking, evaluating, analyzing, questioning, doing, practicing, and redeciding are the basics of behavior change. The cognitive behavioral approaches are based on the assumption that a reorganization of one's self-statements will result in a corresponding reorganization of one's behavior.

Key concepts. REBT holds that although emotional disturbance is rooted in childhood, people keep repeating irrational and illogical beliefs. Emotional problems are the result of one's beliefs, not events, and these beliefs need to be challenged. Clients are taught that the events of life themselves do not disturb us; rather, our interpretation of events is what is critical.

Therapeutic goals. The goal of REBT is to eliminate a self-defeating outlook on life, to reduce unhealthy emotional responses, and to acquire a more rational and tolerant philosophy. Two main goals of REBT are to assist clients in the process of achieving unconditional self-acceptance and to learn unconditional acceptance of others. To accomplish these goals, REBT offers clients practical ways to identify their underlying faulty beliefs, to critically evaluate these beliefs, and to replace them with constructive beliefs.

Therapeutic relationship. Therapy is a process of reeducation, and the therapist functions largely as a teacher in active and directive ways. As clients begin to understand how they continue to contribute to their problems, they need to actively practice changing their self-defeating behavior and converting it to rational behavior.

Techniques. REBT utilizes a wide range of cognitive, emotive, and behavioral methods with most clients. This approach blends techniques to change clients' patterns of thinking, feeling, and acting. Techniques are designed to induce clients to critically examine their present beliefs and behavior. REBT focuses on specific techniques for changing a client's self-defeating thoughts in concrete situations. In addition to modifying beliefs, REBT helps clients see how their beliefs influence what they feel and what they do. From a cognitive perspective, REBT demonstrates to clients that their beliefs and self-talk keep them disturbed. Although this approach does not give priority to feelings, as clients explore what they are thinking and how they are acting, feelings often surface. When feelings do emerge, they can be addressed.

Multicultural applications. Some factors that make REBT effective in working with diverse client populations include tailoring treatment to each individual, addressing the role of the external environment, the active and directive role of the therapist, the emphasis on education, relying on empirical evidence, the focus on present behavior, and the brevity of the approach. REBT practitioners function as teachers; clients acquire a wide range of skills they can use in dealing with the problems of living. This educational focus appeals to many clients who are interested in learning practical and effective methods of bringing about change.

Contributions. REBT is a comprehensive, integrative approach to therapy aimed at changing disturbances in thinking, feeling, and behaving. REBT has taught us how people can change their emotions by changing the content of their thinking. Counseling is brief and places value on active practice in experimenting with new behavior so that insight is carried into doing.

Suggestions for further reading. A useful book for an overview of this approach is *Rational Emotive Behavior Therapy* (Ellis & Ellis, 2011).

Cognitive Therapy

Overview and basic assumptions. Aaron Beck is a pioneer of cognitive therapy who made important contributions in understanding and treating disorders such as depression and anxiety. **Cognitive therapy** (CT) rests on the premise that cognitions are the major determinants of how we feel and act. CT assumes that the internal dialogue of clients plays a major role in their behavior. The ways in which individuals monitor and instruct themselves and interpret events shed light on the dynamics of disorders such as depression and anxiety.

Key concepts. According to CT, psychological problems stem from commonplace processes such as faulty thinking, making incorrect inferences on the basis of inadequate or incorrect information, and failing to distinguish between fantasy and reality. Cognitive therapy consists of changing dysfunctional emotions and behaviors by modifying inaccurate and dysfunctional thinking.

Therapeutic goals. The goal of CT is to change the way clients think by using their automatic thoughts to reach the core schemata and begin to introduce the idea of schema restructuring. Changes in beliefs and thought processes tend to result in changes in the way people feel and how they behave. Clients in CT are encouraged to gather and weigh the evidence in support of their beliefs. Through the collaborative therapeutic effort, they learn to discriminate between their own thoughts and the events that occur in reality.

Therapeutic relationship. CT emphasizes a collaborative effort by both therapist and client to frame the client's conclusions in the form of a testable hypothesis. Cognitive therapists are continuously active and deliberately interactive with the client; they also strive to engage the client's active participation and collaboration throughout all phases of therapy.

Techniques. CT emphasizes a Socratic dialogue to help clients discover their misconceptions for themselves. Through a process of guided discovery, the therapist functions as a catalyst and guide who helps clients understand the connection between their thinking and the ways they feel and act. Cognitive therapists teach clients how to be their own therapist. This includes educating clients about the nature and course of their problems, about how CT works, and how their thinking influences their emotions and behaviors. Techniques in CT are designed to identify and test the client's misconceptions and faulty assumptions. Homework is often used, which is tailored to the client's specific problems and arises out of the collaborative therapeutic relationship. Homework is generally presented as an experiment, and clients are encouraged to create their own self-help assignments as a way to keep working on issues addressed in their therapy sessions.

Multicultural applications. CT is culturally sensitive in that it uses the individual's belief system, or worldview, as part of the method of self-change.

The collaborative nature of CT offers clients the structure many clients want, yet the therapist still strives to enlist clients' active participation in the therapeutic process. Because of the way CT is practiced, with emphasis on enlisting the full participation of clients, it is ideally suited to working with clients from diverse backgrounds.

Contributions. CT has been demonstrated to be effective in the treatment of anxiety, phobias, and depression. This approach has received a great deal of attention by clinical researchers. Many specific cognitive techniques have been supported by empirical evidence as being useful in teaching clients ways to change their belief systems.

Suggestions for further reading. If you are interested in further reading on integrating cognitive therapy into a comprehensive approach, consult J. Beck (2005, 2011), Dobson and Dobson (2017), Ellis and Ellis (2011), Kazantzis, Dattilio, and Dobson (2017), Meichenbaum (2012, 2017), Sperry and Sperry (2018), and Vernon and Doyle (2018). For a general treatment of cognitive perspectives, see Beck and Weishaar (2019, chap. 7) and Corey (2021, chap. 10).

Choice Theory/Reality Therapy

Overview and basic assumptions. **Choice theory** rests on the assumption that humans are internally motivated and behave to control the world around them according to some purpose within them. Choice theory, which is the underlying philosophy of the practice of reality therapy, provides a framework that explains the why and how of human behavior. Founded and developed by William Glasser in the 1960s, **reality therapy** posits that people are responsible for what they do. Based on existential principles, reality therapy holds that we choose our own destiny. Reality therapy is based on the assumption that human beings are motivated to change (1) when they determine that their current behavior is not getting them what they want and (2) when they believe they can choose other behaviors that will get them closer to what they want. Clients are expected to make an assessment of their current behavior to determine specific ways they may want to change.

Key concepts. The core concept of this approach is that behavior is our best attempt to control our perceptions of the external world so they fit our internal world. **Total behavior** includes four inseparable but distinct components—*acting, thinking, feeling,* and the *physiology* that accompanies our actions. A key concept of reality therapy and choice theory is that no matter how dire our circumstances may be, we always have a choice. The key to changing a total behavior is through *acting* and *thinking,* for these aspects of total behavior are easier to change than are the *feeling* and *physiology* components. An emphasis of reality therapy is on assuming personal responsibility and on dealing with the present.

Therapeutic goals. The overall goal of this approach is to help people find better ways to meet their needs for survival, love and belonging, power, freedom, and fun. Changes in behavior should result in the satisfaction of basic needs. Clients are expected to make a self-evaluation of what they are doing, thinking, and feeling to assess whether this is getting them what they want and to assist them in finding a better way to function.

Therapeutic relationship. The therapist initiates the therapeutic process by becoming involved with the client and creating a supportive and challenging relationship. Practitioners teach clients how to make significant connections with others. Throughout therapy the counselor avoids criticism, refuses to accept clients' excuses for not following through with agreed-upon plans, and does not easily give up on clients. Instead, counselors continue to ask clients to evaluate the effectiveness of what they are choosing to determine if better choices may be possible.

Techniques. The practice of reality therapy can best be conceptualized as the **cycle of counseling**, which consists of two major components: (1) the counseling environment and (2) specific procedures that lead to change in behavior. Reality therapy is active, directive, and didactic. Skillful questioning and various behavioral techniques are employed to help clients make a comprehensive self-evaluation.

Some of the specific procedures in the practice of reality therapy have been developed by Robert Wubbolding (2011, 2017). These procedures are summarized in the **WDEP model**, which refers to the following clusters of strategies:

W = wants: exploring wants, needs, and perceptions
D = direction and doing: focusing on what clients are doing and the direction that this is taking them
E = evaluation: challenging clients to make an evaluation of their total behavior
P = planning and commitment: assisting clients in formulating realistic plans and making a commitment to carry them out

Multicultural applications. Reality therapists demonstrate their respect for the cultural values of their clients by helping them explore how satisfying their current behavior is both to themselves and to others. After clients make this self-assessment, they identify those areas of living that are not working for them. Clients are then in a position to formulate specific and realistic plans that are consistent with their cultural values.

Contributions. As a short-term approach, reality therapy can be applied to a wide range of clients. Reality therapy consists of simple, clear concepts that are easily understood by many in the human services field, and the principles can be used by parents, teachers, and clergy. As a positive and action-oriented approach, it appeals to a variety of clients who are typically viewed as difficult to treat. This approach teaches clients to focus on what they are able and willing to do in the present to change their behavior.

Suggestions for further reading. The most current book on reality therapy is *Reality Therapy and Self-Evaluation: The Key to Client Change* (Wubbolding, 2017). For further discussion of reality therapy and choice theory, see Corey (2021, chap. 11), Glasser (1998, 2001), Neukrug (2018, chap. 11), and Wubbolding (2011, 2013, 2016, 2017).

LO6 Mindfulness and Acceptance Therapies

Mindfulness and acceptance are cutting-edge therapeutic approaches often referred to as the *third wave of behavior therapy*. These third-generation behavior therapies center around four core themes: (1) an expanded view of psychological health, (2) a broad view of acceptable therapeutic outcomes, (3) mindfulness and acceptance, and (4) designing a life worth living. The mindfulness and acceptance therapies are expected to increase in popularity in the future (Prochaska & Norcross, 2018). Mindfulness-based therapies are effective treatments for stress disorders and may be even more effective when combined with therapeutic lifestyle changes such as exercise, time in nature, diet and nutrition, recreation, providing service to others, relationships, relaxation, and spiritual involvement (Walsh & Vaughan, 2019).

Contemporary developments in the cognitive behavioral tradition include four major approaches: (1) dialectical behavior therapy (DBT), which has become a recognized treatment for borderline personality disorder; (2) mindfulness-based stress reduction (MBSR), which applies mindfulness techniques to coping with stress and promoting physical and psychological health; (3) mindfulness-based cognitive therapy (MBCT), aimed primarily at treating depression; and (4) acceptance and commitment therapy (ACT), which encourages clients to accept unpleasant sensations rather than attempting to control or change them. All of these mindfulness-based approaches have been subjected to empirical scrutiny, which is a hallmark of the behavioral tradition.

For an in-depth discussion of the role of mindfulness in psychotherapeutic practice, see *Acceptance and Mindfulness in Cognitive Behavior Therapy: Understanding and Applying the New Therapies* (Herbert & Forman, 2011); *Mindfulness and Psychotherapy* (Germer, Siegel, & Fulton, 2013); *Wisdom and Compassion in Psychotherapy: Deepening Mindfulness in Clinical Practice* (Germer & Siegel, 2012), and *The Mindfulness Solution: Everyday Practices for Everyday Problems* (Siegel, 2010).

Dialectical behavior therapy. Dialectical behavior therapy (DBT) was developed by Marsha Linehan (1993a, 1993b), who wanted to alleviate emotional suffering for those who were considering suicide. Now DBT is considered a key approach for treating individuals diagnosed with borderline personality disorder. DBT has been proven effective in treating a wide range of disorders, including anxiety disorders, depression, substance use disorder, posttraumatic stress disorder, eating disorders, and nonsuicidal self-injury (Linehan, 2015).

Dialectical behavior therapists emphasize a strong therapeutic alliance, which occurs by establishing a structured, predictable therapeutic environment. A general goal of DBT is to decrease ineffective coping behaviors and increase effective behaviors through skills training and generalizing these skills to daily life. When clients begin DBT, they are asked to identify some specific goals in life that would make life worth living (Kelly & Robinson, 2018).

Mindfulness, the unfolding of experience moment by moment, is a fundamental skill in DBT that enables individuals to be aware of and accept

---

This section is adapted from *The Art of Integrative Counseling* (Corey, 2019, chap. 8) and *Theory and Practice of Counseling and Psychotherapy* (Corey, 2021, chap. 9).

the world as it is and to avoid evaluation and judgment. Through mindfulness, clients learn to embrace and tolerate the intense emotions they experience when facing distressing situations. Clients are encouraged to accept and experience emotions as they are rather than attempting to change them. *Acceptance,* which involves receiving our present experience without judgment, but with curiosity and compassion, facilitates progress by allowing the client to appreciate the value of living in the moment (Germer, 2013; Kelly & Robinson, 2018).

For a more detailed discussion of DBT, see *DBT Skills Training Manual* (Linehan, 2015).

Mindfulness-based stress reduction. The essence of mindfulness-based stress reduction (MBSR) is realizing that much of our distress and suffering results from continually wanting things to be different than they actually are in reality. MBSR assists people in learning how to live more fully in the present instead of ruminating about the past or being overly concerned about the future. Mindfulness meditation clears the mind and calms the body, which enables individuals to focus on here-and-now awareness in a nonjudgmental way. The emphasis is on *what is* rather than on *what if.*

The MBSR program is designed to teach participants to relate to external and internal sources of stress in constructive ways; individuals strive to develop an ongoing commitment to cultivate its principles in the present. Clients are encouraged to bring mindfulness into all of their daily activities; this informal practice includes being mindful when standing, walking, eating, and doing chores. Acquiring a mindful way of being is not a simple behavioral technique; it is a way of being that we develop over time as we deepen our focus through disciplined practice. We can gain a great deal by establishing even short periods of time for focusing and quiet reflection. Mindfulness practice can have significant effects on how we approach each day. For mindfulness to generalize beyond the therapy office, mindfulness practices must become integrated in daily living.

For an extensive discussion of mindfulness and acceptance, see *Acceptance and Mindfulness in Cognitive Behavior Therapy: Understanding and Applying the New Therapies* (Herbert & Forman, 2011).

Mindfulness-based cognitive therapy. Mindfulness-based cognitive therapy (MBCT) is a comprehensive integration of the principles and skills of mindfulness applied to the treatment of depression. MBCT uses acceptance techniques to promote resilience and to prevent recurrences of depressive episodes (Antony, 2019). The brevity of MBCT makes this approach an efficient and cost-effective treatment. The program integrates techniques from MBSR with teaching cognitive behavior skills to clients. The primary aim is to change clients' awareness of and relation to their negative thoughts.

As we develop the skills of mindfulness, our thinking becomes clearer and we are better able to increase our awareness of the world around us. The attitudes and behavior of the MBCT practitioner are critical in helping clients acquire an accepting way of being and discarding self-critical and judgmental habits.

For a more detailed review of MBCT, see *Mindfulness-Based Cognitive Therapy for Depression* (Segal, Williams, & Teasdale, 2013).

Acceptance and commitment therapy. Acceptance and commitment therapy (ACT) is an empirically based psychological intervention that uses acceptance and mindfulness strategies together with commitment and behavior change strategies to foster psychological flexibility. ACT is not a technique; it is an approach to developing and applying interventions within a psychological flexibility model. Acceptance and commitment therapists help clients accept life's difficulties and move in a committed manner. The main goal of ACT is to help clients remain attuned to the present moment and persist in a value-consistent behavior change that will lead to desired outcomes. Acceptance and commitment therapists teach clients to notice, accept, and even embrace their full range of thoughts and feelings.

There is little emphasis on changing the content of clients' thoughts. Instead, the emphasis is on *acceptance* (nonjudgmental awareness) of their cognitions. The goal is for individuals to become aware of and examine their thoughts. Clients accept their thinking as it is and aim to reorient their relationship with their thought processes. As clients examine their thoughts, their reactions to and relationship with their own thinking is viewed as an alternative to restructuring the content of their thinking.

The main role of the acceptance and commitment therapist is to assist clients in becoming more fully themselves so they can begin to live a more vital life consistent with their values (Hayes & Lillis, 2012). Values imply living in a meaningful way as well as reflecting and choosing life goals (Podina & David, 2018). Toward that goal, practitioners might ask clients these questions: What do you want your life to stand for? What do you truly and deeply care about? What kind of life do you want to live? Therapists and clients collaboratively establish treatment goals as clients become more aware of their values, choose values they want to live by, and take action to match their behavior to their values (Antony, 2019). A commitment to action is essential, and clients are asked to make mindful decisions about what they are willing to do to live a valued and meaningful life. Concrete homework and behavioral exercises are two ways clients can commit to action. It is the role of clients to determine the values that will provide them with a meaningful life; it is not the therapist's role to choose values for clients.

For more on ACT, see *Acceptance and Commitment Therapy* (Hayes & Lillis, 2012) and *Acceptance and Commitment Therapy: The Process and Practice of Mindful Change* (Hayes, Strosahl, & Wilson, 2011).

LO7 Postmodern Approaches

This section describes four of the main **postmodern approaches**, solution-focused brief therapy, motivational interviewing, narrative therapy, and feminist therapy. In these approaches, the therapist disavows the role of expert, preferring a more collaborative and consultative stance. Solution-focused brief therapy, motivational interviewing, and narrative therapy are based on the optimistic assumption that people are healthy, competent, resourceful, and possess the ability to construct solutions and alternative stories that can enhance their lives. Feminist therapy focuses on issues of diversity, the complexity of sexism, and the centrality of social context in understanding gender issues.

Solution-Focused Brief Therapy

Overview and basic assumptions. **Solution-focused brief therapy** (SFBT) is based on the assumption that the therapist is not the expert on a client's life; rather, it is the client who is the expert. This approach emphasizes clients' strengths, resources, previous successes, and their ability to deal with their concerns and move toward their preferred outcomes. Complex problems do not necessarily require complex solutions, and the therapist helps clients recognize the competencies they already possess. Change is constant and inevitable, and small changes pave the way for large increments of change. Attention is given to what clients are doing that is working and to helping them build on their potential and resources.

Key concepts. A central concept of SFBT includes a movement from talking about problems to talking about and constructing solutions. The therapeutic process focuses on the client's desired future rather than on past problems. Therapy is kept simple and brief. Therapists conclude work as soon as possible, and they tend to treat every session as if it were the last. There are exceptions to every problem, and by talking about these exceptions, clients are able to conquer what seem to be major problems in a brief period of time.

Therapeutic goals. The solution-focused model emphasizes the role of clients in establishing their own goals and preferences. This is done when a climate of mutual respect, dialogue, inquiry, and affirmation are a part of the therapeutic process. Working together in a collaborative relationship, both therapist and client develop useful and meaningful treatment goals, and ultimately clients construct meaningful goals that will lead to a better future.

Therapeutic relationship. SFBT is a collaborative venture; the therapist strives to carry out therapy *with* an individual, rather than doing therapy *on* an individual. Therapists recognize that clients are the primary interpreters of their own experiences. Solution-focused therapists adopt a "not knowing" position, or a nonexpert stance, as a way to put clients in the position of being the experts about their own lives. The therapist-as-expert is replaced by the client-as-expert. By adopting a respectful position of curiosity and "not knowing," the therapist is informed by the client of the nature of the work that needs to be done. Together the client and the therapist establish clear, specific, realistic, and personally meaningful goals that will guide the therapy process. This spirit of collaboration opens up a range of possibilities for present and future change.

Techniques. Solution-focused brief therapists use a range of techniques. Some therapists ask the client to externalize the problem and focus on strengths or unused resources. Others challenge clients to discover solutions that might work. Techniques focus on the future and how best to solve problems rather than on understanding the cause of problems. SFBT techniques that are frequently used include pretherapy change, exception questions, the miracle question, scaling questions, homework, and summary feedback.

Solution-focused brief therapists often ask clients at the first session, "What have you done since you called for an appointment that has made a difference in your problem?" Asking about **pretherapy change** tends to encourage clients to rely less on the therapist and more on their own resources to reach their goals.

Exception questions direct clients to those times in their lives when their problems did not exist or when the problem was less severe. Exploring exceptions offers clients opportunities for discovering resources, engaging strengths, and creating possible solutions.

The **miracle question** allows clients to describe life without the problem. This question involves a future focus that encourages clients to consider a different kind of life than one dominated by a particular problem. The miracle question focuses clients on searching for solutions. Examples are "How will you know when things are better?" and "What will be some of the things you will notice when life is better?"

Scaling questions require clients to specify improvement on a particular dimension on a scale of 1 to 10. Clients can be asked this question: "On a scale of 1 to 10, with 1 being the worst and 10 being the best, how would you rate your satisfaction with your work now?" This technique enables clients to see progress being made in specific steps and degrees.

Therapists may provide **summary feedback** in the form of genuine affirmations or pointing out particular strengths that clients have demonstrated.

Multicultural applications. Solution-focused therapists learn from their clients about their experiential world rather than approaching clients with a preconceived notion about their worldview. The nonpathologizing stance taken by solution-focused practitioners moves away from dwelling on what is wrong with a person to emphasizing creative possibilities. The emphasis is on prevention and education rather than on remediation. Instead of aiming to make change happen, the SFBT practitioner attempts to create an atmosphere of understanding and acceptance that allows a diverse range of individuals to utilize their resources for making constructive changes. The attitudes of solution-focused therapists are conducive to establishing collaborative therapeutic partnerships with a diverse range of client populations.

Contributions. A key contribution of SFBT is the optimistic orientation that views people as being competent and able to create better solutions. Problems are viewed as ordinary difficulties and challenges of life. SFBT offers effective ways to work with client resistance and reluctance. A strength of solution-focused brief therapy is the use of questioning, especially future-oriented questions that challenge clients to think about how they might solve potential problems.

Suggestions for further reading. For a further discussion of solution-focused brief therapy, see Corey (2021, chap. 13), Cormier, Nurius, and Osborn (2017, chap. 10), Grothaus, Runyan, and Sacco-Bene (2019, chap. 7), Murphy (2015), Neukrug (2018, chap. 13), and Prochaska and Norcross (2018, chap. 15).

Motivational Interviewing

Overview and basic assumptions. **Motivational interviewing (MI)** is a humanistic, client-centered, psychosocial, directive counseling approach that was developed by William R. Miller and Stephen Rollnick in the early 1980s. The underlying assumption is that clients want to be healthy and desire positive change. MI is based on the premise that individuals have within themselves the capacity to generate intrinsic motivation to change. Responsibility for change rests with clients, and the therapist and client share a sense of hope and optimism that change is possible. Once individuals believe that they have the capacity to change and heal, new possibilities open up for them.

Key concepts. MI is rooted in the philosophy of person-centered therapy, but with a "twist." Unlike the nondirective and unstructured person-centered approach, MI is deliberately directive. When clients exhibit resistance to counseling goals, MI counselors work to reduce client ambivalence about change and to increase intrinsic motivation.

Therapeutic goals. People who seek therapy often experience ambivalence about change, and their motivation may ebb and flow during the course of therapy. Reluctance, or ambivalence to change, is viewed as normal and is an expected part of the therapeutic process. By honoring clients' stories, recognizing clients' strengths and preferences, and enhancing intrinsic motivation, MI provides multiple ways to address the impasses clients often experience during the change process. MI stresses client self-responsibility and promotes an invitational style for working with clients to generate alternative solutions to behavioral problems. MI practitioners believe in clients' abilities, strengths, resources, and competencies, and therapists guide individuals in taking the steps necessary to bring about change based on their personal goals and values. Practitioners assist clients in becoming their own advocates for change and the primary agents of change in their lives.

Therapeutic relationship. The therapeutic relationship is as important in achieving successful outcomes as the specific theoretical model or school of psychotherapy from which the therapist operates. MI therapists emphasize the relational context of therapy, which is known as the **MI spirit**, and establish collaborative partnerships with clients, drawing on clients' ideas and resources, actively engaging clients in a conversation about change, and recognizing that all choices ultimately rest with clients. MI practitioners encourage individuals to explore their concerns and fears about changing and strive to build intrinsic motivation. MI therapists avoid arguing with clients, avoid assuming a confrontational stance, reframe resistance as a healthy response, express empathy, and listen reflectively. MI practitioners do not view clients as opponents to be defeated but as allies who play a major role in their present and future success.

Techniques. MI involves a complex set of skills that are used flexibly, based on what the client is saying and doing in the moment. Asking open-ended questions, employing reflective listening, exploring client goals and values, affirming and supporting the client, responding to resistance without confrontation, asking permission before giving advice, emphasizing personal choice, encouraging client autonomy, and eliciting and reinforcing *change talk* are characteristic techniques used in MI. Motivational interviewing involves a great deal more than simply asking questions; it requires keen listening to help therapists discover ways to activate clients' own motivations for change and desire to adhere to treatment.

Multicultural applications. Therapists practicing MI strive to experience the world from the client's perspective without judgment or criticism. MI emphasizes reflective listening, which is a way for practitioners to better understand the subjective world of clients. Demonstrating empathy is foundational in creating a safe climate for clients to explore their ambivalence for change. When clients are slow to change, it may be assumed that they have compelling reasons to remain as they are as well as having reasons to change. Some of these reasons may be associated with a client's cultural background and cultural values. This stance of understanding the client's world is basic to applying MI in multicultural situations.

Contributions. Practitioners operating from an MI orientation support clients' self-efficacy, mainly by encouraging them to use their own resources to take necessary actions that can lead to success in changing. MI clinicians strive to enhance client agency about change and emphasize the right and inherent ability of clients to formulate their own goals and to make their own decisions. MI focuses on present and future conditions and empowers clients to find ways to achieve their goals. MI has an impressive record of well-conducted empirical studies confirming its value in working with a range of client problems and in a variety of settings.

Suggestions for further reading. An excellent resource for an in-depth look at motivational interviewing is *Motivational Interviewing: Helping People Change* (Miller & Rollnick, 2013). See also Cormier, Nurius, and Osborn (2017, chap. 10) and Iarussi (2019).

Narrative Therapy

Overview and basic assumptions. **Narrative therapy** is based partly on examining the stories that people tell and understanding the meaning of the story. Each of these stories is true for the individual who is telling the story; there is no absolute reality. Narrative therapists strive to avoid making assumptions about people out of respect for each client's unique story and cultural heritage.

Key concepts. Some key concepts of narrative therapy include a discussion of how a problem has been disrupting, dominating, or discouraging the person. The therapist attempts to separate clients from their problems so they do not adopt a fixed view of their identity. This approach focuses on changing the narrative clients have associated with events and invites clients to view their stories from different perspectives, eventually co-creating an alternative life story. Clients are asked to find evidence to support a new view of themselves in which they are competent enough to escape the dominance of a problem. Clients are encouraged to consider what kind of future they could expect if they were competent.

Therapeutic goals. Narrative therapists invite clients to describe their experience in fresh language, which tends to open new vistas of what is possible. The heart of the therapeutic process from the perspective of narrative therapy involves identifying how societal standards and expectations are internalized by people in ways that constrain and narrow the kind of life they are capable of living. Narrative therapists collaborate with clients to help them experience a heightened sense of agency or ability to act in the world.

Therapeutic relationship. Narrative therapy emphasizes the quality of the therapeutic relationship and the creative use of techniques within this relationship. Narrative therapists do not assume that they have special knowledge about the lives of clients. Clients are the primary interpreters of their own experiences. In the narrative approach, therapists seek to understand clients' lived experience and avoid efforts to predict, interpret, or pathologize. Through a systematic process of careful listening, coupled with curious, persistent, and respectful questioning, therapists work collaboratively with clients to explore the impact of the problem and what they are doing to reduce its effects. Through this process, client and therapist co-construct enlivening alternative stories.

Techniques. Narrative therapy's most distinctive feature is captured by the statement, "The person is not the problem, but the problem is the problem." Narrative therapists engage clients in *externalizing conversations* that are aimed at separating the problem from the person's identity. The assumption is that clients can develop alternative and more constructive stories once they have separated themselves from their problem-saturated story.

Multicultural applications. With the emphasis on multiple realities and the assumption that what is perceived to be true is the product of social construction, narrative therapy is a good fit with diverse worldviews. Narrative therapists operate on the premise that problems are identified within social, cultural, political, and relational contexts rather than existing within individuals. Clients do not need to change their essential selves; rather, they are challenged to change the stories they have about themselves in relation to the dominant culture.

Contributions. As narrative therapists listen to clients' stories, they pay attention to details that demonstrate clients' competence in taking a stand against an oppressive problem. Problems are not viewed as pathological manifestations but as ordinary difficulties and challenges of life. In the practice of narrative therapy, there is no recipe, no set agenda, and no formula to follow that will ensure a desired outcome. This therapeutic approach encourages practitioners to use creativity when working with clients.

Suggestions for further reading. For a further treatment of narrative therapy, see *Narrative Counseling in Schools: Powerful and Brief* (Winslade & Monk, 2007). See also Winslade and Del Corso (2019).

Feminist Therapy

Overview and basic assumptions. The basic premise of **feminist therapy** is that gender-role expectations profoundly influence our identity from birth onward. Feminist therapists have challenged the male-oriented assumptions regarding what constitutes a mentally healthy individual. Clients are encouraged to increase their awareness of how deeply gender-role socialization is ingrained in adult personality. A basic assumption of this approach is that an individual's problems cannot be understood by focusing solely on the individual's internal dynamics; rather, contextual factors surrounding diversity and the complexity of sexism must be considered.

The underlying philosophy of feminist theory is gender neutral, flexible, interactional, and life-span-oriented.

Key concepts. A key concept of feminist therapy is that societal gender-role messages influence how individuals view themselves and behave. Contemporary feminist therapy is based on the assumption that gender cannot be considered apart from other identity areas such as race, ethnicity, class, and sexual orientation. Problematic symptoms are viewed as coping or survival strategies rather than as evidence of pathology. Diagnosis of distress becomes secondary to identification and assessment of strengths, skills, and resources. Although individuals are not to blame for personal problems largely caused by dysfunctional social environments, they are responsible for working toward change.

Therapeutic goals. Feminist therapists assist clients in identifying the impact of socialization patterns so clients can critically evaluate and modify early messages pertaining to appropriate gender-role behavior. Feminist therapists believe gender is central to therapeutic practice and that understanding a client's problems requires adopting a sociocultural perspective. Therapy goals focus on six issues: equality, balancing independence and interdependence, self-nurturance, empowerment, social change, and valuing and affirming diversity. Both individual transformation and societal changes are crucial goals of therapy. At the individual level, therapists work to help women and men recognize, claim, and embrace their personal power. As a consciously political enterprise, another goal is social transformation.

Therapeutic relationship. The therapeutic relationship is based on empowerment, deliberately equalizing the power base between client and therapist. The therapist works to demystify therapy and to include the client as an active partner in the assessment and treatment process. Therapists teach clients to recognize how gender-role expectations influence how they define themselves and how they relate to others.

Techniques. In feminist therapy, techniques are drawn from psychodynamic approaches, cognitive behavior therapy, mindfulness-based approaches, and humanistic therapies. Techniques include the use of therapeutic contracts, homework, bibliotherapy, therapist self-disclosure, role playing, cognitive restructuring, reframing, relabeling, and assertiveness training. In addition, feminist procedures include gender-role analysis and intervention, power analysis and intervention, and social action.

Multicultural applications. Feminist therapy and multicultural perspectives have a great deal in common. The feminist perspective on power in relationships has application for understanding power inequities due to racial and cultural factors. Neither feminist therapy nor multicultural perspectives focus exclusively on individual change. Instead, both approaches emphasize direct action for social change as a part of the role of therapists. Many of the social action and political strategies that call attention to oppressed groups have equal relevance for women and for other marginalized groups. Both feminist therapists and multicultural therapists have worked to establish policies that lessen the opportunities for discrimination of all types—gender, race, culture, sexual orientation, ability, religion, and age.

Contributions. A key contribution of feminist therapy is the potential for integration of feminist therapy principles and concepts with other therapeutic systems. Therapists of any orientation can infuse feminist practices in their work if they conduct therapy with a positive, egalitarian attitude toward both women and men and are willing to confront patriarchal systems. Building community, providing authentic mutual empathic relationships, creating a sense of social awareness, and the emphasis on social change are all significant strengths of this approach.

Suggestions for further reading. For a useful presentation of feminist therapy, see *Feminist Therapy* (Brown, 2018). See also Remer (2013) and Corey (2021, chap. 12).

LO8 Family Systems Perspective

Family therapy involves a conceptual shift from individual dynamics to interaction within the system. A **family systems perspective** views the family as a functioning unit and as an entity unto itself that adds up to more than the sum of its members. By focusing on the internal dynamics of an individual without adequately considering interpersonal dynamics, only an incomplete picture of that individual is revealed. Family therapists subscribe to the basic notion that families are systems and that a treatment approach that comprehensively addresses the other family members as well as the "identified" client is required. Although a systems orientation does not preclude dealing with the dynamics within the individual, this approach broadens the traditional emphasis. It is not possible to accurately assess an individual's concerns without observing the interaction of the other family members as well as the broader context in the community and in society.

Family therapy is more than an approach to working with a family; it is a perspective that sheds light on the individual's and the family's development over time. It also provides a lens through which to view connections in the world. It takes into consideration the influence of an individual's neighborhood, community, church, work environment, school, and other systems. Indeed, the family systems perspective holds that significant change within an individual is not likely to be made or maintained unless the client's network of intimate relationships is taken into account.

Family Systems Therapy

Overview and basic assumptions. Family systems approaches rest on the assumption that individuals are best understood through assessing the interactions of the entire family. It is also grounded on the assumptions that a client's problematic behavior may (1) serve a function or purpose for the family; (2) be a function of the family's inability to operate productively, especially during developmental transitions; or (3) be a symptom of dysfunctional patterns handed down across generations. All these assumptions challenge traditional individual therapy frameworks for conceptualizing human problems and their formation.

One of the systemic principles is that symptoms are an expression of a dysfunction within the family system—not the individual—and dysfunctions are often passed across several generations. The family provides the context for understanding how individuals behave. Actions by any individual family member will influence all the other members, and their reactions will have a reciprocal effect on the individual.

Key concepts. Family therapy is a diverse field with respect to concepts, techniques, and approaches. The key concepts presented here address some of the themes that unite the many different systemic approaches.

Family therapy tends to be brief because families who seek professional help typically want resolution of some problematic symptom. In addition to being short-term, solution-focused, and action-oriented, family therapy tends to deal with present interactions. One way in which it differs from many individual therapies is its emphasis on how current family relationships contribute to the development and maintenance of symptoms.

Almost all of the family therapies are concerned with here-and-now interactions in the family system. By dealing with interactions in the here-and-now, patterns that have existed over time can be changed. The family therapy perspective emphasizes verbal and nonverbal communication. Family therapists have a keen interest in the process of family interaction and in teaching patterns of communication.

Therapeutic goals. Family or relationship therapy is aimed at helping the members change the patterns of relationships that are not working well and helping the family create new ways of interacting. The general goal is to bring about a change within a system, predicated on the assumption that if a system changes so will the individuals within the system. The specific goals are determined by the practitioner's specific orientation or by a collaborative process between the family and the therapist.

An integrative approach to the practice of family therapy must include guiding principles that help organize goals, interactions, observations, and ways to promote change. Some theories focus on perceptual and cognitive change, others deal mainly with changing feelings, and others emphasize behavioral change.

Therapeutic relationship. Family therapists function as models, teachers, and coaches. Although the skills of the therapist are crucial, the therapist's ability to establish rapport and create a working relationship with all family members is what counts. What most approaches have in common is their commitment to helping family members learn new and more effective ways of interacting.

For Bitter (2014), the relationship a practitioner creates with a family is far more important than the techniques he or she employs. Bitter identifies the following personal characteristics and orientations of effective family practitioners: presence; acceptance, interest, and caring; assertiveness and confidence; courage and risk-taking; openness to change; paying attention to goals and purposes of a family; working in patterns; appreciating the influence of diversity; being sincerely interested in the welfare of others; tending to the spirit of the family and its members; and involvement, engagement, and satisfaction in working with families. These personal characteristics influence the manner in which techniques are delivered.

Techniques. Diverse techniques are available to family therapists, but the intervention strategies they employ are best considered in conjunction with their own personal characteristics. It is imperative that therapists use skills and techniques that fit their personality and that are appropriate for the goals of therapy. Techniques are tools for achieving therapeutic goals, yet these intervention strategies do not make a family therapist.

Faced with the demands of clinical practice, practitioners need to be flexible in selecting intervention strategies that will meet specific therapeutic objectives and contribute to specific outcomes. The majority of family therapists integrate concepts and techniques from various theoretical orientations to produce their own blend of methods based on their training, personality, and the population of families they serve. Family therapy is moving toward integration. Many therapy procedures can be borrowed from various models, depending on what is likely to work best with a given family. The central consideration is what is in the best interests of the family.

Today family therapists explore both the individual culture of the family and the larger culture to which the family belongs. They look for ways in which culture can inform their work with a family. Therapeutic interventions are no longer applied universally, regardless of the culture involved, but rather are designed to complement the family system within the larger community of which it is a part.

Multicultural applications. Many cultures value interdependence over independence, and this is a key strength of the family systems approach. When working with clients who especially value grandparents, parents, and aunts and uncles in some form of cooperative family unit, it is easy to see that family approaches have a distinct advantage over individual therapy. By understanding and appreciating the diversity of family systems, the therapist can contextualize family experiences in relation to the larger culture of which they are now a part.

Contributions. One of the key contributions of the family systems approach is that neither the individual nor the family is blamed for a particular dysfunction. Rather than blaming either the "identified patient" or a family, the entire family has an opportunity to examine the multiple perspectives and interaction patterns that characterize the unit and to participate in finding solutions. The family is empowered through the process of identifying and exploring internal, developmental, and purposeful interaction patterns. At the same time, a systems perspective recognizes that individuals and families are affected by external forces and systems. If change is to occur in families or within individuals, therapists must be aware of as many systems of influence as possible.

Suggestions for further reading. For further discussion of family systems therapy, see *Theory and Practice of Family Therapy and Counseling* (Bitter, 2014) and Corey (2021, chap. 14).

LO9 An Integrative Approach to the Helping Process

An **integrative model** refers to a perspective based on concepts and techniques drawn from various theoretical approaches. One reason for the current trend toward an integrative approach to the helping process is the recognition that no single theory is comprehensive enough to account for the complexities of human behavior when the full range of client types and their specific problems are taken into consideration. Most practitioners now are open to an integrative perspective drawn from several theories and a diverse range of techniques (Norcross & Beutler, 2019; Norcross & Goldfried, 2019). Each theory has its unique contributions and its own domain of expertise. By acknowledging the strengths and weaknesses of particular theories, practitioners have some basis to begin developing a counseling model that fits them. Norcross and Beutler (2019) contend that "psychotherapy should be flexibly tailored to the unique needs and contexts of the individual client, not universally applied as one size fits all" (p. 531).

We encourage you to remain open to the value inherent in each of the theories of counseling. All the theories described in this chapter have some unique contributions as well as some limitations. Study all the contemporary theories to determine which concepts and techniques you can incorporate into your approach to practice. You will need to have a basic knowledge of various theoretical systems and counseling techniques to work effectively with diverse client populations in various settings. Functioning exclusively within the parameters of one theory may not provide you with the therapeutic flexibility that you need to deal creatively with the complexities associated with diverse client populations.

Each theory represents a different vantage point from which to look at human behavior, but no one theory has the total truth. Because there is no "correct" theoretical approach, it is well for you to search for an approach that fits who you are and to think in terms of working toward an integrated approach that addresses thinking, feeling, and behaving. To develop an integrative approach you need to be thoroughly grounded in a number of theories, be open to the idea that these theories can be unified in some ways, and be willing to continually test your hypotheses to determine how well they are working.

Creating an integrative approach to practice is a complex task. You cannot simply pick techniques from theories in a haphazard manner. If you merely pick and choose without a rationale, it is likely that your selections will reflect your biases and preconceived ideas. The kind of integration we are suggesting is based on common factors across therapeutic schools. However, blending theoretical constructs is more demanding than utilizing diverse techniques from different schools. If you attempt to blend theoretical constructs from different orientations in your own integrative model, these concepts must be compatible. At its best, integration is a creative synthesis of the unique contributions of diverse approaches, dynamically integrating concepts and techniques that fit the uniqueness of your personality and style.

If you are currently a counselor-in-training, it is unrealistic to expect that you will already have an integrated and well-defined theoretical model. An integrative perspective is the product of a great deal of reading, study, clinical practice, research, and theorizing. With time and reflective study, the goal is to develop a consistent conceptual framework that you can use as a basis for selecting from the multiple techniques to which you will eventually be exposed.

Both theory and research need to be considered in developing your way of working with clients. Today, there is an increasing demand in most agencies for practitioners to use techniques that are supported by research. The therapeutic relationship, the therapist's personality and therapeutic style, the client, and environmental factors are all vital contributors to the success of treatment. The therapy relationship acts in concert with the techniques a practitioner uses, client characteristics, and other therapist qualities in determining effectiveness. An understanding of effective psychotherapy considers all of these factors and how they work together to produce benefit to the client. When all of these factors are considered, evidence-based practice is more meaningful (Norcross & Lambert, 2019).

If your clients do not respond to a particular approach, adjust the therapy accordingly. Even with the same client, you will likely need to adapt your methods at different phases of therapy. Therapists need to be competent in providing multiple treatment approaches to accommodate variability in clients' characteristics, attitudes, values, and preferences (Wampold, 2010). Regardless of your theoretical approach, you must decide *what* techniques and procedures to utilize, *when* to use them, and with *which* clients. For counseling to be effective, techniques and procedures must be used in a manner that is consistent with clients' values, worldview, life experiences, and cultural background. Some techniques may be contraindicated because of clients' socialization. Clients' responsiveness (or lack of it) to certain techniques is a critical barometer in judging the effectiveness of these methods.

The therapist as a person and the quality of the therapeutic relationship are of primary importance with respect to therapy outcomes. The therapy relationship accounts for client improvement as much as the particular treatment method. Researchers have repeatedly demonstrated the healing impact of the personal dimensions in psychotherapy (Norcross & Lambert, 2019; Wampold & Imel, 2015).

Be open to respecting practices from across the psychotherapy spectrum, and avoid using techniques in a rigid or "cookbook" way. Techniques and methods are merely tools to assist you in effectively reaching your clients. Tailoring the therapy relationship to specific client characteristics enhances the effectiveness of the therapy process (Norcross & Lambert, 2019). Personalize your techniques so they fit your therapeutic style and the needs of your clients, and be open to feedback from your clients about how well your techniques are working for them.

An integrative approach values all theories that work effectively and places emphasis on the client's experiences to determine which methods to employ (Eubanks, Goldfried, & Norcross, 2019). Developing your personalized approach that guides your practice is a lifelong endeavor that you will refine with experience. The challenge is to think and practice in an integrative manner—but to do so critically.

Using Mindfulness and Acceptance in an Integrative Approach

The third wave therapeutic approaches share common views regarding assisting clients in choosing values they want to live by, establishing specific goals, and taking steps to achieve their goals. Both the behavior therapies and the mindfulness and acceptance therapies are grounded on behavioral concepts and key therapeutic strategies for accomplishing their purposes, and these techniques are based on empirical data.

The goals of mindfulness-based interventions can be integrated into most approaches to therapy. These goals include improved concentration, increased focus, a greater sense of executive control, awareness of valued choices, reduction of negative thoughts and emotions, and general emotional resilience (Pantaleno & Sisti, 2018). These newer approaches emphasize experiential learning, in-session practice, learning from feedback, completing between-sessions assignments, and applying what is learned in the program to challenging situations encountered outside of the sessions. These third wave approaches bridge the gap between the humanistic and relationship-oriented therapies and traditional cognitive behavior models.

LO10 The Future of Psychotherapy Integration

A Delphi poll examining trends in the psychotherapy field indicates that the top six therapeutic approaches predicted to increase over the next decade include mindfulness therapies, cognitive behavior therapies, integrative psychotherapy, multicultural therapies, motivational interviewing, and dialectical behavior therapy (Prochaska & Norcross, 2018). Approaches most likely to decrease in popularity are classical psychoanalysis, Jungian therapy, Adlerian therapy, and transactional analysis. The humanistic therapies (person-centered, existential, and Gestalt therapy) were also expected to decrease in popularity. With respect to therapy formats, psychoeducational groups, couples therapy, and group therapy are predicted to continue their popularity. Short-term therapies will increase in usage, and longer-term therapies are on their way out.

In the past 40 years, psychotherapy integration has grown into a well-established movement in the mental health field. Integration is the modal theoretical orientation for practitioners in most countries and will become more international and interdisciplinary going forward (Eubanks, Goldfried, & Norcross, 2019). There is a growing recognition that counseling is most effective when contributions from various approaches are integrated. Clinical practice should be based on the best available research integrated with a practitioner's expertise and applied within the context of the needs of the client.

Psychotherapy integration has been based on theoretical and clinical foundations to date, but evidence-based practice (EBP) will become the organizing force for integration in the future and is expected to guide all forms of health care (Norcross & Goldfried, 2019; Norcross, Hogan, Koocher, & Maggio, 2017). Prochaska and Norcross (2018) state that "EBP's will exert a profound impact on mental health practice, training, and policy" (p. 446). Integrative therapies offer the evidence and responsiveness to meet the needs of individual clients in their unique contexts and "are intellectually vibrant, clinically popular, and demonstrably effective" (Norcross, Goldfried, & Arigo, 2016, p. 124).

Of necessity, this discussion of the various theoretical orientations has been brief. A comprehensive look at various perspectives on psychotherapy integration is presented in the *Handbook of Psychotherapy Integration* (Norcross & Goldfried, 2019). The contributors in this edited volume will give you a sense of the direction being taken by the psychotherapy integration movement. For a practical approach to thinking and practicing from an integrative perspective, see *The Art of Integrative Counseling* (Corey, 2019). The following resources include a theory chapter on integration of therapies: Corey (2021, chap. 15); Norcross, Goldfried, and Arigo (2016); Prochaska and Norcross (2018, chaps. 17 & 18); and Wedding and Corsini (2019, chap. 14).

By Way of Review

- A theoretical orientation that integrates thinking, feeling, and behaving provides the basis for developing interventions that can be used flexibly with clients at various stages of the helping process.
- A theory can be very practical in the sense that it can guide interventions.
- Because there is no one "right" theoretical approach, you would do well to consider adopting an approach that is congruent with your personality and values.
- Before you can integrate the theories, you first must study the various theories in depth. It is not possible to integrate that which you do not know.
- Psychodynamic theories provide a foundation upon which many of the contemporary theories have been designed.
- Experiential therapies are based on the therapist developing a quality relationship with clients. In many respects, the relationship-oriented therapies are grounded on the assumption that clients are the experts on their own lives. The therapist functions as a facilitator to help clients tap into their internal resources.
- Cognitive behavioral therapies emphasize how thinking influences emotions and behavior. These approaches stress the value of taking action if change is desired.
- Contemporary developments in the cognitive behavioral tradition fall under the umbrella of third wave approaches. The mindfulness-based approaches—dialectical behavior therapy, mindfulness-based stress reduction, mindfulness-based cognitive therapy, and acceptance and commitment therapy—have all been subjected to empirical scrutiny.
- The postmodern approaches are based on the optimistic assumption that people are healthy, competent, resourceful, and possess the ability to construct solutions and alternative stories that can enhance their lives. Individuals, not therapists, are seen as the experts on their lives.
- An assumption of the systems approach is that change in any one part of the system affects all parts of that system.
- A family systems perspective provides a lens through which to view connections in the world by taking into consideration the influence of an individual's family, neighborhood, community, church, school, and work environment.
- No single theory is comprehensive enough to account for the complexities of human behavior when the full range of client types and their specific problems are taken into consideration. Most counselors are leaning toward integration of several theories today.

- Evidence-based practice is expected to be part of all forms of health care in the coming years.
- Study many of the contemporary theories to determine which concepts and techniques you can incorporate into your approach to practice. A basic knowledge of various theoretical systems and counseling techniques is required to work effectively with diverse client populations in various settings.

What Will You Do Now?

1. In small groups explore how you might answer this question if it were posed to you in a job interview: "What is your theoretical orientation, and how do you think this will influence the way you work with diverse client populations?"
2. Review the different theories described and reflect on what concepts of the various theories you could apply to your personal life. How can you use some of these approaches to better understand yourself?
3. As a small group exercise, discuss some the following aspects of the various theories presented:
   - The role of the helper
   - Key concepts you would most want to borrow from each theory
   - Techniques that you find useful from each theory
   - View of the client–counselor relationship
   - Major contributions of each theory
4. In small groups, take some time to discuss what you need to know and specific skills you need to have to be able to work effectively with families. If you were asked by your supervisor in your fieldwork placement to join him or her in conducting family sessions in the agency, what would be your response?

CHAPTER 8

Ethical and Legal Issues Facing Helpers

Learning Objectives

1. Describe what is involved in ethical decision making.
2. Explain the difference between law and ethics.
3. Identify the purposes that codes of ethics serve.
4. Explain how to address unethical behavior by colleagues.
5. Recognize the steps in working through an ethical dilemma.
6. Explain what is involved in the informed consent process.
7. Discuss how confidentiality and privacy form the foundation for a therapeutic relationship.
8. Explain the legal and the ethical aspects of confidentiality in couples and family therapy.
9. Describe the role and limitations of confidentiality in groups.
10. Discuss how confidentiality and privacy apply to technology.
11. Explain the difference between progress notes and process notes.
12. Identify the key ethical issues involved in managed care.
13. List risk management practices that can prevent ethical and legal problems.

Focus Questions

1. What ethical issues most concern you at this stage in your education? Why?
2. When you are faced with an ethical dilemma, what ideas do you have about how you would go about resolving the dilemma?
3. What are the main purposes of the codes of ethics for helping professionals? How can you use the codes of ethics to guide your ethical decision making?
4. There are limits to confidentiality in any helping relationship. If you were a client in therapy, what would you want to know about the purposes and limitations of confidentiality?
5. What concerns do you see in the use of technology in counseling, especially with respect to a client's privacy?
6. What do you consider to be the most important components of informed consent? If you were a client in therapy, what information would you want about the process?

7. What are some of your ideas regarding how you could best go about obtaining informed consent from your clients?
8. In keeping records on your clients, what do you think is most important to document?
9. Do you have concerns about staying out of trouble with a licensure board? What steps can you take to decrease the chances of being involved in a malpractice suit?
10. What ethical concerns might you have that are associated with distance counseling, technology, and social media?

Aim of the Chapter

Regardless of the specific helping profession you decide on, you will face ethical dilemmas. Part of becoming a competent practitioner involves being able to apply the ethics code of your professional organization to practical situations in your work. In this chapter, we introduce you to an array of ethical and legal concerns you may encounter, including informed consent, confidentiality and privacy, documentation and keeping records, and malpractice and risk management. Establishing appropriate boundaries is also a key ethical issue, and it is the subject of Chapter 9. We hope the material presented here will help you prepare to deal effectively with ethical dilemmas whenever they arise in your work with clients.

There has been an increased interest in ethics in the mental health professions during the past few decades. Articles pertaining to ethical and legal issues in the helping field are common in professional journals, and many books have been written about professional ethics. Most undergraduate and graduate programs include a discussion of these topics in various courses, with separate courses in ethical and legal issues now required in most graduate programs.

Inventory of Ethical Issues

What are some of your major concerns about ethical practice? Perhaps at this point you have not even raised this question. For each statement in this inventory, indicate the response that most closely identifies your beliefs and attitudes. Use the following code:

5 = I *strongly agree* with this statement.
4 = I *agree* with this statement.
3 = I am *undecided* about this statement.
2 = I *disagree* with this statement.
1 = I *strongly disagree* with this statement.

____ 1. When an ethical concern arises, the best way to address it is to refer to the code of ethics.

____ 2. If I were faced with an ethical dilemma in one of my cases, I would take the initiative to seek guidance from one of my professors or supervisors.

____ 3. It would be hard for me to refer a client to another professional, even if I felt this was in the client's best interest.

____ 4. I do not have enough time to keep detailed clinical records on my clients and document everything that goes on in the helping process.

____ 5. It would be difficult for me to decide when I had to break confidentiality.

____ 6. If I were uncertain about keeping a client's confidence, I would want to discuss this with my client.

____ 7. It is my responsibility to resolve any ethical dilemmas that arise, and I would not involve my client in this decision-making process.

____ 8. I am uncertain about how to resolve ethical dilemmas.

____ 9. I lack confidence in my ability to discuss informed consent with clients.

____ 10. I am not at all certain that I know what to do if a client poses a danger to self or to others.

____ 11. I am uncomfortable with the prospect of using technology in my work as a helper.

____ 12. I am uncertain what actions to take in situations where there is a duty to warn and protect others.

____ 13. What constitutes ethical practice is very much a concern of mine.

____ 14. I know the steps I am likely to take if I become aware of unethical behavior on the part of my colleagues.

____ 15. I am concerned about the possibility of becoming involved in a malpractice suit as a result of something I do or don't do as a helper.

Once you have finished this inventory, spend a few minutes reflecting on the specific issues of most concern to you. This reflection can help you read the chapter more actively and formulate ethical questions. Identify a few of the areas in which you are uncertain about your position, and discuss these ambiguities in class.

LO1 Ethical Decision Making

Ethical practice involves far more than merely knowing and following a professional code of ethics. In dealing with ethical dilemmas, you will rarely find clear-cut answers. Most of the problems are complex and defy simple solutions. Making ethical decisions involves acquiring a tolerance for dealing with gray areas and for coping with ambiguity. Although knowing the ethical standards of your profession is essential, this knowledge alone is not sufficient. Ethics codes are not dogmatic; however, they do provide guidance in assisting you in making the best possible decisions for the benefit of your clients and yourself. Regulations and procedures vary among agencies. It is essential to understand the specific policies and practices of the agency or institution where you work as well as know the relevant laws and regulations in your state.

In our teaching we find that students often begin an ethics course with the expectation that they will get definitive answers to some of the questions raised in their fieldwork. They typically do not think they will have to engage in personal and professional self-exploration to find the best course of action. We tell our students that the purpose of an ethics course is to assist them in developing the resources to deal intelligently with ethical dilemmas they are likely to encounter.

Consider the example of Gerlinde, who became aware of unethical practices in a community agency where she was an intern. She and other interns were expected to take on some difficult clients. She realized that doing so would mean that she was clearly practicing beyond the boundaries of her competence. To make the situation worse, supervision at the agency was not always available. Her superior was overextended and not able to provide regular supervision. In her fieldwork seminar on campus, she learned that supervisors are ethically and legally responsible for what interns do. Gerlinde had some trouble deciding what to do. She did not want to change placements in the middle of the semester, yet she was struggling with the appropriateness of confronting her supervisor about the situation. Unclear about how to proceed, she made an appointment with her fieldwork professor on campus to discuss her concerns.

In consultation with her professor, Gerlinde explored a number of alternatives. She might approach her agency supervisor herself and be more assertive in getting an appointment. Another option could be a meeting with her agency supervisor and her professor to explore the situation. It might be decided that this particular agency was inappropriate for students. What was important was that Gerlinde knew she could get help in dealing with her problem. Sometimes students who are in similar predicaments arrive too quickly at the conclusion that they will merely tolerate circumstances as they are rather than deal with an uncomfortable situation.

At the beginning of the course, Gerlinde thought that clear answers were available for the variety of situations that would surface. By the end of the semester, she was learning to appreciate that ethics codes are not laws; they are standards that provide guidance in dealing with a range of ethical dilemmas. She had also learned the value of initiating the consultation process in ethical decision making.

Another example involves interpreting the ethical standard that the client's welfare should be the primary consideration in the therapeutic relationship. Consider the case of a client who is talking about her struggles in an alcoholic family. As the therapist listens, he is reminded painfully of the alcohol addiction of his own parents. He wonders whether he should tell this to his client. Why would he want to make this disclosure? Will his disclosure meet his own needs or the needs of the client? How will he know whether the disclosure will help or hinder the client?

Ethical issues in the helping field are often complex and multifaceted, and they defy simplistic solutions. There are gray areas that require decision-making skills. Thinking about ethical issues and learning to make wise decisions is an ongoing process that requires an open mind.

A key question is this: "What is the ethical thing to do?" Some practitioners focus almost exclusively on laws, regulations, and codes of ethics, but this extremely rule-bound approach can have a negative influence on the quality of the professional relationship. A rule-bound approach to ethics is limited in providing meaningful help to practitioners striving to practice at the highest level of ethical functioning. Another mistake helpers may make is to disproportionately pay attention to their personal values and underplay any consideration of laws, rules, regulations, and ethical standards.

LO2 Law and Ethics

Laws and ethics codes provide guidelines for acceptable professional practice, yet neither offers clear-cut answers to most situational problems. **Law** defines the minimum standards society will tolerate; these standards are enforced by government agencies. All of the codes of ethics state that practitioners must act in accordance with relevant federal and state statutes and government regulations. It is critical that practitioners be able to identify legal problems as they arise in their work. Sometimes practitioners are not sure that they have a legal problem; others may not know what to do once a legal issue has been identified (Remley & Herlihy, 2020). When confronted with a legal issue, consult a lawyer to determine which course of action to take. Many professional associations have attorneys who are familiar with both legal and clinical issues, and members of these associations can be called upon for consultations. Many of the situations helpers encounter that involve ethical and professional judgment will also have legal implications.

Unlike law, **ethics** represents aspirational goals, or the maximum or ideal standards set by the profession. Ethical standards are enforced largely by professional associations. Codes of ethics are conceptually broad in nature and generally are subject to interpretation by practitioners. Ethical standards serve as a form of protection for the client, but they also help counselors ensure their own self-care. For example, counselors sometimes struggle with setting limits around being helpful to others. Out of a personal need to ease the pain and suffering of clients who are overwhelmed by their life circumstances coupled with the need to be needed, some clinicians may be inclined to overstep boundaries by fostering client dependence and taking too much responsibility for clients' progress. Having clear guidelines in place can help both counselors and clients to establish appropriate and healthy boundaries. By doing too much in the name of helping, a counselor may unintentionally convey the message to clients that they would not be making progress if it were not for the efforts of the helper. Ethical standards exist in part to remind counselors that their job is to empower clients to learn to take charge of their own lives and to expand their capacity to grow and develop.

Knowledge of the ethics codes and legal guidelines applicable to a helper's practice is essential for practicing ethically and for minimizing legal liability. As a helper, not only must you follow the ethics codes of your profession but you must also know your state's laws and your legal responsibilities. However, merely becoming familiar with local and state laws that govern your profession is not enough to enable you to make sound decisions. Your professional judgment will play a key role in resolving cases, from both an ethical and a legal perspective.

You may encounter a situation in which there is a conflict between the law and ethical practice. In such cases, fulfilling both ethical and legal obligations can demand a great deal of reflection on your part as well as consultation with other professionals. For example, at times ethical standards may conflict with legal standards and requirements for working with minors. Counselors may want to honor a minor's ethical right to confidentiality, yet they may also encounter a parent's demand for information that a particular state law allows

(Wheeler & Bertram, 2019). Some areas that may be governed by law include confidentiality, parental consent, informed consent, protection of client welfare, and civil rights of institutionalized people. Because most helpers do not possess detailed legal knowledge, it is a good idea for helpers to obtain legal consultation about the procedures they use in their practice. Awareness of legal rights and responsibilities as they pertain to helping relationships protects clients and shields practitioners from needless lawsuits arising from negligence or ignorance.

Laws and ethics codes, by their very nature, tend to be reactive, emerging from what has occurred rather than anticipating what may occur. It is not wise to limit your behavior to merely obeying statutes and following ethical standards. Some professionals think mainly about practicing in ways that will protect them from a malpractice suit by their clients. If this legal perspective assumes primacy, helpers may limit their work with clients out of fear of a possible lawsuit and fail to provide effective services. Although it is essential to do what you can to avoid a malpractice action, do not let this overshadow your work as an ethical practitioner. Do not let your behavior be determined mainly by *fear-based ethics.* Instead, do your best to develop an attitude of *concern-based ethics* early in your training program, and strive for the highest level of ethical care for those with whom you work (Corey, Corey, & Corey, 2019).

Understanding the difference between mandatory ethics and aspirational ethics is key to striving for the highest level of ethical practice. **Mandatory ethics** describes a level of ethical functioning wherein counselors act in compliance with minimal standards, acknowledging the basic rules of practice. **Aspirational ethics** goes beyond these minimal standards of practice and entails an understanding of the spirit behind the code and the principles on which the code rests. Practitioners who comply with mandatory ethics are generally safe from legal action in courts of law or professional censure by state licensure boards. Those who practice aspirational ethics go further and reflect on the effects their interventions may have on the welfare of their clients. An example of aspirational ethics is providing services for no fees (pro bono) for those in the community who cannot afford needed services. It is important that you acquire an aspirational approach to your practice at the beginning of your professional program. Keep in mind that the basic purpose of practicing ethically is to advance the welfare of your clients.

LO3 Professional Codes and Ethical Decision Making

Various professional organizations have established codes of ethics that provide broad guidelines for professional helpers. These codes are not static; they are revised as new concerns arise. Some of the professional mental health organizations that have formulated codes of ethics are the National Association of Social Workers (NASW, 2017), the American Psychological Association (APA, 2017a), the American Counseling Association (ACA, 2014), the American Mental Health Counselors Association (AMHCA, 2015), the American School Counselor Association (ASCA, 2016), the American Association for Marriage and Family Therapy (AAMFT, 2015), and the National Organization for Human Services (NOHS, 2015). Herlihy and Corey (2015a) identify several purposes that codes of ethics serve:

- Codes of ethics educate helpers about sound ethical practice. The application of these codes to particular situations demands a keen ethical sensitivity.
- Codes of ethics provide a mechanism for professional accountability. The ultimate purpose of a code of ethics is to protect the public.
- Codes of ethics serve as catalysts for improving practice. Codes provide the foundation for critically examining both the letter and the spirit of ethical principles.

Ethics codes are necessary, but not sufficient, for the exercise of ethical responsibility. Although you have or will become familiar with the ethics codes of your specialization, you must still develop a personal ethical stance that will govern your practice. You have the ongoing task of examining your clinical practices to determine whether you are acting as ethically as you might. Ethics codes do not convey ultimate truth, nor do they make decisions for you.

In making ethical decisions, it will be necessary for you to grapple with the gray areas, raise questions, discuss your ethical concerns with colleagues, and monitor your own behavior. Reflection, collaboration, and consultation can guide your inquiry, but ultimately you must have the courage to make a decision without being certain of the outcome. When dealing with the uniqueness of each client, it is up to you to apply ethics codes to specific situations and to engage in a process of ethical decision making in determining the best course of action.

If you conscientiously practice in accordance with accepted ethics codes, you have some measure of protection in case of litigation. Documenting your actions and ethical decision-making process is an important safeguard. Compliance with or violation of ethics codes of conduct may be admissible as evidence in some legal proceedings. In a lawsuit, your conduct would probably be judged in comparison with that of other professionals with similar qualifications and duties.

The NASW *Code of Ethics* (NASW, 2017) states that an ethics code cannot guarantee ethical behavior, nor can it resolve all ethical issues or disputes, nor can it capture the complexity involved in making responsible choices within a moral community. Instead, the code identifies values, ethical principles, and ethical standards to which professionals should aspire and by which their actions can be judged. The code reinforces the idea that ethical decision making is a process. The American Psychological Association's *Code of Ethics* (APA, 2017a) makes it clear that the code neither provides all the answers nor specifically addresses every dilemma that may confront a practitioner.

The practical application of ethics codes is often difficult. The issues you will encounter as a helper will require not only an understanding of the codes for your profession but also an educated interpretation of these codes in real-life situations.

Codes of Ethics of the Various Professional Organizations

We suggest that you devote some time to reviewing the codes of ethics of two or more of the professional organizations. Examine the assets and limitations of these codes and notice similarities between them. What aspects of the codes do you find most useful? If your practice goes against a specific ethics code, be aware that you must have a rationale for your course of action. Realize also that there are consequences for violating the ethics code of your profession.

You can secure a copy of the codes of ethics of the different professional organizations by going to their websites:

1. **American Counseling Association (ACA):** *ACA Code of Ethics*, ©2014 Visit www.counseling.org/ for more information on this organization.
2. **National Board for Certified Counselors (NBCC):** *Code of Ethics*, ©2016 Visit www.nbcc.org/ for more information on this organization.
3. **Commission on Rehabilitation Counselor Certification (CRCC):** *Code of Professional Ethics for Rehabilitation Counselors*, ©2017 Visit www.crccertification.com/ for more information on this organization.
4. **Association for Addiction Professionals (NAADAC):** *Code of Ethics*, ©2016 Visit www.naadac.org/ for more information on this organization.
5. **Canadian Counselling and Psychotherapy Association (CCPA):** *Code of Ethics*, ©2007 Visit http://www.ccpa-accp.ca/ for more information on this organization.
6. **American School Counselor Association (ASCA):** *Ethical Standards for School Counselors*, ©2016 Visit www.schoolcounselor.org/ for more information on this organization.
7. **American Psychological Association (APA):** *Ethical Principles of Psychologists and Code of Conduct*, ©2017 Visit www.apa.org/ for more information on this organization.
8. **American Psychiatric Association (APA):** *The Principles of Medical Ethics With Annotations Especially Applicable to Psychiatry*, ©2013 Visit www.psych.org/ for more information on this organization.
9. **American Group Psychotherapy Association (AGPA):** *AGPA and IBCGP Guidelines for Ethics*, ©2002 Visit www.groupsinc.org/ for more information on this organization.
10. **American Mental Health Counselors Association (AMHCA):** *Code of Ethics*, ©2015 Visit www.amhca.org/ for more information on this organization.
11. **American Association for Marriage and Family Therapy (AAMFT):** *Code of Ethics*, ©2015 Visit www.aamft.org/ for more information on this organization.
12. **International Association of Marriage and Family Counselors (IAMFC):** *IAMFC Code of Ethics*, ©2017 Visit www.iamfc.org/ for more information on this organization.
13. **Association for Specialists in Group Work (ASGW):** *Best Practice Guidelines*, ©2008 Visit www.asgw.org/ for more information on this organization.
14. **National Association of Social Workers (NASW):** *Code of Ethics*, ©2017 Visit www.socialworkers.org/ for more information on this organization.
15. **National Organization for Human Services (NOHS):** *Ethical Standards of Human Service Professionals*, ©2015 Visit www.nationalhumanservices.org/ for more information on this organization.
16. **American Music Therapy Association (AMTA):** *Code of Ethics*, ©2015 Visit www.musictherapy.org/ for more information on this organization.

17. **British Association for Counselling and Psychotherapy (BACP):** *Ethical Framework for Good Practice in Counselling and Psychotherapy,* ©2013 Visit www.bacp.co.uk for more information on this organization.

Recognizing Unethical Behavior in Yourself

It is easier to see the shortcomings of others and to judge their behavior than to develop an attitude of honest self-examination. You can control your own professional behavior far more easily than you can that of your colleagues, so the proper focus is to look honestly at what you are doing. Helpers have a tendency to think in terms of gross ethical violations, such as sexual misconduct, but overlook more subtle ways of being unethical. Consider for a moment these two scenarios, and ask yourself the degree to which you could picture yourself in each situation:

- You tell your clients that they can call (or text) you if they have a concern, and you give them your home phone number. One of your clients texts you frequently, often late at night. He tells you how appreciative he is of your offer that he can text you. Might you be flattered by being needed? Could you see yourself as fostering client dependency out of your need to be needed?
- A client who is in private therapy with you is ambivalent about continuing counseling sessions. She wonders whether it is time to terminate. Things are rather tight financially for you right now, and several other clients have recently terminated. Would you be inclined to support her decision? Might you be inclined to encourage her to continue, partly for financial reasons?

LO4 Unethical Behavior by Colleagues

You may occasionally encounter colleagues who appear to be behaving in unethical and unprofessional ways. Professional codes of conduct generally state that in such cases the most prudent action is to approach the colleague and share your concerns directly in an attempt to rectify the situation. If this step fails, you are then expected to make use of procedures established by your professional organization, such as reporting the colleague. In cases of egregious offenses, such as sexual exploitation of clients or general incompetence, informal measures are not enough. Depending on the nature of the complaint and the outcome of the discussion, reporting a colleague to a professional board is one of several options open to you.

Although most codes of ethics place the responsibility for addressing problems of competence or unethical behavior of colleagues on the members of their profession, Johnson, Barnett, Elman, Forrest, and Kaslow (2012) state that mental health professionals are reluctant to address these problems. Professionals admit they might not directly approach a colleague they believe is functioning below thresholds for competence or behaving unethically, even though they have an ethical duty to address the situation.

Koocher and Keith-Spiegel (2016) discuss the role of informal peer monitoring as a way to assume responsibility for watching out for each other. When ethically questionable acts are identified, informal peer monitoring provides an opportunity for corrective interventions. Actions can be taken directly by confronting a colleague or indirectly by advising clients on how to proceed when they have concerns about another professional's actions. Maintaining open communication in a supervision or consultation group where colleagues periodically check with one another for feedback is a proactive method of engaging in informal peer monitoring. This method fosters a supportive and respectful environment that promotes professionalism while assisting helpers to avoid the slippery slope of unethical behaviors. It is important to remember that the vast majority of people entering the helping professions do not do so with the intent of committing unethical or illegal acts.

Reflect for a few minutes on being in each of the following situations. What would you do in each case?

- A colleague frequently talks about his clients in inappropriate ways in places where others are able to hear him. The colleague says that joking about his clients is his way of "letting off steam" and preventing him from taking life too seriously.
- A couple of female clients have told you that they were sexually seduced by another counselor at the agency where you work. In their counseling sessions with you, they are dealing with their anger over having been taken advantage of by this counselor. What are the legal and ethical ramifications of this situation for you?
- A colleague has several times initiated social contacts with her clients. She believes this practice is acceptable because she sees her clients as consenting adults. Furthermore, she contends that time spent socializing with these clients gives her insights into issues with which she can productively work in the therapy sessions.
- You see that one of your colleagues is practicing beyond what appears to be the scope of his competence and training. This person is unwilling to seek additional training and is not receiving adequate supervision. He maintains that the best way to learn to work with unfamiliar problems that clients present is simply to learn by doing.

The various ethics codes generally address the matter of how to respond to unethical behavior of colleagues. For example, the Commission on Rehabilitation Counselor Certification (CRCC, 2017) provides this standard:

> When rehabilitation counselors have reason to believe that another rehabilitation counselor is violating or has violated an ethical standard, they attempt to resolve the issue informally with the other rehabilitation counselor if feasible and provided such action does not violate confidentiality rights that may be involved. (L.2.c.)

Certainly, dealing with the unethical behavior of colleagues demands a measure of courage. If these people are in a position of power, you are obviously vulnerable. Even in the case of peers, such confrontations usually are difficult and require honesty and a willingness to deliver a difficult message. Here is one way to approach a colleague about the possibility of practicing beyond her competence level:

> Helen, I have a concern that I wish to discuss with you, and I hope you can hear me nondefensively. I have the utmost respect for you, and I value our relationship. I am concerned about you taking on the new client with anorexia.

I know you like a challenge. However, from what you have shared in the past, neither you nor your supervisor has had training with eating disorders. This is an area that requires special training because of the complexities of working with this disorder and the potential of anorexia being life-threatening. I hope you reflect on the effects of practicing beyond the scope of your competence. What are your thoughts and reactions to what I have said?

If you were the recipient of this feedback about your competence in dealing with a client's problem, how would you respond? Would it depend on the relationship you had with this colleague? Would you be inclined to change your course of action and refer the client because of your lack of training in this area?

LO5 An Ethical Decision-Making Model

The American Counseling Association's (2014) *Code of Ethics* states that when counselors encounter an ethical dilemma they are expected to carefully consider an ethical decision-making process. Various ethical decision-making models can guide you in working through ethical dilemmas, and it is a good idea to understand at least one model that you can apply in thinking about ethical practice. Having a systematic way of examining difficult ethical dilemmas increases your chances of making sound ethical decisions. We cannot overemphasize the importance of seeking consultation when deciding on the best course of action. It is good to consult with more than one colleague or supervisor; doing so can help you see various dimensions of a problem. Responsible and ethical practice requires you to do the following:

- Base your actions on informed, sound, and responsible judgment.
- Consult with colleagues or seek supervision.
- Keep your knowledge and skills current.
- Engage in a continual process of self-examination.

As much as possible, and when appropriate, include your client in the ethical decision-making process. Make ethical decisions *with* clients, not simply *for* them. Respecting the autonomy of your clients implies that you do not decide for them, nor do you foster dependent attitudes and behaviors.

The ethical decision-making model we present here includes clients as collaborators whenever possible. Because you are making decisions about what is best for clients' welfare, explain the nature of the ethical dilemma that pertains to them. From a feminist therapy perspective, ethical decision making calls for involving the client at every stage of the therapeutic process, which is based on the feminist principle that power should be equalized in the therapeutic relationship (Brown, 2018).

The procedural steps we describe should not be thought of as a simplified and linear way to reach a resolution on ethical matters. It has been our experience that the application of these steps generally stimulates self-reflection and encourages discussion. Following these systematic steps will help you think through ethical problems.

1. *Identify the problem or dilemma.* Gather as much information as you can to clarify the situation you are facing. You might ask yourself these questions: Is this an ethical, legal, professional, or clinical problem? Is it a combination of more than one of these? If there are legal dimensions to the problem, seek

legal consultation. Remember that many ethical dilemmas are complex; examine the problem from various perspectives and avoid looking for a one-dimensional solution. Ethical dilemmas often do not have "right" or "wrong" answers, so you will be challenged to deal with ambiguity. It may be helpful to seek consultation to determine whether there actually is an ethical concern—or to identify the exact nature of the problem. Including your client begins at this initial step and should continue throughout the process of working through an ethical problem. Documenting your decisions and actions should also be done at all stages of counseling.

2. *Identify the potential issues involved.* After the information is collected, list and describe the critical issues and discard the irrelevant ones. Evaluate the rights, responsibilities, and welfare of all those who are affected by the situation. Good reasons can be presented that support various sides of a given issue, and different ethical principles may indicate different courses of action. Consider the cultural context of the situation, including any relevant cultural dimensions of the client's situation. Ask yourself these questions: How can I best promote client independence and self-determination? What actions have the least chance of bringing harm to a client? What decision will best safeguard the welfare of the client? How can I create a trusting and therapeutic climate in which clients can find their own solutions?
3. *Apply the relevant ethics code.* Once you have a clearer picture of the nature of the problem, review the code of ethics to see if the issue is addressed. When applying ethical standards to specific cases, you need to carefully read the code and understand the implications of the standards. Rather than making a decision to act on the basis of a single standard, look for all the standards that pertain to a situation. If there are specific and clear guidelines, following them may resolve the problem. However, if the problem is more complex and a resolution is not apparent, you may need to employ additional steps to resolve the problem. Ask yourself whether the standards of your professional organization offer a possible solution to the problem. Consider whether your own values and ethics are consistent with or in conflict with the relevant codes. If you are in disagreement with a particular standard, do you have a rationale to support your position? Your state or national professional association may be able to provide you with guidance in resolving a dilemma. Such associations often make legal counsel available to their members.
4. *Know the applicable laws and regulations.* It is important for you to keep up to date on relevant state and federal laws. This is especially true in matters of keeping or divulging confidentiality, reporting child or elder abuse, dealing with issues pertaining to danger to self or others, parental rights, record keeping, assessment, and diagnosis. In addition, be sure you understand the current rules and regulations of the agency or organization where you work.
5. *Obtain consultation.* It is generally helpful to consult with one or more colleagues or with a supervisor or other expert to obtain a different perspective on the problem. Do not limit yourself to individuals who share your orientation. Poor ethical decisions often result from an inability to view a situation objectively. Prejudices, biases, personal needs, or emotional

investment can distort the perception of the dilemma (Koocher & Keith-Spiegel, 2016). Consider the emotions you are experiencing as you assess the situation. Consultation can help you determine how you may be influenced by feelings such as fear and self-doubt (Herlihy & Corey, 2015a). If there is a legal question, seek legal counsel. After you present your assessment of the situation and your ideas of how you might proceed, ask for feedback on your analysis. Reflect on questions such as these:

- What kinds of questions do you want to ask of those with whom you consult?
- How can you use the consultation process as an opportunity to test the justification of a course of action you are inclined to take?
- Are you considering all of the ethical, clinical, and legal issues involved in the case?
- Are there any questions you are afraid to ask?

Consultation can help you think about information or circumstances that you may have overlooked. It is imperative to document the nature of your consultation, including the suggestions provided by those with whom you consulted.

6. *Consider possible and probable courses of action.* Brainstorm as many possible courses of action as you can. In doing so, ask colleagues to help you generate potential courses of action. By listing a wide variety of courses of action, you may identify a possibility that looks most useful to you. Evaluate each option with reference to the potential consequences for all parties involved. Eliminate those options that do not promise to give the desired results or that may have problematic consequences. As you think about the many possibilities for action, discuss these options with your client, if or when appropriate, as well as with other professionals. Care needs to be taken to ensure that the client does not become the "helper" when the client is included in these discussions. Determine which of the remaining options or combination of options is best suited to the situation. A good guideline in choosing your course of action would be the degree to which you would feel comfortable knowing your actions would be published in the newspaper, posted on the Internet, or mentioned in the news on radio or television. If your answer is "no," you have reason to reconsider your selected course of action.
7. *Explore the consequences of various decisions.* Ponder the implications of each course of action for the client, for others who might be affected by the decision, and for you as the counselor. Again, a discussion with your client about consequences for him or her can be most important, when appropriate. Realize that there are likely to be multiple outcomes, rather than a single desired outcome in dealing with an ethical dilemma. Continue brainstorming and reflecting on other options as well as consulting with colleagues who may see possibilities that have not occurred to you (Remley & Herlihy, 2020). Review the consequences of key decisions to determine if any new ethical problems might arise. If so, go back to the beginning and reevaluate each step of the process.

8. *Decide on the best course of action.* In making the best decision, carefully consider the information you have received from various sources. The more obvious the dilemma, the clearer is the course of action; the more subtle the dilemma, the more difficult the decision will be. In carrying out your plan, realize that other professionals might choose different courses of action in the same situation. However, you can only act in accordance with the best information you have. After you carry out your course of action, it is wise to follow up on the situation to evaluate whether your actions had the anticipated effect and consequences (Herlihy & Corey, 2015a). Determine the outcomes and see if any further action is needed. Reflecting on your assessment of the situation and the actions you took is good practice if you are to learn from your experience. Wheeler and Bertram (2019) recommend careful documentation of the ethical decision-making process you used in arriving at a course of action, including the options you considered and ruled out. It is important to document the outcome and to include any additional actions that were taken to resolve the issue. This is where reviewing your notes can be particularly helpful in assessing the process. To obtain the most accurate picture, involve your client in this process, when appropriate.

Even if you follow a systematic model such as the one we have described, you may still experience some anxiety about whether you made the best possible decision in a given case. Many ethical issues are controversial, and some involve blending ethics and the law. An important sign of your good faith is your willingness to share concerns or struggles with colleagues, supervisors, and fellow students. It is essential that you keep abreast of the laws that affect your practice, maintain awareness of new developments in your field, and reflect on ways that your values will influence your practice. Developing a sense of professional and ethical responsibility is a task never completely finished.

Case example: Applying the eight-step ethical decision-making model to the case of Bob.

To illustrate how a helper might navigate the process of working through complex ethical issues, we present the case of Bob and apply the eight-step ethical decision-making model to his situation. As you review this case and Bob's ultimate decision, what are your reactions? If you were in his shoes, would you follow the same course of action? Why or why not? Can you think of any additional factors that might influence your decision if you were the intern faced with this dilemma?

The case of Bob. Bob is a counseling intern working at a community mental health agency. He has considerable experience working with clients with various disabilities. He felt inspired to work with individuals with disabilities because his brother has Down syndrome. Other than his personal experience with people with disabilities, he has had no formal training working with clients with autism. Joseph, a client with autism, has just been referred to him. Joseph's presenting concerns are wanting to improve his interpersonal relationships, anxiety, and depression. Bob is unsure about accepting this client due to the fact that he lacks formal training in working with clients with autism, and he is concerned about the ethics of practicing beyond the scope of his competence.

Applying the eight steps. Step 1: *Identify the problem or dilemma.* The dilemma is whether or not Bob has the competence to engage in counseling with an individual with autism. This is both an ethical and a clinical problem.

Step 2: *Identify the potential issues involved.* The ethical component centers around Bob practicing beyond the scope of his competence and training. Bob's inexperience with autism could lead him to an intervention that is counterproductive for someone with autistic traits, resulting in regression of previous behavioral gains.

Joseph's concerns seem to encompass environmental issues not specifically related to autism. Bob has a lot of experience working with Joseph's presenting concerns of interpersonal relationship problems, anxiety, and depression. Bob has excellent counseling skills, a desire to work with this population, and a considerable amount of experience personally and professionally with people with disabilities, which could guide him to refer Joseph if he determined that Joseph could be best served by a specialist.

A number of clinical issues also must be considered. Joseph is not defined by his autism—it is only a part of who he is. How would Joseph feel knowing that Bob had referred him elsewhere because he has autism? In addition, Bob is aware that services at his agency are low-cost, whereas therapists in private practice in his area who specialize in autism charge substantially higher fees. Joseph may simply go without counseling if he cannot afford counseling with one of these specialists.

Step 3: *Apply the relevant ethics code.* The *ACA Code of Ethics* (ACA, 2014) states the following on the boundaries of professional competence:

> Counselors practice only within the boundaries of their competence, based on their education, training, supervised experience, state and national professional credentials, and appropriate professional experience. Whereas multicultural counseling competency is required across all counseling specialties, counselors gain knowledge, personal awareness, sensitivity, dispositions, and skills pertinent to being a culturally competent counselor in working with a diverse client population. (Standard C.2.a.)

Bob wonders if a therapist needs to be specifically trained in working with clients with autism. If so, just how much training does Bob need to be competent? If Bob does accept Joseph as a client, he would need to seek consultation or supervision from a colleague more knowledgeable about autism.

Step 4: *Know the applicable laws and regulations.* There are no laws on this issue per se, such as those for abuse, but there are laws against discrimination of individuals with disabilities. If Bob refers Joseph solely on the basis of his autism, could this be viewed as discriminatory?

Step 5: *Obtain consultation.* Bob brings this ethical dilemma to his supervisor and supervision group. His supervisor has experience supervising interns working with clients with autism, and she encourages him to work with Joseph under her supervision. The supervisor suggests that Bob take a continuing education class on autism. In addition, Bob consults with an independent private practice therapist who specializes in autism who concedes that it would not be unethical for Bob to treat Joseph given these conditions. However, the therapist wonders whether Joseph would receive the best quality of care possible given

Bob's lack of clinical experience with autism. Bob documents all the advice from the consultations.

Step 6: *Consider possible and probable courses of action:* One course of action is to refer Joseph to private practitioners in the community who specialize in autism spectrum disorders. Another possible course of action is for Bob to accept Joseph as a client while Bob obtains continuing education relevant to autism. During this time, Bob's supervisor would closely monitor his progress and effectiveness when working with Joseph. A third course of action is for Bob to place Joseph's name on a waiting list for a therapist with training in autism spectrum disorders rather than taking on this client himself.

Step 7: *Explore the consequences of the various decisions.* Referring Joseph to a private practice therapist who specializes in clients with autism spectrum disorders would be ideal if Joseph can afford this service. If Joseph cannot afford the private practice fees, he will not receive any services. In that case, Joseph's presenting concerns will go untreated, leading to worsening symptoms and decreased quality of life. If Bob works with Joseph under supervision, Bob would gain experience with clients with autism, and Joseph would be able to address the issues he is bringing to counseling. Placing Joseph on a waiting list for a therapist with training in autism would delay Joseph's treatment for an unspecified period of time until the colleague has an opening in his caseload. Similar to the first option, a worsening of symptoms is probable due to this delay.

Step 8: *Decide on the best course of action.* Bob carefully considers all relevant aspects of this ethical dilemma and decides to speak to Joseph about his concerns. Bob has an open discussion with Joseph explaining his inexperience and that he will work with Joseph under supervision. Bob provides Joseph with an adequate amount of information for Joseph to make an informed decision about his treatment. Bob takes the advice of his supervisor to get more training and signs up for a continuing education class, receives some training on autism from a colleague, and works closely with his supervisor. He also collaborates with Joseph and discloses that although he has been obtaining more education in this area there are others with more experience. Both parties agree to the counseling relationship, and Bob continues his education, supervision, and consultations with his colleagues.

LO6 Informed Consent

For most clients, asking for formal or professional help is a new experience. They are often unclear about what is expected of them and what they should expect from the helper. The ethics codes of the various professional organizations require that clients be given adequate information to make informed choices about entering and continuing in the therapeutic relationship. A good way to safeguard the rights of clients is to develop procedures to help them make informed choices. **Informed consent** involves the right of clients to be informed about what their relationship with you will entail and to make autonomous decisions pertaining to it. Informed consent enables your clients to decide whether to participate in the helping relationship with you. The **informed consent document** defines boundaries and clarifies the nature of the basic counseling relationship between counselor and client. Informed consent for treatment is a powerful clinical, legal, and ethical tool (Wheeler & Bertram, 2019). Through the informed consent process, you are giving your clients an opportunity to raise questions and to explore the expectations they have in working with you.

Part of ethical practice is having a discussion with clients about their rights. Clients are often unaware of their rights, and they may unquestioningly accept whatever their therapist says or does. How can you teach your clients about their rights and responsibilities from the outset of the helping relationship? Asking clients to sign a form at the initial session does not discharge your duty toward informed consent. Although it is imperative that you secure informed consent at the outset of a helping relationship, realize that clients may not remember all that you tell them. Active informed consent is an ongoing process in the counseling relationship, not a single event (Wheeler & Bertram, 2019).

In addition to discussing the main points of your informed consent policies with clients in the first session, we also suggest that you develop a comprehensive written statement to give to clients at the first session. Clients can take this statement home to read before the next session. In this way clients have a basis for asking questions and valuable time is saved. It is important to have clients sign the document indicating an understanding of these policies and procedures.

Describing informed consent involves a delicate balance between telling clients too little and overwhelming them with too much information at once. Educating clients about the therapeutic process is an ongoing endeavor. Do not assume that clients clearly understand what they are told initially about the helping process. The more clients know about how the helping process works, including the roles of both client and practitioner, the more they will benefit from this professional relationship. By alerting clients to their rights and responsibilities, the practitioner is encouraging a sense of autonomy and personal power. Be sure to use clear and understandable language when you are discussing informed consent matters with clients. Furthermore, you need to take into account cultural implications of informed consent procedures and communicate in ways that are culturally sensitive. For instance, suppose your client is a refugee who experienced persecution in her country. She may have concerns that information she shares privately with you will be disclosed to others, and she understandably may have reservations about meeting with you if you do not clearly explain confidentiality and its limits. Clients from collectivistic cultures may have a different view of professional boundaries, and you may need to take time to educate these clients about the therapeutic relationship (Bemak & Chung, 2015; Chung & Bemak, 2012).

Although most professionals agree on the ethical duty to provide clients with relevant information about the helping process, there is not much consensus about what should be revealed and in what manner. Studies of therapists' informed consent practices have found considerable variability in the breadth and depth of the informed consent given to clients (Barnett, Wise, et al., 2007). In deciding what you would most want to tell a client, consider these questions:

- What are the goals of the helping relationship?
- What services are you able and willing to provide?

- What do you expect of your client? What can your client expect of you?
- What are the risks and benefits of helping strategies that are likely to be employed?
- What do you want to tell your client about yourself?
- What are your qualifications as the provider of the services?
- What are the financial considerations? Do you offer a sliding scale for clients who cannot afford your fee? Do you accept private insurance for your services?
- What is the estimated duration of the professional relationship? How will termination be handled?
- What are the limitations of confidentiality? When does the law require mandatory reporting?
- Under what circumstances are you likely to consult with a supervisor or other colleagues about the case?
- Are there any alternatives to the approaches you might suggest?

If you are part of a managed behavioral health care program, you will also need to explain to your clients the number of sessions allowed, the limitations of confidentiality, and the narrower scope of short-term interventions.

Case example: Providing just enough information.

During the initial interview, Simone asks the counselor, Allen, how long she might need to be in therapy. Allen tells Simone that the process will take a minimum of 1 year of weekly sessions. She expresses dismay at such a lengthy process. Allen says that this is the way he works and explains that in his experience significant change is a slow process that demands a great deal of work. He tells Simone that if she cannot commit to this time period he would be willing to give her a referral.

Your stance. Consider what you would do if Simone came to you for counseling. Explore the following questions:

- Does Allen have an ethical and a professional obligation to explain his rationale for the 1 year of therapy?
- Would an ethical course involve Allen exploring alternatives to his approach to therapy, such as briefer therapy?
- Would it be ethical for Allen to accept clients under a managed care system or with an insurance provider that paid for only a very limited number of sessions?

Discussion. When clients finally make an appointment, they are often anxious to get help on some pressing problem. Talking about the informed consent process in great detail could dampen the client's inclination to return for further sessions. Yet it is a mistake to withhold important information that clients need if they are to make wise choices. *What* and *how much* to tell a client is determined in part by the client. It is a good practice for helpers to employ an educational approach, encouraging clients' questions about evaluation or treatment and offering useful feedback as the helping process progresses. By providing your clients with adequate information, you are increasing the chances that they will become active participants and carry their share of the responsibilities in the relationship.

LO7 Confidentiality and Privacy

The helping relationship is built on a foundation of trust. If clients do not trust their counselor, they are unlikely to engage in significant self-disclosure and self-exploration. Trust is largely measured by the degree to which clients feel assured that what they say will be listened to and kept confidential. Mental health professionals have a dual ethical and legal responsibility to safeguard clients from unauthorized disclosures of information given in the context of the helping relationship. Helpers must not disclose this information except when required by law or authorized by the client to do so.

To explore all aspects of their lives without fear that these disclosures will be released outside the therapy room, clients need reasonable assurance that their confidentiality will be maintained. No effective therapy can occur unless clients trust that what they say is confidential. Counselors are ethically obligated to clearly assist clients in appreciating the meaning of confidentiality in language they can understand and in using an approach that respects the cultural experiences of the client (Barnett & Johnson, 2015).

Confidentiality is one of the most basic ethical obligations, yet it is also one of the most problematic issues for many practitioners. Helpers increasingly confront confidentiality issues that are created by complex legal requirements, new technologies, health care service delivery systems, and a culture that places increasing emphasis on consumer rights.

Although your clients have every right to expect that their relationship with you will remain confidential, your obligation to safeguard client disclosures is not absolute. You need to develop the legal knowledge and an ethical sense for when you *must* break confidentiality. All of the professional codes state that clients have a right to know about any limitations of confidentiality from the outset. This matter should be spelled out for clients in their informed consent, ideally in both written and verbal form. Mandated reporting issues should be clearly explained prior to any client disclosures to help ensure that clients understand exactly when you may need to report child or elder abuse or suicidal or homicidal suspicions. When clients have this information early, the chances of preserving the therapeutic relationship are improved when mandated reporting incidences occur. It is a good idea to discuss the following points with your clients (Herlihy & Corey, 2015c):

- Do not reveal confidential information without client consent, or without sound legal or ethical justification.
- Some clients may want confidential information shared with members of their family or community.
- At times, it is permissible to share information with others in the interest of providing the best possible services to the client.
- Confidential information may also be discussed with other helping professionals when the client requests it or gives permission.
- Confidentiality is not an absolute, and other obligations may override the helper's pledge. For example, it is required that confidentiality be breached to protect someone who is in danger.
- Confidentiality cannot be guaranteed when the client is a minor or when counseling couples, families, or groups.

- Confidentiality can be compromised if a client's records are subpoenaed.
- At the outset of a professional relationship, practitioners should clarify what, when, how, and with whom information can be shared.
- When counselors assume the role of advocate, client confidentiality may be breached. Ethical dilemmas can occur when clients are unwilling to give consent for the counselor to advocate on their behalf.
- Confidentiality may be compromised if client records are stored via cloud computing and during other electronic communication.

State law specifies the circumstances under which confidentiality must be compromised. You may have to reveal information when there is clear and imminent danger that clients will bring harm to others or to themselves. Know the laws in your state as there may be options other than breaking confidentiality available to you. Not all states have the same laws, but all states have mandatory reporting laws for incest and child abuse, and most states have mandatory reporting laws for elder abuse and dependent adult abuse. You are expected to know how to assess signs of abuse and neglect. All states require reporting child abuse or neglect if it results in physical injury. In addition, you are expected to take action when clients are likely to harm themselves or others. If a client is suicidal, you have a responsibility to do what you can to protect this person.

Human services professionals are vulnerable to lawsuits if they improperly handle confidentiality issues, so it behooves you to know the laws of your state or jurisdiction, to follow them, and to be aware of the ethical standards of your profession. Seek help from your professional organization when dealing with complex ethical dilemmas.

To sharpen your thinking about issues surrounding confidentiality, think about what you would do in these cases:

- *Child abuse.* Two young girls are brought to a community agency by their aunt, who has gained custody of them in the last few months. One girl, age 11, is quite verbal, but the other, 13, is not. As they begin to talk and you ask about their history, they tell you of aunts and uncles who attempted to touch one of them and of an aunt who severely beat them. The 11-year-old tells of a suicide attempt by her sister after one such beating. If you were working with these girls, what action would you take and why?
- *An alternative form of medicine or elder abuse?* A 69-year-old client who has been having difficulty with her jealous and controlling son enters her counselor's office for her weekly session. The counselor notices that her client has bruises on her neck and upper back. When asked about these marks on her skin, her client quickly replies that she is undergoing cupping therapy for a respiratory condition. The counselor is left wondering whether her client is being straightforward with her or whether she is covering up for her son. If you were the counselor in this case, how would you proceed?
- *Runaway plan.* A student intern works with pupils in an elementary school. She says to the children in a group, "Everything you say here will stay here." Then a boy reveals a detailed plan to run away from home. The counselor, who has not talked about the exceptions to confidentiality with the children, does not know what to do. If she reports the boy, he may feel betrayed. If she does not report him, she may face a malpractice action for having failed to notify the parents. What might you suggest to her if she came to consult with you about this case?

- *Students' violation of confidentiality.* You are a counselor intern in a local agency. You are part of a training group of students that meets weekly to discuss cases. One day, while you are having lunch in a restaurant with some of the students, they begin to discuss their cases in detail, mentioning names and details of the clients loudly enough for others in the restaurant to overhear. What would you do in this situation?

It is tempting to talk about your clients and their stories, especially as others are usually curious about what you do. It may give you a sense of importance to be able to tell interesting anecdotes. You may talk more than you should when you feel overwhelmed by your clients and need to unburden yourself. As a professional helper, you must learn how to talk about clients and how to report without breaking confidentiality. Clients should know that confidentiality cannot be guaranteed absolutely, but they should have your assurance that you will avoid talking about them except when the law requires you to disclose information or it is professionally necessary to do so.

LO8 Confidentiality in Couples and Family Therapy

Confidentiality is also a key ethical issue in the practice of couples and family therapy. Generally speaking, from a *legal* perspective, confidentiality as applied to couples counseling, family therapy, group counseling, and counseling minors has limitations. However, from an *ethical* perspective, confidentiality is of the utmost importance and must be discussed so all parties are aware of what confidentiality involves in these forms of counseling. When practitioners work with couples and families, confidentiality issues can become extremely complex and may involve determining who is the client, providing informed consent, and handling relational matters in an individual context (James Bitter, personal communication, December 21, 2018). Some helpers contend that whatever information they get from one family member should never be divulged to the other members. By contrast, other helpers have a policy of refusing to keep any information private within the family. Their assumption is that secrets are counterproductive to helping family members be open with one another. These helpers encourage bringing all secrets out into the open. It is essential that you be clear in your own mind about how you will deal with disclosures obtained from family members and that you let your clients know your policy before they enter into a professional relationship with you.

Case example: Concealing information in couples counseling.

Owen is involved in individual therapy, and later his wife, Flora, attends some of the sessions for marriage counseling. Owen discloses to the therapist that he became involved in a sexual relationship with a man a few months previously. He does not want his wife to know for fear that she will divorce him. In a later session in which the therapist is seeing the couple, Flora complains that she feels neglected and wonders if her husband is really committed to working on their marriage. She says that she is willing to continue marital counseling as long as she is sure that he wants to stay in the marriage and devote his efforts to working through their difficulties. The therapist knows about the extramarital relationship but decides to say nothing about it in the joint session and maintains that it is the husband's decision whether to mention it.

Your stance. What do you think of the therapist's ethical decision in this situation? If you were involved in a somewhat similar situation, what might you do differently? Are you concerned about his withholding this information from Flora?

Discussion. Without question, this therapist is faced with a difficult situation. We wonder how confidentiality was initially explained to Owen during the informed consent process, and whether Flora also was given this information later when she joined Owen in marriage counseling. Did this therapist tell Owen that Flora would not be privy to any information he revealed in private sessions if she joined him for sessions? Did Flora understand that as well? If the therapist clearly stated in her informed consent document that information presented would not be withheld from either person, these clients would have understood the potential ramifications of their disclosures and Owen might not have disclosed information about his extramarital relationship to the counselor. When working with couples and families, it is imperative to be clear from the outset about how sensitive disclosures will be handled.

LO9 Confidentiality in Group Counseling

When you lead a group, you will have to consider some special ethical, legal, and professional aspects of confidentiality. In a group setting, you must disclose the limitations of confidentiality. Because so many more people are privy to information shared in the group, you cannot guarantee confidentiality because you cannot control what the members do or say outside of the sessions. You should explain that legal privilege (confidentiality) does not apply to group treatment, unless provided by state statute (Association for Specialists in Group Work [ASGW], 2008). Group practitioners owe it to their members to specify at the outset the limits of confidentiality, and in mandatory groups they should inform members of any reporting procedures required of them. Members should also be aware of any required documentation or record keeping procedures that may have an impact on confidentiality. Even if you continually emphasize to the members how essential it is to maintain confidentiality, there is still the possibility that some of them will talk inappropriately to others about what has been shared in the group. The group leader has the responsibility for explaining how confidentiality can be broken, even without intending to do so. It is a good practice to remind the participants from time to time of how confidences can be breeched inadvertently and in subtle ways.

Confidentiality is essential if members are to develop a sense of safety in a group, which is basic to being willing to engage in risk-taking. Early in a group's life, the group leader can provide guidelines for maintaining the confidential nature of the group. The leader can emphasize to members that it is their responsibility to continually make the group safe by addressing their concerns regarding how their disclosures will be treated. Members can be encouraged to bring up any fears about possible breaches of confidentiality, and these concerns can be openly explored in the group.

In institutions, agencies, and schools, where group members know and have frequent contact with one another and with one another's associates outside of the group, confidentiality becomes especially critical and also more difficult to maintain. Group counselors are responsible for addressing the parameters of online behavior through informed consent and are advised to establish ground rules whereby members agree not to post pictures, comments, or any type of confidential information about other members online. Developing rules that address the use of online discussion outside of the group should be part of the informed consent process and part of the discussion about group norms governing the group.

Confidentiality in School Counseling

In the context of school counseling, protection of confidentiality and privacy is a major concern. Children and adolescent clients have a right to know what information will and will not be kept confidential from their first contact with a school counselor. In cases involving minors who are unable to give informed consent, the parents or guardians will need to provide this informed consent and may need to be included in the counseling process. Parents and guardians have some legal right to request information about counseling sessions, as do school personnel, but this should be done in a manner that will minimize intrusion of the child's or adolescent's privacy and in a way that demonstrates respect for the student. School counselors must clearly inform the students they see of the limitations of confidentiality and how and when confidential information may be shared.

The *ASCA Ethical Standards for School Counselors* (2016) addresses key parameters of confidentiality:

> School counselors recognize their primary ethical obligation for confidentiality is to the students but balance that obligation with an understanding of parents'/guardians' legal and inherent rights to be the guiding voice in their children's lives. School counselors understand the need to balance students' ethical rights to make choices, their capacity to give consent or assent, and parental or familial legal rights and responsibilities to make decisions on their child's behalf. (A.2.f.)

When minor clients pose a danger to themselves or to others, school counselors must breach confidentiality. From both an ethical and legal perspective, any threat of suicide or of violence to others must be taken very seriously. Even if the risk of suicide is remote, the possibility may be enough to establish a duty to contact the parents and inform them of the potential for suicidal behavior. Courts have found that the burden involved in making a telephone call is minor considering the risk of harm to a student who is suicidal. In short, school personnel are advised to take every precaution to protect the student. The same is true in all cases where there is a potential for violent acts. This is especially relevant in light of the increasing number of school shootings in recent years. Some potential tragedies have been averted because a teacher or a student took action when concerned about the violent intentions expressed by a student.

Continuing education is of the utmost importance, as is your willingness to seek appropriate consultation when you become aware of students who are at risk. You can be held legally accountable only for a judgment that is clearly negligent in light of the standard of care of other professionals with similar education and experience. As long as you act in an ethical and reasonable manner, you should not be overly concerned about legal sanctions related to student suicide or harm to others.

Case example: Informing parents and respecting confidentiality.

Conrad, a 17-year-old high school senior, was referred to a psychologist, Andy, by his high school counselor for an evaluation for depression. Conrad currently lives at home with his parents and two younger siblings. He stated during the intake that for the past 2 years he has struggled academically and socially and has felt depressed for most of this time. His grades have suffered, and he has become more socially withdrawn. As a coping mechanism, he writes and plays music in his room. He plans to remain home following graduation and will attend community college. Andy has met with Conrad for a total of four sessions, and he has been very responsive to talk therapy. Following the last session, Andy received a telephone message from Conrad's mother wanting an update on his progress and to share some information that she thinks is pertinent to his case.

Andy tells Conrad that his mother left a telephone message and that she seems to be interested in his progress. Conrad is not sure if he wants Andy to speak with his mother because he doesn't trust what his mother might share with Andy.

Your stance. What are the legal and ethical issues to examine? How do you navigate the needs of the client and the needs of his parents to be informed? Can you think of interventions that could be helpful to Conrad and his parents?

Discussion. Andy might discuss with Conrad the possibility of inviting both of his parents to a session. This approach would empower Conrad to remain active and in charge of his treatment decisions, and it would prevent trust issues from occurring between Conrad and Andy. Before Conrad's parents attend a session, however, it would be worthwhile for Andy to explore with Conrad his concerns about what his mother might disclose about him. What is Conrad's fear? Is he concerned that his mother might reveal something that would shed a negative light on him or his family? This exploration could lead to some meaningful and productive therapeutic work.

LO10 Confidentiality and Privacy in a Technological World

One of the most dramatic changes in the counseling profession over the last decade has been the use of technology in counseling services (Jencius, 2015). Counseling codes of ethics have not been able to keep pace with the rapid development of electronic communication, and a host of ethical and legal issues are associated with various new technologies. Section H of the recently revised *ACA Code of Ethics* (ACA, 2014) contains standards with regard to the use of technology, relationships established through computer-mediated communication, and social media as a delivery platform. Major subsections in Section H address competency to provide services and the laws associated with distance counseling, components of informed consent and security (confidentiality, limitations, and security), client verification, the distance counseling relationship (access, accessibility, professional boundaries), maintenance of records and accessibility of websites, and aspects of the use of social media.

There are a host of ways to violate a client's privacy through the inappropriate use of various forms of technology. Although the use of encryption software is important, confidentiality simply cannot be guaranteed. This is arguably one of the great challenges of practicing counseling in this era of electronic communication. Communication by electronic means is fraught with potential privacy problems.

Counselors and their clients should carefully consider privacy issues before agreeing to send e-mail messages to clients' workplaces or homes. A good policy is to limit e-mail exchanges to basic information such as an appointment time. Tran-Lien (2012) recommends that counselors who plan to exchange e-mails with their clients provide clients with a statement (as part of the informed consent process) that details guidelines and the limitations on the use of e-mail, the potential risks to confidentiality, and the expected turnaround time. She suggests that "communicating with your clients via e-mail can be done, but careful consideration should be given to the guidelines and relevant legal and ethical issues" (p. 22). Both the challenges and the safeguards in using e-mail as a mode of communication should be clearly explained.

Although privacy and confidentiality of clients has long been a central issue, with electronic transactions things have become more complex. The **Health Insurance Portability and Accountability Act (HIPAA)** of 1996 was passed by Congress to promote standardization and efficiency in the health care industry. HIPAA is a federal law that contains detailed provisions regarding client privacy, informed consent, and transfer of records. Counselors are required to provide clients with a clear written explanation of how health information is used and kept (Remley & Herlihy, 2020).

The **HIPAA privacy rule** was designed to give patients more rights and more control over their health information. Patients must be informed of their rights and are required to sign the appropriate forms authorizing a health care provider to obtain and provide information to other health care providers. The HIPAA privacy rule, which applies to both paper and electronic transmissions of protected health information by covered entities, was developed out of the concern that transmission of health care information through electronic means could lead to widespread gaps in the protection of client confidentiality (Wheeler & Bertram, 2019). The new privacy regulations protect patients by limiting the ways that practitioners can use patients' medical information and other individually identifiable health information. The privacy rule requires health plans to establish policies and procedures to protect the confidentiality of protected health information about their patients.

Most of us have become so accustomed to relying on technology that careful thought is not always given to subtle ways that privacy can be violated. It is of the utmost importance to use caution and pay attention to ways that you could unintentionally breach the privacy of your clients when using various forms of communication. As a part of the informed consent process, it is wise to discuss with your clients the potential problems of privacy regarding a wide range of technology and to take preventive measures so that both you and your clients have an understanding and agreement about these important concerns. Consider the following case pertaining to privacy issues in an agency setting.

Case example: Privacy issues and telecommunications.

The agency you work for establishes a call center to take calls from clients and to schedule appointments for them. One of their new policies is to call clients to remind them of their upcoming appointment. A particular client has stated clearly that she does not want her husband to know that she is coming for counseling. However, a call center phone representative calls her residence to remind her of her next appointment, and in the process her husband gets the message about her upcoming appointment for counseling.

Your stance. Do you see an ethical issue pertaining to privacy or confidentiality in this case? How would you reconcile agency policy and client privacy in a situation such as this? How would you handle the client's phone call to you complaining about what has happened?

Discussion. Although this breach of confidentiality was unintentional and resulted from a lapse in communication between agency staff and the call center, the ramifications of this ethical violation may be serious. This client may have any number of reasons for wanting to conceal from her husband the fact that she is in counseling. She has every right to complain about this breach of privacy. It is important for the therapist to hear her concerns without reacting defensively and to apologize on behalf of the agency for this error.

This case example illustrates how easily breaches of confidentiality can happen if you do not exercise caution. It is a good practice to discuss during the initial contact how the client prefers to be reached so that confidentiality is honored. It is of paramount importance that agency staff take every measure to protect clients' privacy.

Privacy in a Small Community

I (Marianne) practiced for many years as a marriage and family therapist in a small community. This situation presented a set of ethical considerations involving safeguarding the privacy of clients. First, it was important that I choose an office that afforded privacy to clients as they entered and left. I considered leasing space in a small professional building in the center of town, but I quickly discovered that people would be uncomfortable making themselves that visible when seeking psychological help. A home office, which was remote from the center of the village, worked out well. However, I had to carefully schedule clients, allowing ample time between sessions so clients who might know each other would not meet in the office. When an office is located within a home, it is essential that a professional atmosphere be provided. Clients have a right to expect privacy and should not have to deal with intrusions by the therapist's family members.

I discussed with my clients the unique variables pertaining to confidentiality in a small community. I informed them that I would not discuss professional concerns with them should we meet at the grocery store or the post office, and I respected their preferences regarding interactions away from the office. Knowing that they were aware that I saw many people from the town, I reassured them that I would not talk with anyone about who my clients were. Another example of protecting my clients' privacy pertained to the manner of depositing checks at the local bank. Because the bank employees knew my profession, it would have been easy for them to identify my clients. Again, I talked with my clients about their preferences. If they had any discomfort about my depositing their checks in the local bank, I arranged to have them deposited elsewhere.

Your Obligation to Protect

Courts have created an exception to confidentiality when the mental health professional has a reasonable basis for believing that clients pose a danger either to themselves or to others. Counselors have a legal as well as an ethical responsibility to protect their clients and others from harm, and they must breach confidentiality when necessary to provide this protection. Wheeler and Bertram (2019) provide this risk management guideline: "The real question for the counselor is how to fulfill his or her legal and ethical duties to protect human life, act in the best interest of the client, and remain protected from potential liability" (p. 151).

Put yourself in this situation: A new client visits you at a college counseling center. He says he was severely abused by his father as a child and is now extremely angry. He is making threats to kill his father and tells you he is armed. How do you proceed? How do you decide whether this client is dangerous? What steps can you think of taking if you determine the client does pose a danger?

Many helpers find it difficult to predict when clients pose a serious threat to others. With more training and supervision, you will learn how to identify and assess the risk factors and warning signs for violence. Predictors of potential violence include a history of violent or aggressive behavior, verbal threats, threatening e-mails or letters, harassment (including sexual harassment and stalking), and possession of a weapon, particularly a firearm ("How to Recognize Students," 2011). Although practitioners are generally not held legally liable for their failure to predict violent behavior of a client, an inadequate assessment of client dangerousness can result in liability for the therapist, harm to third parties, and inappropriate breaches of client confidentiality. Helping professionals faced with potentially dangerous clients should take specific steps designed to protect the public and to minimize their own liability. They should take careful histories, advise clients of the limits of confidentiality, keep accurate notes of threats and other client statements, seek consultation, and document steps they have taken to protect others.

It is extremely difficult to decide when breaching confidentiality to protect potential victims is justified. Mental health professionals are obligated to disclose when legal requirements demand it, and they must be familiar with the laws of their state regarding the duty to protect because state laws differ (Herlihy & Corey, 2015c). Practitioners are advised to consult with a supervisor, a colleague, or an attorney because they may be subject to liability for either failing to warn and protect those entitled to warnings or warning those who are not entitled. Most states either permit or require therapists to breach confidentiality to protect victims. In light of a number of court cases, mental health professionals have become increasingly conscious of a double duty—to protect other people from potentially dangerous clients and to protect clients from themselves. The responsibility to protect the public from potentially violent clients entails liability for civil damages when professionals neglect this duty by failing to diagnose or predict dangerousness, failing to protect potential victims of violent behavior, failing to commit dangerous individuals, and prematurely discharging dangerous clients from a hospital.

HIV issues. One of the more controversial ethical dilemmas pertaining to a helper's duty to warn and protect others involves working with people who have AIDS, or are HIV-positive, and who may be putting others at risk. As a helper, you may need to balance your client's right to confidentiality against warning a third party who may be at risk of being infected due to your client's HIV status.

At this time, there is no *legal* duty to warn, and it will take a court decision to resolve the legal questions. In the meantime, practitioners who work with HIV-positive clients will continue to wrestle with the *ethical* issues in deciding on a course of action with their clients. It is difficult to identify who in particular is at risk and to assess the degree to which individuals who have intimate relationships with people with HIV are in serious and foreseeable harm. Disclosure requires a careful decision, and helpers should not take action until they have confirmed the diagnosis and have ascertained that the client has not informed the third party and has no intentions of doing so in the immediate future. It is critical that helpers know their state laws concerning the disclosure of disease status when considering what to do. The *ACA Code of Ethics* (ACA, 2014, Standard B.2.c.) gives practitioners *permission* to breach confidentiality in respect to contagious life-threatening diseases, but it does not state that they have a *duty* to warn, for such a provision could leave them vulnerable to a malpractice suit. We know several colleagues who have specialized in seeing people with HIV for many years, and they claim that they have never broken confidentiality in this kind of case. They contend that there are many alternatives to breaking confidentiality and warning a third party.

Case example: Duty to inform and protect others.

One of your male clients discloses to you that he is HIV-positive, but he says nothing about his sexual practices with a partner or partners. At a later session, he discloses that he is not monogamous and that one of his partners is unaware of his condition. He has been engaging in unprotected sex with this person for some time, and he sees no point in either disclosing his condition or changing his sexual practices.

Your stance. What might you do in this case? How useful is the ACA guideline in determining your course of action? Would you initially address possible disclosure of information with others as part of the informed consent process? Why or why not? What do you see as your ethical and legal duty? How might you resolve potential conflicts between ethical and legal actions? How would you go about making your decision?

Discussion. Breaching confidentiality should be the last resort and should be considered only after less intrusive measures have failed (Corey, Corey, & Corey, 2019). First, try to help the client see the value of disclosing his HIV-positive status to his unsuspecting partner. Mental health professionals are not legally bound to uphold the "duty to protect" in cases involving HIV infection, and helpers' legal responsibilities for protecting sexual partners of HIV-positive clients remain unclear. Seek guidance from your state public health department, an attorney who specializes in these matters, colleagues who are experienced in ethical decision making, and your professional organization (Wheeler & Bertram, 2019). When consulting with others about how to proceed and determining a course of action, it is important to omit identifying information to protect your client's privacy.

Harm to self. In addition to the duty to warn and to protect others from harm, helpers have a duty to protect clients who are likely to harm themselves. Many therapists inform their clients that they have an ethical and legal responsibility to break confidentiality when they have good reason to suspect suicidal behavior. Even if clients take the position that they are free to do with their lives what they want, therapists have a legal duty to protect them. The difficulty lies in determining when a client is serious about ending his or her life by suicide.

Although some practitioners may object to using coercive methods in preventing suicide out of their desire to honor the client's right to self-determination, many mental health workers believe most suicides can be prevented if those who work with suicidal clients learn to recognize, evaluate, and intervene effectively in crisis situations. Clients in crisis may feel temporary hopelessness, but their potential for suicide can be greatly reduced if they are given help in coping with the immediate problem. Help clients differentiate between wanting to end their life and wanting to end their emotional pain and suffering. More often than not, the pain and suffering feels overwhelming, and recognizing this provides the opportunity for hope and therapeutic intervention. It is generally held that once mental health professionals determine that a significant risk does exist, appropriate action is necessary. Practitioners who fail to act to prevent suicide can be held liable.

The codes of ethics of professional associations are in agreement that helpers must actively attempt to prevent suicide. When assessing the lethality of a threat and determining whether further intervention is necessary, consider these issues:

- Is there a plan?
- Is clinical depression present?
- Does the individual demonstrate helplessness or hopelessness?
- Has there been a sudden and often dramatic change in mood or behavior?
- Has the person attempted suicide in the past?
- Is the person seriously considering taking his or her life?
- Does the person have the means available?
- Is a mental illness present?
- What kind of emotional support is available in the family, at home, or elsewhere?

If clients do not voluntarily self-disclose intentions to harm themselves, counselors may need to ask directly. Factors that could increase clients' risk for self-harm include severe mental illness, substance abuse, recent loss, and acute medical conditions (Bongar & Sullivan, 2013). If it is determined that a client is at risk of suicide, it is the helper's ethical responsibility to take action outside the session. Possible interventions might include informing the parents, spouse, physician, or another significant person in the client's life. Helpers who do not think they can work competently with a client should seek supervision from a professional who has these skills or make the appropriate referral. Consultation helps to ensure that counselors are practicing up to the standards of care, making informed decisions about the exceptions to confidentiality, and accessing all current treatment options. It is extremely important that helpers appropriately document their assessment process, consultation activity, and treatment plan, including which interventions were chosen, the rationale for the decision, and why certain treatment options were not chosen (Werth & Stroup, 2015).

Case example: Protecting a depressed client.

A client is depressed and talks about putting an end to his life. He tells you that he is bringing this topic up only because he trusts you, and he insists that you not mention the conversation to anyone. He wants to talk about how desperate he feels, and he wants you to understand him and ultimately to accept whatever decision he makes.

Your stance. Consider your ethical and legal obligations in this case. What would you say to him? How would you proceed?

Discussion. This case is a good reminder of the importance of discussing the limits of confidentiality at the outset of counseling, including the need to breach confidentiality when a client is in danger of self-harm. In this case, you may discover that the client does not have a plan or the intent to commit suicide, and talking with him may be cathartic and healing. Provide a list of resources the client can access if his suicidal feelings persist.

If talking with the client increases your concern, conduct a lethality assessment to determine if this client has a plan and the means and intent to carry out his plan. If he does, you are ethically obligated to breach confidentiality despite his objections. Clients should understand that the helper is obligated to take suicidal talk seriously and may have to take action to protect the client. Ultimately, it is better to have a client who is alive and angry than one who has completed the act of suicide. Anger can be processed and worked through, but there is no opportunity for a better outcome once a client has ended his or her life.

Case example: Acting on an informant's knowledge.

A college counselor receives an e-mail message from a friend of a current client, Sadie. The friend wants to remain anonymous. The message reveals that Sadie is suicidal and already has a detailed plan to carry out suicide. The counselor telephones Sadie and asks her to come over to the counseling center as soon as possible.

Your stance. Do you believe counselors have an ethical obligation to respond to e-mail messages? Was the college counselor inappropriate in calling Sadie for an emergency session in response to an e-mail from her friend? Does the counselor have a duty to warn Sadie's family members? Do you think it was sufficient for the counselor to call the emergency session with Sadie?

Discussion. Suicidal threats need to be treated with extreme care and taken seriously. Sharing the information that was provided in the e-mail from a concerned friend, the counselor communicates to Sadie that this matter cannot be taken lightly. The counselor is behaving ethically by following up with Sadie and conducting a lethality assessment. The counselor has the right and responsibility to inform Sadie that a concerned friend contacted the counselor and is aware of Sadie's detailed suicide plan. The counselor may also deem it necessary to contact Sadie's parents after discussing this issue with Sadie. To protect Sadie's right to privacy, the counselor cannot communicate with the concerned friend who sounded the alert in this case.

LO11 Documentation and Keeping Records

From an ethical, legal, and clinical perspective, you are responsible to keep adequate records on your clients. It is considered below the standard of care to fail to keep current records for all your professional contacts. Many state licensing laws and regulations establish minimum guidelines for maintaining client records, but more often it is up to the discretion of the clinician to determine the content of records (Knapp & VandeCreek, 2012).

Record keeping serves multiple purposes. From a *clinical* perspective, record keeping provides a history that you can use in reviewing the course of treatment. Maintaining client records has a dual purpose: (a) to provide the best service possible for clients, and (b) to provide evidence of a level of care commensurate with the standards of the profession. From a *legal* perspective, state or federal law may require keeping a record, and maintaining adequate clinical records can provide an excellent defense against malpractice claims. Accurate, relevant, and timely documentation is useful as a risk management strategy.

Practitioners keep two kinds of client records. **Progress notes**, or the client's clinical records, are required by law. These notes are *behavioral* in nature and address what people say and do. Progress notes contain client identifying information, the client's history, reason for seeking treatment, and documentation pertaining to the informed consent process; objective findings from the most recent physical examination; intake sheet; documentation of referrals to other providers, when appropriate; client's diagnosis, functional status, prognosis, symptoms, treatment goals, treatment plan, consequences, progress toward meeting goals, and alternative treatments; types of services provided; precise times and dates of appointments made and kept; and termination summary. Your client's clinical record should *never* be altered after you have documented information into the record. It is a good idea to enter notes into a client's record as soon as possible after a session and sign and date the entry.

Process notes, or psychotherapy notes, are different from progress notes. Process notes deal with client reactions such as transference and the therapist's subjective impressions of a client. These notes are not meant to be readily disclosed to others. They are intended for the use of the practitioners who created them. Information that is essential for treatment should not be included in the process notes. For example, exclude from process notes the diagnosis, treatment plan, symptoms, prognosis, and progress. It is important to note that the law requires clinicians to keep a separate clinical record (progress notes) on all clients, but the law *does not* require keeping psychotherapy (process) notes.

From both an ethical and legal perspective, it is of the utmost importance that you store client records in a secure place and take steps to maintain the privacy of your clients' records. The length of time you are required to keep a client's records is determined by state law and the policies of your agency. Even when the record is discarded in a safe manner, a summary of a client's treatment should be retained. Although this may seem rather straightforward, the emergence of advanced technologies such as cloud computing have made the storage and protection of client data a complex matter.

Realize that clients have a legal right to view their clinical record, or a summary of their record. A client's record is not the place for your personal opinions or personal reactions to the client, and record keeping should reflect professionalism. If a client misses a session, it is a good practice to document the reasons. In writing client notes, it is important to use clear behavioral language. Focus on describing specific and concrete behavior and avoid jargon. When you write notes on your client, always assume that these records may be read by others. Although professional documentation is expected to be thorough, it is best to keep notes as concise as possible.

Be mindful of the dictum, "If you did not document it, then it did not happen." Record client and helper behavior that is clinically relevant. Include in clinical records interventions used, client responses to treatment strategies, the evolving treatment plan, and any follow-up measures taken. It is a wise policy for you to document your actions in crisis situations such as cases involving potential danger of harm to self, others, or physical property. However, it is not in the best interests of clients for you to be more concerned about record keeping as a self-protective strategy than you are to providing quality services to your clients.

Competent record keeping practices serve both the client and the counselor. Wheeler and Bertram (2019) suggest that practitioners who fail to maintain adequate clinical records put themselves at risk for malpractice suits because such failure breaches the standard of care expected of mental health practitioners. They add: "Well-organized and well-documented client counseling records are the most effective tool counselors have for establishing client treatment plans, ensuring continuity of care in the event of absence, and proving that quality care was provided" (p. 153).

LO12 Ethical Issues in a Managed Care Environment

In recent years a transformation has occurred in the delivery of helping services. As Cummings (1995) points out, there is a shift in values and a fundamental redefinition of the role of mental health practitioners in the transition from the traditional fee-for-service model to the **managed care model**, which is characterized by time-limited interventions, cost-effective methods, careful monitoring of services, and preventive more than curative strategies. This shift has implications for how you might view your role as a helper and how you may be expected to develop skills in brief interventions.

Key Ethical Issues

Helpers in a managed care system clearly have divided loyalties between doing what is best for the client and keeping their commitment to a system that demands cost containment through a reliance on short-term interventions. Many times, clients need more than the very brief interventions that are available. It is important that the welfare of the client is not put on the back burner in the interests of preserving the financial integrity of the managed care system.

Managed care demands that practitioners adopt a set of values congruent with limited interventions that mainly treat symptoms. This could raise ethical issues for practitioners who value growth and actualization more than remedial, short-term, solution-focused strategies. Those who work in a managed care context face a number of ethical issues that revolve around these concerns: informed consent, confidentiality, abandonment, utilization review, and competence.

Informed consent. Informed consent is an ongoing process that assumes particular importance under a managed care system. Prior to entering into a professional relationship with you, your clients have a right to know that a managed care company may request a diagnosis, results on any tests given, a wide range of clinical information, treatment plans, and perhaps even the entire clinical record.

From an ethical perspective, clients have a right to know that the focus on cost containment may have an adverse impact on the quality of care available to them. Clients have a right to know that other forms of treatment, possibly ones that may be more helpful, are being denied to them solely for cost-containment reasons. They have a right to know if you are versed in brief therapy, that an outside person is likely to judge what kind of treatment will be given and how many sessions will be allowed, the specific limitations of the plan they are participating in, and who decides the time of termination of therapy.

Confidentiality. Although confidentiality has traditionally been considered to be an ethical and legal duty imposed on helping professionals to protect client disclosures, managed care has redefined the scope of confidentiality. Because managed care providers take an active role in treatment planning, client confidentiality is compromised. Although there have always been exceptions to confidentiality, the demand for client information inherent in a managed care framework far exceeds previous limitations to confidentiality to the extent that the confidential nature of the therapist–client relationship is threatened.

Clients should be aware that the managed care plan may require practitioners to reveal sensitive client information to a third party who is in a position to authorize initial or additional treatment. Practitioners can no longer assure their clients of confidential treatment at any level because they have no control over confidential information once it leaves their offices. Because of these restrictions on confidentiality, helpers must inform clients from the outset about the relevant limits of confidentiality under their managed care policy.

Abandonment. The codes of ethics of the various professional organizations state that mental health practitioners do not abandon clients. Traditionally, the matter of termination of therapy is a collaborative effort involving both the client and the helper. Ethically, professional helpers must not abandon their clients, and they have a responsibility to render competent services. Under managed care, many critical decisions are made for the client and the practitioner by the program, and termination generally does not come out of a collaborative process but from company policy. Clients may have a sense of abandonment if their treatment ends abruptly. It is a helper's responsibility to inform clients that the request for additional sessions may or may not be granted by the managed care company. Managed care guidelines often limit treatment to a specific number of sessions annually with lifetime cost caps. Clients may be denied the care they need if it extends beyond their benefits and they are unable to pay for additional care.

Utilization review. Under managed care programs, all treatment is monitored by someone other than the practitioner. **Utilization review** refers to the use of predefined criteria to evaluate treatment necessity, appropriateness of therapeutic intervention, and therapy effectiveness. This process can take place before, during, and after treatment (Cooper & Gottlieb, 2000).

Competence. Those who work in a managed care system need to have special knowledge and skills competencies to deliver a variety of brief services in a flexible and holistic manner with a diverse range of client populations and client problems. This requires helpers to acquire an eclectic or integrative theoretical orientation. Mental health practitioners are forced to become more proficient in time-limited treatment approaches. Treatment plans need to be formulated rapidly, goals must be limited in scope, and the emphasis must be on attaining results. If helpers are not trained in brief treatment methods, and if clients will not be well served by a limited number of sessions, then helpers need to have skills in making appropriate referrals.

Legal Aspects of Managed Care

Practitioners are ultimately responsible to their clients, even if the decisions are made by the managed care system. Legally, practitioners employed by managed care units are not exempt from malpractice suits if clients claim that they did not receive the standard of care they required. Professionals cannot use the limitations of the managed care plan as a shield for failing to render crisis intervention services, make appropriate referrals, or request additional services from the plan. Practitioners are sometimes caught in conflicting roles when they attempt to offer what the client needs versus what is covered by the managed care plan. Increasingly, mental health providers may feel pressure by third-party payers to limit the amount of care provided to the degree that the needs of clients may be compromised (Koocher & Keith-Spiegel, 2016). Regardless of the structure underlying the delivery of services, ethical practice requires that practitioners put the best interests of their client first.

Trends in Managed Care

Many of you will be faced with finding a way to maintain your integrity while working within the constraints imposed by managed care programs. Accountability is being given increased emphasis in many work settings. Managed care requires that agencies and practitioners be accountable by demonstrating the efficacy of the services they provide. Increasingly, you will be expected to quickly assess the salient problems of your clients, provide a diagnosis, formulate a short-term treatment approach, and demonstrate the degree to which your interventions are effective.

Malpractice and Risk Management

Malpractice is generally defined as the failure to render proper service, through ignorance or negligence, resulting in injury or loss to the client. Malpractice is a legal concept involving negligence that results in injury or loss to the client. **Professional negligence** consists of departing from the usual standard of practice or not exercising due care in fulfilling one's responsibilities (Corey, Corey, & Corey, 2019). The primary problem in a negligence suit is determining which **standards of care** apply to determine whether a clinician has breached a duty to a client. Practitioners are judged according to the standards that are commonly accepted by the profession; that is, whether a reasonably prudent counselor in a similar circumstance would have acted in the same manner (Wheeler & Bertram, 2019). You are expected to abide by legal standards and adhere to the ethics codes of your profession in providing care to your clients. Unless you take due care and act in good faith, you are liable to a civil lawsuit for failing to do your duty as provided by law. Malpractice lawsuits against mental health professionals have increased over the past decade, yet the total number of these lawsuits is relatively small (Remley & Herlihy, 2020). The best defense against becoming embroiled in a malpractice suit or having a complaint filed with the licensing board is to practice quality client care and to establish and maintain respectful and effective relationships with your clients.

For a malpractice suit to be filed against you, these four conditions must be present: (1) you must have a duty to the client (there must be a professional relationship between you and another person); (2) you must have acted in a negligent or improper manner or have deviated from the "standard of care" by not providing the expected level of services; (3) your client must have suffered harm or injury, which must be demonstrated; and (4) there must be a causal relationship between that negligence and the damage claimed by the client (Corey, Corey, & Corey, 2019).

Grounds for Malpractice Actions

Grounds for malpractice actions vary in the helping professions. Malpractice is typically found in the following kinds of situations: (1) the procedure used by the practitioner was not within the realm of accepted professional practice; (2) the practitioner employed a technique that he or she was not trained to use; (3) the professional did not follow standard counseling procedures, which resulted in harm to the client; (4) the therapist failed to warn others about and protect them from a violent client; (5) informed consent to treatment was not obtained or not documented; or (6) the professional did not explain the possible consequences of the treatment (Wheeler & Bertram, 2019). Professional journals reveal an increase in citations for the abuse of alcohol and drugs because of the possibility of impairment. Driving under the influence is a serious offense and there are dire consequences imposed by many licensing boards for licensed practitioners who are convicted of a DUI offense.

As a student, you may think that you have no worries about being sued for malpractice. Unfortunately, student practitioners are vulnerable to such legal action. At this time in your professional development, you might well give serious consideration to ways in which you can lessen your chances of being sued for failing to practice in a professional manner. The reality of today is that even if you abide by the ethics codes of your profession and practice within the boundaries of the law, you can still be accused of wrongdoing. Even if the suit does not succeed, it is likely to be highly stressful, and it can take a toll on you in terms of time, energy, and money. You will have to spend many hours preparing and supplying documents and responding to requests for information. The best defense against becoming embroiled in a malpractice action is to practice quality client care and to know and follow the ethical standards of your profession.

Case example: Who is to blame?

The counselor did a risk assessment of a teenage client that did not show suicidal intent, and the client initially denied any suicidal impulses. The client takes the step of suicide despite the therapist's assessment and his best efforts to be of help. The child's parents fault the therapist for not having known more and done more to prevent this final action.

Your stance. Consider your own stance on the duty to protect. Do you have to be able to predict a possible suicide? Assuming that you are able to identify a suicidal client, will you always know the best course of action to take?

Discussion. Although you do not have to prove that you are a perfect being, you do have to demonstrate that you possess and exercised the knowledge and skill required for the services you provided. You must be able to demonstrate that you acted in good faith, that you have been willing to seek supervision and consultation when needed, and that you have practiced within your competence. You are also expected to produce documentation to support your claims.

Ways to Prevent Malpractice Suits

It should be clear that you would be wise to know your limitations in working with clients, to accept them, and to act only within the scope of your competence. Never hesitate to seek consultation, regardless of your professional experience. Consultation with colleagues often sheds light on a subject by providing a new and different perspective. Even if you are able to make wise decisions, it is validating to get support for your position from other professionals. If you are involved in litigation, it will be helpful to be able to demonstrate that your interventions were in accord with the standard of care exercised by other practitioners. It cannot be emphasized enough that adequate documentation is essential in defending yourself in any malpractice action. If you employ unusual therapeutic techniques with little rationale behind them, you are likely to find yourself the loser in a civil action. Contending that you were following your instincts and doing what "felt right" is not likely to get you very far if you are asked to defend your therapeutic practices.

LO13 Risk Management

Risk management is the practice of focusing on the identification, evaluation, and treatment of problems that may injure clients, lead to filing of an ethics complaint to a licensing board, or lead to a malpractice action. One of the best precautions against malpractice is personal and professional honesty and openness with clients. Providing quality professional services to clients is the best preventive step you can take. You need to know your limitations and remain open to seeking consultation in difficult cases, and, of course, it is essential that you document the nature of any consultations.

If you want a guarantee that you will not be sued for professional negligence, you probably should think about another career. There are no absolute protections in the mental health professions, but some risk management practices can significantly decrease your chances of becoming involved in a legal action. As important as risk management strategies are, it can be a mistake to focus on them too much. Birrell and Bruns (2016) suggest that ethics is better viewed from a relational engagement approach rather than a risk management perspective: counselors need to open themselves to authentic mutuality so that "ethics becomes relational and alive and fully integrated into each moment of the clinical encounter" (p. 396).

When considering ways to implement risk management practices, keep in mind the quality of the relationship between you and your clients. Here are some additional guidelines:

- Make use of informed consent procedures. Do not attempt to mystify the helping process; professional honesty and openness with clients will go a long way in establishing genuine trust.
- Consider ways to define contracts with your clients that clearly structure the helping relationship. Clarify your role with your clients. What are your clients coming to you for? How can you best help them obtain their goals?
- Because you can be sued for abandonment, take steps to provide coverage for emergencies when you are going away.
- Restrict your practice to client populations for which you are prepared by virtue of your education, training, and experience. Refer clients who are clearly not within the scope of your competence and take steps to maintain your competence.
- Keep up-to-date and accurate records of clients and carefully document a client's treatment plan. Develop a diagnostic profile, and keep relevant notes on each client.
- Become aware of local and state laws that limit your practice, as well as the policies of the agency for which you work. Keep abreast of legal and ethical developments by becoming involved in professional organizations.
- Be aware of the limits of confidentiality, and clearly communicate these to your clients. Attempt to obtain written consent whenever disclosure becomes necessary.
- Report any case of suspected child, elder, or dependent adult abuse as required by law.
- If you make a professional determination that a client is a danger to self or others, take the necessary steps to protect the client or others from harm. Document the actions you have taken.
- If you conduct online counseling, make sure you know the true identity and location of your clients in the event of an emergency (e.g., a suicidal crisis).
- If you are a provider of remote services or online counseling, demonstrate competence in both the services you offer and the technology you are using to deliver services.

- Treat your clients with respect by attending carefully to your language and your behavior. Present information to your clients in clear language, and be sure they understand the information. This practice generally leads to good relationships.
- Obtain written parental consent when working with minors. This is generally a good practice, even if not required by state law.
- When in doubt about a situation, consult with colleagues and document the discussions. Consultation shows that you have a commitment to sound practice and that you are willing to learn from other professionals to further the best interests of your clients.
- Find sources of ongoing supervision.
- If you are working with high-risk clients, consult and document the nature of the consultation.
- Establish and maintain appropriate professional boundaries. Learn to anticipate problems and set ground rules.
- Pay attention to how you react to your clients and monitor your countertransference.
- Avoiding imposing your values on your clients and avoid making decisions for them.
- Before engaging in any multiple relationships, seek consultation and talk with your client about the potential advantages and disadvantages of such a relationship.
- Do not engage in sexual or romantic relationships with current or former clients or with current supervisees or students.
- Have a clear rationale for the techniques you use. Be able to intelligently and concisely discuss the theoretical underpinnings of your procedures.
- Have a clear standard of care that can be applied to your services, and communicate this standard to your clients.
- Do not promise clients anything that you cannot deliver. Help them realize that their effort and commitment will be key factors in determining the outcomes of the helping process.
- If you work for an agency or institution, have a contract that specifies the employer's legal liability for your professional functioning.
- Abide by the policies of the institution that employs you. If you disagree with certain policies, first attempt to find out the reasons for them. Then see if it is possible to work within the framework of institutional policies.
- At the outset of therapy, clearly define issues pertaining to fees. Adhere to billing regulations and paperwork requirements as prescribed.
- Make it a practice to assess the progress your clients are making, and teach them how to evaluate their progress toward their goals.
- Let your clients know that they have the right to terminate professional services at any time they choose. The reasons for a client's termination should be documented.
- Carry malpractice insurance. Students are not protected against malpractice suits. Student liability policies are offered through many professional organizations at modest prices.

These guidelines will mitigate the chances of a malpractice suit or an ethics complaint to a licensing board. Wilkinson, Smith, and Wimberly (2019) present findings of the types of ethical violations across state counseling licensing boards for professional counselors. The most frequent types of ethical violations included failure to comply with the appropriate amount of continuing education, dual relationships, and misrepresentation of credentials. In addition to these violations, other areas that led to disciplinary action by a licensing board include documentation, note-taking, billing practices, practicing while impaired, legal arrests, and the failure to obtain informed consent. We encourage you to continually assess your practices and keep up to date on legal, ethical, and community standards affecting your work setting and client populations. The best way to reduce the chance of an ethics complaint or a malpractice suit is to know the ethical and legal standards and to follow them.

A Word of Caution

Students sometimes burden themselves with the unrealistic expectation that they should have clear answers for the ethical issues we raise in this chapter. Quite the contrary is true. Indeed, seasoned professionals are aware that the complex nature of their work with people defies neat and absolute answers. They have an appreciation of the necessity for continuing learning, for ongoing consultation and supervision, and for remaining humble.

Our intention has not been to overwhelm you but to stimulate you to develop habits of thinking and acting that will enhance your ability to base your practice on ethical and professional principles. Working in the helping professions is sometimes a risky as well as a rewarding venture. Although you may make mistakes from time to time, be willing to acknowledge those mistakes and learn from them. Make full use of supervision; you will not only learn from what may seem like mistakes but you will also minimize the chances of harming clients.

Do not be frozen with anxiety over needing to know everything at all times—or be afraid to intervene for fear of becoming embroiled in a lawsuit. Perhaps the best way to prevent a malpractice action is by having a sincere interest in doing what is going to benefit your client. Ask yourself these questions throughout your professional career: *What* am I doing, and *why* am I doing it? Would I be doing the same thing if my colleagues were observing me?

By Way of Review

- One of the trends in the helping professions is an increased interest in ethical and professional practice. This trend stems, at least in part, from a rise in malpractice actions against mental health practitioners.
- Ethical decision making is a continuing process. Issues that you look at as a student can be examined from another perspective as you gain experience in your professional specialty.
- It is essential that you be familiar with the professional codes of ethics. However, knowledge of ethical standards is not sufficient in solving ethical problems.
- Becoming an ethical practitioner involves an integration of both personal and professional ethics. Recognize that unethical acts are often subtle and unintended. Maintain a stance of honest self-exploration to ensure ethical behavior.

- Ethical issues rarely have clear-cut answers. Ethical dilemmas, by their very nature, involve the application of professional judgment on your part.
- Routinely utilize a systematic ethical decision-making process such as the eight-step model provided in this chapter or another one that you personally devise. This type of system encourages objectivity, research, analysis, collaboration, and documentation—all of which are important elements in effective and ethical practices.
- Ultimately, you will have to make many difficult decisions as a practitioner. Responsible practice entails basing your actions on informed, sound, and responsible judgment. Be open to consulting with colleagues and supervisors throughout your professional career.
- Many clients have not even thought about their rights or responsibilities. As a helper, you can do much to safeguard your clients by developing informed consent procedures to help them make wise choices.
- Confidentiality is the cornerstone of the helping relationship. Although clients have a right to expect that what they talk about with you in the professional relationship will remain private, there are times when you will have to breach confidentiality. Clients have a right to know from the outset of the relationship the specific grounds for divulging confidences. It is essential that you know and follow the laws pertaining to confidentiality.
- Confidentiality is limited when you work with couples, families, groups, and minors. These limitations should be discussed in your informed consent process.
- At times you will have a professional and legal obligation to warn or to protect clients. It is essential that you know your duties in this area.
- Your job is to teach clients how to help themselves and thus decrease their need to continue seeing you. Encouraging dependency in your clients is unethical, and it does not lead to client empowerment.
- It is essential to keep adequate clinical records for all clients. Documentation is critical, both for the client's benefit and for the protection of the professional rendering the services.
- If you rely on advanced technologies such as cloud computing for the storage and protection of client data, be aware of the ethical complexities involved.
- Be cognizant of the relevant legal and ethical issues if you communicate with clients via e-mail or online.
- Helpers who work in a managed care setting inform their clients about the services available and about potential limitations on the helping relationship due to the focus on cost-effective methods.
- Take an ethics course or, at the very least, read a book on professional ethics, and attend professional conferences and workshops dealing with ethics and the law.
- Understand what can lead to becoming involved in a malpractice suit, and learn practical ways to lessen the chances of this happening.

What Will You Do Now?

1. Find at least one person in the helping professions to interview about ethical issues in practice. Focus on the major ethical problem that this person has faced. How did this helper deal with this ethical concern? What are their concerns, if any, about malpractice suits?
2. Identify an ethical issue that you may encounter as a practitioner and create a resource list based on that topic. Include Internet resources, phone numbers for local agencies and hospitals, and books and articles on that topic. If this is part of a class assignment, each student should select a different ethical issue or topic. When you have completed the assignment, share your resource list with other students, and ask them to share their lists with you.
3. Think about a particular ethical dilemma that you have experienced in one of your field placements. How did you deal with the situation? If you could replay the situation, would you do anything differently?
4. Identify what you consider to be the most pressing ethical issue you expect to face, and write about your concerns and ideas in your journal. If you are involved in fieldwork, keep journal entries about any potential ethical dilemmas and bring your concerns to your supervision sessions or class meetings. Write down specific ways for you to increase your likelihood of becoming an ethical practitioner. What can you do now to move in this direction?
5. Structure a class debate around the arguments for and against suicide prevention. Consider debating a specific case of a client who is terminally ill with cancer and decides to end his life because of his suffering and because there is no hope of getting better. Divide the class into teams for an exchange on the therapist's responsibility to prevent this suicide.
6. In small groups discuss specific circumstances in which you would break confidentiality, and see whether you can agree on some general guidelines. In your groups, explore ways you might teach clients about the purposes of confidentiality and the legal restrictions on it. Discuss how you would do this in various situations, such as school counseling, group work, couples and family counseling, and counseling with minors.
7. Identify some forms of technology that you might be inclined to use in your counseling practice (such as e-mail, texting, Facebook, and other forms of social media). In small groups, discuss specific ethical issues associated with each form of technology you might employ. What are some safeguards you can take to protect clients' confidentiality and privacy?
8. For the full bibliographic entry for each of the sources listed here, consult the References at the back of the book. A useful guide to legal and ethical practice is Wheeler and Bertram (2019). A practical and positive approach to ethical practice is found in Knapp and VandeCreek (2012). For a casebook geared to the 2014 *ACA Code of Ethics*, see Herlihy and Corey (2015a). For practical desk references for interpreting and applying ACA ethics codes, see Barnett and Johnson (2015). For a useful discussion of duty to protect issues pertaining to harm to others, harm to self, and end-of-life decisions, see Werth, Welfel, and Benjamin (2009). For a book on ethics in counseling practice, see Remley and Herlihy (2020) and Corey, Corey, and Corey (2019).

9. We recommend that you familiarize yourself with the basic standards for ethical practice of the various mental health professions. Refer to the list of websites provided in this chapter or see Chapter 1, which has contact information for various professional organizations.

Ethics in Action Video Exercises

10. In video role play 1, Counseling Adolescents: Teen Pregnancy, in Part One (Ethical Decision Making) the client is a 13-year-old who just found out she is pregnant. She begs the counselor not to tell her parents. In this situation, what are the rights of the minor client? What rights do the parents have for access to certain information? What ethical and legal issues are involved in this case? What role would parental consent laws play in this case? What kind of informed consent process would you implement if you were counseling minors?

CHAPTER 9

Managing Boundary Issues

Learning Objectives

1. Complete a self-assessment on managing boundaries.
2. State the ethical guidelines regarding multiple relationships.
3. Differentiate between boundary crossings and boundary violations.
4. Describe boundaries from a cultural perspective.
5. Explain the ethical challenges in managing multiple relationships in small communities.
6. List four guidelines for setting boundaries.
7. Explain the ethical aspects of combining professional and personal relationships.
8. Identify the importance of boundaries in social media.
9. Explain the pros and cons of bartering for professional services.
10. Formulate guidelines on giving and accepting gifts in helping relationships.
11. Articulate guidelines for dealing with sexual attractions in therapeutic relationships.
12. Recognize the ethical and legal aspects of sexual relationships with current clients.
13. Recognize the ethical and legal aspects of sexual relationships with former clients.

Focus Questions

1. What problems might you expect to encounter in establishing boundaries with your clients?
2. If a client lost her job and could no longer afford to pay you for counseling services, would you be willing to enter into a bartering arrangement if she suggested bartering as an alternative to terminating her sessions? What other alternatives might you suggest?
3. If a client offered you a gift at the termination session and explained how important it was to him that you accept this gift as a token of his appreciation for your help, what would you be inclined to do?
4. How might the client's cultural background influence boundaries in the therapeutic relationship? How might your own cultural background influence your own boundaries in both personal and professional domains?

5. What kinds of multiple relationships do you believe are problematic, and why? Can you think of any multiple relationships that you might be willing to engage in with a counseling client?
6. How might you deal with unavoidable multiple relationships with your clients?
7. If a client were interested in forming a social relationship with you, what would you say? If this person were a former client, would that make a difference?
8. If a *current* client wanted to keep in touch with you by Facebook, what would be your stance? Would you agree to keep in contact with a *former* client via Facebook or some other form of social media?
9. If a client expressed his or her sexual attraction to you, what would you be likely to do or say? What would you do if *you* experienced sexual attraction to a client?
10. What ethical, legal, and clinical issues would you consider before entering a multiple relationship (social, sexual, business, professional) with a *former* client?

Aim of the Chapter

Regardless of which helping profession you enter, you will be faced with learning to define and maintain appropriate boundaries with your clients. If you are not able to establish and maintain good boundaries in your personal life, you may have trouble with boundaries in your professional life. In this chapter, we introduce you to an array of ethical concerns that helpers encounter in keeping relationships professional with their clients. In many ways, the topics covered in this chapter are a continuation of the discussion of ethical decision making in Chapter 8. Learning to deal with a range of boundary concerns is a key ethical and clinical issue that practitioners in all settings must address. Research shows how critical it is for helpers to learn to establish clear yet flexible boundaries. One of the most frequently used and effective self-care strategies is setting boundaries (Norcross & VandenBos, 2018).

Multiple relationship issues cannot be resolved with ethics codes alone. Helpers need to consider all of the ethical and clinical dimensions involved in a range of boundary concerns (Corey, Corey, & Corey, 2019). Good judgment, the willingness to reflect on our practices, and being aware of our motivations are critical dimensions of being an ethical practitioner. Mental health professionals oftentimes get into trouble by not heeding warning signs in their relationships with clients. Helpers may not have paid sufficient attention to potential problems involved in boundary crossings and may innocently cross boundaries that lead to problems for both the client and themselves.

The underlying theme of this chapter is the need for helpers to be honest and self-searching in determining the impact of their behavior on clients. Some of the issues and cases we present may seem clear-cut, but others are not. Resolving the ethical dilemmas we pose requires personal and professional maturity and a willingness to continue questioning our motivations.

LO1 Self-Inventory on Managing Boundaries

What are some of your major concerns about establishing appropriate boundaries with clients? Perhaps you have not yet raised or reflected on this question. We hope you will broaden your awareness of the importance of creating and maintaining appropriate boundaries in the helping relationship. For each of the following statements, indicate the response that most closely identifies your beliefs and attitudes. Use this code:

5 = I *strongly agree* with this statement.
4 = I *agree* with this statement.
3 = I am *undecided* about this statement.
2 = I *disagree* with this statement.
1 = I *strongly disagree* with this statement.

____ 1. It will be relatively easy for me to establish clear and firm boundaries with my clients.

____ 2. At times I am concerned about my ability to keep relationships with my clients professional.

____ 3. I am not sure how I would respond to a *current* client who wanted some form of social involvement with me.

____ 4. I might be willing to consider a social relationship with a *former* client if both of us were interested in meeting on a social basis.

____ 5. I think my training has prepared me to deal with sexual attractions in the helping relationship.

____ 6. Because multiple relationships are so widespread, they should not be considered as either inappropriate or unethical in all circumstances but should be decided on a case-by-case basis.

____ 7. Multiple relationships are almost always problematic and therefore should be considered unethical.

____ 8. If I were a truly ethical professional, I would never be sexually attracted to a client.

____ 9. If I were counseling a client who was sexually attracted to me, I would be inclined to refer this client to another counselor.

____ 10. I would be open to bartering my therapeutic services for goods if a client could not afford my fees.

____ 11. Bartering can easily sour a therapeutic relationship, so I would explore other options with the client.

____ 12. Sexual involvement with a client is never ethical, even after therapy has ended.

____ 13. I would never accept a gift from a client because doing so constitutes crossing appropriate boundaries.

____ 14. It is essential to consider the cultural context in deciding on the appropriateness of bartering, accepting gifts, and the helper assuming multiple roles with a client.

____ 15. I would have no trouble accepting a close friend as a client if we had a clear understanding of how our personal relationship could be separated from our professional one.

Once you have finished this inventory, spend a few minutes reflecting on any ethical concerns you have at this time on any of these topics. Identify a few of the areas where you are uncertain about your position, and bring this ambiguity up in class discussions.

LO2 Multiple Relationships and the Codes of Ethics

Ethical problems are often raised when helpers blend their professional relationship and another kind of relationship with a client. **Multiple relationships** occur when professionals assume two or more roles simultaneously or sequentially with a person seeking their help. Helpers establish a multiple relationship whenever they have another, significantly different relationship from the professional one they have with one of their clients, students, or supervisees. In these situations, the potential for a conflict of interest and for exploiting those seeking help cannot be ignored.

The terms *dual relationships* and *multiple relationships* (APA, 2017a) have been used interchangeably, and some codes of ethics continue to use both terms. In this chapter, we use the term *multiple relationships.* The scope of multiple relationships may involve assuming more than one professional role (such as instructor or supervisor and therapist) or blending a professional and a nonprofessional relationship (such as counselor and business partner). Other multiple relationships result from providing therapy to a relative or a friend's relative, socializing with clients, becoming emotionally or sexually involved with a client or former client, borrowing money from a client, or loaning money to a client. Mental health professionals must learn how to effectively and ethically manage multiple relationships, including dealing with the power differential that is a basic part of most professional relationships, managing boundary issues, and striving to avoid the misuse of power (Herlihy & Corey, 2015b). The argument to abstain from boundary crossings or multiple relationships is based on the *possibility* of helpers misusing their power to influence and exploit clients for their own benefit and to the detriment of their clients (Zur, 2007, 2017). Some helpers do place their personal needs above the needs of their clients by engaging in more than one role with clients to meet their own financial, social, or emotional needs. However, most helpers enter into multiple relationships out of a desire to meet the needs of their clients. From our perspective, a blanket condemnation of engaging in multiple relationships and performing multiple roles is not justified.

The blanket prohibition on multiple relationships has been replaced in recent years with cautions against taking advantage of the power differential in the therapeutic relationship and exploiting the client. Helpers today acknowledge that some boundary crossings may be beneficial. An increasing number of helping professionals now agree that flexible boundaries can be clinically helpful when applied ethically and that boundary crossings need to be evaluated on a case-by-case basis (Herlihy & Corey, 2015b).

The various codes of ethics deal specifically with setting appropriate boundaries, recognizing potential conflicts of interest, and taking steps to manage multiple relationships. Examples of codes of ethics that address managing boundaries and multiple relationships include: the American Counseling Association (ACA, 2014), the American Psychological Association (APA, 2017a), the American Association for Marriage and Family Therapy (AAMFT, 2015), the American Mental Health Counselors Association (AMHCA, 2015), the Commission on Rehabilitation Counselor Certification (CRCC, 2017), the National Association of Social Workers (NASW, 2017), the National Organization for Human Services (NOHS, 2015), and the National Board for Certified Counselors (NBCC, 2016). Although ethics codes such as these may function as guidelines, multiple relationships are frequently not a clear-cut matter. Ethical reasoning and judgment come into play when ethics codes are applied to specific situations. Consider the following examples of ethics codes addressing multiple relationships and managing boundaries.

The *ACA Code of Ethics* (ACA, 2014) describes special circumstances in which the usual boundaries might be extended:

> Counselors consider the risks and benefits of extending current counseling relationships beyond conventional parameters. Examples include attending a client's formal ceremony (e.g., a wedding/commitment ceremony or graduation), purchasing a service or product provided by a client (excepting unrestricted bartering), and visiting a client's ill family member in the hospital. In extending these boundaries, counselors take appropriate professional precautions such as informed consent, consultation, supervision, and documentation to ensure that judgment is not impaired and no harm occurs. (Standard A.6.b.)

NASW's *Code of Ethics* (2017) focuses on the risk of exploitation or potential harm to clients:

> Social workers should not engage in dual or multiple relationships with clients or former clients in which there is a risk of exploitation or potential harm to the client. In instances when dual or multiple relationships are unavoidable, social workers should take steps to protect clients and are responsible for setting clear, appropriate, and culturally sensitive boundaries. (Dual or multiple relationships occur when social workers relate to clients in more than one relationship, whether professional, social, or business. Dual or multiple relationships can occur simultaneously or consecutively.) (1.06.c.)

The APA (2017a) code states that multiple relationships that are unlikely to cause impairment or risk exploitation or harm are not unethical:

> A psychologist refrains from entering into a multiple relationship if the multiple relationship could reasonably be expected to impair the psychologist's objectivity, competence, or effectiveness in performing his or her functions as a psychologist, or otherwise risks exploitation or harm to the person with whom the professional relationship exists. (3.05)

Zur (2007, 2014, 2017) observes that none of the codes of ethics of any of the professional organizations refer to boundary considerations such as home visits, meeting outside the office, self-disclosure, home office, and nonsexual touch.

Home-based therapy has been used extensively with ethnic minority populations, mainly because many of these individuals have difficulty trusting traditional mental health professionals. For some clients, home-based therapy may be their only way to access services, due to mobility issues, transportation problems, or other barriers that make it difficult for them to travel. Going outside the office can decrease suspicion and build trust. Making a home visit gives the counselor a firsthand view of the client's home, neighborhood, and community. Amanda Connell (2015) addresses some of the challenges she has faced in maintaining boundaries when providing in-home services to clients. She has found that confidentiality and privacy can be compromised because other people are often present in the home during sessions. When no caregiver is present, clients may make numerous requests for personal assistance that is outside the scope of the helper's professional role. Connell strives to set clear boundaries and remind clients of the purpose of the session while acting in a compassionate and humane manner.

The codes of ethics of most professional organizations warn of the potential problems of multiple relationships but do not prohibit such relationships. Flexible guidelines regarding multiple relationships emphasize the importance of considering context in making ethical decisions. Nonsexual multiple relationships are not inherently unethical, and most ethics codes acknowledge that some multiple relationships are unavoidable. When multiple relationships harm clients, or have the significant *potential* to harm or exploit clients, they are unethical.

LO3 The Multiple Relationship Controversy

The helping professions have become increasingly concerned about the ethics of multiple relationships. During the 1980s, the issue of sexual dual relationships was given considerable attention in the professional literature. There is no doubt that sexual dual relationships are unethical, and all of the ethics codes of the professional organizations prohibit sexual relationships between client and therapist. This prohibition extends at least 2 to 5 years after termination of a professional relationship. Furthermore, most codes of ethics warn against any activities on the helper's part that could lead to the risk of exploitation.

Nonsexual multiple relationships came under increased scrutiny in the 1990s. Examples of nonsexual multiple relationships that are problematic and inappropriate include accepting clients who are family members or friends, combining the roles of supervisor and therapist, forming business arrangements with therapy clients, or combining personal counseling with consultation or supervision. However, not all nonsexual multiple relationships are inappropriate or unethical.

Multiple relationships and taking on multiple roles tend to be complex and involve many shades of gray. However, helpers cannot always perform a single role when working with clients or in the community, nor is it always desirable that they limit themselves to one role. Helpers will be challenged to balance multiple roles in their professional relationships throughout their careers. Herlihy and Corey (2015b) conclude that there is no clear consensus among practitioners regarding nonsexual multiple relationships in counseling. Practitioners are responsible for monitoring themselves and examining their motivations for engaging in such relationships. They should be cautious about entering into more than one role with a client unless there is sound clinical justification for doing this.

Interpersonal boundaries are fluid; they may change over time and may be redefined as counselors and clients continue to work together. Zur (2014, 2017) identifies dual roles that do *not* constitute multiple relationships: making a home visit, accepting small gifts from clients, attending a graduation ceremony or a wedding, accompanying a client to a dreaded medical appointment, playing basketball with an adolescent client, going for a walk with a client, and flying with a client who suffers from fear of flying. These incidents might best be considered **boundary crossings**—which occur when counselors shift their usual boundaries to respond to the needs of a client in a given situation. Such crossings are departures from standard practice that could potentially benefit clients.

An absolute avoidance of all boundary crossings is neither desirable nor possible (Barnett, 2017a). However, even though boundary crossings may not be harmful to clients, these crossings can lead to blurring of professional roles and can result in multiple relationships that do have a potential to be harmful. A **boundary violation** is a serious breach that causes harm to the client. It is critical to take steps to prevent boundary crossings from becoming boundary violations.

Barnett (Barnett, Lazarus, Vasquez, Moorehead-Slaughter, & Johnson, 2007) states that even well-intentioned clinicians must thoughtfully reflect on their actions to determine when crossing a boundary may result in a boundary violation. Failing to practice in accordance with prevailing community standards, as well as other variables such as the role of the client's diagnosis, history with trauma or oppression, values, and culture, can result in a well-intentioned action being perceived as a boundary violation. For instance, a client who was sexually abused as a child may perceive a mere touch on the shoulder by her therapist as a boundary violation. This simple action, intended as a gesture of support, could lead the client to feel uncomfortable in the therapeutic relationship—a place that should feel like a safe haven.

Not all multiple relationships can be avoided, some are mandated, and some helping professionals believe these relationships are not necessarily harmful, unethical, or unprofessional (Herlihy & Corey, 2015b; Zur 2007, 2014, 2017). Johnson and Johnson (2017) claim that in military settings multiple relationships are often unavoidable and mandated. To be effective in military psychology, clinicians must assume they will encounter clients in unexpected ways in a small base or on a ship. Johnson and Johnson assert that "multiple relationships in the military can actually improve morale, lower stigma about seeking professional assistance, and improve real-time access to care" (p. 53). They add that "multiple relationships with clients rarely cause harm, particularly when the psychologist demonstrates comfort with these interactions and remains attuned to the client's best interests" (p. 53).

Barnett (2017a) believes that a rigid risk-avoidance application of boundaries can result in harm to the client by creating a sterile climate that does not promote a positive therapeutic alliance. Pope and Vasquez (2016) point out that refusing to engage in boundary crossings may be both a lost opportunity and harmful to clients.

LO4 A Cultural Perspective on Boundaries

Traditional views of boundaries often need to be considered in a more flexible and expanded light when counselors are involved in working in the community and in social justice advocacy. In counseling across cultures, it is essential that practitioners acquire cultural competency, which takes into consideration cultural dimensions of professional relationships. Social justice and advocacy entails adopting a broader framework, focusing on societal factors rather than on the dynamics of the individual. Counselors who are not aware of cultural dynamics and their impact on clients risk engaging in unethical practice (Lee, 2015).

Speight (2012) calls for a reexamination of the traditional perspective on understanding boundaries, boundary crossings, and the client–counselor relationship. Many African American clients expect a warm, reciprocal, and understanding relationship and perceive therapists' objective detachment as a sign of not being involved. When working with multicultural clients, boundary crossings may be culturally consistent. Speight proposes the concept of *solidarity*, which is based on the ties within a community that unite people, as a culturally congruent way of understanding, defining, and managing boundaries. "Solidarity between myself and my clients both allowed and required me to be myself, to give primacy to the real relationship, to establish close boundaries, and to act in clients' best interests" (p. 147). By embracing a broader understanding of boundaries, Speight is able to be genuine and close in her therapeutic relationships without being inappropriate or unprofessional. She encourages clinicians to be mindful of the fine line between boundaries that are too close and those that are too distant. Speight recommends that counselors learn to tolerate complexity and to develop role flexibility in therapeutic situations.

LO5 Multiple Relationships and Boundary Issues in Small Communities

Boundary crossings are everyday realities faced by therapists who live and practice in small communities. Helpers who work in rural communities have greater challenges in dealing with multiple relationships than those who work in urban areas. It is likely that practitioners in rural communities will regularly be involved in multiple relationships, and counselors have the task of exercising good judgment about which multiple relationships to avoid, which to enter into, and for those entered into, how to ethically manage them (Barnett, 2017b).

Schank and Skovholt (1997) conducted interviews with psychologists who live and practice in rural areas and small communities and found that all of the psychologists in their study acknowledged concerns involving professional boundaries. Some of the major themes were the reality of overlapping social or business relationships, the effects of overlapping social relationships on members of the psychologist's own family, and the dilemma of working with more than one family member as clients or with clients who have friendships with other clients. Although the psychologists knew the content of the ethics codes, they admitted that they often struggled in choosing how to apply those codes to the ethical dilemmas they faced in rural practices. Although some time has passed since this study was conducted, the findings remain relevant today.

Unique ethical dilemmas often confront counselors in rural practice. The local pharmacist, physician, mechanic, banker, small business owner, teacher, or beautician might be a client of a particular helper. Rural professionals may see clients in the local store and ponder whether to acknowledge the person in the presence of others. If counselors are in local organizations such as the Chamber of Commerce or if they attend the same church, they may worry about conflicts with some fellow members who are also clients. They may be concerned if clients have children in the same school who are friends with their children or are on the same sports team. There is also the problem of mixing business with the therapeutic endeavor in rural communities. For example, if a therapist shops for a new tractor, he or she risks violating the letter of the ethics code if the only person in town who sells tractors happens to be a client. However, if the therapist were to buy a tractor elsewhere, this could strain relationships with the client because of the value rural communities place on loyalty to local merchants. Or consider clients who wish to barter goods or services for counseling services. Some communities operate substantially on swaps rather than on a cash economy. In rural settings, helpers typically play multiple roles and are likely to experience more difficulties maintaining clear boundaries than do their colleagues who practice in urban areas. Due to the demands that rural practitioners face, consultation with peers and colleagues is recommended to help prevent burnout. When a therapist's coworker has a relationship with one of the therapist's clients (e.g., the client may be the teacher of the coworker's child), seeking consultation from professionals outside the shared work environment and perhaps even outside the small community may be necessary.

Establishing Personal and Professional Boundaries

We find it useful to frame the discussion of multiple relationships within the context of boundaries. If you have developed clear boundaries in your personal life, you are less likely to have trouble with multiple relationships professionally. If your boundaries are poorly defined or if you attempt to blend roles that do not mix well, such as therapy and friendship or therapy and business, you are likely to stumble into ethical dilemmas.

We appreciate Lazarus's (2001, 2015) reasonable perspective on therapeutic boundaries. Lazarus contends that a general prohibition against multiple relationships has led to unfair and inconsistent decisions by state licensing boards, brought sanctions against practitioners who have done no harm, and often impeded a practitioner's ability to perform optimum work with a client. Lazarus contends that some well-intentioned ethical standards can be transformed into artificial boundaries that result in destructive prohibitions and undermine clinical effectiveness. Moreover, he believes some multiple relationships can enhance treatment outcomes. Lazarus argues for a case-by-case, nondogmatic evaluation of boundary questions that involves a selective process of deciding when it may be appropriate to enter into a secondary relationship. He contends that it is essential to consider individual client differences rather than to be subjugated to rigid standards. Lazarus (2015) believes that a "safe connection between therapist and client should be the overriding aim because this, not strict boundaries, will protect clients from abuse" (p. 31). From his perspective, great benefits can accrue when therapists are willing to think and venture outside the proverbial box.

Lazarus (2001) admits that some well-intentioned guidelines can backfire. He has socialized with some clients, played tennis with others, taken walks with some, respectfully accepted small gifts, and given gifts (usually books) to some of his clients. Lazarus makes it clear that he is opposed to any form of disparagement, exploitation, abuse, harassment, or sexual contact with clients. He sees certain boundaries as being essential but calls for a process of negotiation in many areas of nonsexual multiple relationships that some would contend are in the forbidden zone. Lazarus (2015) emphasizes that transcending boundaries should not be undertaken without serious consideration. He believes that a clear rationale for crossing a boundary is necessary, roles and expectations should be quite clear, and possible power differentials must be kept in mind.

LO6 Guidelines for Setting Boundaries

Although there are divergent viewpoints on multiple relationships, most professionals will agree that blending the roles of counselor and employee or counselor and lover is not appropriate. Whenever helpers play multiple roles, there is a potential for a conflict of interests, loss of objectivity, and exploitation of individuals who have sought help. Ethical practitioners must take appropriate precautions to ensure that the best interests of their clients are maintained. Several of the ethics codes emphasize the importance of informed consent, ongoing discussion with the client, and documenting any discussions in the client's record. Herlihy and Corey (2015b) provide these guidelines for professionals operating in more than one role:

- Set healthy boundaries from the outset. In your informed consent document, it is wise to state your policy pertaining to professional versus social or business relationships.
- Involve clients in setting the boundaries of the professional relationship. Discuss with clients what you expect of them and what they can expect of you.
- Informed consent is essential when you are playing more than one role with a client. Clients have a right to know about any potential risks associated with multiple relationships. Informed consent and discussion of unforeseen problems and conflicts is an ongoing process.
- Consultation with colleagues is most useful in obtaining an objective perspective and identifying unanticipated difficulties. If you are functioning in more than one role or engaging in multiple relationships, it is a good policy to consult on a regular basis.
- When multiple relationships are particularly problematic, or when there is a high degree of risk for harm, it is wise to work under supervision.
- It is essential that counselor educators and supervisors discuss with students and supervisees topics such as dealing with balance of power issues, boundary concerns, appropriate limits, purposes of the relationship, potential for abusing power, and subtle ways in which harm can result from engaging in multiple and sometimes conflicting roles.

- From a legal perspective, it is good practice to document any discussions about multiple relationships with your clients. Include in your notes any actions you have taken to minimize the risk of harm.
- If necessary, refer the client to another professional.

The controversy surrounding nonsexual multiple relationships is likely to continue. As with any complex ethical issue, complete agreement may not be reached. Prohibiting all forms of multiple relationships does not seem to be the best answer to the problem of exploitation of clients. Therapists should avoid crossing boundaries if doing so would likely harm the client or would be expected to impair the therapist's objectivity, judgment, competence, or interfere with his or her therapeutic effectiveness (Zur, 2017). Helping professionals need to clarify their stance on a host of boundary issues they will face in their practice and develop a systematic way of making ethical decisions. Zur (2014, 2017) believes it is of the utmost importance to consider multiple relationships in context. What is appropriate, unavoidable, and ethical in one context may be inappropriate, avoidable, and unethical in another context.

Herlihy and Corey (2015b) present a decision-making model that can be applied when helpers are confronted with multiple relationship issues. If the potential multiple relationship is *unavoidable,* helpers would do well to (1) secure informed consent of clients, (2) seek consultation, (3) engage in an ongoing discussion with the client, (4) document and monitor their practices, and (5) obtain supervision. If the potential multiple relationship is *avoidable,* helpers should first assess the potential benefits and risks in the case, and this should be discussed with the client. If the benefits outweigh the risks, the multiple relationship may be justified. However, if the risks outweigh the benefits, helpers might decline to enter the relationship, explain the rationale to the client, and, if necessary, offer a referral to another professional.

In your struggle to determine what constitutes appropriate boundaries, you are likely to find that some blending of roles is inevitable in certain situations. Therefore, it is crucial to learn how to manage boundaries, how to keep boundary crossings from turning into boundary violations, and how to develop safeguards that will prevent exploitation of clients. Even seasoned professionals are often challenged to follow the most ethical course when it comes to crossing boundaries and establishing appropriate roles. Managing multiple relationships can be even more challenging to students, trainees, and inexperienced helpers. For those with relatively little clinical experience, the wisest course might well be to avoid engaging in multiple relationships whenever possible. Think about these general themes and the guidelines we have discussed, and apply them to each situation presented in this chapter. Ask yourself how you would proceed in resolving any ethical dilemmas over conflicting roles with your clients.

LO7 Combining Personal and Professional Relationships

You may be tempted to form social relationships with clients who admire you excessively and who invite you to develop a friendship. This lure can be especially strong if you like your client and if you have a limited circle of friends. You may also be afraid to deal with your clients' potential feelings of rejection if you tell them that a personal or social relationship is not possible.

Factors to Consider in Balancing a Professional and a Personal Relationship

Balancing a professional and a personal relationship with a client is complex. As a helper, you may not be inclined to challenge clients you consider as friends lest you endanger your personal relationship with them. Or you may experience difficulty in separating yourself from your clients. Even if you are able to maintain your objectivity, provide an optimal balance between confrontation and support, and still be a therapeutic agent, your clients may have difficulty keeping the two relationships separate. One factor to consider is that no matter how you look at this issue, the relationship is bound to be unequal. As a helper, you are likely to be doing more of the listening and giving. In an equal friendship, both partners are typically giving and receiving.

At times, social interactions between helpers and their clients may occur. When you find yourself in this position, here are some questions to ponder: Does the social relationship get in the way of working effectively with my client? Does the social relationship get in the client's way of working with me? Am I retaining enough objectivity to determine any possible negative effects? We do have concerns about helpers who rely on their clients to make social and personal contacts. If most of your social acquaintances are people whom you serve professionally, we question whether you are using your role as a helper to meet your personal needs.

Case example: Going to lunch with a client.

A therapist (Yoana) has been seeing a client for some time. The male client (Joel) asks Yoana if she would be willing to meet for lunch. When asked about the reason for the out-of-office meeting, Joel says that he would like to talk in an informal setting and would like to take Yoana to lunch as an expression of appreciation for the help she has provided. The situation is complicated by the fact that one of Joel's personal issues is the fear of being rejected. Joel tells Yoana that he is taking a risk with this invitation.

Your stance. How would you handle this situation? Would it make a difference whether the client was of the same or the opposite sex? Would your own feelings toward the client influence your decision?

Discussion. Some clinicians never meet with clients outside of the office setting, and others feel comfortable interacting with clients in less formal surroundings. What makes this particular situation difficult is that Yoana and Joel have had an established contract to meet in a formal setting for quite some time, and Joel has taken the initiative to change the contract. Yoana must consider the motivation behind this invitation. Joel's desire to take Yoana to lunch may simply reflect his appreciation for the help she has provided, as he revealed, but it may indicate a developing attraction he has toward Yoana. Unquestionably, taking this action required courage for Joel who fears rejection, and Yoana may feel some degree of pressure to accept his invitation. Nevertheless, accepting his lunch invitation may lead Joel to misinterpret her intentions. If Yoana is attracted to Joel, this could potentially take her down a slippery slope, resulting in a boundary violation. Yoana must evaluate the implications of this invitation and her response on the therapeutic relationship she has with Joel.

Case example: Attending group functions outside of therapy.

Derek has been facilitating a men's group in an agency setting. The members discuss how men in our culture are isolated, and to deal with this isolation they decide to establish a once a month potluck meeting outside of the regular weekly group meeting time at the agency. They invite Derek to join them in this out-of-group meeting.

Your stance. Do you think it is appropriate for Derek to attend these potlucks? What are your ethical concerns about this situation? What are the pros and cons of socializing with group members? How would you respond to them, and why? Would your gender make a difference in your decision?

Discussion. Helpers need to be aware of the potential pitfalls of socializing with clients. If Derek consumes alcohol at the potluck, knowing that several group members are recovering alcoholics, this may affect how they view him and his professionalism. Derek would do well to assess his underlying needs and motivations before accepting this invitation. It is quite possible that Derek would maintain his professional demeanor at these potlucks. However, if he regards these events as an extension of his workday, he may begin to resent the extra time required, and his negative feelings might become apparent to group members. This case illustrates that something as seemingly straightforward as an invitation to a potluck dinner can be ethically complex.

The Cultural Context in the Intersection of Personal and Professional Relationships

The cultural context can play a role in evaluating the appropriateness of blending friendships with a helping relationship. In writing about multiple relationships from an African perspective, Parham and Caldwell (2015) question the conventional ethical standards that discourage multiple relationships and claim that such standards can prove to be an obstacle or hindrance in counseling African American clients. From an African perspective, the helping relationship is not limited to the office nor does it always fit into the 50-minute hour for a session. Instead, counseling involves multiple activities that might include conversation, playful activities, laughter, shared meals and cooking experiences, laughter, travel, rituals and ceremony, singing or drumming, storytelling, writing, and touching. Parham and Caldwell view each of these activities as having the potential to bring a "healing focus" to helping experiences.

In a similar spirit, Sue and Capodilupo (2015) make it clear that some cultural groups value multiple relationships with helping professionals. In some Asian cultures, it is believed that personal matters are best discussed with a relative or a friend. Self-disclosing to a stranger (a professional helper) is considered taboo and a violation of familial and cultural values. Sue and Capodilupo point out that some Asian clients may prefer to have the traditional helping role evolve into a more personal one.

Machuca (2015), a Latino counselor who works with Latino clients, writes about the importance of considering the cultural context in effective counseling. With Latino clients, a practitioner needs to understand their need for personal warmth, the desire to relate to a counselor on a more personal level, comfort with touching, and more flexible time limits for counseling sessions. Clients in a Latino culture often expect their counselor to attend social and family events, accept a gift as a sign of appreciation, and engage in personal self-disclosures. Machuca emphasizes that addressing boundary issues with Latino clients requires counselors to make a special effort to accommodate clients' cultural values and preferences beyond what is allowed for in a more rigid and traditional approach to counseling. Boundary crossing in this cultural context provides opportunities to create effective therapeutic relationships. "As an immigrant Latino counselor, walking the acculturation path alongside my clients has helped me to appreciate the importance of being flexible" (p. 103).

In some ethnic and racially diverse communities, Bemak and Chung (2015) have found that the relationship is expected to expand beyond the formal, 50-minute session. When counselors share aspects of their personal lives, they cultivate trust and openness with these clients. Bemak and Chung contend that counselors who do not "self-disclose may create mistrust, loss of counselor credibility, client feelings of being unsafe, potential harm to the client, and premature termination" (p. 87).

Socializing With Former Clients

Making friends with *former* clients is not addressed in the various ethics codes. Although social interactions with former clients may not be unethical, the practice may be unwise. The safest policy is to avoid developing social relationships with former clients. In the long run, former clients may need you more as a therapist at some future time than as a friend. If you develop a friendship with a former client, he or she is no longer eligible to use your professional services.

Very often the imbalance of power between counselor and client remains. Even in the social relationship, you may be seen as the provider of help, or you may behave as the person in the helping role. This imbalance of power may change very slowly or not at all (Herlihy & Corey, 2015a). You need to be aware of your own motivations, as well as the motivations of your clients, before allowing a professional relationship to evolve into a personal one. If you are in the habit of developing relationships with former clients, you may find yourself overextended and come to resent the relationships you sought out or to which you consented. What is central in this situation is your ability to establish clear boundaries regarding what you are willing to do and not do.

LO8 Social Media and Boundaries

Kolmes (2017) writes that online multiple roles and relationships between clients and therapists are becoming increasingly common. These multiple relationships include social, professional, and business relationships, and all of them can present new challenges for a therapist. From an ethical perspective, we need to understand the nature of these multiple relationships, when they may become problematic, and when they are a part of the therapeutic process. An example of a problematic multiple relationship is requesting online reviews or testimonials from either current clients or former clients. According to Kolmes, asking clients to participate in marketing a therapist's business is inviting them into a business multiple role with the professional. Kolmes believes that multiple relationships via social media and the Internet potentially may have both positive and negative impacts. "Some multiple relationships may be beneficial to the therapeutic relationship if they are well managed by a sensitive and thoughtful clinician. They can even offer opportunities to enhance the clinical relationship. Other multiple roles may erode the therapy relationship in a variety of ways" (pp. 186–187). The task for practitioners who participate in social media with clients is to develop a social media policy. Kolmes claims that a policy statement can reduce confusion and provide clients with guidelines pertaining to social media. "Simply thinking through your policies to create such a document offers the opportunity to review your ethics code and explore your own thinking on what you want your approach to be" (p. 192).

Increasingly, clients or former clients want to become friends with their counselor via the Internet. It is not unusual for a mental health professional to receive a "friend request" from a client or former client (Reamer, 2017). For helping professionals who are considering using Facebook, Twitter, or some other form of social media, a host of ethical concerns about boundaries, dual relationships, and privacy are raised. Helping professionals are encountering increasing challenges in the digital age, and Reamer (2013) describes the boundary confusion that can ensue if a social worker "friends" clients:

> Clients who have access to social workers' social networking sites may learn a great deal of personal information about their social worker (such as information about the social worker's family and relationships, political views, social activities, and religion), which may introduce complex transference and countertransference issues in the professional–client relationship. (p. 168)

Although "friending" a client is ethically problematic, Reamer (2013) underscores that denying a friend request on a social networking site may inadvertently result in the client feeling rejected. Reamer (2017) recommends that practitioners create separate personal and professional social media and websites in order to establish clear boundaries and to avoid inappropriate multiple relationships.

Reamer (2017) addresses the unprecedented ethical and risk-management challenges involved in multiple relationships in a digital world. Digital technology poses a host of ethical issues, a few of which relate to the blending of boundaries in both clients' and therapists' personal and professional lives and changes in the complex intersection between privacy and openness. Reamer agrees that digital technology in the mental health field is here to stay, and he emphasizes the need for helpers to cultivate sensible guidelines that facilitate responsible efforts to provide psychological services. The development of digital technology calls for "sound ethical judgment and careful risk management, especially related to novel forms of both intentional and unanticipated multiple relationships" (p. 205).

Spotts-De Lazzer (2012) claims that practitioners have to translate traditional ethics when it comes to social media and offers the following recommendations to help counselors manage a presence on Facebook:

- Limit what is shared online.
- Include clear social networking policies as part of the informed consent process.
- Regularly update protective settings because Facebook is constantly changing.

The *ACA Code of Ethics* (ACA, 2014) emphasizes informed consent and the need for counselors to develop a social media policy. This revised code emphasizes the virtual relationship between counselor and client and suggests ways for counselors to maintain a safe virtual presence (Jencius, 2015). The *Code of Ethics* of the National Board for Certified Counselors (NBCC, 2016) standard on the use of digital technology states: "Counselors who use social media for professional purposes shall limit information posted to that which does not create multiple relationships or which may threaten client confidentiality" (Standard 21).

What questions would you explore before becoming involved in social media with former clients? What are your thoughts about developing online friendships with present or former clients? Would you be willing to form such personal or social relationships with clients? Would you agree to keep in contact with a former client via some form of social media? Why or why not? What issues would you want to discuss with a former client before entering into a personal relationship?

LO9 Bartering in Counseling

Helpers who engage in bartering, or exchanging goods or services for counseling services, are often motivated by benevolent reasons, typically to help clients who are unable to afford professional counseling. Clients may suggest a barter arrangement—for example, cleaning house for the helper, performing secretarial services, or doing other personal work. Clients can easily be put in a bind when they are in a position to learn personal information about their counselor. This can interfere with the counselor–client relationship.

Bartering is an accepted practice in many cultures, but bartering for counseling services can be especially problematic. Clients may believe their counseling is not progressing well and resent the helper for not following through on his or her agreement. Likewise, helpers may be dissatisfied with the lack of timeliness or the quality of goods and services delivered by clients, which can lead to resentment and ultimately interfere with the therapeutic relationship.

Ethical Dimensions of Bartering

Most professional ethics codes have a specific standard pertaining to bartering. Although bartering is not prohibited outright, limitations to the practice are defined. The ethics codes of the ACA (2014), APA (2017a), NASW (2017), CRCC (2017), AMHCA (2015), NBCC (2016), and AAMFT (2015) all specify that bartering may be ethical only under these conditions: if the client requests it; if it is not clinically contraindicated; if it is not exploitative; if it does not increase the risk of harm; and if the arrangement is entered into with full informed consent.

In some cultures and in certain communities, bartering is an accepted practice. Bartering is an example of a multiple relationship that we think allows some room for helpers to use their professional judgment and to consider the cultural context in which they practice. Bemak and Chung (2015) note that in many cultures bartering is a valuable alternative to the traditional form of payment. They stress that bartering must be thoroughly arranged on a case-by-case basis, keeping in mind the cultural context and specific situations of each client. Forester-Miller and Moody (2015) address the difficulties involved in avoiding overlapping relationships in rural communities and remind counselors that values and beliefs may vary significantly between urban dwellers and their rural counterparts. They suggest that counselors need to ensure that they are not imposing values that come from a cultural perspective different from that of their clients. Forester-Miller describes her experience providing therapy in the Appalachian culture, where individuals pride themselves on being able to provide for themselves and their loved ones. She once provided counseling for an adolescent girl whose single-parent mother could not afford her usual fee, nor could she afford to pay a reduced fee, as even a small amount would be a drain on this family's resources. When Forester-Miller informed the mother that she would be willing to see her daughter for free, the mother stated that this would not be acceptable to her. However, she asked the counselor if she would accept a quilt she had made as payment for counseling the daughter. The mother and the counselor discussed the monetary value of the quilt and decided to use this as payment for a specified number of counseling sessions. This proved to be a good solution because it enabled the adolescent girl to receive needed counseling services and gave the mother an opportunity to maintain her dignity by paying her own way.

If you are considering some form of bartering in lieu of payment for your professional services, consult with experienced colleagues or a supervisor. This type of consultation is likely to reveal alternatives that you and your client have not considered. After reflecting on the relevant issues involved in a situation and consulting others, we highly recommend a straightforward discussion with your client about the pros and cons of bartering in your particular situation. This collaborative discussion with your client, as well as the opinions of others, might assist you in identifying potential problems associated with certain kinds of proposed bartering arrangements. Ongoing consultation and discussion of cases, especially in matters pertaining to boundaries and multiple roles, provide a context for understanding the implications of certain practices. Of course, all of the discussions with those whom you consult and with your clients should be documented.

Before bartering is entered into, both parties should talk about the arrangement, gain a clear understanding of the exchange, come to an agreement, and this agreement should be entered into the client's record. A good practice is for the helper and the client to collaboratively assess risks and benefits for a particular situation and decide after careful discussion. It is also important that potential problems that might develop be discussed. The client may not realize the potential conflicts and problems involved in bartering. It is the counselor's responsibility to identify the potential problems and risks in bartering. Perhaps the safest course to follow as a general rule is to refrain from accepting goods or services in exchange for professional services because of the potential for conflicts, exploitation, and strain on the helping relationship.

Legal Aspects of Bartering

Bartering is not prohibited by ethics or law. As a helper, you may face situations in which you will need to decide whether you will use bartering as an alternative, especially when clients can no longer afford to pay for services. If you were to consult with Robert Woody, a counselor educator and an attorney, he would likely advise you to stay clear of any bartering arrangements. Woody (1998) argues against the use of bartering for psychological services, saying that a case could be made that bartering is below the minimum standard of practice. If you enter into a bartering agreement with your client, you will have the burden of proof to demonstrate (a) that the bartering arrangement is in the best interests of your client; (b) that it is reasonable, equitable, and undertaken without undue influence; and (c) that it does not get in the way of providing quality psychological services to your client. Because bartering is so fraught with risks for both client and therapist, Woody believes prudence dictates that it should be an option of last resort.

Other Perspectives on Bartering

Koocher and Keith-Spiegel (2016) suggest that bartering can be a reasonable and humanitarian practice when people require psychological services but do not have insurance coverage and are experiencing financial difficulty. Although bartering arrangements may prove satisfactory to both parties, they advise practitioners to use caution in situations involving exchanging therapy for goods. Thomas (2002) views bartering as a legitimate means of helping a person with financial difficulties. He maintains that bartering should not be ruled out simply because of the slight chance that a client might initiate a lawsuit against the therapist. Venturing into any multiple relationship requires careful thought and judgment, and the vast majority of professional work should be paid by the usual monetary means. When this is not possible due to a client's economic situation, Thomas believes allowances should be made so that psychological services might be available. Bartering is one way of providing help to those in financial straights who do not qualify for insurance reimbursement. Thomas recommends a written contract that spells out the nature of the agreement between therapist and client, and this agreement should be reviewed regularly.

Case example: Bartering for therapy services.

For several months Carol has been counseling Wayne, who has consistently paid for her services and who is currently making excellent progress in counseling. Wayne comes to a session very depressed because he lost his job as an auto mechanic at a large dealership. He can see no way of continuing to see Carol because of his other pressing financial commitments. He proposes that he do a complete engine overhaul on Carol's vintage car as a way of paying for some counseling sessions. He asks if Carol would be willing to go along with this arrangement because he really does not want to interrupt counseling at this point.

Your stance. Would you be inclined to enter into some form of bartering arrangement with Wayne? Why or why not? Besides bartering, what other options might you present to Wayne? Would you consider seeing him without payment due to his circumstances? Consider what you would do as you address the following issues:

- Would your decision be dependent on whether you were practicing in a large urban area or a rural area?
- How might you take the cultural context into consideration when making your decision?

- If you engaged in this exchange of services and Wayne did not do a good job on the engine, how might this affect your work with Wayne?
- If you told Wayne that you did not feel comfortable bartering and he responded that he felt you were abandoning him in a time of need, how might you respond?

Discussion. Because Wayne proposed the idea of bartering for services, it would not be unethical for Carol to agree to this arrangement if she is comfortable with the idea. To ensure that their therapeutic work would not get derailed by this new arrangement, Carol and Wayne need to candidly discuss the possible pitfalls of bartering before reaching an agreement. Carol might point out to Wayne that he could feel resentful if the work on her vintage car ended up taking more time than he originally expected. He might also feel greater pressure to do a "perfect job" to please his therapist. Carol may wonder how she would feel if Wayne's work was substandard and she had to pay someone else to fix her car later. By discussing potential problems with bartering, Carol would be providing her client with informed consent and keeping his best interests in mind. If they decided to move forward with this plan, they would need to specify the terms of the arrangement, including their plan for addressing any challenges that may arise. If Wayne is hesitant to pursue this arrangement after hearing Carol's concerns, Carol needs to provide an acceptable alternative so Wayne can continue to receive services. Perhaps she would agree to provide pro bono services to him for a limited time until he found another job, or lower her fee and offer him a deferred payment plan.

LO10 Giving and Accepting Gifts in the Therapeutic Relationship

Several of the professional codes of ethics specifically address the topic of giving or receiving gifts in the therapeutic relationship. The ethics code of the American Association for Marriage and Family Therapy (AAMFT, 2015) contains this standard:

> Marriage and family therapists attend to cultural norms when considering whether to accept gifts from or give gifts to clients. Marriage and family therapists consider the potential effects that receiving or giving gifts may have on clients and on the integrity and efficacy of the therapeutic relationship. (3.9)

The *ACA Code of Ethics* (ACA, 2014) also has a standard on receiving gifts:

> Counselors understand the challenges of accepting gifts from clients and recognize that in some cultures, small gifts are a token of respect and gratitude. When determining whether to accept a gift from clients, counselors take into account the therapeutic relationship, the monetary value of the gift, the client's motivation for giving the gift, and the counselor's motivation for wanting to accept or decline the gift. (Standard A.10.f.)

The National Board for Certified Counselors (2016) takes this position on accepting gifts in their *Code of Ethics*:

> NCCs shall not accept gifts from clients except in cases when it is culturally appropriate or therapeutically relevant because of the potential confusion that may arise. NCCs shall consider the value of the gift and the effect on the therapeutic relationship when contemplating acceptance. This consideration shall be documented in the client's record. (Standard 4)

Bemak and Chung (2015) state that many cultures have well-established principles regarding gift exchanges. For a helping professional to reject a reasonable gift, or at times withhold giving a gift, can be perceived as insulting and as a rejection of the client's culture. Bemak and Chung acknowledge that the expense and appropriateness of the gift must be considered, yet helpers also need to be aware of the cultural norms and the importance of showing respect by and to the client through the gift. Lavish gifts certainly present an ethical problem, but you might have mixed feelings about accepting a small gift from a client or giving a client such a gift. Accepting certain kinds of gifts (highly personal items) would be inappropriate and require an exploration of the client's motivation. Some practitioners include a policy statement that they do not accept gifts from clients in their informed consent document. Our preference is to evaluate the circumstances of each case because a number of factors need to be considered. Several of the ethics codes identify specific factors to consider when accepting gifts: the therapeutic relationship, the motivation of giving, the counselor's motivation for receiving or declining the gift, cultural norms, and the value of the gift.

Here are some questions you might explore in deciding whether to accept a gift from a client:

- *What is the monetary value of the gift?* Most helping professionals would probably agree that accepting a very expensive gift is inappropriate and unethical. It also could be problematic if a client offered tickets to the theater and wanted you to accompany him or her to this event.
- *At what phase in the helping process is the offering of a gift occurring?* It makes a difference if a client wants to give you a gift during the early stage of the relationship or whether this occurs at the termination of the professional relationship. Small gifts given by either client or therapist as part of a termination process may be appropriate and valuable from a clinical perspective. It is more problematic to accept a gift at an early stage of a counseling relationship because doing so may be a forerunner to relaxing needed boundaries.
- *What are the clinical implications of accepting or rejecting the gift?* It is important to know when accepting a gift from a client is clinically contraindicated, and you should be willing to explore this with your client. You would also want to explore with the client his or her motivation for presenting you with a gift. A client might be seeking your approval, in which case the main motivation for giving you a gift is to please you. Accepting the gift without adequate discussion would not be helping your client in the long run. Helpers should carefully consider the risk-benefit ratio as it applies to accepting or not accepting a gift, or as it applies to giving or not giving clients gifts.

- *What are the cultural implications of offering a gift?* In working with culturally diverse client populations, counselors sometimes find that they need to engage in boundary crossing to enhance the counseling relationship. The cultural context does play a role in evaluating the appropriateness of accepting a gift from a client. Giving gifts has different meanings in various cultures. In some cultures, if you were not to accept a gift, it is likely that your client would feel insulted. For example, an Asian client may offer a gift to show gratitude and respect and to seal a relationship. Although such actions are culturally appropriate, some helpers believe accepting the gift would distort boundaries, change the relationship, and create a conflict of interest.

Brown and Trangsrud (2008) surveyed practitioners to assess their ethical decision making regarding accepting or declining gifts from clients. Those who participated in the survey indicated they were more likely to accept gifts from clients if the gift was inexpensive, was culturally appropriate, and was given as a sign of appreciation at the end of treatment. They were more likely to decline gifts that were expensive, that were offered during treatment rather than at the end of treatment, and that had sentimental or coercive value. Clearly cultural considerations are important when weighing the benefits of accepting the gift against the risk of jeopardizing the therapeutic relationship by refusing the gift.

If you find a pattern of clients wanting to give you gifts, reflect on the possibility that you might be, in some way, promoting a sense of indebtedness on your clients' part. If, however, it is rare that clients offer you a gift, you still need to determine a therapeutic way to address the situation. Consider what you feel comfortable doing and what is in the best interests of your client. If you decide not to accept the gift, we recommend that you discuss your reasons with your client. An open discussion is more fruitful and sensitive than simply giving your client a rule or a policy. As is the case with discussions about bartering, it is wise to document your reasons either for accepting or not accepting a gift from a client.

Case example: Giving and receiving gifts.

A Chinese client, Lin, presents her therapist with a piece of jewelry after five therapy sessions, and it is likely that they will continue for another five sessions. Lin says she is grateful for all that the therapist is doing for her and that it would mean a lot to her for the therapist to accept this jewelry, which has been in her family for many years. This is her way of expressing her appreciation.

Your stance. Consider your stance on giving or receiving gifts in the client–therapist relationship. Do you see a difference between accepting a gift during the therapy or at the end of therapy? What aspects would you want to explore with Lin before accepting or refusing her gift? To what extent would you consider Lin's cultural background and the meaning giving a gift holds for her in making your decision?

Discussion. This situation must be handled delicately. Given this client's cultural background, it is quite possible that she would feel offended if her therapist did not accept her gift. If Lin's motives for presenting the gift are genuine and transparent and the jewelry is relatively inexpensive (even if it has sentimental value), it may be appropriate for the therapist to accept it. On the other hand, if Lin's motives seem more convoluted, which a competent therapist would be able to detect by the fifth session, it would be important for the therapist to explore the underlying meaning of Lin's gift. If the gift was extremely costly—an heirloom that should remain in Lin's family—the therapist would need to find a tactful way of declining the gift. She might say "Lin, I appreciate your generosity, but I am uncomfortable in accepting this gift. This piece of jewelry is exquisite, and it belongs in your family. I want you to know that your gratitude is accepted and does not need to be underscored with this special gift."

LO11 Dealing With Sexual Attractions

Some helpers feel guilty over an attraction toward a client, and they feel uncomfortable if they sense that a client is attracted to them. There is a tendency to treat sexual feelings as if they shouldn't exist, which makes it difficult for helpers to recognize and accept them. Typical reactions to sexual feelings in the helping relationship include surprise, startle, and shock; guilt; anxiety about unresolved personal issues; fear of losing control; fear of being criticized; frustration at not being able to speak openly; frustration at not being able to make sexual contact; confusion about tasks; confusion about boundaries and roles; confusion about actions; and fear over frustrating the client's demands.

In their seminal work, *Sexual Feelings in Psychotherapy,* Pope, Sonne, and Holroyd (1993) break the silence surrounding the taboo of acknowledging and dealing with sexual feelings in therapy and offer these guidelines:

- Exploring helpers' sexual feelings and reactions should be a key aspect of training programs and continuing professional development.
- Sexual feelings must be clearly distinguished from sexual intimacies with clients.
- It is never permissible for helpers to exploit clients.
- Most helpers have experienced sexual attraction to a client, which can result in their feeling anxious, guilty, or confused.
- It is essential that helpers do not avoid recognizing and dealing with sexual attraction in the helping relationship.
- Helpers are best able to explore their feelings in a context with others that is safe, nonjudgmental, and supportive.
- Understanding sexual feelings is not a simple matter, which means that helpers need to be willing to engage in a personal, complex, and often unpredictable process of exploration.

Being emotionally or sexually attracted does not mean that you are guilty of therapeutic errors or that you are perverse. It is important, however, that you acknowledge your feelings (but not to a client) and avoid developing inappropriate sexual intimacies with a client. Although transient sexual feelings are normal, intense preoccupation with clients is problematic.

Part of learning how to deal effectively with emotional reactions or attractions to clients involves recognizing your own feelings and taking steps to minimize the chances of an attraction interfering with the client's welfare. Simply experiencing sexual attraction to a client, without acting on it, makes the majority of therapists feel guilty, anxious, and confused (Pope & Wedding, 2014). Given these reactions, it is not surprising that many therapists want to hide rather than to acknowledge and deal with sexual feelings by consulting a colleague or a supervisor, or by bringing this matter to their own therapy.

Koocher and Keith-Spiegel (2016) advise therapists to discuss feelings of sexual attraction toward a client with another therapist, an experienced and trusted colleague, or an approachable supervisor. Getting a fresh perspective on the situation can help therapists clarify the risk, become aware of their vulnerabilities, and explore some options on how to proceed. Seeking professional consultation is always a good idea, but we caution against sharing your feelings of attraction with your client directly. Such disclosures often detract from the work of therapy and may be a confusing burden for the client. In a survey on counselors' perceptions of ethical behaviors, Neukrug and Milliken (2011) found that 89.7% of the 535 ACA members polled believed it was unethical to inform clients about their attraction to them. It is the helper's responsibility to manage his or her feelings toward clients and maintain appropriate boundaries with clients by setting clear limits.

As you read the case examples that follow, consider what you would do in each situation.

Case example: A therapist's attraction to a client.

A single female colleague of yours tells you that she is having a problem with one of her female clients, to whom she is very much attracted. She finds herself willing to run overtime in the sessions. If she were not a client, your colleague confides to you that she would most likely ask this person out for a date. Your colleague is wondering if she should terminate the professional relationship and begin a personal one. She has shared with her client that she is sexually attracted to her, and the client admits finding her attractive too.

Your stance. Your colleague comes to you for your suggestions on how she should proceed. What would you say to her? What do you think you would do if you found yourself in a similar situation?

Discussion. This situation is problematic because the therapist is beginning to act on her feelings. The therapist behaved inappropriately by directly sharing her sexual feelings with this client, which complicates the matter further. Even if they terminate the professional relationship in order to pursue a personal one, there is a clear power differential between them. Pursuing a sexual relationship would be damaging to the client. The client has been put in an awkward position. If the client does not reciprocate those feelings, she may feel too uncomfortable to continue the therapeutic relationship. If the client admits to finding the therapist attractive, the client is in a vulnerable position. You must directly share your concerns regarding the potential ethical and legal repercussions that could ensue for your colleague due to her self-serving decisions that may have harmed this client.

Case example: A client's attraction to a therapist.

In a counseling session, one of your clients discloses finding you "sexually attractive." The client seems uncomfortable making this admission and now asks what you are thinking and feeling.

Your stance. If you heard this, how do you imagine it would affect you? What might you say in response to your client's concern?

Discussion. Given the emotional intimacy of the therapeutic relationship, some clients may develop an attraction to their therapist. By creating the optimal caring and safe environment necessary for therapeutic work to be done, therapists may present the illusion of being the "ideal" partner. It is important to remember that the therapist knows intimate details about the client, but that the reverse is not true. Clients may be attracted to you even though they know very little about your life, and this attraction may be rooted in transference. If you find yourself in this situation, be compassionate and sensitive as you explore the meaning of your client's projections pertaining to you, but also be clear in communicating appropriate boundaries. Processing this issue with the client may be an uncomfortable task, but if handled adeptly, it may deepen the client's insight and self-awareness.

Case example: Discussing sexual feelings.

One of your clients describes in detail sexual feelings and fantasies. As you listen, you begin to feel uncomfortable. The client notices this and asks, "Did I say something that I shouldn't have?"

Your stance. How would you respond to this client's question? Would you pursue this issue in your own therapy or talk with colleagues to gain some perspective on your own feelings? How much of this would you share with your client?

Discussion. We find that helpers-in-training often have difficulty talking openly about sexuality. For many, this discomfort stems from early injunctions in their family of origin about sexuality and from societal taboos. When clients bring up concerns pertaining to their sexuality, you need to be prepared to hear their concerns. As illustrated in this brief scenario, the client may end up feeling a sense of shame or embarrassment if he or she detects that you are uncomfortable with this topic. You hold the power in the relationship, so it is important for you to work through your own discomfort without burdening the client. Even if the nature of the client's sexual fantasies seems deviant from a clinical perspective and causes you to feel alarmed, you must deal with your reactions in a professional and therapeutic manner.

Training in Managing Attractions

Seeking help from a colleague, supervision, or personal therapy can give students and trainees access to guidance, education, and support in managing their feelings of attraction toward clients. Peer supervision groups are ideal places to discuss sexual feelings about clients. Deliberate attention to sexuality issues during training is essential for the development of competent mental health professionals.

In light of the challenges of dealing with sexual attractions in the helping process, Herlihy and Corey (2015b) recommend that training programs place increased emphasis on the issue of sexual attraction. Helpers need to be assured that their feelings are natural and that with awareness they can learn to provide professional assistance to clients, even if they might experience sexual attraction at times. Herlihy and Corey stress the value of counselors learning to monitor their countertransference, consulting with colleagues, and being alert to the subtle ways that sexual attractions can cross the boundary into inappropriate multiple relationships. We recommend Irvin Yalom's (1997) book, *Lying on the Couch: A Novel,* for an interesting case and discourse on the slippery slope of sexual attraction between therapist and client.

LO12 Sexual Relationships With Current Clients

Sexual misconduct is one of the major causes for malpractice actions against mental health providers. Those who have studied the sexual relationships between helpers and clients generally report that such misconduct is more widespread than is commonly believed. Studies demonstrate that sexual contact in the helping relationship can potentially cause severe harm to clients (Knapp & VandeCreek, 2003). Most mental health professionals take the position that erotic contact with clients is totally inappropriate and is an exploitation of the relationship by the therapist. The ethics codes of virtually all of the various professional organizations view sexual contact with clients as unprofessional, unethical, and clinically harmful.

Sexual relationships with clients carry serious consequences in both ethical and legal terms. These consequences include being the target of a lawsuit, being convicted of a felony, having a license revoked, being expelled from a professional organization, losing insurance coverage, and losing a job. Therapists may also be placed on probation, be required to undergo their own psychotherapy, be closely monitored if they are allowed to resume their practice, and be required to obtain supervised practice.

Here is one example of a therapist's sexual misconduct (California Association of Marriage and Family Therapists [CAMFT], 2010, pp. 55–57). A licensed marriage and family therapist was charged with committing sexual misconduct and gross negligence. When his client, a woman with a history of alcohol dependency and psychologically abusive relationships with men, revealed her sexual attraction to him, this therapist disclosed his mutual attraction to her and did not attempt to redirect her feelings or discuss the transference issue. He talked about his sexual fantasies in their sessions and expressed disappointment that they were prevented from having sex. He also revealed personal details about himself, and they would talk on the phone at night and on weekends, sometimes in a flirtatious fashion. After receiving feedback from her Alcoholics Anonymous sponsor about this relationship, the client began to understand that her therapist was harming her, and she shared her confusion about their relationship directly with her therapist. He did not respond well, which left the client feeling distraught, and he made no attempts to counsel her or refer her to a different therapist.

As you read this, you may think that you would never become involved in sexual misconduct with any of your clients. The chances are that those practitioners who have engaged in sexual intimacies with clients made the same assumption. Realize that you are not immune to the possibility of becoming sexually involved with those you help. Remain alert to your own needs and motivations and how they could get in the way of your work when you find yourself attracted to a client.

Clients are usually with you for a short time, and they are probably seeing the best side of you. You are likely to receive respect and adulation and to be perceived as someone who has no faults. This unconditional admiration can be very seductive, especially for beginning helpers, and you may come to depend on this feedback too much. If clients tell you how understanding and how different you are from anyone else they have met, it may be difficult to resist believing what they say. You are heading for trouble as a helper if you cannot keep the feelings that your clients express to you in proper perspective. Without self-awareness and honesty, you may direct the sessions toward meeting your needs and may eventually become sexually involved.

The reason erotic contact is unethical centers on the power that helpers have by virtue of their professional role. Because clients are talking about very personal aspects of their lives and making themselves highly vulnerable, it is easy to betray this trust by exploiting clients for helpers' own personal motives. Sexual contact is also unethical because it fosters dependency and makes objectivity on the part of the helper impossible. But perhaps the most important argument against sexual involvement with clients is that most clients report harm as a result. Clients typically become resentful and angry at having been sexually exploited and abandoned and generally feel stuck with both unresolved problems and unresolved feelings relating to the traumatic experience.

LO13 Sexual Relationships With Former Clients

Most of the codes of ethics of the various professions do not currently have an absolute ban on sexual relationships after the end of a professional relationship, but helpers are cautioned against forming romantic relationships with former clients for a specified time period, usually 2 to 5 years after termination. However, this does not imply that such relationships with clients are ethical or professional after the specified number of years has elapsed. The ethics codes of the ACA (2014), NASW (2017), CRCC (2017), AAMFT (2015), and APA (2017a) are quite specific about conditions pertaining to relationships with former clients. For example, it is not considered ethical to terminate with a client because of an attraction, wait the time period, and then begin a romantic relationship. Even after 2 to 5 years, it is incumbent on helpers to examine their motivations, to continually consider what is best for the former client, and to be extremely careful to avoid any form of exploitation.

In the exceptional circumstance of a sexual relationship with a former client, the burden of demonstrating that there has been no exploitation clearly rests with the practitioner. The factors that must be considered include the amount of time that has passed since termination of therapy; the nature and duration of therapy; the circumstances surrounding termination of the helper–client relationship; the client's personal history; the client's competence and mental status; the foreseeable likelihood of harm to the client or others; and any statements or actions of the helper suggesting a romantic relationship after terminating the professional relationship.

Almost all practitioners agree that termination of a helping relationship, in and of itself, does not justify changing the professional relationship to a sexual one. If a helper were to consider getting romantically involved with a former client after 5 years had passed, it would be wise to consult with a colleague or seek a therapy session conjointly with the former client to explore mutual transferences and expectations. Helpers must remain aware of the potential harm that can result from sexual intimacies that occur after termination, of the aspects of the therapy relationships that can influence the new relationship, and of the continuing power differential (Herlihy & Corey, 2015b).

By Way of Review

- A multiple relationship may occur whenever you interact with a client in more than one capacity. Be aware of your position of power and avoid even the appearance of conflict of interest.
- The codes of ethics of most professional organizations warn of the potential problems of multiple relationships, yet most codes do not prohibit all such relationships.
- Helpers are faced with the challenge of learning how to effectively and ethically manage multiple relationships, including dealing with the power differential that is a basic part of most professional relationships, managing boundary issues, and striving to avoid the misuse of power.
- It helps to keep your relationships with your clients on a professional, rather than a personal, basis. Mixing social relationships with professional relationships often works against the best interests of both the client and the helper.
- Traditional views of boundaries often need to be considered in an expanded light when counselors work in the community and advocate for social justice.
- Helpers who work in rural communities face unique challenges in managing boundaries and multiple relationships. Some multiple relationships cannot be avoided, and helpers must exercise good judgment in establishing ethical boundaries for these relationships.
- Exercise prudence in using social media. Be aware of the problems inherent in friending clients on Facebook. Keep up with the rapid developments in technology that can raise new issues related to professional boundaries.
- It is a good idea to avoid bartering, except when this is the best available option and when it is the cultural norm. Exchanging services can lead to resentment on both your part and your client's.
- In deciding whether to accept a gift from a client, consider the cultural context, the client's motivations for offering a gift, and the stage of the helping process.
- Sexual attractions are a normal part of helping relationships. It is important to learn how to recognize these attractions and to develop strategies to deal with them appropriately and effectively.

- Sexual misconduct is one of the leading causes of malpractice actions against mental health providers. Sexual intimacies between helpers and clients are unethical for a number of reasons. One of the main reasons is that they entail an abuse of power and trust and usually cause harm to clients.

What Will You Do Now?

1. Some say that multiple relationships are inevitable, pervasive, and unavoidable and have the potential to be either beneficial or harmful. In small groups explore both the potential benefits and the risks of multiple relationships. Come up with guidelines as a group for how you might assess the balance between the benefits and risks of multiple relationships.
2. Review the discussion on sexual relationships with former clients. Form two teams and debate the issue of whether sexual and romantic relationships with former clients should be allowed a specific length of time after termination of the counseling relationship.
3. Assume that you are a member of a committee with the task of revising an ethics code. What input would you have regarding the appropriateness of social, sexual, business, and professional relationships with former clients? Should these relationships be considered unethical under some or most circumstances? Can you think of exceptions? Can you think of situations in which you might accept a social invitation from a former client? Would you see it as appropriate to engage in a business relationship with a former client? Can you think of any situations in which you might form a personal relationship with a former client?
4. In small groups spend some time discussing what you learned about the importance of creating personal and professional boundaries. What difficulties might you expect to encounter in establishing and maintaining certain boundaries with some clients?
5. What impact does culture have on the boundaries that helpers establish with their clients? Break into dyads and discuss how your own cultural background might influence your perception of appropriate therapeutic boundaries.
6. In small groups, discuss how you anticipate you will respond to friend requests from clients who are using social networking sites such as Facebook. Debate the pros and cons of using social media in your work as a helper.
7. For the full bibliographic entry for each of the sources listed here, consult the References at the back of the book. For a treatment of many facets of the multiple relationship controversy, see Herlihy and Corey (2015b) and Zur (2007, 2017).

Ethics in Action Video Exercises

8. Using Part III of the DVD/Workbook *Ethics in Action* or online program (boundary issues), bring your completed responses to the self-inventory to class for discussion.

9. In video role play 14, Therapy Outside of the Office: The Picnic, the client (Lucia) would like to meet with the counselor (John) at the park down the street for their counseling sessions so she can get to know him better and feel closer to him. She could bring a lunch for a picnic. John is concerned about creating an environment that would help Lucia the most, and she says "that [meeting in the park] would really help me." Through role playing, demonstrate how you would establish and maintain boundaries with Lucia if she were your client. Under what conditions would you consider counseling a client outside the office?
10. In video role play 15, Beyond the Office Contact: The Wedding, the client (Richard) wants his counselor (Suzanne) to come to his wedding and reception. He stresses that her attendance would mean a lot to him. Suzanne is uncomfortable about going to the reception, but she agrees to attend the marriage ceremony. Through role playing, demonstrate how you might deal with your client's request to attend his wedding and reception.
11. In video role play 16, Social Relationships with Clients: The Friendship, at the last therapy session the client (Charlae) says she would like to continue their relationship because they have so much in common and she has shared things with the counselor (Natalie) that she has not discussed with anyone else. Natalie informs Charlae that this puts her in a difficult situation and she feels awkward. Charlae says, "What if we just go jogging together a couple of mornings a week?" Assume your client would like to meet with you socially and this is the final therapy session. Set up a role-playing exercise showing how you would handle a client's request to develop a social relationship with you once the professional relationship is terminated.
12. In video role play 17, Counselor Sexual Attraction to Client: Crossing the Line, the counselor (Conrad) shares with the client (Suzanne) that he has been thinking about her a lot and that he is attracted to her. Suzanne responds with, "You are kidding, right?" She says she came to him because she was having problems with men taking advantage of her and not respecting her. She has bared her soul to him, and now she feels devalued. Suzanne suggests possibly seeing another counselor, but Conrad thinks they can work it out. What are your thoughts about the way the counselor shared his feelings with the client? If you were sexually attracted to a client, what course of action would you follow?
13. In video role play 18, Client Sexual Attraction to Counselor: The Disclosure, the client (Gary) discloses his attraction to his counselor (LeAnne). The counselor attempts to deal with his attraction therapeutically by focusing on how his attraction might be a theme in his life and how it is related to issues he has pursued in counseling, especially his relationships with women. Role-play this situation by showing how you would deal with a client who admits to being sexually attracted to you.

14. In video role play 19, Bartering: Manicuring for Therapy, the client states she can no longer afford to pay for therapy but that she does not like to think about terminating. The counselor (Natalie) takes the initiative of suggesting a bartering arrangement, indicating she would be open to trading manicures and haircuts for therapy services. Discuss the ethical issues involved in this case. What is your stance on bartering for counseling?
15. In video role play 20, Bartering: The Architect, the client (Janice) lost her job and can no longer pay for counseling sessions. She suggests providing architecture services for work on his house. The counselor (Jerry) suggests they discuss the pros and cons and that he wants to be sure that this is in her best interests. He mentions the code of ethics that discourages bartering. Jerry talks about issues of value and timeliness of services. Put yourself into this scene. Assume your client lost her job and could no longer pay for therapy. She suggests a bartering arrangement for some goods or services you value. Role play how you would deal with her. What issues would you want to explore with your client?
16. In video role play 21, Gift Giving: The Vase, the client (Sally) is grateful for her counselor's (Charlae) help and wants to give her a vase. Sally informs the therapist that giving gifts is a part of the Chinese culture. Charlae discusses her dilemma with wanting to accept the gift, but also the fact that the ethics codes discourage her from accepting gifts from clients. Sally says she would feel rejected if her gift to Charlae is not accepted. Role-play this situation and demonstrate ways of either accepting or not accepting the gift. Discuss guidelines you would use to determine your decision.
17. In video role play 22, Gift Giving: Tickets for Therapy, the client (John) shows his appreciation for his counselor (Marianne) by giving her tickets to the theater. John says, "I got tickets for you so you can go and enjoy it and have a good time." Marianne talks about why she cannot accept the tickets, in spite of the fact that she is very appreciative of his gesture. Put yourself in the counselor's place. What issues would you explore with John? Might you accept the tickets under any circumstances? Why or why not? Demonstrate, through role playing, what you would say to the client.

CHAPTER 10

Getting the Most From Your Fieldwork and Supervision

Learning Objectives

1. List ways to secure a quality fieldwork placement.
2. Discuss the knowledge and skills required for successful job performance.
3. List five ways to profit from a fieldwork experience.
4. Discuss the challenges involved in working with differences.
5. Explore ways of getting the most from supervision.
6. Identify the characteristics of an effective supervisor.
7. Explore ways to deal with supervision that is less than ideal.
8. Explain the value of group supervision.
9. Discuss ethical issues involved in blending personal therapy with supervision.

Focus Questions

1. What specific steps can you take to maximize your learning from fieldwork placements?
2. How can you better profit from your supervision? If you are not getting the quality of supervision you need, what actions could you take? How comfortable would you be taking these actions?
3. What are some self-doubts you may have in thinking about a fieldwork experience? What can you do to challenge your doubts?
4. What specific steps can you take to confront any difficulties you are experiencing in your field placement?
5. In meetings with your supervisor, what attitudes and behaviors of yours are most likely to lead to maximizing your learning?
6. What would you look for in a field placement? What kinds of questions would you ask before accepting an assignment?
7. What personal characteristics do you think are associated with an effective supervisor?
8. What would you want to know about what is expected of you from your supervisor? What do you expect of a supervisor?
9. How would it be for you to work with a supervisor whose worldview is very different from your own? How might you handle differences of opinion between you and your supervisor that result from having different worldviews?
10. How would you go about securing a quality fieldwork placement?

Aim of the Chapter

Some trainees may have had field experience prior to entering their undergraduate or graduate training programs, but many have not. Whether you have had field experience or not, it is natural for you to experience the gamut of emotions as you anticipate your fieldwork experience. Many beginning helpers feel nervous and scared when starting this phase of their training. If you are plagued with feelings of self-doubt and excitement simultaneously, you can be assured that you are not alone. Once you become acclimated to your fieldwork placement, it is likely that your self-confidence and competence will develop, especially if you are determined to get the most out of your experience.

You will get far more from your program of studies and your fieldwork activities by assuming an *active stance.* Rather than concentrating on what you cannot do, think of what you *can do* and the advantages of taking a more active role in all aspects of your educational program. In this chapter, we encourage you to think about what you can do to ensure that you will be involved in meaningful fieldwork placements and that you will do what it takes to receive adequate supervision.

Self-Inventory on Being a Supervisee

Complete the following self-inventory as a way of focusing your thinking on the beliefs and attitudes pertaining to being a supervisee. As you read each statement, decide the degree to which it most closely identifies your perspective on supervision. Use this code:

3 = This statement is true for me.
2 = This statement is not true for me.
1 = I am undecided.

____ 1. In securing a fieldwork placement, I place a high priority on getting adequate supervision and being able to work with a diverse range of clients.

____ 2. I believe in treating my fieldwork placement like a job.

____ 3. I am willing to think and act in a self-directed way by involving myself in a variety of activities.

____ 4. I am clear in my own mind about what I expect from my supervisor, and I am willing to discuss my goals and expectations with a supervisor from the outset.

____ 5. It is important that I talk with my supervisor about my concerns about making mistakes and that I remain open to learning from mistakes.

____ 6. I am willing to assume an active role in my supervision and to prepare myself before each meeting with my supervisor.

____ 7. If I were to have difficulty in my relationship with my supervisor, I would discuss this with the supervisor.

____ 8. I am willing to take steps to get the best supervision possible.

____ 9. In the supervisory relationship, it is appropriate to identify my personal problems that may be interfering with effectively working with my clients.

____ 10. To get the most from my supervision, I am willing to challenge myself by talking about any difficulties I am encountering in my placement.

Making the Most of Your Fieldwork

In the helping professions of counseling, social work, psychology, and couples and family therapy, most graduate programs have fieldwork and internship placements at their core. Most undergraduate programs in human services have a comprehensive fieldwork component, which is often the heart of the program. These activities provide a bridge between theory and practice. Actual experience in a field placement gives students opportunities to learn firsthand about paperwork, agency policies and procedures, and the challenge of working with a wide range of client populations and problems. These are some of the goals of a typical fieldwork instruction program:

- Provide students with knowledge of the varied approaches and methods used in human services programs
- Help students extend self-awareness and achieve a sense of professional identity
- Broaden students' sociocultural understanding of the individual, the family, the community, and relevant social systems, and strengthen students' commitment to social justice advocacy
- Assist students in recognizing and respecting cultural diversity and offer ways to use this understanding in practice
- Help students expand their awareness of professional role relationships within their organization as well as the agency's role in the community

Before you can meaningfully participate in fieldwork and internship placements, you need theory courses, specific knowledge, and a range of helping skills. You can enhance your academic learning by volunteering to work in a community agency. It is the combination of academic coursework, fieldwork placement, skills training, and personal development that makes for a sound program.

LO1 Securing a Quality Fieldwork Placement

If your program selects placements for students, finding a fieldwork placement on your own may not be possible. However, if you have some choice in selecting the place where you will be gaining supervised practical experience, do what you can to secure the best placement possible. First, do your homework; thoroughly investigate the websites of prospective agencies and become familiar with each agency's mission and goals, services, and fieldwork/internship opportunities. Each agency or fieldwork site may require a slightly different application procedure, so be sure to follow any guidelines listed on their website. You will surely leave a better impression with agency staff if you adhere to their application process and follow their guidelines. Seek out peers who were placed at the agency you are interested in, and ask them about their experience. If you are granted an interview, you will have the opportunity to ask more specific questions about the placement. Here are some questions you might ask:

- How does the agency and professional staff view the role of interns? Are they viewed as members of the team or more as peripheral observers?
- What would be my specific responsibilities as an intern or practicum student?
- Are there any special skills or requirements for the placement?

- To whom would I report? Who would supervise me? How many hours per week would I meet for supervision?
- Are there training or staff development opportunities at the agency? What kinds of training might I receive prior to and during my placement?
- Is there any videotaping equipment available?
- Would I be covered by the agency for malpractice liability?
- What are some typical concerns my clients might face?

Sometimes students seek placements that are expedient, convenient, and not very challenging. We hope you will do what you can to secure a meaningful placement that will enhance your learning. This can take considerable thought, time, and preparation on your part. Strive for a placement where you will receive adequate supervision and where you will be able to profit from learning how to cope with a variety of problems that clients bring to the agency.

Due to budget cuts, high-quality internships and field placements are becoming increasingly competitive. We are aware of a situation in which three counseling students went to great lengths to secure a meaningful placement. They were determined to obtain internships at an agency that was so popular that they only rarely had openings. The students explored the agency's existing services and looked for gaps in community service needs that matched the students' individual interests and skill sets. Then each student went to the manager of the agency and proposed ideas on how to expand the services provided based on community needs. The manager was very open to the new ideas and hired all three interns immediately: one was bilingual and provided counseling in Spanish; one was hearing impaired and made counseling services in sign language available to members of the deaf and hard of hearing community; and one had a background with people with various disabilities and created a program for in-home counseling for people with severe disabilities as well as groups and services for their family members. The programs these interns created have flourished, giving them the satisfaction and fulfillment of delivering services to individuals who were previously unable to obtain counseling.

If you are employed at a community agency and want to use the agency for your fieldwork placement, we suggest that you branch out to get as much variety as possible in your placements. For instance, if you work part-time in the adolescent eating disorders division of a psychiatric hospital, challenge yourself to work with a different client population at the hospital, such as geriatric patients with dementia. If you already have volunteer or paid work experience in a particular setting, try doing something different for your internship: do different tasks, occupy a different role, or work with another client population. Your fieldwork experience should provide you with a variety of settings in which to work and also with various supervising environments. A wide range of opportunities exists within most agencies. Secure training in areas new to you as a way to acquire new knowledge and skills. Internships and supervised fieldwork placements provide practical experiences that can help you learn how to work meaningfully within a system. The more practical supervised experience you can get the better. The time spent in internships and fieldwork placements serves as the foundation for future work. Choosing a variety of placement settings and populations enables you to discover your strengths with some populations and learn about areas that interest you less.

When we talk with graduates of human services programs, they typically mention that they found their current job as a result of contacts they established at their fieldwork placement. In fact, most graduates report wishing they had been able to participate in even more fieldwork activities. Some regret not having had a broader range of experience in their internships. We recommend that you visit as many sites as possible before making your selection, if that is allowed in your program. Review job descriptions, ask site supervisors if it would be possible (or appropriate) to speak with current or past interns about their experiences at the site, and arrange interviews with selected agencies.

LO2 Knowledge and Skills Required for Successful Job Performance

When we asked practitioners about the skills they most need in their present jobs, they listed counseling skills, supervisory skills, consulting skills, communication skills, the ability to interact with different levels of management, the ability to write a proposal, organizational skills, the ability to deal with crisis intervention, and networking skills. A number of professionals pointed out the value of self-exploratory experiences, especially groups aimed at personal and interpersonal growth. These therapeutic experiences gave them opportunities to look at themselves and to deal with their own feelings and problems, activities that were seen as especially helpful in preparing them to relate to clients. Even those professionals who were primarily engaged in the administration of human services programs commented on the value of self-awareness and the understanding of interpersonal dynamics as tools they used in their managerial functions. Those in management pointed out that they would not be able to develop and coordinate their programs if they did not know how to work effectively with people.

A view from community agencies. As part of the self-study program conducted by our Human Services Department at the university, community agencies that offer fieldwork placements to our students were contacted and asked a number of questions regarding what they were looking for in hiring employees as well as their views on other relevant issues. Here are some of the questions we posed to agency personnel along with a representative sample of their responses to these questions.

1. What special knowledge and skills do our students need in order to work effectively at your agency?
   - Ability to work with diverse cultures
   - An understanding of ethics and confidentiality issues
   - Ability to connect with others
   - Resourcefulness and ability to direct and give referrals
   - Listening skills, case management skills, and counseling skills
   - Ability to be proactive rather than reactive

2. What knowledge, skills, and competencies do you consider most important for employees in your agency?
   - A good deal of independence combined with responsible reporting of treatment plans, incidents, and therapeutic progress
   - Sound judgment and problem-solving skills
   - Ability to identify and maintain clear personal and professional boundaries
   - An outreach person who can organize a program from start to finish
   - Must be creative, adaptable, and open-minded with an eagerness to serve the community in a nonjudgmental way
   - Awareness and acceptance of cultural diversity, including the immigrant experience
   - Self-motivated and hard-working
   - Good organizational skills
   - Ability to work with a disabled population in an educational environment
   - Flexibility and ability to work as a team
   - Good problem-solving skills and a good innovator

LO3 How to Profit From Your Fieldwork Experiences

For a variety of reasons, at times students do not derive the maximum benefit from fieldwork and supervision. Here are some practical strategies for getting the most value out of your fieldwork placements:

- Do not limit yourself to one kind of population, seek a variety of placements. Stretch your boundaries to discover where your talents lie and the kind of population you would eventually like to serve. Through your internships you may learn what you do not want to do as well as what you would like to do. Some students who initially want to practice counseling exclusively later find themselves in the role of administrator or supervisor.
- Attend courses, workshops, and webinars that will prepare you for the type of work expected of you in your placement. These opportunities can be a useful resource for staying on the cutting edge of new developments with specialized populations.
- Let yourself fit into the agency rather than trying to make the agency fit you. Be open to learning from the staff and the clients who come to the agency. Attempt to suspend your preconceived judgments about what you should be learning and focus instead on the lessons that are available to you. Learn as much as you can about the politics of the agency by talking with people who work there, by attending staff meetings, and by asking questions.
- Be aware of the toll that your work can have on you both emotionally and physically. Certain aspects of your own life may surface as you become involved with clients, and this can lead to some anxiety. Consider the value of personal therapy as a part of self-care.
- Your personal relationships are likely to be affected by your involvement in your fieldwork. As you gain experience in your work, your growth and

changes may not always be appreciated by those with whom you are close. You may face difficulties if your partner or significant others are not growing with you.

- Practice within the boundaries of your training, and put yourself in situations where you will be able to obtain supervised experience.
- Work toward becoming flexible in applying techniques with different client populations, but do so under supervision. Be open to fitting your theory to your clients rather than your clients to your theory. Adapt your communication approach and relationship style to meet clients needs and diverse backgrounds. Although it is important to learn therapeutic skills and techniques, they should be applied in culturally appropriate ways.
- Do not write off as a waste of time a placement that you do not particularly like. At least you are learning that working in a particular agency or with a specific clientele may not be what you want for a career.
- Make connections in the community. Use community resources and draw on support systems beyond your placement. Talk to other professionals in the field, ask fellow students about their connections in the community, and develop a network of contacts. This kind of networking may well lead to a range of job opportunities.
- Keep a journal and record your observations, experiences, concerns, and personal reactions to your work. Your journal is an excellent way to stay focused on yourself as well as to keep track of what you are doing with clients.
- Be open to trying new things. If you have not worked with a family, for example, observe a family session or, if possible, work with a supervisor who is counseling a family. Do not make the mistake of concluding that if you do not succeed perfectly in a new endeavor you are a dismal failure. Give yourself room to learn by doing, and recognize the value of your supervised experience.
- Look for ways to apply what you are learning in your academic courses to your experiences in the field. For example, one professional recalls having taken abnormal psychology as part of her graduate program and also having served as an intern in an institution for people with mental illness. She was able to see some of the concepts she was studying in the behavior the patients exhibited.
- Be prepared to adjust your expectations. It is unlikely that you will be asked to provide direct services to clients before the agency staff get to know you. You will probably start your fieldwork in an observing role. However, be aware that some agencies may give interns jobs without adequate preparation.
- Treat your field placement like a job. Approach fieldwork in much the same way as you would if you were employed by the agency. Demonstrate responsibility, dress professionally and act appropriately, be on time for your appointments and meetings, follow through with your commitments, and strive to do your best.
- When you are at your field placement, be fully present and avoid distractions. Supervisors and agency staff may become frustrated with interns who are constantly reaching for their cell phones and texting.

- Learn as much as you can about the structure of the agency where you are placed. Ask about agency policies, about the way programs are administered, and about management of the staff. At some point, you may be involved in the administrative aspects of a social program.
- Talk to people on the staff to learn about their roles and how they view the agency.
- Try to gain a global perspective of the agency as well as seeing it as clients might view it. Learn how agency systems work, and assess how you can work successfully within the system. Identify others in the agency who are successfully working within the system: talk to them, learn from them, and use them as a support system. Find out what keeps them motivated to do a good job.
- Think and act in a self-directed way by involving yourself in a variety of activities. Take the initiative to get involved in meaningful assignments.

LO4 The Challenge of Working With Differences

As we have suggested, it is a good idea to seek a placement where you will be expected to work with a variety of client populations and settings. By working with diverse populations, you can explore your interests and develop new ones. If you focus narrowly on the population or problem area you have chosen as a specialization, you are likely to close off many avenues of learning and limit yourself professionally.

As a part of your fieldwork for internship placement, you usually receive on-the-job training and supervision. Your coworkers and supervisors are in a position to teach you some interventions in working with clients. More important than knowing how to work with a specific population or a specific problem is having a general background of knowledge and skills and being open to acquiring more specific abilities.

Helping someone different from you. One of our colleagues told us that her client who was paralyzed became upset and angry when she said to him, "I understand how you feel." His reply was: "How would you know? You can walk out of here, and I can't." On reflection, our colleague thought that a better response might have been the following: "You're right, I don't fully understand your situation. I can imagine your frustration and pain over being paralyzed at such a young age. But I haven't been in your situation, so I don't know what you're thinking and feeling. I want to be open to understanding what it is like for you, and I will make a great effort to attend to your feelings about being paralyzed."

Some interns make the mistake of clinging to the conviction that to help a person they must have had the same life experience. A male clinician may doubt his capacity to effectively counsel an adolescent girl who is struggling with what she wants to do about a pregnancy. A helper may doubt that she can work with a client of a different race. Or a practitioner who has not experienced trauma may wonder about her ability to empathize with clients who have had pain and trauma in their lives. A helper who works with people with addictions may doubt his ability to effectively reach his clients if he has not had an addiction problem. When these helpers are confronted by a client, they often backtrack and become apologetic. We hope that you can see the value of drawing on your own life experience in working with clients who are different from you. You may not have had the same problem, but you have some experience with pain.

It is a mistake to try to ignore others' differences. Clinicians who do not acknowledge differences in their clients run the risk of alienating them and even causing them unintentional harm. Connecting on an emotional level is an effective way to work with clients whose life experiences are different from yours. For example, a client going through a divorce may feel a sense of loss. We have all experienced loss of some kind—death of a loved one, end of a relationship, or losing a job—and it is this experience of loss that enables us to empathize with our client's pain. It is more important to be able to understand the client's world than to have had an identical problem. It is crucial that we realize that some of our clients will view the world from a different perspective than we do.

LO5 Benefiting From Your Supervision

Most professionals question their competence at certain times and in certain situations. We hope you can be patient with your feelings of incompetence rather than denying your concerns. The purpose of your supervised fieldwork is to provide you with a varied and meaningful learning opportunity. This is a place where you can acquire specific knowledge and where you can develop the skills to translate the theories you have learned into practice. Be clear in your own mind about what you expect from your supervisors, and discuss your desires with them from the outset.

Maximize your time in supervision. Supervision is a required component of most training programs, and you will obtain the maximum benefit from your experience in supervision if you understand the roles, functions, and responsibilities of supervision. Prepare to assume an active role in your supervision and develop a collaborative relationship with your supervisor. You will get the most from your supervision if you take the initiative as a supervisee. Here are a few suggestions for benefiting from your supervision:

- Know the general purpose of supervision.
- Recognize that different supervisors will attempt to achieve the purpose of supervision in a variety of ways.
- Accept that a certain level of anxiety is normal to the supervision process.
- Clarify any aspects of your contract with your supervisor regarding the content of the supervision sessions.
- Be active in seeking the clinical experiences you desire.
- Be as honest and open as possible during your supervision sessions.
- If you are not able to select your supervisor, do your best to work within the framework of the supervisory style of the supervisor assigned to you.
- Clarify for yourself what you most want and need from supervision, and inform your supervisor of your needs.
- Take the time to prepare for your supervision session by identifying questions you want to explore and by bringing in examples you want to discuss with your supervisor.

- Do related research and reading between sessions to enhance your work with clients.
- If you are having trouble with colleagues or fellow supervisees, bring these matters into supervision.
- Ask your supervisor for feedback about both your strengths and areas where you need to improve.
- Be open to various forms of supervision, including live supervision, group supervision, and videotaping.
- Talk about insecurities and anxieties you have that pertain to your work.
- Provide feedback to your supervisor about what you find helpful or unhelpful in your supervision sessions.

Be Open to Multiple Sources of Learning

Be open to learning and to feedback not only from supervisors but also from teachers, peers, colleagues, and clients. Take advantage of your role: as a student, you are not expected to know everything. Internalizing this understanding can be freeing. If you understand that making mistakes provides you with an opportunity for self-reflection, critical thinking, and, ultimately, learning and change, you will be less likely to feel frozen in an attempt to avoid making mistakes. Talk openly with your supervisor about your presumed mistakes and discuss what to do in various situations when you are uncertain of your abilities. Believing that you must already have the knowledge and skills you need to be successful puts undue pressure on you; this attitude can get in the way of your ability to learn and prevent you from asking for help from your supervisors, peers, and clients.

In our training of group facilitators we typically find that the students approach workshops with considerable anxiety over looking incompetent in the eyes of their peers and supervisors. Early in the workshop we tell them this: "Be as active as you can. Stretch yourself past the point at which you typically stop. No matter what happens, there is something to be learned."

When we give students these instructions, they usually react with relief and acknowledge feeling much less anxious. We let them know that we understand and empathize with their difficulty in being observed by their peers and by supervisors. It is not possible to escape from being watched by clients, supervisors, and coworkers. Being observed live or through some form of media tends to be anxiety-provoking, but it is one of the best ways to learn and improve. Your internship or field placement may be one of the few times when your work is so closely observed; this is a great opportunity for growth and learning. Talking about your experience of being observed allows you to be in control of this process rather than being controlled by what others might think of you. Students often find it helpful to openly share their fears. Paradoxically, your fears are often diminished by simply acknowledging them.

Dealing With Challenges and Self-Doubts

Trainees may be unsure, apologetic, and unwilling to credit themselves with the ability to be helpful. Ask yourself how you typically deal with any self-doubts you may have about your ability as a helper. Consider how you might deal with a client who challenged you. At the initial session, your client is surprised at your age. "How can you help me?" he asks. "You look so young, and I wonder if you have the experience to help me." Assume that this challenge reflects your own fears and doubts. Can you imagine saying any of the following things silently to yourself?

- "He's right. There are many years separating us. I wonder if I can understand his situation?"
- "This man's attitude annoys me. I feel judged before he even had a chance to know me."
- "I don't feel comfortable with this confrontation, but I don't want to back down. I feel like letting him know that even though we differ in age we might have many similarities in our struggles. I'd like an opportunity to at least explore whether we can form a relationship."

Certainly as individuals we are all affected when someone challenges us, yet we need to learn how to deal with these situations. Helping is not about proving that we are "right." By staying focused on the best interests of our clients, we can address any challenges in a direct and honest manner. If you feel that you might have done something more effectively or sensitively, it helps to simply acknowledge this.

You Are Not Expected to Know Everything

Be willing to admit a lack of knowledge or understanding about a situation with both your supervisor and your clients. Don't be afraid to say you don't know something and to ask for help, and certainly do not pretend to possess knowledge that you do not have. You are at your placement to learn, not because you already have all the knowledge and skills you need. If you feel intimidated because you do not have the ability to effectively attend to a client's problem, you can say something like this: "Maria, I don't have all the answers, but I am confident that together we can figure things out and come up with a solution that works well for you. With your permission, I will consult with my supervisor to see if she has any ideas or options that we have not thought about yet. Ultimately, the best solution will be the one that you are most comfortable with." Your role as helper is not to provide solutions or to give advice but to teach clients how to examine options and apply problem-solving skills.

Think Out Loud

In working with both students and professionals, we often find that they keep many powerful reactions to themselves. We typically encourage our trainees to talk out loud rather than engaging in an internal monologue. Telling us what they were thinking but not saying helps them to get unstuck. Most of the time we find that what they are not saying could be extremely helpful to them and to their clients if they were to share it. In a recent workshop, one trainee, Victoria, was quiet throughout the group session. The supervisor asked Victoria what was going on. She replied, "I feel inhibited in following my hunches, and I fear that you might be judging me and not liking what you see." Her supervisor encouraged her to more frequently say aloud these kinds of thoughts. Victoria reported that by simply making this statement she felt much less self-conscious and less frightened over her supervisor's reactions.

In another instance, Lee continually suggested one exercise after another during a group training session. Later, when Lee was asked why he had introduced so many different exercises in such a short session, he replied: "Well, the group seemed to be going nowhere. People seemed to lack energy, and I felt responsible for making something happen! I was hoping to bring the group alive by trying some interactive exercises." We told Lee that it would have been good to describe what he saw happening in the group rather than trying techniques without explaining what was going on. We are not suggesting that you express every fleeting reaction you have to your clients, but in your supervision meetings it is wise to talk about unrehearsed material. That which is kept hidden tends to have power over us. What do you think Lee could have said instead of moving from one exercise to the next?

Finding Your Voice While Listening to Others

We have observed that some trainees limit their own development by trying too hard to copy the style of a supervisor or teacher. You are likely to observe supervisors whom you respect, and you may try to adopt their style. It is important, however, to avoid becoming a copy of another person. To get the most from your supervision, try different styles, but continually evaluate what works for you and what does not.

You might ask yourself: "What fits my belief system, both personal and theoretical? Do I have any conflicts between the theory or application of my supervisor's way and my own?" If you pay too much attention to another person, you are likely to blur your own unique approach to helping people. The more experience you gain, the easier it will become to listen to your own intuitive voice and to respect your inner hunches. Eventually, you will have less need to look to outside experts.

A Focus of Supervision

Some approaches to supervision emphasize the client's dynamics and teach you strategies for intervening in specific problems. Others focus on your dynamics as a helper and as a person and on your behavior in relation to your client. In our opinion, comprehensive supervision takes both of these elements into consideration. You need to understand models of helping clients, and you need to understand yourself if you hope to form truly therapeutic alliances. If your supervision is focused solely on what your client is doing or on teaching you specific techniques for what to do next, we think your supervision will be lacking a significant dimension. A critical focus for discussion in supervision sessions is the degree to which you are as present as possible for your clients. If you are overly concerned about what to do about a client's problem, this concern is likely to distract you from making connections with the person. A useful focus of supervision is the quality of the relationship between you and your clients. In supervision, you can talk about what you are experiencing as you work with different clients. This focus will reveal a good deal about both you and your clients.

Our Style of Supervision

When we supervise, we pay attention to the relationship between our supervisees and ourselves, as well as the dynamics and relationships between supervisees and their clients. Here we see a parallel process operating between a practice model and a supervisory model. Through this **parallel process**, supervisees can learn ways to conceptualize what they are doing with their clients by reflecting on what they are learning about interpersonal dynamics in the supervisory relationship.

Rather than placing emphasis exclusively on assessing and treating a client's problems, we are very concerned with the interpersonal aspects that are emerging between the supervisee and his or her clients. In our view, supervisors do well to look beyond the cases that trainees bring to the supervisory sessions and focus on the interpersonal dimensions.

In our role as supervisors we attempt to help our supervisees develop their own insights and refine their clinical hunches. Rather than placing the emphasis on direct teaching with supervisees by giving them information, we strive to help them learn how to conceptualize a case and think about how they are likely to proceed with a given client and why. Instead of using our words with supervisees' clients, we hope supervisees will discover their own words and find their own voice. Our style of supervision is reflected by the following questions we typically explore:

- Are you addressing any difficulties you may be having with me (as your supervisor)?
- What are you wanting to say to your clients?
- What direction do you think is most appropriate to take with your clients?
- How are you affected by your clients?
- How is your behavior affecting them?
- Which clients are difficult for you to work with, and what might this say about you?
- How are your values manifested by the way you interact with your clients?
- How might our relationship, in these supervisory sessions, mirror your relationships with your clients?
- Are you feeling free enough to bring into these supervisory sessions any difficulties you are having with your clients?

Many of the points we are making about supervision reflect our particular philosophy and style of supervision. Other styles of supervision may operate from a different set of assumptions. From what you have read in this section, consider these questions: What style of supervision do you think would be most useful for you at this stage of your development? What kind of supervisor do you think would be the most difficult for you to work with, and why? If it were impractical to change positions or change supervisors, what strategies could you use in constructively dealing with this supervisor?

Get the Supervision You Deserve

The assertion skills you practice in getting adequate supervision will be useful in your relationships with both clients and colleagues. Being assertive does not mean being aggressive. An aggressive approach will needlessly put others on the defensive.

Being passive is not useful either because your supervisor will have no idea what you want or need. Being aggressive or passive will shut you off from many opportunities to learn.

Get a clear picture of how you want to spend your time in an agency. Identifying what you want may not be easy, especially if this is your first fieldwork placement. You can begin by thinking about what you would most like to learn and what skills you would like to acquire. A placement typically involves a written contract signed by the student and the supervisor of the agency. This contract usually spells out the number of hours to be worked per week, the activities that will be performed, the learning objectives, the opportunities for training, the expectations for the intern, and the expectations for the supervisor. A written supervisory contract also typically addresses the number and frequency of supervision sessions, as well as guidelines for how both supervisor and supervisee should prepare for each session. Before signing your contract with your supervisor, discuss in some detail what you want and the kinds of opportunities available to you. In collaboration with your supervisor, identify what you would like to experience and learn. Although you may not always get what you want, if you have a clear idea of what that is, you will have a better chance of obtaining it.

It helps to realize that supervisors have many demands on them. As their client load grows and pressures increase, they may not initiate the regular supervision sessions that you have been promised. Furthermore, some practitioners do not volunteer to become supervisors but are told that they should add interns to their already heavy workload. At times their training in supervision is minimal, and they find they must take continuing education coursework to learn how to effectively supervise. If you are able to understand the predicament of your supervisors, you are more likely to be able to establish a basis of communication with them. Within a climate of open communication, you can let your supervisor know that you need help. If you have a difficult case, you can say something like this: "I really think I am at an impasse with Kristen. For several weeks now, we have made little progress. Every suggestion I make seems to go nowhere. I suggested termination, and she got angry with me. Now I don't know what to do. Can I meet with you to talk about some alternatives?" By being clear, specific, and persistent, you are more likely to have your needs met.

After you have gained some fieldwork experience, you will still need support and guidance, along with feedback from your supervisors, but you can profit from experiences that will demand more intuition and skill. Most important is establishing regular communication between you and your supervisor. This is particularly difficult in cases where you perceive your supervision to be inadequate, a topic we explore shortly. Your program is responsible for providing you with regular and competent supervision. As an intern, you deserve to have a meaningful supervision experience.

Case example: Duties outside an intern's area of competence.

A supervisor asks an intern to counsel a family, consisting of mother, father, and two young boys. The supervisor tells the intern that the parents are primarily interested in learning how to manage their problem children and want to learn disciplinary techniques. In the supervisor's view, a more important problem consists of the conflicts between the wife and husband. The intern has had very little coursework or training in working with families and lacks the competencies to do family counseling.

Your stance. If you were the trainee in this situation, what might you do? Might you give into pressure from the supervisor, especially with the offer of some supervision? How could you look for ways on the job to acquire the knowledge base that would enable you to work with a family? How would you like to be able to respond to this supervisor?

It is important to let your supervisor know of your concerns so the two of you can talk about alternatives. Consider the following dialogue, and think about how you might say some of the same or different things as this trainee.

Supervisor: We are short on personnel in the agency, and we really need you to work with some families.

Trainee: I am surprised that you think I would be able to see families. Yet at this stage of my professional development, I am going to have to decline.

Supervisor: Look, it is you or no treatment at all. Most of us have hesitations when we begin working with new populations. Just jump in and get involved.

Trainee: In my case it is more than feeling anxious and having self-doubts. I have yet to take a single course in family therapy. It just does not seem ethical for me to undertake this task now.

Supervisor: Well, I don't want you to do something that doesn't seem ethical to you. But I would be available for supervision, so you won't be without any guidance.

Trainee: I appreciate your offer for supervision. Perhaps I could observe your work with a family, with their permission of course, and then we could talk about your interventions after the session.

Supervisor: If I had the time that would be great, but that would be adding one more thing to an already overbooked schedule.

Trainee: After I take the family therapy course next semester, perhaps I'll be in a better position to assist in this kind of work. For now, I need to work within my own limits.

Discussion. This case example is realistic in the sense that some organizations use interns as relatively "free" staff. The problem is not so much using interns to fill critical service needs but being unwilling to provide adequate supervision for trainees. Student interns do need some minimal theoretical foundation and knowledge competencies in working with families before they are able to effectively participate in actual clinical work with families. Certainly, when trainees are moving into a new area, they will need to acquire practical skills that will enable them to work effectively in this new setting. Good supervision enables trainees to apply their knowledge while acquiring these intervention strategies. If trainees take on work that is new for them, they can learn and gain competence through supervision.

LO6 The Effective Supervisor

Although there is no one right way of conducting clinical supervision, there are established standards for counseling supervisors. The Association for Counselor Education and Supervision (ACES, 2011) developed a comprehensive *Best Practices in Clinical Supervision* document that address areas such as informed consent, goal setting, providing supervisees with ongoing feedback, conducting supervision, the supervisory relationship, diversity and advocacy considerations, documentation, supervision format, and the supervisory role. The best practice guidelines support supervisors in their work and clarify most aspects of the supervisory process. These guidelines are designed to help supervisors (1) observe ethical and legal protection of clients' and supervisees' rights; (2) provide training for supervisees in ways that are consistent with clients' welfare and requirements of the program; and (3) establish policies, procedures, and standards for implementing programs. The supervisor's main functions are to teach trainees, to foster their personal and professional development, and to assist in the provision of the effective delivery of counseling services.

Based on input from practicing clinical supervisors, Corey, Haynes, Moulton, and Muratori (2010) compiled this list of personal characteristics of an effective supervisor:

- Is aware of clinical, legal, and ethical issues
- Possesses good clinical skills
- Behaviorally demonstrates empathy, respect, genuineness, and listening
- Establishes an accepting supervisory climate
- Creates a supervisory relationship characterized by trust and respect
- Is flexible in determining the developmental level of the supervisee and providing supervision methods that will best serve the training needs of the supervisee
- Has a sense of humor
- Develops clear boundaries
- Encourages appropriate risk-taking on the part of supervisees
- Supports a collaborative supervisory process
- Respects the knowledge that supervisees bring to the supervisory relationship
- Appreciates individual differences among supervisees and differing opinions about theoretical viewpoints
- Is open, approachable, and supportive
- Has a keen interest in training and supervision
- Shows sensitivity to the anxieties and vulnerabilities of supervisees
- Values supervision as a "protected" time
- Provides honest and constructive feedback

In a nutshell, good supervisors tend to be available, accessible, affable, and able.

The picture of the effective supervisor that emerges from the research is derived primarily from findings regarding supervisee satisfactions and preferences. The effective supervisor is one the supervisees respond to positively and are able to trust. The general picture of the effective supervisor is a technically competent professional with good human relations skills and effective organizational and managerial skills (Corey et al., 2010).

Barnett, Cornish, Goodyear, and Lichtenberg (2007) report that numerous studies have found that the quality of the supervisory relationship is a key component in determining outcomes, much as it is for the client–therapist relationship. Effective clinical supervisors provide constructive feedback to their supervisees in a supporting and nonjudgmental environment. They are well trained, knowledgeable, and skilled in the practice of clinical supervision. They limit their supervision to those areas in which they are competent, and they delegate portions of supervision when necessary to make sure that supervisees receive the best quality of supervision possible.

You may meet and work with supervisors who demonstrate effectiveness and others who seem ill equipped to do what is expected of them. Some may be as insecure in their supervisory role as you are in your new role as an intern. We hope that you will remember that getting the most from supervision is a shared responsibility between you and your supervisor.

LO7 Dealing With Supervision That Is Less Than Ideal

From time to time you may encounter supervision that is far from ideal. How can you recognize inadequate supervision? What can you do to ensure that you get the quality of supervision you need and have a right to expect?

Accepting different styles of supervision. You can benefit from learning how to function under a range of supervisory styles, both now as a student and later as a helping professional. One supervisor may believe confrontation is a way to cut through a client's defenses. Another may provide frequent advice for clients and promote a problem-solving orientation for client problems. Some supervisors foster a supportive and positive orientation with clients exclusively. Some supervisors may work very hard at establishing collegial relationships with their interns, whereas others may be more directive and professionally distant. Be open to supervisors with various orientations and styles, and be open to incorporating some of their viewpoints in your practices. Do not be too quick to criticize a style different from yours, but consider it as an opportunity for learning. As a supervisee, recognize that at different stages in your professional development you may require different styles of supervision.

Understand and appreciate the responsibility of your supervisor. If you have trouble with a supervisor, the answer is not finding a new one. You can learn a great deal by working with supervisors who have perspectives different from yours and from supervisors who may initially appear to be difficult for you to make contact with. When you experience conflicts with a supervisor, it is a good idea to talk about these conflicts and do all that you can to work them out. Rather than telling yourself that your supervisor will not be cooperative, assume that he or she will be open to your quests and suggestions. Remember that your supervisor is the person who bears responsibility for your work with clients. Later, when you accept a position in an agency, you typically will not have the option of changing supervisors. What is more, you often do not choose who your coworkers will be. It is important to learn the interpersonal skills necessary in working out differences.

Realize that your supervisor is legally and ethically responsible for all of your actions as a supervisee. This is known as **vicarious liability**. You are not expected to assume *final* responsibility for your clients. Supervisors are legally expected to carry the decision-making responsibility and liability. Polychronis and Brown (2016) broaden the concept of vicarious liability to encompass the legal doctrine of **strict liability**, which holds clinical supervisors responsible for supervisees' actions in a professional realm without any need to establish that supervisors were negligent or careless in their supervisory duties. Even supervisors who provide exemplary supervision may bear legal responsibility for any wrong caused by a supervisee. Supervisors who practice in jurisdictions that apply the strict liability standard to clinical supervision are especially vulnerable and need to engage in vigorous risk-management strategies to protect themselves. Knowing this may help you put the supervisory relationship into perspective.

Solving problems in your supervision. You may encounter a number of problems in working with a supervisor. Communication may not be open or encouraged. Some supervisors may poorly define what they expect of you. Some may fail to show up for appointments. Others may delegate their responsibilities to their secretary. There is also the supervisor who is insecure but disguises this insecurity by being overly controlling and autocratic. Some supervisors put too much responsibility on an intern too soon or delegate menial work. Supervisors may be guilty of unethical practices. One supervisor had her supervisee do her work and then wrote up the proceedings as though she had seen the client. Some supervisors misuse power through a need to be seen as always being right. Others give little feedback, keeping the student intern in the dark and offering very little direction. Although most supervisors have good intentions and strive to provide quality supervision, some of them feel overwhelmed with the multitude of responsibilities expected of them. This can lead to supervisors not being attentive to those in their charge.

Supervisory roles and functions themselves can be detrimental to efforts to create an open relationship. Supervisors are responsible for your work with clients and will evaluate you. It is understandable that you might be anxious about being observed and evaluated. It may help to accept that performance anxiety goes with the territory of being a supervisee. However, you can face and deal with your fears rather than allowing yourself to be caught up in performance expectations.

If you are very dissatisfied with your supervisor and believe that you are not getting the quality of supervision you have a right to receive, consider discussing this with the supervisor in question as an initial step. If you decide this is not a good alternative, bring the matter to your university supervisor for help in exploring your options.

Informed Consent in Supervision

Informed consent is a basic part of the supervisory relationship (ACES, 2011). It is now considered the standard of practice to incorporate clear informed consent material for supervisees, both orally and in writing. The goal of informed consent is to enhance the quality of the supervision experience. It is beneficial to discuss the rights of supervisees from the beginning of the supervisory relationship, in much the same way as the rights of clients are addressed early in the therapy process. Supervisors are expected to engage in sound informed consent practices from the beginning of a supervisory experience (ACES, 2011). When supervisees know what to expect in all aspects of their supervision and what they need to do to achieve success, they are empowered to make decisions and become active participants in the supervisory process. In addition, misunderstandings are minimized, and both parties are more likely to experience satisfaction in their respective roles. If your fieldwork supervisor does not provide you with an informed consent document (usually a supervision contract), you should consult with your university supervisor to support you in obtaining the appropriate supervisory informed consent from your field placement.

Student supervisees may not be aware that they should be receiving regular supervisory feedback. Many states require written supervision session documents, which demonstrate that supervisors are fulfilling their responsibilities by providing feedback to supervisees. As a best practice, supervisors provide ongoing formative evaluations on a weekly basis. At minimum, supervisors should provide their supervisees with a midterm evaluation of their progress and emphasize areas of focus for the time remaining at the field placement. Regular written evaluations can protect both supervisees and supervisors from misunderstandings. Supervisors who provide feedback only at the end of the semester leave supervisees feeling that they did not have adequate feedback to make necessary adjustments to improve their performance. Ideally, the methods of evaluation and the time frames for supervision are outlined in the supervision contract.

LO8 Participating in Group Supervision

The value of group supervision is sometimes overlooked. In groups, trainees benefit by listening to others and by discussing cases with their peers as well as with a supervisor. Our approach is to combine individual and group supervision when this is practical and possible. **Group supervision** is a time-efficient and unique format that assists trainees in developing skills in conceptualizing cases and in implementing a variety of treatment interventions. If you participate in group supervision, you learn not only from your supervisor but also from fellow trainees. You learn that you are not alone with your anxiety and concerns surrounding clinical work, and you are exposed to different perspectives of the helping relationship.

In group supervision you will have many opportunities to role-play challenging clients and to try on a variety of helper roles in a given situation. Role playing offers many possibilities, not only for you to become aware of potential countertransference issues but as a way to acquire alternative perspectives in working with clients you sometimes perceive as being "difficult." You can assume the role of your client by "becoming" the client while the supervisor demonstrates other approaches for dealing with your client. Later, the supervisor can switch roles and become the client while you try another way of dealing with your client. Of course, in a group context your peers can assume various roles, which can enhance learning. Role-playing techniques tend to bring to life a situation that all can witness, as opposed to merely talking about problems with clients.

The group supervision model is enhanced when you make the process a personal one. You can do this by focusing on your own reactions and sharing them in your supervision group. What clients trigger you? What clients do you hope won't show up next week? What clients threaten you? What clients do you like more than others? By focusing on your relationships with your clients and your own dynamics, you can increase your self-awareness through the feedback you get from others in the group.

It is also helpful to explore your values and attitudes in conjunction with your supervision. If you become aware of a tendency to seek gratitude or approval from clients, for example, it could be useful to explore your own need for approval and your fear of rejection, either in your own personal therapy or in a group supervision session.

Multiple Roles and Relationships in Supervision

The ACES (2011) *Best Practices in Clinical Supervision* document states that clinical supervisors are expected to possess the personal and professional maturity to play multiple roles. **Multiple-role relationships** in supervision occur when a supervisor has concurrent or consecutive professional or nonprofessional relationships with a supervisee in addition to the supervisor–supervisee relationship. Multiple roles and relationships are common in clinical supervision, and although they are often unavoidable, they also have the potential to be problematic. It is the ethical responsibility of supervisors to carefully manage these relationships so they do not result in harm to or exploitation of supervisees. Supervisors need to clarify their roles and to distinguish between flexible and rigid boundaries. If the supervisor does not maintain objectivity, the supervisee will not be able to make maximum use of the process.

The *Code of Ethics* of the ACA (2014) deals directly and clearly with boundary issues in teaching and supervisory relationships. It is the responsibility of clinical supervisors to create and maintain appropriate relationship boundaries with supervisees:

> Counselor educators are aware of the power differential in the relationship between faculty and students. If they believe a nonprofessional relationship with a student may be potentially beneficial to the student, they take precautions similar to those taken by counselors when working with clients. (Standard F.10.f.)

Those who teach or supervise students in the helping professions have an obligation to trainees to openly discuss appropriate boundaries and to work with trainees to help them understand how to balance multiple roles and manage multiple relationships. It is critical for supervisors to serve as effective role models in establishing and maintaining appropriate boundaries (Austin, Austin, Muratori, & Corey, 2017).

Freedom From Sexual Harassment

One of the most egregious boundary violations in supervision involves sexual harassment and sexual relationships in the supervisory relationship. Those who are in charge of supervising trainees must avoid engaging in sexual relationships with trainees and avoid subjecting trainees to any form of sexual harassment. If the supervisory relationship evolves into a romantic one, the entire supervisory process is seriously compromised, with the supervisee sooner or later likely to allege exploitation. You have a right to expect a learning environment free from sexual harassment, both in the classroom and at your field placement. You should not be expected to deal with situations involving unwanted sexual advances from those who function in teaching or supervisory roles. However, you need to know what to do in the event that you are faced with sexual harassment. Most agencies and institutions of higher education have specific policies regarding sexual harassment, as well as procedures to follow to report such abuse through offices of equity and inclusion or Title IX officers. Find out what the procedures are at your institution, and be prepared to use them should the need arise.

LO9 Supervision Versus Personal Therapy

Another boundary concern pertains to blending supervision and personal therapy. Supervisors play multiple roles in the supervision process, functioning as teachers, consultants, mentors, and, at times, counselors. This complexity of roles means that the boundaries are always changing. It may not be possible for supervisors to function in a singular role, so supervisors must demonstrate responsible behavior in managing multiple roles and relationships. Because clinical supervision often includes personal and professional concerns that have an impact on the helping relationship, discussion of the supervisee's thoughts and feelings often occurs during a supervision session. A supervisor has the responsibility of helping trainees identify how their personal dynamics are likely to influence their work with clients, but supervision should address trainees' personal concerns only to the extent that they may impede or facilitate their ability to effectively work with clients. Although it is not appropriate to turn supervisory sessions into therapy sessions, the supervisory process can be therapeutic and growth producing.

Supervisory relationships have qualities in common with instructor–student and therapist–client relationships. In all of these professional relationships, it is the professional who occupies the position of power. Thus it is the professional's responsibility to establish and maintain appropriate boundaries and to explore with the trainee ways to prevent potential problems associated with boundary issues and with managing multiple roles and relationships. If problems do arise, the professional has the responsibility to take steps to resolve them in an ethical manner (Corey, Corey, & Corey, 2019).

Supervision is one way in which you can learn how to apply your knowledge and skills to particular clinical situations. It is of the utmost importance that you receive regular feedback so that you have a basis for honing your skills. Although supervision aims at honing the skills of trainees, the welfare of the clients served by trainees is the primary consideration. Supervisors must balance protection of client welfare with their responsibility for increasing competence and professional development of the supervisee.

Supervisors are in a good position to recognize some of your blocks and countertransferences. They can help you identify attitudes, feelings, and behaviors that could interfere with your handling of certain clients. If further exploration is needed, and if your difficulties with certain clients are rooted in your own dynamics, a supervisor may encourage you to get involved in personal therapy. This does not mean that you are personally unfit for the profession. Getting involved in the lives of clients is likely to open up some of your own psychological wounds, and unresolved conflicts are likely to surface. We strongly encourage personal therapy along with your supervision as an ideal combination (provided your supervisor and your therapist are not the same person). This arrangement prevents blurring of boundaries and allows the proper focus to be either on working with clients (in supervision) or on dealing with your personal issues (in personal therapy).

By Way of Review

- Your fieldwork courses are likely to be among the most important experiences you will have in your program. Select these experiences wisely and arrange for a variety of field placements. Realize that these placements can help you decide on your professional specialization.
- To learn about prospective field placements, explore the websites of local agencies and become familiar with the services offered as well as their mission/philosophy and internship opportunities.
- Treat your field placement like a job, even if you don't get paid for your internship. Arrive on time, dress appropriately, and behave professionally in your interactions with your supervisor, the other interns, agency staff, and clients.
- Although it is good to do your best, do not try to be a perfect intern. Fieldwork experiences are designed to teach you about the skills of helping, and you can learn much from your mistakes.
- Learn how to ask for what you need from your supervisor. It is important that you learn your limits and communicate them effectively to your supervisor. Know the difference between being assertive and aggressive in communicating your needs.
- Supervisors have different styles, and no one way is right. You can learn a great deal from various supervisors.
- The ideal supervisor may be hard to find. Supervisors are sometimes assigned to this role with little preparation or training. If your supervision is inadequate, be assertive in doing something about it by taking an active stance in asking for what you need from your supervisor.
- Even though supervision is similar to therapy in some ways, there are important differences. Supervision sessions should not evolve into personal therapy sessions.
- Sexual relationships between supervisors and supervisees (or professors and students) are unethical because of the harm that they typically do to supervisees (or students). Such relationships represent a clear misuse of power and also confound the supervisory or learning process.

What Will You Do Now?

1. If you have a supervisor (for your fieldwork or in your job), make up a short list of questions that you would like to discuss with him or her. What would you like to gain from supervision?
2. As the time approaches to look for an internship, explore several websites and make it a point to visit several community agencies where you might work as an intern. Interview the director of the agency or the supervisors who make decisions about accepting fieldwork students. Learn to ask questions that will help you select a placement that will teach you about various client populations and a range of problems. Each student in your class could visit just one agency and then present the findings to the rest of the class.
3. Reflect on some of the following issues and use this as a basis for your journal writing. Remember to write whatever comes to mind rather than censoring your thoughts and the flow of your writing. If you do not have the time to commit to keeping a journal, use the following issues as the basis of small group discussions in class.
   - Write about the kind of learner you see yourself as being. What does the concept of active learning imply to you? How can you become a more active learner as you read this book and take this course?
   - Write about the ideal kind of fieldwork experience you would like to obtain. What can you do to get that kind of field placement?
   - If you are already in a field placement, write briefly about the work you are doing. What are your reactions to the staff at the agency? How are you being affected by your clients? Are any personal issues emerging as a result of your work with clients? What are you learning about yourself?
   - If you are in supervision currently, what is most satisfying about it? What kind of relationship do you have with your supervisor? What ideas do you have for improving the quality of your supervision sessions?
4. The full bibliographic entry for each of these sources can be found in the References at the back of the book. For a comprehensive book on clinical supervision, see Bernard and Goodyear (2014); for a practical approach to doing and making use of supervision, see Corey, Haynes, Moulton, and Muratori (2010). Useful introductory texts in the human services field include Neukrug (2016a) and Woodside and McClam (2019). Kiser's (2012) human services internship handbook describes how to get the most from your internship experience. For an excellent treatment of the successful internship, see Sweitzer and King (2014).

CHAPTER 11

Working With Groups

Learning Objectives

1. Describe the types of groups and considerations that affect conducting groups in varied settings.
2. Discuss the value of group work.
3. Identify the main tasks of group leaders at each stage of a group.
4. Identify the key multicultural and social justice themes in groups.
5. Identify a few advantages and disadvantages of the coleadership model of groups.
6. Describe the potential value of participating in a group experience.
7. List the key points in helping members get the most from a group experience.

Focus Questions

1. Have you participated in a therapeutic group? If so, what was this experience like for you? What did it teach you about group process and group dynamics? about leading groups? about being a member? about yourself?
2. What value do you see in group work for meeting the needs of the various client populations you hope to serve?
3. What kind of group would you most like to organize? What would be your goals for the group?
4. What specific actions would you take to start your group? What colleagues or other sources would you consult to get this group started?
5. What personal qualities do you have that could help or hinder you as a group leader?
6. What knowledge and skills do you think you need to acquire to be able to lead groups effectively?
7. What characteristics would you look for when selecting a person to colead a group with you?
8. What ethical concerns do you need to address in setting up or facilitating a group?

Aim of the Chapter

Group work is recognized as the appropriate modality to be used most frequently in school and agency settings for a variety of client populations. Your supervisor or the director of your agency may ask you to start a specific kind of group. You may feel unprepared to organize and lead a group, or you may be unclear about the value of groups for special client populations. This chapter introduces you to the unique value of group work. We present a perspective on group process and provide an introduction to how groups can be useful in various settings. We discuss the skills you will need to organize and facilitate groups for the diverse client populations you will serve. This chapter provides an overview of group work, but it is not sufficient to equip you to lead groups on your own without supervision from a person who is skilled in doing group work. This chapter also highlights some of the major advantages of your becoming involved as a member in a therapeutic group.

Group Work as the Treatment of Choice

In the past two decades, group work has been enjoying a resurgence of interest. In the 1960s and 1970s encounter groups and personal-growth groups were considered one pathway for making human connections and for moving toward greater self-actualization. Today the focus has changed, and structured groups to remediate or prevent problems for specific client populations are most in demand. Short-term groups are the treatment of choice for trauma reactions, adjustment problems, and existential concerns. Therapy groups are most effective if they are closed, short-term, homogeneous, and process-centered (Shapiro, Peltz, & Bernadett-Shapiro, 2019). Barlow (2008) reports that group therapy is no longer viewed as a second-choice form of treatment; it is as effective as individual treatment and, in some cases, is more effective. From our perspective, groups are the treatment of choice for many client populations. Groups provide a natural laboratory and a sense of community that demonstrate to people that they are not alone in their struggles and that there is hope for making changes and creating a better life. Groups are highly effective, and they offer unique opportunities for new learning. Groups have the power to move people in creative and more life-giving directions.

Brief group counseling is beneficial for both economic and theoretical reasons. Group approaches fit well into the managed care scene because groups can be designed to provide brief, cost-effective treatments. In this type of setting, the group is definitely time limited, and will have fairly narrow goals. Many time-limited groups are aimed at symptomatic relief, teaching participants problem-solving strategies and interpersonal skills. Brief group counseling is popular in both community agencies and school settings because of the realistic time constraints and the ability of a brief format to be incorporated into both educational and therapeutic programs. Practitioners of brief group therapy must set clear and realistic treatment goals with the members, establish a clear focus within the group structure, maintain an active therapist role, and be able to work effectively within a limited time frame.

The interpersonal learning that occurs in groups can accelerate personal changes, but groups do not represent the only approach to helping clients understand and cope with their problems. Practitioners need to assess whether clients are better served in a group or in some other form of therapy. In some cases, groups may be the most appropriate intervention in a client's life. In other cases, group work may be used as a supplementary form of treatment or as the next step a client takes after completing some individual counseling. Although groups have much to offer, designing and facilitating groups in a variety of settings is a complex undertaking. Most client populations can benefit from a properly designed group with a qualified leader or coleaders, a topic we discuss in more detail later in this chapter.

LO1 Various Types of Groups

Groups differ with respect to goals, techniques used, the role of the leader, training requirements, and the participants involved. The range of groups designed to help people cope with specific problems or those aimed at particular client populations is limited only by a practitioner's imagination. We find that such special groups are mushrooming and that they frequently arise from the needs of a particular group or from the interests of the professional who is designing them.

Many groups have both an educational and a therapeutic dimension. These groups are often short-term, have some degree of structure, deal with a particular population, and focus on a specific theme. They can serve a number of purposes, such as giving information, sharing common concerns, teaching coping skills, helping people practice effective interpersonal communication, teaching problem-solving techniques, and assisting people once they leave the group.

Eventually, as a part of your job as a professional helper, you may be asked to set up and lead one or more groups. Depending on the age and population with which you work, you are likely to find yourself looking for resources to help you design a group. Many creative groups have been designed to meet the special needs of particular populations.

Structured groups, sometimes referred to as **psychoeducational groups**, generally have an educational focus and are designed to deal with an information deficit in a certain area. The emphasis is on providing information to prevent an array of educational deficits and psychological problems. Psychoeducational groups are useful for a broad range of problems, including stress management, substance abuse and sobriety issues, interpersonal violence, anger management, and behavioral problems. Structured groups are common when working with court mandated clients who are expected to learn strategies for dealing with some specific psychological difficulties. The aim is not to open up the emotional or interpersonal processes of the participants but to teach skills for more effective living. These groups are increasingly common in agencies, health care settings, schools, and college counseling centers. Structured groups also can be useful in enhancing or building on members' existing skills through behavioral rehearsal, skills training, and cognitive exploration. Psychoeducational groups may focus on stress management, coping skills, social skills, intimate partner violence, anger management, behavioral problems, bullying, managing relationships and ending relationships, and parenting skills.

Another type of group is the **counseling group**, which focuses on interpersonal process and problem-solving strategies and attends to conscious thoughts, feelings, and behavior. A counseling group helps participants resolve problems in living or dealing with developmental concerns. This kind of group also uses interactive feedback and support methods in a here-and-now time frame. Members of a counseling group are guided in understanding the interpersonal nature of their problems. With an emphasis on discovering inner personal strengths and constructively dealing with barriers that are preventing optimal development, members develop interpersonal skills that enable them to better cope with both current difficulties and future problems.

The counseling group becomes a microcosm of society, with a membership that is diverse but that shares common problems. The group process provides a sample of reality, with the struggles that people experience in the group resembling their conflicts in daily life. Participants learn to respect differences in cultures and values and discover that, on a deep level, they are more alike than different. Although participants' individual circumstances may differ, their pain and struggles are often similar.

From time to time societal problems present the need for group work with special populations. For example, with the growth of social media, cyberbullying has expanded, and victims can benefit from a group experience. The MeToo movement has brought women's struggles with sexual abuse and sexual harassment into the light of day. Women now want to process their long hidden feelings from such treatment, and a group can support this work. Finally, the numbers of students and family members who lost a child or adolescent in a school shooting incident is tragically increasing each year. These survivors also can benefit from a group experience with others who grapple with their grief and fears as a result of this trauma.

In reality, the kinds of groups you might design are a function of both your interests and the needs of your work setting. For most client populations, a support or structured group can be organized to combine educational and therapeutic aims. Once you determine some areas of need within the community or at the agency where you work, you and your coworkers can launch short-term groups to address these needs.

LO2 The Value of Group Work

Many of the problems for which people seek professional assistance are rooted in interpersonal difficulties. People have trouble forming and maintaining intimate relationships, and they sometimes feel they have few options for changing their predictable patterns. They may be at a loss in how to live well with the ones they love. Groups provide a natural laboratory that enable people to acquire skills for interpersonal living. Groups provide a sense of community, which can be an antidote to the impersonal world in which many individuals live. Group counseling provides a powerful place for healing. Participants can rewrite old scripts that no longer serve them and practice new ways of being in relation to others. Groups are powerful because participants can experience some of their long-term problems being played out in the group sessions. At the same time, a group gives members opportunities to try out more effective ways of behaving and responding to their problems, which can result in a corrective emotional experience.

Through the unfolding of the group process, members observe how others interact, and they learn something about themselves by joining in the interaction. The group experience serves as a living laboratory; it becomes a mirror in which members see themselves as they are. For instance, Luigi tends to keep himself isolated in the group, and in many ways he makes it difficult for others to get close to him. Through the feedback of other members and the leader, he has a chance to learn about his part in contributing to his own isolation, not only in the group but also in his everyday life. The safety of the group affords him opportunities to experiment with being different. Instead of ignoring his feelings, he can begin to express them. Rather than being immediately defensive, he can open himself to really hearing others. He can experiment with reaching out to others and asking for what he wants. Others in the group profit from Luigi's work because it enables them to understand the ways they are like him.

Groups offer a forum in which members reveal their confusion, anger, helplessness, guilt, resentment, depression, and anxiety. By expressing and exploring their feelings, members are able to see the similarity of human struggles. This has been referred to as *universality*. Those group members who have difficulty in expressing their feelings are likely to learn by listening to others who are able to express the range of their emotions. For example, Carola has adopted a stoic attitude, thinking that her situation will be more tolerable if she contains her feelings. She may not realize the stress to which she is subjecting herself by doing this. As she begins to express her concerns, she may realize that others experience some of her pain and that she is not alone in the way she feels. Her sharing can help lower the walls that keep her isolated.

Some universal human themes typically become apparent through a group experience. For example, in existential-oriented groups, it is quite common for group members to address the themes of loneliness, meaninglessness, and struggles that are an inevitable part of being human. In addition, the differences that do exist within the group can become catalysts for growth among group members. Clients may be separated by differences in age, gender, ability/disability, sexual orientation, religious affiliation, socioeconomic status, social and cultural background, worldview, and life experience. Yet as people risk revealing their deeper life concerns and feelings, they begin to recognize similarities with other group members. Although the circumstances leading to pain over disappointment may be different for each person, the emotions associated with certain events have a universal quality.

In groups composed of people with a common concern, such as a support group for women survivors of incest, the shared feelings are often even more intense. Before joining the support group, these women probably felt alone in their feelings of hurt, sadness, fright, guilt, resentment, and anger. As each woman reveals her story and her feelings about her situation, others are able to identify and come to understand a pattern that unites them. The bonding that builds within the group creates an atmosphere in which the women can see more clearly how they have been affected by incest. It also leads to insights into how their earlier experiences have set the stage for the way they now think, feel, and behave. Members are often at different stages in their healing process, and the group enables members to see what they have achieved and where they can do more work.

Groups offer hope to members that a different kind of life is possible. For example, recovering alcoholics and addicts abusing other substances can find groups to be a tremendous source of support and healing. When these clients were abusing substances, they believed they were powerless to change and were without hope. But the modeling of others who are learning to take control of their lives one day at a time is living proof that there is hope for a better life. Having hope that change is possible can lead individuals to significant lifestyle changes; Alcoholics Anonymous is one example of this idea in action.

The acceptance that develops in a group can be a powerful healing force. In a group for children of divorce, compassion and support are given not only by the leader but also by other children. Individuals within this group are able to be vulnerable when they sense that what concerns them has importance for others too.

Groups have particular value for people who have experienced a traumatic situation or for people who are coping with loss. Talking about their emotional reactions and listening to others who have been through a similar kind of situation can be healing. Professionals who work with trauma survivors are affected by the pain shared by their clients, and this repeated exposure can have an adverse affect on helpers. Too often helpers who engage in crisis work keep their feelings locked inside. A group experience enables these first responders to debrief and share their experience of vicarious trauma, which can be instrumental in their own healing (see Chapter 14).

Groups for Veterans and People in the Military

Active duty service members in the military, veterans, and their families deal with stresses that most of us do not face. This brief discussion of a group for veterans is based on the work of Mark Stebnicki (2016b) in counseling military personnel. We have summarized many of Stebnicki's ideas and adapted his work with people in the military to illustrate how a group could provide therapeutic outcomes for this population and how the unique properties of a group contribute to healing.

For group work practitioners to succeed in designing and facilitating a group for military veterans and their family members, it is necessary for them to understand the military culture. Active duty service members and veterans are subjected to pressures and demands that are very different from those experienced by civilian populations. Those in the military must cope with repeated separations from their family and friends. They are always on call, are trained to have total focus on their mission, and are prepared to protect the life and safety of others around them. This close-knit group of men and women creates an extended family rarely found in other work environments.

The psychosocial adjustments to trauma are quite different for civilians and for military personnel. Civilians have early access to mental health services after a traumatic event. Those in the military who witness catastrophic injury or death on the battlefield must continue to perform physically, emotionally, and mentally despite this trauma to protect their lives and the lives of fellow service members. Their focus must be on the "mission" at all times. When engaged in fighting enemy combatants, they must put their emotions on hold. Because they cannot begin the grieving process directly following their trauma, they may not experience the full range of posttraumatic stress symptoms until they return from deployment or transition from active duty to civilian life.

Civilians typically do not experience any stigma when seeking professional assistance after a traumatic event. In contrast, active service members rarely seek counseling because of the stigma attached to mental health issues. Active duty service members who seek counseling may lose their security clearance, may not be promoted, and may be seen as weak or unfit for duty by their unit members. It is an occupational risk for many military service members to be given a posttraumatic stress disorder (PTSD) diagnosis and other co-occurring mental health conditions (such as depression, anxiety, or substance use disorders) because of the perception of those in command that they may be medically unfit for duty, which will have a negative impact on their career. However, military veterans attempting to gain a disability rating from the VA system must have a good record documenting their medical, physical, and mental health conditions while in the service.

Both men and women who have served in the military are at risk of acquiring chronic and persistent health-related conditions. A group for military personnel can be a viable alternative to individual psychological treatment. Labeling their mental health issues as *posttraumatic stress symptoms* can help normalize the condition and diffuse the emphasis on the "disorder" of PTSD. Group practitioners who understand the unique demands faced by those in the military and who understand the military culture are in a good position to create a group that can be healing for the participants. It is critical to understand that some veterans will not do well in group therapy because group discussions may focus more on "war stories," which can retraumatize the individual. It is important for the counselor to assess the risks and benefits of group therapy for each military member.

A group experience allows participants to talk about deeply personal matters that they have kept to themselves. They can share their pain and fears over being exposed to combat operational stress, express their survivors' guilt, and put words to feelings that they had to bury in order to adapt and survive. Although they cannot change the traumatic situations they have faced, in the safety of a group they can allow themselves to talk about these events. The scars of the trauma experience will not disappear, but the acceptance, compassion, caring, empathy, and mutual understanding offer hope to veterans that they can be survivors and can lead healthy civilian lives. The universality of themes within a group provides the healing capacity as veterans realize that they are not alone.

For a more detailed discussion of military counseling, see Stebnicki (2016b, 2017). A wide variety of groups for specific populations can be developed. For descriptions of groups designed for different settings and age groups, see *Groups: Process and Practice* (M. Corey, Corey, & Corey, 2018).

A Bereavement Group

Groups can begin serendipitously as a response to a particular need in the community. Sherry Cormier shares her experience in creating and facilitating a bereavement group and explains how this group was formed.

> Recently, after giving a talk about my new book on loss and grief at a local senior center, it became apparent that the small group of participants had intense unprocessed grief over their losses. When I mentioned the importance of processing their grief in some kind of support group, I was told that the only available community group met once monthly and this did not serve their needs. As a result, I volunteered my services as a certified bereavement trauma specialist to return to the senior center on a weekly basis to facilitate a bereavement support counseling group.
>
> We have continued to meet weekly for the past three months including the holiday season, which is often a treacherous time for grief survivors. As a grief survivor myself, I am well aware that while loss is universal, grief is individualized and very isolating. Grievers feel awkward and self-conscious around non-grievers because we don't want to burden others with the intensity of our emotions of sadness and sorrow. A bereavement support group is a safe container for grievers to share their stories of loss and to express their emotions with others who are receptive listeners. The bereavement group gives grief survivors a place to digest and process their losses. In this particular group, the members have shared many different positive and negative coping strategies with one another, have bonded with each other, and have demonstrated paths of growth and resilience. Many of them are doing things they never thought they could do such as juggling finances, selling a home singlehandedly, or finding new employment. These new behaviors are helping them manage their sadness better and feel more empowered as they journey with a new identity following a significant and often traumatic loss.

This description of a bereavement group is but one example of the value of groups in assisting people with existential concerns and life themes. In *Sweet Sorrow: Finding Enduring Wholeness After Loss and Grief*, Sherry Cormier (2018) discloses her own personal journey through painful losses. She shares her professional expertise as a mental health practitioner in dealing with grief and provides many helpful resources to assist others in coping with their losses. Cormier emphasizes the fact that there is no universal time frame for working through losses. Grief work is more of a personal journey than a destination at which we arrive.

The Value of Feedback in Groups

A distinct advantage of groups is the opportunity for learning from the feedback of many others. **Feedback** occurs when both members and leaders share with each other their personal reactions about one another. If reactions are given with sensitivity and respect, members come to realize the ways in which their behavior affects others. The process of interpersonal feedback shows people how they contribute to both favorable and unfavorable outcomes, and it also gives them new possibilities for relating to others. The group leader's role is to create a climate of safety within the group that allows for an honest exchange of feedback and to establish norms that help members give and receive feedback with care and compassion.

Difficult-to-hear feedback must be timed well and given in a nonjudgmental way, otherwise the person receiving it is likely to become defensive and not take in what others have to say. If members give one another their reactions and perceptions honestly and with care, participants are able to hear how they affect others. This feedback can be useful to the member who is exploring a problem, attempting to resolve a difficult situation, or experimenting with different ways of behaving. Leaders model giving effective feedback and encourage members to engage in valuable feedback exchanges (Stockton, Morran, & Chang, 2014).

LO3 Stages of a Group and Tasks of Group Leaders

If you expect to lead groups, understanding the typical patterns during different stages of a group will give you a valuable perspective and help you predict problems and intervene in appropriate and timely ways. Knowledge of the critical turning points in a group can guide you in helping participants mobilize their resources to successfully meet the tasks facing them at each stage. Your tasks as a group worker are different for each of the stages.

The stages of a group include the pregroup, initial, transition, working, and final stages. These stages in the life of a group do not generally flow neatly and predictably in the order described in this section. In actuality there is considerable overlap between the stages. Groups ebb and flow, and both members and leaders need to pay attention to the factors that affect the direction a group takes. We begin with a brief description of each of the stages in the life of a group.

Pregroup Stage

The **pregroup stage** consists of all the factors involved in the formation of a group. Careful thought and planning are necessary to lay a solid foundation for any group. Long before the first group meeting, the leader will have designed a proposal for a group, attracted members, and screened and selected members for the group.

Initial Stage

The **initial stage** of a group is a time of orientation and exploration. At the initial sessions members tend to present dimensions of themselves that they consider socially acceptable. This phase is generally characterized by a certain degree of anxiety and insecurity about the structure of the group. Members are tentative because they are discovering and testing limits and are wondering whether they will be accepted. Typically, members bring to the group certain expectations, concerns, and anxieties, and it is vital that they be allowed to express them openly. As members get to know one another and learn how the group functions, they develop the norms that will govern the group, explore fears and expectations pertaining to the group, identify personal goals, clarify personal themes they want to explore, and determine if this group is a safe place.

The manner in which the leader deals with the reactions of members largely determines the degree of trust that develops. Group leaders have the general role of helping the members form a community where they can learn from one another. They carry out this role by teaching members from the beginning of a group to focus on the here-and-now, by modeling appropriate group behavior, and by assisting members in establishing personal goals. Group leaders have many tasks during the initial phase of a group, including the following:

- Teach participants how the group works.
- Address matters of informed consent.
- Develop ground rules and set norms.
- Assist members in expressing their fears and expectations and work toward the development of trust.
- Be open with the members and be psychologically present for them.
- Provide a degree of structuring that will neither increase member dependence nor promote excessive floundering.
- Help members establish concrete personal goals.
- Deal openly with members' concerns and questions.
- Teach members basic interpersonal skills such as active listening and responding.

Transition Stage

Before group members can interact at the depths they are capable of, the group generally goes through a **transition stage**. During this stage, members deal with anxiety, reluctance, defensiveness, and conflict, and the leader's task is to help members learn how to begin working on the concerns that brought them to the group. Leaders can help members come to recognize and accept their fear and defensiveness yet, at the same time, challenge them to work through their anxieties and any reluctance they may be experiencing. Members decide whether to take risks and bring out into the open ways they may be holding back, either because of what they might think of themselves or what others could think of them.

Perhaps the central task that leaders face during the transition phase is the need to intervene in the group in a sensitive manner and at the appropriate time. The basic task is to provide both the encouragement and the challenge necessary for the members to face and resolve the conflicts that exist within the group and their own defenses against anxiety and resistance. Major tasks that leaders perform during the transition phase include the following:

- Teach group members the importance of recognizing and expressing their anxieties.
- Help participants recognize the ways in which they react defensively and create a climate in which they can deal with this defensiveness openly.
- Provide a model for the members by dealing with them directly, respectfully, and honestly.
- Encourage members to express reactions that pertain to here-and-now happenings in the sessions.

Working Stage

The **working stage** is characterized by productiveness, which builds on the effective work done in the initial and transition stages. Mutuality and self-exploration increase, and the group focuses on making behavioral changes. In actual practice the transition stage and the working stage merge with each other, and there are individual differences among members at all of the stages of a group. During the working stage, the group may return to earlier themes of trust, conflict, and reluctance to participate. Productive work occurs at all stages of a group, not just at the working stage, but the quality and depth of the work takes different forms at various developmental phases of the group.

The central leadership functions at the working stage include the following:

- Provide systematic reinforcement of desired group behaviors that foster cohesion and productive work.
- Look for common themes among members.
- Provide opportunities for members to give one another constructive feedback.
- Continue to model appropriate behavior, especially caring confrontation, and disclose ongoing reactions to the group.
- Support the members' willingness to take risks and assist them in carrying this behavior into their daily living.
- Assist members in developing specific homework assignments as practical ways of making changes.
- Focus on the importance of translating insight into action.

Final Stage

The **final stage** is a time to further identify what was learned and to decide how this new learning can become part of daily living. Group activities include terminating, summarizing, and integrating and interpreting the group experience. As the group is ending, the focus is on conceptualization and bringing closure to the group experience. During the termination process, the group will deal with feelings of separation, address unfinished concerns of members, review the group experience, engage in practicing new behaviors that members may want to take into their daily life, design action plans, identify strategies for coping with relapse, and build a supportive network. If the group has been therapeutic, the members will be able to extend their learning outside the group despite experiencing a sense of sadness and loss as the group ends.

The group leader's central tasks during the ending phase are to provide a structure that allows participants to clarify the meaning of their experiences in the group and to assist members in generalizing their learning from the group to everyday situations. Neglecting the process of termination can leave members with unfinished work, which limits their ability to use what they learned from a group experience. The ending of a group often triggers other losses members have experienced, and grieving may be part of this process.

For an illustration of the stages of an actual group, see the DVD program "Evolution of a Group" in *Groups in Action: Evolution and Challenges—DVD and Workbook* (Corey, Corey, & Haynes, 2014).

Developing Skills as a Group Leader

Many institutions now use groups as their primary approach in helping clients resolve their problems. If you hope to set up and facilitate groups, you must obtain the necessary knowledge and skills to lead groups effectively. Supervised training is an indispensable element in becoming a competent group leader. You are faced with an ethical dilemma if a supervisor asks you to design or lead certain kinds of groups without supervision when you have not had the proper educational preparation. Although you do not need to be an expert when you begin to facilitate groups, you should seek the guidance of experienced group workers.

Effective group leaders are aware of group processes and know how to tap the healing forces within a group. Leading a group is far more complex than working on an individual basis with clients. In addition to the basic skills for individual counseling, group leadership skills include helping members create trust, linking members' work, teaching members how to give and receive feedback, facilitating disclosure and risk-taking, intervening to block counterproductive group behavior, identifying common themes, setting up role-playing situations that help members enact and explore their struggles, and preparing members for termination.

Leadership Skills in Working With Challenging or Reluctant Group Members

One of the major group leadership skills you need to develop is the ability to intervene effectively when you encounter defensiveness in a group member. It is essential that you not only learn to recognize and deal with members' defenses, but also that you become aware of your own reactions to the defensive behaviors exhibited by members, some of which may include being threatened by what you perceive as a challenge to your leadership role; anger over the members' lack of cooperation and enthusiasm; feelings of inadequacy; and anxiety over the slow pace of the group.

One of the most powerful ways to intervene when you are experiencing intense feelings over what you perceive as defensiveness is to deal with your own feelings and possible defensive reactions to the situation. If you ignore your reactions, you are leaving yourself out of the interactions that occur in the group. Furthermore, by giving the members your reactions, you are modeling a direct style of dealing with conflict and problematic situations rather than bypassing them. Your own thoughts, feelings, and observations can be the most powerful resource you have in dealing with defensive behavior. When you share your reactions pertaining to what is going on in the group without blaming or criticizing the members for deficiencies, you are letting the members experience an honest and constructive interaction with you.

Although it is understandable that you will want to learn how to handle "problem members" and the disruption of the group that they can cause, the emphasis should be on actual *behaviors* rather than on labeling members. It is helpful to understand problem behaviors as manifestations of protecting the self, which most participants may display at one time or another during the history of a group.

As the leader of a group, it is your task to educate members to involve themselves in productive group behaviors that will maximize the benefits of their group experience. In working with problematic behaviors displayed by group members, you need to be mindful of how your interventions can either decrease or escalate these behaviors. Some of the following interventions are appropriate when dealing with difficult behaviors of group members. If you keep these points in mind, you have a good chance of effectively dealing with difficult situations:

- Do not dismiss or put members down.
- Educate the members about how the group works. Strive to be honest with members rather than mystifying the process.
- Encourage members to explore their defensiveness rather than demanding they give up their ways of protecting themselves.
- Challenge group members in a caring and respectful way to do things that may be painful and difficult.
- Do not retreat from conflict in a group.
- Provide a balance between support and challenge.
- Invite group members to state how they are personally affected by problematic behaviors of other members while blocking judgments, evaluations, and criticisms.

In working with group members whom you perceive as difficult, you might ask yourself these questions: What am I doing to contribute to any defensiveness or resistance that I am encountering in the group? Does the client remind me of anyone in my personal life? These questions can help you examine and understand how your personal reactions might be contributing to the client's defensive behaviors. It is good to remind yourself that the very reason people seek a group is to assist them in finding more effective ways of expressing themselves and dealing with others. For examples of how to deal with a variety of challenging group members, see the DVD program "Challenges Facing Group Leaders" in *Groups in Action: Evolution and Challenges—DVD and Workbook* (Corey, Corey, & Haynes, 2014).

The Ethical and Professional Group Leader

The "Best Practice Guidelines" (Association for Specialists in Group Work, 2008) provide group workers with suggestions aimed at increasing ethical and professional behavior. The following overview describes some of the qualities that we believe reflect these standards.

You first spend time thinking about what you most want to accomplish through a group format. If you intend to colead your group, take the time before you meet potential members to discuss with your coleader general group goals and an overall plan for getting your group into motion. You will not be getting a group together unless you believe your group has real potential for making a difference to those who join.

The next step is to provide information to prospective group candidates. Realizing that some of the people who need your group the most may be reluctant to seek your services, make some provisions for outreach to get the word out to a particular target population that could most benefit. Screen prospective group members and develop a set of criteria for selecting members. In the screening sessions, select members whose needs and goals are compatible with the goals of the group, those who will not impede the group process, and those whose well-being will not be jeopardized by the group experience. Explore with the members the risks of potential life changes, and help them explore their readiness to face these possibilities. In short, before the group ever meets, you are laying a foundation and preparing members for a successful learning experience.

Once the group begins to meet, it is a good practice to assess the degree to which its purposes are being met. If you are coleading the group, arrange to meet with your colleague regularly to coordinate your efforts. Ideally, these meetings will take place both before and after each group session.

Because you are aware that confidentiality is the cornerstone of any group, make sure that the participants know what it implies and encourage them to bring up any concerns they might have about maintaining confidences. Make some effort to teach members how to become active participants so that they can get the most from the group sessions and can apply their newly acquired interpersonal skills in everyday living.

Confidentiality is necessary if members are to develop a sense of safety in a group, which is basic to being willing to engage in risk-taking. Throughout the life of a group, provide guidelines for maintaining the confidential nature of the group. Explain to the members how confidentiality can be broken, even without intending to do so. Emphasize that it is members' responsibility to continually make the group safe by addressing their concerns regarding how their disclosures will be treated.

You cannot guarantee confidentiality in a group setting because you cannot control what the members do or do not keep private. Members have a right to know that legal privilege (confidentiality) does not apply to group treatment unless provided by state statute (ASGW, 2008). You owe it to the members to specify at the outset the limits of confidentiality.

If you have an open group, one characterized by changing membership, help members who are ready to leave the group integrate their learning, and encourage those who are staying to talk about their feelings about losing a member. As new members join, attend to them so that they will be able to make use of the group resources. Although members ultimately have the right to leave a group, discuss with them the possible risks of leaving prematurely, and encourage them to discuss their reasons for wanting to terminate. If your group is made up of involuntary members, take steps to enlist their cooperation and their continuation on a voluntary basis.

It is important to understand the ways in which your values and needs may have an impact on the group process. Exert care to avoid coercing participants to change in ways they have not chosen. It is equally important to protect members' rights against coercion and undue pressure from other participants. Make it a practice to teach the members that the purpose of the group is to help them find their own answers rather than yielding to pressure from others.

For the duration of the group, monitor your behavior and become aware of what you are modeling to the members. A part of ethical practice involves teaching members how to evaluate their progress in meeting their goals, and in designing follow-up procedures. Evaluation is an ongoing process throughout the life of a group and can benefit both members and the leader. By monitoring the progress of each group member through systematic data collection, you can make adjustments to your way of facilitating the group so members benefit from this experience.

Just as you prepare members for entering a group, it is useful to prepare them for termination from the group in the most efficient period of time. Members can profit from your guidance in pulling together what they have learned from their group experience and in developing an action plan to use after they leave the group. If you have knowledge about the resources within your community, you are in a position to assist members in finding any professional assistance they need once they leave a group.

LO4 Multicultural and Social Justice Themes in Groups

Each person is a member of many different cultures. Recognize and respect diversity within the group and encourage members to be sensitive to how differences in culture, ethnicity, socioeconomic status, language, religion, age, sexual orientation, disability, and gender might influence the group process. In some cultures, individuals are not encouraged to express their feelings openly, to talk about their personal problems with people whom they do not know well, or to give their personal reactions to others. Group counselors need to be aware that reluctance or hesitation to participate fully in a group may reflect members' cultural background rather than being a manifestation of an uncooperative attitude. Culture can be considered as a lens through which life is perceived.

Oftentimes members who are immigrants have allegiance to their home culture but find certain aspects of their new culture appealing. These members may experience conflicts in their attempt to integrate the values from the two cultures in which they live. These core struggles can be productively explored in an accepting group if you and other members respect this cultural conflict. If you are a diversity-sensitive group practitioner, the techniques you employ will be appropriate to the cultural background and needs of the members in your group.

The Western cultural values that underpin our view of helping may pose a challenge for Asians, Latinos/as, and African Americans who are more familiar with a collectivistic culture. For example, open exploration of intimate emotional issues may conflict with the values of some Latino/a members who consider the expression of intense emotions to be private and only to be shared within their family. In addition, Latinos/as may approach people carefully and cautiously because of their negative experiences in society at large (Torres-Rivera, Torres Fernandez, & Hendricks, 2014). Some African American clients may experience difficulty in a group if they are expected to make deeply personal disclosures too quickly or if they are expected to talk about their family. By being aware of the cultural background of African American clients, group leaders can incorporate their cultural values into group work (Steen, Shi, & Hockersmith, 2014). Many Asian cultures stress self-reliance, which could make it difficult for individuals from these cultures to ask for help from others. Asian clients often remain quiet regarding their personal problems or turn to family members for help (Chung & Bemak, 2014). The goals, structure, and techniques used in a group may need to be modified to make a group culturally appropriate and therapeutically useful for these members.

It is critical that you recognize the limits of your multicultural competence and expertise when working with a diverse range of group members. It is not necessary to know everything about the cultural background of all of the members in your groups, but you must have a basic knowledge of how culture affects group process. There is a good deal to be said for inviting members to identify what they deem to be significant aspects of their culture. As a microcosm of society, groups provide a context for addressing issues of power, privilege, discrimination, social injustice, and oppression. If these themes emerge in a group and are not addressed, members are deprived of an opportunity to explore cultural values and biases, to raise their awareness of these injustices, and to learn to deal with them. Group leaders should encourage open discussion of what are often referred to as "difficult conversations."

Multicultural and social justice themes are intertwined in the practice of group work. Developing cultural competence enables practitioners to appreciate and manage diverse worldviews. In addition to becoming competent in working with diverse client populations, becoming an effective group leader involves acquiring basic social justice and advocacy competencies. The ASGW (2012) *Multicultural and Social Justice Competence Principles for Group Workers* specifically addresses the scope of competence in both multicultural and social justice areas and includes the following:

- Group counselors discuss why social justice and advocacy issues are important in a group and how these issues influence the practice of group work.
- Group counselors see their responsibility to address issues of status, privilege, and oppression that arise in their groups; they provide a climate of safety that allows for an open discussion of these personal topics.
- Group counselors conduct a cultural assessment of each group member within the context of their presenting concerns. They assess members' cultural identity, acculturation level, and the role that oppression and culture played in the development and evaluation of symptoms.
- Group counselors are concerned with empowerment and build on the strengths of each group member and the resources of the group as a whole.
- Group counselors promote egalitarianism by educating group members about their rights and assisting them in assuming an active role in bringing about social change as well as individual change.

Encourage open discussion of cultural diversity and social justice considerations, especially issues of power and privilege, to deepen members' awareness of social justice. For a description of social justice and advocacy competencies that can be applied to group work, see *ACA Advocacy Competencies: A Social Justice Framework for Counselors* (Ratts, Toporek, & Lewis, 2010) and *Multicultural and Social Justice Counseling Competencies: A Blueprint for the Profession* (Ratts & Butler, 2019).

LO5 Working With Coleaders

In our practice of group work, in teaching and supervising group practitioners, and in conducting group-process workshops for students and professionals, we favor working as a team. When forming a coleadership team, it is important that the two leaders have some say in deciding whether to work together. Although our preference is for the coleadership model, this is not the only acceptable model of group leadership. Many people facilitate a group alone quite effectively. Realistically, there are many institutional barriers to the practice of coleadership of groups. Budgetary concerns are an ever-increasing barrier to cofacilitated groups. An agency administrator is likely to ask the question, "Why should we pay two staff members to facilitate a group that could be led by one person?"

There are a number of advantages to coleading groups for all concerned: the group members can gain from the perspectives of two leaders; depending on their styles, the coleaders can each bring a unique focus to the session and can complement each other's facilitation; and the coleaders can process what is occurring in the group and plan for future sessions. One of the advantages of coleading is that it can help you identify and work with countertransference that emerges within the group. As you recall from Chapter 5, countertransference can distort your objectivity to the extent that it interferes with effective counseling. For example, your coleader may typically react with great impatience to men who are reluctant to express their feelings. You may be better able to make contact with such a man. You can also help your coleader identify his or her reactions and attachments to a certain member in your private meetings outside of the group.

Along with the advantages of coleadership, there are also some disadvantages. Coleader relationships can complicate the group process, which raises potential ethical issues. For example, a power struggle or other difficulties may develop between coleaders, which is likely to have a negative impact on the progress of a group. It can be somewhat demanding for group leaders to establish and maintain a good working relationship, yet doing so is necessary for a successful group.

In their study of competency concerns in coleader relationships, Okech and Kline (2006) found that effective coleader relationships require a commitment to establishing and maintaining these relationships. Coleaders who are not communicating effectively tend to spend an inordinate amount of time within the group on their relationship issues. It is important that group leaders deal with these issues outside of group so their dynamics do not interfere with the group's work. Okech and Kline's study underscores the importance of coleaders being committed to recognizing and working through issues that interfere with their ability to work effectively in the group.

The choice of a coleader is crucial, and it involves far more than attraction and liking. Their functioning as a dyad affects the dynamics of the group, either positively or negatively. If the coleaders are not working effectively together, the group will likely suffer. Unresolved conflicts between the leaders often result in splitting within the group. If the leaders' energies are directed at competing with each other or at some other power struggle or hidden agenda, there is little chance that the group will be effective. Each of the leaders should be secure enough that the group won't have to suffer as one or both of them try to impress each other. We surely do not think it is essential that coleaders always agree or share the same perceptions or interpretations; in fact, a group can be given vitality if coleaders feel trusting enough to express their differences of opinion. Mutual respect and the ability to establish a relationship based on trust, cooperation, and support are most important. We emphasize the value of coleaders spending some time together immediately following a group session to assess what has happened. Similarly, they should meet at least briefly before each session to talk about anything that might affect their functioning in the group.

LO6 Consider a Group Experience for Yourself

Now that you have learned the value of group approaches in your professional work, we ask you to consider the value of experiencing a group as a participant. One of the best ways to learn how to facilitate a group is to actively participate in a small group as a member. The majority of group counseling courses in graduate programs include an experiential group training experience. The experiential growth group combines elements of experiential learning and personal development. The Council for Accreditation of Counseling and Related Educational Programs (CACREP, 2016) requires 10 hours of direct experience as a participant in a small group. This requirement is most often met by incorporating an experiential group as a part of the group counseling course.

Zhu (2018) reviewed the literature on experiential groups in counselor education and concluded that there is solid evidence that students benefit from participating in an experiential growth group and generally appreciate the value of the small group experience. A major benefit to students who participate in an experiential group is the opportunity to identify personal characteristics that might enhance or inhibit their ability to function as group counselors. Conducting experiential group training activities as a part of group work instruction involves fully informed consent on the part of students and a high level of competence on the part of the instructor. Matters such as confidentiality, privacy, managing multiple roles and relationships, and providing safeguards to address potential pitfalls of experiential group work are of the utmost importance (Corey, Corey, Muratori, Austin, & Austin, 2017).

If you participate in experiential groups as a part of your training, you can use your experience for personal change and also for working on concerns you have as a helper. Other members can help you take an honest look at yourself and help you to better understand how you come across to others. Your own honesty about who you are is the most significant factor in your ability to change. It is up to you to make any group you enter personally meaningful. Take a few moments to reflect on your openness to being a group member. How willing are you to define goals that will enable you to participate actively and fully in learning about yourself and others? Would you be willing to recognize your own vulnerabilities and to reveal them in the context of the group?

In Chapter 5 we discussed dealing with the transference reactions your clients may have, as well as ways of recognizing any countertransference reactions you may have to them. An experiential growth group is an ideal place to explore your feelings toward clients and the effects they have on you. By becoming aware of blind spots that make it difficult for you to be objective, you can identify potential sources of countertransference (Corey et al., 2017). A group experience that is connected to your training program may not be an appropriate place to work through unfinished business from your past, but it can serve you by sensitizing you to how your vulnerabilities could interfere with your work as a helper. For instance, assume that you become aware of being uncomfortable and seeking approval when you are in the company of older people, much like you did with your parents. You will probably need to work outside the group in your own therapy to understand your vulnerability and to heal in this area, but the group can draw your attention to this way of responding. In a group, you can learn about your defensiveness when you feel vulnerable, and this awareness of your own defenses can be extremely useful in teaching you how to work with clients that you perceive as being difficult.

One of our colleagues (Kristin) tells us that she felt extremely anxious the first time she coled an incest survivors' group. Kristin remembers saying to herself, "What if they ask me if I was molested? Will they believe I can help them if I tell them I wasn't? How will I be able to handle the painful things I'm going to hear?" She worked on these concerns both in her supervision and with her coleader, who also shared many of these concerns. As the group progressed, it didn't take long for Kristin to realize that there were many ways for her to relate to and be helpful to the members. Her initial fears did not paralyze her because she was able to express them and work through them outside of the group.

You do not have to be psychologically impaired to profit from a group experience designed for personal growth. Your willingness to seek input from others and to accept feedback can start a pattern that will encourage you to continue seeking out others when the demands on you in your helping role are great. Being in a group as a part of your program provides an avenue for talking about the feelings, fears, and uncertainties that characterize the developing helper you are becoming. Your capacity to receive constructive feedback from others can better equip you to give quality service to clients. If you are a reluctant group participant yourself, you will probably have trouble inspiring others, especially clients who seem reluctant. If you are able to become an involved group member yourself, you can use this experience later in teaching members in your groups how to make the most of their group experience.

LO7 Teaching Group Members How to Get the Most From a Group Experience

We are convinced that those who participate in groups will get more from the experience if they are given some instructions on how to become involved participants. We offer some recommendations for group members here that you can use to teach members in a group you are facilitating how to best participate. For a more detailed discussion, we refer you to *Group Techniques* (Corey, Corey, Callanan, & Russell, 2015) and to *Groups: Process and Practice* (M. Corey, Corey, & Corey, 2018).

1. Recognize that trust is not something that just happens in a group; you have a role in creating this climate of trust. If you are aware of anything getting in the way of a sense of safety, share your hesitations with the group.
2. Commit yourself to getting something from your group by focusing on your personal goals. Before each meeting, think about how you can get involved, what personal concerns you want to explore, and other ways to use the time in group meaningfully.
3. Don't be so committed to your agenda that you cannot work with other issues that frequently come up spontaneously in the life of a group.
4. If the work other members are doing is affecting you, it is important to let them know in what ways you are being affected. If you are able to identify with the struggles of others, it generally helps both you and them to share your feelings and thoughts.
5. Express persistent feelings that you are having that pertain to what is emerging in the group in the here-and-now. For example, if you have difficulty sharing yourself personally in your group, let others know what makes it hard for you to self-disclose.
6. Decide for yourself what, how much, and when you will disclose personal facets of yourself. However, others will not have a basis for knowing you unless you tell them about yourself.
7. Avoid getting lost and overwhelming others with detailed information about you or your history. Disclose struggles that are significant to you at this time in your life, especially as these concerns pertain to what others in the group are exploring.
8. Practice your attending and listening skills. If you can give others your attention and understanding, you are contributing a great deal to the group process.
9. Try to challenge yourself if you judge that you are "taking too much group time for yourself." If you become overly concerned about measuring your participation, you will inhibit your spontaneity and hold yourself back.
10. Use your group as a place to experiment with new behaviors. Allow yourself to try out different ways of being to determine ways that you may want to change.
11. Understand that making changes will not be instantaneous. You can also expect some setbacks. Keep track of the progress you are making. Give yourself credit for what you are willing to try and for the subtle changes you can see yourself making.
12. Be aware of using questions as your main style of interacting. If you are inclined to ask a question, let others know what prompted you to ask the question.
13. Avoid giving advice. If you become aware of wanting to tell others what to do, reveal to them what your investment is in giving this advice. Learn to speak *for* yourself and *about* yourself.
14. Concentrate on making personal and direct statements to others in your group rather than providing interpretations and asking questions.

15. In giving feedback to others, avoid categorizing or labeling them. Instead of telling others who or what they are, tell them what you are observing and how this is affecting you.
16. Pay attention to any consistent feedback you might receive from others in your group. Take in what you are hearing and consider their input to determine how what they are saying fits for you, especially in your life away from group.
17. Respect your defenses and understand that they have served a purpose for you. However, when you become aware of feeling or acting defensively in your group, challenge your defenses by seeing what will occur if you become less guarded.
18. Provide support for others by expressing your care for them, but do not quickly intervene by trying to comfort others when they are experiencing feelings, such as expressing pain over an event. Let them know how their pain is affecting you.
19. Take responsibility for what you are accomplishing in your group. Spend some time thinking about what is taking place in these meetings and evaluating the degree to which you are attaining your goals. If you are not satisfied with your group experience, look at what you can do to make the group a more meaningful experience.
20. Be aware of respecting and maintaining the confidentiality of what goes on inside your group. Keep in mind how easy it might be to inadvertently betray the confidences of others. Make it a practice not to talk about what others are doing in your group or what they are experiencing. If you have any concerns that what you are disclosing is not staying within the group, be willing to bring this matter up in a session.
21. Keep a personal journal in which you record impressions of your own explorations and learning in your group. A journal will be invaluable in keeping track of your progress and noting changes in your ways of thinking, feeling, and acting.

By Way of Review

- For many target populations and certain purposes, groups are the treatment of choice, not a second-rate approach to helping people change.
- A group process can lead to self-acceptance, deeper understanding of oneself, and change. Some of the values of a group experience are learning that one is not alone, receiving feedback from many sources, gaining opportunities for experimenting with new behavior, and using the group as an interpersonal laboratory.
- Become familiar with the stages of development of groups so that interventions are effective and meet the needs of the group. Group development includes the pregroup and initial, transition, working, and final stages.

- Helpers are expected to follow ethical guidelines in forming and conducting group sessions. It is important to know the limits of your competency if you are asked to work with groups.
- Multicultural and social justice themes are intertwined in the practice of group work. Effective group work addresses diversity within a group and encourages members to explore topics such as power, privilege, and oppression as they surface in a group.
- Skills in working with groups can be acquired and refined. These skills can be applied to working with a wide array of special populations in a variety of settings. Becoming an effective group leader involves acquiring basic social justice and advocacy competencies.
- As a student in a training program, you have a great deal to gain from groups in your personal and professional development. If you expect to make group work a part of your practice, training and supervision are essential.

What Will You Do Now?

1. Investigate the services that are offered in a local community agency or facility. Ask about how the groups are organized, what services are available to special client groups, and what outcomes these groups have had. If you are doing fieldwork in an agency now, inquire about group work.
2. If a group experience is not part of your training program, join a group in your college or university, in the community, or through private practice. Even if you decide not to join a group, this exercise can be useful in learning about community resources.
3. If you are working in an agency or if you have a fieldwork placement, see whether you can observe a group. Of course, both the group members and the leader would have to agree before you could visit a session. The purpose of this visit is to acquaint you with the potential of groups for meeting the needs of various client populations.
4. If you are currently involved in a group, or have been in a group in the past, in your journal describe the kind of group member that you are (or were). What might this teach you about your ability to lead or colead groups? You might also write about your concerns or fears in doing group work. Let yourself brainstorm as you write about the possible advantages of working with people in groups. Think about your interests, and see if you can identify some general ideas for ways to employ small groups as a vehicle for branching out from your interests.

5. If you are interested in learning more about group counseling, four professional organizations (each with journals shown in parentheses) are useful resources:
   - APA's Division 49, the Society for Group Psychology and Group Psychotherapy (*Group Dynamics: Theory, Research, and Practice*)
   - American Group Psychotherapy Association (*International Journal of Group Psychotherapy*)
   - Association for Specialists in Group Work (*Journal for Specialists in Group Work*)
   - American Society for Group Psychotherapy and Psychodrama (*Journal of Group Psychotherapy, Psychodrama, & Sociometry*)

   These organizations regularly sponsor conferences, which provide opportunities for networking with colleagues and for learning what is new in group work.
6. For the full bibliographic entry for each of the sources listed here, consult the References at the back of the book. For a practical handbook on the evolution of a group and key group process issues at each stage, see M. Corey, Corey, and Corey (2018). For a practical book on ways of creating, implementing, and evaluating techniques for therapeutic groups, see Corey, Corey, Callanan, and Russell (2015). For a useful treatment of group skills and strategies, see Jacobs, Schimmel, Masson, and Harvill (2016). For a comprehensive discussion of time-limited group counseling, see Shapiro, Peltz, and Bernadett-Shapiro (2019). Consult Yalom (2005) for an in-depth treatment of theoretical and practical issues dealing with interpersonal therapy groups. For an overview of 11 major theories of group counseling, with practical applications to various groups, see Corey (2016). For an educational video program showing the Coreys coleading two different groups, see *Groups in Action: Evolution and Challenges—DVD and Workbook* (Corey, Corey, & Haynes, 2014).

CHAPTER 12

Working in the Community

Learning Objectives

1. Explain why a community perspective is important to the professional helper.
2. Briefly discuss the alternative roles of professional helpers in the community.
3. Describe what is involved in outreach work.
4. Identify a few ways professional helpers can educate the community.
5. Identify five specific skills for mobilizing community resources.

Focus Questions

1. What interests do you have that could lead to your involvement in the local community? As a helper, what are some roles you may want to play in your community?
2. Many helpers direct their efforts to helping clients understand factors within themselves that contribute to their problems. Others focus on the environmental factors that may be influencing an individual's problems. What advantages do you see in combining both individual and environmental perspectives?
3. If you were to educate your community about pressing social problems, which ones would you emphasize? What resources would you recommend to community members who were experiencing these particular social problems?
4. Outreach work is a basic community intervention. If you were working in a community agency, what group would you consider targeting for outreach services and why?
5. What challenges do you expect to face as a community worker with respect to delivering services to diverse clients? What kinds of helping roles might you have to assume as a worker in the community?
6. What do you understand by the term *social activism*? What steps can you take to become a social activist?

Aim of the Chapter

By addressing the causes of problems within the community, helpers can improve the lives of many individuals rather than helping one person at a time. There is a need for mental health workers to focus on prevention, as the following story demonstrates.

> **Moving Upstream**
>
> While walking along the banks of a river, a passerby notices that someone in the water is drowning. After pulling the person ashore, the rescuer notices another person in the river in need of help. Before long the river is filled with drowning people, and more rescuers are required to assist the initial rescuer. Unfortunately, some people are not saved and some people fall back into the river after they have been pulled ashore. At this time, one of the rescuers starts walking upstream. "Where are you going?" the other rescuers ask disconcerted. The upstream rescuer replies, "I'm going upstream to see why so many people keep falling into the river." As it turns out, the bridge leading across the river upstream has a hole through which people are falling. The upstream rescuer realizes that fixing the hole in the bridge will prevent many people from ever falling into the river in the first place. (Cohen & Chehimi, 2010, p. 5)

Too often we pay primary attention to the interior world of the individual client without examining how the community and the system contribute to the client's problem. As this story illustrates, an individual focus may limit our effectiveness.

For professional helpers to foster real and lasting changes, many argue that they must have an impact on the total milieu of people's lives. Working with people who come for individual counseling is one way professionals can use their helping skills, but helpers can foster change in both individuals and the community if they use a systems approach. The aspirations and difficulties of individual clients are intertwined with those of many other people in a community system. By focusing on the capabilities and strengths within a community, helpers can empower people in the community.

The aim of this chapter is to help you recognize how the external environment is affecting your clients. We cannot treat individuals in isolation from the context of their lives because the community has an impact on how individuals think, feel, and act. As helpers, we have a responsibility to address the social, political, and environmental conditions that create problems for the individuals who come to see us.

LO1 The Community Perspective

What is a community, and how will you find members of it? In *Promoting Community Change*, Mark Homan (2016) captures the spirit of **community** in this definition:

> A community is a number of people who share a distinct location, belief, interest, activity, or other characteristic that clearly identifies their commonality and differentiates them from those not sharing it. This common distinction is sufficiently evident that members of the community are able to recognize it,

> even though they may not currently have this recognition. Effectively acting on their recognition may lead members to more complete personal and mutual development. (p. 133)

A **community agency** includes any institution—public or private, nonprofit or for-profit—designed to provide a wide range of social and psychological services to the community. Likewise, the term **community workers** describes a diverse pool of human services workers and community health workers with varying levels of education and training whose primary duties revolve around serving individuals within their community and serving the community as a whole.

Community **change agents** play an active role in creating community programs and agencies from the bottom up. They base their efforts on the needs of the members of the community in which they work. By listening to your clients, you will become aware of environmental factors that limit the changes many of your clients want to make, or believe they can make, in their lives. You will hear your clients' aspirations and begin to recognize some of the roadblocks to their success. You may not specialize in community interventions, but you can still play a significant role in helping to bring changes to the community you serve.

The first step in becoming a community change agent is to become aware of the communities that touch your clients' lives. Answer the following questions, keeping your clients' communities in mind:

- How are the human services needs in this community met?
- What are some of the special needs of low-income people, and what local, state, and federal resources exist to help them?
- In this community, where can people go for the social and psychological services they need?
- What forces within the community do you see as contributing to the problems individuals and groups are experiencing?
- What assets and resources are available to empower people in the community?
- What institutional barriers serve to deter individuals from gaining equitable access and participation in the community and in society?

The traditional approach to understanding and treating human problems focuses on resolution of internal conflicts as a pathway to individual change. In contrast, the community approach focuses on changing environmental factors that create individual problems and tapping into the forces that can strengthen the entire community. A **community orientation** requires helpers to design interventions that go beyond the office. It takes a paradigm shift for helpers trained in individual helping models to learn to identify the community as the client. The community itself may be the most appropriate focus of attention for resolving some issues because resources, strengths, and the ability to find solutions lie within the community. When addressing unmet community needs, helpers must work closely with community members to identify and develop community resources and employ measures that ultimately strengthen the community.

To illustrate this paradigm shift, consider the case of a young student who is experiencing academic failure due to excessive absences from school. The counselor could work to increase this student's attendance at school by enlisting the help of the boy's family to support him in achieving this goal. A community counselor would expand her inquiry to consider the larger picture and, in partnership with the family, identify systemic factors that contribute to the student's absenteeism and academic problems. Perhaps this boy misses school to care for his younger siblings while his parents work. By actively working to develop affordable day care options in the community, the community counselor could help this family as well as many others in the community who face similar concerns.

By adhering to traditional roles, Chung and Bemak (2012) suggest that practitioners are maintaining and reinforcing the status quo, which results in politically supporting the social injustices, inequalities, and discriminatory treatment of certain groups of people. Chung and Bemak contend that advocacy is an ethical and moral obligation for an effective mental health professional.

The Scope of the Community Approach

The helping process does not take place in a vacuum. Human services specialists develop intervention strategies that deal with the societal factors that adversely affect the lives of many diverse members of the community. This is in keeping with the traditional social work perspective of working with the "person in the environment." A process that considers both individual and environmental factors is consistent with the **community mental health movement**, which began in the 1950s and was based on the premise that human problems result primarily from failures in the social system. The community mental health perspective is relevant to all communities, but it is particularly relevant to historically marginalized, oppressed, and underserved communities. Community work requires that practitioners learn a range of skills, including connecting people with others in their community, developing leadership skills, empowering community members, providing client advocacy, and promoting a culture of learning.

Client Advocacy and a Social Justice Perspective

Many of the problems people face are the result of being disenfranchised as individuals or as members of a group from systems that withhold valued resources from them. Culturally skilled community workers particularly understand how the sociopolitical influences impinge on the experiences of people from diverse cultural groups. These workers strive to ameliorate social injustices that adversely affect the mental health of people in oppressed and marginalized groups in contemporary society (Crethar, Torres Rivera, & Nash, 2008). Many community workers believe that all people are equally entitled to high-quality treatment programs. Consequently, community workers advocate for services for people of all ages and backgrounds and with all types of problems regardless of their ability to pay for these services.

Helpers must demonstrate a willingness to deal with clients' economic survival needs from the outset. Before people can be motivated toward growth and actualization, their basic needs must be met. People who are homeless or who are struggling to feed themselves and their children need to move out of crisis mode before they are likely to benefit from self-exploration and personal growth. Generally speaking, stabilization precedes exploration.

Stabilization often includes a whole spectrum of environmental factors such as housing, food, money, legal concerns, substance detoxification, medication management, child care, practical coping strategies, and social supports. For example, a woman abused by her husband has a greater immediate need for medical treatment and a safe shelter than for counseling to explore whether her family of origin contributed to her acceptance of an abusive relationship. The client may also need to develop assertiveness skills and to process self-esteem issues, but the timing and hierarchy of needs necessitates careful consideration to achieve the most effective outcomes. Likewise, a newly sober client may require assistance with obtaining a sober living environment, a concrete relapse prevention plan, 12-step meeting referrals, and learning new coping strategies prior to exploring the correlations between his childhood abuse and his current addiction. If the client needs stabilization, then the full scope of needs should be assessed and addressed.

A shift in thinking toward client advocacy is gaining recognition in the counseling profession. Homan (2016) stresses that we need to change the conditions that affect people rather than trying to change the people who are affected by the conditions. He believes that all human services workers are called upon to work for change when there are injustices in the system. If we are interested in changing societal conditions, Hogan (2013) believes we must first work on better understanding ourselves as cultural beings. We need to recognize that our personal cultural framework is the starting point for how we engage the world and for the methods we use in our professional work. By understanding our personal culture, Hogan believes we can build a foundation for engaging in meaningful dialogue in a culturally diverse environment.

Helpers need to develop an awareness of their own beliefs and attitudes regarding social issues and marginalized populations, understand the scope of their knowledge, and strive to increase their level of skill when intervening and adopting multiple roles. Multicultural competence is essential in understanding the cultural relevance and appropriateness of advocacy interventions as counselors bring their own attitudes and beliefs to the sociopolitical history of their communities. For comprehensive discussions of social justice and systems changes as applied to working with diverse client populations, see *Social Justice Counseling: The Next Steps Beyond Multiculturalism* (Chung & Bemak, 2012) and *Counseling for Social Justice* (Lee, 2018a).

Multiple Roles of Community Workers

Helpers with a community orientation are committed to making society a better place by challenging systemic inequities. Ideally, all helping professionals are committed to promoting change on both individual and community levels; however, practitioners do not all have the same areas of interest and expertise. Community intervention calls for practitioners who (a) are familiar with resources within the community; (b) have a basic knowledge of the cultural background of their clients; (c) are able to use contextual and strength-based perspectives that can be adapted to all facets of their work; (d) are able to alter the types of strategies and services they use with clients; (e) are able to implement programs, techniques, and concepts among a broad range of people;

(f) are able to prepare clients to be their own self-advocates; and (g) have the ability to connect with the community and to connect community members with each other (Lewis, Lewis, Daniels, & D'Andrea, 2011).

Stepping Outside of the Office and Into the Community

Helpers in private practice or in an agency setting can go outside of their offices and do some work in their community (Kottler, Englar-Carlson, & Carlson, 2013). Practitioners can help create ripples within segments of the community even in small ways if they are committed to becoming grassroots change agents. For example, a community worker might organize a community event, such as a 5K walk, aimed at raising awareness of a particular problem such as suicide or domestic violence. Bemak (2013) illustrates how he is engaged in community action in counseling on a broader scale and writes about the concept of counselors without borders. Counselors have traveled to various places in the world where there are critical needs due to a natural disaster. This kind of community action is very different from traditional counseling done in an office setting.

By creating opportunities for community members to develop skills and abilities that contribute to the vitality of their community, community workers help to develop the community, not merely attend to some of its problems. This elevates the quality of life in the community and expands the members' capacity to confront current and future challenges. The work of community change is often the work of small groups. That is, within the community groups with whom you are working there will likely be a smaller group of people who take an active part in change efforts. Most of the work of this group will be done in a small group context. In Chapter 11 we emphasized the importance of small group approaches for human services workers. In functioning as a change agent within the community, small group skills are essential and powerful.

LO2 Various Perspectives on the Roles of Helper

Conventional approaches to therapy are sometimes criticized for placing undue responsibility on the client for his or her plight. At the extreme, some interventions place the major responsibility for client problems entirely on the individual without regard for environmental factors that may be contributing to the problem. The helping professions must recognize that many problems—prejudice, oppression, and discrimination—reside outside, not within, the person. Community-oriented work emphasizes the necessity of recognizing and dealing with environmental conditions that often create problems for diverse client groups. Helpers are encouraged to embrace the roles of environmental change agents and sociopolitical activists to reform social systems and to ameliorate unnecessary suffering. To do this, helpers need to acquire new professional roles in delivering a broad range of services aimed at promoting the mental health of people from diverse groups and backgrounds (Crethar et al., 2008).

Alternative Roles to Traditional Helping Models

Atkinson (2004) suggests that it is appropriate for community workers to assume some or all of the following alternative roles to traditional helping models as needed to benefit clients: (1) advocate, (2) change agent, (3) consultant, (4) adviser, (5) facilitator of indigenous support systems, and (6) facilitator of indigenous healing methods. These alternative roles embody fundamental principles of social justice and activism that are aimed at client empowerment. In selecting a role and strategies to use with racial or ethnic minority clients, it is useful to take into account the client's level of acculturation, the etiology of the problem, and the goal of counseling. Becoming an advocate for empowerment requires a high level of commitment. Assuming any of these alternate roles involves a shift from focusing exclusively on individuals to working for social change. Let's briefly examine these alternative helper roles.

1. **Advocate**. Because ethnic minority clients are often oppressed by the dominant society, helpers can speak on their behalf. Helpers especially need to function as advocates for clients who are low in acculturation, people who need remediation of a problem resulting from discrimination and oppression, and disenfranchised individuals whose backgrounds make it difficult for them to utilize professional services. Crethar and colleagues (2008) define **advocacy** as "proactive efforts carried out by counseling professionals in response to institutional, systemic, and cultural impediments to their clients' well-being" (p. 274). Helpers function in an advocacy role when they use their skills in helping clients to effectively deal with institutional barriers that impede their personal, social, academic, or career goals.

   Client advocacy should be carried out by practitioners who have multicultural competence. Helpers can get involved in social and political activism to help client groups learn how to overcome barriers and empower themselves (Lee, 2013a). Practitioners are called upon to act *with* and *on behalf of* their clients and others in the community. To illustrate this, a counselor working with a group of traumatized veterans who served in Iraq and Afghanistan may encourage these clients to join her in a public awareness campaign to educate the community about Post-Traumatic Stress Disorder (PTSD). It may be empowering for these veterans to share their stories and to encourage others in the community who are not seeking treatment to reach out for support.

2. **Change agent**. Functioning in this role, community workers do what they can to confront and bring about change within the system that contributes to, if not creates, the problems clients face. In the role of change agents, helpers assist clients in recognizing oppressive forces in the community as a source of their problem and also teach clients strategies for dealing with these forces.

   The main purpose of community change is to foster healthy communities. A change agent recognizes that healthy communities produce healthy people. As systemic change agents, community workers assist clients in developing power, particularly political power, to bring about change in the clients' social and physical environment. When operating in the role of a change agent, community workers must sometimes educate organizations to change their culture to meet the needs of the community (Homan, 2016).

For example, a counselor might meet with local employers to educate them about sexual harassment in the workplace and provide employees with gender sensitivity training.

3. **Consultant.** Operating as consultants, helpers can encourage individuals from diverse cultures to learn useful skills to interact successfully with various forces within their community. In this role, the client and the helper cooperate in addressing unhealthy forces within the system. As consultants, helpers can work with clients from diverse racial, ethnic, sexual/affectional, ability, gender, and cultural backgrounds to design preventive programs to reduce the negative impact of racism and oppression. A helper who has expertise on the needs of the gay, lesbian, bisexual, and transgender population may be hired by an organization as a consultant to help the administrators change the heterosexist and homophobic workplace culture to one that is more accepting and tolerant.
4. **Adviser.** This role is similar to that of consultant. It differs in that the community worker as adviser initiates the discussion with clients about ways to deal with environmental problems that contribute to their personal problems. For example, recent immigrants may need advice on immigration paperwork, coping with problems they will face in the job market, problems that their children may encounter at school, and resources for the acquisition of language skills. Helpers need to acquire knowledge about these topics and know when and where to refer clients for further assistance.
5. **Facilitator of indigenous support systems.** Many ethnically diverse clients, people in rural environments, and older people would not consider seeking professional counseling or therapy. Instead, they may turn to help from family members, close friends, or social support systems within their own communities. Community workers can play an important role by encouraging clients to make full use of resources within their own communities, including community centers, churches, extended families, neighborhood social networks, friendship networks, and advocacy groups. Community workers can work with church leaders in influencing social policy and community change.
6. **Facilitator of indigenous healing systems.** In many cultures, human services professionals have little hope of reaching individuals with problems due to their mistrust of traditional mental health approaches and professionals. If helpers are aware of the kinds of healing resources that exist within a client's culture (indigenous resources), they can refer a client to a folk or spiritual healer from his or her culture. At times, it may be difficult for helpers to adopt the worldview of their clients. In such instances, it could be helpful to work collaboratively with an indigenous healer (such as religious leaders and institutions, energy healers, and respected community leaders). Chung and Bemak (2012) describe a Somali client who had witnessed the murder of several family members before coming to the United States. In addition to working with a counselor, this client benefited from meeting with an indigenous healer who performed a ritual to "appease the spirits of the deceased family members" (p. 90). The client and the healer then read passages from the Koran, ate certain foods, and burned incense to complete the ceremony. Becoming a culturally competent helper requires

being open to indigenous health and healing practices. Helpers who develop an understanding of indigenous healing systems are likely to find that this profoundly affects their practice in working with others.

School Counselors as Social Justice Advocates and Change Agents

Taking on the role of change agent in the school setting involves a number of challenges. Bemak and Chung (2008) describe many school counselors as being caught in the "nice counselor syndrome," promoting peace and interpersonal harmony at any cost, which tends to uphold the status quo. These school counselors are not prepared to deal with inequity, unfair treatment, and the lack of access to opportunities and resources. Bemak and Chung outline a number of ways to avoid or move beyond the nice counselor syndrome and become effective social justice advocates and organizational change agents in schools. Here are a few of their recommendations:

- Expect to experience some interpersonal conflict in expanding your professional role and breaking away from the nice counselor syndrome.
- Recognize both the personal and professional obstacles to redefining the counselor's role and becoming a social justice advocate and a change agent in a school.
- Appreciate the necessity of coping with uncertainty, ambiguity, and anxiety, which are often part of the change process.
- Recognize that it takes courage to speak out and to take personal and professional risks to ensure that all students have the opportunity to obtain a quality education.
- Consider the role of change agent in school counseling as a professional imperative rather than as a professional option.

Bemak and Chung (2008) believe school counselors must assume new professional roles if they are to address the inequities and injustices that adversely affect many young people in public schools.

Community Intervention

A way of conceptualizing the community counseling model is through the various forms of services helpers might offer: (1) direct client services, (2) indirect client services, (3) direct community services, and (4) indirect community services (Lewis et al., 2011). We explore each of these services in more detail in the following discussion.

Direct client services focus on *outreach activities* to a population that might be at risk for developing mental health problems. Community workers provide help to clients either facing crises or dealing with ongoing stressors that impair their coping ability. Target populations for such programs are school dropouts, alcohol and drug abusers of all ages, people who are homeless, victims and perpetrators of child and elder abuse, suicidal individuals, victims of violent crimes, older people, individuals with AIDS, and adolescent mothers. By reaching out to schools and communities, helpers can offer a variety of personal, career, and family counseling services to at-risk groups (Lewis et al., 2011).

Indirect client services consist of *client advocacy,* which involves active intervention for and with an individual or a group. The community agency works to empower disenfranchised groups that have become split off from the mainstream community. These include, but are not limited to, the unemployed, the homeless, older people, individuals with disabilities, and people living with AIDS. Helpers need to become advocates, speaking up on their clients' behalf and actively intervening in their clients' situation. Helpers identify factors that negatively affect their clients and take action, often in collaboration with others, to bring about needed changes (Lewis et al., 2011). The advocacy process is best conceived of as a way to assist groups who typically do not have power to move in the direction of acquiring tools to find and use resources, both within the community and within themselves.

Direct community services in the form of *preventive education* are geared to the population at large. Examples of these programs include life planning workshops, the creative use of leisure, and training in interpersonal skills. Because the emphasis is on prevention, these programs help people develop a wider range of competencies.

Indirect community services are attempts to *change the social environment* to meet the needs of the population as a whole and are carried out by influencing public policy. Community intervention deals with the victims of poverty, sexism, and racism, which typically leave people feeling powerless. The focus is on promoting systemic change by working closely with those in the community who develop public policy. For example, a community worker might focus on helping to shape policies at the local, state, or national level that support people with disabilities in finding satisfactory employment and that safeguard their rights in the workplace.

See "Counseling Survivors of Hurricane Katrina" (Herlihy & James, 2018) for an example of community interventions when working with disaster victims. This essay demonstrates ways of meeting the needs of a community following a natural disaster.

LO3 Outreach

As mental health professionals have become more aware of the need to provide services to a wider population, effective outreach strategies have received increased attention. These strategies are particularly useful for reaching ethnic minorities because of the traditional mistrust of primarily White mental health professionals who have often been seen as mislabeling people from diverse groups and excluding them from services.

As discussed in Chapter 4, if practitioners hope to reach and effectively deal with a cultural group different from their own, they must acquire a broad understanding of culturally diverse client populations. It is essential that culturally competent helpers use intervention techniques that are consistent with the life experiences and cultural values of diverse groups in the community if they hope to succeed in their outreach efforts (Lee & Park, 2013).

The outreach model differs from the traditional model used in the helping professions in the sense that the community worker does not wait for people to come in for help. Instead, the worker reaches out to the community with a coordinated package of preventive mental health services aimed at improving the psychological health of people throughout the life cycle.

The outreach approach includes developmental and educational efforts, such as skills training, stress management training, education of the community about mental health and the benefits of counseling, and consultation in a variety of settings. These efforts must be made in a way that makes sense to the community, not just the practitioner. For instance, a helper might establish a health and wellness program for older adults that is held at a convenient location in the community, such as at a senior center. A program that emphasizes successful aging might involve activities that clients would benefit from such as the creative arts as well as have a focus on maintaining a healthy lifestyle, stress reduction, resilience and positive thinking, and social support. If people in the community do not utilize services, it is appropriate to question the value of the services or the appropriateness of the way these services are delivered. Community workers need to be willing to learn *from* and *with* the community when organizing services.

You do not have to be all things to potential clients in the community. If you work in a community agency, you will most likely be part of a team working with individual clients. The case management approach involves a number of helping professionals, each with a different specialty. Managed care systems also utilize a team approach, so you need to learn how to build collaborative relationships with the members of a professional team at your agency. Once a need is identified within a community, a group of workers has more power to reach client groups than does a single worker functioning in isolation.

An Outreach Program in Schools

During one of my first internships I (Marianne) worked in an elementary school as a juvenile diversion counselor, helping children between the ages of 6 and 11 who had come to the attention of school authorities for various types of problematic behavior. This program was aimed at preventing relatively small problems from becoming more serious problems and also keeping older children out of the juvenile court system. I had some supervision from a psychologist, but it was up to me to design a program to work with these children. I formed several groups for children of similar ages to provide group counseling at the school. Although the group counseling was helpful, I quickly realized it was necessary to go beyond the school setting to deal effectively with the children's difficulties. I instituted an outreach program to make connections in the community to assist these children. Interventions that made a significant difference in the behavior of these children involved these community resources:

- I visited the classroom, the playground, and, in some cases, the children's homes to observe their behavior before making assumptions about what these children needed.
- I consulted with the principal, teachers, and school nurse to form a team to develop ways to most effectively help the children.
- I contacted the parents and let them know who I was and how I would be working with their children. I invited them to be involved as much as possible in helping their children.

- With the permission of the parents, I recruited college student volunteers to tutor the children who had academic problems and acted out because of their problems. These college students were taking child psychology courses and were required to complete 10 hours of fieldwork with children, so they also benefited from this work.
- Several of the parents agreed to permit their children to participate in fun outings away from school such as swimming parties or a trip to the mountains for hiking.
- I discovered that some children were habitually truant because they were embarrassed about not having "nice" clothes to wear. I was able to find resources in the community to provide for the needs of these children.

Feedback from parents, children, and school officials confirmed that this program was effective in preventing the development of major problems for these children. The program was implemented by other counselors who were also employed by the juvenile diversion system.

LO4 Educating the Community

There are many reasons people do not make use of available resources: they may not be aware of them; they may not be able to afford these services; they may have misconceptions about the nature and purpose of counseling; they may be reluctant to recognize their problems; they may believe that they should be able to take charge of their own lives; they may believe professional helpers are attempting to control their lives; they may perceive that these services are not intended for them because they view such services as culturally insensitive; or they may believe they are not worthy to receive services.

Practical limiting factors also may make it difficult to access community services. For example, if clients are required to travel to the agency to receive services, community members without access to transportation cannot participate in your programs. A lack of adequate or affordable child care is another significant limiting factor. Whenever possible, find creative ways to mitigate barriers to treatment. Providing in-home counseling, on-site child care services, or arranging for clients to access city transit systems are some ways to increase access to programs. Think about creating satellite groups by borrowing space from another community resource. For instance, if enrollment is low in your caregiver support group and the location seems to be a barrier, investigate the possibility of using a room in a library, at a community activity center, a church, or any public building that is more centrally located than your agency. Be creative in your endeavors to provide and expand services to the community.

Demystifying the Notion of Mental Illness

One goal of the community approach is to educate the public and attempt to change the attitudes of the community toward mental health programs. Perhaps the most important task in this area is to demystify the notion of mental illness. Many people still cling to misconceptions and archaic notions of mental illness. Professionals face a real challenge in combating these faulty notions. Helpers also need to be able to present the array of services they offer to the community in terms that the target groups can understand. Many people still consider seeking any form of professional psychological treatment as something only for those who are seriously mentally ill. Some think professional helpers have answers to every problem a client brings to the agency. Others hold the belief that professional help is only for the weak or for those who simply cannot solve their own problems. Unless professionals actively promote helping services in a way that is understandable, acceptable, and culturally appropriate to the community at large, many people who could benefit from professional help may not seek it. Educating the community can awaken people to the resources that are available to assist and empower them.

Hogan (2013, chap. 5) identified some tasks that practitioners might be involved in when educating the community:

- Support the needs of minority groups in the community.
- Actively reach out to people with special needs and initiate programs aimed at preventing problems rather than merely treating them.
- Draw on and improve the skills of community workers and laypeople to help meet the many different needs of clients and discover and use the many abilities of clients.
- Develop strategies to deal effectively with poverty, drug and alcohol abuse, child sexual/physical abuse, child neglect, and intimate partner violence.
- Develop strategies that will empower the disenfranchised in the community.

Influencing Policymakers

The need for community-based programs is compounded by problems of contemporary society such as poverty, homelessness, crime, drive-by shootings, gang activities, absent parents, AIDS, divorce, child abuse, intimate partner violence, unemployment, tension and stress, alienation, addictions to drugs and alcohol, delinquency, and neglect of older people. These are just a few of the major challenges communities need to address in preventing and treating human problems. Community helpers can shape social policy by working within the sociopolitical arena to instigate change. For instance, research into the prevention of AIDS has come about largely through lobbying efforts and political pressure. For systemic change and social transformation to occur, Waller (2013) believes we must be willing to get out of the office and get involved with the community: "My social justice action tends to focus on changing policies within a system that impact the community rather than just an individual" (p. 93).

Although it is not realistic to expect that you will have in-depth knowledge of the range of problems confronting a community, you can have a general knowledge of these problems and familiarize yourself with resources valuable to people with specific needs. In working in a community, you will probably be part of a team of human services professionals. Professional training programs have a responsibility to prepare helpers to become competent advocates for at-risk individuals and groups and to teach students the skills they will need to influence policymaking.

Community workers can easily feel overwhelmed, and community agencies are often underfunded and understaffed. Without adequate funding, creative programs remain on the drawing board, and agencies resort to crisis work, treating rather than preventing problems. Because helpers are frequently overworked and have many conflicting demands on their time, it may be difficult for them to do much work in the areas of education, influencing policymakers, outreach, and advocacy. However, helpers must find a way to legitimize the use of time for these activities. One way community workers can initiate change is by organizing within an agency and developing a collective voice.

LO5 Mobilizing Community Resources

In *Promoting Community Change: Making It Happen in the Real World,* Homan (2016) suggests that if you want to assume an active role in mobilizing the resources within a community it is useful to have certain knowledge and skills. To maximize your efforts in a community, Homan suggests honing your skills in these areas:

- Achieve credibility and standing within the community.
- Promote meaningful involvement of members of the community being served in community change efforts.
- Develop and build on the strengths or capabilities of members of the community.
- Know your target, your issue, your troops, and your resources.
- Identify the stakeholders, those who are potential allies and opponents.
- Establish and maintain a personal network, especially involving people who may be in a position to assist client groups.
- Understand the transferability of skills used in working with individual clients to working with the community.
- Understand planning and its relationship to action.
- Acknowledge that power is used to maintain or change conditions within the community.
- Learn that power *with* is more appropriate than power *over.*
- Assist the community to declare its needs in a way that enables people to act on them.
- Keep people who are involved in the change effort connected to one another.
- Make sure that your strategies and tactics fit the situation.
- Understand that people must *feel* something before they will *do* something.
- Use the "cycle of empowerment": involvement, communication, decisions, action.
- Listen as assertively as you speak.
- Assume responsibility for instigating change.
- Avoid setting arbitrary limits on yourself. Believe in your own capabilities.
- Commit yourself to learning—about yourself, your community, your issue, your strategies and tactics.
- Focus on the commonalities among community members rather than on their differences.
- Remember that it's not only "they" who need to change but "we" who must change what we are doing.
- Accept the reality of certain problems or conditions without letting these barriers stop productive efforts.
- Address ethical issues in the delivery of services.
- Believe in the rights of members of the community to lead full and satisfying lives.

Recognizing Community Members as the Experts

The most successful programs include community members in determining the direction their communities need to take. As a community worker, you will assume an active role, but remember that it is the community members themselves who are the "experts" on their own needs. Recognizing community members as the experts fosters a sense of empowerment. Your main job is to help community members develop their capacities to strengthen their own community. Just as individual clients are encouraged to find their own solutions and to recognize their strengths, you can do a great deal in assisting members of a community to discover both their internal and external resources in addressing their problems. Facilitate connections within the community and help individuals learn to use available resources to effect the changes they desire.

Some uncertainty is natural when you are trying to decide how you can make a difference in your community. Remind yourself of the skills you have to help you analyze situations and build relationships. It is also important to recognize that idealism can be a valuable asset. Like any other asset, it is strengthened when put into practice. Oftentimes therapists believe that making a difference requires something radical such as a monumental community event organized and funded by the therapist alone. It is worth remembering that making a difference can start with a small daily gesture in your community that has a positive effect on another's life.

Working With Diverse Populations in the Community

We encourage you to think about diverse groups, especially neglected or marginalized client groups, within your community and see how you could mobilize community resources to meet their needs. Any program that you design must incorporate ways of reaching out to the target population as well as ways for potential clients to gain access to your services. Learn to work *with* the community as well as *for* the community. The American Psychological Association (2017b) addresses implementation of culturally adaptive interventions in the community: "Psychologists seek to promote culturally adaptive interventions and advocacy within and across systems, including prevention, early intervention, and recovery" (Guideline 6).

When working with a target group in the community, first clarify your own knowledge and the principles that will be foundational to your work. Regardless of the client population, begin by answering these questions.

- What specific populations in your community are most in need of help? What kind of help do they need?
- To what degree do you understand the special needs of these target groups? What resources and capabilities of the community can be brought to bear on resolving the plight of a target group?
- What are your assumptions and attitudes toward this target group? What possible prejudices, biases, and stereotypes might you harbor toward this group?
- Identify some of your fears or concerns in working with this client group. How will you deal with your own fears?

- What ideas do you have for developing educational programs in your community to provide services to specific client groups?
- How might you deal with the strong reactions of those within the community who may be shocked that you are working with such unpopular client populations?
- In what ways might society stigmatize at-risk groups such as people who are homeless? people who abuse substances? veterans? children from alcoholic families? those who are unemployed?
- In what ways might individuals within certain groups continue to stigmatize themselves?
- As a helper, how can you remove stigmas that block effective programs?

Take a moment to reflect on what you have read about the community approach. Think of your educational background, level of professional training, and work experiences. If you plan to go into the human services field, you are likely to spend some time working in a community agency setting, and you will be working with many different groups within the community. If you were working in such a setting at this time, how prepared are you, both personally and academically, to assume a broader view of helping that encompasses being an agent for change within the community?

Social Activism and Making a Difference

In "Making a Difference," Rob Waters (2004) profiles the work of five community-oriented therapists who became social activists. These five "citizen-therapists" exemplify people who are deeply engaged in their own communities and who are actively working to promote change. Each of these therapists has taken a different path to change the community, yet each of them has been motivated by the question, "How can I make a difference?"

Ramon Rojano (cited in Waters, 2004) is convinced that therapists must become active agents of social change. Rojano, a psychiatrist working primarily with rich Anglo Americans, shifted his focus to work in a child guidance clinic with Latinos/as and African Americans. He quickly realized that traditional psychotherapy approaches for dealing with a family's psychological needs were pointless unless he addressed poverty, violence, and the social and economic crises that were part of the lives of these family members. Referring to his approach as "community family therapy," Rojano is now an advocate for better mental health systems for the poor.

Diane Sollee (cited in Waters, 2004) is a leader in the marriage education movement. Part of her work has involved seminars aimed at training people to become marriage educators, who have the task of teaching basic communication skills to couples. To avoid becoming identified with any political faction, Sollee has refused to accept funding from anyone. The core of her work is providing couples with the information and skills they need to succeed in their marriage and family life.

Kenneth Hardy (cited in Waters, 2004) is a family therapist who over the years has developed projects in schools, churches, corporations, and the United States military to help groups deal with diversity issues. Hardy's goal is to help people acknowledge the reality of social injustice and the inequalities of race, gender, and social class in ways that help develop a true understanding of diversity. In his professional work, Hardy has focused increasingly on those who are disenfranchised and disempowered.

Jack Saul (cited in Waters, 2004) is the director of New York University's International Trauma Studies program, and he is committed to helping people survive disaster. Saul contends that "collective suffering requires a collective response" (p. 40). In disaster situations, Saul believes therapists need to think in broader terms and develop models for mobilizing a community's own resources for healing. Currently, Saul is devoting his energies to developing community resources for healing the 6,000 Liberian refugees living on Staten Island. He operates largely behind the scenes to help organize drop-in centers, job-placement programs, and family support programs that bring together various community leaders. Saul says, "The key thing in doing this kind of work is to bring your therapeutic skills to the community in a way that promotes the community's own capacities, without becoming too central" (p. 41).

Barbara Lee, a graduate of the School of Social Welfare at the University of California at Berkeley, has been a member of Congress in Washington, D.C. since 1998 (cited in Waters, 2004). Lee has learned that she is able to have the widest possible impact by exercising political power. Lee brings a clinician's perspective to bear on running her congressional office, and she and her staff advocate for low-income people. Lee cosponsored a bill that authorized AIDS relief to Africa, which was signed into law by President Bush in 2003. This achievement is but one example of what Lee means when she says, "I didn't go into politics to be part of the system, but to change the system, to shake it up and make things better" (p. 43).

These five social activists have demonstrated that systems can be changed and that communities have a built-in capacity for healing. Helpers who adopt a social activist and social justice perspective do not restrict themselves to thinking in terms of remediation of problems in individual clients' lives. They are concerned with implementing preventive strategies aimed at fostering systemic changes in their clients' environmental contexts (Crethar et al., 2008).

By Way of Review

- The community perspective emphasizes social change rather than merely helping people adapt to their circumstances.
- It is not useful to focus on individual client treatment and neglect the institutional or social conditions that contribute to an individual's problems. A process that considers both the internal conflicts of the individual and the social factors within the community will provide a balanced perspective for helpers.
- It is essential that training programs prepare students to assume a proactive stance toward community intervention, especially with reference to early prevention approaches for at-risk groups in the community.
- A comprehensive community counseling program has four aspects. Direct client services focus on outreach activities for at-risk groups in the community. Direct community services in the form of preventive education are geared to the population at large. Indirect client services consist of

intervening actively for an individual or a group via client advocacy. Indirect community services focus on influencing policymakers and bringing about positive changes within the community.

- Helpers need to assume an advocacy role for disenfranchised clients whose background makes it difficult for them to utilize professional assistance.
- Helpers who work in the community will be expected to develop the skills necessary to engage in outreach, provide education to community members, assume an advocacy role, and influence policymakers.
- The nice counselor syndrome occurs when helpers promote peace and interpersonal harmony at any cost, which tends to entrench the status quo.
- You do not have to be all things to potential clients in the community. If you work in a community agency, you will most likely be part of a team working with individual clients.
- Social activism is a powerful way to make a significant difference in the community.
- Each of us has the power and ability to make a difference.

What Will You Do Now?

1. Select an at-risk population in your community. As a class project, you and several classmates can explore strategies for advocating for a particular client population by using a community approach. What can be done to awaken people in your community to the needs of the at-risk group you have identified?
2. Explore the kinds of outreach work you might be inclined to do in your own community. If you have a field placement or a job in a community agency, what ideas do you have for outreach projects? What mental health professionals in your community, or faculty members at your college, have the expertise to provide you with direction in meeting critical needs of certain client groups? How might you and fellow students combine your talents and efforts to develop a program for reaching a neglected segment of your community? What agencies and resources within your community could you use in developing such an outreach project? Briefly describe the components of your program. Your program does not have to involve a grand design; even a small change can help individuals who might never ask for assistance.
3. Draft a grant proposal, on your own or as a course assignment, for the outreach program you described in the previous assignment.
4. For the full bibliographic entry for each of the sources listed here, consult the References at the back of the book. Homan (2016) views the community as the client and offers the basic knowledge and skills needed to face the challenge of community change. See Lewis, Lewis, Daniels, and D'Andrea (2011) for a comprehensive description of the community counseling perspective. Chung and Bemak (2012) do an excellent job of showing how to apply a social justice approach in the community. Lee's (2018a) edited book covers a range of topics related to the community, including becoming an agent of social change. For a variety of perspectives illustrating how therapists have taken helping beyond the traditional 50-minute hour and into the community, see Kottler, Englar-Carlson, and Carlson (2013).

CHAPTER 13

Stress, Burnout, and Self-Care

Learning Objectives

1. Describe the A-B-C theory as a cognitive method.
2. Identify three cognitive distortions.
3. Describe how an agency environment is sometimes stressful.
4. Describe individual factors that can contribute to burnout.
5. Describe how burnout can lead to impairment.
6. Identify two strategies to prevent burnout.
7. Explain the implications of the concept of self-care as an ethical mandate.
8. Identify five key therapeutic lifestyle changes.
9. Describe how mindfulness can be a path to self-care.
10. Explain how self-compassion is related to caring about others.
11. Establish your own wellness strategies and self-care plan of action.

Focus Questions

1. To what degree are you willing to seek help from others when you experience difficulties?
2. What are your major stressors, both at home and at work?
3. What specific strategies do you use to cope with stress in your personal life? in your professional or academic life?
4. It has been said that either you control stress or stress controls you. How would you apply this maxim to yourself at this time in your life?
5. Are you aware of any self-defeating attitudes and beliefs you may hold? To what extent do you engage in self-defeating internal dialogues?
6. If you have experienced burnout, what have you done about it?
7. What do you do to decrease the likelihood that you will experience burnout?
8. How do you retain your vitality?
9. How satisfied are you with your self-care practices? What are some of the major changes you are willing to make?
10. Self-care is not a luxury; it is an ethical mandate. What are your thoughts about this message?

Aim of the Chapter

In your career as a professional helper, you may be looking forward to helping people resolve problems they face and to assisting them in dealing constructively with pain in their lives. You may be thinking about the satisfaction that comes with knowing that you can be an agent of change for your clients and that you are taking part in making the world a better place as a social justice advocate. There are many rewards associated with being a helper, and we encourage you to bring your enthusiasm and idealism to your work. At the same time, be aware of the potential stress involved in your work and how these stressors may affect you. Our aim in this chapter is to share ideas for managing stress more effectively so you can prevent burnout and can develop self-care practices that will keep you vital both personally and professionally.

A major part of this chapter addresses factors that contribute to stress. It is unrealistic to think that you can have a stress-free personal or professional life, but stress can be managed. You can recognize the signs of stress and make decisions about how to think, feel, and behave in stressful situations. You can become aware of ineffective reactions to stress and learn constructive ways of coping with it. In short, you can learn to manage and control stress rather than being controlled by it.

When you enter the profession and begin practicing full time, new stresses will emerge from the nature of your work and from professional role expectations. If you work in the field of crisis counseling (see Chapter 14), you can expect to experience stressors on a frequent basis. Too often, helpers in a training program are not given enough warning about the potential hazards of the helping professions. Becoming aware of sources of stress and learning strategies to cope with stress will enable you to maintain your optimism and belief in what you are doing in the service of others.

In this chapter, the emphasis is on developing attitudes, thought patterns, and specific action plans to help you maintain your devotion to and enthusiasm for your career choice. We also discuss the effects of stress and how prolonged stress can lead to burnout and professional impairment. Retaining vitality as a person and as a professional requires self-care, and we discuss how your strengths can help you deal effectively with the stresses you experience. Read this chapter in a personal way and reflect on how you plan to take care of yourself so you are able to make a significant difference in the lives of others throughout your career.

Individual Sources of Stress for Helpers

The sources of work-related stress for helping professionals fall into two categories: individual and environmental. To understand stress, you must understand both the external realities that tend to produce stress and the ways you contribute to your stress by your perceptions and interpretations of reality. If you personalize and internalize these stressors, you will diminish your effectiveness as helper.

Individual stressors can be discovered by examining your attitudes and personal characteristics as a helper. Think about client behaviors (as well as behaviors of colleagues and supervisors) that would make the following situations stressful for you. Look over the checklist of behaviors and rate them according to this scale:

1 = This would be *highly stressful* to me.
2 = This would be *moderately stressful* to me.
3 = This would be *mildly stressful* to me.
4 = This would *not be a source of stress* to me.

____ 1. I am seeing a client who seems unmotivated and is coming to the sessions only because he was ordered to attend.

____ 2. One of my clients wants to terminate counseling, but I don't think she is ready for termination.

____ 3. A client is very depressed, sees very little hope that life will get better, yet keeps asking me for help.

____ 4. One of my clients makes suicidal threats, and I have every reason to take his threats seriously.

____ 5. A colleague in my agency is upset with me for not adequately supporting her at meetings.

____ 6. A client with a history of violent outbursts expresses intense anger about his ex-wife during sessions, and I am concerned that he may violate the restraining order she filed and harm her.

____ 7. A colleague at my agency is frequently critical of my work at case conference meetings.

____ 8. A client to whom I am attracted tells me that she (he) is sexually attracted to me.

____ 9. My client is very demanding and wants to contact me at home for advice on how to deal with every new problem that arises.

____ 10. My supervisor at my place of work does not give me the recognition and appreciation that I deserve.

Once you have made your ratings, assess the patterns that emerge. What specific behaviors seem to be the most stressful for you? How does this stress affect you?

Cognitive Approaches to Stress Management

Our beliefs largely determine how we interpret events. Therefore, events themselves are not necessarily the cause of our stress; it is the meaning we give to these events that influences how stress affects us. Founded by Albert Ellis, **rational emotive behavior therapy** (REBT) is a theory of personality and psychotherapy that places emphasis on the role thinking plays in influencing feelings and behavior. **Cognitive therapists** help people become aware of their cognitions—the dialogue that goes on within us—and how their thinking affects how they feel and act. The cognitive approaches offer specific strategies to clients for challenging and changing self-defeating cognitions and for developing sound thinking that leads to less stressful living. In this section, we draw heavily from the writings of Albert Ellis and other cognitive therapists, especially Aaron Beck, in presenting the strategies cognitive therapists use that can help you manage stress.

We are all prone at some time to engage in self-defeating thinking and ineffective self-talk. If we recognize the nature of our faulty beliefs and understand how they lead to problems, we can begin the process of defusing these self-defeating cognitions. Because we have the capacity to escalate the stress we experience, we also have the means to lessen it. Cognitive strategies can be employed to retain vitality on both personal and professional levels. In discussing these strategies, the examples provided are geared primarily to situations that you are likely to eventually encounter in your work as a helping professional.

LO1 The A-B-C Theory

Ellis developed the **A-B-C theory of irrational thinking** (Ellis, 2001b; Ellis & Ellis, 2019). This theory explains the relationship among events, beliefs, and feelings. According to Ellis, our interpretations of events are frequently more important than what occurs in reality. He labels *A* an Activating event, *B* one's Belief system, and *C* the emotional Consequence. Consider the situation of going through an interview. Let's imagine the worst outcome: The director of the agency interviewed you and said that you lack the necessary experience for a placement in this agency. You do not get the job you wanted. The activating event (A) in this case is the situation of being rejected. The emotional consequences (C) you experience may include feeling depressed, hurt, and maybe even devastated. Chances are that you hold what Ellis would term "irrational beliefs" about not having been accepted for the position. Ellis would say that your beliefs (B) about this rejection might include some combination of the following thoughts: "It is horrible that I didn't get this job, and it proves that I'm incompetent." "I must succeed at every important endeavor." "This rejection means I'm a failure."

REBT and other cognitive behavioral therapies are grounded on the premise that emotional and behavioral disturbances are originally learned by the incorporation of irrational beliefs from significant others during our childhood, as well as by our own creative invention of inflexible thinking. We actively and continually reinforce these false beliefs by the processes of autosuggestion and self-repetition (Ellis, 2001b; Ellis & Ellis, 2019). It is largely our own repetition of these faulty thoughts, rather than a parent's repetition, that keeps dysfunctional attitudes alive within us.

To complete Ellis's (Ellis, 2001b; Ellis & Ellis, 2019) A-B-C model, consider *D* (Disputing), which is the process of actively disputing irrational beliefs. If we are successful in this process of disputing and in substituting constructive thinking for faulty thinking, we can create new effects (*E*). This provides us with a basis for thinking, feeling, and acting differently. Revisiting our interview example, instead of feeling depressed about not being offered the job and feeling like a failure, we can put it in a new perspective and feel appropriately disappointed with our ego left intact. Challenging the irrational idea that we are incompetent simply because we did not get one position may help us to feel better, which in turn may help us to move forward more quickly and actively pursue other possibilities. By changing our beliefs, we also change our feelings and quite possibly our actions, which is a useful way of reducing stress.

REBT (Ellis, 2001b, 2004b; Ellis & Ellis, 2019) is based on the premise that we have the power to control our emotional destiny. When we are upset, it is well to look to our hidden dogmatic "musts" and our absolutist "shoulds." We have the ability to observe how our *shoulds* and *musts* largely *create* our destructive feelings and behaviors. We have the power to change these demands into strong *preferences* instead of unrealistic commands.

Identifying Self-Defeating Internal Dialogue

Those of us who are human services providers often incorporate a wide range of dysfunctional beliefs that impair our capacity to function effectively when people seek our assistance. At times, we may distort the processing of information, which can easily lead to faulty assumptions and misconceptions. As helpers, we can complicate our life by believing that we *must* be all-knowing and perfect. If we feel depressed or agitated about the job we are doing, it is most important that we examine our basic assumptions and beliefs to determine how they are influencing what we are doing and how we are feeling. As we become more aware of our faulty thinking, we are in a position to change these patterns into constructive ways of thinking (Ellis & Ellis, 2019).

Our negative thoughts tend to produce stress. By becoming aware of the quality of our language, we can get some idea of how our self-talk influences us. Here are some examples of negative thinking:

- I *must* act competently in all situations, and I need to win people's approval.
- If I make a mistake, it *proves* I am a failure.
- I *feel driven* to perform well at all times. If I'm ever less than perfect, I am inadequate.
- I *should* always put the interests of other people before my own.
- I *ought* to be available when anybody needs me. If I'm not, this shows that I'm not a caring person.
- If a client discontinues, I *must have* done something wrong.
- If clients are in pain, I *should* always be able to alleviate their pain.

Statements such as these can be repeated endlessly in our self-talk, and as you can see, most of these statements refer to feelings of inadequacy, a nagging belief that we should be more, and a chronic sense of self-doubt. By assuming the major share of responsibility for our clients, we relieve them of the responsibility to direct their own lives, and in addition create stress for ourselves. Reread these faulty belief statements, and underline the statements that you hear yourself making. Do you tend to make other related statements, especially with regard to your role in assuming responsibility for being the "perfect" helper? What are some examples of things you say to yourself that create stress for you?

LO2 Changing Distorted and Self-Defeating Thinking

Most stress results from beliefs about the way life is or should be. For example, the pressures to perform outstandingly well as a student are greatly exacerbated by self-talk such as "I *must* do all my academic work perfectly." You can use cognitive techniques to change your self-defeating beliefs about living up to these unrealistic expectations. You will experience less stress if you monitor your self-talk so you can recognize your faulty beliefs. Once you identify beliefs that create stress for you, use cognitive techniques to modify those beliefs.

Aaron T. Beck developed an approach known as **cognitive therapy** (CT) as a result of his research on depression. Beck's observations of depressed clients revealed that their interpretation of certain life events had a negative bias, which contributed to their cognitive distortions (Beck, 1976). CT has a number of similarities to both rational emotive behavior therapy and behavior therapy. All of these therapies are active, directive, time-limited, present-centered, problem-oriented, collaborative, structured, and empirical. They emphasize homework and require explicit identification of problems and the situations in which they occur (Beck & Weishaar, 2019). Cognitive therapy perceives psychological problems as stemming from commonplace processes such as faulty thinking, making incorrect inferences on the basis of inadequate or incorrect information, and failing to distinguish between fantasy and reality. A number of systematic errors in reasoning may lead to faulty assumptions and misconceptions, collectively referred to as **cognitive distortions** (Beck & Weishaar, 2019). Let's examine a few of these distortions.

- **Arbitrary inferences** refer to making conclusions without supporting and relevant evidence. This includes "catastrophizing," or thinking of the absolute worst scenario and outcomes for most situations. You might begin your first practicum placement with the conviction that neither your supervisors nor your clients will like you. You may be convinced that you somehow just managed to get into your graduate program by accident, and you are certain now that you do not have the skills to be successful in your practicum placement.
- **Selective abstraction** consists of forming conclusions based on an isolated detail of an event. In this process, other information is ignored, and the significance of the total context is missed. The assumption is that the events that matter are those dealing with failure and deprivation. As a student, you might measure your worth by what you do not know and your weaknesses, not by your successes.
- **Overgeneralization** is a process of holding extreme beliefs on the basis of a single incident and applying them inappropriately to dissimilar events or settings. If you have difficulty working with one adolescent in a practicum, for example, you might conclude that you will not be effective in counseling any adolescents. You might also conclude that you will not be effective in working with *any* clients, and this idea can spill over into feeling ineffective in your personal relationships!
- **Magnification** and **minimization** consist of perceiving a case or situation in a greater or lesser light than it truly deserves. You might make this cognitive error by assuming that even minor mistakes you make in counseling a client in your internship placement could easily create a crisis for the individual and might result in psychological damage.
- **Personalization** is a tendency for individuals to relate external events to themselves, even when there is no basis for making this connection. If a client does not return for a second counseling session, you are convinced that this absence is due to your "inadequate performance" during the initial session.

- **Dichotomous thinking** involves thinking and interpreting in all-or-nothing terms, or categorizing experiences in either/or extremes. You might give yourself no latitude for being a learner. As a student, you are not expected to know everything. You might view yourself as either being the perfectly competent student or as a total failure if you are not at all times highly skilled and always know what to do with a client.

The most direct way to change dysfunctional emotions and behaviors is to modify faulty assumptions and inaccurate beliefs. Cognitive therapy teaches people how to identify their cognitive errors and biases in information processing, and CT guides them in modifying core beliefs that promote faulty conclusions (Beck & Weishaar, 2019). Cognitive behavior therapists help people become aware of their dialogue within and how their thinking affects how they feel and act. They learn the influence that cognition has on their feelings and behaviors and even on environmental events. A unifying theme of all cognitive approaches is identifying dysfunctional beliefs and replacing them with more reality-oriented, constructive self-statements.

Review the common cognitive distortions we have discussed, and think about statements you might be inclined to make that contain these errors. How often do you create stress in yourself with such thoughts? After you have identified a few core self-defeating beliefs, begin to challenge them through a process of critical evaluation. One method for disputing unfounded beliefs is illustrated in these examples of a dysfunctional belief, a disputation, and a constructive belief.

Self-Statement: I should always be available for anyone who needs me.

Disputation: Why must I always be available? It would be good for me to stop telling myself that if I am not always there when a client wants me, I am not a caring person.

Constructive Belief: Although I want to be responsible, I also want to set limits.

Self-Statement: I should be able to do everything well. Either I'm the perfect helper, or I am worthless.

Disputation: Where did I pick up this belief? Does it make any sense that I should always do everything well? Can I do some things less than perfectly and still be outstanding in other areas?

Constructive Belief: Although I like doing well, I can at times accept imperfection in myself. I can tolerate mistakes. I do not have to be perfect to be capable. Perfection is an unrealistic ideal.

Self-Statement: I should always put the interests of other people before my own.

Disputation: Can I have self-interests and still be interested in others?

Constructive Belief: I can't show more interest in others than I have for myself. If I don't take care of myself, the chances are that I'll not be able to help others take care of themselves.

Awareness is the first step in self-change, followed by learning how to deal with self-defeating thinking. However, merely identifying faulty beliefs and learning to make functional statements will not alone ensure change. For change to occur, *action* is absolutely necessary. You need to test reality and act on your new thoughts and beliefs. Rather than avoiding trying new things, you might seek out some of these new ventures and take the risk of being less than perfect.

Environmental Sources of Stress for Helpers

In addition to personal, or internal, sources of stress, external factors also create stress in helpers. **Environmental** sources of stress include the physical aspects of the work setting or the structure of the position itself. A major stressor is the reality of having too much to do in too little time. Other environmental stresses are organizational politics, restrictions imposed by insurance companies, unrealistic demands by the agency or institution, overly large caseloads, an overwhelming amount of paperwork, critical coworkers, cutbacks in programs, and lack of proper supervision. Managed care programs demand that helpers address critical needs of individual clients and families within a few sessions. Helpers often feel personally responsible to provide the level of care that is necessary, and attempting to accomplish the impossible in an unrealistically short time can be highly stressful. Helpers who work in school settings are also under tremendous pressure and stress. They may have extremely large caseloads of students to serve and are accountable to several stakeholders: school administrators, colleagues, parents, and most important, the students. Like counselors practicing in mental health settings, school counselors have to deal with highly restrictive parameters and unrealistic expectations set out by administrative policies.

Another potential environmental stressor is the quality of your working relationships with colleagues. Dealing with coworkers and supervisors can be a source either of support or of stress. Some of your coworkers may be difficult to get along with because of their negative personality traits or toxic behaviors. Some events can be extremely stressful, such as legal actions, financial pressures, major life transitions, threats of layoffs, and change of job responsibilities. Certain client behaviors, such as suicidal or homicidal threats or attempts and severe depression, are highly stressful. Other client-induced stresses include anger toward the helper, aggression and hostility, apathy or lack of motivation, a client's premature termination, and lack of client cooperation. Landrum, Knight, and Flynn (2012) examined the link between staff members' stress and client engagement in substance abuse treatment facilities and discovered that higher organizational stress is associated with lower client engagement. A stressful work environment may lead to burnout among the staff, but it also may have a negative impact on clients. The following case example illustrates how stress can take its toll on a helper who faces many demands.

Case example: An overburdened counselor.

Wendy works in a very busy county social service agency and carries a large caseload. The agency is understaffed, and she is constantly asked to take on more clients than she can adequately serve. When Wendy is asked to take on extra work, she has a difficult time saying "no." She likes being seen as a hard worker by her colleagues. She skips meals, works overtime to complete paperwork, functions on only a few hours of sleep each night, and worries about how her schedule is affecting her family. At a recent physical examination, Wendy's physician prescribed blood pressure medication and cautioned that her health is at risk. Although Wendy is aware of her stressful situation, she does not see any way to change it. Her husband has a severe disability, and she is the sole provider for the family. In addition, her supervisor is also overworked and has no time to deal with Wendy's problems.

Your stance. If Wendy consulted with you, what would you suggest she do? If you were in Wendy's situation, what would you do? What ethical issues, if any, do you see in this case?

Discussion. Wendy derives satisfaction from being viewed by her colleagues and supervisor as a hard worker and a dedicated employee, which is one payoff she receives from maintaining such a stressful workload. However, if Wendy does not begin to set limits to her overwhelming job responsibilities, she may pay an even higher price for neglecting her personal needs. If Wendy sought your professional advice as a consultant, you could remind her that learning to set limits is part of her ethical responsibility. By continually taking on more than she can handle, she will have increasing difficulty maintaining quality care for her existing clients. This could result in harm to her clients, potentially jeopardizing her career. If Wendy does not exercise some self-care, she may burn out and become so ill that she can no longer work at all. As a consultant to Wendy, you might encourage her to challenge the irrational belief that she must *always* accept every new responsibility in order to be seen as a hard working, competent person. She can be reminded that she is a person who has limits.

LO3 Stress in an Agency Environment

Retaining your power and vitality within an agency setting can be challenging. A rehabilitation counselor who works with veterans told us of the stress he experiences as a result of the demands placed on him by his agency to see more clients in a shorter amount of time. He feels pressured to "close a case quickly and efficiently," yet his clients often want more from him than he can give. In fact, he reports that many of his clients see him as uncaring because he does not give them enough time. What he did not tell his clients was that he would have liked to spend more time with them. Instead, he took on full responsibility for how his clients were reacting, and he typically felt unappreciated by both his staff and his clients. Had he said more to his clients about what he was thinking and feeling, they would have had a basis to perceive him differently.

During the initial years of employment as a professional helper in an organization, it is common to experience a high level of stress and anxiety.

Many helpers have reported frustration and disappointment over their job's unexpected stressors and demands. We asked former students who had entered the helping professions to identify some of the main frustrations and stresses they were facing. Most often they identified the slowness of the system, the resistance of administrators and fellow staff members to new ideas, and unrealistic expectations and demands. One woman in her mid-20s made this comment:

> I get frustrated with the slow process of the system. New ideas are often overlooked. Because of my age, I sometimes have difficulty gaining credibility. My biggest source of dissatisfaction, however, is watching children that I have worked with and have seen improve go back into the system (or family) and regress to where they started.

A young social worker observed, "My greatest frustration is with the administration and its lack of support, common purpose, or teamwork." And a woman who was managing a volunteer staff of student interns had this to report:

> I am most frustrated when the staff is resistant to new ideas. Dealing with governmental bureaucracy is another major source of stress. They make it very difficult to get things done.

Agencies often make unrealistic demands, especially insisting that problems be solved quickly. For those who work with clients sent by the courts or those on probation, for instance, the helper is under pressure to see that behavioral changes take place in a specified time so that more people can be seen, which means more funding.

Retain Power and Vitality

We cannot prescribe a universal method for getting along in the agency where you work. We can, however, present some strategies we have found helpful that may be appropriate strategies for you. It is best to devise your own strategies to cope with the stresses associated with being part of an organization.

During a job interview ask questions about the requirements and expectations of the position. Accepting a position with an agency entails agreeing to work within a certain philosophical framework. By asking relevant questions, you begin to assume a stance of responsibility: you are exploring how much you want a particular job and what you are willing to give up to get it.

In our experience, established organizations tend to resist major attempts at change. Realize that small and subtle changes can be quite significant. When you attempt radical policy changes, you may be overwhelmed and be at a loss of where to begin. If you focus instead on making changes within the scope of your position, you stand a better chance of succeeding. Study the reasons for the policies of the organization for which you work. Perhaps there are good reasons certain rules have been established. However, if a policy does not seem to be in the best interest of your clients, you can begin to question the assumptions on which the policy is based and formulate new ideas, which can potentially influence the development of a new and improved policy. We live in a data-driven world today, and accountability is of supreme importance. Be sure to back up your ideas with research to demonstrate that your ideas are credible. Forming alliances with colleagues can put you in a better position to bring about change than operating in isolation.

Establish Priorities and Cultivate Support

We have found it helpful to first determine what we *most* want to accomplish in a given position. By reflecting on our priorities, we can decide which compromises we can make without compromising our integrity and which positions we are not willing to negotiate. Knowing what we consider to be most important puts us in a much better position to ask for what we want. In addition, good communication with directors and supervisors is essential.

One essential element in learning how to work effectively in any organization is to realize that *you* are a vital part of that system. Your relationships with other staff members are a central part of the system, and working with your colleagues will most likely enhance your effectiveness. Colleagues can be nourishing and supportive, and your interactions with them can give you a fresh perspective on some of your activities. Furthermore, genuine relationships with your coworkers can be a way of gaining influence.

Although interactions with others in the institution can be energizing, they also can be draining and be a chronic source of stress. Instead of developing support groups within an agency, some people form cliques, harbor unspoken hostility, and generally refuse to confront the conflicts or frictions that keep the staff divided. There are often hidden agendas at staff meetings, resulting in discussion of superficial matters while real issues remain unaddressed. We want to underscore the importance of finding ways to establish working relationships that enrich your professional life instead of draining your energy. If you feel isolated, take the initiative to interact with others on the staff who appear productive and positive and who are not drawn into dysfunctional workplace dynamics.

LO4 Understanding Burnout

People in many different careers experience burnout, but those in the helping professions are especially vulnerable because of the nature of their involvement with people in need. If you increase your awareness of the early warning signs of burnout and develop practical strategies for staving it off, you will be better able to respond effectively to the challenges your work presents. When stresses are not coped with effectively, the end result can be burnout.

Mental health professionals are likely to get a potent dose of stress on a daily basis simply by listening to their clients' experiences. Helpers may be especially challenged by the number of clients who are presenting with symptoms of trauma. When compared to earlier years, Foreman (2018) states that counselors now report higher numbers of traumatized clients in their caseloads. Foreman cautions practitioners to recognize that they are at greater risk for developing vicarious traumatization and for becoming impaired if they have a large number of clients who have experienced trauma.

Counselors are likely to encounter a range of other stressors that simply are part of the terrain of their jobs. These include dealing with high-risk clients; keeping up with written reports and client notes; dealing with the demands and internal politics of agencies, school systems, or other institutions; facing financial pressures; dealing with insurance companies; encountering risks of ethics complaints; working in isolation; managing value conflicts with clients; and learning to leave work at the office—just to name a few. Stress and the inevitable burnout that typically results from inadequately dealing with chronic stress is a major ethical issue facing helping professionals. The goal is to replace ineffective coping strategies with constructive ways to control stress. You can learn to control stress rather than being controlled by it.

Mental health practitioners are not immune from the pressures and stresses we all experience in everyday life. This wide variety of personal challenges may include the death of loved ones; interpersonal conflicts with family members and others; divorce and custody battles; financial problems; physical and mental health issues; racism, sexism, and other forms of discrimination; and struggles finding a healthy work–life balance. In "The Hurting Counselor," Gregory Moffatt (2018) draws on his own experience of the stress associated with a personal crisis to illustrate how a crisis can be debilitating for counselors, especially if they have not establishing strong self-care patterns. Moffatt described how separation from his wife affected his teaching, his counseling practice, as well as all aspects of his personal life. Believing that a personal crisis would not be a part of his life, he had not developed an effective self-care plan, even though he understood the value of self-care. Moffatt indicated that his self-care habits were weak at best, but he *did* exercise regularly, which helped a great deal. However, he slept poorly and typically did not eat breakfast or lunch.

Moffatt's personal crisis ended in reconciliation, but the lessons he learned were costly. Moffatt offered the following advice to help counselors avoid burnout when stressful events in one's personal life seem overwhelming.

- Find a counselor before you need one. Don't allow shame and embarrassment stop you from seeking a personal counselor at various times in your life.
- Seek supervision as a check on your personal and professional competence.
- Eat right, sleep right, and get reasonable exercise.
- Don't forget about the value of recreation and play. Research demonstrates the benefits of play; recreation often helps people manage stress more effectively.
- When you are experiencing a personal crisis, recognize that you cannot expect yourself to function at a high level. Know your limits, both personally and professionally.

Moffatt's key message is that taking good care of yourself is not only healthy for you but will help you better serve your clients. He courageously shared his hard journey as a way for readers to avoid some of his mistakes: "I hope that, with better preparation than I made for myself, you can be prepared to weather the inevitable storms on your own horizons" (p. 56).

The Path to Burnout

Burnout is a state of physical, emotional, and mental exhaustion that results from constant or repeated emotional pressure associated with an intense, long-term involvement with people. Burnout is characterized by feelings of helplessness and hopelessness and by a negative view of self and negative attitudes toward work, life, and other people. Burnout results in personal feelings of depression, loss of morale, feelings of isolation, depersonalization, reduced productivity, and a decreased capacity to cope. The path to burnout is often associated with people working in systems or in community agencies and experiencing the stresses that are a part of this work.

Burnout is the end result of constant and long-term involvement with people with intense needs and is a state of mental, emotional, and physiological exhaustion. Factors that lead to a path toward burnout include work overload, poor working conditions, lack of control, lack of support, insufficient reward, breakdown of community, unfairness, and significant value conflicts. Maslach (2015) conceptualizes the dimensions of burnout along a continuum: exhaustion versus energy, cynicisms versus involvement, and inefficacy versus efficacy. Stress is a key factor resulting in exhaustion, negative responses to work and workers can lead to cynicism, and inefficacy is a manifestation of a negative response to one's accomplishments. Burnout is an ongoing process that begins slowly and progresses through several developmental stages. In the beginning of a helping career, practitioners are often motivated by a high sense of idealism. As they experience the inevitable frustrations and stresses of being a professional helper, their idealism may tend to wane.

Ethical dilemmas, the threat of ethical violations, and being vulnerable to malpractice complaints also can be extremely stressful. Mullen, Morris, and Lord (2017) studied the relationship between practicing counselors' experiences with ethical dilemmas and their stress and burnout. Concerned about the well-being of counselors who encounter ethical dilemmas, Mullen and colleagues suggest that counselors consider the collateral costs of facing and managing ethical situations and acknowledge the stress resulting from such experiences. They note that it is important for practitioners to accept and deal with their emotional responses to the ethical problems they encounter, and they recommend incorporating coping strategies to mitigate the personal effects of stress that is part of their work.

A study conducted by Lent and Schwartz (2012) demonstrated that community mental health outpatient counselors reported significantly greater burnout rates than did counselors working in inpatient settings. With the emphasis in this kind of work on giving to others, there is often not enough focus on self-care. Vilardaga and his colleagues (2011) identified a host of difficult conditions that are a path to burnout among addiction and mental health counselors: funding cuts, restrictions on the delivery of services, changing certification and licensure standards, mandated clients, special needs clients, low salaries, staff turnover, agency upheaval, and limited career opportunities. The potential for burnout is also great for helpers in private practice who have little interchange with fellow professionals, have demanding or disturbed clients, or have few vital interests outside of work.

Skovholt (2001, 2012a) distinguishes between two kinds of burnout: meaning burnout and caring burnout. If you are experiencing **meaning burnout**, your work in caring for others no longer gives you sufficient meaning and purpose in life. The meaning of your work has been lost, and the existential purpose for your work is not apparent. If you are experiencing **caring burnout**, your professional attachments are draining your energy. Caring burnout is the result of a cumulative depletion of your energy to the extent that you are left without a spark. Skovholt (2012a) suggests that counselors need "to learn to be both present and separate and also to be able to strategically attach, detach, and reattach" (p. 128). A meta-analysis of 17 studies revealed that overinvolvement with clients was the major predictor of symptoms of burnout (Norcross & VandenBos, 2018). By applying some of the principles of the cognitive approaches to your personal and professional life, you can learn how to effectively both engage with your clients and also how to detach from them.

Those who work with people need to see that what they do is worthwhile, yet the nature of their profession is such that they often do not see immediate or concrete results. This lack of reinforcement can have a debilitating effect as counselors begin to wonder whether anything they do makes a difference. When helpers find it increasingly difficult to be fully present for their clients and catch themselves responding in rehearsed and detached ways, burnout is not far away.

Work-related stress can result in serious psychological, physical, and behavioral disorders. A growing body of research reveals the negative toll exacted from mental health professionals in symptoms such as moderate depression, mild anxiety, emotional exhaustion, and disturbed relationships. Norcross and VandenBos (2018) remind us that we need to recognize the hazards of the helping professions if we hope to develop effective self-care strategies: "Psychotherapist self-care begins with recognizing and preparing for the inevitable hazards of the undertaking. Understanding its various liabilities demystifies the process and enables us to effectively cope with its downside" (p. 39). Norcross and VandenBos point out that burnout does not necessarily lead to professional impairment. Burnout can be stopped and can be reversed, and they emphasize that proactive self-care can prevent burnout. Helpers must be vigilant for the signs of burnout, and they need to engage in self-care to avoid eventually becoming impaired practitioners. A supervisor can play a key role in assisting trainees in developing an ongoing practice of self-assessment and self-care that will reduce the risk of burnout and impairment (Stebnicki, 2017).

Some Individual Factors Contributing to Burnout

Helpers can play a role in contributing to their own burnout. Certain personality traits and characteristics can increase your risk for burnout. Some individual factors such as a compelling need for approval, feeling unappreciated, striving for unrealistically high goals, feeling high levels of unresolved anxiety, and having a negative or pessimistic attitude can increase your risk for burnout.

Feeling needed. In Chapter 1 we talked about the helper's need to be needed. This need can work for or against you. There is a considerable expenditure of energy in thinking about and taking care of those who need you. As you are starting out and building a practice, you may be flattered that people seek your help. Indeed, it feels affirming to be sought after and needed. Some helpers have a difficult time taking a vacation, especially when they are convinced that their clients cannot function without them. These helpers forget that they, too, have needs, which are probably not being met because their involvement and commitment to others has overwhelmed their life. There are limits to how much you can take on without paying a price in terms of your physical, mental, and emotional health. Strong and healthy boundaries are an important element of self-care that serve as a buffer against burnout.

Feeling unappreciated. A major theme of helpers suffering from burnout is that they do not feel recognized for who they are or what they do, that they receive little positive feedback, and that their dedication is not appreciated. You may be sincerely devoted to helping others, yet your efforts may seem meager at times. You will hear more often about what you are failing to do and about your deficiencies than about what you have done well. If appreciation is lacking on the job, it is difficult over a period of time to know whether what you are doing really makes a difference to anyone. This process tends to erode both your ideals and your enthusiasm, which leads to demoralization.

Feeling overwhelmed. At times you may be expected to carry a heavy workload, and the demands to see more clients, to provide an increasing number of services, and to do more in less time can contribute to a sense of disillusionment. Caseloads may be unrealistically high in some agencies, and no matter how efficient you are, it may not be possible to do all that is expected of you. You may feel alone and isolated and believe that nobody understands or cares. If you are also overwhelmed with family and other outside responsibilities, these feelings may expand to encompass your whole life.

Feeling discouraged. An important factor in burnout is whether your ideals are working for or against you. In our experience, those who set unrealistically high goals for themselves also tend to have high expectations of others. As long as helpers feel satisfied by their efforts, their energy level remains high. Most health professionals were initially attracted to their careers in large part because of their hope of making a significant difference in the lives of others. One sign of burnout is the dulling of these ideals and the loss of involvement and passion. When helpers' efforts are not recognized, they are likely to become discouraged.

The problem of tarnished idealism increases as you come into contact with cynical colleagues who are threatened by your enthusiasm. It is difficult to stay creative and excited when those around you are continually undermining your efforts to make a difference. If you constantly hear that your proposals for change will not work and if you are without real support for your ideas, your belief that you can make a difference may disappear. If you receive an abundance of negative reactions from others, you may become self-critical and wonder whether you are making any difference to those you are supposedly helping. Being critical of and unkind to yourself often leads to being critical of and unkind to others.

If you work in a toxic environment, you would do well to actively seek some source of support either in your job setting or away from it. It is not likely that the agency will create this support for you. You could ask colleagues to join you in making the time for regular meetings aimed at providing mutual support. Balancing idealism with realism is essential for survival as a helping professional.

Continuous contact with clients who are unappreciative, upset, and depressed often leads helpers to view all recipients in helping relationships in negative terms. Those working with highly demanding client populations may be particularly vulnerable to becoming discouraged and to developing burnout. Utilizing a burnout inventory designed by Maslach, Jackson, and Leiter (1996), a group of researchers examined demographic and work-related correlates of job burnout among eating disorder treatment providers (Warren, Schafer, Crowley, & Olivardia, 2013). They discovered that "over 45% of participants reported that treatment resistance, ego-syntonicity, high relapse rates, worry about patient survival, emotional drain, lack of appropriate financial reimbursement, and extra hours spent working contributed to feeling burned out *somewhat* to *very much*" (p. 1). Discouraged practitioners may care less, begin to make derogatory comments about their clients, ignore them, and want to move away from them. Dehumanized responses are a core ingredient of burnout.

LO5 The Impaired Professional

If burnout is not addressed, it will probably lead to the helper becoming an impaired practitioner. Impairment can be viewed as the presence of an illness or severe psychological depletion that is likely to block a professional from being able to deliver effective services, which results in the helper consistently functioning below acceptable practice standards. A number of other factors can negatively influence a professional's effectiveness, both personally and professionally, including addictions, substance abuse, and physical illness. **Impaired professionals** are unable to effectively cope with stressful events, and they are unable to adequately carry out their professional duties. Those practitioners whose inner conflicts are consistently activated by client material may respond by trying to stabilize themselves rather than facilitating the growth of their clients.

Impaired practitioners clearly contribute to the suffering of their clients rather than alleviating it. Because a common characteristic of impairment is denial, professional colleagues may need to confront the behavior of an impaired counselor in a respectful and sensitive manner. Caring colleagues can be instrumental in helping impaired practitioners break through their denial.

Ethics Codes on Impairment

It is an ethical imperative that impaired professionals recognize and deal with their impairment. Most of the ethics codes of the various professions specifically address the ethical dimensions of professional impairment and mention self-care as an ethical imperative. The *Code of Ethics* of the National Association of Social Workers (NASW, 2017) emphasizes carrying out one's professional responsibility in a competent way:

> Social workers should not allow their personal problems, psychosocial distress, legal problems, substance abuse, or mental health difficulties to interfere with their professional judgment and performance or to jeopardize the best interests of people for whom they have a professional responsibility (4.05a.).

The American Counseling Association (ACA, 2014) offers these steps for helpers to follow in dealing with impairment:

> Counselors monitor themselves for signs of impairment from their own physical, mental, or emotional problems and refrain from offering or providing professional services when impaired. They seek assistance for problems that reach the level of professional impairment, and, if necessary, they limit, suspend, or terminate their professional responsibilities until it is determined that they may safely resume their work. Counselors assist colleagues or supervisors in recognizing their own

> professional impairment and provide consultation and assistance when warranted with colleagues or supervisors showing signs of impairment and intervene as appropriate to prevent imminent harm to clients. (C.2.g.)

The American Psychological Association (2017a) calls for monitoring the impact of one's personal problems:

> When psychologists become aware of personal problems that may interfere with their performing work-related duties adequately, they take appropriate measures, such as obtaining professional consultation or assistance, and determine whether they should limit, suspend, or terminate their work-related duties. (2.06.b.)

The American Association for Marriage and Family Therapy (AAMFT, 2015) standard requires helpers to monitor their own behavior:

> Marriage and family therapists seek appropriate professional assistance for issues that may impair their work performance or clinical judgment. (3.3.)

A common theme of ethics codes for mental health practitioners is that helpers must monitor their own behavior and be aware of how their personal problems could interfere with their ability to perform their professional activities. Professional burnout is an internal phenomenon that becomes obvious to others only in its advanced stages; therefore, take special care to recognize your own limits. Ideally, practitioners themselves will realize that they need help and take steps to deal with problems that are keeping them stuck in dysfunctional patterns. But you do not need to do this alone; reach out to your colleagues as a source of support. In addition, explore the valuable resources your agency may have available to help you maintain your effectiveness.

LO6 Strategies to Prevent Burnout

Many paths are available to combat burnout and prevent impairment. You can do much personally to lessen the chances of becoming impaired or to restore yourself. How you approach your tasks and what you get from doing them are more important than how much you are doing. Ultimately, whether you experience burnout depends on how well you monitor the effects that the stresses of your work have on you and the choices you make to deal with stress both internally and externally.

We would be remiss if we did not mention that organizations have the power and the resources to do a great deal to prevent burnout. Agencies can provide child care at the job site, create support groups, offer counseling for staff members, and give workers opportunities for physical exercise during breaks. Creating a positive work environment enhances worker productivity. When helpers feel that the organization is concerned for their well-being, they tend to have positive feelings about themselves and others in their workplace.

You Have Control Over Yourself

As was mentioned earlier in this chapter, you can contribute to creating your own stress by the interpretation you give to events. Although you cannot always control these events, especially if you have had to endure oppressive conditions, you can control how you respond to them and the stance you take toward them. Taking precautions to mitigate stressors contributing to burnout may result in reduced absenteeism, less sense of fatigue, greater quality of care with clients, and higher job satisfaction (Lent & Schwartz, 2012). It is crucial that you become attuned to the warning signals that you are being depleted, and take seriously your own need for nurturing and for recognition. Kottler (2017) points out that we may notice when a colleague has lost energy and is displaying classic signs of burnout, but it is more difficult for many mental health professionals to recognize the signs and symptoms of burnout in themselves. Here are some tips to prevent burnout by proactively engaging in taking care of yourself on all levels.

- Examine your behavior to determine if what you are doing is working for you. Ask yourself: "Is what I am doing really what I want to be doing? If not, why am I continuing in this direction?" "Is what I am doing sustainable, or if I continue at this pace, will I eventually face burnout?" Once you have answered some of these questions, decide what actions you are willing to take to get what you want.
- Look at your expectations to determine whether they are realistic. Temper your ideals with reality to avoid continual frustration.
- Remind yourself that just because you *can* do something does not mean you *should* do something.
- You may expect that you can be all things to all people, and you must always to be available for anyone who needs you. Regardless of how much you have to offer others, there is a limit to what you can give and what clients will accept. Identify your limits and learn to work within them.
- Find other sources of meaning outside of work and your educational program. Do you derive meaning in your life from spirituality or involvement in faith-based activities? Is it important for you to connect with nature or to get involved in activities aimed at protecting the environment? Do you find pleasure and meaning in developing new talents or skills and taking courses in new subject areas to stretch your mind? These activities and interests can help you at least temporarily escape from job stresses and develop some balance in your life.
- Pay attention to what your body, mind, and spirit need in order to reduce stress. This might include a combination of physical activity, good nutrition, adequate rest and relaxation, contact with friends and loved ones, and some form of mindfulness practice.
- There may be some unpleasant aspects of your job or your educational program that are difficult to change, but you can approach your work differently. Find some way to rearrange your schedule to reduce your stress.
- Adopt an "Attitude of Gratitude" (an Alcoholics Anonymous saying). Actively seek things to feel grateful or appreciative about, however small. Practicing gratitude is associated with better physical and emotional well-being (Cormier, 2018). An attitude of gratitude shifts us from a narrow-minded focus on faults and lack to a wider perspective of benefit and abundance (Dalai Lama & Tutu, 2016).
- Learn the art of positivity and practice reframing frustrating circumstances, interactions, or events in positive terms.

- It is easy to become overwhelmed by thinking of all the things that you feel powerless to change. Instead, focus on the aspects of your work or your practicum placement that you have the power to change.
- The companionship of colleagues or fellow students can be a great asset, and they can provide you with new information, insights, and perspectives. Take the initiative and create a support group so that your colleagues or fellow students have the opportunity to listen to one another and to provide help.
- Recognize the early signs of burnout and take remedial action. It is best to direct your energies toward preventing this condition rather than treating it.

You can do much personally to lessen the chances of becoming impaired or to restore yourself. Seek variety in what you are doing on a daily basis. Engaging in diverse personal and professional activities can increase your vitality.

A couple that we know, both social workers employed at an agency, remind themselves continually not to become overwhelmed by myriad demands and not to lose sight of why they remain at their workplace. They accept that they cannot do everything they want to do. They are creative in finding ways to vary their activities. They work with children and adults, colead groups, supervise interns and professionals, teach, administer programs, and give in-service presentations. They have developed a tolerant perspective when agency staff acts in a petty way, partly by having a sense of humor. They both assess their priorities and maintain limits. To be sure, this is not a simple matter; it involves a commitment to self-assessment and an openness to change. In some instances, the ultimate solution may be to change jobs.

Take Action to Change: Designing an Action Plan

You cannot give and give without replenishing your reserve. But simply recognizing that you cannot be a universal giver is not enough; you need an action plan and the commitment to carry out this plan. An effective action plan helps you manage stress in your life. Wubbolding (2017) applies reality therapy techniques to creating an action plan that produces positive results. Wubbolding identifies these characteristics as a path to help you attain your goals:

- Good plans are realistically doable, positive rather than negative, and dependent on you rather than on others. Although plans need to be specific, concrete, and measurable, they should be flexible and open to revision.
- Plans involve process-centered activities such as getting into an exercise program, beginning the practice of meditation, choosing nutritious food, participating in some kind of community service, and taking up music.
- Good plans describe a positive course of action or specify what actions you are willing to take. Even small plans can help you take significant steps toward desired changes.
- Plans are carried out as soon as possible: "What are you willing to do today to begin to better manage your stress?"
- Effective plans can be revised as needed. After you have implemented your plan, it is useful to evaluate it and make any revisions that you deem necessary.

How might you be able to apply the characteristics of an effective plan to your own life? Evaluate your present level of self-care, and consider specific changes you most want to make. Ask yourself, "What plans can I make now that will result in a more satisfying life?" After identifying what you want your self-care program to look like, devise a plan to help you attain the results you want.

Staying Alive Personally and Professionally

What can you do to promote wellness in your life from a holistic perspective? Skovholt and Trotter-Mathison (2016) note that those in the helping professions are experts at one-way caring in their professional work, and they ask us to reflect on the number of one-way caring relationships in our personal life. They encourage helpers to find a balance in their personal life to the imbalance of too many one-way caring professional relationships.

LO7 Self-Care Is Not a Luxury; It Is an Ethical Mandate

If counselors do not practice psychological self-care, eventually they will not have the stamina required to be present with their clients. Skovholt (2012a, 2016) emphasizes that becoming a resilient practitioner is about wellness, which is a necessary state of being if we expect to have the energy it takes to work effectively with clients. To be able to commit to making a difference in the lives of clients, we need to nourish ourselves. It will be difficult to maintain our vitality if we do not find ways to consistently practice self-care. Norcross and VandenBos (2018) state that "self-care is not a narcissistic luxury to be fulfilled as time permits; it is a human requisite, a clinical necessity, and an ethical imperative" (p. 15). Simply put, *self-care is not a luxury; it is an ethical mandate.* If we are drained and depleted, we will not have much to give to those who need our time and our presence. Wise and Barnett (2016) emphasize that we must be willing to take steps to protect our effective functioning if we are to provide our clients with the competent services they deserve.

Factors widely believed to contribute to a helper's ability to function well include self-awareness and monitoring; support from peers, spouses, friends, mentors, and colleagues; strong values; and a balanced life that allows time for family and friends. People who are well are committed to creating a lifestyle that contributes to taking care of their physical selves, challenging themselves intellectually, expressing the full range of their emotions, finding rewarding interpersonal relationships, and searching for a meaning that will give direction to their lives. This holistic approach to well-being requires that we pay attention to the specific aspects of our lifestyle, including how we work and play, how we relax, how and what we eat, how we think and feel, how we keep physically fit, our exercise habits, our relationships with self and others, our values and beliefs, and our spiritual practices. To the degree that we ignore or neglect one or more of these areas, we pay a price in terms of optimal functioning.

Striving for Wellness as a Way of Life

Wellness entails a lifestyle choice and involves a lifelong process of self-care, which is the result of a conscious commitment to care for ourselves in all ways. Wellness encompasses more than the absence of illness. It is best conceived as a holistic approach to health over the life span. The goal is to develop a variety of self-care strategies that address the various dimensions of human functioning. Norcross and VandenBos (2018) believe that "psychotherapists should avail themselves of multiple self-care strategies unencumbered by theoretical dictates" (p. 12).

Wellness as a way of life involves identifying personal goals, prioritizing your goals and values, identifying any barriers that might prevent you from reaching your goals, making an action plan, and then committing yourself to following through on your plans to reach your goals. This sounds like a simple pathway to health, but many of us find it difficult to put this plan into action. Achieving wellness requires effort, and the results are often slow. Wellness is not a one-time decision; it is a process of making a series of decisions that lead to zest, peace, vitality, and happiness in our whole being (Corey, Muratori, Austin, & Austin, 2018).

More broadly, self-care counseling may provide needed help for many clients. In *Wellness Counseling: A Holistic Approach to Prevention and Intervention*, Ohrt, Clarke, and Conley (2019) describe a strength- and prevention-based program concerned about the whole person (mind, body, spirit, emotion, and connection). Their purpose is to (a) provide a theoretical background and empirical support for wellness counseling, (b) explore current trends in wellness, (c) present strategies for the clinical application of wellness concepts, and (d) describe ways that wellness counseling fits for specific populations and settings. Wellness counseling is applicable across the life span and is applicable to a wide range of concerns that clients bring to therapy. "Maintaining wellness at the forefront of counseling may aid in reducing the stigma of receiving counseling, potentially resulting in more people seeking and receiving services" (p. 5). Wellness counseling is versatile; it is transtheoretical and honors the change process.

Wellness in Older Adulthood

Lifestyle choices made earlier in life have an impact on the degree of wellness we achieve during later stages of life. Fullen (2019) states that wellness in older adulthood is best understood in a multidimensional and holistic framework. Based on extensive reviews of scholarly literature, Fullen describes a framework of eight dimensions of wellness that can be used to guide both wellness-informed clinical practice and future empirical research on wellness in older adulthood:

1. *Developmental wellness* involves cultivating a healthy, realistic attitude about growing older. Surviving late into the life span can require believing that life continues to have value into later life.
2. *Cognitive wellness* entails factors such as the need for control, self-efficacy, and engaging in activities that promote brain health and lifelong learning. Resilience is a malleable trait that is associated with cognitive wellness.
3. *Physical wellness* is an important predictor of subjective well-being during later life. This dimension includes diet and exercise, as well as the extent to which people perceive that they are taking care of their physical well-being.
4. *Emotional wellness* is a key factor that allows older adults to maintain hope and to experience resilience in facing the challenges associated with aging. The quality of life is enhanced by the ability to cope adequately with stressors during later years.

5. *Spiritual wellness* encompasses the human need for meaning in life. It has been shown that older adults who derive meaning from religion or a spiritual sense have higher ratings of life satisfaction, self-esteem, optimism, and an enhanced sense of subjective well-being.
6. *Relational wellness* entails the need for relationships with friends, partners, family members, and others. Meaningful relationships provide a sense of mattering to others and give older adults an opportunity to offer support to others.
7. *Vocational wellness* relates to finding one's calling for each phase of older adulthood. Even though formal work may end, many older people find meaning through part-time work, volunteering, and continued work. When older adults are able to use their talents to give to others, they may enter into a new calling that provides an ongoing sense of purpose.
8. *Contextual wellness* refers to financial considerations and living environments. Not having adequate finances can negatively affect the quality of life. Older adults often face the challenges of a new living context. When the context is supportive, older adults stand a better chance of experiencing a higher sense of life quality.

Fullen contends that wellness in adulthood is best defined subjectively by older adults. Rather than viewing objective wellness as a fixed entity, it is preferable to promote holistic wellness in a way that is collaborative, flexible, and attuned to individual differences. A lifespan perspective considers the continuity of habits pertaining to well-being at the various stages of life. If you are committed to a healthy way of living during your earlier years, the likelihood of enjoying life as you age will be greatly enhanced.

LO8 Therapeutic Lifestyle Changes That Promote Wellness

Ample research and clinical evidence support the value of the following therapeutic lifestyle changes: exercise, nutrition and diet, time in nature, relationships, recreation, relaxation, stress management, religious or spiritual involvement, and service to others. Roger Walsh (2011) provides a comprehensive review of these ***therapeutic lifestyle changes*** (TLCs) that promote wellness for therapy clients. Walsh contends that TLCs are sometimes as effective as psychotherapy or pharmacotherapy, and TLCs offer significant therapeutic advantages such as enhancing health and well-being. It is critical for mental health providers to incorporate proactive self-care in their daily living as well. Many TLCs are enjoyable and may become healthy self-sustaining life patterns.

LO9 Mindfulness as a Path to Self-Care

Mindfulness is "awareness of present experience with acceptance" (Siegel, 2010, p. 27). It is the opposite of multitasking. Through mindfulness practice we can learn to focus on one thing at a time and bring our attention back to the present moment when distractions arise. By being aware of our thoughts, emotions, and sensations as they arise within us, we can reduce our reactivity to distressing emotions and thoughts, leading to a more adaptive mode of consciousness (Brown, Marquis, & Guiffrida, 2013). Mindfulness involves developing an attitude of curiosity and compassion to present experience without judgment. Through mindfulness practice, we can train ourselves to intentionally focus on our present experience rather than dwelling on the past or being preoccupied with the future. Living in the present allows us to gain full awareness of whatever actions we are engaged in and to be fully present when we are with another person. Mindfulness is not limited to periods of formal practice; rather, it is meant to become a way of life that we can practice in daily life (Corey, Corey, & Muratori, 2018).

Through the practice of mindfulness, helping professionals are able to learn the pathway to compassion, which embodies the personal characteristics associated with therapeutic presence. Mindfulness improves memory, mental flexibility, and concentration and is a route to reducing compassion fatigue and burnout. Because mindfulness involves suspending judgment, it increases recognition of the positives in life. Mindfulness also increases intuition, insight, empathy, and compassion (Hays, 2014). Accumulating research confirms the multiple self-care benefits of mindfulness for mental health professionals (Norcross & VandenBos, 2018).

An excellent resource to learn more about applying mindfulness to daily life is *The Mindfulness Solution: Everyday Practices for Everyday Problems* (Siegel, 2010). For more on this topic, see *The Healing Power of Mindfulness: A New Way of Being* (Kabat-Zinn, 2018).

Meditation

Meditation is a process of directing our attention to a single focus as a way of centering ourselves by increasing our internal awareness. This practice sharpens our concentration and our thinking patterns with the goal of eliminating mental distractions and relaxing the body. Basically, meditation is simply being still, paying attention to our thoughts, and trying to clear and settle our mind. Meditation is an exercise in noticing our thoughts and feelings, acknowledging that they are simply thoughts and feelings, and gently directing our attention back to our breathing (Hays, 2014).

By narrowing our focus of attention, we often gain an enhanced sense of being. There are many health benefits of meditation, including clearing our mind, reducing stress and anxiety, and bringing joy into our day. The Dalai Lama has said that even 10 minutes of meditation on the well-being of others can help to increase their joy. "When we close our heart, we cannot be joyful. When we have the courage to live with an open heart, we are able to feel our pain and the pain of others, but we are also able to experience more joy" (Dalai Lama & Tutu, 2016, p. 251). Meditation helps to cleanse the mind of distractions and enables us to perceive reality more clearly (Corey, Corey, & Muratori, 2018).

For more on what science teaches us about meditation, see *Altered Traits: Science Reveals How Meditation Changes Your Mind, Brain, and Body* by Daniel Goleman and Richard Davidson (2017). The authors present what meditation can do for people and how to get the most out of the practice.

Breathing and Relaxation

One of the best ways to stop our frantic pace and multitasking is by learning and practicing proper ways of breathing. Breathing is an effective way to control agitation, fear, anxiety, and anger. Take a few moments now to become aware of your breathing. Although breathing is our most natural instinct, many of us have forgotten how to breathe properly. Simply breathe slowly and deeply, in and out, and focus on what it feels and sounds like. Relearning the correct way to breathe can have a significant impact on your well-being and can contribute to your ability to relax. When you are able to breathe properly, you are able to relax more fully (Corey, Corey, & Muratori, 2018). Breathing is a key part of both mindfulness and meditation.

LO10 Self-Compassion as a Route to Caring About Others

Being self-critical increases our stress, hampers productivity, and gets in the way of enjoying life. Self-compassion can enhance our own well-being and the therapeutic relationships we establish with our clients. **Self-compassion** involves developing attitudes of caring, being nonjudgmental, being accepting, and being kind to ourselves. "Through self-compassion we become an inner ally instead of an inner enemy" (Neff & Germer, 2018, p. 9). Neff's (2011) work on self-compassion strongly suggests that people who are more self-compassionate lead healthier, more productive lives than those who are self-critical. They experience greater well-being, which involves more happiness, life satisfaction, self-confidence, and physical health. The key is to strive to be self-accepting and to set realistic and meaningful personal goals. Patsiopoulos and Buchanan (2011) state, "Our hope is that the practice of self-compassion by counselors will facilitate compassionate and healing workplace environments, in which counselors care for themselves and each other, while providing quality client care" (p. 306).

Learning self-compassion and being accepting of ourselves is a starting point for making life changes. To treat others kindly, we must first be kind to ourselves. If we are able to create a compassionate way of being for ourselves, we stand a good chance of demonstrating compassion toward our clients. Norcross and VandenBos (2018) write that "self-compassion soothes our inner critical voice, reorients us toward positivity, builds empathy for patients, and facilitates healing for all involved" (p. 175). Our critical and judgmental voice causes us havoc. A powerful tool for countering this critical voice is to strive for acquiring a compassionate voice, which opens the heart and mind to positive possibilities, for both ourselves and for others (Hays, 2014).

If you are interested in reading more about self-compassion, see *Self-Compassion: Stop Beating Up on Yourself and Leave Insecurity Behind* (Neff, 2011). See also Neff and Germer's (2018) workbook, *The Mindful Self-Compassion Workbook.*

Physical Activity as a Way of Caring for Ourselves

One of the most important things we can do for ourselves to promote general wellness is to build physical activity and regular exercise into our daily lives. Regular exercise is a central aspect to achieving physical fitness and maintaining wellness.

It helps prevent disease, promotes health, prolongs and enhances life, and is a means of reducing the negative aspects of stress. Understanding stress from a cognitive perspective is very useful, but physical activity and exercise can be of the utmost importance in caring for ourselves, both physically and emotionally. The psychological benefits of exercise include enhanced self-efficacy and self-esteem and also interruption of negative thoughts and rumination (Walsh, 2011). If we have depressed moods, simply analyzing our cognitions is not enough. If we hope to change our mood, doing some kind of physical activity is generally necessary. Indeed, there is abundant literature on physical activity as a key approach to stress management and general overall health.

Although we may be aware of the benefits of exercise, many of us tell ourselves and others that we are simply too busy to take the time for physical exercise. Engaging in exercise is one aspect of our lives that we can control. We suggest that you find something suitable for your age, physical condition, and life circumstances and something that you want to make a consistent part of your life. Many studies suggest that exercise can help people deal with mental health issues and boost well-being, but there are risks. Too much exercise may negatively affect mental health (Cohut, 2018). Design a plan that is right for you and that will minimize the risks and maximize the gains to your overall wellness. If you select a form of exercise that you enjoy, you are likely to make a commitment to engaging in this practice on a regular basis. Doing so can be instrumental in changing your life.

Diet and Nutrition

Considerable evidence points to the key role that nutrition plays in mental and physical health (Walsh, 2011). Although it is easy to feel overwhelmed by the information currently available about diet and nutrition, we need to become informed consumers in determining how we will nourish ourselves. If our primary diet is poor, we will not have the energy to meet the demands of everyday life. Irregular and inconsistent eating patterns are a nutritional problem for many. If you find developing healthy eating patterns to be a challenge, you might consider a consultation with a nutritionist. Healthy nutritional habits do not have to take a great deal of time. By learning how to eat wisely and well, how to manage our weight, and how to become physically fit, we can begin a lifelong process toward wellness. By establishing healthy eating habits, we increase our ability to maintain the vitality that is necessary for us to provide quality care to our clients (Corey, Muratori, Austin, & Austin, 2018).

Being in Nature

Urbanization and technology often distance us from the natural world. Immersing yourself in nature provides numerous benefits as a path toward enhancing both physical and mental health. Nature can be used as a therapeutic partner. Phillips (2018) suggests that counselors consider ways to bring nature into the therapeutic endeavor and claims that "counselors don't have to be extreme adventure guides to help clients experience some of the mental and emotional health benefits of reconnecting with nature" (p. 26).

Engaging with nature is an ideal way to manage stress and to promote well-being. It enhances self-esteem, elevates mood, and promotes relaxation. Walsh (2011) asserts that nature calms the body and mind, reduces stress, removes mental trivia, and calls to mind what matters most in life. Walsh reminds us that being in nature offers the gift of silence. He points out that in the global rush of urbanization and technology it is imperative that mental health professionals advocate for spending time in nature. The Dalai Lama suggests that wellness and happiness are enhanced and supported when we spend at least 30 minutes a day in nature. The more time we spend in nature, the better we feel.

Relationships and Well-Being

How we respond internally to our circumstances and our beliefs are directly related to our self-care and our effectiveness in our professional roles. Our ability to care for others will be limited if we neglect to care for ourselves. The individuals we choose to have in our lives have a profound effect on our worldview and on our professional work. Good relationships are central to both physical and psychological well-being (Walsh, 2011). Establishing relationships that are fulfilling and supportive can positively influence our level of well-being. Hays (2014) sees healthy relationships as the core of self-care and states "that healthy, mutually satisfying relationships are among the most powerful contributors to well-being" (p. 10).

Religious/Spiritual Involvement and Meaning in Life

Religious and spiritual involvement can be a vital component of self-care and can help you put life in perspective. A growing body of scientific evidence reveals that faith and spirituality can provide an inner source of strength and calmness and enhance your sense of well-being (Hales, 2017). Walsh (2011) identifies religious and spiritual involvement as a significant aspect of lifestyle that mental health practitioners would do well to consider, both for their own life and in their work with clients. He asserts that religious and spiritual concerns are vitally important to most people who come to therapy and that religious or spiritual practices are a major means of coping with stress. Walsh notes that religious and spiritual involvement is most likely to be beneficial in therapy when it centers on themes such as love, acceptance, and forgiveness.

There is plenty of evidence of religion being a divisive force rather than a unifying one. The Dalai Lama (2001) contends that the ultimate goal of all religions is to produce better human beings who will demonstrate caring and acceptance of others. Despite our differences, we can strive to make this world a better place by treating one another with compassion and kindness. The Dalai Lama talks about core spiritual values that include qualities of goodness, love, compassion, tolerance, patience, contentment, forgiveness, human warmth, caring, and kindness toward oneself. We would do well to reflect on these ideas to determine how we can incorporate these actions as a part of our care of self and care for others.

For a more detailed treatment of spirituality as a pathway to meaning, see *Fulfilled: How the Science of Spirituality Can Help You Live a Happier, More Meaningful Life* by Anna Yusim (2017). The author integrates the tenets of Western medicine, psychology, and neurobiology with some spiritual principles she learned in her own personal journey to fulfillment.

Providing Service to Others as a Lifestyle Pattern

Service to others is one of the therapeutic lifestyle changes that can enhance the quality of our lives (Walsh, 2011). Perhaps you gravitated toward counseling in the first place because you derived satisfaction and fulfillment from helping people navigate their struggles. Adlerian psychologists refer to social interest as a sign of mental health. Adlerians contend that we need to go beyond the narrow confines of self by concerning ourselves with reaching out to others. Making a difference in the lives of others is a motivating force for many in the helping professions.

As part of your self-care, reflect on the service that you would like to provide to your clients and think about the difference you can potentially make in their lives. We can become overwhelmed with keeping up with the responsibilities involved in being part of the helping professions. It can help to engage in self-reflection about the positive changes that we can make in our own way. You may need to place boundaries on how much you are "serving" others for the sake of preserving your own wellness, but many of you may become energized by the notion of seeking out opportunities to provide service to others in new ways.

The Role of Recreation in Self-Care

Finding enjoyment through activities that are not related to our work is a key to our well-being and is a means of reducing stress and preventing burnout. Enjoyable recreational activities, and the positive emotions that ensue, foster a range of physical and psychological benefits (Walsh, 2011). As much as you may feel invested in your work, you are likely to compromise your effectiveness as a helper if you rarely take breaks and fail to develop other interests. Even rewarding work takes energy, and most of us need a life outside of work to derive personal satisfaction. Recreation involves creating new interests that become our path to vitality. A challenge many of us face is balancing work, family, and leisure pursuits. We need to remind ourselves to pause long enough to savor and enjoy experiences that nurture and rejuvenate us. With some imagination, we can identify activities that not only provide a time out from work but enhance our relationships with others (Corey, Muratori, Austin, & Austin, 2018).

LO11 Designing a Personal Strategy for Self-Care and Wellness

Learning to cope with personal and professional sources of stress generally involves making some fundamental changes in your lifestyle. At this point, take some time to ask yourself what basic changes, if any, you want to make to promote your wellness. What is your personal strategy for self-care?

Use the following suggestions to stimulate you to think of additional methods of preventing or treating burnout. After you think about each suggestion, rate each one using the following code:

3 = This approach would be *very meaningful* to me.
2 = This approach would have *some value* for me.
1 = This approach would have *little value* for me.

____ 1. Pursue paths to self-care such as mindfulness, meditation, and deep relaxation.
____ 2. Take time to experience nature.
____ 3. Find other interests outside of my work.
____ 4. Attend to my health and wellness from a holistic perspective.
____ 5. Determine whether what I am doing is meaningful or draining.
____ 6. Take time for myself to do some of the things that I enjoy.
____ 7. Read stimulating books, and do some personal writing.
____ 8. Vary the activities in my work environment.
____ 9. Find nourishment with family and friends.
____ 10. Take short breaks during the day.
____ 11. Use meditation as a way to keep focused and anchored in the present moment.
____ 12. Develop a regular exercise program.
____ 13. Establish healthy nutrition and eating patterns.
____ 14. Make time for sleep and rest.
____ 15. Find and maintain balance in my life.
____ 16. Learn my limits, and learn to set limits with others.
____ 17. Do things to bring happiness to others.
____ 18. Discover what I am passionate about in life and actively pursue it.
____ 19. Live life consciously and purposefully.
____ 20. Treat myself with the same love and compassion that I so readily give to others.

Recognizing that you are on a path toward impairment demands a high level of honesty. You need to be alert to subtle indications and then be willing to take action to remedy a situation that will inevitably result in burnout. Reflect on ways in which you can take care of yourself while being a helper to others. We cannot emphasize enough how important it is that you act on the awareness you have gained from your reflections.

Our Personal Experiences With Self-Care

We would like to share with you our own struggles with burnout and some measures we use to take care of ourselves. First of all, even though we are aware of the dangers of burnout, we are not immune to it. At different times throughout our professional lives, we have wondered about the meaning of our work. We have come to realize that the answer does not lie merely in cutting out activities that we don't enjoy. Much of what we do professionally we like very much, and we have to remind ourselves that we cannot accept all the attractive projects that may interest us. The psychological and financial rewards, however tempting, do not always compensate for the emotional and physical depletion that results from an overscheduled professional life. For example, there was a period of time when we scheduled too many counseling groups in a given year. Although these groups were professionally rewarding, it took a great deal of energy to organize and facilitate them. We eventually began to reduce the number of groups we conducted. In another instance, we became aware that too many of our "vacations" were coupled with professional commitments such as giving a workshop or attending a convention. Although we see this mixture as a good balance, we nevertheless realized that we missed real vacations that were separate from any professional commitments.

Another way in which we attempt to prevent burnout and to take care of ourselves is to pay attention to the early signals that we are overextending ourselves. We involve ourselves in diverse projects and engage in a variety of professional tasks, all of which are enjoyable and rewarding to us. However, we recognized that we could not do all of them at the same time. Besides offering our services to others, we recognize our need for input from others in the field, and we attend workshops and conferences for our own personal and professional development. Being active at professional conferences is not only a way to give to others but a way for us to make significant contact with colleagues and to learn from them. Being aware of the demands that our profession puts on us, we are highly conscious of living a healthy lifestyle. Therefore, we pay attention to our nutritional habits, and no matter how busy we are, we make the time that we need for adequate rest and regular exercise. We are both committed to a consistent exercise program on a daily basis, a practice that we find rejuvenating. As part of our lifestyle, we made the decision to live in a remote mountain community. But this remoteness and our busy schedules kept us, at times, from seeing our friends and colleagues. We had to realize that we could easily separate ourselves too much from relationships that were much needed and a source of joy and support for us.

By Way of Review

- One of the hazards of the helping professions is that helpers are typically not very good at asking for help for themselves.
- Sensitize yourself to both the external and internal factors that contribute to your experience of stress.
- It is next to impossible to eliminate stress from your life; the crucial question is, "To what extent does stress control you, or do you control stress?"
- Self-monitoring is the first step in developing an effective stress management program. If you recognize situations that lead to stress, you can make decisions about how to think, feel, and behave in response to these situations.
- Some of the most useful ways of managing stress are the cognitive approaches. These include changing your distorted self-talk, learning time management skills, and applying them to daily life in a systematic fashion.

- Learning to recognize and cope with the reality of professional burnout is essential for your survival as a helper. Intense involvement with people over a period of time can lead to physical and psychological exhaustion.
- There is no single cause of burnout; rather, a combination of individual, interpersonal, and organizational factors can lead to burnout. Understanding these factors can help you learn how to prevent or cope with burnout.
- Burnout can be the result of the many demands placed on you by an agency. It is important to learn specific ways of surviving with dignity in an agency setting.
- Just as there are many sources of burnout, there are multiple ways to prevent burnout.
- Coping with stress effectively is a way to lessen the chances of becoming an impaired helper.
- Self-care is not a luxury, it is an ethical mandate.
- A self-care program entails being attentive to the physical, emotional, mental, social, and spiritual dimensions of human functioning.
- Physical activity is a way not only to survive but to thrive. An exercise program is an effective route to managing stress and to helping you retain your vitality.
- Mindfulness practice is one form of self-care that can be extremely useful, both personally and professionally.
- Helpers who are more self-compassionate lead healthier, more productive lives than those who are self-critical.
- Wellness is a process of making choices that lead to a healthy lifestyle. This involves choosing a way of life that leads to zest, peace, vitality, and happiness.

What Will You Do Now?

1. Make a list of some of the environmental factors that are most stressful in your life. Once you have identified external stressors, write in your journal about how you might deal with them differently. What can you do now to minimize at least some of these sources of stress? Develop a plan of action, and try it out for at least a week. Consider making a contract with someone so that you will be accountable for acting to reduce stress in your life.
2. Identify a few of the warning signs that you are not taking care of yourself. What are some specific steps that you are willing to consider in taking better care of yourself?
3. We encourage you to take an honest look at the factors in your life that are most likely to cause burnout. A common denominator in many cases of burnout is the question of *responsibility.* In what ways could your assumption of an inordinate degree of responsibility contribute to burnout?
4. If you have trouble doing everything that you want with the time you have available, consider trying the time management strategies described. Keep a written record of what you do in the coming week. At the end of the week, add up the hours you are spending on personal, social, job, and academic activities. Review your activities, and ask yourself if you are spending the time you have in meaningful ways.

5. Arrange an interview with a practicing professional, and ask this person these questions: "What are some of the major stresses you face in your work?" "What are some ways you deal with these stresses?" "What are your thoughts on preventing burnout?"
6. Self-care and self-renewal involve a balanced attention to our physical, emotional, mental, social, and spiritual dimensions. Identify some specific ways you can achieve greater balance in your life to continue your self-renewal process. In your journal, write down some ideas about patterns that you may want to change to enhance the balance in your life. Then make an action plan that will assist you in coping with stress by using some of the strategies discussed in this chapter.
7. For the full bibliographic entry for each of the sources listed here, consult the References at the back of the book. Useful sources on burnout and self-care strategies can be found in Skovholt (2001, 2012a), and Skovholt and Trotter-Mathison (2016). See Kottler (2017) for discussions of how stress affects the personal and professional lives of helpers. For two well-written books on self-care, see Corey, Muratori, Austin, and Austin (2018) and Norcross and VandenBos (2018). For an excellent treatment of empathy fatigue and what you can do to prevent it, see Stebnicki (2008). See Corey, Corey, and Muratori (2018) for ideas on self-renewal and retaining your vitality. See Neff (2011) and Neff and Germer (2018) for a treatment of self-compassion.

CHAPTER 14

Managing Crisis: Personally and Professionally

by Robert Haynes,* Marianne Schneider Corey, and Gerald Corey

Learning Objectives

1. Describe some ways that crises affect people emotionally.
2. Describe the characteristics of empathy fatigue.
3. Identify factors that influence a crisis response.
4. Explain the role of resilience in coping with crisis situations.
5. Discuss the cognitive, emotional, and behavioral components involved in managing a crisis.
6. Differentiate between first-order intervention and second-order intervention.
7. List five guidelines for working with clients in a crisis situation.
8. Identify four personal qualities required to work in the field of disaster mental health.

Focus Questions

1. How well do you handle crises in your life? Are you able to approach them with resolve and determination, or do you tend to become overwhelmed and frustrated?
2. What major personal crises have you encountered? Some examples are the death of someone close to you, divorce, illness, bankruptcy, home foreclosure, and family crises. How did you cope with them? Do you have a plan to resolve any unfinished business you have related to these crises?
3. If you have encountered a natural disaster (such as a fire, flood, earthquake, or superstorm), how well did you handle the aftermath?
4. How important is your self-talk in handling both your own and your clients' crises? Are you aware of your self-talk in highly stressful situations and how it does or does not help you?
5. To what degree do you see yourself as a resilient individual? Do you tend to recover quickly following stressful events, or do those events get you down and sap your energy for an extended period?

---

*We invited Robert Haynes, a colleague and friend, to take the leading role in coauthoring and revising this chapter. He is a licensed clinical psychologist with a professional interest and expertise in the area of crisis intervention. He published a self-help book on managing crisis situations and is coauthoring (with Michelle Muratori) a workbook for counselors and clients in coping with stress.

6. How would you go about helping a client become more resilient in his or her life? Do you think you have to be resilient yourself to help a client develop resilience?
7. What training and preparation do you need to become prepared to work with individuals and communities that have experienced floods, hurricanes, earthquakes, mass shootings, or bombings?
8. Crisis intervention is a short-term helping strategy that has particular relevance for dealing with many of the problems individuals in a community face. What do you think the most challenging aspects of crisis intervention would be in community work?
9. Could you see yourself working in the specialty area of disaster mental health? If so, what draws you to this specialty area? If not, what about this work concerns you most?

Aim of the Chapter

One of the most popular emerging subfields in the helping professions is disaster mental health counseling. This movement is placing counseling professionals at the forefront of disaster response efforts. A disaster can occur in the most unexpected setting and at the most unexpected time, and it is important for helpers to be prepared to deal with clients in crisis. Many of our trainees have reported feeling overwhelmed with the demands of crisis work. You owe it to these individuals to acquire basic knowledge and skills in practicing crisis intervention. This chapter provides a brief introduction to this highly specialized field, but you will need further coursework and training in this area prior to obtaining your degree.

This chapter includes an understanding of how crisis situations affect individuals, a plan for learning to better handle crises in your own life, and a system that can be applied to help clients cope with crises in their lives. We also discuss the critical role resilience plays in managing crises and provide an overview of the development of crisis intervention in the community mental health system. The chapter concludes with a discussion of how counselors, psychologists, and social workers have embarked on working in this specialty area in mental health.

LO1 How Crises Affect Us

We all experience **stress** in our lives and our work—a feeling of strain and pressure that can originate from external or internal sources. Our stress may be acute or chronic. For most events, we can subjectively assign a score from 1 (very low) to 10 (extremely high) to the level of stress we feel. Stressful events at the higher end of the scale are defined as **crises**, "the perception or experiencing of an event or situation as an intolerable difficulty that exceeds the person's current resources and coping mechanisms" (James & Gilliland, 2017, p. 9). Another definition of a **crisis** is "a highly distressful event or time when people are overwhelmed and cannot function with normal coping skills" (Webber & Mascari, 2018, p. 4). According to the United Nations International

Strategy for Disaster Reduction (2009), a **disaster** can be defined as "a serious disruption of the functioning of society, causing widespread human, material, or environmental losses which exceed the ability of affected society to cope using only its own resources" (p. 9). *Crisis intervention* was first described by Caplan (1964) as a model for intervention that followed a stressful life event. The literature poses multiple definitions of the term "disaster" classified by categories, types, and etiologies, which include *natural, person-made,* and *technological disasters*. Crises and disasters are distinct events, and counselors may be called upon to respond to either or both in the course of their careers. Over the past couple of decades, and in particular since 9/11, advances have been made in the disaster mental health counseling field.

The Federal Emergency Management Agency (FEMA) provides standardized training in responding to emergencies, and the Council for Accreditation of Counseling and Related Educational Programs (CACREP, 2016) has adopted disaster, trauma counseling, and crisis competencies as key skills for counselors-in-training and in practice. Disaster and trauma counseling is no longer the exclusive domain of those who specialize in disaster and trauma counseling. Responding to people who are affected by disasters and mass violence has become a part of every counselor's scope of practice (Mascari & Webber, 2018). As a beginning helper, you may or may not have entertained the idea of working professionally in the disaster mental health counseling field. However, it is highly likely that you will encounter clients who are disaster survivors or who have experienced traumatic events. Even if you do not intend to specialize in this area of practice, is important to be prepared if the unthinkable happens.

Think about a crisis you have experienced in your life. How did you react? Were you able to remain calm and think clearly about a resolution? Was your response effective and systematic, or were your thoughts and actions disorganized and random? If you have worked as a helper, think about a crisis you encountered in a counseling situation. How did you react? Was it stressful for you? What were your thoughts and emotions surrounding the situation? Did you feel that you were helpful to the client? How might you have handled the situation better? What impact did this particular counseling situation have on you personally? How you have reacted to crises provides a benchmark for what you are likely to do in future crises. Reacting, recovering, and quickly developing and implementing an action plan can be difficult. What do you think you need to learn as a helper to improve your ability to help a client deal effectively with a crisis?

The personal toll of engaging in crisis work can have a tremendous impact on helpers. The key to our survival in the long term is to be able to balance a caring and empathic therapeutic style with the ability to distance ourselves from the impact on our personal life at the end of the day. When you begin your career, it is normal to "take home" these concerns, but over time that can have a detrimental effect.

Sometimes helpers worry that they cannot do enough when they are working in crisis situations. What we can do for clients is to respect and acknowledge what they are facing and let them tell their story. As clients tell their stories, we need to listen to understand what they are going through from their perspective. As clients express themselves, it is important that we also make an assessment of their immediate situation and discover what coping resources are available to them. Our willingness to fully connect with others as they strive to put their lives back together can be healing and is necessary. We get a sense of where our clients want to go and what options for action they would consider. During our initial encounter with a client in crisis, we can give the gift of presence by what we say and by reflecting genuine caring and a deep sense of compassion. Presence is powerful and often transcends what we can actually do to change the situation.

LO2 Stress and Emotional Fatigue Can Lead to Burnout

Helpers may be called upon to assist people in many different kinds of crisis situations, and they are not immune to the long-term effects of this intense and critical work. **Vicarious trauma** can have a negative impact on helpers both personally and professionally. *Vicarious traumatization* occurs as a result of chronic exposure to client trauma when the helper begins to take on the client's trauma-related symptoms (James & Gilliland, 2017). Professionals who listen to clients' stories of trauma, horror, and extreme loss often become overwhelmed and may begin to experience fears, pains, losses, and sufferings similar to those of their clients. Simply hearing about the crisis or trauma over and over again can have adverse effects on the helper. The helper may begin to view the world, others, and relationships differently and perhaps more cynically. New counselors and counselors-in-training appear to be most susceptible to experiencing vicarious trauma.

Crisis intervention and other frontline mental health workers experience sources of stress that often lead to **burnout**. Some of these stress factors include lacking full involvement in the decision-making process related to their work; feeling that their abilities are not being fully utilized on the job; feeling unvalued or unsupported by their colleagues; being taxed by regulations, procedures, and paperwork; and being exposed to discomfort and dangers in their work setting. One young social worker did crisis intervention primarily with the family members of murder victims. Although she showed concern and empathy for her clients, the nature of her work affected her so much that she was planning to change jobs. Like other crisis workers, she learned that burnout is an occupational hazard. The importance of self-care for helpers who are involved in any kind of crisis work cannot be overemphasized. Self-care requires a plan to learn and practice activities that sustain energy and increase hope (see Chapter 13). Although each caregiver's action plan is unique, regular self-care routines are essential to maintaining the vitality necessary to carry out helpers' demanding professional work (Gentry, Webber, & Baranowsky, 2018).

Helping professionals who observe and work with people who have experienced traumatic events may suffer from **compassion fatigue**, a stress-related syndrome that results from the cumulative drain on the helper's capacity to care for others (Figley, 1995). Compassion fatigue involves the negative feelings associated with offering help to clients who are experiencing crises. Compassion fatigue can be treated, and it can also be prevented by acquiring specific skills and practices that augment resiliency in caregivers (Gentry et al., 2018). As noted in Chapter 1, your personal needs and motivations for becoming a helper must be examined, not just while in training but throughout your career to avoid the pitfalls of burnout or compassion fatigue (see Linley & Joseph, 2007; Skovholt, 2012b; Smith, 2007; Stebnicki, 2008).

Living in the age of globalization and social media, it is difficult to avoid the constant bombardment of stressful news about local, national, and international events. It can be exhausting for mental health professionals to have to process their own reactions to major stressful events occurring in the world, and then to spend so much time each week helping their clients process their reactions to the same events. The stress generated by listening to multiple stories of trauma that clients bring to therapy may lead to a deterioration of the counselor's resiliency or coping abilities over time. Stebnicki (2008, 2016a, 2017) calls this **empathy fatigue**, a condition that shares some similarities with compassion fatigue, vicarious trauma, and burnout. Although similar to compassion fatigue, empathy fatigue is more specifically a focus for counselors who care for clients every day and eventually wear down. Stebnicki (2017) believes that helpers who are psychologically present for their clients often pay a physical and emotional price of being profoundly affected by clients' stories that are saturated with themes of daily extraordinary stress, grief, loss, anxiety, depression, and traumatic stress. Practitioners who experience empathy fatigue may be heading toward professional burnout. Stebnicki emphasizes the importance of counselors preparing their mind, body, and spirit to help them become more resilient in working with people in distress. Skovholt (2012a) believes that counselors need to achieve *empathy balance*, being able to enter the client's world without getting lost in that world. Too little empathy results in the absence of caring, but too much empathy may result in practitioners losing themselves in the stories of their clients.

Peter R. Teahen, a mental health counselor, served on a team with a nurse and a dentist that was sent to a critical care unit in a Port-au-Prince hospital following the devastating 2010 Haiti earthquake (Tarvydas, Levers, & Teahen, 2018). Referring to the conditions in the 50-bed ward as "nightmarish at best," Teahen recalls this harrowing experience:

> The first hours were extremely difficult for me as I withered under the oppressive heat and humidity and became drenched as my sweat flowed. As we worked in the dark, we listened to cries of pain, begs for care, and adults crying for their mothers. I found myself several times trying to control my emotions when providing care. The small children were reminding me of my own grandchildren. I provided care to an older woman, with no family, who I knew would soon die. . . . After 3 hours, I physically and emotionally surrendered and walked out the front door and was followed quickly by the dentist. We both looked at each other and admitted we could not do what was being asked of us and accepted that we were in "over our heads." (pp. 102–103)

For the next 25 minutes, Teahen seriously contemplated abandoning his task, but due to the extreme shortage of medical staff, he ultimately decided to go back inside to care for his patients. He and his team were undoubtedly stretched beyond their capacity, yet they persisted despite lacking the resources they needed. As Teahen and his colleague put it, "if not us, then who?" In reflecting upon this experience, he wonders how he would have lived with himself if he had chosen to abandon his responsibilities. Disaster and trauma work require courage and commitment.

Because this intense work can take a toll on helpers if they are not vigilant about self-care, it is essential that efforts be made to replenish oneself on a consistent basis. Spending quality time with friends outside the crisis intervention and counseling field can provide a much needed break. In addition, joining a group of peers doing the same work can be an effective way of dealing with the emotions that often surface. If we are carrying around excess psychological pain, the crises of our clients can soon become our crises. It is absolutely essential that we remain sensitive to the ways in which this work is affecting us personally. If we forget to take care of ourselves, we can be certain that we will not be able to function very long in the demanding work of helping others through their crises. We will have become stuck in the quagmire of our own crisis. The best prevention for many of the maladies we are likely to encounter is to actively participate in a program of professional renewal and long-term self-care. (See Chapter 13 for a discussion of burnout and self-care strategies.) Specific standards pertaining to self-care appear in the ethics codes for helping professionals as an ethical requirement to ensure that helpers are able to provide effective services to all clients.

Crisis Situations Are Common in Counseling

A recent college graduate with a degree in psychology described her first counselor work setting and the first client she encountered. Regina went to work at a day treatment center for children with severe behavioral disorders. She thought the experience would be valuable in gaining clinical experience and that the experience would fortify her application to graduate school. Her first student was Tyler, a 7-year-old adoptee who was likeable enough but had violent episodes and suffered from the effects of fetal alcohol syndrome. Regina developed a positive relationship with Tyler, but the first time she saw him become enraged she was overwhelmed. At one point in her work with Tyler, she had to help restrain him for his own protection, and he bit her during that episode. Regina was referred for HIV testing as a result of the bite, which was quite severe. Nothing in her college classes had prepared her for that experience with Tyler and never did she think she could become HIV-positive as a result of working at the school. This was an eye-opener for Regina and helped her face the reality and complexity of working in the real world of counseling as well as the emotional toll this work can have.

Over the course of your professional career, you will come into contact with clients who are dealing with crises in their lives of varying degrees of severity. Some situations may seem more manageable than others. Think about the range of crises you may encounter in your role as a helper and the impact that a crisis could have on an individual's life. You need to acquire the knowledge and skills of a trauma-informed counselor to assist your clients who are coping with crises. Envision yourself as the helper in these situations:

- Mia comes in for counseling because she is considering leaving her husband of 8 years. He hit her once, but lately he has become more verbally hostile and has threatened her physically if she leaves him. He has never hit their children, but his increased drinking and irrational thinking have Mia scared for herself and her children.
- Jaleel is a 16-year-old high school junior who has been referred to you by a school counselor. He has talked with the counselor about feeling depressed and has had suicidal thoughts. The referring counselor believes Jaleel needs professional counseling. In your first session with Jaleel, he states, "Life just doesn't seem worth living anymore. I don't have any friends and my girlfriend just broke up with me."
- Sammy has come to you for grief counseling. Her best friend was shot and killed in a mass shooting at the local shopping mall, and she is distraught and terrified for her own safety.
- A shooting occurred on the middle school sports field yesterday. One teacher received a minor injury, but the entire school population has been affected by the shooting. As the school counselor, your job is to provide debriefing services to three of those homeroom classes today.

Do you think you have the emotional capacity to provide assistance to these clients? What if you were working with all of these clients at the same time? Would any one of these situations seem more difficult than the others? How can you minimize the emotional toll of this work? If you found this work to be exceedingly stressful, what could you do to take care of yourself?

LO3 Understanding Our Response to Crisis

Natural events that are beyond our control do not elicit the same reaction and emotional response as human-caused events; we react differently when someone is killed in a shooting than when someone is killed in a tornado or an earthquake. Although we may feel angry at the circumstances and powerless when a natural disaster strikes, we tend to feel anger, assign blame, and might even want some kind of revenge for the perpetrator of a violent act. It is important to identify the source of these crises and recognize how various kinds of crises affect us.

An unexpected event brings about the most psychological disruption. Anticipated crises, such as upcoming financial difficulties, provide an opportunity for us to plan our strategy in advance. Brief events, such as worry about an upcoming annual physical exam or a job interview, tend to be quickly resolved. But a diagnosis of cancer at the annual physical exam can become a very stressful long-term crisis that is much more difficult to confront.

Although we can identify some typical responses to crisis, individual reactions vary significantly from one person to the next. A minor crisis might affect us significantly, whereas a major disaster may not. Generally speaking, crises involving physical injury or death have the greatest impact. In addition, the closer we are to the crisis situation and to the people involved, the more frightened we are and the more traumatic our reaction is likely to be. Seeing the destruction from a wildfire in another state on television has less impact than being in the midst of the wildfire and facing mandatory evacuation.

Professional helpers work with a variety of clients and experience situations that can take a toll on us personally and professionally. We need to be prepared cognitively and emotionally for these events, and we need to have the knowledge and skills necessary to help clients in crisis. Here are some factors that may influence your crisis response.

1. Your current life situation and level of stress influence how you are able to work with your client's crisis. Stress reactions to a crisis involve physiological, emotional, and cognitive components. If you are going through a divorce, facing serious financial problems, or dealing with your child's behavioral problems, you may be less effective in handling your own daily crises and those of your client.
2. Previous crises in your life may trigger reactions to current crises. If you have successfully worked through a crisis in the past and believe you will be able to do so in the future, that expectation most likely enhances your ability to succeed simply because you have the experience and success to back it up. On the other hand, if you have not dealt successfully with crisis situations in the past, you may question your ability to handle highly stressful situations when they do occur.
3. A common reaction in a crisis is the feeling of disbelief and disorientation. Most people can overcome those reactions, but in more serious crises some individuals may become immobilized and unable to respond.
4. Another common reaction to crisis is the fight or flight reaction we experience, which involves an increase in heart rate, breathing rate, muscle tension, and blood pressure. Our hearing and vision go on high alert. This is the body's emergency response system, but in today's stress-filled world, this stress response may be activated many times a day, leading to fatigue, exhaustion, an inability to cope, and eventually to physical disorders and illnesses. Effective crisis management will help us make this fight or flight reaction work for us as a mobilizing force and minimize the time this system is activated. Our own inner self-talk can affect this physiological process.
5. The neurochemistry of the stress response involves more neurotransmitters, hormones, and cortical areas of the brain than was previously known (James & Gilliland, 2017). It has also been found that continual exposure to stressful situations—such as the work of first responders or military personnel in a war zone—can cause permanent changes in the brain. This unrelieved continuous hyperarousal may well play a role in posttraumatic stress disorder. Experiencing severe stress and crisis can have emotional, physiological, and neurobiological effects on the human body.
6. Cognitive and problem-solving abilities may be significantly reduced in an extreme crisis. In a crisis, we usually react with emotion—fear, anger, disbelief—and our thinking processes take a back seat. Anxiety may result in distortions in perception and a loss of problem-solving skills. Evaluating and restructuring our thinking can greatly assist us in managing crisis situations.

In summary, we can expect some kind of an emotional reaction to a crisis, and we can expect to recover with time. Our ability to effectively handle a crisis has to do with how well we have been able to manage ourselves in the past, how we perceive the situation, and how well prepared and practiced we are to handle the current situation. Life presents us with small crises on a daily basis, and this is the practice ground on which we can learn to cope with crises of greater magnitude.

LO4 The Role of Resilience

Resilience is the ability of an individual to cope with and bounce back from extraordinary stressful and adverse events. When people cope with a crisis, a disaster, or a traumatic event, they may discover strengths they did not believe they had. Terms commonly used when referring to resilience are "hardiness," "resourcefulness," and "mental toughness." Resilience can be seen as a set of learned behaviors that are largely dependent on the beliefs of individuals about their ability to cope effectively with difficult situations. Resilience is largely a process that occurs when people react successfully to crisis situations. Resilient individuals are able to act in adaptive ways to crisis and traumatic situations. According to Stebnicki (2017), resilient people are not immune to stress and temporary self-doubt, but they can adapt to a crisis situation and bounce back from adversity better than those who are less resilient. They often can be transformed into a new depth of understanding, find a purpose in life, and develop a peaceful resolve. Stebnicki states that individuals who exhibit resilience tend to have the following characteristics:

- Are positive thinkers, have an internal locus of control, and are self-directed and self-motivated
- Choose healthy emotions, behaviors, and thoughts
- Have faith in themselves and their abilities, are highly confident, and believe they can affect a positive outcome for self and others
- Take self-responsibility and seek opportunities to make intentional conscious choices
- Demonstrate persistence with tasks they take on and know how to achieve their life goals
- Take healthy risks, are reality driven and flexible, and are willing to try new things to enhance their mind, body, and spirit
- Exhibit attitudes of tolerance, openness, and respect for different ways of solving problems

Meichenbaum (2012) takes the position that it is possible to achieve positive growth by facing, working through, and sharing painful experiences. Individuals, groups, and communities can become stronger and develop deeper relationships following stressful life events. Meichenbaum states that resilience is a multidimensional concept that includes the following factors:

- Adapt to adversity and challenging life experiences
- Successfully cope with stressful life events
- Recover quickly from misfortune
- Endure traumatic events without lasting harm
- Adapt to the situation and overcome difficulties

Posttraumatic Growth

Posttraumatic growth (PTG) can flow from posttraumatic stress situations. Some people are able to move through the pain and healing after experiencing a trauma and become stronger. Trauma can be a springboard for transformation and life changes, enabling people not just to survive a traumatic incident but to grow from it (Calhoun & Tedeschi, 2013; Hays, 2014; James & Gilliland, 2017). Posttraumatic growth goes one step beyond resilience; it encompasses unexpected positive changes that *can* result from a traumatic situation. Letting go of the old and accepting new ways signals transformation of the traumatic event from posttraumatic stress to posttraumatic growth (Cormier, 2018).

Calhoun and Tedeschi's (2013) research with grief survivors, prisoners of war, veterans with Post-Traumatic Stress Disorder (PTSD), and those who have become paralyzed after accidents shows growth in five specific areas: increased personal strength, more depth in personal relationships, an increased appreciation of life, an awareness of new possibilities, and a different relationship to spirituality. Instead of remaining victims of tragedy, many people are able to triumph over extreme life circumstances. Individuals find inner strengths and resources they barely knew they possessed, which frequently include survival skills, self-acceptance, resilience, empathy, compassion, and a deeper understanding of life (Cormier, 2018). PTG is the result of a successful struggle to cope with and make meaning of a traumatic event, and it involves a shift in how one views the world, accepting what cannot be changed. The American Psychological Association's (2017b) *Multicultural Guidelines* provides this standard for helpers:

> Psychologists actively strive to take a strength-based approach when working with individuals, families, groups, communities, and organizations that seeks to build resilience and decrease trauma within the sociocultural context. (Guideline 10)

In these turbulent global times, Cormier (2018) points out that traumatic events may occur within a family, a group, a community, or a country.

Some experts have noted that, as a human race, we are survivors. We may complain loudly about the little annoyances in life, but when we are in extreme situations, we demonstrate amazing resilience. We all hope that in a major crisis we will remain calm, develop and implement an action plan, and remain optimistic and hopeful. Some experience horrible situations and cope adequately, whereas others encounter a minor crisis and feel helpless. We can improve upon our past behaviors and develop resilience so we are better able to help ourselves and our clients in crises.

For a compelling account of posttraumatic growth following the experience of loss, we recommend Sherry Cormier's (2018) book, *Sweet Sorrow*.

How Can We Become More Resilient?

Resilience can work for us by helping us look forward with confidence and focus on problem resolution. Resilience helps us maintain an attitude of optimism and hopefulness. Some of us are inherently resilient individuals, but we all can practice and implement new skills to become more resilient. First and foremost is developing solid relationships with family and friends. Community-based groups or faith-based groups also provide social help and support, and many feel strengthened and fortified by helping others through community involvement. Connection to others and social support are extremely important in developing and maintaining resilience. Herlihy and James (2018) identify some lessons for counselors in the aftermath of a multisystemic disaster such as Hurricane Katrina.

Counseling interventions are more effective when they are community-based, and Herlihy and James recommend establishing and facilitating neighborhood groups as a means of providing understanding and emotional support to survivors of a disaster. Such groups can establish connections and reduce isolation, create mutual support networks, and share information about how to obtain resources to aid in recovery.

Second, we can spend some time reflecting on our existing strengths as we learn how to expand them while developing new strengths. Carol Dweck (2006) described this as a "growth mind-set" wherein people move beyond their baseline of intelligence and talents through a commitment to practice and learning. Those stuck in a "fixed mind-set" don't believe they can learn more and don't strive to accomplish more. Resilient individuals rely on hope and optimism to move forward.

Third, we can identify and work toward our life goals. We might take on one goal at a time and see what happens when we take small steps toward accomplishing it. Recognizing what we can change and what we cannot change is an important step in setting goals. We may not be able to change what has happened, but we can change how we view, react, and respond to the event. Suffering often results from not being able to accept what is. We can review past successes with coping or overcoming crises, and build on those successes for future crises. The human spirit is resilient, adaptable, and capable of great accomplishments.

Fourth, we can learn from life and from adversities and mistakes. Rather than being critical of ourselves for our choices, we can reframe poor choices as opportunities for growth. We can design our personalized self-care plan and commit to practicing self-care consistently (Corey, Muratori, Austin, & Austin, 2018; also see Chapter 13).

Finally, a major factor in developing and maintaining resilience is the role of our belief system and our self-talk. Our belief in our ability to cope with crises is essential to being a resilient person. Resilient individuals are strong, confident, and determined, and they believe in their ability to solve problems. Resilience helps us function better than expected when faced with adversity. We can strive to develop resilience in our own lives as well as assist our clients in doing the same.

LO5 Cognitive, Emotional, and Behavioral Components of a Crisis

In *Take Control of Life's Crises Today! A Practical Guide* (Haynes, 2014), readers are introduced to the essence of how to better handle life crises. There are three general components in the process of dealing with a crisis: cognitive (thinking and self-talk), emotional (feelings and reactions), and behavioral (plan of action).

Cognitive Components

In Chapter 13 we discussed the cognitive behavioral approaches to managing stress and evaluating how your cognitions and self-talk influence your feelings and behaviors. **Self-talk** is the nearly constant internal monologue we engage in at a conscious or semiconscious level. When our self-talk is irrational and inaccurate, we feel stressed and upset and have trouble making decisions. Here is an example of negative self-talk: "I cannot figure out what is going on with this client, I am at a loss about how to handle their suicidal thoughts, I must be a lousy counselor, I don't know what to do, and I just can't be of help." This self-talk can be a path toward failure. Positive questions such as these can lead to solving problems: "What is going on here? How can I best manage this? What do I need to know about this situation? Is there an imminent danger? How can I best ensure safety of the client?" When we look forward and focus on what we can do, we have a much better chance of navigating successfully through the crisis.

How can I help this client? In private practice I (Bob) was seeing a client (Colleen) who was having marital and family issues. During one session Colleen reported that she had taken aspirin because she was feeling poorly but was not quite sure how many she had taken. My self-talk went like this: "Is this a medical emergency? Is she just stringing me along for attention? Is she at risk of dying? What if I don't do the right thing? What if I don't act and she dies? Could I be held liable? Could I lose my license? This is just a mess." Clearly, this self-talk was not working toward a solution to the problem. In fact, it was creating doubt and fear, which was unproductive. I consciously shifted my self-talk and began to develop a plan of action: "Ask more about what she took, when she took it, what her thinking was as she was taking the aspirin. Is she demonstrating any signs of suicidal thoughts? Are physiological symptoms present? I could take her to the hospital or I could call an ambulance. Should I call her husband first to see if he can take her? I should question Colleen more to determine specifically how many aspirin she has taken. If I cannot determine that, I will call paramedics and have her taken to the hospital and then call her husband. I have to do what will provide for the safety of my client first, and deal with the effects of that decision later." These are thoughts that flew through my mind in a matter of a few seconds, and I was able to move my thinking from self-doubt and confusion to formulating a plan and moving ahead for the good of the client. The outcome was that, with Colleen's consent, I called her husband and then 911 for an ambulance. She was hospitalized, had her stomach pumped, then spent several days in the psychiatric unit for evaluation for suicide risk.

Begin to examine your self-talk and see how it works for you or against you and your problem-solving ability. As we change our thinking, our self-talk affects what we are doing and how we are feeling. This is true in everyday life and in your work as a helper. Let's take a more detailed look at how you can engage in more productive self-talk.

Managing Your Self-Talk

Step 1: Learn to recognize your self-talk. Focus on that conversation that is going on in your head all the time. Does it seem to work for you, or are you sabotaging yourself? Your self-talk may be so automatic that you barely notice it is happening, so try to raise your awareness of it throughout the day. Pay attention to your self-talk while you are counseling a client, and see if it influences the assessment and intervention you provide.

Step 2: Carefully study your self-talk patterns. Is your self-talk more positive or negative? Do you use phrases such as "I don't have a clue about what is going on with my client" or "It is just too difficult for me to talk about this client's situation" or "I'm lost, I guess I should refer this client on to another counselor." In moments like this, refocus on problem-solving self-talk and become your own internal crisis coach and guide yourself to help your client. You might say to yourself: "Look at the situation, what caused it, and what do I need to do to resolve this" or "This is a little overwhelming, but focus on how this is affecting the client and how I can help her manage the situation" or "What are the pros and cons of the various solutions? Which one has the best chance of succeeding?" or "What are the ethical and legal implications of various courses of action?"

Keeping a log is a productive way to become more aware of your self-talk and how it does or does not work for you. You could take a **time sample**, recording your self-talk for 15 minutes at the same time each day for several days. Our thoughts are so automatic that we tend not to notice them, so you will have to work at becoming more aware. You might also consider logging your self-talk following **specific situations**, such as having a consultation session with a supervisor or counseling a client. Using the log can help you analyze and begin to modify your self-talk. Write a brief summary of the situation and the content of your self-talk, including your first thoughts and your resulting emotions. After you have logged your self-talk, look at the patterns of your thinking and see where you might want to change those patterns to allow them to work better for you at managing the situation successfully.

Step 3: Modify your self-talk. Now that you have a better understanding of your self-talk patterns, you are ready to learn how to change those patterns. Analyze the objective facts of the situation you have logged. What did you say to yourself? Did that help or hinder resolving the situation? Are you distorting the facts (such as exaggerating or minimizing the circumstances), or did you assess the situation accurately? What could you have said to yourself that might have affected the outcome more positively? Try out new self-talk language. Work at toning down your critical self-talk and shifting to self-accepting and self-compassionate sentences. See what works for you, what does not, and how your self-talk improves your ability to better manage a situation.

Step 4: Practice and implement your new self-talk skills. Practice is the best way to improve your new self-talk patterns. Be patient and give yourself time to try on new ways of thinking. You will need plenty of practice modifying and implementing more effective self-talk that will work for you in crisis situations. Applying your new self-talk will help you build confidence, and you will eventually use this self-talk automatically, which will help you become better prepared to handle crises.

Step 5: Evaluate your new skills. Evaluate how these new skills are working for you and modify as necessary. Apply these fine-tuned skills in everyday life, then use them in your training and work as a helper. Listen to your self-talk while you are working with a client, meeting with a supervisor, or participating in a group training experience.

Emotional Components

We have the ability to affect the intensity of the emotions we experience. Our emotions can be intense, and we may feel that we are out of control. Some of that self-talk might involve any of the following:

- "I'm too upset to make a decision."
- "Why do these situations always happen to me?"
- "This supervisor is driving me crazy—I can't learn a thing in this environment."
- "I can't stand working with this person."

We can use our self-talk in a productive manner to help us move from our emotional reaction and take action. Our own inner voice and self-talk can have a dramatic calming effect. Some examples of calming self-talk are:

- "I know I'm upset and shaken, but I need to deal with the facts of this situation."
- "I will calm down now and focus on what needs to be accomplished."
- "I don't need to worry about how I've handled past situations right now. I just need to stay in the present."

Consider this example of how self-talk can have a positive impact. Olivia is a social worker for a local hospice provider. On a daily basis she deals with death and dying, and the impact of that on clients' families and friends. If she becomes absorbed in the pain and suffering of her clients, it would be easy for her self-talk to become depressed, down, and discouraged. Instead, Olivia focuses on how much she is helping her clients' loved ones and friends by locating resources for them and the comfort they find in the services and counsel she provides. She focuses her self-talk on the positive effects of her work, which helps her remain upbeat.

For some individuals, the emotional response to a crisis or a series of crises, such as in wartime, may lead to emotional dysregulation. The individual's emotional state of arousal may be so intense and overwhelming that dysfunctional coping strategies such as dissociation, denial, or avoidance of acknowledging emotions are chosen. In that case, emotional regulation must be reestablished before further work on recovering from the crisis can be accomplished. Techniques for restoring emotional regulation include relaxation training, cognitive therapy, meditation, anxiety management, and stress inoculation. In some instances, when there is a great deal of emotional dysregulation, medication may be warranted.

At times our emotions may impede our problem-solving abilities, but we need to attempt to recover from our emotional reaction as quickly as possible and put what we have practiced into operation. If, for example, someone were to try to rob us on the street, fear, anger, and fight or flight reactions all may occur almost automatically. Having a plan of action in mind (discussed in more detail in the next section) can be helpful in these situations.

Practicing and rehearsing our problem-solving action plan for various situations will improve our ability to respond effectively in a real crisis and help us manage our emotions. Mentally preparing how we would handle various crisis situations will help us when those situations actually occur. We cannot anticipate every possible crisis that might occur in counseling, but we can identify and think about our response to the various types of situations we may encounter: suicidal talk, psychotic talk and behavior, reporting abuse of various kinds, discussion of divorce, aggressive or hostile talk and behavior from a client, and discussion of repressed memories.

Behavioral Components

Our behavioral action plan in a crisis involves assessing the situation, considering the various courses of action, and implementing the best course of action. Managing our emotions and practicing effective self-talk will influence how we carry out our course of action. The practice and mental rehearsal of potential problems combine to make us more effective in working with people in crisis.

A behavioral action plan involves these systematic steps, which help us to take action:

- Observe the situation and gather necessary information.
- Assess various courses of action to solve the problem.
- Choose and implement the best plan of action.
- Evaluate how well the plan worked.
- Modify the plan as needed.

Applying a problem-solving method is a good way to approach a crisis situation. Having this problem-solving formula in your repertoire can help in any crisis situation, whether it is a personal crisis or a crisis in counseling.

The problem-solving approach: Walking you through the process. A shooting occurred at the high school an hour ago, and you have been called in to provide crisis counseling for students who witnessed the incident. A problem-solving approach will help to guide you through the process. You begin by meeting with all of the students together as a group to conduct a psychological triage to assess how they are reacting to the event. You gather information, asking each one what they saw and heard, what their first thought was, what it was like for them, and how they are doing now. Depending on the information they disclose, you assess the various courses of action available. That might include conducting a brief session now to educate them as to what they might experience over the next hours and days, scheduling a follow-up debriefing session in a day or two, identifying those students who are having a more severe reaction and referring them for individual counseling, and notifying parents. Your next step is to implement those action plans that best fit each student's individual needs. Some will need more intensive counseling, and others will need very little follow-up. You contact parents as necessary and as required by the school protocol. Over time, you will evaluate the various courses of action and how they are or are not working for those students. This will likely result in modifying and refining certain interventions.

We now turn to consideration of the knowledge and skills helpers will need as they engage in the work of crisis intervention and disaster mental health. We examine the roles of crisis workers and describe the services provided by counseling professionals in disaster mental health. We also look at different facets of crisis intervention work.

LO6 Crisis Intervention Work

Crisis intervention is a community-based approach to helping individuals, groups, and communities with a variety of crises in their lives. Crisis intervention is one of the main models utilized in community agency work. You will learn methods of dealing with a variety of crisis situations in your supervised field placements, and you will likely have many opportunities to practice these skills. The crisis intervention model developed by Kanel (2018) is linked to community-based mental health programs. The community mental health movement emphasizes prevention programs, and much of crisis intervention theory is based on interventions aimed at minimizing psychological impairment and promoting psychological health. In some communities, crisis teams meet regularly to update information and work out procedures for responding to crisis situations. It is clear that those in the helping professions need to have the knowledge, skills, and training to provide immediate assessment, intervention, referral, and follow-up.

Crisis intervention is a short-term approach to helping that is the treatment of choice when clients are experiencing a state of acute psychological disequilibrium. Individuals in crisis, or a community that is faced with a crisis, are temporarily disrupted cognitively, emotionally, and behaviorally, and they are in need of immediate and skilled help. This helping process should last as long as it typically takes people to bounce back to their previous level of functioning, which is generally up to 6 weeks.

Helping Clients Examine Their Options

Clients in crisis may feel immobilized and may fail to examine the options available to them. In fact, they may not see any options. Effective helping involves teaching clients to recognize that there are alternatives, some of which are better than others. James and Gilliland (2017, p. 54) describe three strategies designed to help clients in crisis consider the options open to them: (1) identify **situational supports**, which include people in the client's life from whom they can draw strength during their crisis; (2) discuss **coping mechanisms**, which are the actions, behaviors, or environmental resources that clients can use in getting through a crisis; and (3) emphasize **positive and constructive thinking patterns**, which includes ways of reframing a situation that can lessen stress and anxiety by substantially changing a client's perspective on a problem. Crisis workers are in a position to examine a number of possibilities for action, and they can help their clients develop a different perspective, especially if clients feel that their situation is hopeless and that they are lacking in choices.

First-Order Intervention

First-order intervention can be thought of as psychological first aid. This level of intervention is carried out by mental health professionals and a network of others such as ministers, judges, police and fire personnel, nurses, paramedics, physicians, school counselors, parole officers, teachers, and a wide range of human services workers.

First-order intervention involves immediate assistance and entails a short-range plan of what to do next. The major goal of this level of intervention is to reestablish an individual's immediate coping capacity. To accomplish this goal, helpers offer support, do what they can to reduce the chances of death, and link people in crisis to other helping resources. In many settings, such as the hospital emergency room or the crisis intervention hot line, the staff must be equipped to handle a wide range of crises. Staff members and nonlicensed workers can be given training to respond quickly and effectively when they initially encounter people in crisis.

Your primary task in crisis intervention is to ensure your clients' safety. Some clients may feel so distraught and so unable to cope with the crisis that they see suicide as their only way out. Suicidal urges may last for only a short time in the face of despair, and it is your job to intervene to prevent any deadly actions. People in crisis frequently provide clues to the depth of their despair. In making an assessment of the client's potential for taking lethal action, it is important to know the appropriate questions to ask as well as to be aware of danger signs. Arranging for referrals is a very important part of this work. You need to evaluate whether you have enough knowledge and skill to assist your clients in crisis. Know your limits and the resources within the community that can serve as a lifeline for people who are experiencing a crisis. If you are involved in crisis intervention with clients, this requires close supervision.

Corey, Corey, and Corey (2019) describe the value of a *safety plan* with clients who pose a high risk for suicide. Written safety plans are best designed collaboratively with clients who are a danger to self. Individuals are asked to list their reasons for living. If they cannot think of any reason to live, this may be diagnostic and indicative for the need of a higher level of care. Clients who have the potential for lethal action are asked to list the names and phone numbers of two people they can call for assistance or just to have a conversation as a distraction from suicidal thoughts. Again, if clients are unable to identify a single person to call, this may be indicative of the need for a higher level of care. Clients are provided with the phone numbers of emergency suicide prevention resources (suicide hotlines, mobile crisis intervention teams) and are advised to go to the nearest emergency room if they try everything on the safety plan and are still feeling suicidal. The safety plan is an intervention used outside of the counseling sessions, and it is provided in writing because clients who are in suicidal crisis often are unable to remember everything that was recommended in the therapy session.

People in crisis can overwhelm themselves with the feeling that everything has to be attended to at once. You can help clients focus on what must be done now and what can wait until later. Clients often feel immobilized to the degree that they cannot see any options. You can calm them and help them identify a network of resources available to them, such as family, friends, and community. Through the process of receiving psychological first aid, people often get the understanding, support, and guidance they need to refrain from harming themselves or others. At this level, one of your tasks is to help clients identify and examine possible routes they can later use to work through the crisis.

For some individuals, a crisis can be resolved through this first level of intervention, especially when the crisis worker can connect the client to community resources that can be utilized throughout the client's life. These community agencies, schools, faith-based organizations, and many other natural support systems existing in the community are a more natural way for people to cope with the many and never-ending stressors (possible precipitating events that often lead to crisis states). First-level crisis intervention creates the opportunity for clients to learn what the community has to offer them in the future when life becomes too difficult for them to manage on their own. These community services create a sense of social connectedness, which is vital for successful management of life's struggles.

Psychological first aid. The task of helpers who offer **psychological first aid** (PFA) is to help individuals tap into any resources available to them to restore a sense of equilibrium, which will eventually enable them to work through their reactions so that they can meet future challenges (James & Gilliland, 2017). The goal of crisis intervention is to increase an individual's functioning to a normal or higher level, which is done by assisting the person in perceiving events differently and by acquiring coping skills (Kanel, 2018). Helpers create support through their attitudes and behaviors. As stated earlier, perhaps what helpers most have to offer is their gift of presence. This is the capacity "to be fully there" for individuals in crisis as they tell their story and seek human connection to guide them to some sense of stability amid the temporary chaos they are experiencing.

Second-Order Intervention

Sometimes, this initial level of intervention does not resolve a client's crisis. The effects of the crisis may linger, and vestiges must be worked through. This is where **second-order intervention**, also known as **crisis therapy**, becomes necessary. This is a short-term therapeutic process that goes beyond immediate coping and aims at crisis resolution and change. The main goals of this level of intervention are to help people in crisis better face their future and to minimize their chances of becoming psychological casualties. It is critical that clients learn from the crisis and that they be given opportunities to work through unfinished business. Ideally, they will be given the assistance that will result in their remaining open to life and to new choices rather than closing themselves off to the vast range of future possibilities.

In crisis counseling, clients are encouraged to express and deal with feelings, some of which may have been repressed. It can be very freeing for clients to express these feelings and convert them into positive emotional energy to be used constructively. Typically, it is feelings that are denied expression (such as guilt or anger) that cause people the most difficulty. Expressing pent-up feelings in itself often facilitates psychological healing.

Another task of second-order crisis intervention consists of helping clients attain a realistic perspective on the crisis event. There is a need to develop an understanding of how the event has affected them, including the meaning of the crisis in their lives. Clients typically must rebuild cognitions that have been damaged by the crisis. Part of the process of crisis therapy involves clients' learning how their thought patterns have resulted in certain behaviors. Clients are helped to cognitively reframe events, which allows for a new range of behavioral possibilities. This advanced phase of crisis work demands a great deal of expertise and is provided by helping professionals who have specialized knowledge and skills.

LO7 Guidelines for Working With Clients in Crisis

The following list is a quick guide to strategies for working with clients in nearly any crisis situation:

- Ensure your clients' safety
- Help clients understand how the crisis might affect them emotionally, cognitively, behaviorally, and spiritually
- Explore and foster resilience
- Encourage client to identify any ways used in the past to cope with difficulties
- Be present, show respect, demonstrate empathy, and give your full attention to clients
- Facilitate clients in "telling their story"
- Monitor for violent, self-destructive, and other dangerous behaviors
- Evaluate existing social supports and help clients connect with appropriate resources
- Help clients successfully cope with managing emotions by identifying and modifying self-talk
- Practice your own action plans and be ready to implement them in intervening in various types of crises
- Help clients develop action plans for managing their own crises
- Learn more about working with crises from supervision, courses, reading, workshops, and consultation with colleagues

Dealing with crisis is an important job for helpers. Be as prepared as you can be to handle your own personal crises and to help clients deal with theirs. A well-trained mental health practitioner has the skills and the personal strength necessary to work with clients while maintaining a positive outlook of hope, support, and encouragement in difficult times.

LO8 Disaster Mental Health Workers

Mental health professionals working in disaster management have commonly been referred to as working in the field of "disaster mental health counseling"; this includes many first responders as well as public health workers. In the last two decades, disaster mental health workers have learned a considerable amount about the psychological effects of various kinds of disasters and effective intervention programs to work with individuals and communities. These helpers work with those who have been involved in fires, floods, war, earthquakes, hurricanes, and tornadoes as well as person-caused disasters such as school shootings, bombings, auto accidents, acts of terrorism, bankruptcies, rape, and murder. Helping professionals are specially trained to move into action when any of these disasters occurs and has widespread psychological effects. Some organizations that are active sponsors in coordinating these services include the American Counseling Association, the American Psychological Association, the National Association of Social Workers, and the American Red Cross.

In disaster mental health work, counselors provide trauma counseling and disaster counseling. **Trauma** means "wound," and a wound can be physical or psychological, or both. Psychological trauma is the direct personal experience of an event, singular or recurring, that completely overwhelms the individual's ability to cope. It usually involves an upheaval in one's view and beliefs about the world and an unsettling loss of security and stability about life (ACA, 2011; Briere & Scott, 2013). **Trauma counseling** uses a variety of psychodynamic, cognitive behavioral, and other therapeutic approaches to help individuals cope with the personal experience and reaction to the trauma event (Briere & Scott, 2013).

Disaster mental health professionals are trained to aid individuals, families, groups, and communities. Psychosocial interventions have become commonplace in the first responder community and in the military to help people deal with the aftereffects of an incident and recover as quickly as possible. Lawson (2015) states that providing services as a disaster mental health counselor is interesting and rewarding, but it poses new challenges because much of the work is performed outside the traditional counseling office. Counselors may provide on-the-spot support, deliver basic services of food and shelter, and offer counseling services informally in shelters where boundaries are blurred and providing informed consent is neither possible nor practical. Counselors must be trained and skilled at working in settings where boundaries and counseling relationships are far different than in the traditional office setting. These counselors are especially vulnerable to vicarious trauma, empathy fatigue, compassion fatigue, and burnout. Training is essential for anyone working in the area of disaster and trauma counseling; it is critical that counselors have a strong and functional support system, seek peer supervision, and take steps to become well-grounded. The work of disaster mental health counseling can be demanding and draining, and it is essential that helpers develop stamina and resilience.

In a disaster, there is both a physical impact and a psychological impact. Consider the terrorist attack on September 11, 2001, that toppled the World Trade Center buildings and damaged the Pentagon. These acts of terrorism were unpredictable, human caused, and intentional. Some 3,000 people were killed and approximately 6,000 were injured. The physical impact affected 9,000 or so individuals, but the psychological impact affected hundreds of millions more. The **physical footprint**, which is the physical area directly affected by the disaster, was limited to New York City, the Pentagon, and an area where one of the planes crashed in Pennsylvania. The **psychological footprint**, which is the geographical area of individuals and communities affected by the event, involved people throughout the United States and around the world. Any of us can remember how we heard about that disaster and how that affected us psychologically in the days and months that followed. You can see from this example how much greater the psychological impact can be in this kind of a disaster. Natural disasters that are somewhat predictable and not human caused, have a much smaller psychological footprint. If we did not live in the path of a hurricane, we watched the news about the storm and its ferocity, but once it passed we typically returned to a normal mode of functioning. These two disasters resulted in very different psychological issues for individuals and communities and required different interventions for varying lengths of time.

We have learned that disasters almost always have psychological consequences. Depending on the type and severity of a disaster, nearly every individual experience's distress, anxiety, and fear. Most will rebound and recover in a period of time without psychological intervention. Others will not, and will need intervention. Psychological intervention can speed the healing and recovery process by helping individuals understand their reactions and learn what they can do to enhance the recovery process.

Disaster mental health counseling involves much more than providing psychological interventions. It requires a global approach, and professionals in all of the helping professions are needed to provide leadership, research, assessment, consultation, training, and intervention for individuals, groups, and communities affected by disasters. The work typically involves dozens of cultures and subgroups in just one large disaster, so an understanding of multicultural issues is critical for counselors in this field. In addition, because of the demanding nature of this work, it is essential that you have learned to handle crises and disasters in your own life in the best way possible so that you can help others without your own countertransference becoming an issue.

Psychologists, social workers, and licensed counselors are all becoming more actively involved in disaster mental health counseling. This work requires a number of identifiable strengths for counselors:

- Knowledge of various kinds of crises and how they affect people.
- Knowledge and training in how to work with the various kinds of crises such as natural disasters, shootings and other crimes, suicidal behavior, substance abuse, and more.
- Familiarity with the relevant codes and laws of the state pertaining to handling crisis behavior such as danger to self and others, reporting abuse, and working with the gravely disabled due to serious mental illness.
- Knowledge of multicultural issues across a range of cultures, ethnicities, religions, sexual orientations, disabilities, and ages. This is especially necessary when working with large groups in a disaster where clients may include a range of people with different backgrounds and experiences.
- Being well grounded as a person and as a helper and being able to separate your needs from the needs of clients in crisis. You must be prepared professionally to work with any number of scenarios and maintain a caring, respecting presence with clients. In addition, you must be prepared emotionally so you can separate yourself from the stories you hear. This kind of stability may be enhanced by your participation in personal counseling designed to help you explore how you can best take care of yourself in your work as a counselor.

If you think you have the qualities required to work in disaster mental health counseling, we encourage you to consider learning more about this important field.

We have introduced you to the developing field of disaster mental health work. We recommend two excellent resources to build upon your learning: *Disaster Mental Health Counseling: Responding to Trauma in a Multicultural Context* (Stebnicki, 2017) and *Disaster Mental Health Counseling: A Guide to Preparing and Responding* (Webber & Mascari, 2018).

By Way of Review

- Counseling is a rich and rewarding profession that often involves helping clients through a crisis.
- One of the best ways to be able to help clients through crises is to be the best prepared you can be to handle crises in your life as well as to practice and prepare for the various kinds of crisis situations for which clients will seek counseling.
- Sometimes the best approach for working with a client in a crisis is for you to be present, to listen, respect the client, and to encourage the client to tell his or her story.
- Self-talk has a significant effect on how we react to and respond to crisis events.
- Resilience is the ability of an individual to cope with and bounce back from stressful and adverse events. Resilience can be fostered and developed, and one of the major ways is to stay connected to family, friends, and community organizations.
- Crisis intervention is one of the main modalities in community agencies. Many at-risk groups are in need of immediate short-term help in working through both situational and developmental crises.
- One of the fastest and most popular emerging subfields in mental health and school counseling, psychology, and social work is that of disaster mental health.
- Working in disaster mental health counseling and crisis intervention on a large scale with groups and communities requires a broad understanding of multicultural issues and differences among groups.

What Will You Do Now?

1. Assume that you are a school counselor and you have learned that a boy in middle school wielded a knife and threatened a number of students in the school. You have been asked to provide training to help teachers address this crisis situation and its psychological impact with their students. What would you do?
2. As a crisis counselor, you have been asked to devise a plan to help citizens in your community recover from a bombing that killed two people; a tornado that devastated part of the town with several injuries but no deaths; or a fire at a local manufacturing plant that killed five and injured dozens. For each scenario consider the following:
   - What would you need to know?
   - Who would you consult with and enlist to help you?
   - How would you evaluate the effectiveness of the intervention?

3. What do you think are the best ways for a crisis counselor to manage the effects of vicarious trauma, empathy fatigue, or burnout? Are there ways to prevent those phenomena from occurring?
4. What do you see as your potential role as a counselor, educator, or consultant in the disaster mental health field? What are your strengths, and what areas do you need to improve upon for that work? What resources would help you to make these improvements?
5. What have you learned from this chapter that would help you cope better with a personal crisis in the future? Which client crises would be particularly challenging for you? What have you learned about working with those client crises? What do you think you need to learn and practice to be better able to handle those crises?
6. Investigate the services available in your community for people in crisis. Look into what is offered at your own college or university. Ask about the crisis services provided by one of your community agencies. Inquire about what is being done to train volunteers for crisis intervention, such as working on a telephone hot line. Consider doing volunteer work in your community as part of a crisis team. Ask about training programs and the possibility of serving as an "on-call" worker in times of special need.
7. For the full bibliographic entry for each of the sources listed here, consult the References at the back of the book. For a practical guide to successfully mastering crises in your own life, see Haynes (2014). For an excellent resource outlining the theory and practice of crisis intervention, see James and Gilliland (2017), and for a practical guide to crisis intervention techniques, see Kanel (2018).

EPILOGUE

Now that you have completed the book, we have a few specific suggestions for consolidating your learning. If you are not inclined to do all of these things, choose the exercises that seem most useful to you. Return to Chapter 1 and once again complete the *Self-Assessment: An Inventory of Your Attitudes and Beliefs About Professional Helping*. You may have taken this inventory as a pretest at the beginning of the course. Now, as the course is ending, you can use this self-inventory again to determine the degree to which your attitudes and beliefs about helping may have changed.

We recommend that you review the key points at the end of each chapter in the *By Way of Review* section to help you consolidate your key learning. Finally, choose one activity from the *What Will You Do Now?* section at the end of each chapter and pursue it on your own.

If this book has been instrumental in giving you some ideas about the kind of helper you want to become, we have met our objectives. We encourage you to dream and to allow yourself to envision the helper you want to become. Remember that the challenges we have presented throughout these chapters do not have to be addressed immediately or all at once. Refrain from being overly ambitious; remember that the "ideal helper" we described in Chapter 1 is just that—an ideal to strive toward. You can begin now to reach your vision by becoming an active and questioning student and by investing yourself in your fieldwork activities. We hope you will become excited by your journey of self-exploration as you learn about the helping professions.

The process of becoming a helper is intrinsically related to the process of becoming a person. We have emphasized the importance of looking at your life and of understanding your motivations. Although it is not essential for you to be problem free, we have stressed the importance of being a model for your clients. Reflect on whether what you do in your own life is what you encourage your clients to do. If you encourage your clients to take the risks that growth entails, it is essential that you do this in your own life.

This is a good time to reflect on the personal meaning this book has for you. Ask yourself these questions: Do you still think the helping professions are for you? What do you think you can bring to your work? How might your work affect your personal life? What are the greatest challenges you expect to face? Do you now have a different perspective on the concerns that were addressed in this book? At this point, what do you see as your major strengths and some of your limitations? What steps could you take to address your limitations? How can you build on your strengths? We hope that you see more clearly how the kind of person you are is vitally linked to the kind of helping professional you will become. We wish our best to you in your continuing journey!

American Association for Marriage and Family Therapy. (2015). *Code of ethics.* Washington, DC: Author.

American Counseling Association. (2011). *Disaster mental health fact sheet 7: Terms to know.* Retrieved from www.counseling.org/docs/trauma-disaster/fact-sheet-7-terms-to-know.pdf

American Counseling Association. (2014). *ACA code of ethics.* Alexandria, VA: Author.

American Group Psychotherapy Association. (2002). *AGPA and IBCGP guidelines for ethics.* Retrieved from http://www.groupsinc.org/home/practice-resources/ethics-in-group-therapy

American Mental Health Counselors Association. (2015). *Code of ethics of the American Mental Health Counselors Association.* Alexandria, VA: Author.

American Mental Health Counselors Association. (2016). *AMHCA standards for the practice of clinical mental health counseling.* Alexandria, VA: Author.

American Music Therapy Association. (2015). *Code of ethics.* Retrieved from www.musictherapy.org/ethics.html

American Psychiatric Association. (2000). *Diagnostic and statistical manual of mental disorders.* (4th ed.). Washington, DC: Author.

American Psychiatric Association. (2013a). *Diagnostic and statistical manual of mental disorders.* (5th ed.). Washington, DC: Author.

American Psychiatric Association. (2013b). *The principles of medical ethics with annotations especially applicable to psychiatry.* Washington, DC: Author.

American Psychological Association. (2003). Guidelines on multicultural education, training, research, practice, and organizational change for psychologists. *American Psychologist, 58*(5), 377–402.

American Psychological Association. (2010). *Ethical principles of psychologists and code of conduct* (2002, Amended June 1, 2010). Retrieved from http://www.apa.org/ethics/code/index.aspx

American Psychological Association. (2017a). *Ethical principles of psychologists and code of conduct.* Retrieved from http://www.apa.org/ethics/code/ethics-code-2017.pdf

American Psychological Association. (2017b). *Multicultural guidelines: An ecological approach to context, identity, and intersectionality.* Retrieved from http://www.apa.org/about/policy/multicultural-guidelines.pdf

American School Counselor Association. (2016). *Ethical standards for school counselors.* Alexandria, VA: Author.

Antony, M. M. (2019). Behavior therapy. In D. Wedding & R. J. Corsini (Eds.), *Current psychotherapies* (11th ed., pp. 199–236). Boston, MA: Cengage Learning.

*Armstrong, T. (2007). *The human odyssey: Navigating the twelve stages of life.* New York: Sterling.

Arredondo, P., Toporek, R., Brown, S., Jones, J., Locke, D., Sanchez, J., & Stadler, H. (1996). Operationalization of multicultural counseling competencies. *Journal of Multicultural Counseling and Development, 24*(1), 42–78.

Association for Addiction Professionals. (2016). *NAADAC code of ethics.* Alexandria, VA: Author.

*Association for Counselor Education and Supervision. (2011). *Best practices in clinical supervision.* Retrieved from www.acesonline.net/wp-content/uploads/2011/10/ACES-Best-Practices-in-clinical-supervision-document-FINAL.pdf

Association for Lesbian, Gay, Bisexual and Transgender Issues in Counseling. (2008). *Competencies for counseling gay, lesbian, bisexual and transgendered (GLBT) clients.* Retrieved from www.algbtic.org/resources/competencies.html

Association for Lesbian, Gay, Bisexual and Transgender Issues in Counseling. (2009). *Competencies for counseling with transgender clients.* Alexandria, VA: Author.

Association for Specialists in Group Work. (2008). Best practice guidelines. *Journal for Specialists in Group Work, 33*(2), 111–117.

Association for Specialists in Group Work. (2012). *Multicultural and social justice competence principles for group workers.* Retrieved from http://www.asgw.org/

*This list contains both references cited and suggestions for further reading. An asterisk (*) before an entry indicates a source that we highly recommend as supplementary reading.

Atkinson, D. R. (2004). *Counseling American minorities* (6th ed.). Boston, MA: McGraw-Hill.

Austin, J., Austin, J., Muratori, M., & Corey, G. (2017). Multiple relationships and multiple roles in higher education: Maintaining multiple roles and relationships in counselor education. In O. Zur (Ed.), *Multiple relationships in psychotherapy and counseling: Unavoidable, common, and mandatory dual relations in therapy* (pp. 165–173). New York, NY: Routledge (Taylor & Francis).

Baldwin, K. D. (2018). Faculty and supervisor roles in gatekeeping. In A. M. Homrich & K. L. Henderson (Eds.). *Gatekeeping in the mental health professions* (pp. 99–125). Alexandria, VA: American Counseling Association.

Barlow, S. H. (2008). Group psychotherapy specialty practice. *Professional Psychology: Research and Practice, 39*(2), 240–244.

Barnett, J. E. (2017a). An introduction to boundaries and multiple relationships for psychotherapists: Issues, challenges, and recommendations. In O. Zur (Ed.), *Multiple relationships in psychotherapy and counseling: Unavoidable, common, and mandatory dual relations in therapy* (pp. 17–29). New York, NY: Routledge (Taylor & Francis).

Barnett, J. E. (2017b). Unavoidable incidental contacts and multiple relationships in rural practice. In O. Zur (Ed.), *Multiple relationships in psychotherapy and counseling: Unavoidable, common, and mandatory dual relations in therapy* (pp. 97–107). New York, NY: Routledge (Taylor & Francis).

Barnett, J. E., Cornish, J. A. E., Goodyear, R. K., & Lichtenberg, J. W. (2007). Commentaries on the ethical and effective practice of clinical supervision. *Professional Psychology: Research and Practice, 38*(3), 268–275.

*Barnett, J. E., & Johnson, W. B. (2008). *Ethics desk reference for psychologists*. Washington, DC: American Psychological Association.

Barnett, J. E., & Johnson, W. B. (2011). Integrating spirituality and religion into psychotherapy: Persistent dilemmas, ethical issues, and a proposed decision-making process. *Ethics and Behavior, 21*(2), 147–164.

*Barnett, J. E., & Johnson, W. B. (2015). *Ethics desk reference for counselors* (2nd ed.). Alexandria, VA: American Counseling Association.

Barnett, J. E., Lazarus, A. A., Vasquez, M. J. T., Moorehead-Slaughter, O., & Johnson, W. B. (2007). Boundary issues and multiple relationships: Fantasy and reality. *Professional Psychology: Research and Practice, 38*(4), 401–410.

Barnett, J. E., Wise, E. H., Johnson-Greene, D., & Bucky, S. F. (2007). Informed consent: Too much of a good thing or not enough? *Professional Psychology: Research and Practice, 38*(2), 179–186.

Beck, A. T. (1976). *Cognitive therapy and the emotional disorders*. New York, NY: New American Library.

Beck, A. T., & Weishaar, M. E. (2019). Cognitive therapy. In D. Wedding & R. J. Corsini (Eds.), *Current psychotherapies* (11th ed., pp. 237–272). Boston, MA: Cengage Learning.

*Beck, J. S. (2005). *Cognitive therapy for challenging problems*. New York, NY: Guilford Press.

*Beck, J. S. (2011). *Cognitive behavior therapy: Basics and beyond* (2nd ed.). New York, NY: Guilford Press.

Bemak, F. (2013). Counselors without borders: Community action in counseling. In J. A. Kottler, M. Englar-Carlson, & J. Carlson (Eds.), *Helping beyond the 50-minute hour: Therapists involved in meaningful social action* (pp. 186–196). New York, NY: Routledge (Taylor & Francis).

Bemak, F., & Chung, R. C-Y. (2007). Training social justice counselors. In C. Lee (Ed.), *Counseling for social justice* (pp. 239–258). Alexandria, VA: American Counseling Association.

Bemak, F., & Chung, R. C-Y. (2008). New professional roles and advocacy strategies for school counselors: A multicultural/social justice perspective to move beyond the nice counselor syndrome. *Journal of Counseling and Development, 86*(3), 372–382.

Bemak, F., & Chung, R. C-Y. (2015). Cultural boundaries, cultural norms, multicultural and social justice perspectives. In B. Herlihy & G. Corey, *Boundary issues in counseling: Multiple roles and responsibilities* (3rd ed., pp. 84–89). Alexandria, VA: American Counseling Association.

*Bemak, F. P., & Conyne, R. K. (Eds.). (2018). *Journeys to professional excellence: Stories of courage, innovation, and risk-taking in the lives of noted psychologists and counselors*. Thousand Oaks, CA: Sage.

*Bernard, J. M., & Goodyear, R. K. (2014). *Fundamentals of clinical supervision* (5th ed.). Upper Saddle River, NJ: Pearson.

Bevacqua, F., & Kurpius, S. E. R. (2013). Counseling students' personal values and attitudes toward euthanasia. *Journal of Mental Health Counseling, 35*(2), 172–188.

Birrell, P. J., & Bruns, C. M. (2016). Ethics and relationship: From risk management to relational engagement. *Journal of Counseling & Development, 94*(4), 391–397.

Bitter, J. R. (1987). Communication and meaning: Satir in Adlerian context. In R. Sherman & D. Dinkmeyer (Eds.), *Systems of family therapy: An Adlerian integration* (pp. 109–142). New York, NY: Brunner/Mazel.

*Bitter, J. R. (2014). *Theory and practice of family therapy and counseling* (2nd ed.). Belmont, CA: Brooks/Cole, Cengage Learning.

*Bongar, B., & Sullivan, G. R. (2013). *The suicidal patient: Clinical and legal standards of care* (3rd ed.). Washington, DC: American Psychological Association.

Briere, J. N., & Scott, C. (2013). *Principles of trauma therapy: A guide to symptoms, evaluation, and treatment* (2nd ed.). Thousand Oaks, CA: Sage.

British Association for Counselling and Psychotherapy. (2013). *Ethical framework for good practice in counselling and psychotherapy*. Retrieved from http://www.bacp.co.uk

Brown, A. P., Marquis, A., & Guiffrida, D. A. (2013). Mindfulness-based interventions. *Journal of Counseling & Development, 91,* 86–104.

Brown, C., & Trangsrud, H. B. (2008). Factors associated with acceptance and decline of client gift giving. *Professional Psychology: Research and Practice, 39*(5), 505–511.

*Brown, L. S. (2018). *Feminist therapy* (2nd ed.). Washington, DC: American Psychological Association.

*Cain, D. J. (2010). *Person-centered psychotherapies.* Washington, DC: American Psychological Association.

*Calhoun, L. G., & Tedeschi, R. G. (2013). *Posttraumatic growth in clinical practice.* New York, NY: Routledge.

California Association of Marriage and Family Therapists. (2010). Disciplinary actions. *The Therapist, 22*(4), 47–57.

California Department of Consumer Affairs. (2011). *Professional therapy never includes sex.* Sacramento, CA: Author.

Canadian Counselling and Psychotherapy Association. (2007). *CCA code of ethics.* Ottawa, Canada: Author.

Caplan, G. (1964). *Principles of preventive psychiatry.* New York, NY: Basic Books.

Capodilupo, C. M., & Sue, D. W. (2013). Microaggressions in counseling and psychotherapy. In D. W. Sue & D. Sue, *Counseling the culturally diverse: Theory and practice* (6th ed., pp. 147–173). New York, NY: Wiley.

Cardemil, E. V., & Battle, C. L. (2003). Guess who's coming to therapy? Getting comfortable with conversations about race and ethnicity in psychotherapy. *Professional Psychology: Research and Practice, 34*(3), 278–286.

*Carlson, J. D., & Englar-Carlson, M. (2017). *Adlerian psychotherapy.* Washington DC: American Psychological Association.

Carlson, J., Watts, R. E., & Maniacci, M. (2006). *Adlerian therapy: Theory and practice.* Washington DC: American Psychological Association.

*Cashwell, C. S., & Young, J. S. (Eds.). (2011). *Integrating spirituality and religion into counseling: A guide to competent practice.* (2nd ed.). Alexandria, VA: American Counseling Association.

Chu, J., Leino, A., Pflum, S., & Sue, S. (2016). A model for the theoretical basis of cultural competency to guide psychotherapy. *Professional Psychology: Research and Practice, 47*(1), 18–29.

*Chung, R. C-Y., & Bemak, F. (2012). *Social justice counseling: The next steps beyond multiculturalism.* Thousand Oaks, CA: Sage.

Chung, R. C-Y., & Bemak, F. (2014). Group counseling with Asians. In J. DeLucia-Waack, C. R. Kalodner, & M. T. Riva (Eds.), *Handbook of group counseling and psychotherapy* (2nd ed., pp. 231–241). Thousand Oaks, CA: Sage.

Cohen, L., & Chehimi, S. (2010). The imperative for primary prevention. In L. Cohen, V. Chávez, & S. Chehimi, *Prevention is primary: Strategies for community well being* (2nd ed.). San Francisco, CA: Jossey Bass.

Cohut, M. (2018). Exercise for mental health: How much is too much? *Medical News Today.* Retrieved from www. medicalnewstoday/com/articles

Commission on Rehabilitation Counselor Certification. (2014). *Scope of practice statement.* Retrieved from http://www.crccertification.com /pages/crc_ccrc_scope_of_practice/43.php

Commission on Rehabilitation Counselor Certification. (2017). *Code of professional ethics for rehabilitation counselors.* Schaumburg, IL: Author.

Connell, A. (2015). Boundary issues and in-home counseling for clients with disabilities. In B. Herlihy & G. Corey, *Boundary issues in counseling: Multiple roles and responsibilities* (3rd ed., pp. 271–272). Alexandria, VA: American Counseling Association.

Cooper, C. C., & Gottlieb, M. C. (2000). Ethical issues with managed care: Challenges facing counseling psychology. *The Counseling Psychologist, 28*(2), 179–236.

*Corey, G. (2010). *Creating your professional path: Lessons from my journey*. Alexandria, VA: American Counseling Association.

*Corey, G. (2013a). *Case approach to counseling and psychotherapy* (8th ed.). Boston, MA: Cengage Learning.

*Corey, G. (2013b). *DVD for Theory and practice of counseling and psychotherapy: The case of Stan and lecturettes.* Belmont, CA: Brooks/Cole, Cengage Learning.

Corey, G. (2015). Eclecticism. In E. Neukrug (Ed.), *The Sage encyclopedia of theory in counseling and psychotherapy* (Vol. 1, pp. 307–310). Thousand Oaks, CA: Sage.

*Corey, G. (2016). *Theory and practice of group counseling* (9th ed.). Boston, MA: Cengage Learning.

*Corey, G. (2019). *The art of integrative counseling* (4th ed.). Alexandria, VA: American Counseling Association.

Corey, G., Corey, M., & Corey, C. (2019). *Issues and ethics in the helping professions* (10th ed.). Boston, MA: Cengage Learning.

*Corey, G. (2021). *Theory and practice of counseling and psychotherapy* (Enhanced 10th ed.). Boston, MA: Cengage Learning.

*Corey, G., Muratori, M., Austin, J., & Austin, J. (2018). *Counselor self-care*. Alexandria, VA: American Counseling Association.

*Corey, G., Corey, M., Muratori, M. (2018). *I never knew I had a choice* (11th ed.). Boston, MA: Cengage Learning.

*Corey, G., Corey, M. S., Muratori, M., Austin, J., & Austin, J. (2017). Multiple relationships and multiple roles in higher education: Teaching group counseling with a didactic and experiential focus. In O. Zur (Ed.), *Multiple relationships in psychotherapy and counseling: Unavoidable, common, and mandatory dual relations in therapy* (pp. 174–182). New York, NY: Routledge (Taylor & Francis).

*Corey, G., Corey, M. S., Callanan, P., & Russell, J. M. (2015). *Group techniques* (4th ed.). Belmont, CA: Brooks/Cole, Cengage Learning.

*Corey, G., Corey, M. S., & Haynes, R. (2014). *Groups in action: Evolution and challenges, DVD and workbook* (2nd ed.). Belmont, CA: Brooks/Cole, Cengage Learning.

*Corey, G., Corey, M. S., & Haynes, R. (2015). *Ethics in action: DVD and workbook* (2nd ed.). Belmont, CA: Brooks/Cole, Cengage Learning.

Corey, G., & Haynes, R. (2013). *DVD for integrative counseling: The case of Ruth and lecturettes.* Belmont, CA: Brooks/Cole, Cengage Learning.

*Corey, G., Haynes, R., Moulton, P., & Muratori, M. (2010). *Clinical supervision in the helping professions: A practical guide* (2nd ed.). Alexandria, VA: American Counseling Association.

*Corey, M. S., Corey, G., & Corey, C. (2018). *Groups: Process and practice* (10th ed.). Boston, MA: Cengage Learning.

*Cormier, S. (2016). *Counseling strategies and interventions for professional helpers* (9th ed.). Boston, MA: Pearson Education.

*Cormier, S. (2018). *Sweet sorrow: Finding enduring wholeness after loss and grief.* New York, NY: Rowman & Littlefield.

*Cormier, S., Nurius, P. S., & Osborn, C. (2017). *Interviewing and change strategies for helpers* (8th ed.). Boston, MA: Cengage Learning.

Cornish, J. A. E., Gorgens, K. A., Monson, S. P., Olkin, R., Palombi, B. J., & Abels, A. V. (2008). Perspectives on ethical practice with people who have disabilities. *Professional Psychology: Research and Practice, 39*(5), 488–497.

Council for Accreditation of Counseling and Related Educational Programs. (2016). *CACREP standards*. Alexandria, VA: Author.

*Craske, M. G. (2017). *Cognitive-behavioral therapy* (2nd ed.). Washington, DC: American Psychological Association.

Crethar, H. C., Torres Rivera, E., & Nash, S. (2008). In search of common threads: Linking multicultural, feminist, and social justice counseling paradigms. *Journal of Counseling and Development, 86*(3), 269–278.

Cummings, N. A. (1995). Impact of managed care on employment and training: A primer for survival. *Professional Psychology: Research and Practice, 26*(1), 10–15.

Dalai Lama. (2001). *An open heart: Practicing compassion in everyday life.* Boston, MA: Little Brown.

*Dalai Lama, & Cutler, H. C. (1998). *The art of happiness: A handbook for living.* New York, NY: Riverhead Books.

*Dalai Lama, & Tutu, D. (2016). *The book of joy: Lasting happiness in a changing world.* New York, NY: Penguin Random House.

Day-Vines, N. L., Wood, S. M., Grothaus, T., Craigen, L., Holman, A., Dotson-Blake, K., & Douglass, M. J. (2007). Broaching the subjects of race, ethnicity, and culture during the counseling process. *Journal of Counseling & Development, 85,* 401–409.

*DeJong, P., & Berg, I. (2013). *Interviewing for solutions* (4th ed.). Belmont, CA: Brooks/Cole, Cengage Learning.

DePoy, E., & Gilson, S. F. (2004). *Rethinking disability: Principles for professional and social change.* Belmont, CA: Brooks/Cole, Cengage Learning.

*Deurzen, E., van. (2010). *Everyday mysteries: A handbook of existential psychotherapy* (2nd ed.). London, United Kingdom: Routledge.

*Deurzen, E., van. (2012). *Existential counselling and psychotherapy in practice* (3rd ed.). London, United Kingdom: Sage.

Dobmeier, R. A., & Reiner, S. M. (2012). Spirituality in the counselor education curriculum: A national survey of student perceptions. *Counseling and Values, 57*(1), 47–65.

*Dobson, D., & Dobson, K. S. (2017). *Evidence-based practice of cognitive-behavioral therapy* (2nd ed.). New York, NY: Guilford Press.

*Dolgoff, R., Loewenberg, F. M., & Harrington, D. (2009). *Ethical decisions for social work practice* (8th ed.). Belmont, CA: Brooks/Cole, Cengage Learning.

Dugger, S. M., & Francis, P. C. (2014). Surviving a lawsuit against a counseling program: Lessons learned from *Ward v. Wilbanks. Journal of Counseling & Development 92*(2), 135–141.

Duncan, B. L., Miller, S. D., & Sparks, J. A. (2004). *The heroic client: A revolutionary way to improve effectiveness through client-directed, outcome-informed therapy.* San Francisco, CA: Jossey-Bass.

Dweck, C. S. (2006). *Mindset: The new psychology of success.* New York, NY: Ballantine Books.

*Egan, G. (2014). *The skilled helper: A problem management and opportunity development approach to helping* (10th ed.). Belmont, CA: Brooks/Cole, Cengage Learning.

*Egan, G., & Reese, R. J. (2019). *The skilled helper: A problem management and opportunity development approach to helping* (11th ed.). Boston, MA: Cengage Learning.

Elkins, D. N. (2009). *Humanistic psychology: A clinical manifesto.* Colorado Springs, CO: University of the Rockies Press.

Elkins, D. N. (2016). *The human elements of psychotherapy: A nonmedical model of emotional healing.* Washington, DC: American Psychological Association.

*Ellis, A. (2001a). *Feeling better, getting better, and staying better.* Atascadero, CA: Impact.

*Ellis, A. (2001b). *Overcoming destructive thoughts, feelings, and behaviors.* Amherst, NY: Prometheus Books.

*Ellis, A. (2004a). *Rational emotive behavior therapy: It works for me—It can work for you.* Amherst, NY: Prometheus Books.

*Ellis, A. (2004b). *The road to tolerance: The philosophy of rational emotive behavior therapy.* Amherst, NY: Prometheus Books.

*Ellis, A., & Ellis, D. J. (2011). *Rational emotive behavior therapy.* Washington, DC: American Psychological Association.

Ellis, A., & Ellis, D. J. (2019). Rational emotive behavior therapy. In D. Wedding & R. J. Corsini (Eds.), *Current psychotherapies* (11th ed., pp. 157–198). Boston, MA: Cengage Learning.

*Englar-Carlson, M., Evans, M. P., & Duffey, T. (2014). *A counselor's guide to working with men.* Alexandria, VA: American Counseling Association.

Erikson, E. (1963). *Childhood and society* (2nd ed.). New York, NY: Norton.

Erikson, E. (1982). *The life cycle completed.* New York, NY: Norton.

Eubanks, C. F., Goldfried, M. R., & Norcross, J. C. (2019). Future directions in psychotherapy integration. In J. C. Norcross & M. R. Goldfried (Eds.), *Handbook of psychotherapy integration* (3rd ed.). New York, NY: Oxford University Press.

Ferguson, A. D. (2016). Cultural issues in counseling lesbians, gays, and bisexuals. In I. Marini & M. A. Stebnicki (Eds.), *The professional counselor's desk reference* (2nd ed., pp. 159–162). New York, NY: Springer.

Figley, C. R. (1995). Compassion fatigue: Toward a new understanding of the costs of caring. In B. H. Stamm (Ed.), *Secondary traumatic stress.* Lutherville, MD: Sidran Press.

Foreman, T. (2018). Wellness, exposure to trauma, and vicarious traumatization: A pilot study. *Journal of Mental Health Counseling, 40*(2), 142–155. doi: 10.17744/mehc.40.2.04

Forester-Miller, H., & Moody, E. E. (2015). Rural communities: Can dual relationships be avoided? In B. Herlihy & G. Corey, *Boundary issues in counseling: Multiple roles and responsibilities* (3rd ed., pp. 251–253). Alexandria, VA: American Counseling Association.

*Frame, M. W. (2003). *Integrating religion and spirituality into counseling: A comprehensive approach.* Belmont, CA: Brooks/Cole, Cengage Learning.

Francis, P. C. (2016). Religion and spirituality in counseling. In I. Marini & M. A. Stebnicki (Eds.), *The professional counselor's desk reference* (2nd ed., pp. 559–564). New York, NY: Springer.

Francis, P. C., & Dugger, S. M. (2014). Special section: Professionalism, ethics, and value-based conflicts in counseling: An introduction to the special section. *Journal of Counseling & Development 92*(2), 131–134.

Fullen, M. C. (2019). Defining wellness in older adulthood: Toward a comprehensive framework. *Journal of Counseling and Development, 97*(1), 62–74.

Gamino, L. A., & Bevins, M. B. (2013). Ethical challenges when counseling clients nearing the end of life. In J. L. Werth Jr. (Ed.), *Counseling clients near the end of life: A practical guide for mental health professionals* (pp. 3–24). New York, NY: Springer.

Gentry, J. E., Webber, J. M., & Baranowsky, A. B. (2018). Compassion fatigue: Our Achilles' Heal. In J. M. Webber & J. B. Mascari (Eds.), *Disaster mental health counseling: A guide to preparing and responding* (4th ed., pp. 79–92). Alexandria, VA: American Counseling Association.

Germer, C. K. (2013). Mindfulness: What is it? What does it matter? In C. K. Germer, R. D. Siegel, & P. R. Fulton (Eds.), *Mindfulness and psychotherapy* (pp. 3–35). New York, NY: Guilford Press.

*Germer, C. K., & Siegel, R. D. (Eds.). (2012). *Wisdom and compassion in psychotherapy: Deepening mindfulness in clinical practice.* New York, NY: Guilford Press.

*Germer, C. K., Siegel, R. D. & Fulton P. R. (Eds.), (2013). *Mindfulness and psychotherapy.* New York, NY: Guilford Press.

Ginicola, M. M., Filmore, J. M., & Smith, C. (2017). Developing competence in working with LGBTQ+ communities: Awareness, knowledge, skills, and action. In M. M. Ginicola, C. Smith, & J. M. Filmore (Eds.), *Affirmative counseling with LGBTQI+ people* (pp. 3–20). Alexandria, VA: American Counseling Association.

Ginicola, M. M., Smith, C., & Filmore, J. M. (Eds.). (2017). *Affirmative counseling with LGBTQI+ people*. Alexandria, VA: American Counseling Association.

Glasser, W. (1998). *Choice theory: A new psychology of personal freedom.* New York, NY: HarperCollins.

Glasser, W. (2001). *Counseling with choice theory: The new reality therapy.* New York, NY: HarperCollins.

*Goldenberg, I., Stanton, M., & Goldenberg, H. (2017). *Family therapy: An overview* (9th ed.). Boston, MA: Cengage Learning.

Goldfried, M. R., Glass, C. R., & Arnkoff, D. B. (2011). Integrative approaches to psychotherapy. In J. C. Norcross, G. R. Vandenbos, & D. K. Freedheim (Eds.), *History of psychotherapy* (2nd ed., pp. 269–296). Washington, DC: American Psychological Association.

*Goleman, D. (1995). *Emotional intelligence*. New York, NY: Bantam Books.

Goleman, D., & Davidson, R. (2017). *Altered traits: Science reveals how meditation changes your mind, brain, and body.* New York, NY: Penguin Books.

Grothaus, T., Runyan, H., & Sacco-Bene, C. (2019). In G. McAuliffe (Ed.), *Positive counseling: A guide to assessing and enhancing client strength and growth* (pp. 173–183). San Diego, CA: Cognella Academic.

*Gutheil, T. G., & Brodsky, A. (2008). *Preventing boundary violations in clinical practice.* New York, NY: Guilford Press.

Hagedorn, W. B., & Moorhead, H. J. H. (2011). Counselor self-awareness: Exploring attitudes, beliefs, and values. In C. S. Cashwell & J. S. Young (Eds.), *Integrating spirituality and religion into counseling: A guide to competent practice* (2nd ed., pp. 71–96). Alexandria, VA: American Counseling Association.

Hales, D. (2017). *An invitation to health: Build your future* (17th ed.). Boston, MA: Cengage Learning.

*Hayes, S. C., & Lillis, J. (2012). *Acceptance and commitment therapy*. Washington, DC: American Psychological Association.

Hayes, S. C., Strosahl, K. D., & Wilson, K. G. (Eds.). (2011). *Acceptance and commitment therapy: The process and practice of mindful change* (2nd ed.). New York, NY: Guilford Press.

*Hays, P. A. (2014). *Creating well-being*. Washington, DC: American Psychological Association.

*Haynes, R. L. (2014). *Take control of life's crises today: A practical guide*. Chula Vista, CA: Aventine Press.

Herbert, J. D., & Forman, E. M. (2011). *Acceptance and mindfulness in cognitive behavior therapy: Understanding and applying the new therapies*. Hoboken, NJ: Wiley.

*Herlihy, B., & Corey, G. (2015a). *ACA ethical standards casebook* (7th ed.). Alexandria, VA: American Counseling Association.

*Herlihy, B., & Corey, G. (2015b). *Boundary issues in counseling: Multiple roles and responsibilities* (3rd ed.). Alexandria, VA: American Counseling Association.

Herlihy, B., & Corey, G. (2015c). Confidentiality. In B. Herlihy & G. Corey, *ACA ethical standards casebook* (7th ed., pp. 169–182). Alexandria, VA: American Counseling Association.

Herlihy, B., & Corey, G. (2015d). Managing value conflicts. In B. Herlihy & G. Corey, *ACA ethical standards casebook* (7th ed., pp. 193–204). Alexandria, VA: American Counseling Association.

Herlihy, B., Hermann, M. A., & Greden, L. R. (2014). Legal and ethical implications of using religious beliefs as the basis for refusing to counsel certain clients. *Journal of Counseling & Development 92*(2), 148–153.

Herlihy, B., & James, A. E. (2018). Counseling survivors of Hurricane Katrina. In J. M. Webber & J. B. Mascari (Eds.), *Disaster mental health counseling: A guide to preparing and responding* (4th ed., pp. 165–175). Alexandria, VA: American Counseling Association Foundation.

Herlihy, B., James, A. E., & Taleri, K. S. (2018). Social justice and counseling ethics. In C. C. Lee (Ed.), *Counseling for social justice* (3rd ed., pp. 205–220). Alexandria, VA: American Counseling Association Foundation.

Hill, C. E., Knox, S., & Pinto-Coelho, K. G. (2019). Self-disclosure and immediacy. In J. C. Norcross & M. J. Lambert (Eds.), *Psychotherapy relationships that work: Evidence-based therapist contributions* (Vol. 1, 3rd ed.). New York, NY: Oxford University Press.

*Hogan, M. (2013). *The four skills of cultural diversity competence: A process for understanding and practice* (4th ed.). Belmont, CA: Brooks/Cole, Cengage Learning.

*Homan, M. (2016). *Promoting community change: Making it happen in the real world* (6th ed.). San Francisco, CA: Cengage Learning.

Homrich, A. M., & Henderson, K. L. (Eds.). (2018). *Gatekeeping in the mental health professions*. Alexandria, VA: American Counseling Association.

How to recognize students who are potentially dangerous. (2011). Johns Hopkins University Counseling Center. Retrieved from http://web.jhu.edu/counselingcenter/worried/recognize

Hoyt, M. F. (2015). Brief therapy. In E. Neukrug (Ed.), *The Sage encyclopedia of theory in counseling and psychotherapy* (Vol. 1, pp. 144–147). Thousand Oaks, CA: Sage.

Iarussi, M. (2019). Motivational interviewing. In G. McAuliffe (Ed.), *Positive counseling: A guide to assessing and enhancing client strength and growth* (pp. 287–305). San Diego, CA: Cognella Academic.

International Association of Marriage and Family Counselors. (2017). *IAMFC Code of Ethics*. Alexandria, VA. Author.

*Ivey, A. E., Ivey, M. B., & Zalaquett, C. P. (2018). *Intentional interviewing and counseling: Facilitating client development in a multicultural society* (9th ed.). Boston, MA: Cengage Learning.

*Jacobs, E. F., Schimmel, S. J. Masson, R. L., & Harvill, R. L. (2016). *Group counseling: Strategies and skills* (8th ed.). Boston, MA: Cengage Learning.

*James, R. K., & Gilliland, B. E. (2017). *Crisis intervention strategies* (8th ed.). Boston, MA: Cengage Learning.

Jencius, M. (2015). Technology, social media, and online counseling. In B. Herlihy & G. Corey, *ACA ethical standards casebook* (7th ed., pp. 245–258). Alexandria, VA: American Counseling Association.

*Johnson, R. (2013). *Spirituality in counseling and psychotherapy: An integrative approach that empowers clients*. Hoboken, NJ: Wiley.

Johnson, W. B., Barnett, J. E., Elman, N. S., Forrest, L., & Kaslow, N. J. (2012). The competent community: Toward a vital reformulation of professional ethics. *American Psychologist, 67*(7), 557–569.

Johnson, W. B., & Johnson, S. J. (2017). Unavoidable and mandated multiple relationships in military settings. In O. Zur (Ed.), *Multiple relationships in psychotherapy and counseling: Unavoidable, common, and mandatory dual relations in therapy* (pp. 49–60). New York, NY: Routledge (Taylor & Francis).

Kabat-Zinn, J. (2003). Mindfulness-based interventions in context: Past, present and future. *Clinical Psychology: Science and Practice, 10*, 144–156.

Kabat-Zinn, J. (2018). *The healing power of mindfulness: A new way of being.* New York, NY: Hachette Books.

Kalkbrenner, M. T., Neukrug, E. S., & Griffith, S. M. (2019). Appraising counselor attendance in counseling: The validation and application of the revised Fit, Stigma, and Value scale. *Journal of Mental Health Counseling, 41*(1), 21–35. doi:10.17744/mehc.41.1.03

*Kanel, K. (2018). *A guide to crisis intervention* (6th ed.). Boston, MA: Cengage Learning.

Kaplan, D. M. (2014). Ethical implications of a critical legal case for the counseling profession: *Ward v. Wilbanks. Journal of Counseling & Development 92*(2), 142–146.

*Kazantzis, N., Dattilio, F. M., & Dobson, K. S. (2017). *The therapeutic relationship in cognitive-behavioral therapy: A clinician's guide.* New York, NY: Guilford Press.

Keeton v. Anderson-Wiley, No. 1:10-CV-00099-JRH-WLB, 733 F. Supp. 2d 1368 (S. D. Ga., Aug. 20, 2010).

Kelly, C., & Robinson, D. M. (2018). Dialectical behavior therapy. In A. Vernon & K. A. Doyle (Eds.), *Cognitive behavior therapies: A guidebook for practitioners* (pp. 209–245). Alexandria, VA: American Counseling Association.

Kerr, M. E., & Bowen, M. (1988). *Family evaluation: An approach based on Bowen theory*. New York, NY: Norton.

*Kiser, P. M. (2012). *The human services internship: Getting the most from your experience* (3rd ed.). Belmont, CA: Brooks/Cole, Cengage Learning.

*Knapp, S., & VandeCreek, L. (2003). *A guide to the 2002 revision of the American Psychological Association's ethics code.* Sarasota, FL: Professional Resource Press.

*Knapp, S. J., & VandeCreek, L. (2012). *Practical ethics for psychologists: A positive approach* (2nd ed.). Washington, DC: American Psychological Association.

Kocet, M. M. (2019). Affirmative counseling with lesbian, gay, bisexual, transgender, queer, questioning, and intersex clients. In C. C. Lee (Ed.), *Multicultural issues in counseling: New approaches to diversity* (5th ed., pp. 169–180). Alexandria, VA: American Counseling Association.

Kocet, M. M., & Herlihy, B. J. (2014). Addressing value-based conflicts within the counseling relationship: A decision-making model. *Journal of Counseling & Development, 92*(2), 180–186.

Kolmes, K. (2012). Social media in the future of professional psychology. *Professional Psychology: Research & Practice, 43*(6), 606–612.

Kolmes, K. (2017). Digital and social media multiple relationships on the Internet. In O. Zur (Ed.), *Multiple relationships in psychotherapy and counseling: Unavoidable, common, and mandatory dual relations in therapy* (pp. 185–195). New York, NY: Routledge (Taylor & Francis).

Kolmes, K., & Taube, D. G. (2016). Client discovery of psychotherapist personal information online. *Professional Psychology: Research and Practice, 47*(2), 147–154.

*Koocher, G. P., & Keith-Spiegel, P. (2016). *Ethics in psychology and the mental health professions: Standards and cases* (4th ed.). New York, NY: Oxford University Press.

Kottler, J. A. (2017). *On being a therapist* (5th ed.). Oxford, NY: Oxford University Press.

Kottler, J. A., & Balkin, R. (2017). *Relationships in counseling and the counselor's life.* Alexandria, VA: American Counseling Association.

Kottler, J. A., & Carlson, J. (2016). *Therapy over 50: Aging issues in psychotherapy and the therapist's life.* New York, NY: Oxford University Press.

*Kottler, J. A., Englar-Carlson, M., & Carlson, J. (Eds.). (2013). *Helping beyond the 50-minute hour: Therapists involved in meaningful social action.* New York, NY: Routledge (Taylor & Francis).

*Kottler, J. A., & Shepard, D. S. (2015). *Introduction to counseling: Voices from the field* (8th ed.). San Francisco, CA: Cengage Learning.

Krebs, P. M., Norcross, J. C., Nicholson, J. M., & Prochaska, J. O. (2019). Stages of change. In J. C. Norcross & B. E. Wampold (Eds.), *Psychotherapy relationships that work: Evidence-based responsiveness* (Vol. 2, 3rd ed.). New York, NY: Oxford University Press.

Kwak, J., & Collet, E. P. (2013). Diversity considerations with clients who are near the end of life. In J. L. Werth Jr. (Ed.), *Counseling clients near the end of life: A practical guide for mental health professionals* (pp. 25–51). New York, NY: Springer.

Landrum, B., Knight, D. K., & Flynn, P. M. (2012). The impact of organizational stress and burnout on client engagement. *Journal of Substance Abuse Treatment, 42,* 222–230.

LaViolette, A. D., & Barnett, O. W. (2014). *It could happen to anyone: Why battered women stay* (3rd ed.). Thousand Oaks, CA: Sage.

Lawson, D. M., & Gaushell, H. (1988). Family autobiography: A useful method for enhancing counselors' personal development. *Counselor Education and Supervision, 28*(2), 162–167.

Lawson, D. M., & Gaushell, H. (1991). Intergenerational family characteristics of counselor trainees. *Counselor Education and Supervision, 30*(4), 309–321.

Lawson, G. (2015). Boundaries in disaster mental health. In B. Herlihy & G. Corey, *Boundary issues in counseling: Multiple roles and responsibilities* (3rd ed., pp. 224–228). Alexandria, VA: American Counseling Association.

Lazarus, A. A. (2001). Not all "dual relationships" are taboo: Some tend to enhance treatment outcomes. *The National Psychologist, 10*(1), 16.

Lazarus, A. A. (2015). Transcending boundaries in psychotherapy. In B. Herlihy & G. Corey, *Boundary issues in counseling: Multiple roles and responsibilities* (3rd ed., pp. 27–31). Alexandria, VA: American Counseling Association.

Ledley, D. R., Marx, B. P., & Heimberg, R. G. (2018). *Making cognitive-behavioral therapy work: Clinical process for new practitioners* (3rd ed.). New York, NY: Guilford Press.

Lee, C. C. (2013a). The cross-cultural encounter: Meeting the challenge of culturally competent counseling. In C. C. Lee (Ed.), *Multicultural issues in counseling: New approaches to diversity* (4th ed., pp. 13–19). Alexandria, VA: American Counseling Association.

Lee, C. C. (2013b). Global literacy: The foundation of culturally competent counseling. In C. C. Lee (Ed.), *Multicultural issues in counseling: New approaches to diversity* (4th ed., pp. 309–312). Alexandria, VA: American Counseling Association.

Lee, C. C. (2015). Social justice and counseling across cultures. In B. Herlihy & G. Corey, *ACA ethical standards casebook* (7th ed., pp. 155–168). Alexandria, VA: American Counseling Association.

*Lee, C. C. (Ed.). (2018a). *Counseling for social justice* (3rd ed.). Alexandria, VA: American Counseling Association Foundation.

Lee, C. C. (2018b). Final thoughts: The counselor as agent of social justice: The process of becoming. In C. C. Lee (Ed.), *Counseling for social justice* (3rd ed., pp. 249–254). Alexandria, VA: American Counseling Association Foundation.

Lee, C. C. (2018c). Training counselors as agents of change: A pedagogy for social justice. In C. C. Lee (Ed.), *Counseling for social justice* (3rd ed., pp. 239–254). Alexandria, VA: American Counseling Association Foundation.

Lee, C. C. (2019a). The cross-cultural encounter: Meeting the challenge of culturally competent counseling. In C. C. Lee (Ed.), *Multicultural issues in counseling: New approaches to diversity* (5th ed., pp. 15–21). Alexandria, VA: American Counseling Association.

Lee, C. C. (2019b). Multicultural competency: A conceptual framework for counseling across cultures. In C. C. Lee (Ed.), *Multicultural issues in counseling: New approaches to diversity* (5th ed., pp. 3–13). Alexandria, VA: American Counseling Association.

Lee, C. C. (Ed.). (2019c). *Multicultural issues in counseling: New approaches to diversity* (5th ed.). Alexandria, VA: American Counseling Association.

Lee, C, C., Baldwin, R., Mamara, S. M., & Quesenberry, L. (2018). Counselors as agents of social justice. In C. C. Lee (Ed.), *Counseling for social justice* (3rd ed., pp. 3–20). Alexandria, VA: American Counseling Association Foundation.

Lee, C. C., & Park, D. (2013). A conceptual framework for counseling across cultures. In C. C. Lee (Ed.), *Multicultural issues in counseling: New approaches to diversity* (4th ed., pp. 3–12). Alexandria, VA: American Counseling Association.

Lee, C. C., & Zalkalne, E. (2019). The culturally competent counselor as an agent of social justice. In C. C. Lee (Ed.), *Multicultural issues in counseling: New approaches to diversity* (5th ed., pp. 273–276). Alexandria, VA: American Counseling Association.

Lent, J., & Schwartz, R. C. (2012). The impact of work setting, demographic characteristics, and personality factors related to burnout among professional counselors. *Journal of Mental Health Counseling, 34*(4), 355–372.

Levenson, H. (2017). *Brief dynamic therapy* (2nd ed.). Washington, DC: American Psychological Association.

*Levitt, D. H., & Moorhead, H. J. H. (Eds.). (2013). *Values and ethics in counseling: Real-life ethical decision making.* New York, NY: Routledge (Taylor & Francis).

*Lewis, J. A., Lewis, M. D., Daniels, J. A., & D'Andrea, M. J. (2011). *Community counseling: A multicultural-social justice perspective* (4th ed.). Belmont, CA: Brooks/Cole, Cengage Learning.

Lim, S-L. (2008). Transformative aspects of genogram work: Perceptions and experiences of graduate students in a counseling training program. *The Family Journal: Counseling and Therapy for Couples and Families, 16*(1), 35–42.

Linehan, M. M. (1993a). *Cognitive-behavioral treatment of borderline personality disorder.* New York, NY: Guilford Press.

Linehan, M. M. (1993b). *Skills training manual for treating borderline personality disorder.* New York, NY: Guilford Press.

Linehan, M. M. (2015). *DBT skills training manual* (2nd ed.). New York, NY: Guilford Press.

Linley, P. A., & Joseph, S. (2007). Therapy work and therapists' positive and negative well-being. *Journal of Social and Clinical Psychology, 26*(3), 385–403.

Machuca, R. (2015). Boundaries issues in counseling Latino clients. In B. Herlihy & G. Corey, *Boundary issues in counseling: Multiple roles and responsibilities* (3rd ed., pp. 100–103). Alexandria, VA: American Counseling Association.

*Mackelprang, R. W., & Salsgiver, R. O. (2009). *Disability: A diversity model approach in human service practice* (2nd ed.). Chicago, IL: Lyceum Books.

Margolin, G. (1982). Ethical and legal considerations in marital and family therapy. *American Psychologist, 37*(3), 788–801.

Marini, I. (2007). Cross-cultural counseling issues of males who sustain a disability. In A. E. Dell Orto & P. W. Power (Eds.), *The psychological and social impact of illness and disability* (5th ed., pp. 194–213). New York, NY: Springer.

Mascari, J. B., & Webber, J. M. (2018). Disaster mental health and trauma counseling: The next decade. In J. M. Webber & J. B. Mascari (Eds.), *Disaster mental health counseling: A guide to preparing and responding* (4th ed., pp. 287–294). Alexandria, VA: American Counseling Association Foundation.

*Maslach, C. (2015). *Burnout: The cost of caring* (2nd ed.). Los Altos, CA: Malor Books.

Maslach, C., Jackson, S. E., & Leiter, M. P. (1996). *Maslach Burnout Inventory* (3rd ed.). Palo Alto, CA: Consulting Psychologists Press.

McAuliffe, G. J. (2019). *Positive counseling: A guide to assessing and enhancing client strength and growth.* San Diego, CA: Cognella Academic.

McGoldrick, M. (2011a). *The genogram journey: Reconnecting with your family.* New York, NY: Norton.

*McGoldrick, M. (2011b). Women and the family life cycle. In M. McGoldrick, B. Carter, & N. Garcia-Preto (Eds.), *The expanded family life cycle: Individual, family, and social perspectives* (4th ed., pp. 42–58). Boston, MA: Allyn & Bacon (Pearson).

McGoldrick, M. (2016). *The genogram casebook: A clinical companion to assessment and intervention.* New York, NY: Norton.

*McGoldrick, M., Carter, B., & Garcia-Preto, N. (Eds.). (2011a). *The expanded family life cycle: Individual, family, and social perspectives* (4th ed.). Boston: Allyn & Bacon (Pearson).

McGoldrick, M., Carter, B., & Garcia-Preto, N. (Eds.). (2011b). Self in context: Human development and the individual life cycle in systemic perspective. In M. McGoldrick, B. Carter, & N. Garcia-Preto (Eds.), *The expanded family life cycle: Individual, family, and social perspectives* (4th ed., pp. 20–41). Boston, MA: Allyn & Bacon.

McGoldrick, M., Gerson, R., & Petry, S. (2008). *Genograms: Assessment and intervention* (3rd ed.). New York, MA: Norton.

McWhirter, P., & Robbins, R. (2014). Group therapy with Native people. In J. DeLucia-Waack, C. R. Kalodner, & M. T. Riva (Eds.), *Handbook of group counseling and psychotherapy* (2nd ed., pp. 209–219). Thousand Oaks, CA: Sage.

Meichenbaum, D. (2012). *Roadmap to resilience: A guide for military, trauma victims and their families.* Clearwater, FL: Institute Press.

Meichenbaum, D. (2017). *The evolution of cognitive behavior therapy: A personal and professional journey with Don Meichenbaum.* New York, NY: Taylor & Francis.

Miller, E., & Marini, I. (2009). Brief psychotherapy. In I. Marini & M. A. Stebnicki (Eds.), *The professional counselor's desk reference* (pp. 379–387). New York, NY: Springer.

*Miller, W. R., & Rollnick, S. (2013). *Motivational interviewing: Helping people change* (3rd ed.). New York, NY: Guilford Press.

Moffat, C. T. (2011). Helping those in need: Human service workers. *Occupational Outlook Quarterly* (Fall), 22–32. Retrieved from https://www.bls.gov/careeroutlook/2011/fall/art03.pdf

Moffatt, G. K. (2018). The hurting counselor. *Counseling Today, 61*(2), 52–56.

Mosak, H., & Shulman, B. (1988). *Life style inventory.* Muncie, IN: Accelerated Development.

Mullen, P. R., Morris, C., & Lord, M. (2017). The experience of ethical dilemmas, burnout, and stress among practicing counselors. *Counseling & Values, 62*(1), 37–56. doi: 10.1002/cvj.12048

Mullenbach, M., & Skovholt, T. M. (2016). Burnout prevention and self-care strategies of expert practitioners. In T. M. Skovholt & M. Trotter-Mathison, *The resilient practitioner* (3rd ed. pp. 231–254). New York, NY: Routledge (Taylor & Francis).

*Murphy, J. J. (2015). *Solution-focused counseling in schools* (3rd ed.). Alexandria, VA: American Counseling Association.

*Murphy, J. J., & Sparks, J. A. (2018). *Strength-based therapy: Distinctive features.* New York, NY: Routledge.

*Naar, S., & Safren, S. A. (2017). *Motivational interviewing and CBT: Combining strategies for maximum effectiveness.* New York, NY: Guilford Press.

*Nagy, T. F. (2011). *Essential ethics for psychologists: A primer for understanding and mastering core issues.* Washington, DC: American Psychological Association.

National Association of Social Workers. (2017). *Code of ethics.* Washington, DC: Author.

National Board for Certified Counselors. (2016). *National Board for Certified Counselors (NBCC) code of ethics.* Retrieved from http://www.nbcc.org/assets/ethics,/nbcc-codeofethics.pdf

National Organization for Human Services. (2015). *Ethical standards for human services professionals.* Portland, OR: Author.

*Neff, K. (2011). *Self-compassion: Stop beating up on yourself and leave insecurity behind.* New York, NY: HarperCollins (William Morrow).

Neff, K., & Germer, C. (2018). *The mindful self-compassion workbook.* New York, NY: Guilford.

Neukrug, E. S. (2016a). *Theory, practice, and trends in human services: An introduction* (6th ed.). Boston, MA: Cengage Learning.

*Neukrug, E. (2016b). *The world of the counselor: An introduction to the counseling profession* (5th ed.). Boston, MA: Cengage Learning.

Neukrug, E. (2018). *Counseling theory and practice* (2nd ed.). San Diego, CA: Cognella Academic.

Neukrug, E., Kalkbrenner, M. T., & Griffith, S. A. (2017). Barriers to counseling among human service professionals: The development and validation of the fit, stigma, & value (FSV) scale. *Journal of Human Services, 37,* 27–40.

Neukrug, E. S., & Milliken, T. (2011). Counselors' perceptions of ethical behaviors. *Journal of Counseling & Development, 89*(2), 206–216.

*Newman, B. M., & Newman, P. R. (2015). *Development through life: A psychosocial approach* (12th ed.). Boston, MA: Cengage Learning.

*Nichols, M. P., & Davis S. D. (2017). *Family therapy: Concepts and methods* (11th ed.). New York, NY: Pearson.

Norcross, J. C. (2000). Psychotherapist self-care: Practitioner-tested, research-informed strategies. *Professional Psychology: Research and Practice, 31*(6), 710–713.

*Norcross, J. C. (2005). The psychotherapist's own psychotherapy: Educating and developing psychologists. *American Psychologist, 60*(8), 840–850.

Norcross, J. C. (2010). The therapeutic relationship. In B. L. Duncan, S. D. Miller, B. E. Wampold, & M. A. Hubble (Eds.), *The heart & soul of change: Delivering what works in therapy* (2nd ed., pp. 113–141). Washington, DC: American Psychological Association.

*Norcross, J. C., & Beutler, L. E. (2019). Integrative psychotherapies. In D. Wedding & R. J. Corsini (Eds.), *Current psychotherapies* (11th ed., pp. 527–560). Boston, MA: Cengage Learning.

*Norcross, J. C., & Goldfried, M. R. (Eds.). (2019). *Handbook of psychotherapy integration* (3rd ed.). New York, NY: Oxford University Press.

*Norcross, J. C., Goldfried, M. R., & Arigo, D. (2016). Integrative theories. In J. C. Norcross, G. R. VandenBos, & D. K. Freedheim (Eds.), *APA handbook of clinical psychology* (Vol. 2, pp. 303–332). Washington, DC: American Psychological Association.

Norcross, J. C., Hogan, T. P., Koocher, G. P., & Maggio, L. A. (2017). *Clinician's guide to evidence-based practices: Behavioral health and addictions* (2nd ed.). New York, NY: Oxford University Press.

*Norcross, J. C., & Lambert, M. J. (Eds.). (2019). *Psychotherapy relationships that work: Evidence-based therapist contributions* (Vol. 1, 3rd ed.). New York, NY: Oxford University Press.

Norcross, J. C., Pfund, R. A., & Prochaska, J. O. (2013). Psychotherapy in 2022: A Delphi poll on its future. *Professional Psychology: Research and Practice, 44*(5), 363–370.

*Norcross, J. C., & VandenBos, G. R. (2018). *Leaving it at the office: A guide to psychotherapist self-care* (2nd ed.). New York, NY: Guilford Press.

*Norcross, J. C., & Wampold, B. E. (Eds.). (2019). *Psychotherapy relationships that work: Evidence-based responsiveness* (Vol. 2, 3rd ed.). New York, NY: Oxford University Press.

*Ohrt, J. H., Clarke, P. B., & Conley, A. H. (2019). *Wellness counseling: A holistic approach to prevention and intervention*. Alexandria, VA: American Counseling Association.

Okech, J. E. A., & Kline, W. B. (2006). Competency concerns in group co-leader relationships. *Journal for Specialists in Group Work, 31*(2), 165–180.

*Okun, B. F., & Kantrowitz, R. E. (2015). *Effective helping: Interviewing and counseling techniques* (8th ed.). San Francisco, CA: Cengage Learning.

Olkin, R. (2016). Disability-affirmative therapy. In I. Marini & M. A. Stebnicki (Eds.), *The professional counselor's desk reference* (2nd ed., pp. 215–223). New York, NY: Springer.

Orlinsky, D. E., & Ronnestad, M. H. (2005). *How psychotherapists develop: A study of therapeutic work and professional growth*. Washington, DC: American Psychological Association.

Orlinsky, D. E., Schofield, M. J., Schroder, T., & Kazantzis, N. (2011). Utilization of personal therapy by psychotherapists: A practice-friendly review and a new study. *Journal of Clinical Psychology, 67*(8), 828–842.

Pantaleno, A., & Sisti, M. (2018). Mindfulness. In A. Vernon & K. A. Doyle (Eds.), *Cognitive behavior therapies: A guidebook for practitioners* (pp. 247–280). Alexandria, VA: American Counseling Association.

*Parham, T. A., & Caldwell, L. D. (2015). Boundaries in the context of a collective community: An African- centered perspective. In B. Herlihy & G. Corey, *Boundary issues in counseling: Multiple roles and responsibilities* (3rd ed., pp. 96–100). Alexandria, VA: American Counseling Association.

Patsiopoulos, A. T., & Buchanan, M. J. (2011). The practice of self-compassion in counseling: A narrative inquiry. *Professional Psychology: Research and Practice, 42*(4), 301–307.

*Pedersen, P. (2000). *A handbook for developing multicultural awareness* (3rd ed.). Alexandria, VA: American Counseling Association.

Pedersen, P. (2008). Ethics, competence, and professional issues in cross-cultural counseling. In P. B. Pedersen, J. G. Draguns, W. J. Lonner, & J. E. Trimble (Eds.), *Counseling across cultures* (6th ed., pp. 5–20). Thousand Oaks, CA: Sage.

Phillips, L. (2018). Using nature as a therapeutic partner. *Counseling Today, 60*(11), 26–33.

Podina, I. R., & David, D. (2018). Acceptance and commitment therapy. In A. Vernon & K. A. Doyle (Eds.), *Cognitive behavior therapies: A guidebook for practitioners* (pp. 177–208). Alexandria, VA: American Counseling Association.

Polychronis, P. D., & Brown, S. G. (2016). The strict liability standard and clinical supervision. *Professional Psychology: Research and Practice, 47*(2), 139–146.

Pope, K. S., Sonne, J. L., & Holroyd, J. (1993). *Sexual feelings in psychotherapy: Explorations for therapists and therapists-in-training*. Washington, DC: American Psychological Association.

*Pope, K. S., & Vasquez, M. J. T. (2016). *Ethics in psychotherapy and counseling: A practical guide for psychologists* (5th ed.). Hoboken, NJ: Wiley.

Pope, K. S., & Wedding, D. (2014). Contemporary challenges and controversies. In D. Wedding & R. J. Corsini (Eds.), *Current psychotherapies* (10th ed., pp. 569–603). Belmont, CA: Brooks/Cole, Cengage Learning.

*Powers, R. L., & Griffith, J. (2012). *The key to psychotherapy: Understanding the self-created individual.* Port Townsend, WA: Adlerian Psychology Associates.

Prochaska, J. O., & Norcross, J. C. (2018). *Systems of psychotherapy: A transtheoretical analysis* (9th ed.). New York, NY: Oxford University Press.

Ratts, M. J., & Butler, S. K. (2019). *Multicultural and social justice counseling competencies: A blueprint for the profession*. Alexandria, VA: American Counseling Association.

Ratts, M. J., Singh, A. A., Nassar-McMillan, S., Butler, S. K., & McCullough, J. R. (2016). Multicultural and social justice counseling competencies: Guidance for the counseling profession. *Journal of Multicultural Counseling and Development, 44,* 28–48.

*Ratts, M. J., Toporek, R. L., & Lewis, J. A. (2010). *ACA advocacy competencies: A social justice framework for counselors*. Alexandria, VA: American Counseling Association.

Reamer, F. G. (2013). Social work in a digital age: Ethical and risk management challenges. *Social Work, 58*(2), 163–172.

Reamer, F. G. (2017). Multiple relationships in a digital world: Unprecedented ethical and risk management challenges. In O. Zur (Ed.), *Multiple relationships in psychotherapy and counseling: Unavoidable, common, and mandatory dual relations in therapy* (pp. 196–206). New York, NY: Routledge (Taylor & Francis).

Remer, P. (2013). Feminist therapy. In J. Frew & M. D. Spiegler (Eds.), *Contemporary psychotherapies for a diverse world* (pp. 339–372). New York, NY: Routledge.

*Remley, T. P., & Herlihy, B. (2020). *Ethical, legal, and professional issues in counseling* (6th ed.). Boston, MA: Pearson.

Robertson, L. A., & Young, M. E. (2011). The revised ASERVIC spirituality competencies. In C. S. Cashwell & J. S. Young (Eds.), *Integrating spirituality and religion into counseling: A guide to competent practice* (2nd ed., pp. 25–42). Alexandria, VA: American Counseling Association.

Ronnestad, M. H., Orlinsky, D. E., & Wiseman, H. (2016). Professional development and personal therapy. In J. Norcross, G. R. VandenBos, & D. K. Freedheim (Eds.), *APA handbook of clinical psychology* (Vol. 5, pp. 223–235). Washington, DC: American Psychological Association.

Roysircar, G., Arredondo, P., Fuertes, J. N., Ponterotto, J. G., & Toporek, R. L. (2003). *Multicultural counseling competencies 2003: Association for multicultural counseling and development.* Alexandria, VA: American Counseling Association.

Safran, J. D., Kriss, A., & Foley, V. K. (2019). Psychodynamic psychotherapies. In D. Wedding & R. J. Corsini (Eds.), *Current psychotherapies* (11th ed., pp. 21–57). Boston, MA: Cengage Learning.

*Sahker, E. (2016). Therapy with the nonreligious: Ethical and clinical considerations. *Professional Psychology: Research and Practice, 47*(4), 295–302.

*Satir, V. (1983). *Conjoint family therapy* (3rd ed.). Palo Alto, CA: Science and Behavior Books.

*Satir, V. (1989). *The new peoplemaking.* Palo Alto, CA: Science and Behavior Books.

Satir, V., & Baldwin, M. (1983). *Satir: Step by step.* Palo Alto, CA: Science and Behavior Books.

Satir, V., Banmen, J., Gerber, J., & Gomori, M. (1991). *The Satir model.* Palo Alto, CA: Science and Behavior Books.

Satir, V., Bitter, J. R., & Krestensen, K. K. (1988). Family reconstruction: The family within—A group experience. *Journal for Specialists in Group Work, 13*(4), 200–208.

Schank, J. A., Helbok, C. M., Haldeman, D. C., & Gallardo, M. E. (2010). Challenges and benefits of ethical small-community practice. *Professional Psychology: Research and Practice, 41*(6), 502–510.

Schank, J. A., & Skovholt, T. M. (1997). Dual-relationship dilemmas of rural and small community psychologists. *Professional Psychology: Research and Practice, 28*(1), 44–49.

Schneider, K. J., & Krug, O. T. (2017). *Existential-humanistic therapy* (2nd ed.). Washington, DC: American Psychological Association.

Schreier, B., Davis, D., & Rodolfa, E. (2005). Diversity-based psychology with lesbian, gay and bisexual patients: Clinical and training issues—Practical actions. *California Department of Consumer Affairs (Board of Psychology), 12,* 1–13.

Segal, Z. V., Williams, J. M. G., & Teasdale, J. D. (2013). *Mindfulness-based cognitive therapy for depression* (2nd ed.). New York, NY: Guilford Press.

Shafranske, E. P., & Sperry, L. (2005). Future directions: Opportunities and challenges. In L. Sperry & E. P. Shafranske (Eds.), *Spiritually oriented psychotherapy* (pp. 351–354). Washington, DC: American Psychological Association.

*Shapiro, J. L., Peltz, L. S., & Bernadett-Shapiro, S. (2019). *Basics of group counseling and psychotherapy: An introductory guide* (2nd ed.). San Diego, CA: Cognella Academic.

Sheperis, D. S., Henning, S. L., & Kocey, M. M. (2016). *Ethical decision making for the 21st century counselor.* Los Angeles, CA: Sage.

Shields, D., Westwood, M., & Kuhl, D. (2019). Counseling military clients: Multicultural competence, challenges, and opportunities. In C. C. Lee (Ed.), *Multicultural issues in counseling: New approaches to diversity* (5th ed., pp. 229–251). Alexandria, VA: American Counseling Association.

Shiles, M. (2009). Discriminatory referrals: Uncovering a potential ethical dilemma facing practitioners. *Ethics & Behavior, 19*(2), 142–155.

*Siegel, R. D. (2010). *The mindfulness solution: Everyday practices for everyday problems.* New York, NY: Guilford Press.

*Skovholt, T. M. (2001). *The resilient practitioner: Burnout prevention and self-care strategies for counselors, therapists, teachers, and health professionals.* Boston, MA: Allyn & Bacon.

*Skovholt, T. M. (2012a). *Becoming a therapist: On the path to mastery.* Hoboken, NJ: Wiley.

Skovholt, T. M. (2012b). The counselor's resilient self. *Turkish Psychological Counseling and Guidance Journal, 4*(38), 137–146.

Skovholt, T. M., & Trotter-Mathison, M. (2016). *The resilient practitioner: Burnout prevention and self-care strategies for the helping professions.* (3rd ed.). New York, NY: Routledge (Taylor & Francis)

Smart, J. (2016). Counseling individuals with disabilities. In I. Marini & M. A. Stebnicki (Eds.), *The professional counselor's desk reference* (2nd ed., pp. 417–421). New York, NY: Springer.

Smart, J. (2019). Counseling individuals with physical, cognitive, and psychiatric disabilities. In C. C. Lee (Ed.), *Multicultural issues in counseling: New approaches to diversity* (5th ed., pp. 181–198). Alexandria, VA: American Counseling Association.

Smith, B. D. (2007). Sifting through trauma: Compassion fatigue and HIV/AIDS. *Clinical Social Work Journal, 35,* 193–198. doi: 10.1007/s10615-007-0096-2

Speight, S. L. (2012). An exploration of boundaries and solidarity in counseling relationships. *The Counseling Psychologist, 40*(1), 133–157.

Sperry, J., & Sperry, L. (2018). *Cognitive behavior therapy in counseling practice.* New York, NJ: Routledge.

Spotts-De Lazzer, A. (2012). Facebook for therapists: Friend or unfriend? *The Therapist, 24*(5), 19–23.

*Stebnicki, M. A. (2008). *Empathy fatigue: Healing the mind, body, and spirit of professional counselors.* New York, NY: Springer.

Stebnicki, M. A. (2009a). A call for integral approaches in the professional identity of rehabilitation counseling: Three specialty areas, one profession. *Rehabilitation Counselor Bulletin, 99*(4), 64–68.

Stebnicki, M. A. (2009b). Empathy fatigue in the counseling profession. In I. Marini & M. A. Stebnicki (Eds.), *The professional counselor's desk reference* (pp. 801–812). New York, NY: Springer.

Stebnicki, M. A. (2009c). Empathy fatigue: Assessing risk factors and cultivating self-care. In I. Marini & M. A. Stebnicki (Eds.), *The professional counselor's desk reference* (pp. 813–830). New York, NY: Springer.

Stebnicki, M. A. (2016a). From empathy fatigue to empathy resiliency. In I. Marini & M. A. Stebnicki (Eds.), *The professional counselor's desk reference* (2nd ed., pp. 533–545). New York, NY: Springer.

Stebnicki, M. A. (2016b). Military counseling. In I. Marini & M. A. Stebnicki (Eds.), *The professional counselor's desk reference* (2nd ed., pp. 499–506). New York, NY: Springer.

Stebnicki, M. A. (2017). *Disaster mental health counseling: Responding to trauma in a multicultural context.* New York, NY: Springer.

Steen, S., Shi, Q., & Hockersmith, W. (2014). Group counseling for African Americans: Research and practice considerations. In J. DeLucia-Waack, C. R. Kalodner, & M. T. Riva (Eds.), *Handbook of group counseling and psychotherapy* (2nd ed., pp. 220–230). Thousand Oaks, CA: Sage.

Stockton, R., Morran, K., & Chang, S. (2014). An overview of current research and best practices for training beginning group leaders. In J. DeLucia-Waack, C. R. Kalodner, & M. T. Riva (Eds.), *Handbook of group counseling and psychotherapy* (2nd ed., pp.133–145). Thousand Oaks, CA: Sage.

Sue, D. W. (2005). Racism and the conspiracy of silence: Presidential address. *The Counseling Psychologist, 33*(1), 100–114.

Sue, D. W., Arredondo, P., & McDavis, R. J. (1992). Multicultural counseling competencies and standards: A call to the profession. *Journal of Counseling and Development, 70*(4), 477–486.

Sue, D. W., Bernier, Y., Durran, A., Feinberg, L., Pedersen, P. B., Smith, E. J., & Vasquez- Nuttal, E. (1982). Position paper: Cross-cultural counseling competencies. *The Counseling Psychologist, 10*(2), 45–52.

Sue, D. W., & Capodilupo. C. M. (2015). Multicultural and community perspectives on multiple relationships. In B. Herlihy & G. Corey, *Boundary issues in counseling: Multiple roles and responsibilities* (3rd ed., pp. 92–95). Alexandria, VA: American Counseling Association.

Sue, D. W., Capodilupo, C. M., Torino, G. C., Bucceri, J. M., Holder, A. M. B., Nadal, K. L., & Esquilin, M. (2007). Racial microaggressions in everyday life: Implications for clinical practice. *American Psychologist, 62*(4), 271–286.

Sue, D. W., Carter, R. T., and colleagues. (1998). *Multicultural counseling competencies: Individual and organizational development*. Thousand Oaks, CA: Sage.

*Sue, D. W., & Sue, D. (2016). *Counseling the culturally diverse: Theory and practice* (7th ed.). New York, NY: Wiley.

*Sweitzer, H. F., & King, M. A. (2014). *The successful internship: Personal, professional, and civic development in experiential learning* (4th ed.). Belmont, CA: Brooks/Cole, Cengage Learning.

Tarvydas, V., Levers, L. L., & Teahen, P. R. (2018). Ethics narratives from lived experiences of disaster and trauma counselors. In J. M. Webber & J. B. Mascari (Eds.), *Disaster mental health counseling: A guide to preparing and responding* (4th ed., pp. 97–107). Alexandria, VA: American Counseling Association Foundation.

Taylor, J. M., & Neimeyer, G. J. (2015). The assessment of lifelong learning in psychologists. *Professional Psychology: Research and Practice, 46*(6), 385–390.

Taylor, J. M., & Neimeyer, G. J. (2016). Continuing education and lifelong learning. In J. Norcross, G. R. VandenBos, & D. K. Freedheim (Eds.), *APA handbook of clinical psychology* (Vol. 5, pp. 135–152). Washington, DC: American Psychological Association.

Tedeschi, R. G., & Calhoun, L. G. (1995). *Trauma and transformation: Growing in the aftermath of suffering.* Thousand Oaks, CA: Sage.

*Teyber, E., & Teyber, F. H. (2017). *Interpersonal process in therapy: An integrative model* (7th ed.). Boston, MA: Cengage Learning.

Thomas, J. L. (2002). Bartering. In A. A. Lazarus & O. Zur (Eds.), *Dual relationships and psychotherapy* (pp. 394–408). New York, NY: Springer.

Torres-Rivera, E., Torres Fernandez, I., & Hendricks, W. A. (2014). Psychoeducational and counseling groups with Latinos/as. In J. DeLucia-Waack, C. R. Kalodner, & M. T. Riva (Eds.), *Handbook of group counseling and psychotherapy* (2nd ed., pp. 242–252). Thousand Oaks, CA: Sage.

Tran-Lien, A. (2012). E-mailing your client: Legal and ethical implications. *The Therapist, 24*(3), 20–22.

*Vernon, A., & Doyle, K. A. (Eds.). (2018). *Cognitive behavior therapies: A guidebook for practitioners.* Alexandria, VA: American Counseling Association.

Vilardaga, R., Luoma, J. B., Hayes, S. C., Pistorello, J., Levin, M. E., Hildebrandt, M. J., . . . Bond, F. (2011). Burnout among the addiction counseling workforce: The differential roles of mindfulness and values-based processes and work-site factors. *Journal of Substance Abuse Treatment, 40,* 323–335.

Waller, B. (2013). Real-life social action in the community. In J. A. Kottler, M. Englar-Carlson, & J. Carlson (Eds.), *Helping beyond the 50-minute hour: Therapists involved in meaningful social action* (pp. 86–95). New York, NY: Routledge (Taylor & Francis).

Walsh, R. (2011). Lifestyle and mental health. *American Psychologist,* 66, 579–592.

Walsh, R., & Vaughan, F. (2019). Mindfulness and other contemplative psychotherapies. In D. Wedding & R. J. Corsini (Eds.), *Current psychotherapies* (11th ed., pp. 429–480). Boston, MA: Cengage Learning.

Wampold, B. E. (2010). *The basics of psychotherapy: An introduction to theory and practice*. Washington, DC: American Psychological Association.

Wampold, B. E., & Imel, Z. E. (2015). *The great psychotherapy debate: The evidence for what makes psychotherapy work* (2nd ed.). New York, NY: Routledge (Taylor & Francis).

Ward v. Wilbanks, No. 09-CV-11237, Doc. 139 (E. D. Mich., Jul. 26, 2010).

Warren, C. S., Schafer, K. J., Crowley, M. E. J., & Olivardia, R. (2013, June 24). Demographic and work-related correlates of job burnout in professional eating disorder treatment providers. *Psychotherapy: Theory, Research, Practice, Training*. Advance online publication. doi: 10.1037/a0028783

Waters, R. (2004). Making a difference: Five therapists who've taken on the wider world. *Psychotherapy Networker, 28*(6), 356–359.

Watts, R. E. (2019). Adlerian therapy as a positive counseling approach. In G. McAuliffe, *Positive counseling: A guide to assessing and enhancing client strength and growth* (pp. 209–231). San Diego, CA: Cognella Academic.

Webber, J. M., & Mascari, J. B. (Eds.). (2018). *Disaster mental health counseling: A guide to preparing and responding* (4th ed.). Alexandria, VA: American Counseling Association Foundation.

Webber, J. M., Mascari, J. B., & Runte, J. K. (2018). Disaster mental health counseling: Skills and strategies. In J. M. Webber & J. B. Mascari (Eds.), *Disaster mental health counseling: A guide to preparing and responding* (4th ed., pp. 23–38). Alexandria, VA: American Counseling Association Foundation.

Wedding, D., & Corsini, R. J. (Eds.). (2019). *Current psychotherapies* (11th ed.). Boston, MA: Cengage Learning.

*Werth, J. L., Jr. (Ed.). (2013a). *Counseling clients near the end of life: A practical guide for mental health professionals.* New York, NY: Springer.

Werth, J. L., Jr. (2013b). Counseling clients who are near the end of life. In J. L. Werth Jr. (Ed.), *Counseling clients near the end of life: A practical guide for mental health professionals* (pp. 101–120). New York, NY: Springer.

Werth, J. L., Jr., & Holdwick, D. J. (2000). A primer on rational suicide and other forms of hastened death. *The Counseling Psychologist, 28*(4), 511–539.

Werth, J. L., Jr., & Stroup, J. (2015). Working with clients who may harm themselves. In B. Herlihy & G. Corey, *ACA ethical standards casebook* (7th ed., pp. 231–244). Alexandria, VA: American Counseling Association.

*Werth, J. L., Jr., Welfel, E. R., & Benjamin, G. A. H. (Eds.). (2009). *The duty to protect: Ethical, legal, and professional considerations for mental health professionals.* Washington, DC: American Psychological Association.

Werth, J. L., Jr., & Whiting, E. L. (2015). Boundary issues and multiple relationships when working with clients with end-of-life concerns. In B. Herlihy & G. Corey, *Boundary issues in counseling: Multiple roles and responsibilities* (3rd ed., pp. 259–265). Alexandria, VA: American Counseling Association.

*Wheeler, A. M., & Bertram, B. (2019). *The counselor and the law: A guide to legal and ethical practice* (8th ed.). Alexandria, VA: American Counseling Association.

Wheeler, G., & Axelsson, L. S. (2015). *Gestalt therapy.* Washington, DC: American Psychological Association.

*Wilcoxon, S. A., Remley, T. P., & Gladding, S. T. (2013). *Ethical, legal, and professional issues in the practice of marriage and family therapy* (Updated 5th ed.). New York, NY: Pearson.

Wilkinson, T., Smith, D., & Wimberly, R. (2019). Trends in ethical complaints leading to professional counseling licensing boards disciplinary actions. *Journal of Counseling and Development, 97*(1), 98–104.

Winslade, J., & Del Corso, J. J. (2019). Narrative therapy. In G. McAuliffe, *Positive counseling: A guide to assessing and enhancing client strength and growth* (pp. 183–208). San Diego, CA: Cognella Academic.

Winslade, J., & Monk, G. (2007). *Narrative counseling in schools: Powerful and brief* (2nd ed.). Thousand Oaks, CA: Corwin Press (Sage).

Wise, E. H., & Barnett, J. E. (2016). Self-care for psychologists. In J. Norcross, G. R. VandenBos, & D. K. Freedheim (Eds.), *APA handbook of clinical psychology* (Vol. 5, pp. 209–222). Washington, DC: American Psychological Association.

Wise, E. H., Bieschke, K. L., Forrest, L., Cohen-Filipic, J., Hathaway, W. L., & Douce, L. A. (2015). Psychology's proactive approach to conscience clause court cases and legislation. *Training and Education in Professional Psychology, 9,* 259–268.

Wise, E. H., Hersh, M. A., & Gibson, C. M. (2012). Ethics, self-care and well-being for psychologists: Re-envisioning the stress-distress continuum. *Professional Psychology: Research and Practice, 43*(5), 487–494.

*Woodside, M., & McClam, T. (2019). *An introduction to human services* (9th ed.). Boston, MA: Cengage Learning.

Woody, R. H. (1998). Bartering for psychological services. *Professional Psychology: Research and Practice, 29*(2), 174–178.

Wrenn, C. G. (1962). The culturally encapsulated counselor. *Harvard Educational Review, 32,* 444–449.

Wrenn, C. G. (1985). Afterword: The culturally encapsulated counselor revisited. In P. Pedersen (Ed.), *Handbook of cross-cultural counseling and therapy* (pp. 323–329). Westport, CT: Greenwood Press.

*Wubbolding, R. E. (2000). *Reality therapy for the 21st century.* Philadelphia, PA: Brunner-Routledge (Taylor & Francis).

*Wubbolding, R. (2011). *Reality therapy: Theories of psychotherapy series.* Washington, DC: American Psychological Association.

Wubbolding, R. E. (2013). Reality therapy. In J. Frew & M. D. Spiegler (Eds.), *Contemporary psychotherapies for a diverse world* (pp. 339–372). New York, NY: Taylor & Francis.

Wubbolding, R. E. (2016). Reality therapy/choice theory. In D. Capuzzi & M. D. Stauffer (Eds.), *Counseling and psychotherapy: Theories and interventions* (6th ed., pp. 311–338). Alexandria, VA: American Counseling Association.

*Wubbolding, R. E. (2017). *Reality therapy and self-evaluation: The key to client change.* Alexandria, VA: American Counseling Association.

*Yalom, I. D. (1997). *Lying on the couch: A novel.* New York, NY: Perennial.

*Yalom, I. D. (2003). *The gift of therapy.* New York, NY: Perennial.

*Yalom, I. D. (with Leszcz, M.). (2005). *The theory and practice of group psychotherapy* (5th ed.). New York, NY: Basic Books.

Young, J. S., & Cashwell, C. S. (2011a). Integrating spirituality and religion into counseling: An introduction. In C. S. Cashwell & J. S. Young (Eds.), *Integrating spirituality and religion into counseling: A guide to competent practice* (2nd ed., pp. 1–24). Alexandria, VA: American Counseling Association.

Young, J. S., & Cashwell, C. S. (2011b). Where do we go from here? In C. S. Cashwell & J. S. Young (Eds.), *Integrating spirituality and religion into counseling: A guide to competent practice* (2nd ed., pp. 279–289). Alexandria, VA: American Counseling Association.

*Young, M. E. (2013). *Learning the art of helping: Building blocks and techniques* (5th ed.). Boston, MA: Pearson.

Younggren, J. N., & Gottlieb, M. C. (2008). Termination and abandonment: History, risk, and risk management. *Professional Psychology: Research and Practice, 39*(5), 498–504.

Younggren, J. N., Harris, E. A., & Martin, J. N. (2016). Malpractice and risk management. In J. Norcross, G. R. VandenBos, & D. K. Freedheim (Eds.), *APA handbook of clinical psychology* (Vol. 5, pp. 395–408). Washington, DC: American Psychological Association.

Yusim, A. (2017). *Fulfilled: How the science of spirituality can help you live a happier, more meaningful life.* New York, NY: Grand Central Life & Style.

Zalaquett, C. P., Fuerth, K. M., Stein, C., Ivey, A. E., & Ivey, M. B. (2008). Reframing the DSM-IV-TR from a multicultural/social justice perspective. *Journal of Counseling and Development, 86*(3), 364–371.

*Zalaquett, C., Ivey, A., & Ivey, M. (2019). *Essential theories of counseling and psychotherapy: Everyday practice in our diverse world.* San Diego, CA: Cognella Academic.

Zhu, P. (2018). Experiential growth groups in counselor education: A review of its pedagogy, research, and ethical dilemmas. *The Journal for Specialists in Group Work, 43*(2), 144–165.

*Zur, O. (2007). *Boundaries in psychotherapy: Ethical and clinical explorations.* Washington, DC: American Psychological Association.

Zur, O. (2014). Not all multiple relationships are created equal: Mapping the maze of 26 types of multiple relationships. *Independent Practitioner, 34*(1), 15–22.

Zur, O. (Ed.). (2017). *Multiple relationships in psychotherapy and counseling: Unavoidable, common, and mandatory dual relations in therapy.* New York, NY: Routledge (Taylor & Francis).

NAME INDEX

SUBJECT INDEX